# France Since 1789

# FRANCE SINCE 1789

### Revised Edition

### Paul A. Gagnon

Harper & Row, Publishers

NEW YORK, EVANSTON, SAN FRANCISCO, LONDON

TO MY PARENTS

*Joseph Eugène*

AND

*Alice Tougas Gagnon*

STANDARD BOOK NUMBER: 06-042222-X

LIBRARY OF CONGRESS CATALOG CARD NUMBER: 73-170621

# CONTENTS

# PREFACE
# TO THE
# REVISED EDITION

I am grateful for this opportunity to continue the story through the end of Charles de Gaulle's presidency. Events in France since the first edition appeared in 1964—events in the whole industrialized world—have been dramatic; dangerous enough to shock men to a new sense of complexity. Their world rushes into a new century, their leaders are apparently not quick to accept changing reality, to admit doubt, or to pose questions squarely to the people or to themselves. Unhappily, de Gaulle's manner tempted men to call him anachronistic, inflexible. His decade of power says otherwise. His personal code of honor was indeed an old one (are there new, innovative ones?) and he was constant to it. Perhaps it was precisely this that allowed him to face new realities unflinchingly, to do and say things much against the view of the world he learned when young. Decolonization of an empire, decentralization of a state, the acceptance of a world revolution and of the human needs of men in other continents—these were not easily to be expected of a bourgeois French Catholic soldier of exalted patriotism, whose schooling ended before the First World War. No more than other men did he see all, nor did he avoid error, arrogance, and cruelty, but we shall be happy to find leaders—in any sphere of life—who so manage to add imagination to honor.

P. A. G.

*Paris, France*
*March, 1971*

# PREFACE

In writing this relatively brief, interpretive history, my first aim has been to offer to readers in modern French civilization a convenient chronology of events, ideas, and men around which to gather their other readings in original sources, in literature, and in the many specialized works now readily available. I also have aimed, without being willfully combative, to invite a dialogue, a continuing debate, over judgments and interpretations of this complicated material.

The organization of the book is conventional, according to political regimes, with analyses of economic, social, religious, intellectual and cultural affairs introduced where they seem most pertinent. The concept of national history is by now also conventional. Yet whatever the virtues of the wider historical approach—and they are many—the fact remains that the most critical human and political dramas are still played out on the national stage, are still shaped by national weaknesses and strengths, national institutions and styles. To study the struggles of the French people in the last two centuries, then, should help us to understand not only the French nation but also the complexities and blemishes of other national histories, and of the human condition in all ages.

In addition to the historical debts I owe to the authors listed in the bibliography, I am particularly, and immeasurably, indebted to the late Donald C. McKay of Harvard, to Theodore C. Caldwell of the University of Massachusetts, and to Theodore M. Pease of Ashfield, for excellence of instruction and example. Special thanks go to Judith Abbott Switky, who checked the manuscript throughout, and to my wife, Mona Harrington, for her wise and indispensable critique of ideas and language.

PAUL A. GAGNON

*Amherst, Massachusetts*
*September, 1963*

# France Since 1789

# THE FRENCH
# REVOLUTION

On the morning of May 4, 1789, Louis XVI, chief of the House of Bourbon and King of France, walked the streets of Versailles to the Church of Saint Louis, named for that royal predecessor so difficult to emulate. With him in grand procession went most of the delegates to the Estates-General, called to assembly for the first time since 1614: nobles and prelates in color, silver, and gold; commons and priests in the dull black costume prescribed by the royal master of ceremonies. There also were Louis' two brothers, who would be the last Kings of France: the Comte de Provence, to be Louis XVIII, and the Comte d'Artois, to be Charles X. The future King of the French, Louis-Philippe, then the young Duc de Chartres, walked in the shadow of his father, the wealthy and ambitious Duc d'Orléans, who within four years, as Philippe-Égalité, was to vote for the death of his cousin, Louis XVI.

Although the country lay in profound economic distress and its government was near bankruptcy, the elections to the Estates had proceeded in good order and expectations of reform and renewal were high, in marchers and spectators alike. Of these, a half million had flooded the town of Versailles, coming from Paris and all the realm, to see for themselves the start of reformation. The occasion demanded pageantry and solemn religious observance, but even in the church appeared signs of harsher things to come. The Bishop of Nancy in his sermon deplored the sufferings of the people and dared to attack the luxury of the court; the commons, in the presence of King, Queen, courtiers, and magnates, dared to applaud. What we now call the French Revolution began with the formal sessions of the following days.

## THE ESTATES-GENERAL

The calling of the Estates-General created a revolutionary situation. It brought to the centers of political action—Versailles and then Paris—a vigorous and talented body of men, of whom the great majority, whether of noble or clerical or common rank, were ill-satisfied with things as they were. The immediate pressures upon Louis XVI to make this admittedly dangerous appeal were financial; the royal treasury was close to bankruptcy. Behind bankruptcy was the failure of absolute monarchy in France. The power wielded by Louis XIV over his subjects, their services and their wealth, had never been absolute according to the exacting standards of our own century. Yet, such as it was, it had declined during his own lifetime and was struck from the hands of his successors. Both Louis XV and Louis XVI aspired to reform, particularly in taxation and administration. In an age of enlightened despots, they were not the least enlightened rulers in Europe; and some of their ministers, like Maupeou and Turgot, were men of extraordinary talent whose plans won them the admiration of the Philosophes. Not enlightenment but despotism was lacking. A monarchy called absolute and regarded as such by the world had found itself powerless to enact reforms indispensable to its own survival.

Since the death of the aged Louis XIV in 1715, the nobles of France, of sword and of robe, had freed themselves from the subservient roles in which the Sun King had cast them. He had himself prepared this resurgence by merely overriding, instead of destroying, their feudal privileges and institutions, by selling hereditary offices in the administration and judiciary, and by imprisoning his successors in the barren isolation of Versailles, surrounded and distracted by their aristocratic courtiers. Since 1715, the nobility had seized an unprecedented monopoly of the high offices in Army, Church, and State. The influence of the wealthiest at court, in the provincial Estates and in the law courts called *parlements,* went largely unchallenged. The last had on several occasions frustrated royal reforms that would have reduced the nobles' privileges and their nearly complete exemption from taxation. When Louis XV and Louis XVI sought to reduce or evade the powers of the *parlements*, the members had rallied public opinion and won even the support of some Philosophes by their appeals to "ancient liberties" and "traditional rights" against "royal despotism." Thus did they defend privilege in the name of liberty and, unwittingly, prepare Frenchmen for a revolution that was to destroy the very privilege they sought to preserve. Unable to move the *parlements*, the crown called in 1787 an Assembly of Notables to gain public support for reforms of the tax system. Again the nobles, lay and clerical, blocked any change and, after a final refusal by the *parlements* in 1788 to register the royal edicts of reform, Louis XVI was left with little choice but to revive the nearly-forgotten elected body of the Estates-General.

The aristocracy encouraged and approved the call. Certain of their control in the First and Second Estates, clergy and nobles, they expected to vote down the Third, the commons, whenever it opposed their interests. To them, the meeting of the Estates-General promised even further control of the crown and an end to attacks on their privileges. Here was a triumph such as the nobility had not enjoyed since the sixteenth century, superb revenge for the frustrations and humiliations inflicted by Richelieu, Mazarin, and Louis XIV. But their apparent victory was short-lived. It lasted six weeks, to the middle of June, 1789, when the Third Estate declared itself the National Assembly and initiative passed to the leaders of the middle class.

The calling of the Estates-General meant something more than a royal surrender to the ambitions of a resurgent nobility. For the King and his chief minister, the cautious Swiss financier Necker, it offered a final opportunity to carry a series of moderate reforms reducing the tax exemptions of nobles and clergy, to the end of restoring royal finances. To gain bourgeois approval, Louis XVI had granted double representation to the Third Estate, making its delegation equal to those of the two higher orders, but reserving the crucial question of vote by order or by head. Since a number of liberal nobles and many of the lower clergy were known to sympathize with the well-known aspirations of the Third Estate, a vote by head would wrest control of events from the privileged classes. This question dominated the months of May and June. In finally obtaining the vote by individual member, the Third Estate won the chance to reform the government and the society of France according to ideals and interests long cherished and long repressed.

The eighteenth century was a time of prosperity for bourgeois Frenchmen. As a class, they had grown apace in numbers, wealth, and education. Ambitious, talented, feeling their strength, they resented all the more their lowly social and political position as well as the remaining obstacles to their economic activity—from the excessive burden of taxes placed upon them by the near-exemption of nobles and clergy to the endless web of tolls, interior customs, and regulations of trade imposed by guilds and arbitrary government. The English political system, with the middle class represented in the House of Commons, had achieved a financial solidity and a security for business that excited their envy. The American Revolution, its success in moderation, only increased their impatience and their hopes in representative government. Their aspirations to social equality quickened as titles and positions of honor were closed to them by the reviving nobility. Deprived in the eighteenth century of the advancement offered under Louis XIV in the seventeenth, many wealthy French commoners saw in representative government a chance to grasp the positions of power their talents deserved. To these long-standing grievances was added, in 1789, an immediate and intolerable danger: a royal declaration of bankruptcy. To the bondholders of France, this was the frightful prospect offered by continuing domination of government by the privileged classes whose wealth lay mainly in land and office. Thus the struggle for control of the Estates-General involved, for many delegates on both sides, the difference between wealth and relative poverty.

Interests alone cannot explain the moods and events of the summer of 1789. Louis XVI's call for elections to the Estates-General had met joyful acclamation. The *cahiers*, petitions of grievance, and the instructions to delegates demonstrated by their very moderation the confidence and hopes of the moment. The French public had been taught by the Philosophes and their followers to expect much from an assembly of its chosen representatives. The ideas of Locke, Montesquieu, Voltaire, the Encyclopedists, and Rousseau were in the air, at city corners and town squares, in cafés, in salons, and even in noble châteaux and the court itself. The call for elections inspired countless public meetings and the production of model *cahiers* and pamphlets of every political hue. Of these, the most famous, and perhaps the most influential, was the Abbé Sieyès' *What Is the Third Estate?* Up to now, said this student of Locke, it has been nothing, but its ability and its work for the common good have earned it the right to be "everything" in the political life of the nation. Recent events had further spread and popularized ideas. In the struggle between *parlements* and King, both sides had appealed to Reason, to general interest, to Natural Right and Natural Law. The revolution of the Americans was already storied to a people who saw themselves playing a glorious role in its success. Popular sovereignty, representative government, liberties of speech, thought, and action, social and civic equality, reformed and refined codes of law and courts, equality in taxation, the abolition of feudal prerogative—all were, in greater or lesser degree, demanded of the King and the Estates-General.

As in any revolution, new ideas and appeals for innovation were matched and, for a time, reinforced by restatements of old ideals, appeals to tradition, and demands for return to a glorious past—however imperfectly recalled. The monarchy of Saint Louis was renowned for its justice, charity, holiness, and forbearance. Let the Bourbons now learn from the thirteenth century. Or, if they preferred, from Bossuet, whose ideal of divine-right kingship required a monarch at the service of all. The Church in Thomas Aquinas' time had been self-denying yet prolific in great art and intellectually alive—a Church wherein a poor young commoner might rise to a bishopric or sainthood. Let the Church, now ruled by wealthy and prideful aristocrats, look back with humility. Let the religious toleration and—pity Louis XVI—the gallantry of Henry IV reign again, together with the glory of the age of Louis XIV, France's cultural dominion of Europe, a fitting accompaniment to her military and diplomatic prowess.

The eighteenth-century monarchy and Church offended national pride, not only because all the world except France seemed to be moving forward to enlightenment, but also because the grandeur of the past was mocked and betrayed. One historian has said that the most dangerous revolutionaries are the conservatives, the pious folk loyal to a real or imagined Golden Age. In the mood of 1789, Louis XVI, his Queen, his courtiers, and the hierarchy of the Church were particularly vulnerable to this sort of righteous attack. A respect for tradition, Edmund Burke's vaunted cure for discontent, was in France more likely to feed resentment against the existing order. During the first crucial months of the Revolution, the best defense of the monarchy was missing; loyalty and something that passed for respect revived only under the cruelest blows. By then it was too late.

Behind the threat of royal bankruptcy lay not only a failure to achieve

basic tax reform but a history of bad judgment, mismanagement, corruption, and extravagance in which the luxury of the court played a
minor, although notorious, part. Marie Antoinette, disliked and distrusted as few queens have been, bore the title of "Madame Deficit."
But the financial disaster went much beyond a young woman's appetite
for jewelry and display; it went back to the immense drains of the aggressive wars of Louis XIV and the dynastic wars of Louis XV, and
forward to the great expense borne by the monarchy in the American
Revolution. In that struggle, England, the old enemy, had been humbled
for the moment, but Louis XVI had undermined his throne. By 1788,
the interest on the public debt took more than half of the annual budget.

At the same time, the glitter of Versailles and the great fortunes
flaunted by a few nobles and prelates confirmed the public impression
of frivolity, favoritism, and unearned privilege. To the laboring masses
of country and town who were buffeted by the economic crisis, such
luxury was the hateful fruit of injustice and oppression. More hateful
still, the happy few seemed oblivious to the misery about them, and
apparently determined to remain so. Had the wretches no bread? "Let
them eat cake!" It mattered little whether or not the Queen had said it;
she and the courtiers appeared capable of no other response. Here, as
in so many cases, what was true was less important than what was believable. Never before had the monarchy been so closely identified in the
public mind with the ignorance and indifference of the magnates. If the
King of France was bankrupt, it seemed to be his own fault and the
fault of the system. Why else would the government be insolvent and
the people bound to poverty, in a land so rich, so favored by nature?

To the representatives of the Third Estate who gathered at Versailles
in 1789, then, there were many reasons for both anger and hope. The
King was ill-suited and ill-advised in his role, but he could be better advised if not controlled; the system was deplorable, but the system could
be changed. The first order of business was to rally those nobles and
churchmen who agreed and, provided the votes were taken by head, to
gain control of the Estates-General and to equip France with a government suited to the modern world, a new regime worthy of the finest days
of the old.

The first formal session of the Estates, on the 5th of May, proved a
disappointment to all sides. The King's speech and Necker's were neutral
and indecisive. Privilege was neither defended nor attacked. On the vital
question of the vote, Louis allowed each house to decide for itself

whether to meet, organize, and vote separately or to join the others. The nobles and clergy chose separate meetings, the latter, however, by a portentously close margin, 133 to 114. The Third Estate met but refused to organize. It adopted a tactic of passive resistance, waiting for desertions from the other orders, or until the King should take its part. This challenge to the feudal constitution of the Estates divided the advisers of the King. The conservatives, headed by Artois and supported by the Queen, urged Louis to hold fast to the vote by order. Others, with Necker, suggested compromise or an outright grant of the vote by head. Historians have blamed Louis XVI for hesitating, for failing to grasp this opportunity to join the Third Estate and to lead the great majority of his people in reform against the privileged few who had stripped the monarchy of its power and popularity. Had he not already made such attempts in the recent past? How much agony might France have been spared if he had accepted at this time the sensible role of constitutional monarch, they ask. But Louis was not the only man unable to perceive the future. And arrayed against Necker's somewhat feeble advice and the King's own interest in limiting the power of the aristocrats were the old traditions and habits of kingly prerogative, a natural distrust of bourgeois motives, an admirable if impolitic loyalty to those he considered his friends, and Louis' regard for his brothers and his wife. The King vacillated and the issue was decided without him.

## THE NATIONAL (CONSTITUENT) ASSEMBLY

On June 17th, after a few of the lower clergy had joined them, the delegates of the Third Estate declared themselves the National Assembly and immediately claimed the power of the purse by decreeing that no taxation would be legal if the Assembly were dissolved. Here was the first clear act of revolution, for it overturned the legal constitution of France as the monarchy had publicly defined it. The response of Louis XVI was typical of his conduct in the few years of life left to him. At first inclined by Necker to seek compromise, he was turned by the Queen and Artois to opposition. On the 20th of June, the Third Estate and its friends found themselves locked out of the customary meeting place. There followed that dramatic act, immortalized and romanticized by the painter David, known to us as the Tennis Court Oath. Drawn up by the moderate Mounier, a leading advocate of constitutional monarchy on the English model, and administered by Bailly, the presiding officer and a senior delegate from Paris, the oath bound the members never to disband until they had given France a constitution. This second show of defiance only strengthened the conservative faction at court. At a royal session of the Estates on June 23rd, the King declared the Third Estate to have acted illegally and ordered the feudal distinction of the three houses preserved.

The great hopes aroused by the previous days were not to be this easily extinguished. The King's plan offering limited reforms from above might have sufficed for May 5th. By the 23rd of June it was too late for him to assume the role of benevolent despot; neither his person nor his entourage suited the piece. At the end of the royal address, the session was dismissed. The Third Estate refused to leave the hall with the privileged orders; the Comte de Mirabeau, a renegade noble elected as a commoner, swore that only bayonets would move the members. Bailly answered the King's master of ceremonies, who demanded that the hall be cleared: "The nation is assembled here, and it takes no orders." Unsure of the armed force at his disposal and threatened by a rumored march of Parisians, Louis surrendered and in the following days urged the nobles and clergy to join the National Assembly. By the 27th of June, some 820 Deputies, including twenty prelates led by the agile Talleyrand, sat in its meetings. Most of the remaining 400 followed within the fortnight. The chances for a peaceful revolution controlled by the privileged classes had now disappeared. All sides recognized that only civil war could save the feudal regime.

Early in July, it appeared that Louis XVI had again changed course. A dozen regiments of foreign mercenary troops converged on Versailles and Paris. The conservative faction had resolved on force; Artois sought to harden the court: "He who wishes an omelette must not shrink from breaking eggs!" By Saturday the 11th of July 30,000 royal troops had gathered, and Necker, still a popular symbol of reform, was dismissed. The National Assembly at Versailles protested helplessly. But one of Paris' many great hours was at hand. The city's 400 electors had continued to meet, after sending their delegation to the Estates in May, and now stood ready to organize the metropolis in defense of the Assembly. Under rumors of approaching troops and of a royal declaration of bankruptcy, bourgeois money—apparently augmented by the Duc d'Orléans—flowed to arm the citizens. Talented managers of the crowd, like the journalist Camille Desmoulins, played the parts that would first earn them fame and later bring them execution. The King's French Guards, assigned to Paris, refused to obey their officers and went over to the people. Their mutiny gave the revolutionaries control of the city, the mark of successful uprising then and later, in Paris, Petrograd, and elsewhere. On the 14th of July, 1789, Paris staged the greatest of her revolutionary "days"; it became a legend and a model for the future.

Men and women of every class joined the Guards, some remaining police, a few hurriedly organized groups of citizen militia, and deserters from other regiments, in erecting barricades at the city gates and in searching out arms and ammunition. The Invalides yielded thousands of firearms to its invaders and the crowd turned back across the river, eastward to the working-class quarter of Saint-Antoine, where the old Bastille dominated the crowded, jumbled tenements. Well-defended, the Bastille might have broken or long delayed the effort of Paris to free herself from the threat of royal force. Ill-defended—with a tiny garrison and unready cannon—it yet cost a hundred lives. The capture was more than the empty symbol some have made it. Legends have been woven of flimsier stuff: the fall of the Bastille defeated Artois and the conservatives at court. The future Charles X now led the first wave of emigration to foreign soil, a choice which may have spared France a civil war in 1789 but which condemned the counterrevolution to an association with foreign intervention.

Louis XVI withdrew his troops, recalled Necker, and rode to Paris on the 17th to signify his peaceful acceptance of the coup. Bailly became mayor of the revolutionary Paris Commune set up by the electors. Lafayette, at thirty-two, assumed command of the National Guard, a militia organized by the middle class as much to protect itself from the masses as from the King's troops. It was on this occasion that he combined the Paris colors of red and blue with the Bourbon white to make the tricolor cockade.

The 17th of July marks the start of the first attempt to solve the political dilemma of revolutionary France: the phase of constitutional monarchy. But the bourgeois leaders of Paris and the Assembly had paid dearly for this chance. They had first excited, and then armed, masses of Parisians whose temper and whose emerging leaders bode ill for the unglamorous and mainly conservative compromise that constitutional monarchy demanded. The seizure of Parisian government by the revolutionary Commune was imitated and—evidence of prior organization—even anticipated in other cities and towns of France. The urban lower classes thus entered upon the scene: new actors with resentments more immediate and aspirations more extreme than those of the elected representatives of the Third Estate at Versailles.

The violence of the 14th, the simultaneous destruction of the royal administration in many parts of France, and the unprecedented departure of noble *émigrés* loosed yet another force, the largest in number and harboring the oldest grievances of all: the peasantry and agricultural laborers of the countryside. In 1789, they numbered 22 million out of a total population of some 26 million. Like the workingmen of the towns, they were not represented by their own in the National Assembly and the summary *cahiers* taken to Versailles contained relatively few of the grievances filling many of the primary *cahiers* of the villages. Although legally free, the peasantry of France labored under endless and extremely odious remnants of feudal restrictions, fees, and taxes. Although many were landowners, they often held but tiny plots whose returns had to be supplemented by cottage industry or paid labor on neighboring lands of the nobility or Church. And below them on the rural scale came the renters, the sharecroppers, and the farm laborers. Together they bore the main burden of taxation, forced labor (*corvée*), and military service. Since 1787, the countryside had suffered in depression, beginning with the bad harvest of that year. Although grain prices had doubled, the subsistence farmer naturally could not share in the profit as his crop did not go to market. On the contrary, he faced higher rental fees, rising prices for his seed and for whatever manufactured goods he required. Rural population growth and the agricultural reforms of the eighteenth century, by closing common pasture and woodlands, had increased the pressures upon him. Side by side with prosperous large-scale farms—possibly as much as one-quarter of the arable land had passed into middle-class hands by 1789—there lived millions of men hungering for land, whose families were enclosed in misery, on the edge of famine.

Historians still debate the sources and spread of the "Great Fear" that passed through the countryside in July of 1789 and then turned to a general peasant insurrection, attacks on châteaux, the burning of feudal records, and in some places the seizure and occupation of the land. This was no mere *Jacquerie*, such as France had seen erupt so often in the past. It was nearly nation-wide and this time there was no organized force ready to put it down. The dissolution of local authority had proceeded swiftly after the 14th of July. The agitation that had surrounded the calling of the Estates and the popular participation in writing *cahiers* had prepared the way for a genuine agrarian revolution. Moreover, the radicalism of the country districts reinforced, and was itself reinforced by, the radicalism of the towns and of Paris. This was the first, and significantly the last, time the two acted in common. The land settlement of the following years turned the bulk of country people into a conservative force. Later revolutionary movements, so confidently launched in republican and radical Paris, were to be dampened or extinguished by the descendants of the peasants who destroyed feudalism in 1789.

The response of the Assembly in Versailles came in the remarkable night session of August 4th and 5th, when the nobles and clergy, led by a small group of liberal aristocrats, surrendered their remaining feudal privileges. Although feudal dues were to be commuted in long-term payments—to preserve the sanctity of private property—payments never were made. The resolutions passed before dawn ended the sitting not only abolished feudal courts, hunting rights, and the other minor but detested privileges of the feudal landlord (be he noble, cleric, or bourgeois) but went on to proclaim the end of inequalities in taxation and justice as well as the end of the special privileges of the provinces. The ground was swept clean of the old regime, notwithstanding the debates on implementation that ensued. The National Assembly was ready, indeed it was now forced, to build a wholly new system of government for France.

## THE DECLARATION OF
## THE RIGHTS OF MAN

On August 27th the Deputies voted the Declaration of the Rights of Man and the Citizen. As an essay in the discovery and expression of new principles of authority by which to govern society, the Declaration emerged—like others before and after it—as an amalgam of ideals, group interests, and reactions to the most vexing circumstances of the recent past. The old regime, if never absolute, had often been arbitrary; henceforth no government authority was to act except in accordance with the letter of public law. Law itself was to be carefully circumscribed, prohibiting "only actions hurtful to society" as defined by the elected representatives of society. The old regime had been hierarchical and privileged; henceforth all men were to be equal before the law and "equally eligible to all honors, places, and employments . . . without any other distinction than that created by their virtues and talents." The old regime had bred a host of privileged courts, councils, guilds, and estates; henceforth no individual or body of men would hold authority except as expressly derived from the nation, "source of all sovereignty." The old regime had enforced intolerance; henceforth no man was to be molested for his opinions, "even" his religious opinions. The clergy and aristocracy had been exempt from the tax collector; henceforth all men were to be taxed and—a phrase the middle class was later to regret—taxed "according to their abilities."

Property-owning became a natural right of man; property was sacred and inviolate, of which no man could be deprived, except in public necessity, and then only after just indemnity. Other safeguards against disorder and radicalism appeared; speech, writing, and publishing were free, but law might define and prevent abuses of these liberties. Notwithstanding these signs of what we have come to consider bourgeois conservatism, and notwithstanding the omission of the people's right of assembly, association, education, work, or relief—the last three were included in the Constitution of 1791, drawn by the same body—the Declaration of the Rights of Man stood and still stands as a tribute to the generous confidence of its framers in the ideas of the eighteenth century and in the example set by the American colonists a few years before. The causes of misfortune and misgovernment were, the deputies said, "ignorance, neglect, or contempt of human rights." These rights were liberty, equality, security, property, and resistance to oppression. Men were born to enjoy them and to rule themselves. Regardless of the failures, violence, and cruelties soon to come, and beyond the aggression and exploitation of the following twenty-five years, the Declaration carried the essential message of the French Revolution to all of Europe and, with our own, to all the world. It expressed the humane aspirations of a triumphant Third Estate. Men still feel its attraction, its strength, and—as did the French bourgeoisie in the years immediately following—its power to afflict those who would reserve its meaning to themselves alone.

The Declaration offered a platform and a justification for widely divergent political forms. As the delegates labored through September to make good their promise of a constitution for France, quarrels arose in the Assembly and the country. As always, men who had readily co-operated to overturn the old fell into dispute over what should take its place. As each constitutional issue emerged, there emerged also a "conservative" and a "liberal" position on it, a Right and a Left—the terms were soon to be commonly used—and often mixtures of both. The former, in the Constituent Assembly and its successors, usually stood for a greater degree of executive power and a lesser role for the Assembly, higher property requirements for suffrage and officeholding, a more cautious approach to civil liberties, and a greater measure of protection for wealth and business enterprise. In sum, they stood for a narrow definition of the Declaration of the Rights of Man.

Their opponents differed mainly in degree and not in kind. The parliamentary struggles of the decade were usually fought within the limits of middle-class ideas and interests. After July 14th and August 4th–5th, most of the delegates who adhered to absolute monarchy or to the feudal regime had emigrated, resigned their seats, or simply failed to appear at the meetings. On the other side, there never developed a Left of the socialist style within the Assemblies. Moreover, from August of 1789 to the end of the Convention in 1795, the social and economic backgrounds of the members remained remarkably consistent. Apart from a small number of liberal nobles and priests and, under the Convention, a tiny handful of peasants and artisans, the delegates were middle-class men. They drew their incomes as landlords, bondholders, bankers, traders, shopkeepers, or civil servants, or from the professions of law, journalism, scholarship, and letters. Only gradually did a group of professional politicians arise—men who supported themselves on the proceeds, proper and improper, of elective office. Finally, the proportion between members of higher income and those of lower remained much the same from 1789 to 1795. Although the leaders of the Right could generally count upon the support of the wealthier and the leaders of the Left on the others, the lines were rarely fixed or predictable. Results depended as often upon the particular issue at hand, the personalities of leaders, pressures from constituents or onlookers, geographic interests, and the rapidly changing events and conditions outside the chamber.

Nevertheless, the Revolution took a steadily leftward course from June of 1789 to the end of 1793. As each new political solution was reached, the Deputies who were content with it joined to defend it and halt the drift to a more radical solution. Yesterday's liberal became to-day's conservative; today's liberal would become tomorrow's conservative, identified in the eyes of the public—especially the petty bourgeoisie of Paris—with reaction and betrayal of the Rights of Man. Many historians, taking the view of Edmund Burke, have blamed the vagueness of the Declaration itself and the entire body of ideology current in France at the time. The best was the enemy of the good, they have said; intoxicated with visions of the ideal society, Frenchmen ignored both history and human nature and tried to do too much too soon. The more pragmatic solution was sacrificed to the ideal, which was unattainable. The result was instability, chaos, and finally terror; and, after terror, the inevitable reaction. So runs the argument: each possible stopping-point, or solution, was swept away by its failure to meet the impossible demands of French ideologues. It has been the thesis of royalist, conservative and, often, English-speaking historians ever since.

The liberal reply has been that ideology was neither so radical nor so important as conservatives believe. The Declaration of the Rights of Man was more cautious than the American Bill of Rights proposed one month later. The two most influential Philosophes, in the opening years of the Revolution, were Voltaire and Montesquieu. Liberal historians have argued that no man ever depended less upon abstract reason than Montesquieu and few less than Voltaire, that both men were concerned with specific abuses and specific reforms, were respectful of authority and deeply suspicious of the masses. Moreover, the liberals contend, the supposed solutions at each successive stage, however desirable they might have been, were not true solutions because they failed to satisfy the urgent practical questions of the day. Each possible stopping-point was swept away not by the impossible demands of ideology but by the impossible circumstances surrounding it—endless difficulties, they add, not to be compared with the relatively manageable problems of the English and American revolutions, which proceeded in isolation and were less burdened with class hatreds left by the old order. Frenchmen were discontent, they conclude, not because each solution failed their ideological tests but because it failed to satisfy their most pressing daily wants, political and economic security.

The facts are complex but they support the thesis of circumstance more clearly than that of ideology. In late September of 1789, Louis XVI still withheld his assent to the decrees of August 4th–5th and to the Declaration of Rights. Rumors spread of a new royal plan to coerce the Assembly with troops; others warned of Louis' intent to flee and promote civil war or foreign intervention. Paris resounded with accusations: royalist officers had trampled upon the tricolor cockade at a banquet attended by the Queen at Versailles; bread shortages were arranged by aristocrats to turn the people against the Assembly; hired assassins threatened the lives of liberal Deputies. Such was the daily fare offered by the Paris press and orators at the political clubs. By the end of September, these repeatedly called for a march of the people to Versailles.

The "October Days" marked the second dramatic intervention on the part of Paris. Behind this action lay the long-accumulated resentments of the urban lower classes. From the petty bourgeoisie, through the artisans to the day laborers, all had suffered grievously from the economic depression then two years old. In a population of about 600,000, the workers of Paris, with their families, numbered nearly 300,000. Added to them were thousands of unemployed from the provinces who had come to the city in the hope of finding relief. Alongside bourgeois affluence, many lived in subhuman conditions, prey to every disease and vice that accompanied the proletariat in the early stages of the industrial and urban revolution. Yet there is little evidence that they shared a class feeling in the Marxist sense, or even any coherent political or economic aims. It is much more likely that the call to the Estates-General and the events of July had aroused in them great hopes for a general improvement in their lives and for the overnight disappearance of oppression. Instead, the continuing economic crisis had brought them only more unemployment, lower wages, higher prices, and a chronic shortage of bread, now more expensive than at any time in the memory of living men. In the previous fifty years, its cost had risen three times as rapidly as wages. Bread riots were common in Paris and other towns in the summer of 1789. By early October, popular misery and the agitation of the city's more radical political leaders set off the remarkable march of the Paris women—led by the formidable ladies of les Halles—to the palace of Versailles. Amid scenes of unprecedented turbulence, barely held in check by Lafayette and the National Guard, the royal family consented to move to Paris. On October 6th, a singing, shouting mob of thousands escorted "the Baker, the Baker's wife, and the Baker's little boy" to the Tuileries. Louis promised to see to the provisioning of the city, and accepted the August resolutions and the Declaration of the Rights of Man. The Assembly took up its residence in the Manège, a riding-school arena near the palace, where the rue de Rivoli now passes the Tuileries gardens. Paris had again forced the issue. Already the center of French economic, social, and cultural life, it now beçame once more the political capital as well, and—although it was not immediately apparent—the arbiter of the Revolution.

## THE CONSTITUTION OF 1791

The following months were relatively quiet; Paris and the provinces settled down, with the help of an ample harvest. The Assembly was free to complete its solution of the problem of government, which emerged as the Constitution of 1791, accepted by Louis XVI in September of that year. Given the divergent political factions contending at the time, the constitution achieved a notable compromise, one to which France returned in 1814, after twenty-three years of strife.

As constitutional monarch, Louis found his powers severely limited. His suspensive veto could, at most, delay legislation for two sessions of the Assembly—four years. He kept the initiative in foreign affairs and formal command of the army, but could not declare war or make peace without the consent of the Assembly. He had no right of dissolution, and his ministers, though answerable to the Assembly for their acts, could not be members of it themselves. A single chamber, to be known as the Legislative Assembly, held complete power over appropriations and initiative in legislation. In another reaction against the previous regime, the national administration was drastically decentralized. Eighty-three departments replaced the bewildering network of royal and feudal administrative units of the past. The intendants, royal officers with wide powers over local affairs, disappeared, their places taken by local officers, locally elected. Control from Paris nearly vanished, greatly weakening the authority of the Legislative Assembly in the crises to come.

In matters of suffrage and eligibility, the Constitution of 1791 was far from democratic. Hitherto, inherited rank and class privilege had determined the role a Frenchman could play in his government. Now it was property alone that mattered. Although nearly half the male citizens of France paid enough taxes to vote, they voted only for electoral bodies composed of very much wealthier men, who in turn elected local and national officers and legislators. Only some 50,000 held enough property to qualify for the electoral colleges. Thus the new privileged class was only one-sixth to one-eighth the number of the privileged nobility and clergy of the old regime. Here was an egregious violation of the spirit of the Declaration of Rights, and an issue that was to divide the constitutional Right from the Left and to disturb French politics for three generations. In the short run, it raised the radical factions in Paris and other cities against the constitution and its creators.

The moderate framers of the constitution, who had appeared radical in the spring of 1789, and who were to be castigated as reactionaries in 1792—men like Bailly, Mirabeau, Lafayette, and Mounier—were unable to preserve their compromise solution. Their failure ruined the prospects of orderly evolution from the old regime to a stable form of representative government in France. First of all, they lacked a king who was willing, or able, to play the role of constitutional monarch. As even the English had found, a century earlier, it was not an easy part to fill. Although Louis XVI was a better prospect than any of the Stuarts, his political naïveté, his sudden turns of heart, and his susceptibility to conservative pressure made him an untrustworthy executive. The royal family's flight to the east in the summer of 1791 all but destroyed the hopes of the moderates.

Even more basic a source of failure was the Constituent Assembly's treatment of the Church. The Civil Constitution of the Clergy, completed in July of 1790, had disastrous effects. Not only did it decide the King on his flight; it raised against the moderates in the Assembly a host of Frenchmen whose religious feelings should have made them the natural allies of moderation. Those who wished the political, economic, and social changes of the Revolution to go no further were irrevocably divided on the question of religion, greatly weakened for their ensuing struggle with the Left.

The problem of the Catholic Church, the oldest institution in France, was extremely complex; yet circumstances conspired to persuade the Deputies that any changes they chose to make would be welcome, or at least acceptable, to laity and clergy alike. The Church, if not religion itself, had been an easy target for the Philosophes in the eighteenth century. It possessed between one-tenth and one-fifth of the landed wealth of the nation before 1789. Privileged and secure in its alliance with the throne and aristocracy, the hierarchy was identified with all the abuses of the old regime, the more so as it usually maintained a discreet silence about them. Injustice, oppression, poverty, illiteracy, corruption, and speculation, the cruelties of social caste—none seemed to arouse the moral sense or critical faculties of the upper clergy, now exclusively noble in birth. Parish priests and churches were frequently left in neglect and poverty by bishops who rarely visited their dioceses, preferring the easy society of Paris or Versailles. Alongside the many who were diligent and religious men, however conservative, were a few whose lives were openly scandalous. After the silencing of the Jansenists and the expulsion of the Jesuits under Louis XV, the field of criticism and ideas was left more than ever open to the Philosophes.

Among the upper classes—even at court—it was fashionable before 1789 either not to take the Church seriously or to join the sport of ridiculing its wealth, its intolerance, and its indifference. The *cahiers*, even those of the clergy, had cried for reform. The lower clergy had been the first to desert the privileged orders in the spring of 1789 and had supported without a murmur the Declaration of the Rights of Man. During the night of August 4th–5th, the Church had given up its tithe; the Assembly had immediately undertaken to support the clergy, raising the income of the lower, reducing that of the prelates. The changes were widely praised. Even the gradual suppression of the monastic orders evoked little reaction; many of the secular clergy approved this elimination of rivals, as they had the attacks on the Jesuits some years before.

The first widespread opposition arose in November of 1789, upon the Assembly's nationalization of the church lands, done to save the government from bankruptcy. Old taxes had been disrupted, new taxes —on land, industry, and commerce—were insufficient, particularly as the economic crisis continued. Borrowing, inflation, and "patriotic gifts" hardly began to solve the treasury's problem. On the basis of the nationalized lands, the government issued *assignats*, paper bills, to pay its debts; and much of the property was put up for sale. The economic and social results of this action greatly benefited the Revolution. Although the *assignats* later suffered a severe inflation, they saved the regime from bankruptcy. More important, the sale of the lands gave thousands of new proprietors a vested interest in the Revolution. Although huge tracts fell into the hands of the already prosperous middle class or were cornered by speculators, title to much of the land ultimately came to rest in the peasantry, creating a large and henceforth conservative class of individual owners.

The reorganization of the Church necessitated by this action was embodied in the Civil Constitution of the Clergy, passed by the Assembly in July of 1790. Each department became a diocese; bishops and priests were to be elected by the citizens; the Pope was deprived of authority over episcopal offices; no papal pronouncements were to be published or preached without the consent of the civil authorities. The terms were logical to an extreme. The royal government had previously designated bishops with little interference from Rome; as in other affairs, it had abused its power by appointing unworthy men on the basis of their noble rank and financial contributions. Now that sovereignty had passed to the people, it was logical that they—like the early Christians, some Deputies said—should make the choice on the basis of known ability. The terms were also Gallican to an extreme. For centuries the French government had asserted increasing authority over Church affairs, denying papal authority in all but matters of dogma. But the legislation was a direct challenge to the Papacy and to the hierarchy of France, both by now assumed to be dangerously counterrevolutionary. In issuing it, the Deputies demonstrated their assumption that they and their more liberal priestly colleagues represented French Catholic opinion, and they gravely overestimated the discord between upper and lower clergy.

The majority of French prelates, either out of hatred for the Revolution or out of concern for the integrity of the Church, opposed the Civil Constitution of the Clergy. Others, with the King, hoped for a major revision of its terms in negotiations between the Assembly and a French church council or between the French government and Rome. On August 24th, 1790, Louis accepted the legislation, while secretly resolving on flight if revisions were refused. The resentment of the Papacy was known, although it issued no public condemnation before April of 1791. Meanwhile the Assembly, aware that contradictory advice was flowing to Rome from the French bishops, took a fatal step. On November 27th, it demanded that all priests and bishops take an oath swearing loyalty to the Revolution, including the Civil Constitution of the Clergy. The Deputies were astonished when two-thirds of the 70,000 priests refused the oath, following the lead of their bishops. In the spring of 1791, Pius VI officially condemned not only the Civil Constitution of the Clergy but all of the principles of the Revolution. The schism between the Catholic Church and the new regime was complete.

Even yet the Assembly was not prepared for what followed. While supporting the "constitutional" clergy, those who had taken the oath, it took no action against the "refractory" or nonjuring priests. The country as a whole took the issue more seriously. Many practicing Catholics, including the King himself, refused to accept the sacraments from the constitutional clergy and found themselves now bound in conscience to oppose the other works of the Revolution. Supporters of the Revolution felt bound in turn to silence the refractory priests who were endangering it. Towns, villages, and even families were violently split. Men who had hitherto been united on the principles and works of the Revolution now held each other in fear and contempt. In the following months and years, resistance brought government persecution of priests and their followers. Persecution only raised more violent resistance. Extreme begat extreme; and Frenchmen who might have desired both Catholicism and Revolution were forced to choose the one, resist and attack the other. In France, liberalism became synonymous with anti-clericalism and then anti-religion. Catholicism was identified with the old regime, not only in France but in all those parts of Europe touched by the Revolution and its ideas. The middle ground, embracing both, was a century in reappearing and is still suspect and contradictory in the eyes of many Catholics and liberals alike.

Those in the Assembly who had sought, and who now welcomed, the schism were probably in the minority: noble clerics of the Right who detested the Revolution, and men of the Center and of the Left who wished not only to destroy a feudal institution but to efface religion itself, at least in its Catholic form. The others, who had misjudged the religious feelings of their countrymen and underestimated the loyalty of the ordinary priests to their bishops, had erred in treating the Church as nothing more than an economic and political problem. Bourgeois men of city and town, they appeared to believe that religion was little more than a fading social habit. That the French Church, for all its outward appearance of decay, remained a spiritual force escaped their understanding. It was a tragic misconception, but one for which the eighteenth-century Church itself must bear a heavy responsibility.

At Easter in 1791, a mob prevented Louis XVI from driving to Saint Cloud, where it was assumed he would receive the sacraments from a refractory priest. In the middle of June, he fled his capital for the eastern frontier, there to raise loyal troops against the Revolution and perhaps to accept the aid of his wife's brother, the Emperor Leopold of Austria. Recognized and captured within sight of safety, the King and Queen were brought back to Paris from Varennes in a harrowing four-day journey, frequently halted by insulting crowds. Lafayette, wary of the radical working-class districts of eastern Paris, took the royal carriage around the northern edge of the city and down the Champs-Élysées. Crowds lining the streets were sullen and silent. Ever suspect, Louis XVI had now made clear his opposition to the work of the Constituent Assembly, both by his flight and by a manifesto he left behind among his papers. Though the Paris radical clubs and newspapers now demanded a republic, the Assembly majority tried to pay no attention. A republic, they feared, would mean their fall and radical control of France. In a last effort to save the constitutional monarchy, they adopted the fiction that Louis had been taken from Paris against his will. The King impassively played out the charade. In September, 1791, the constitution was voted, Louis accepted it, and the Constituent Assembly was at an end. The new assembly, the Legislative, met on October 1st and its make-up reflected a new political situation.

## THE LEGISLATIVE ASSEMBLY

The Right, as it was composed in the Constituent Assembly, was no longer represented in the Legislative Assembly. In its place now sat the constitutional Monarchists—followers of Lafayette and Sieyès. Mirabeau was dead, having spent the last few months of his life in the pay of the King, though probably holding to his own version of a representative monarchy. Bailly, the Mayor of Paris, could be counted upon for support, as could most of the units of the National Guard, at least for the moment. Of the 745 members of the new Assembly, about one-third belonged to the political club called the Feuillants, which had broken from the original Jacobin club (so called because the Paris group met in a former Jacobin monastery) when the latter turned republican in its program. The new Right suffered not only from discredit over the religious question and the behavior of the King, but also from a lack of organized support in the country. Local politics were already dominated by the Jacobin societies, from which Feuillants were on occasion physically expelled. The latter were also weakened by the loss of their experienced parliamentary leaders; the members of the Constituent Assembly had disqualified themselves from sitting in the Legislative. Moreover, their press failed to compete in either numbers or appeal with fiercely democratic sheets like Marat's *Ami du Peuple*. To the radical political activists of Paris, who often filled the galleries of the Assembly with organized claques, the Feuillants were suspect as aristocratic or bourgeois men of wealth who sought only security for themselves behind a traitorous king and a severely restricted suffrage.

The new Left was Jacobin and republican, led by a group called Brissotins, after their chief, Brissot, a choleric and romantic figure who had lived in England and America. Others of the group, like the orator Vergniaud, were natives of the Gironde and hence called Girondins. Their policy was to discredit the monarchy, to punish the *émigrés* and the refractory clergy, and to lead France into a republic. Supported for the moment by the Jacobin clubs and republican leaders like Danton, Robespierre, and Marat, the Left in general suffered less than the Right from the self-denying ordinance passed by the previous assembly. The new Center, forming the majority of the Legislative Assembly, was an uncommitted mass, determined for a variety of reasons that nothing of the Revolution thus far should be undone (this was to be decisive when war came), but not itself likely to press for republic or monarchy. As it turned out, it moved with the dominant current of the moment and that was, in the following months, the current of Paris.

Despite their disadvantages, the Feuillants held both Paris and the Assembly in check from the return of the King until March of 1792. Soon after the capture of Louis, a meeting of Republicans on the Champ de Mars had been forcibly dispersed, with over forty killed. Bailly, the Municipal Council, Lafayette, and the National Guard had cooperated to arrest a number of radicals and to close their newspapers, but the victory was not followed up. The Jacobins and the leaders of the poorer Paris *sections*, or wards, never forgave their one-time heroes. Under the leadership of Danton and others, the Jacobins worked successfully during the ensuing year to capture control of the Parisian municipal government and command of the National Guard.

The final blow to constitutional monarchy was the coming of the war in the spring of 1792. War, as always, polarized opinion and swept away what remained of the spirit of compromise and moderation. Whoever appeared to stand for throne or altar was attacked as an ally of the crowned heads of Europe, bent on destroying the Revolution. Men rightly suspected the Queen of encouraging foreign invasion, in collusion with the most reactionary of the *émigrés*, Artois. The European monarchs had at first little interest in restoring Louis XVI to a stable throne, much less to absolute power. Confusion and weakness in France freed their hands for the game of power diplomacy, particularly in Poland. The Declaration of Pillnitz in August, 1791, by the King of Prussia and Leopold of Austria, was an empty gesture. The sovereigns of Europe were "interested" in the fate of Louis XVI; provided all agreed —Leopold knew they would not—the powers would join to help him restore a solid monarchy. Marie Antoinette felt betrayed, but the French revolutionists, aroused by the Brissotins, took the declaration seriously. The Left, with the nearly sole exception of Robespierre, now opened its campaign for "a war of peoples against kings." What remained of the royalist Right—no longer in the Assembly but in the Ministry and the court—likewise saw in war a chance to capture power. The revolutionary forces, they reasoned, would collapse before the disciplined armies of Europe—particularly the Prussian—and France would beg her King to take absolute power and save her from conquest.

This familiar mating of extremes, under the rising clamor for war, had the desired effect. The Feuillants lost their majority in March of 1792. Brissot imposed a Ministry led by the opportunist General Dumouriez and on April 20th France declared war on Austria. The cautious Leopold II was dead. In his place was Marie Antoinette's nephew, Francis II, more impressed than his father by the danger of revolutionary sentiment at home and more confident in his ability to lead a crusade against its source in France. Prussia, goaded by German princes on the Rhine, some of whose feudal holdings had been abolished by the Constituent Assembly—in Alsace, where jurisdictions overlapped—sent an army under the renowned Duke of Brunswick. Frederick William confidently awaited victory and the annexation of Alsace and Lorraine. Fears of revolution spreading in Europe—stirred by the *émigrés* and, among others, Edmund Burke—combined with hopes for territorial aggrandizement to set the European sovereigns on the march against what appeared to be, and for a time was, a weak and demoralized French army.

In France, the war brought down the Feuillants, the monarchy, and the Legislative Assembly itself in rapid order. Nationalist and revolutionary feelings, united by the threat of invasion, exploded into a second French Revolution. On August 3rd, Paris received the news of the Brunswick Manifesto, in which the European allies foolishly threatened the entire city with reprisal if harm came to the King and Queen. It appeared to confirm all suspicions of royal treachery, further discredited the constitutional Monarchists, and opened the way for the most determined enemies of the regime. Popular excitement, anger, and fear rose with rumors of panic, defeat, and surrender (or treason) in the armies on the frontier. The recurring bread shortages and rising prices of late summer embittered the poorer quarters of the city. The press, now led in its violence by the extremist Hébert's *Père Duchesne*, waged a campaign of general denunciation of royalist and clerical plots which it saw everywhere poised to "stab the people in the back." Paris prepared for its third great "day" of revolution in as many years.

The year-long campaign of the Jacobins to gain control of the city government and the National Guard bore fruit on the night of August 9th, when a revolutionary committee ousted the legal Commune of Paris and placed one of their own, the brewer Santerre, at the head of the Guard. The active members were lower-middle-class men, shopkeepers and artisans, who called not only for the end of monarchy, but for universal suffrage and a direct political role for themselves. Their best-known figure was Danton, although he may have followed more than led in the actions of August 9th and 10th. The movement easily enlisted the aid of provincial Jacobin and Guard leaders, who had remained behind in Paris after the annual celebration of Bastille Day, as well as a body of citizen soldiers from Marseilles on their way through Paris to the front. These soon made good the promise of their fiery anthem, the Marseillaise. On August 10, 1792, they joined an armed mob that stormed the Tuileries, massacred the Swiss Guard, and imprisoned the royal family. The Left had attained its object; the constitutional monarchy was dead. But even in their hour of triumph the Girondins had lost the initiative to the radicals of Paris. In bringing war, Brissot and his followers had loosed the tiger. The fall of Louis XVI meant the end of the Legislative Assembly, which had given them their majority. The Girondins had no choice but to declare the constitution void and call for new elections, by universal manhood suffrage, to a new Constituent Assembly. The Republic was assured, but a new Left was rising, this time based on the revolutionary Paris Commune.

## THE CONVENTION

The Convention, named after its American counterpart, met on September 22, 1792, in an atmosphere of violence and fear. Events had moved quickly. Longwy and Verdun were lost to the enemy; there were redoubled accusations of treachery, especially when Lafayette fled to the Austrian camp. By early September, hundreds of political arrests had crowded the prisons with accused royalists and aristocrats. Amid rumors of planned outbreaks by the prisoners, to join with "foreigners" infiltrating the capital, small bands of armed extremists constituted themselves judges and executioners and moved from prison to prison, massacring the inmates. Between the 2nd and 10th of September some 1200 helpless victims perished, many of them common criminals, vagrants, and prostitutes. The Paris Commune officially deplored the acts, but did nothing, for several of its members were instigators. The minister Roland, whose wife was the self-appointed conscience of the Girondins, found patriotic excuses, as did other members of the party. Danton, Minister of Justice, Santerre, commander of the National Guard, and Marat, who led the city's Vigilance Committee in overseeing the prisons, found ways of applauding the acts they had done much to incite. The September massacres blackened the Revolution in the English-speaking world and deepened the fissures in all of European society.

When the Convention met, the Gironde—now the new Right—and its allies had elected enough members to organize the Chamber. Opposite them, taking seats high up on the left of the gloomy riding school, was the "Mountain," led by the Jacobins of Paris and those provincials, like Robespierre, who had endeared themselves to the city's activists by the purity of their democratic ideals, the fury of their anti-Royalist orations. The struggle between the parties began almost at once, the Jacobins more and more confident of their strength in Paris, emboldened by the applause of the press and the galleries. The Girondins depended upon support from the countryside, which they overestimated, and their successful prosecution of the war. On the 20th of September, the first victory of the revolutionary armies, at Valmy in the Argonne, forced the Prussian invaders to withdraw across the Rhine. The action itself was an indecisive cannonade; the Prussians suffered more from dysentery and lack of supplies. But the French armies had held their ground for the first time; and Dumouriez, identified with Brissot, became a hero. His victory over the Austrians in Belgium, at Jemappes in November, seemed to insure the Girondist ascendancy.

French victories in the field encouraged the Deputies, on November 19, 1792, to declare revolutionary war on all the "despots" of Europe, and to offer French aid to all peoples struggling for liberty. The Convention annexed Savoy and Belgium to France. French armies held the entire left bank of the Rhine and openly challenged English commerce by opening the Scheldt to free trade. England, already provoked by the conquest of Belgium and French threats to Holland, retaliated by seizing French merchant ships. Pitt, who had clung to neutrality against the sardonic gibes of Edmund Burke, was further pushed to war by the execution of Louis XVI in January, 1793. In Paris, Brissot and the Girondins, under pressure from the Jacobins, showed their crusading fervor by declaring war on England and Holland on February 1, 1793.

The contest between Gironde and Mountain for leadership of the Revolution sprang from personal rivalries and factional ambitions as much as from differences over means and ends. In such a struggle, the Girondins lacked organization and leaders skilled in political tactics, both in Paris and at the local level. Ever ready with the proper words, they lacked political thrust and stamina. No one ever expressed the ideals of 1789 more honestly than Condorcet, more powerfully than Vergniaud, more appealingly than Madame Roland. Their disdain for mere partisan conformity did them honor; but in a partisan battle with men eager to prove them unrepublican, every nuance or qualification could be exploited. During and after the trial of the King, the Girondins tried to postpone, and then to escape responsibility for, the sentence of death on which the Jacobins insisted. The fact that most of the Girondist leaders ultimately voted with the regicides did nothing to allay the suspicions of Jacobin Paris.

On January 16th–17th, Louis XVI was condemned to death by the margin of a single vote—the Bourbons could ever after claim that it was Philippe-Égalité's—and execution was set for the 21st. Early that morning, the King was taken to the Place de la Révolution, now Place de la Concorde, where the guillotine stood in the midst of an immense crowd of spectators. His last words were snuffed out by the drums of Santerre's Guards. Like Charles I, Louis died bravely and in that way, if in few others, served the cause of royalism well.

By the spring of 1793, the tide of war had turned and with it the political fortunes of the Girondins. In March and April, Dumouriez was defeated in Belgium, and, failing in an attempt to rally his army in the counterrevolutionary cause of the child Louis XVII, he went over to the Austrians. Brissot and his friends suffered in guilt by association. Soon afterward, the left bank of the Rhine was lost. The great provincial revolt of the Vendée broke out, stirred by the persecution of nonjuring priests and by the forced levy of troops for the front, though its circumstances were complex and involved at least as much local rivalries between countryside and town, between embittered artisans and revolutionary bourgeois, between small farmers and large. The Vendée was nonetheless seen as an attack on all revolutionary France, and once more Paris fell into agitation. To the fears of military defeat and civil war were added the violent demands of the workers for economic controls. Bread riots again erupted and the *sections* organized for action. The Jacobins quickly took their part, and, under the pressure of events and the presence of the mob, carried the votes of the center Deputies (called *The Plain* by the radicals) for a stringent new war program. It was at this point, before the purge of the Girondins, that much of the machinery of the Terror appeared.

The Left demanded price, wage, and currency controls; the requisitioning of food and materials; and exemplary punishments for hoarders, speculators, and smugglers. Later denounced as socialist by the enemies of the Jacobins, these measures were but early versions of wartime economic controls now familiar to much of the modern world. Although middle-class men themselves, the Jacobins took the opportunity to denounce the Girondins as tools of the wealthy and the profiteers, as careerists who heartlessly put their dogma of laissez-faire over the human needs of patriots. In March of 1793, a revolutionary tribunal was created to judge political crimes quickly and without appeal. In April came the first Committee of Public Safety—a war cabinet—with Danton at its head. His reputation as destroyer of the monarchy and organizer of the revolutionary armies was never higher. In the interests of the nation's security and his own, he made a brief attempt to reconcile the factions of Gironde and Mountain. He succeeded only in compromising his popularity with the Left, which sensed the tide in its favor and would be content only with a purge of the Convention and the downfall of its Girondist rivals.

The affair was quickly managed. With the encouragement of the Commune and the cooperation of the National Guard, now in the hands of the dependable Hanriot, a mob surrounded the Convention on June 2, 1793, and demanded the arrest of the "reactionary" Girondins. Under less physical pressure, the majority of Deputies might still have refused and saved legal government. Instead, they voted the arrest of thirty Girondist leaders. Soon many in the Right and Center resigned their seats and left Paris. The Mountain easily dominated the rump Convention and set about to organize its dictatorial control of

France. The show trial of the Girondins, staged in late October, was as vicious, silly, and obscurantist as any twentieth-century witch hunt or totalitarian purge. They were accused of every low act, from arranging Charlotte Corday's murder of Marat to personal immorality and petty thievery. All who had not escaped in June were executed, including Madame Roland. Her husband, still at large, committed suicide, as did Condorcet.

The fall of the Girondins marked the leftward extreme of the French Revolution, leaving control in the hands of a new Committee of Public Safety whose spokesman after July was Robespierre. The Committee and its allies in the Convention governed with the support of the lower middle class and artisans of Paris. In general, the same layers of society dominated the Jacobin clubs and communal governments throughout France. The regime was never socialist, though under pressure of war and economic dislocation it was willing, or forced, to appear more radical and egalitarian than many of its leaders would have preferred. Many wealthier Frenchmen were politically disabled by their earlier associations with Feuillants or Girondins and took little public part during the year that followed. But private property was not disturbed unless its owners emigrated or could be convicted of treason. Bondholders, though losing through inflation, had little reason to fear repudiation of the state debt. In sum, the bourgeoisie survived the Jacobin dictatorship and were ready, on its fall, to resume active control of affairs.

The lasting changes wrought by the Jacobin year were not economic and social, but political. Decentralization of government, one of the most prized aims of the *cahiers* and quickly accomplished in 1789, was reversed. The Girondin attempt to preserve local autonomy had made little sense in a wartime crisis, particularly as many departments were in revolt against the policies of the Convention. And it had only weakened them in their struggle with the Mountain by earning them the enmity of Paris. War and civil war, more than the ideas of Rousseau, defeated Montesquieu's ideal of multiple local bodies acting as buffers between the central government and the individual, preserving islets of freedom and encouraging popular participation in civic affairs and self-government. War ended the chances for decentralized government in France, a nation rich in local traditions, capable of the most fruitful variety. Apart from the other reasons for their fall, the Girondins' political solution—the dispersal of public authority—did not fit the circumstances of the day, any more than had the Feuillants' solution of constitutional monarchy without a monarch willing to be constitutional.

The circumstances facing the Jacobins in the summer of 1793 could hardly have been more perilous. The allied armies, although proceeding slowly, seemed everywhere victorious. The peasant revolt of the Vendée, reinforced by British and *émigré* agents, resisted all attempts to put it down. The fleeing Girondins had helped to raise Lyons, Bordeaux and Marseilles against Paris. The British had captured the seaport of Toulon. In Paris itself, more radical elements threatened yet another leftward coup. The answer of the Committee of Public Safety was a series of rigorous and repressive measures collectively known as the Reign of Terror.

## THE TERROR

In substance—Robespierre failed to see it at the end—the Terror was a wartime emergency government. In style and symbol and in occasional episodes it was one version of Rousseau's republic of virtue, a version that has done little honor to his memory. As an emergency dictatorship, the Terror was a success as history judges matters. The Dantonist Committee of Public Safety had sought a compromise peace; both it and its policy were swept out in July of 1793. The Mountain insisted on all-out war and found in the engineer Lazare Carnot an "Organizer of Victory." Aided by countless and now nameless patriots, Carnot and Prieur de la Côte d'Or put together the armies, the munitions, and many of the methods which carried the tricolor across all Europe in the next twenty years. In August the Committee decreed the *levée-en-masse,* calling the entire people to total war: all unmarried men between 18 and 25 to be soldiers; women and children and husbands to make munitions, uniforms and bandages; even the old men were to be carried to village squares, there to "rouse the courage of the fighting men, and hatred for kings." The Committee sent its own representatives to the provinces, with coercive powers to force obedience to its decrees, and to the armies, to watch over the zeal of officers. By the spring of 1794, French soldiers had reached the unprecedented number of 800,000. Like Danton, Carnot demanded audacity in tactics—to rush in masses, slash through, and rush again, without counting the cost. Bonaparte made his career in this army, as did most of his marshals—Ney,

Murat, Augereau, Soult, Davout, Marmont, Bernadotte, and Masséna. By the end of 1793, partly because of the divisions and selfish interests of the allies, France was clear of foreign troops. The revolts in the Vendée and Lyons were crushed. In 1794, France took the offensive, reconquered Belgium and the left bank of the Rhine, and penetrated the Alps and the Pyrenees.

To civil affairs the Committee applied the same determination, but with less obvious success. The Jacobin constitution of 1793 was never in effect, though its uncompromising democracy was to serve as a model for later years. As long as war lasted, government was to be left in the hands of the Convention, delegating its powers to the Committees of Public Safety and General Security. It achieved what was the most effective centralization of political power yet seen in France. The twelve who ruled the Committee of Public Safety were able, energetic, and, for several months, united in their work. By a law of December, 1793, all local authorities were placed under their direction. Their direct representatives in the provinces held far more power, and were more closely supervised from the capital, than the intendants of the old regime. The Committee of General Security commanded all the police of the nation, with unlimited powers to search out the slacker and the subversive. Yet in many departments this machinery barely achieved a truce and had the greatest difficulty in procuring men and supplies for the war.

It had, understandably, even less success in enforcing controls over prices and wages. The laws of the *maximum*, passed in September of 1793, encountered all of the ingenious obstacles and evasions familiar to our own times, and lacked the men and methods to overcome them. Yet unquestionably some good was done; food supplies were relatively well maintained and the *assignat* remained stable in value for that single year. The later laws of Ventôse (February–March, 1794) by which the property of "enemies of the people" was to be distributed to the poor, were in effect too short a time to have appreciable results. It is doubtful that Robespierre or his disciple Saint-Just contemplated an attack on private property in general, but something had to be done to meet a new threat from the Left.

Throughout 1793, working-class leaders like the fiery, republican priest Jacques Roux continued to denounce businessmen and property owners and castigated both Girondins and Jacobins for their favoritism to employers. Despite their show of concern for laboring men, the Jacobins had retained the Le Chapelier law of 1791, which forbade all associations for economic purposes, all collective petitions, and all strikes and picketing. As always, the legislation proved far more effective—and the authorities far more zealous—in stifling labor unions than employers' combinations. Likewise, it appeared that wage ceilings were easier to enforce than price ceilings. And employers were gratified to find that the Committee of Public Safety was ready to impress workers to break strikes on several occasions. By the winter of 1793–1794, the Committee felt it necessary to act against the new Left, now partly proletarian in make-up. Roux had been in prison since September; the government rounded up other leaders of the *enragés,* the have-nots of Paris and the provinces. At the same time, it arrested the leading Hébertists, named for the violent anti-Christian Jacques Hébert. Both groups were charged with plotting "counterrevolution" and guillotined in March of 1794.

Danton, alarmed by the *enragés'* agitation, and concerned for the safety of his friends in Paris, had returned from a brief retirement to aid the Committee in what he saw as a relaxation of the Terror. But in April Robespierre and his associates turned to attack their rivals on the Right, on charges of corruption, profiteering, and conspiracy with foreign financiers. Danton, whose popularity Robespierre envied and whose unorthodoxy he distrusted, perished with Desmoulins and others who had called for an end to the dictatorship.

The Robespierre faction had now eliminated its chief rivals and the way seemed clear to establish forever Rousseau's republic of virtue. In this, if not in the more mundane work of the Committee, Robespierre himself was the prime mover, assisted by young Saint-Just and the cripple, Couthon. Maximilien Robespierre had been educated in the law and the Philosophes as a bright young scholarship student from Artois. Elected to the Estates-General in 1789, he gained the reputation of an earnest and honest reformer, with driving energy and a gift for prepared oratory that made him a favorite among the petty bourgeois of the Paris Jacobin club. The triumph of the Mountain allowed him to turn his humanitarian zeal to action on a national scale. No other prominent leader in the Revolution was so clearly a believer in the "heavenly city," the possibility of attaining political and social perfection through the exercise of reason and virtue. For him, politics was not an art of the possible, a changing game of trial and error, but a science of the single and exclusive right, which men, naturally virtuous, could discover and practice if they only stood aloof from special interests and looked deeply into their consciences. There—and in the rational study of history and society—they would find the general will, the natural law of human behavior. Any state led by men who grasped it could never, by definition, be oppressive, for the general will was merely the collective expression of each individual's own true or inner will, if he could but see it. Yet in the imperfect society left by the old regime, innumerable local and selfish interests, factions, and cults stood between the individual and his vision of what was right for all and thus for himself. For Robespierre and his followers, the mission of the Terror was to clear the ground of these obstructions, to act as "the despotism of liberty directed against tyranny."

Unquestionably the Robespierrists felt themselves to be right. It was their strength and the source of their cruelty. Here was the meaning of their leader's vaunted incorruptibility. He had achieved, in their eyes and his own, that secular celibacy, the freedom from unworthy ties, which enabled a man to see clearly, unselfishly, the greater good. The reforms of the year of Robespierre were designed to create a wholly new environment, enabling all Frenchmen to know as surely as he the natural law and to practice virtue unhampered by the relics of the past.

Some of the reforms were unexceptionable and deservedly survived the revolutionary years: the metric system of measurements, the abolition of slavery in the colonies, and the decree of free and universal education. Other changes, some sponsored by the government and many more apparently spontaneous (or commercial), were little more than fads. Yet they suggest the mood and style of the day, later depicted by Anatole France in his novel *The Gods Are Athirst*. Kings and queens disappeared from playing cards, to be replaced by decently republican figures. Children's names underwent easily imaginable transformations; Louis became rare, Gracchus abounded. Good republican men eschewed the powdered hair and knee breeches (*culottes*) of the old regime and appeared *sans-culotte,* in long trousers and in that careful disarray which has become traditional for conformist rebels. For the virtuous republican woman, the high-necked white robe of the Roman Republic replaced, for a notably short time, the décolletage of previous styles. Some of this merely reflected, of course, the customary tastes of the lower classes of Paris and the provinces.

More serious were the attempts to mold the minds of citizens through the schools, the press, and the arts. Although censorship and indoctrination had appeared in various forms prior to 1793, they had been haphazard, much mixed in ideology and local in inception and enforcement. Only in the Terror was there a central government determined to police a nation and having a coherent dogma to propound. Teachers, where schools were still open, were chosen for their Jacobin orthodoxy rather than for their erudition. The year of Terror silenced the great and clamorous variety of newspapers, pamphlets, and periodicals which had appeared since 1788. Only dull official, and edifying Jacobin, sheets remained. The theater was on the one hand censored and on the other stuffed with works of Jacobin social significance.

Among the most curious, yet most significant, of Jacobin reforms was the revolutionary calendar decreed in October of 1793. The Year I was dated back to September 22, 1792, the first day of the Republic. Each week had ten days, which was logically metric, obscured the Christian Sunday, and gladdened employers. The months bore names describing seasonal weather or work: Vendémiaire, Grape Harvest; Ventôse, Windy; Thermidor, including parts of July and August, Heat. The calendar was bound up with the anti-Christian enthusiasm of the more extreme Jacobins, who had begun even in 1789 to surround themselves with a bewildering variety of civic and patriotic cults and ceremonies. By 1793 the most determined de-Christianizers led attacks on churches and believers in many areas. Much of the damage done to medieval churches (not all, for there were other revolutions and city-planners to come) dates from this period. Robespierre himself disliked their fanaticism on political grounds, fearing needless provocation of Frenchmen and foreigners alike. He also sought to create a religion of his own, the worship of a Supreme Being; this allowed a belief in God and the immortality of the soul, which he vainly hoped might reconcile Christians and anti-Christians. His part in its pretentious inauguration in June of 1794 only brought suspicion and raillery down upon him.

The most memorable symbol of the Reign of Terror was the guillotine. Although less than half of the 40,000 Frenchmen who were victims of the Jacobin dictatorship perished beneath its blade, most of the best-known did. Royalists, Feuillants, Girondins, *enragés,* Hébertists, and Dantonists followed each other to execution. Finally, as 1794 wore on, came Jacobins of the Mountain who had hitherto been exempt. As the foreign danger receded and civil insurrections were beaten down, the tempo of trials and executions continued to mount. Its wider justification ended, the Terror became an instrument of sectarian epuration, the punishment of those who betrayed too little faith in the republic of virtue. On June 10, 1794 (22 Prairial), Robespierre and Couthon offered a new law which further loosened judicial procedures, made death the only punishment, and threatened the parliamentary immunity of the Deputies. Fear gave it a majority, but now both the Convention and the Committee of Public Safety were divided within themselves.

After the great French victory of June 26th, at Fleurus in Belgium, there seemed less need than ever for the rigors appropriate to defeat and encirclement. The wealthy, the employers, and the merchants resented economic controls and feared the laws of Ventôse, which seemed to presage a collectivist turn. The poor and the laborers suffered again the annual shortages, made worse by the stifling heat of July, and bitterly opposed the Committee's attempts to stiffen controls on wages and on discipline in the workshops. Attempts on the lives of Robespierre and his collaborators brought vicious reprisals, without trial. Men as prominent as Carnot feared for their lives.

## THERMIDOR

During July, Robespierre's enemies combined against him in the Convention, their attack managed by Barras, Fouché, and Tallien, who had been among the most cruelly repressive of the Jacobin Deputies on missions to the provinces. Robespierre's speech in the Assembly on July 26th denounced a "new conspiracy" in the broadest terms; it only alarmed the members, who still feared his power over the Commune, the Jacobin club, and the *sections,* and stiffened their resolve to be rid of him. On the next day, 9 Thermidor (July 27, 1794), as Robespierre and Saint-Just rose to attack their enemies in the Convention, they were shouted down by a well-coached group of Terrorists and moderates, now united in fear and political ambition. The Convention voted the arrest of Robespierre and his men, placing them in the custody of the Committee of General Security. To meet the expected insurrection, Barras raised an armed force from the wealthier sections and some of the National Guard. That night, the Commune secured Robespierre's release but it failed to gather enough loyal Jacobins and *sans-culottes* to control the streets, although the workers' *sections* sent more men than might have been expected, given the Commune's treatment of their interests and leaders. Robespierre, outlawed by the Convention, was recaptured at the Hôtel de Ville and carried off to the guillotine. His brother Augustin, Couthon, Saint-Just, Hanriot, and over ninety others, mostly members of the Commune, followed him to execution in one of the bloodiest days of the Revolution.

Thermidor has passed into several languages, signifying a time of reaction and relaxation, the end of revolution. Although the men who led the attack on Robespierre had little intention of relaxing the Terror —several were more Terrorist than he—the Incorruptible had so much come to stand for all the machinery and atmosphere of the Jacobin year that his fall made relaxation a political necessity. Public clamor rose at once and the Convention acceded to its demands. The Paris Commune, already physically liquidated, was not replaced. Henceforth, the city was ruled not by its own chosen leaders but by committees of the Convention, that is, by delegates from all of France. The reign of Paris, dating from the October days of 1789, was at an end.

Moderates crept back to their seats in the Convention. Once-fiery Jacobins like Barras, Tallien, and Fouché showed their talent for repentance by leading the new majority in destroying the engines of the Terror. The two great comittees lost their wide powers and were diluted, brought to obedience by monthly elections. Amnesties freed hundreds of the victims of the Robespierrists, and the Revolutionary Tribunal was reorganized and directed against its former masters. The notorious Carrier, held responsible for the mass drownings at Nantes, died by the guillotine. The celebrated prosecutor of the Terror, Fouquier-Tinville, followed soon after, accompanied by those jurors of the Jacobin tribunal who had not fled in time.

None were better qualified than the ex-Terrorists to break the power of the Jacobin network they themselves had helped to build. In November of 1794, the Paris Jacobin club was closed after an invasion by young toughs encouraged by the Thermidorean leaders. The Convention purged provincial administrations, suspended the local revolutionary committees, and forbade the Jacobin clubs to correspond or to act in concert. As Marat's remains were hustled out of the Panthéon in February of 1795 (only five months after they had been ceremoniously deposited there), the Girondist Deputies regained their seats in the Convention and tipped the balance still more to the Right.

By then a spiteful anti-Jacobin reaction was in full cry. Bands of "Gilded Youth" roamed the streets of Paris—avoiding, to be sure, the inhospitable workers' districts—and assaulted Jacobins or any others they chose to label Jacobin. The enthusiasts, who a few months earlier had affected Jacobin simplicity, now paraded their disdain of the late puritanism in garish costumes and flippant manners which they supposed to be redolent of the old regime. The newly freed press and theater abruptly and profitably reverted to un-Jacobin frivolities and anti-Jacobin ridicule. In print and on stage, caricature Robespierres exuded hypocrisy and villainy. The virtues of poverty, purity, and republican fervor were proclaimed to be as out of date as the liberty cap and the plebeian *carmagnole*. Released from fear and tension, those who could afford it turned conspicuous self-indulgence into an occupation. From the spectator sports of tribunal and guillotine they moved to the pleasures of the table, gambling, and dance, the last now graced by the semi-nude fashions in vogue with the idle ladies of Thermidor. The leaders of style were Thérèse Tallien, named "Our Lady of Thermidor," the widow Josephine Beauharnais, and the wives and mistresses of the newly rich whose profits had escaped the watchful Robespierrists. The center of talk, for those who counted and for those who, like the lean young General Bonaparte, wanted to count, shifted from the austere Jacobin clubs to the salons in which these ladies tried to revive some of the charms of the old regime and, as at Madame de Staël's, some of its intellectual precocity. The war continued, but its battles were safely distant and the upper layers of Parisian society were setting a standard for many postwar euphorias to come.

Then, as in more recent Thermidors, the retreat of danger brought down the system of economic controls so much resented by the commercial interests. The laws of Ventôse, designed by Saint-Just to rescue the indigent, were expunged and the seized lands returned to their liberated owners or sold to the best-connected bidders. The Convention abolished the *maximum* laws in December of 1794, just as the annual food shortages began to appear. Prices soared, but wages and employment lost ground as the unusually severe winter hobbled production and trade in all goods. Speculation and monopoly went uncontrolled; the nearly bankrupt government printed new *assignats* to pay its most pressing bills. From all these pressures an inflation resulted that was nearly to destroy the value of all paper money in France.

The urban workers and the poor suffered from the disappearance of private and religious charities which the government, despite its promises, was unable to replace. Although the Convention requisitioned foodstuffs and attempted to ration bread in the cities, its efforts were of little help. Thousands died of the effects of malnutrition and cold. The new regime, by its reversal of Jacobin policies, by its apparent impotence and irresponsibility in economic affairs, managed in a few short months to revive among the have-nots of the cities a nostalgia for the days of Robespierre. Men who a year before had resented the economic policies of the Terror were now reconfirmed in their Jacobinism and infuriated by what appeared to them as a heartless and self-indulgent oligarchy amassing wealth by the manipulation of human need.

Twice in the spring of 1795, the poor of Paris rose in futile attempts to recapture what was already a legendary past. On April 1st (12 Germinal) a mob of women and children invaded the Convention, which was at the moment trying Jacobins of the Terror, including Barère, who had been an author of the *maximum*. They demanded bread, work, and the Constitution of 1793. But they had no leaders or armed support, and the Convention, defended by bourgeois units of the National Guard, was not impressed. After scattering the rioters, it voted to deport to the "dry guillotine" of Guiana those Jacobins who could be accused of instigating them.

Again on the 20th of May (1 Prairial) a large force of workers and their families cleared the Convention of all but a few Montagnard Deputies, who reluctantly voted all their demands, including the Constitution of 1793. The National Guard intervened once more and for the first time since 1789 regular troops marched in to occupy Paris and forcibly disarm the workers' Faubourg Saint-Antoine. The kind of revolution waged by the people in 1789 and 1792 was no longer possible. Paris of the Left, disorganized and leaderless, was overborne by superior force. The Convention decreed the Constitution of 1793 abolished forever and condemned hundreds of insurgents to death or deportation, including six Jacobin Deputies who had dared to conspire with the "new Terror."

The Thermidoreans seemed to be ushering in the counterrevolution. In the Pacification of La Jaunaye, they had already in February of 1795 come to terms with the Royalist rebels in the west, granting them a complete amnesty, the end of conscription, religious freedom, the return of refractory priests, and even indemnities to the leaders. Royalists and *émigrés* were released and given back their lands; many joined local administrations. Controls over Catholic worship were everywhere relaxed. A "White Terror" rolled through the south and west, with murder and torture of Jacobins, of their families and friends, and of new owners of nationalized lands. While the Convention was in part unwilling and in practice unable to stop these excesses, its leaders had no intention of allowing a Royalist seizure of political power. Even the Girondins who sat on the Right had, after all, voted the death of Louis XVI. Their aim was not counterrevolution but the creation of a moderate republic in the interest of property owners and of their own political careers.

Fortunately for the Thermidoreans, the Royalists largely crippled themselves. In June of 1795 the boy Louis XVII died in a Paris prison and the constitutional Monarchists who wished to turn back no further than 1791 lost their principal hope. From Verona, the Comte de Provence as Louis XVIII issued a totally uncompromising proclamation demanding the return of the old regime, with all its traditional privileges for King, Church, and nobility. The *émigrés,* supported by English gold, would hear of no accommodations and Provence had not yet developed that blend of guile and compromise that preserved his throne after 1814. In June of 1795, the long-expected military expedition of the *émigrés* from England landed at Quiberon Bay in Brittany. Pitt, whose political sense told him that only a limited monarchy could now succeed in France, gave only nominal support. The invaders suffered from all the internal divisions, jealousies, and ineptitudes that have since come to appear typical of such efforts. They failed to coordinate their actions with the experienced rebels on the spot, whose Royalist orthodoxy they suspected. The republican General Hoche easily defeated them and executed over 700 of the invaders who failed to regain their ships. Only then, characteristically, did the Vendée rise again and the Convention open a military campaign in the west that lasted through the year.

With dangers from Left and Right uppermost in their minds, the committees of the Convention proceeded to draw up the Constitution of the Year III, designed to make France safe for moderate bourgeois republicanism. As in 1791, the vote went only to those citizens who paid direct taxes, and to the soldiers. With the poor, the priests, and the *émigrés* eliminated, this left some 5 million out of 7 million French males eligible. It was a much larger number of primary voters than in 1791, but the property requirement for eligibility to the electoral colleges was set so high that only 20,000 Frenchmen fulfilled them. This provision, said one of the drafters, guaranteed "government by the best," by the educated, propertied men who had the greatest personal interest in a stable society. Yet by itself the constitution produced no rigid oligarchy. The widely shifting majorities of the next four years proved the system capable, according to the popular mood, of electing assemblies of Royalist, moderate, and even Jacobin temper. Contrary to the Constitution of 1793, no right of rebellion was recognized, nor any right of the poor to state aid. The citizen found himself confronted with a list of duties to his nation and to the property of his betters that ill-accorded with the pure revolutionary slogans still popular with orators in the Convention. For the first time, a bicameral legislature appeared: a Council of Five Hundred to initiate and debate bills, and a Council of Ancients, 250 men over 40 and sobered by marriage, to vote them. Beginning in 1797, one-third of the Deputies was to be renewed each year. The executive power rested in a Directory of five men with experience as officials or legislators, chosen by the Ancients, one to retire each year.

The Thermidoreans were well aware of the dangers to their own political careers in the constitution they had drawn. Together with the possibility of a resurgence from the Right or the Left, they had nearly as much to fear from moderates, new men likely to supplant the unpopular Conventionnels and to make life uncomfortable for the assorted ex-Jacobins, ex-Terrorists, profiteers, and office-seekers who had beaten Robespierre. Partly for these reasons and also to avoid the consequences of the National Assembly's self-denying ordinance of 1791, they decreed that two-thirds of the membership of the new assemblies was to consist of Deputies in the Convention. Although the new constitution won general approval in the plebiscite of August, the supplementary two-thirds decree passed by the narrowest of margins and only because many negative votes were simply ignored. Paris had overwhelmingly rejected it. The Right, which had expected, perhaps too optimistically, a victory in the first elections, was enraged. And the press and spokesmen of all factions derided *les perpétuels* who dared frustrate the will of the people. The Convention once more found itself in the midst of a hostile city. Through September of 1795 Royalist agitators worked to build an alliance of the discontented—this time among the more prosperous *sections*—and to prepare an insurrection against the assembly at the Tuileries.

# THE EMPIRE
# OF FRANCE

In the small hours of October 5, 1795 (13 Vendémiaire), Major Joachim Murat and his cavalry barely won a race with a battalion of insurgents on foot, and rushed the cannon of the Sablons camp to the beleaguered Convention at the Tuileries. Barras—again hastily appointed as General of the Interior to save the Convention as he had done in Thermidor—posted his troops in the narrow streets leading to the palace from the rue Saint-Honoré, whence the armed *sections* of the Right Bank would launch their attack. So short of fighting men was the Convention—perhaps 4000 against five times that number—that the Committee of Public Safety released and armed over a thousand of its Jacobin prisoners to bolster the defense. The ragged veterans of the Terror bore the brunt of the fighting at the Church of Saint-Roch until Bonaparte's artillery broke the rebel *sections'* will to battle. The Directory, offspring of the Convention, was saved in a short day's fight and the young Corsican general had made his name. The manner of victory was typical of the adventures to come, for both the regime and the man.

## THE DIRECTORY

The Directory is frequently passed over in relatively few words by historians who are seemingly impatient to leap from the austere heroic of the Terror to the grandeur of Napoleon's Empire. Yet its events and complexities, however tawdry, are among the most instructive in modern French history. The Directory was the fourth attempted solution to France's revolutionary condition, proposed by the Thermidoreans to achieve continuity for themselves and their policies. It has suffered from an extremely bad press, beginning in its own day and underscored by Bonapartist propaganda after 1799. Although its dismal reputation was in large part deserved, the men who took control of France's constitutional Republic at the end of October faced difficulties of an unprecedented order. The economy, the administration, the courts, and the police lay in near-chaos. Government revenue had fallen to the vanishing point, and with it all public services. Everywhere rose the loud and contradictory demands of every group in French society, envenomed against the government and one another by the fears, hatreds, and frustrations born of six years of revolution, war and civil strife.

To their extraordinary tasks none of the five Directors brought extraordinary gifts of statesmanship or breadth of mind. But—with the exception of the Gascon Barras, dubbed the "King of the Rotten," an indolent and unscrupulous ex-noble whose tastes for pleasure and political intrigue were equally notorious—they were relatively honest and hard-working men. Carnot, the Organizer of Victory, was the best known, and Reubell, an Alsatian lawyer, was probably the most energetic and dedicated republican. Letourneur and La Reveillière-Lépeaux generally followed Carnot and Reubell, respectively. For the first year they succeeded rather well in working harmoniously with each other and with the Councils, in which there were many able men and more disinterested patriots than the common reputation of the regime suggests.

Their aim was recovery, reconciliation, and stability on a center of republican moderation, and their best hope lay in drawing to themselves and their acts the support of the middle classes and at least the passive acquiescence of the peasantry. In this they had only marginal success. Lack of confidence in the permanence of the regime and lack of respect for the *perpétuels* hurt them from the start. Taxes were evaded, bond issues were ignored (except by speculators), and even a forced loan in 1796 was a failure. The Directory has been called a triumph of the bourgeoisie. This is misleading at best. The middle classes, in whose name the Directory claimed to rule, had many grievances against it. The inflation let loose in Thermidor continued unabated, ruining countless creditors, pensioners, and *rentiers* while enriching those few opportunists well-connected enough to take advantage of the collapsing *assignats* by buying national lands. Inside information, favoritism in war contracts, graft, and monopoly made fortunes for the few at the expense of all. In the government, the grand corruption of men like Barras and Talleyrand was an open scandal. Even more demoralizing to Frenchmen, perhaps, was the ubiquitous venality and petty graft of civil servants on all levels, who were plagued by low wages usually paid in next-to-worthless paper money.

The peasants were angered by the government's requisition of food (in return for depreciated paper) to feed the urban poor, who were in their turn angered by constant scarcity. The producers could only seek to recoup their losses by raising prices on private sales, another source of inflation. By 1796, production of all goods had fallen so low that those who could afford it would buy anything at any price. Profit lay so obviously in commerce that middlemen proliferated. The Directory lamented the many productive hands which turned to trade, further shortening the supply of goods and raising the price to consumers—a problem destined to burden the French economy to the present day. Although both the Convention and the Directory occasionally sought to restrict the most flagrant speculation—thus annoying even those who prospered—the results were meager and the Directory undermined its own efforts by its lavish handling of army contractors and moneylenders. The fall of the *assignat* (0.025 percent in 1796) and its successor, the *mandat territorial,* embittered both the creditors, who were paid in worthless paper, and the debtors, who were caught by the government's return to metallic currency in February of 1797. The Directory's frantic attempts to adjust values, to assuage debtor and creditor alike, only gave it the appearance of heartless toying with the fate of all. In the autumn of 1797, the government in effect repudiated two-thirds of the national debt, ruining thousands of bondholders and further undermining the confidence of those classes whose support the Directory needed most.

The exigencies of war and depression prevented the Directory, as they had the Convention before it, from allowing the free operation of laissez-faire principles so much desired by the bourgeoisie. The *maximum,* of course, remained abolished, as did the practice of requisitioning other than foodstuffs. Likewise, the government arsenals and foundries of Jacobin days were turned over to private enterprise—or rather, to that public subsidization of private profit so familiar to modern nations at war. But a high tariff was raised in 1796 against British trade; and, while it helped some fledgling French industries, it earned the resentment of traders and financiers who had hoped for better days. It was from these that the peace party, including Carnot and (while it was profitable) Talleyrand, gained support in 1796 and 1797. The war and the tariff slowed French economic recovery under the Directory, cutting off raw materials in such vital industries as silk. The government's efforts to compensate for these losses anticipated Napoleon's but were even less effective; subsidies, roads, canals, and technical assistance all suffered from lack of funds. In short, the bourgeoisie had little cause for positive enthusiasm in the years 1795–1799. It suffered the Directory through fear of the only alternatives that seemed possible until nearly the end of the century: the Jacobin Left and the Royalist Right.

In 1796 came the first threat of reversion to social democracy, or something worse. The continuing misery of the poor and the workers, amid the deceptive affluence of what passed for polite society under the Directory, stirred an alliance of Parisian Jacobins and proletarian activists to launch the "Conspiracy of Equals." Under the leadership of François-Noël "Gracchus" Babeuf, who is accepted by the Marxists as the first true socialist of the French Revolution, a comparatively small band of conspirators planned a *coup d'état* against the Directory. Babeuf's ideas, like those of his associate, the Tuscan Philippe Buonarroti, went well beyond the small-town druggist's paradise of Robespierrist equality among petty bourgeois and prosperous artisans. They envisaged the collective ownership and equal sharing of property in all forms. Thermidor and its aftermath had convinced them that class exploitation and conflict were inevitable until the power of the state should intervene to abolish private property and its evils. Their immediate program, however, was more modest. In deference to their Jacobin allies, they called merely for the return of the Constitution of 1793 and increased government attention to the needs of the lower classes.

The conspirators attempted to subvert the soldiers at the camp of Grenelle with the aid of funds from a few prosperous Jacobins. Betrayed by police spies in their midst, the plotters failed and were seized in May of 1796. Babeuf was executed a year later and Buonarroti was jailed for a time—one of many imprisonments and exiles for this remarkable man, who wandered over Europe as one of the first professional revolutionaries of the modern world. The ideas of *Babouvisme,* transmitted in Buonarroti's writings and ceaseless underground activities, were to influence many French republicans and socialists in the nineteenth century, among them Louis Blanc and Auguste Blanqui.

In the year between the arrest and execution of Babeuf, the Directory took every opportunity to repress and discredit the Left and its ideas. It is doubtful that such zeal was necessary. Babeuf's doctrine had found little mass enthusiasm; the leadership of the proletarian Left had been decimated by Robespierre, that of the Jacobin Left by Thermidor. In any case, Paris was firmly in control of armed forces obedient to the Directors. To meet these changed conditions, the Babouvists had developed new tactics: secret and disciplined cells, anonymous agents, infiltration of other societies and clubs, hidden caches of arms, subversion of police and troops. Although a failure in 1796, the new style of revolution was destined to a long and often successful role in European history, from the Carbonari to the Leninists.

The greater danger to the Directory was on the Right. During its attack on the Jacobins and Babeuf, the government had relaxed its persecution of priests, émigrés, and conservatives. These proceeded to take full advantage of the regime's unpopularity. Forming clubs and political committees in many parts of France—in Paris, the Clichy Club—a loose alliance of conservatives, constitutional Monarchists, and outright Royalists won a clear-cut victory in the first elections to the Councils in April of 1797. Only a dozen perpétuels were reelected, out of 216 who were candidates. The new majority was united on only two points: disdain for the Thermidorean careerists in the inner circle of government and society, and a desire for peace with England and Austria. In both, they evidently had broad support in public opinion. Among the Directors, Carnot and Barthélemy (who had replaced Letourneur) favored concessions to end the war, and hoped to oust the triumvirate of Barras, Reubell, and La Reveillière-Lépeaux in favor of more conservative men.

The new majority did not endanger the Republic. Its bourgeois members feared a Bourbon restoration as much as they desired peace. But their reform program endangered the careers of Barras and his associates and their peace policy endangered the gains that General Bonaparte had made in northern Italy. Barras' strategy—to divide and discredit his opponents—was only too well abetted by the conduct of the extreme Royalists. During the summer, the boldness of returning émigrés irritated the moderates and constitutional Monarchists in the Councils. Their public approval of attacks on owners of national lands, their flaunting of British financial support, were followed by foolish and uncompromising utterances from Louis XVIII. The Royalists in the Councils prepared indictments of the Directors. General Pichegru, President of the Five Hundred, was in the pay of the Bourbons and intrigued with Royalist officers to bring the restoration. What had begun as the electorate's healthy discontent with the Directory now assumed the look of a Royalist plot. Its chances for success were remote, but the three Directors seized upon it as a pretext to purge the Councils of their political enemies. Bonaparte had sent them General Augereau to insure military control of the capital. On the morning of 18 Fructidor (September 4, 1797), Paris was occupied by Augereau's loyal troops and the triumvirate announced its discovery of a conspiracy against the Republic. The electoral results in 49 departments were nullified, unseating almost 200 Deputies. Carnot fled; Barthélemy, Pichegru, and other leaders of the opposition were sent to Guiana along with several priests who had been active in the electoral campaign. Military tribunals condemned hundreds of suspects throughout the country. The coup of Fructidor preserved the Thermidorean trimmers, but they were now ruling under virtual military dictatorship and were more than ever in debt to the army, and to Bonaparte in particular.

The tack to the Left which followed these events included a rigid censorship of the press, theater, and books, renewed suppression of Catholic worship, and a revival of such Jacobin devices as the revolutionary calendar and republican civic services on the tenth day—everything, that is, but the substance of Jacobinism. There was no move toward political or social democracy, no rehabilitation of Jacobin leaders to disturb the bourgeoisie, whose recent defection at the polls had brought the crisis about. The Directors were wholly aware of their own unpopularity in a deeply divided country. Their original attempts to follow a middle course, to achieve stability through moderation, had failed in a society eager for repose but not yet ready for compromise. Thus they practiced not moderation but trimming and vacillation. Staying in the middle of the road and protecting their own careers and fortunes necessitated more and more frequent and harsh attacks alternately on Left and Right, which only eroded their own already narrow base of popular support.

Nothing illustrates more clearly the dilemma of the Thermidoreans than their policy toward the Catholic Church. Under the Terror, public worship was forbidden and even the constitutional clergy was attacked. Thermidor, although largely the work of such fervent anti-Christians as

Tallien, Barras, and Fouché, brought a relaxation of religious persecution, and the Convention's peace with the Vendée in early 1795 included freedom of religion. The Thermidoreans then proceeded to extend a limited toleration to all of France in the law of 3 Ventôse III (February 21, 1795). This law formally recognized the separation of Church and State, the logical sequel of the law of September, 1794, which had ended government support to all religious bodies. In theory, all cults were free to worship, all priests—refractory as well as constitutional—were free to officiate. In practice, the government retained title to all churches and most remained closed to Catholic services; public processions, clerical garb, Sunday closings were forbidden. But the leftist risings of Germinal and Prairial in 1795 produced further concessions to religion; the law of May 30th reopened the churches for use by all cults, republican and Catholic, on condition that priests take an oath of "submission" to the laws of the Republic.

This oath and the others that followed it opened a debate within the French Catholic community which persisted throughout the next century. On the one hand were those who believed that spiritual and temporal affairs, religion and politics, could be separated, that the form of government and even its philosophy should be of no concern to the priest. They asserted that religion could flourish under any regime, even one largely hostile, if the clergy refrained from political action and the government on its part allowed a decent minimum of freedom to worship. The chief spokesman for this point of view was the Abbé Emery of Paris. He and those who agreed with him were the forerunners of French liberal Catholicism; only in the late nineteenth century, in the papacy of Leo XIII, did their position find support from Rome. On the other side, led by the *émigré* bishops, were those who refused to admit neutrality in political questions, who doubted that Catholicism could coexist with a government dominated by an Enlightenment philosophy of man and society. They asserted that the clergy and the faithful owed allegiance only to a regime essentially Catholic and should actively work, in this case, for a Bourbon restoration.

For a short time, the Abbé Emery seemed to prevail. In the summer of 1795, the majority of French priests, both constitutional and refractory, took the oath of submission to the Republic. The *émigré* bishops protested, carrying with them a group of clerical intransigents devoted to the monarchy. Now the clergy was split into three factions, having already divided over the Civil Constitution. The intransigents were no less hostile to the "submissive" than the refractory priests had been to the "constitutional," refusing to recognize the validity of baptisms or marriages performed by men they called traitors. Unfortunately for the liberals—and for the experiment of separation—the subsequent religious policy of the Directory only strengthened the intransigents by making compromise seem impossible. From October of 1795 to its demise in 1799, it alternated between grudging toleration and severe repression of Catholicism. When threatened from the Left, the Directors sought allies on the Right by appeasement of Catholics; a revival of the Right was answered by persecution.

After the Royalist-led uprising of Vendémiaire in the fall of 1795, the government returned to a policy of harassment of all clergy and imposed a second oath, this time of "obedience" to the laws of the Republic. Conversely, the Babouvist conspiracy of 1796 ushered in, with the approval of a frightened bourgeoisie, another phase of relaxation which saw the abolition of all the anti-clerical laws remaining from the Terror. Finally, the *coup d'état* of Fructidor in 1797 resulted in yet another reversal, a vigorous anti-Catholic campaign which lasted until the advent of Bonaparte. The Royalist sympathies of the *émigré* clergy who returned after the Babeuf episode and their aggressive role in the elections of 1797 brought down upon all the clergy the most violent measures the Directory could enforce. The civil rights of priests were suspended, dozens were executed, hundreds transported to penal colonies. The government closed churches and sold them, at purposely low prices, to anti-clericals who would turn them to other uses or dismantle them. Over four hundred were lost in this way, including the great abbey church of Cluny, which was demolished for building materials. A minority of liberal priests sought in vain to temper the anti-clerical storm by taking an oath, dictated by the Directory, to "hate royalty." The intransigents heaped scorn upon them, and Royalist missionaries, organizing secret worship as in the days of the Terror, denounced them as heretics.

Meanwhile, the Directors tried positive means to educate Frenchmen to republican orthodoxy. The civic services of the *décadi* received new funds and instructions from Paris to popularize their programs. La Reveillière-Lépeaux sponsored a new cult of Reason called theophilanthropy. Neither enjoyed much success. The government's better efforts lay in education. It established central secondary schools in the chief towns of the departments, to substitute the study of republican ideas and institutions for that of religion. Despite their frankly political aims, many of these schools achieved high standards of instruction and their destruction by Napoleon was a grievous loss to French education. Despite the attitude of Paris, clerical instruction often persisted in the lower schools or, as in Stendhal's Grenoble, by private tutoring. Thus began the legendary confrontation between anti-clerical schoolmaster and Catholic priest that has enlivened French history and literature ever since.

Only the weakness of the Directory and the independence of its local administrators prevented something like a new Terror in religious affairs after 1797. The experiment of separation broke upon the hatreds left by the past. There could be no separation of Church and State without compromise, without a Church whose clergy was loyal to the State. Not even the most moderate bourgeois government could have accepted a Church dominated by prelates dedicated to restoring the old regime. And not even the clerical peasantry of the Vendée desired to return to feudal conditions. No accommodation seemed possible until the Church cut itself loose from the uncompromising Louis XVIII—or until the Royalists, together with the Church, accepted the end of feudal privilege and the land settlement of the Revolution. Paradoxically, the very weakness of the government discouraged any compromise. Both Left and Right expected its fall and their own triumph in all matters. Only a strong regime, giving an appearance of permanence, could force the mutual concessions necessary for a true separation of Church and State. But when that strength appeared with Napoleon, he chose instead to bind them together again.

## WAR AND CONQUEST

Despite its many projects and controversial acts, the Directory was mired in *immobilisme*. Prior impetus and other active forces dominated the four years of its life. Of the latter, the army was the most influential. Of mainly rural origin, the soldiers distrusted both extremes. The Royalists were allied with the enemy and would restore feudalism; the radicals of the cities lived by requisition from the farms and, like Saint-Just or Babeuf, dreamed of destroying private ownership. Generally republican in sentiment, the army of France was yet growing away from the rest of society. The slowing of conscription and its campaigns on foreign soil made it into a professional force increasingly loyal to its successful generals rather than to French civil officials, undistinguished and remote.

The overwhelming fact of the Directory's life was war. New prestige and power attached to the men who fought it and profited from it. The heroes of the day were not political figures like Mirabeau, Danton, or Robespierre but victorious generals like Hoche, Masséna, and Bonaparte. War discouraged whatever toleration might have been possible in French society. Liberty for difference of opinion, for human error or simple foolishness, for humanitarian impulse, was narrowed by the real and imagined needs of a country in arms. War and its problems held the main attention of the Directors, drained the treasury, and enriched the oligarchy of politicians and suppliers. Moreover, war had changed its character since the embattled days of the Terror. By 1795, France was no longer in danger; neither was she any longer in revolution. War had passed beyond defense and through a brief flurry of crusade into imperialism. By the middle of 1795, France had founded her satellite empire in Europe, four years before Bonaparte took power in Paris.

At the peace negotiations at Basel in April of 1795, Prussia had been preoccupied by the impending partition of Poland and consented to French annexation of the left bank of the Rhine. In return, secret provisions promised France's support for Prussian compensation among the minor and ecclesiastical princes of the Holy Roman Empire. This alone guaranteed difficulty in the near future with Austria and the Papacy. In May at The Hague, Holland delivered three provinces, a large indemnity, and guarantee of free navigation on the Rhine and the Scheldt. In addition, she was forced into an alliance against England, which brought her heavy commercial and colonial losses. In October, the Constitution of the Year III provided for the administration of Belgium as an integral part of France. Thus the Republic had attained and even surpassed the old ambition of the "natural frontiers," and seized territories much beyond France's traditional and cultural boundaries. Whatever Frenchmen might tell themselves, their foreign policy henceforth would be imperialistic in the eyes of most Europeans.

War or peace, a "greater" France or a smaller, became major issues between the Directors and their opponents on the Right. Royalists of all degrees and conservative bourgeois members of the Councils demanded peace, even at the price of withdrawals from conquered positions to appease Austria and England. The Directors felt bound to oppose them. In a society that had little else to cheer it, republican victories allowed

Barras and his friends to take refuge in patriotism. More important were the revenues to be gained for their impoverished government. The Councils consistently refused to levy sufficient taxes, both Right and Left seeking to force favorable policies by withholding appropriations. To carry out their program, even to survive, the Directors depended on the fruits of conquest and corruption. They bribed moneylenders with swollen rates of interest and favorable sales of national property; they promised army contractors a share in the spoils of conquered territory. In some cases, the suppliers of money and arms held what amounted to tax-farming authority in French satellites. Thus the Directors' wars and the generals who won them were essential to their political power as well as to their personal fortunes. After Fructidor, the support of the generals was more vital than ever; Bonaparte in particular was able to conduct French foreign policy in Italy without referring to Paris.

For his part in saving the Directory in Vendémiaire, the 27-year-old Corsican received the command of the Army of Italy in 1796. Only Austria and England remained at war with France, and Austria was to be humbled by a double offensive through southern Germany and northern Italy. Jourdan and Moreau failed in their campaigns north of the Alps, but Bonaparte enjoyed a series of brilliant successes in Italy and in April of 1797 was approaching Vienna. The Austrians dragged the peace negotiations through the summer, hoping for more favorable terms from the peace party which had won a majority in the Councils at Paris. But the Directors' successful coup of Fructidor, made possible by Bonaparte's dispatch of Augereau, forced the Austrian Emperor to accept the treaty of Campo Formio. In it, he recognized French sovereignty over Belgium and the left bank of the Rhine. In secret clauses directly contrary to those at Basel, Bonaparte promised that Austria but not Prussia should be compensated in the Germanies; and in a crowning act of cynicism he handed over to Austria the decaying but hitherto independent Venetian Republic, which he had attacked, occupied, and plundered—on his own and without the least provocation— in return for Austrian recognition of French conquests in northern Italy. Out of these, Napoleon constructed the Cisalpine Republic, supported his army from its countryside, and sent wagonloads of treasure and art to the Directors in Paris. Northern Italy, which the Directory had seen only as a theater of war against Austria, was now part of the French Empire, and the government in Paris was forced into an Italian policy it did not want and a truce with Austria that was patently unstable. The old Italian dreams of Charles VIII and Francis I were even more dangerous and less justified by national interest than expansion to the Rhine. But the Directory, trapped by its dependence upon Bonaparte, had no choice. It could not repudiate its most popular general and would not deny itself a share in the glory and the loot.

England alone remained of the first coalition, her finances severely strained by war, but still impregnable behind the Channel and her fleet. Anglo-French peace negotiations had broken down after the coup of Fructidor unseated the advocates of concessions in Paris. Talleyrand, who had become Foreign Minister before Fructidor and who had hoped to win personal profits from his exertions at the conference table (the Americans were ungentlemanly enough to publish his methods to the world after the XYZ affair), turned with the tide, attaching himself to the more aggressive Directors. Although he had opposed Bonaparte's treatment of Venetia and doubted the wisdom of Campo Formio, his letters to the Corsican proconsul in Italy were increasingly flattering. It was in their letters that the plan for striking at England through Egypt was elaborated. Such a campaign was hardly a bolt from the blue. French interest in the eastern Mediterranean was as old as the Crusades; in the late eighteenth-century the Turkish Empire already appeared loose enough to dismember. Likewise, French activity in India had already brought one struggle with the British, and ministers of the old regime had frequently talked of Egypt and the Isthmus of Suez as the natural path to the East. With Talleyrand's active promotion, Bonaparte was appointed Commander of the Army of the East in April of 1798.

The spectacular campaign in Egypt culminated in the battle of the Pyramids on July 21, 1798, where Bonaparte routed the picturesque Mameluke cavalry and captured Cairo. But ten days later, Horatio Nelson found the French fleet at Aboukir, destroyed it, and left the Army of the East without supplies and reinforcements. The Sultan refused to be dismembered and declared war on France. Bonaparte's march into Syria ended in defeat, plague, and a hasty withdrawal to Egypt. In July of 1799, he and Murat annihilated the army of the Turks at Aboukir, but the great dream of eastern empire had evaporated. Upon receiving news that the Directory was in danger at home, Bonaparte abandoned his army (its remnants were repatriated by the Treaty of Amiens in 1801) and sailed through Nelson's scattered fleet to France.

The failure of the Egyptian expedition did little to diminish Bonaparte's reputation, much to the disappointment of those politicians who had hoped to rid themselves of this formidable rival. On the contrary, the push to the East resulted in the second coalition and the reopening of general war on France, a war whose effects ultimately brought down the Directory itself. By 1799, Turkey and England had been joined by Russia and Austria in grand alliance against imperialist France. Apart from the attack on Egypt, the Directory had provoked the allies by further aggression in Europe. In Holland, French guns had set up the Batavian Republic, in Switzerland the Helvetic Republic, and in Italy, the Roman Republic, which expelled Pius VI. In December, 1798, the French overran Piedmont, sending the King in flight to Sardinia, and in January of 1799 French troops took command of a revolt in the Kingdom of Naples and turned it into the Parthenopean Republic.

In all, the pattern of French rule was consistent: a government modeled after the Directory, protected and dominated by French troops, and staffed by a minority of natives who were revolutionaries or opportunists and sometimes both. In all, the French took large indemnities in every form of wealth and partially introduced the anti-feudal reforms of the Revolution. The Directory made feeble efforts to restrain the appetites of its generals for plunder, but its agents were either rebuffed and sent away or settled down to make their own fortunes. In most cases French officials displayed little more interest in liberty, equality, or fraternity in their new territories than did their uneasy masters at home. Even among those peoples who had most reason to welcome a change of government, as in Italy, native patriotism grew in direct proportion to French exploitation.

In 1799, the entire string of Italian republics was swept away by allied victories, and by fall only Genoa remained in French hands. But Masséna managed to stop the Austrians and Russians in Switzerland and an English-Russian invasion of Holland failed in October. Although all Europe but Prussia was ranged against France, she was still in control of Holland, Belgium, and the left bank of the Rhine. The internal effects of the war were more dangerous to the Directory than the military situation. The elections of 1799, from which many conservatives abstained out of disgust over Fructidor, brought a Jacobin majority to the Councils. At once, the Jacobins proclaimed the nation in danger and proceeded to vote measures reminiscent of the Terror: increased taxes and conscription, a forced loan, and a law of hostages which threatened the families of anyone accused of disloyalty. From the newly opened Jacobin club, the Society of Friends of Liberty and Equality which met, appropriately, at the Manège, the Left demanded a return to the Constitution of 1793. By the end of June, 1799, all of the Directors but the pliant Barras had been purged by the Councils and in their places sat men thought to be favorable to a democratic republic.

## THE ADVENT OF BONAPARTE

The Directory of the Thermidoreans was overthrown, then, by a revived Jacobin party. But the Left was unable to organize and preserve its victory. The Jacobins lacked effective leadership and, more significantly, they lacked influence with the police and soldiers who held Paris helpless in their grasp. The moderates and conservatives who had so despised the late Directors quickly rallied to restore a regime favorable to their own interests. The Abbé Sieyès, whose disdain for the Directory had been mistaken for Jacobinism, emerged as the most active of the new Directors. Around him gathered a group of moderates and Thermidoreans eager to create a government of authority. Sieyès' famous formula, combining authority from above and confidence from below, meant a revision of the constitution to strengthen the executive. But legal revision would take time and anything might emerge from the coming elections of 1800. What was needed was a general who would support a coup and then keep order while the political system was remade according to Sieyès' prescription.

Under the threat of a reviving Jacobinism, and with new Royalist troubles in the west, the plotters had little difficulty in finding allies. Among the Directors, Sieyès secured the help of Roger-Ducos and bought the consent of Barras. Fouché, as Minister of Police, prepared the way by closing the Jacobin club and harassing its press. In the Council of Ancients, a majority could be found for a constitutional change, though not necessarily for an illegal change and clearly not for a military dictatorship. The Council of Five Hundred was the most important obstacle. But the self-styled Jacobin Lucien Bonaparte had been elected its presiding officer and was prepared to use his post to whatever advantage might be possible. Talleyrand acted as emissary to Napoleon Bonaparte, who had landed at Fréjus on October 9, 1799. The thirty-year-old general was the most flamboyant and the most ambitious officer that Sieyès could have chosen. But his earlier choice, Joubert, had been killed in Italy that summer and others, like Bernadotte, who was Minister of War, were too republican to be relied upon. Bonaparte was popular and he had assured Talleyrand of his sincere desire for sane and stable government. All agreed that it was to be a strong, non-Jacobin, center regime capable of meeting all dangers, domestic and foreign, without disturbing the interests of the bourgeoisie—Thermidor with a sword. War contractors like the wealthy Ouvrard supplied the needed funds.

By November of 1799, French victories in Holland and Italy had removed the threat of invasion. The Royalist uprisings had failed and Sieyès had succeeded in nullifying most of the Councils' emergency laws. The immediate crisis was past. But the memories of Terror and White Terror and the fears of Left and Right were real enough. Sieyès easily persuaded the necessary notables in the Council of the Ancients that a Terrorist plot was threatening society, the more so as a Jacobin victory seemed likely in the elections of 1800. On 18 Brumaire (November 9, 1799) a rump of the Ancients moved the Councils to Saint Cloud, "for safety." The conspirators themselves were now safe from the unpredictable Paris mood. Bonaparte received command of the troops in the district; Sieyès, Barras, and Roger-Ducos resigned and the other two Directors, Gohier and Moulin, were confined to Luxembourg Palace. The Directory had disappeared and the way was open for an emergency government.

On 19 Brumaire, Bonaparte's troops surrounded the meeting halls at Saint Cloud. But when he appeared before the Five Hundred to ask for emergency powers, he was furiously denounced and ejected from the Chamber. The Deputies would have outlawed him had not his brother Lucien delayed a vote and then summoned the Guard to clear the room of "traitors" who would attack a general of France; the constitutional Republic expired in a hasty flight of Deputies. That night a remnant of the Councils voted power to three men, called Consuls, to prepare a new constitution: Roger-Ducos, Sieyès, and Bonaparte. Few of them doubted who would rule France. Edmund Burke's educated guess had predicted rightly the fate of the Revolution; the fifth solution was military dictatorship.

The coup of Brumaire was accepted peacefully by the nation as a whole. For Frenchmen who had never lived under its occupation, the army had something heroic, clean, and healthy about it, a promise of relief from the rottenness of the Directory. It was not the only time that something approaching a puritan reaction was to benefit a military authoritarian come to rescue the innocent and right-thinking from unwholesome politicians. The Directory had few mourners. Unlike each of the earlier phases of the Revolution, it was never exalted as a model by later parties contending for power. But its devices and stratagems were timeless, and endured.

The Directory's bad press was partly due to the preoccupation of contemporary observers with the pungent high life of Thermidorean society. But Paris, with its elegant thugs and brazen ladies, was not all France. Compared with the strife of the Terror, much of the country enjoyed a measure of recuperation, a breathing time. What looked like, and often was, self-indulgence, reaction, and the grossest profiteering was also a time of rest and revival for millions of common men on the land. Those with something to sell—apart from their own labor—did not fare badly from inflation and many a plot of land was quickly paid for in depreciated paper willingly handed over for food. Thermidor and the Directory have been compared with the American Jazz Age following World War I. The comparison is justified in at least one way: the masses of common people who did the two nations' work shared little in the splendor or the rot.

It is said that Napoleon Bonaparte created order out of chaos; better, perhaps, to say that he found a desire for order, even plans for order, and gave them power. For the Directory not only had established an empire and a method of governing it, but had sketched out the main institutions that Napoleon's regime was to live by. The loose and quarrelsome alliance of bourgeois moderates and political careerists who made the Directory knew what they wanted: a uniform and productive tax system that yet would not discomfit property owners; internal peace and improvements in transport and communications; laws and courts both honest and consistent; a stable and respected currency; government encouragement of production and trade combined with government discouragement of expensive social innovations on behalf of the poor, whether idle or working; a national system of sober education. The Directory had prepared all of these ingredients of bourgeois liberalism, had even inherited some in being, such as the ample restrictions on working-class association and on public charity. After Fructidor, it had made a modest start on education, justice, tax, and currency reform. Bonaparte brought all these to fruition—albeit very much in his own style—and completed the foundation of the bourgeois French state.

The man who at thirty became First Consul of the French Republic was born on Assumption Day, 1769, at Ajaccio, a year after the feeble Genoese Republic sold its rebellious island to France, and five months after the forces of Louis XV crushed the native Corsican uprising led by Pasquale Paoli. As a son of the lesser nobility, Napoleon Bonaparte received a scholarship to the royal military school at Brienne, studied a year at the École Militaire in Paris, and in 1785 was commissioned second lieutenant of artillery. Like many others who have won fame in politics and the other arts, he was in these early years an outsider. His stature, his speech, his manners, and his poverty set him apart. In turn, he had contempt for many of his classmates, the frivolous sons of privileged nobles, and for the obtuse inefficiency of the royal government. Books sharpened his antipathy and revealed what men of ability could do when times were right. His quick mind and excellent memory fed on histories of the ancient empires, the heroes of Plutarch, and the greater days of France under Charlemagne and Louis XIV; to these he added the Philosophes, Montesquieu, Mably, Voltaire, and that other outsider, Rousseau. Almost too soon, the Revolution of 1789 opened his way to fortune and unequaled glory.

His ambition led him back to Corsica, where he failed in his first political adventure. Paoli, fighting for an independent Corsica, defeated Napoleon's attempt to seize Ajaccio in 1792 at the head of a band of pro-French volunteers, and again in 1793. Returning to France, Bonaparte paraded his Jacobinism, was promoted to major of artillery, and won the favor of Robespierre's brother Augustin. In December of 1793, he placed his batteries so well at the siege of British-held Toulon that his superior, General du Teil, gave him credit for a share in the victory. At twenty-four, he was a brigadier and planning an offensive in Italy when Robespierre's sudden fall threatened his career. But in Thermidorean Paris he attached himself to Barras, the last man to quibble over another's past associations. Vendémiaire brought him the rank of major general and the hand of Josephine, widow of the guillotined General Beauharnais and one of Barras' mistresses. Within four days of their marriage, Napoleon Bonaparte rode off to Italy and the command of the southern campaign against the Austrian Empire. Victory in Italy and the treaty of Campo Formio made him a national hero. Some in Paris no doubt felt relief on his departure for Egypt and rejoiced at his failure there, but Napoleon's luck held and what should have been a fiasco shed an exotic luster upon the young soldier. His return meant the end of the Directory and the beginning of a fifteen-year adventure that would close the Revolution and leave ineradicable marks on the mind and body of France.

## NAPOLEON AND FRANCE

Abbé Sieyès' project for the new constitution cast its author in the role of an omniscient Grand Elector who would choose all of the senior officials for the perfect regime. In choosing Bonaparte as his sword, he had elected far less and far more than he had foreseen. Napoleon rejected Sieyès' constitution and substituted one in which the First Consul held all power in his own hands. Sieyès and Roger-Ducos were induced to resign, their places taken by Lebrun and Cambacérès, competent men but content to serve as silent partners. The Constitution of the Year VIII (December, 1799) embodied Sieyès' theory of "authority from above, confidence from below" behind the façade of popular sovereignty. Universal manhood suffrage—except for domestic servants and criminals—meant only that ordinary Frenchmen could list "trustworthy citizens" from whom the First Consul could, in effect, choose all government officials from judges to Deputies. The Corps Législatif could vote on bills but neither initiate nor discuss them. The Tribunate might discuss but could not vote. The Senate in theory vetoed bills and advised the executive; in practice it helped to distribute offices to deserving supporters.

The most active body, the only one destined to preserve its functions (and, after Napoleon, to enlarge them), was the Council of State. This panel of carefully chosen experts—Sieyès advised Napoleon in their appointment—prepared legislation and supervised the entire machinery of government from the work of the ministers who headed the executive departments down to that of petty local officials. It became the heart and head of the bureaucracy and has remained so to this day, a power unto itself whenever the elected government of France has lacked the vigor to restrain it. Extraordinarily useful to all governments and a guarantor of continuity in troubled times, it has often obstructed needed changes in better times. It was the epitome of what Napoleon proudly called his "blocks of granite," institutions so solid that no future political storm could level them. Through it moved Napoleon's most distinguished officials, drawn from all political factions so long as their loyalty and competence were demonstrated to his satisfaction. The Council of State was the Empire in miniature, from its personnel to its efficient inflexibility.

The remains of local government, which had enjoyed a temporary revival under the Directory's uncertain hand, were swept away. Napoleon capped the long and often-interrupted process of centralization in France that dated from Louis the Fat and before. The executive in Paris chose the prefects, subprefects, and mayors. The elected local Councils of Notables met only fifteen days each year, just long enough to incur popular blame for dividing among the communes the direct tax assessments whose total was decreed from Paris. The powers, wisdom, and loyalty of Napoleon's prefects have no doubt been exaggerated, but the system was an obvious improvement and has persisted. Like the Council of State, it has more often been accused of rigidity than of laxity or corruption, but its stifling effect on local political experience and initiative has been immeasurable.

Of Napoleon's monoliths, the codes of law were perhaps the most impressive to his generation. The Civil Code of 1804, afterward known as the Code Napoléon, drew upon the earlier work of the revolutionary assemblies. Cambacérès had submitted drafts to both the Convention and the Directory and again helped in the later stages. Napoleon himself often intervened, usually in behalf of strict paternal authority in family and state. In one brief volume, which was translated into most European languages, the principles of civil equality, religious toleration, and liberty of private property were carried through Europe by conquest and example. In whole or part it survived Napoleon's fall in much of Europe, its usefulness recognized by authorities that were neither revolutionary nor enlightened. Together with a Code of Procedure, a Code of Commerce, and a stern Criminal Code, it offered a great advance over the tangle of contradictory and arbitrary practices of the old regimes. But it did not fulfill the ideals of the more liberal Philosophes.

Apart from the Civil Code's discrimination against women and minors in most matters, it deprived workmen of equal treatment in court. Article 1781 declared that the master's word would be taken against the worker's on the rate and payment of wages. The Penal Code of 1810 reinforced the Le Chapelier law of 1791, forbidding associations of employers and employees but reserving the harsher penalties for the latter. Likewise, no principle of civil equality prevailed against the return of slavery to the French colonies in 1802. Torture remained permissible in some cases of criminal procedure and, throughout the courts, the advantage lay with the prosecution and the State against the defense and the accused individual.

The codes, like the rest of Napoleon's domestic program, reflected his own view of the good society: order and stability underpinning national power wielded by men who were firm, competent, and patriotic, that is, loyal to him. He had no faith in the common run of men and his memory of Louis XVI's humiliation at the hands of the mob in 1792 filled him with aversion for democracy. After ten years of disorder, Frenchmen appeared ready to accept a diminution of liberty—which for most of them had never been real—in return for security. Napoleon thus enjoyed the advantages of Henry IV and Louis XIV after the religious wars and the Fronde, and his program for order was more far-reaching than either's could have been. On the negative, ostensibly short-run side, he employed police repression, exemplary justice, and censorship to stifle opposition in all forms; on the positive side, a campaign to reconcile Frenchmen to each other and to himself through religion, education, public honors, economic well-being, and national glory.

Joseph Fouché, ex-Oratorian brother, ex-Hébertist, ex-Terrorist, ex-Thermidorean, won his reward for Brumaire in the Ministry of Police. His spies were reputed to be everywhere, an impression he did nothing to diminish. Night arrests, intercepted mail, and refined methods of interrogation uncovered plots that were real and others that were only convenient. In 1800, Royalists led by Georges Cadoudal of the Vendée narrowly missed Napoleon with a bomb. But it was the unwary Jacobins who suffered; dozens whom Napoleon feared were sent to die in Guiana. In 1803, Cadoudal tried again but was caught and executed; General Pichegru was implicated and died by strangulation in his cell. Now Napoleon struck at the Right. The young Royalist Duc d'Enghien of Bourbon-Condé was kidnaped from his home in Baden, outside French territory, and murdered at Vincennes, innocent in the eyes of all, including his captors. Disturbances—they hardly qualified as revolts— in the Royalist back country met quick repression. Opposition in word was no less efficiently stifled. Only 13 of over 70 Paris newspapers survived the decree of April, 1800, and they were allowed to print only what was favorable to Napoleon. All but three perished before the Empire fell. Books and the theater were similarly cleansed of disturbing thought. Benjamin Constant and 20 others were purged from the Tribunate for questioning the quality of justice in political trials. Even the salons felt Bonaparte's rigor; the voluble Madame de Staël was banished from Paris for not appreciating enough the new model society.

For the formation of right thoughts, there were two more "blocks of granite": a new system of education and a docile Catholic Church. Napoleon had no religious belief but a political belief in religion as necessary to social peace; society meant inequality of wealth and the masses of men would accept it only with the hope of eternal equality to come. Once reconciled to the regime, he boasted, his priests would join his police in generating contentment. Peace with the Church would deprive his Bourbon enemies of their exclusive claims to God's approval and thus to the loyalty of bishops, priests, and millions of Frenchmen who had shown their tenacity of faith. Napoleon would employ no less a power than the Pope against the Royalist hierarchy on one hand and the minority of liberal clergy on the other. Negotiations with Pius VII ended with agreement in 1801. In 1802, over the objections of Royalist clericals and Jacobin anti-clericals, and to the dismay of Protestants, Jews, and those few liberal Catholics who preferred separation, Napoleon announced his Concordat with Rome.

Vital to Napoleon's interests was the Pope's concession to him of the power to name new bishops, who would then be consecrated by the Holy See. Barring a serious quarrel between the two authorities—for the Pope gained the right to demand the resignation of bishops—this provision brought the Church in France under the control of a self-styled republican government solemnly accepted by Rome as properly Catholic. Another concession, fully as vital, won the Pope's assent to the earlier nationalization of Church property. The bourgeois and peasant owners were thus relieved of fears that had haunted them for a decade. Pius VII, hard-pressed by French victories in northern Italy, gained little in return save for his satisfaction in ending the schism, in seeing the eldest daughter of the Church return to orthodoxy. Catholic worship, including processions, was again to be free and public. The Sabbath and the Gregorian calendar were revived, seminaries reopened, and religious orders, including the Jesuits, returned to France. Catholicism was declared to be the religion of "the great majority of French citizens"—and of the Consuls.

As in the Civil Constitution of the Clergy, the government paid the salaries of all priests and also of the Protestant and Jewish clergy. Toleration of all sects was guaranteed, but the sermons and publications of all were as rigorously censored as the government could manage. A set of Organic Articles added by Napoleon after the signing took more than full advantage of the Concordat's Article 16, in which the Pope recognized in the First Consul "the same rights and prerogatives which the old government enjoyed," that is, the Gallican autonomy of the Church in France, won by Louis XIV in 1682. No papal bulls, no papal legates, no decrees of "foreign" councils were to be admitted without prior approval of the State; all clerical and religious matters were to be minutely regulated by the government and its prefects.

Quarrels soon arose over Napoleon's choice of prelates and his restrictions on religious ceremonies and education. Official interference discredited Bonapartist Gallicanism among the clergy and the end result was a strengthening of papal prestige, a turning of French Catholics to appeals "over the mountain" (ultra-montanism) to Rome. Pius VII was a simple but tenacious man. Amid growing exasperation on both sides, he refused to give up his neutrality in foreign affairs. Napoleon responded in 1809 by annexing the Papal States, blandly reclaiming the "fiefs" granted by his predecessor Charlemagne, and denouncing the Pope's temporal power as alien to the "simplicity, charity, and truth of the faith" as Jesus Christ had founded it. Pius refused to consecrate Napoleon's appointed bishops and in 1809 excommunicated the Emperor. His reward was arrest and imprisonment at the Palace of Fontainebleau. By 1814, on Napoleon's fall, the Papacy enjoyed the sympathy and subservience of the French clergy, which was—despite and because of all Napoleon's efforts—more Royalist than ever.

The Concordat has been blamed for many of the weaknesses of the French Church in the nineteenth century and for the growth of anti-clericalism in French society, up to what most historians agree was a Catholic revival after 1905, when the Third Republic legislated the separation of Church and State. Either too docilely tied to the ruling elite, as under the Bourbons (1814–1830) and the Second Empire (1852–1870), or given to an exaggerated ultra-montanism under less friendly regimes, the Church in France often neglected the complex problems of its own rapidly changing society and the human needs of men, particularly in the new urban centers. Undoubtedly its close association with turbulent and vindictive French politics seriously compromised its spiritual authority. And, as under the old regime, it is difficult to say whether official favor or official hostility was more harmful to its essential mission. Yet the Concordat was not alone responsible. The new spiritual and social vigor which accompanied—and, significantly, preceded—its abrogation in 1905 resulted as much from a change in the character of the Papacy and from new men and new views in the French hierarchy. Napoleon had no interest in the spiritual quality of the Church and no desire to see churchmen meddling in social questions. If the Concordat failed to win him the loyalty of the French Church, the fault lay less with its terms than with his quest for total authority in every realm of human life.

In education as elsewhere, Napoleon's influence meant greater paternalism and centralization. Only primary education was left to local control. The greater prosperity of the nation and the return of the clergy reversed to some extent the decay these schools had suffered during the preceding decade. But without financial support from Paris, primary education was nowhere adequate to the need, and the rate of literacy barely progressed. For the sons of the wealthy and the favored, and some few thousand holders of scholarships for the talented, Napoleon organized a highly centralized system of secondary schools called *lycées*. These replaced the Directory's promising Central Schools and featured a stern classical curriculum, accompanied by military drill, uniforms, and soldierly etiquette. In 1808 appeared the Imperial University, a government bureau whose Grand Master was theoretically the absolute dictator of education on all levels. In practice, it meant a needless rigidity of curricula and, under the Catholic Royalist Louis Fontane, increased authority of the bishops in education.

The Empire continuued, in some aspects of higher education, the brilliant beginnings of the old regime and the Convention. In 1793, the latter had enlarged the functions of the Jardin du Roi and renamed it the Museum of Natural History. It offered research and instruction in the natural sciences under such men as Cuvier, Saint-Hilaire, Lamarck, Lagrange, and Laplace. The royal schools of engineering and mining were reopened and grouped around the new (1795) École Polytechnique, destined to provide France and Europe with thousands of well-trained scientists and engineers. Napoleon injected new funds, if not at first new life, into the Convention's École Normale Supérieure, ostensibly for the training of teachers but also one source of France's intellectual elite ever since. In 1795 the Convention had also created the Institut de France, which replaced the seven royal academies. Napoleon's contribution here was characteristic. He revived the conservative Académie Française and closed the Institut's section in moral and political science. The Collège de France, formerly the Collège Royal, offered public lectures on various subjects throughout the Revolution. These subjects were severely restricted by Napoleon, who sought only what he conceived to be of practical utility to the Empire.

Napoleon's attempts to organize education as indoctrination—there was even a saccharine, pseudo-Christian "Imperial Catechism" teaching loyalty to the Emperor—and to impose an army-like discipline on teachers and students gave an outward appearance of loyal orthodoxy and did provide large numbers of civil and military technicians. Whether these are enough to sustain any society is another question. Napoleon later admitted that the men of 1812 were not the men of 1792; it has been taken as an indictment of his own drill-sergeant's idea of education. More surely he was himself no longer the lean and imaginative youth of '92, and in 1812 there was no new Bonaparte to rescue the old from his complacency. If there had lived, somewhere in France, a bright and bitter young man who believed Plutarch and Rousseau, he would have fared badly in the schools, the bureaucracy, and even the army of the Empire. By 1812, "careers open to talent" was barely half a principle, applied mainly to those who were content with more of the same.

In the Consulate and early Empire, careers abounded not only in the army, the bureaucracy, and in the French governments of the conquered territories, but also in an economy that was reviving and, for a time, prosperous. Napoleon at first appeared to fulfill the dearest hopes of the bourgeois businessmen who had lost patience with the Directory. His minister Gaudin brought a high degree of order into government finances. The Directory's plan for a centralized system of tax collection was put into practice. To a relatively more efficient gathering of direct taxes—French governments have rarely succceeded in realizing the potential revenue from higher incomes—Napoleon progressively added indirect taxes on salt and wine and extended the system of urban customs (octrois) that the Revolution had only temporarily abolished. Internal peace made commerce safer, and a network of new roads speeded trade as well as military transport. Canals, harbor improvements, government buildings, and other public works, together with the endless needs of the armies, stirred the economy, reduced unemployment, and involved less official corruption than Frenchmen had recently been accustomed to. Technical schools, prizes for inventions, and industrial exhibitions promised much. In 1800 Napoleon founded the Bank of

France, to stabilize the currency and extend credit for economic expansion. These it did, but its private control by two hundred of the wealthiest financiers made it a power for concentration rather than dispersal of opportunity for new enterprise. The Bank was another monolith, destined to exert its inflexible power down to the twentieth century. The law codes favored business and private property; government subsidies and protective tariffs were extended. Brumaire appeared for a moment to have been the middle class's most adroit investment.

Napoleon Bonaparte, however, was more than a soldierly figurehead for a businessman's government. Economic strength was to him a means to higher, or at least more glorious, ends. Whether his wars are called offensive or defensive, the comfortable principles of laissez-faire could not survive them. Yet even in the year of peace following the Treaty of Amiens with England in 1802, his ideas were clearly more mercantilist than had recently been the fashion. His regulation of manufactures, of exports and imports, his attempts to organize a closed system of colonial exploitation, were akin to Colbert's and less flexible in practice.

The resumption of war brought with it the famous Continental System, by which he hoped to ruin British prosperity by excluding British goods from Europe; it went far beyond the moderate tariffs that advocates of laissez-faire have found so easy to accept. Its effects on France's own economy were pleasing to only a minor segment of the business community and after 1810 a general economic decline made businessmen welcome the fall of the man they had helped to raise in 1799. The blockade cut France off from raw materials and overseas outlets, while Napoleon's ultra-nationalist policies spoiled French chances of recouping within a free European economy. His new order did not envisage a united European market but French industrial hegemony. European resentment and retaliation not only crippled the Continental System but harassed French industry and commerce at every turn. Exporters of wine and luxury goods suffered greatly. Wool, silk, and cotton enjoyed early bursts of affluence but declined again, partly for lack of raw materials. On the other hand, coal, metals, and chemicals made steady progress and the encouragement of beet sugar production made France self-sufficient in this vital food. These gains survived Napoleon's fall but only at the cost of high protective tariffs which were not materially reduced until the 1850's. Overall, French production grew steadily but slowly; France was not yet in her industrial revolution. Only the needs

—and rewards—of military expansion and the effects of public works sustained prosperity and full employment until 1810. The ensuing depression was part of Napoleon's debacle.

## NAPOLEON AND EUROPE

The impact of Napoleonic ideas and institutions on France was decisive and their effects are evident today. But Napoleon the man is remembered as the Emperor on horseback who pursued, overtook, and then lost a dream of glory, as the central figure in a drama of lurid splendor and terrible futility. He is pictured not as founding a bank, worrying an article of law, bargaining with a Pope, squabbling with a Fouché or a Talleyrand, but crowning himself at Notre Dame, leaping the Alps, humiliating the Hapsburgs at Austerlitz and the Prussians at Jena, captivating Alexander I on the raft at Tilsit—or raging alone in an empty Moscow set afire, parting from the Old Guard at Fontainebleau, crushed at Waterloo, sunk in revery on Saint Helena. His was a most substantial pageant and, though it faded nonetheless, it made a legend that has defied time, common sense, and the sober judgments of historians.

When Napoleon became First Consul, the second coalition was still in the field, although weakened by Russia's withdrawal in October of 1799. Napoleon's Christmas letters to England and Austria urged peace, a peace demanded by public clamor in France and necessary to the consolidation of his personal power. The letters were ignored; Austria was enjoying too much success in Italy. Her armies routed Masséna's and besieged Genoa in the spring of 1800. Nothing would bring peace but war. It was to be Carnot's plan once again. Moreau led an army across the Rhine and through southern Germany; Napoleon dragged his cannon in hollow logs across the Saint-Bernard Pass, entered Milan on the 2nd of June, and proclaimed again his Cisalpine Republic. But two days later, Genoa, piled with corpses from famine and disease, surrendered to the Austrians. During an anxious fortnight, the trimmers who had made Brumaire awaited news of the man they had chosen and considered possible replacements. Then came word of Marengo, where Desaix and his corps saved Napoleon's badly deployed army from retreat and won unexpected victory. Desaix died on the field; Napoleon sped home to receive the cheers of all Paris, on Bastille Day,

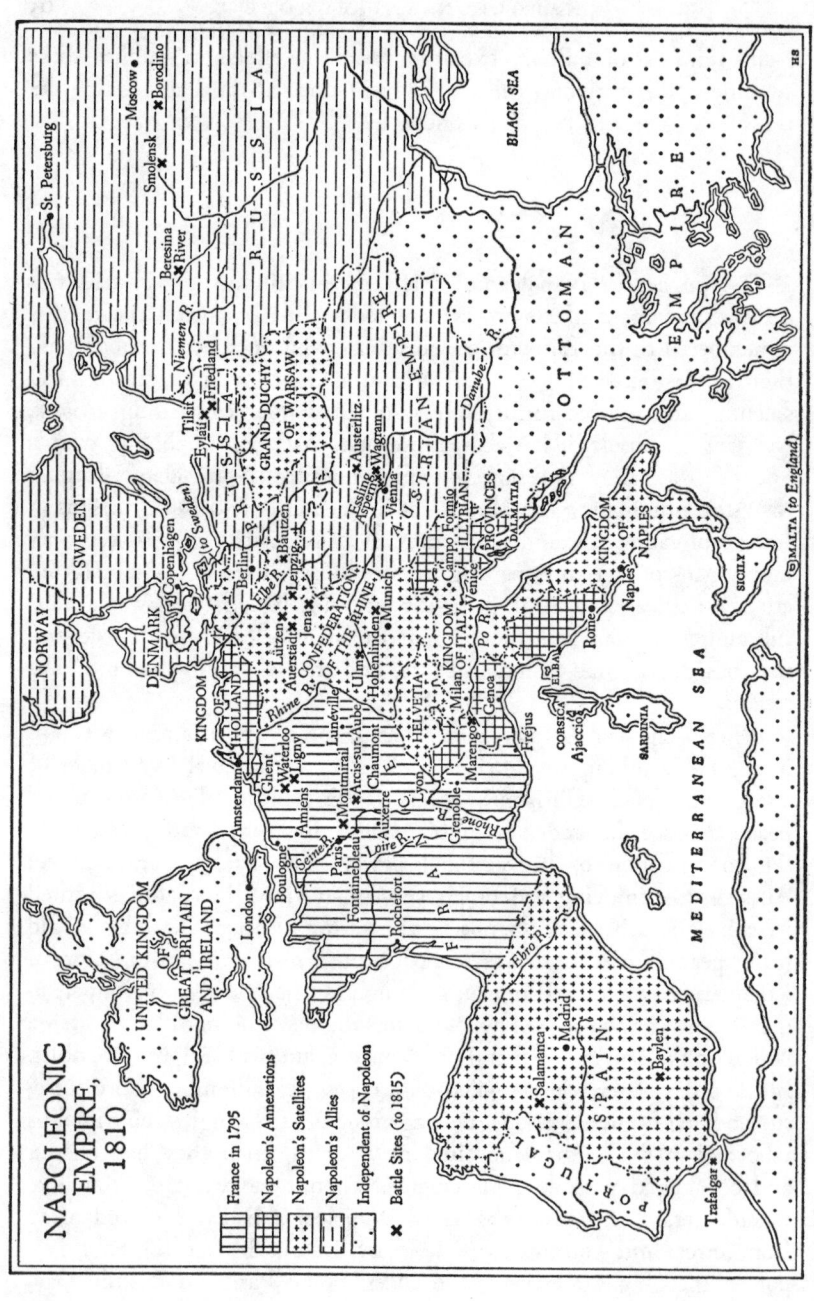

1800. Moreau occupied Munich in July, then defeated the Austrians at Hohenlinden on December 3rd. In January MacDonald and Brune struck Austria from the south and forced the Emperor to make peace.

The Treaty of Lunéville, February 9, 1801, reaffirmed Napoleon's gains at Campo Formio and all but broke Vienna's power in the Holy Roman Empire. Along with recognition of the "independent" republics of Italy, Switzerland, and Holland, Austria accepted the principle of French help to the dispossessed German princes on the left bank of the Rhine in arranging compensation in the Germanies. When war returned, Napoleon was to have his excuse for remaking the map of Central Europe. Meanwhile Talleyrand made a personal fortune in helping German princes despoil each other and unravel what was left of the Empire.

In March, 1802, the Treaty of Amiens ended hostilities with England and for the first time in ten years France was at peace. French troops had surrendered Malta in 1800; the remnants of Bonaparte's Army of the East gave up Egypt in 1801. England had made her point in the Mediterranean and now, financially strained and eager to resume normal trade with the Continent, she conceded far more than her negotiators had offered at Lille five years before. Not only were no questions raised over French conquests in Europe, but Britain surrendered all of her own overseas conquests except Trinidad, which had been Spain's, and Ceylon, which had been Holland's. Even the Cape of Good Hope was returned to France's Dutch satellite and there was no guarantee of English commerce with French-held Europe. In return, France gave up Egypt to Turkey, Malta to the Knights of Saint John—both already lost in any case—and evacuated Naples. It was, like the Concordat, too much of a victory for Napoleon. English patriots were embittered and English traders aghast. The English will to resist was reborn almost at once, and Napoleon shortly proceeded to make another clash unavoidable.

The year of Amiens was the zenith of the Consulate and, where France's deepest interests were concerned, of Napoleon's entire reign. Peace with all Europe, renewed trade, the development of Napoleon's most solid instruments of political and economic welfare, from the law codes down to the importation of new industrial machinery, promised a way out of thirteen years' turbulence. Napoleon was never more popular. Talleyrand, echoing others, wrote that "the most ambitious man could ask no more for his country." But France was not Napoleon's country; for him, all Europe hardly sufficed. Men have long argued his motives and the nature of his ambition. True Royalists and true Republicans (and many English-speaking authors who are not, cannot be, either) have seen only the supreme *condottiere,* literally mad with passion for personal power and glory. Pious Bonapartists accept Napoleon's testament from Saint Helena: he fought to give Europe, and especially the little man, the perfection of liberty, equality, and fraternity. Most historians, working with the evidence of what he did, rather than what he said or what others said about him, reject these extremes. Even this leaves room for nearly total disagreement; deeds alone are only partial proof of man's intent. But for now, deeds must suffice as clues to inner fact.

After victory in the field and at the conference table, Napoleon was ready to take the step that bound France's destiny to his own. He made himself Consul for life. The prefects worked to insure a proper plebiscite, but the majority would have been substantial in any case. On August 2, 1802, some 3.5 million answered Yes; 8300, No. The hired sword of the Thermidoreans was now their dictator and held all of France as his instrument. The Senate, well bribed, agreed to alter the constitution; Bonaparte won the right to choose his successor, to amend the constitution, to make treaties, to dissolve the Assemblies—all with the approval of the Senate, which he could enlarge as he wished with men of his own choice.

In the same year, Napoleon reached out to build a new colonial empire. Louisiana, ceded by Spain in 1800, was to serve as the base for French power in the western hemisphere. The guardian of the Republic began by restoring the old regime to the French West Indies, revoking the Convention's abolition of slavery and the slave trade, reestablishing French monopoly of trade. A French army seized the liberal Haitian Negro leader Toussaint L'Ouverture and sent him to France and execution. French forces quickly took control over all the islands of the group. But yellow fever and the ferocity of Toussaint's devoted followers took 20,000 French lives in Haiti, and the threat of war with England induced Napoleon to sell Louisiana to the United States government in 1803. Of more direct interest to the former commander of the Army of the East, and more alarming to Englishmen who felt confident of their power in the Atlantic, were French aims in the Mediterranean. Napoleon's agents publicly boasted of their activities in Greece, Turkey, and Egypt; and in Paris the controlled press spoke of reconquering the road to India. In answer, the London press helped its government to justify the continued occupation of Malta, in violation of the Treaty of Amiens. This was the ostensible cause of the war that followed.

On the Continent, Napoleon used the year of peace to bolster his political and economic position. He made himself president of the Cisalpine (now Italian) Republic, annexed Piedmont directly to France, forced an alliance on the Helvetic Confederation of Switzerland, and enlarged the French garrisons at Dutch and Italian ports. All of these acts violated the letter or spirit of the Treaties of Lunéville and Amiens. And all ignored the bounds of what has been called the gentleman's diplomacy of the eighteenth century. Napoleon brusquely refused to discuss or to recognize the interests of other powers in French aggrandizement. They were not offered a share in the spoils. Worse, the English were not to share even in the trade. The French high-tariff law of April, 1803, betrayed Napoleon's aim to close all ports under his control to British commerce. Negotiations between the two powers, in which Napoleon took a polite but evasive line, ended in an ultimatum from the exasperated English, demanding French evacuation of Holland and a delay in British evacuation of Malta. War resumed in May, 1803, fittingly, with the British seizing French colonies and blockading French ports and Napoleon redoubling his efforts to exclude British goods from Europe.

While the crowned heads of the third coalition gathered their forces, Napoleon founded a dynasty in France. The Cadoudal-Pichegru conspiracy served as an added excuse for solidifying the rule of the man who stood "between France and upheaval." But for many Frenchmen it was neither surprising nor shocking for Napoleon to take the title of Emperor. In the midst of *émigré* intrigue (Napoleon had accused Artois of keeping sixty assassins in Paris), and under the threat of war, which in the past had meant a resurgence of Jacobinism, who would deny that Bonaparte alone could keep France safe? Among the prominent, only Carnot denied it. Fouché, who had briefly opposed the consulship for life, now pushed the Senate to declare Napoleon hereditary Emperor on May 4, 1804, "in the interest of the State." The wording of the constitution was changed accordingly; there was little need to change the substance. The plebiscite, its figures altered to improve on those of 1802, showed the usual 3.5 million for and only 2500 against.

Napoleon dutifully made a pilgrimage to Charlemagne's tomb at Aix-la-Chapelle, but there would be no pilgrimage to Rome. Instead, Pius

VII was summoned to Paris for the coronation of the Emperor. Neither was there to be feigned Carolingian modesty; on December 2, 1804, in the splendidly decorated Cathedral of Notre Dame, Napoleon received the crown from the Pope and placed it on his own head. David produced his lavish and idealized canvas of the Bonaparte clan turned dynasty. His rough sketch of Marie Antoinette on her way to the guillotine has more life. The coronation painting reveals the stiff pomp of the court etiquette which settled upon the Tuileries, complete with officers and ladies of the old regime to teach upstarts and their wives how to simulate nobility. Titles were as heavy as the new court costumes: Joseph Bonaparte was Grand Elector; Louis, Grand Constable; Murat, Grand Admiral; Cambacérès, Arch-Chancellor. Partly to allay their lingering republicanism, sixteen generals became Marshals of France. By a law of 1808, the highest officials became Princes, their elder sons Dukes; there appeared 400 Counts, 1000 Barons, and all were rewarded with suitable purses and lands. The new nobility mingled with the old, now returning in large numbers to positions of dignity and, for a few, of power. Like the earlier Legion of Honor, the new chivalry was Napoleon's attempt to rally men of all backgrounds and political preferences to peaceful coexistence in his service. The court of Enlightened France was a splendid production meant to dazzle Europe; for ten years, Napoleon's power made it all believable.

The conflict that followed the breakdown of Amiens deserves the title of the first world war, its battles fought from New Orleans to Moscow by mass armies and navies, propaganda and subversion, economic and military collisions almost worthy of the twentieth century. It was for the allies a war to make Europe safe for the old regime and the world open to British commerce. But also, as it progressed, it became a war of all parties in all countries to free themselves from Napoleon's power to impose his will on them and on what they saw, more or less clearly, as their national futures. That Napoleon was able to withstand and often to defeat his enemies for ten years was proof of the weakness of coalitions, the negative and self-seeking attitudes of the allied governments toward each other and toward their own peoples, the mediocrity of the political and military leadership cast up by the monarchical systems of Europe, and the ordinary incapacity of men to meet quickly any challenge that is novel in style and scope. It was also proof of France's strength, endurance, and discipline, of Napoleon's many-sided ability, of his generals' skill, of their soldiers' willingness to fight, and, not least, of the attraction for many Europeans in the ideas and institutions of the French imperium.

In 1804, France was the second most populous state in Europe—some 28 million people against Italy's 17 million, England's 15, Spain's 11, Belgium's 3, and Holland's 2. With Belgium and the left bank of the Rhine ("greater France"), the French population probably equaled Russia's, and the Russians were widely scattered under a far less efficient government. French industry was well behind England's, yet it was adequate to equip—but not quickly to reequip—the armies of that day, and France was self-sufficient in all the basic necessities of life. The armies first created by the Committee of Public Safety had reached the peak of their effectiveness. The Grand Army that stood across the Channel from England in 1805 numbered 200,000 men, of whom half were veterans of several campaigns. In the years that followed, Napoleon raised a million men from France alone; and until the Russian campaign of 1812, the recruits were well leavened with disciplined cadres of experienced fighters. The French general officers had long and varied battle experience unmatched by that of their opponents. Moreover, they had brought into tested practice the theories of the eighteenth-century masters Saxe, Bourcet, and Guibert, whose tactics and strategy were both more flexible and more sparing of human life than any since employed in large-scale warfare.

In July, 1805, Russia and Austria joined Great Britain in the third coalition. Napoleon abandoned for the moment his preparations for the second Norman Conquest and turned the Grand Army from Boulogne to a quick march on Austria. Meanwhile, Nelson's victory at Trafalgar (October 21, 1805) over the combined French and Spanish fleets ended the chances of even momentary French control over the Channel. England was safe from invasion and Napoleon was spared for the moment the temptation of fighting two wars at once, of seeking dominion at sea as on the land.

The campaign of 1805 illustrates most of the methods Napoleon employed to crush his enemies. The ragged armies of the Revolution had lacked the wooden marching precision of the monarchies' professionals. Walking freely, they covered two miles to the enemy's one and needed less time for rest. Poor in supplies, they had lived off the land, dispensing with cumbersome wagon trains. Napoleon had used these advantages in Italy; in October of 1805 seven corps crossed Europe in three weeks and captured an Austrian army at Ulm before the Russians had begun to arrive. The dispersal of units for battle strategy as well as for long marches was worked out in the writings of Bourcet and Guibert. At Austerlitz, north of Vienna, Napoleon deceived the Austrians and Russians by marching divisions 50 miles in two days, then reconcentrating them for attack where the enemy expected him least. As in Italy and Egypt, he addressed his troops before the battle, confiding his plans and winning their admiration. On December 2, 1805, he won his greatest victory, losing 9000 dead and wounded of his 70,000, his foes 30,000 of their 80,000. It was not so brilliant as Hohenlinden, where Moreau had lost still fewer, but it was a fitting anniversary of the Emperor's coronation. The low casualties and the relatively undamaged country through which his armies marched hid for the moment the two worst defects of the French military system: a barbarously ineffective medical corps and slipshod means of supply. Two other factors helped. Prussia, though angered by a violation of her neutrality, failed to intervene; the inexperienced Russian command obligingly entered Napoleon's trap before Austrian forces from Italy could reach the scene.

## THE FRENCH IMPERIUM

Austerlitz brought down the third coalition. Russia accepted an armistice; Austria signed the Treaty of Pressburg, giving Venetia to Napoleon's Kingdom of Italy and ceding valuable lands to the minor German states of Bavaria, Württemberg, and Baden. In July, 1806, Napoleon organized most of Germany except Prussia and Austria into the Confederation of the Rhine, under his protection, thereby more than fulfilling the grandest dreams of Richelieu and Louis XIV. The Holy Roman Empire, he announced, was dead; in August, Francis II laid aside his thousand-year-old title and became simply the Emperor of Austria.

Prussia could no longer ignore Napoleon's affronts to her power and prestige in the Germanies. With appeals to the spirit of Frederick the Great, she sent the old Duke of Brunswick against the French with an army barely worthy of the eighteenth century. At Jena and Auerstadt, Napoleon and Davout destroyed it in twin battles (October 14, 1806) and the French staged a victory march through Berlin. Only East Prussia escaped occupation. But now Russia, embroiled in war with a Turkish government encouraged by French agents, reentered the conflict. At

Eylau, Napoleon suffered a bloody stalemate (February, 1807). After months of refitting at winter quarters in Poland, his larger forces defeated an ineptly led Russian army at Friedland in June, driving it across the Niemen. Under an armistice, the Russian Tsar and the French Emperor met on a neutral raft moored in the middle of the river and, amid assurances of mutual admiration, arranged the Treaties of Tilsit.

Prussia, whose King was left out of their talks, suffered most from the agreement signed in early July of 1807. She lost her Polish lands to a new Grand Duchy of Warsaw ruled by Napoleon's ally, the King of Saxony. Her lands west of the Elbe went to a new Kingdom of Westphalia to be ruled by Napoleon's brother Jerome. Prussia agreed to limit her army to 42,000 men, to pay a heavy indemnity and the costs of occupation, and to close her ports to British trade. Napoleon's triumph was complete, but the hidden cost was high: the rise of a fierce Prussian nationalism awaiting the moment for revenge. Napoleon and Alexander divided the hegemony of Europe between themselves: the former in the center and west, which meant Russian recognition of every French advance including that into Poland; the Tsar in the "east," which was his already, and a share in the Ottoman Empire, which was not yet dismembered and whose demise Napoleon was determined should benefit no one but himself. Russia also agreed to join the economic boycott of England and even to declare war if the British refused to make peace with France on Napoleon's terms.

Tilsit marked the zenith of the Napoleonic Empire. On the Continent Napoleon was unchallenged and proceeded to consolidate his political power from Amsterdam to Naples, from the Niemen to the Channel. But his main preoccupation was England; to break her and to advance French prosperity, he fastened the Continental System on conquered Europe. The Berlin Decrees of 1806, the Milan Decrees of 1807, excluding British and most neutral ships from European ports, were met by the British Orders in Council, better enforced by a fleet that sealed French ships in their harbors. England remained free to deal with the rest of the world; French trade on the Continent was crippled by short-sighted discrimination against others' products. Throughout, England maintained a substantial trade with Europe, aided by the laxity of Napoleon's allies (including his brother Louis, pro-Dutch King of Holland), the connivance of his agents, who were in any case never numerous enough, and smuggling, which Napoleon himself progressively accepted and licensed. Finally, his Trianon tariff of 1810 established high revenue customs on colonial products, diverting to the French treasury the profits hitherto gained by smugglers. Though driven to these expedients, and faced with severe crises in several French industries, Napoleon nevertheless refused to admit the failure of the Continental System. While French contractors bought English shoes and clothing for the French armies, the Emperor redoubled the penalties on others caught with English or English-shipped products. In a Europe plagued with shortages of all kinds, French authorities staged wholesale burnings of confiscated goods. They inspired only bitterness and disgust, particularly among those Europeans who might otherwise have welcomed French rule—the middle and poorer classes.

Napoleon's reorganization and reform of the lands under direct French control varied greatly according to local conditions. Nowhere, of course, was there real political liberty, and everywhere were high taxes, conscription, and confiscations of land and treasure—all to benefit France. French police and secret agents stifled critics and hunted down opponents. Resistance often meant indiscriminate reprisals that fell on all and only stirred more resistance. But side by side with the old familiar face of foreign military occupation worked the apostles of a new order. An able corps of French administrators, helped by natives (usually bourgeois) who had much to gain from the disappearance of their former rulers, labored to establish those reforms of the Revolution that Napoleon had allowed to France. They destroyed feudal and clerical rule, including the Inquisition, and substituted the new codes of law, centralized government—including the forms if not the substance of representative institutions—public works, and, where possible, a paternal concern for education, public health, and poor relief.

In the early years, Napoleon's proportion of reform to exploitation was an improvement on the Directory's. But the necessities of war and the economic struggle with England in turn increased the demands he made on his subjects—often over the protests of his own local rulers: Louis in Holland, Murat in Naples, and his stepson Eugène Beauharnais in Milan. Even in Italy and the Rhineland, where previous misgovernment had created a strong pro-French feeling, privations and wounded pride stirred resistance and discredited the collaborationists. Enthusiasm for liberalism and nationalism, first fed and then frustrated by the conquering French, hastened the downfall of Napoleon's Empire but also opened the way to reaction. Whether a victorious Napoleon, at peace with his enemies, would ever have allowed the liberal, federated Europe of equal and autonomous states he so often promised can never be known. After 1807, his military fortunes changed.

The fateful invasion of Spain (March, 1808) began with Napoleon's desire to seize and partition Portugal, the ally of England, and to close a breach in the Continental System. He also desired to end the misrule of the degenerate Spanish Bourbons and to extend to Spain his imperial reorganization of European society. But Catholic Spaniards were not eager to be reformed by the despoiler of the Pope and the scourge of the Inquisition; liberal Spaniards resented military dictatorship and the imposition of brother Joseph as King; patriotic Spaniards hated the presence of foreign troops, the imprisonment of their favorite, the royal prince Ferdinand, and the arrogance of Napoleon, whose alliance had cost them so many naval and colonial losses at the hands of the English. On May 2, 1808, Madrid staged a futile revolt against Murat's troops. French reprisal was bloody and the news of the Dos de Mayo rang through Spain, raising everywhere fierce bands of guerrilla insurgents. In July, the French General Dupont feebly surrendered 20,000 men to the Spaniards at Baylen; Napoleon raged over the "first stain" on imperial France's military record. In August Junot surrendered to a British force under Arthur Wellesley, the future Duke of Wellington. Napoleon dashed into Spain with 200,000 men recalled from Germany, drove the Spanish armies from the field, and placed Joseph on his throne in Madrid. But the war in Spain was a war of the people, aided in their resistance by the mountainous, intractable Spanish land. From 1808 to 1813, Wellington and the Spanish guerrillas inflicted heavy losses and Napoleon was forced to keep 300,000 men across the Pyrenees, far from the decisive battlefields of Central and Eastern Europe.

Leaving his armies to bleed on this futile second front, he returned to Paris, where he knew that the Peninsular War was sapping his prestige and that Fouché and Talleyrand had already discussed possible successors. More than ever, he needed to be constantly victorious. Austria was rearming under the able leadership of Archduke Charles, brother of Francis I. As in Prussia, her humiliation had given way to a sentimental nationalist revival and in April, 1809, she declared war. This time Napoleon's march eastward was not so swift and his army was diluted with untrained recruits. After early victories in Bavaria, he was defeated in May at Aspern and Essling, losing 50,000 effectives. Prussian patriots implored Frederick William to intervene, but in July Napoleon recovered the superiority of numbers and outlasted the Archduke Charles at the savage and clumsily fought battle of Wagram. In October, Austria accepted the Treaty of Vienna (Schönbrunn) which gave Salzburg to Bavaria, western Galicia to the Grand Duchy of Warsaw, eastern Galicia to Russia, and the port of Trieste with its surrounding territory to France (the Illyrian Provinces, administered as part of France herself).

The settlement marked the outermost extension of the Empire, but Napoleon was now increasingly concerned with its duration. Austria yielded one more prize. Archduchess Marie Louise, the eighteen-year-old daughter of Francis I, was chosen as Napoleon's second wife, with the single purpose of producing an heir. His marriage to Josephine, who had borne him no children, was annulled by an obsequious church court of Paris. The son of the French Revolution married the niece of Marie Antoinette on April 1, 1810, and in March, 1811, there was born the heir, called the King of Rome. For Napoleon the political and nuptial alliance with Austria seemed to insure his Empire. To Metternich, newly arrived to power in Vienna, it was merely a tactic enabling Austria to prepare for the day when the rest of Europe would be ready to join her in bringing down the usurper.

## DECLINE AND DEFEAT

Outwardly the Empire of France never appeared more dazzling than in 1810. Yet historians and biographers agree that the man at the center of it all began at that moment to show signs of mental and physical decline. Only forty-one, Napoleon had driven himself mercilessly for twenty years, carrying alone responsibilities beyond those of any of his contemporaries and of most world leaders since. He had tried to manage all things, down to surprising detail, in battle, intrigue, politics, administration, religion, law, and diplomacy. How much there was an actual loss of energy or mental acuity is impossible to say. Napoleon was less and less patient of delay or criticism, more tense and volatile, yet slower in decision and execution. Even in battle, since Austerlitz, he often relied more on sheer mass and frontal attack than on maneuver and finesse. Imperious and aloof, he appeared to take less notice of others, of their advice and warnings on the policies he now pursued.

Apart from whatever personal decline he may have suffered, apart from the delays and diversions of his brief infatuation with the demanding young Marie Louise, two measurable facts stand out. Napoleon was more alone than ever; his difficulties were more perplexing than ever. He had lost or discarded the services of many able men and was justly disappointed in the work of those who remained. His brothers, except for Lucien, whom he had turned out during the Consulate, were mediocre men made worse by his own interference in their domains. Moreau, too able and a political rival, was exiled in 1804; Bernadotte, sent to Sweden as Crown Prince in 1810; Fouché and Talleyrand, both removed from power as too independent, too eager to plan for the future.

To face mounting problems, Napoleon relied on lesser men. In 1810 began the economic crises that brought unemployment, financial instability, and the desperate expedients that wrecked the Continental System. The Spanish wound drained blood, treasure, and morale, more and more difficult to replenish. The reequipment of the armies was beyond French industry, the training of recruits beyond the energies of complacent officers and jaded veterans. Desertion and draft evasion grew serious. The conquered territories now yielded less booty and required more troops and agents to restrain their rising discontent. Catholics resented the imprisonment of the Pope, liberals the brutal stifling of opinion, businessmen the decline of profits and the rise in taxes, peasants the conscription of their sons, workingmen the spreading unemployment and the usual shortage of relief. Yet France remained inert and obedient, even under the disheartening news that Napoleon was marching on Russia.

With a sea of troubles rising, an army wasting in Spain, and England unsubdued, Napoleon struck eastward in an unreasoning gamble to rid himself of his autocratic rival. Alexander had remained aloof from Napoleon's troubles in Austria, had refused him the hand of a Russian princess, had violated the Continental System, and had raised tariffs against French goods. In April of 1812, he signed the Treaty of Saint Petersburg with Bernadotte of Sweden, who promised an army for operations in Germany if Russia and France should go to war. In May, Alexander managed to extricate himself from war with Turkey despite French insistence that the Sultan continue the struggle.

That Napoleon should have resented these acts is understandable; that he should have seen them as justifying war with Russia, half a continent away, is proof of his ambition, his overwhelming self-confidence, his fatal inability to measure the power of men and circumstance. Since 1807, he had himself pursued policies directly contrary to his quiet assurances at Tilsit. He had added Galicia to the Duchy of Warsaw in

1809, presaging a restored Kingdom of Poland, a threat to Alexander's Lithuanian lands. He had continued French intrigue in Turkey for influence in the Balkans and the Middle East. He had annexed the Duchy of Oldenburg, ruled by Alexander's uncle, retained French troops in Prussia to the Niemen, occupied Danzig, and built military depots in Poland. His tone with the Tsar, a proud and sensitive man under fire from his own people for submitting too much, was increasingly peremptory. Russian aristocrats detested the revolutionary, Russian liberals the tyrant, and Russian traders the author of the devastating Continental System. Napoleon hoped that a mere show of force would induce Alexander to submit again, but Russians were ready for war and an end to surrender.

In February of 1812, Napoleon forced an alliance on Prussia, gaining 20,000 men for his army; Austria followed suit in March with 30,000 more. Neither desired war with Russia, but neither welcomed Alexander's plan to restore Poland under his own authority. Between two giants, they had little choice but to follow whichever was stronger at the moment. When Napoleon crossed the Niemen in June, his army of over 400,000 was less than half French. There were great, but muddled, efforts to organize supply convoys of food and munitions; even in the first weeks these broke down under the weight of such enormous numbers. The troops quickly resorted to pillage, alienating the Lithuanian peasants who had been expected to rally to their liberators—a first and significant defeat. As the armies pushed on through the heat of July, the Russians—greatly outnumbered—fell back and resorted to scorching the earth, leaving empty villages and barren fields. Not heat but hunger cut down Napoleon's armies, and hunger's companion, disease. Only a decisive victory could bring Alexander to terms, but Napoleon was denied it. Smolensk was defended in August only by a Russian rear guard. Against his officers' advice, Napoleon refused to make winter quarters there and pushed on to Moscow. At Borodino, sixty miles from Moscow, Russian pride gave him his battle, but it was a draw that cost him 30,000 troops and the Russians 50,000. Only the devotees of Tolstoy claim to know what happened. Whether Fate, a common cold, or the fears of a man 1500 miles from home prevailed, Napoleon did not send in the Imperial Guard at what seemed a crucial moment. Both sides claimed victory, but the Russians withdrew, leaving an open road to their old capital.

After the burning of Moscow, and the futile demands on Alexander,

Napoleon ordered retreat on October 18th. Hunger drained his men of strength to resist the lowering cold, the mud, the unceasing attacks. Crossing the Beresina under fire from both banks cost 20,000 men, a fearful revelation of war's cowardice, heroism, and lunacy. In the middle of December, only a sixth of the Grand Army was left to recross the Niemen; some 250,000 died in Russia; the rest were prisoners, and deserters. Napoleon had dashed ahead alone to Paris two weeks before, to build another army and face all of Europe rising against him. Under his still efficient bureaucracy and their fears of the alternatives to his rule, Frenchmen obeyed and in 1813 he marched into Germany with 200,000 men. In February, Prussia had joined the advancing Russians. Napoleon defeated their armies at Lützen and Bautzen in May, but his refusal to give up any of his conquests brought Austria into war against him in August. Despite his inexperienced troops and their meager supplies, Napoleon won a last victory at Dresden in the same month. But by October he was outnumbered, and at Leipzig, between the 16th and 19th, the allies overwhelmed the French army (Battle of the Nations).

Napoleon crossed the Rhine into France on November 7, 1813, and hurried to Paris to organize resistance at home. Wellington had crossed the Pyrenees a month before and was advancing on Bordeaux. In December the allies were in Switzerland, Holland, and on the Rhine. For a moment they slowed, divided among themselves and afraid of reawakening the spirit of Valmy. But that spirit was exhausted; as the allies advanced in early 1814, French cities and towns tamely surrendered to small detachments. In February, Napoleon again fought well, winning a series of engagements with an army outnumbered three to one. He still hoped for one miraculous battle that would force his enemies to negotiation on his own terms. For the first time in twenty years, he was ignored. In March, Castlereagh brought the allies together (with the aid of a £5 million subsidy) in the Treaty of Chaumont, which bound them to a twenty-year alliance and temporarily quieted the disputes already arising over the future of Polish and German lands. In late March, Napoleon lost the battle of Arcis-sur-Aube, then failed to rouse the population of the eastern departments to resistance. Schwarzenberg and Blücher simply bypassed him. The allied armies took the heights of Montmartre on the 30th of March and the next day moved into Paris, encamping near the half-built Arc de Triomphe.

As early as 1807, Talleyrand had assured the Tsar behind Napoleon's back that true Frenchmen did not share the imperial dream. Now he received Alexander into his own house and urged upon him a restoration of the Bourbons. Napoleon was at Fontainebleau when his Senate, under the threats of Alexander and the arguments of Talleyrand, deposed him on April 3rd. His offer to abdicate in favor of the infant King of Rome was refused and on the 6th the Senate summoned the Count of Provence to the restored throne of France as Louis XVIII. On the 11th, Napoleon formally abdicated, for himself and his dynasty. The Allies granted him sovereignty over the island of Elba, 86 square miles of land lying between Tuscany and his native Corsica. After a sentimental farewell to the Old Guard at Fontainebleau, the great adventurer was escorted southward to Fréjus, where he had landed from Egypt in 1799, and sailed to his exile on a British man-of-war.

## THE REVOLUTIONARY LEGACY

In eras of liberal enthusiasm, it was necessary to suggest that the French Revolution did not entirely renew France and Europe, did not erase a past that was unmixed folly and open a clear road to human progress. In more conservative times, the suggestion must be turned about; despite confusion, error, and the cruelest suffering, the French Revolution was not a failure. A new society emerged by 1814, not so far from the dreams of 1789 as the pessimists would have it. The Revolution did not prevent, and it probably stimulated, a century of splendid and varied work in every sphere of French life. Its achievements—above all, in the raising of human expectations—prepared the slow, unsteady advance of liberty. It did not bring affluence, efficiency, or repose—these are not, in any case, the promises of liberty—but it left a society in which more and more Frenchmen could live and work according to their individual tastes.

In outward physical appearance, France in 1814 seemed little changed from the country Louis XVIII had last seen twenty-five years before. In reality, the changes that were only beginning when he took flight had directly touched the lives of most Frenchmen in nearly everything that matters to men. From a hodgepodge of innumerable and overlapping units and layers of feudal, royal, provincial, economic, judicial, and ecclesiastical jurisdictions, they had stepped into a unitary society and were subject only to the authority of a central government which delegated very few of its powers to local bodies. For most of their public concerns, including taxation, they dealt with an official who was responsible not to a local noble, a private tax farmer, an abbot or bishop, but to a central bureaucracy in Paris. If they were wealthy or notable enough, they might enjoy the privilege of some slight voice in naming a man who represented them at the capital and who might exercise some influence over that bureaucracy.

At the very beginning and under the proposed Jacobin Constitution of 1793, it appeared that most or all men might have the power to choose their representatives in Paris. But universal suffrage was allowed only for Napoleon's plebiscites, in which men expressed not so much a choice as varying mixtures of confidence and fear. During most of the twenty-five years, the prosperous alone were admitted to political power. This rule by notables was to continue, with slight interruptions, for another two generations. But the principle of representative self-government, proclaimed in 1789, was never denied; and the promise, the logic, of the system implied that political privilege would be broadened, property requirements lowered, as education was extended to all classes. The principle and the expectation were unshakable and these alone marked a fundamental change in French political life. The following century showed that they could not be ignored for long without violent consequences.

Frenchmen were now subject to a single system of justice and were equal before the law. The social and religious discrimination of the old regime, once the very essence of the legal system, was now illegal. Noble, cleric, bourgeois, peasant, laborer (except when his claims clashed with his employer's), Catholic, Protestant, Jew, and unbeliever had the right of equal treatment under laws that were public, uniform, and broadly based on the Declaration of the Rights of Man. Napoleon's codes and the practice of his judges had given French law a turn toward the authoritarian. But all men, again excepting the workers, were equal under its rigors as well as its benefits. In many cases, they had the right to trial by jury and appeal to higher courts. The expectation, if not always the practice, of civil equality was universal. If many Frenchmen still deferred to their betters, it was a matter of habit, of practical (often proprietal) circumstance, or of genuine respect, not of law.

Taxation, likewise, was uniform and centrally regulated. All of the hated feudal and ecclesiastical fees had disappeared, as had many of the indirect taxes on necessities. Direct levies on property and income, without class distinction, were legislated by the representatives of the electors, if not of the people. After Thermidor, persistent tax evasion and tax loopholes were allowed to the wealthy and influential. These violations of the ideals of 1789 were to hobble public finances in a basically rich country and to discredit bourgeois government in the eyes of other Frenchmen. Here, together with the absence of local self-government, was a source of modern French *incivisme,* the lack of that public spirit upon which Anglo-Saxons have until recently prided themselves. The bourgeois notable was not alone in evading his fiscal responsibilities. Returning nobles did not need the spirit of Thermidor to exercise their ancient right of tax evasion, and the peasants had centuries of practical experience at the game. In times of government need, as under the Directory and Napoleon, indirect taxes mounted inexorably and their weight, as always, bore on the unpropertied classes of country and town. But the Revolution did abolish the demoralizing multiplicity of taxes as well as the most arbitrary and flagrant injustices. Both government and people fared better in 1814 than in 1788.

In economics, as in other fields, the Revolution opened careers to talent, and especially if the talent had capital at its disposal. France became a single market, with uniform business laws, weights, measures, and currency. Restraint or regulation of trade and manufacturing by feudal, church, or royal authority had disappeared, as had the guilds and all but a tiny number of associations of workingmen. Napoleon's programs of public works and the numberless restrictions of the Continental System notwithstanding, the Revolution liberated private capitalism. By 1814 the only meaningful restrictions on business enterprise were those arranged by other businessmen, through control over sources of credit, through monopoly and combinations acquiesced in by their allies in government. Direct government intervention was limited to what the middle class could call constructive violations of laissez-faire: tariffs, subsidies, state aid to research, invention, and technical training, along with strict enforcement of laws forbidding unions, strikes, and collective bargaining. The upper bourgeoisie, which with certain liberal nobles and revolutionary politicians, had dominated events before the Terror, was now a conservative force.

The land settlement of the Revolution created many new middle-class fortunes. It also greatly enlarged the class of peasant owners and of free tenants maintaining family farms. These, too, were men conservative in their politics no less than in their agricultural methods. Those with less reason to be satisfied, the sharecroppers and landless laborers who worked the farms of the bourgeoisie and of those nobles who retained their property, did not become a political force for a generation or more. In effect, the Revolution gave proprietorship, or the reasonable hope of proprietorship in the future, to millions of Frenchmen on the land. What they expected from Paris was continued security for their gains and a proper concern for their interests when these were threatened by natural disaster or foreign competition.

The Revolution left other, less material, expectations of liberty, equality, and fraternity. Liberty of worship and official tolerance of all religious beliefs were won, though it was a century before the abrogation of the Concordat began to soften the quarrels between clericals and anti-clericals. Legislation alone could not end private discrimination against Protestants and Jews. Liberty of speech, of movement, and of the press were much restricted from 1792, but no public power, not even Napoleon, dared deny them as principles. Equality of wealth had never been the object of any but a few. Equality of opportunity in employment, government service, and education was, of course, only partially attained, and thus all the more prized. In brief—despite the shortcomings of practice—liberty and equality became sacred words, which even conservatives henceforth had to brandish in justifying policies that denied them both.

The Revolution also acclaimed fraternity, which had meant many things to many men. To the hopeful at Versailles in 1789, it meant the generous condescension of the privileged in behalf of the majority. To the celebrants of July 14, 1790, at the great festival on the Champ de Mars, it meant the rough and sentimental camaraderie of the crowds, embracing each other across the lines of class and region. To the Rousseauists, fraternity was the idyllic brotherhood of all citizens, purified by their common consent to practice republican virtue. War brought other meanings: a fierce patriotism that progressively excluded and anathematized fellow Frenchmen who opposed the impulse of the moment; a messianic determination to join all Europeans who would take arms for liberty from tyrants. By 1799, crusading ardor had cooled, but national pride of conquest remained, particularly in the armies and among the veterans of the revolutionary campaigns.

Patriotism in revolutionary times, however, divided Frenchmen as much as it united them. Mass conscription, which called men from all classes into common struggles and common danger, encouraged in some a vague collectivism. Veterans who had risked their lives for the goods of all claimed the right to share in these goods, and despised the Directory and its favorites, who were indifferent to such claims. It was only one of many resentments which all groups of Frenchmen nursed against their government and against each other in 1799. If liberty and equality were badly fulfilled, fraternity survived the revolutionary decade hardly at all. Class against class, region against region, priest and *émigré* against republican and new proprietor, Frenchmen of all persuasions saw their particular version of the "true France" endangered. Thus, patriotic ardor only widened the gulfs that ten years of passionate struggle had produced, and which the Directory seemed powerless to bridge.

## THE IMPERIAL LEGACY

Napoleon's greatest legacy to France was the restoration of a measure of fraternity among the French. It was not a product of his amazing conquests. Doubtless Frenchmen felt a collective pride in being the imperial masters of Europe and some still saw themselves as missionaries of the revolutionary gospel. But Napoleon's wars were probably more popular after his death than in 1805 and certainly more than in 1812. At the end, his soaring ambitions in Europe endangered French unity and the Hundred Days very nearly destroyed it. Other, less spectacular, achievements worked to reknit French society: the domestic programs of the Consulate and early Empire, and the appearance of solidity that Napoleon's government maintained for more than ten years. Thus the Sword of Thermidor did what he had been chosen to do. He remade and enlarged the Center—anti-Jacobin and anti-Royalist—and gave it more numbers and more confidence than it had enjoyed even in 1790. The restoration of internal peace gratified all Frenchmen and especially those with property or purses to lose. New confidence quieted mutual fears and hatreds. In this respect, nothing was more vital than the Concordat, which allowed moderate Catholics to accept the Revolution and settled the question of national property. Napoleon believed he had deprived the Bourbons of their foremost allies; in reality, he had cut the Gordian Knot that bound them to sterile counterrevolution and enabled them to make peace with the purchasers of national lands while keeping the alliance of the Church. No other single act did so much to bring together the elite of notables that was to govern France in the next thirty years.

Napoleon deliberately appealed to the old nobility to serve his cause, using them side by side with Jacobins, Thermidoreans, rough soldier comrades of Italy and Egypt, businessmen, career politicians, and experts drawn from every field. One historian has pictured them early in their forced coexistence, regarding each other with smirks that barely concealed their snarls. But snarls were less deadly than swords; and a generation later, as new social dangers entered from the Left, they were to clasp each other firmly. Under the piecemeal amnesties humanely, and profitably, arranged by Fouché, émigrés returned home and discovered that they could live with the Revolution and its supporters. For fourteen years they had no choice; this was Napoleon's greatest legacy to a nation torn by hatred.

His bridging of the chasms opened by the Revolution and his revival of the Center did not insure the success of representative government but they were indispensable prerequisites for its trial. A man who despised debate and distrusted the people, who failed to construct a political system combining liberty with order, nevertheless prepared the way for genuine constitutional government. It was a passive preparation; the Empire offered no meaningful parliamentary experience. Napoleon had merely pacified France—in every sense of the word. Apathy greeted the Bourbons and they would have to work well to make their compromise succeed. But apathy was better than hatred and civil war. Beneath the defeat and disgrace of 1814, there rested solid gains and a far better chance for political stability than had existed in 1799.

Other legacies of the Napoleonic era were not so beneficial: for the French people, a million men dead and disabled from battle and disease, with the immeasurable losses of mind, spirit, and energy that no society can sustain with impunity; to French law, administration, and education, a lasting inflexibility; to French economic development, an intrenchment of the plutocracy and fifteen added years of wartime delay in economic progress otherwise decreed by invention and the Revolution's unprecedented release of human talent and human energy. To the French patriot the Empire left a recurring appetite for military glory and military solutions of foreign problems. To the French army it left the dangerous and costly military dogma that grew out of Napoleon's later campaigns: faith in the massed offensive and, paradoxically, the abandonment of the eighteenth-century strategists' adaptability to circumstance; also, less serious but hardly negligible, a reborn and intensified concern for color and show, spit and polish.

The Napoleonic armies were typical of the Empire period as a whole; a memorable display and drama masked the harsher realities. If the Empire of Napoleon became, even before his death in 1821, an object of nostalgia, the reason lay partly in its style. It was natural that a great *condottiere* should seek to embellish his reign and legitimatize his dynasty by employing the arts in his service. Yet even here Napoleon expressed his absolutism. It was not enough, as in Renaissance Italy, to patronize artists who worked independently at unique creations, shedding luster on their patron through sheer excellence, or even to dictate the work of some and let others go free, as Louis XIV had done. Artists, architects, and designers glorified the Empire and the Emperor in the most direct manner, from the gargantuan paintings of victories to the inscription of Napoleon's initial on every visible object.

The Empire style was neither original nor great art. It was solid, large, magnificent, and it was everywhere and into everything, at least in Paris. In short, it was impressive and interesting particularly to those who either resented or did not know the art of the past. It was also synthetic and eclectic, therefore all the more appropriate to the Empire itself. For in both reality and art, Napoleon deliberately manufactured his imperial style from four distinct traditions: the Revolution, enlightened despotism, the Carolingian Empire, and the ancient Empires of Rome and Alexander.

To match Napoleon's imperial conquests, there were his great codes of law, his caesaropapism, his roads, his aqueducts, his Legion of Honor and—continuing the fad of classicism that flourished in the previous decade—the eagles, fasces, laurel wreaths, busts, furniture, and utensils of Etruscan, Greek, and Roman derivation. On a larger scale, the heavy temples of the Bourse and the Madeleine, the Vendôme column in Trajan's style, the triumphal arches of the Carrousel and the more-than-Roman Étoile. David and Gros, the most prominent artists of the day, evoked Alexander, Caesar, Charlemagne in giant canvases of Napoleon crowned, victorious, ever heroic, whether with Pope, marshals, or army corps, in cathedrals, battles, and processions.

Matching the enlightened despot's central control of government, his councils of experts, fiscal and economic reforms, his rationalism and paternalism were the trappings of European monarchy: dynastic insignia, court ceremony and costume, titles and honors, and the dazzling uniforms of the Imperial Guard and other elite regiments. Along with the revolutionary's civil equality, his professions of liberty and popular sovereignty, his patriotic enthusiasm, came the tricolor standards, the drab little gray overcoat, the simple black hat with its penny cockade, and those other, humbler paintings: Napoleon joking with his soldiers, comforting the wounded, bouncing children on his knee, and—surely the apogee—Napoleon quietly taking the place of a sleeping sentry. These last were more common, to be sure, after his exile to Saint Helena, where he composed his final legacy to the French: the Bonapartist myth, with himself as son and servant of the democratic revolution.

Napoleon Bonaparte was a master showman. His own histrionic talent is evident in the harangues to the troops in Italy and Egypt, the self-crowning at Notre Dame, the farewell at Fontainebleau, the baring of his breast to the troops sent to arrest him in the Hundred Days. The Empire style was a stage setting, with all the most diverting props in place; little wonder that it gives an aura of melodrama, a flavor of the theater loft and the curio shop. Even today, Paris testifies to its success: a street map is a recital of Napoleon's marshals and their victories; the garish splendor of his tomb is an object of pilgrimage; every museum has its lines of battle flags, uniforms, weapons, panoramas, and mementos; his Arc de Triomphe—which some may insist belongs more properly to the soldiers of 1914–1918—dominates an entire quarter of the metropolis. As theater it impresses. As historical artifact it both reveals and conceals the meaning of an era.

Few great works of art or of letters appeared during the years of Revolution and Empire. The Emperor patronized science and technology as productive of material power and progress, but disdained the original in art, literature, and thought. The sensationist philosophers Destutt de Tracy, Volney, and Cabanis were in official disfavor. Chateaubriand, Constant, and Madame de Staël were suspect, held at arm's length for most of his reign. Thinkers won favor only when they served the State, edifying loyal citizens of a regime that possessed the truth and needed no speculation. Napoleon sought to mold French minds to a tidy pattern. It was a vain attempt. The generation then young produced men of genius in every field; their works appeared after 1814. Stendhal, Hugo, Vigny, Lamartine, Michelet, Delacroix were younger contemporaries of Napoleon. The Revolution and Empire have been blamed for the paucity of creative works in their time, yet the arts seem to flourish more often according to their own inner developments (and to the inexplicable appearance of genius) than according to the political atmosphere of any period. The gentle and brilliant André Chenier was guillotined by the Terror, it is true. But he was an exception, both in his promise and in his fate. The effects of the twenty-five years were less direct, less measurable; millions were too busy to create, tens of thousands died too soon.

By 1814, France had a new society but had not yet found a political system to govern it. Unlike the English and American revolutions, the French Revolution left no single political tradition to its heirs. In the realm of ideas, the old regime itself was not dead; a privileged, hierarchical, and clerical monarchy still seemed possible and desirable to men who gladly accepted the title of Ultra-Royalists. Bonapartists drew hope from Napoleon's testament of Saint Helena—a curious mixture of personal authority, political democracy, state guarantees of economic justice, and, of course, national glory. Bonapartism was to grow important, less on its own than in reaction to its rivals, in the decades to come. The third tradition to develop and survive was Jacobin democracy, a popular, progressively social, republicanism which had as its charter the Constitution of 1793 and as its inspiration such names as Danton and Robespierre. The fourth political legacy of the Revolution, and the one most alive in 1814, was the compromise embodied in the Constitution of 1791, a constitutional monarchy, roughly on the English pattern, with representative parliamentary institutions in the hands of those educated and prosperous citizens who in France went by the name of "notables." From 1814 to 1848, this solution to France's political problem was to have its opportunity.

# THE CONSTITUTIONAL MONARCHIES

Louis XVIII embarked on HMS *Royal Sovereign* at Dover on April 24, 1814, with the acclaim of London crowds still ringing in his ears. As the Prince-Regent bade him farewell, English forts and warships thundered their salute to the man whose reign all hoped would keep the peace so dearly won in over twenty years of war. His reception in France was equally enthusiastic. Along the road to Paris, at Boulogne, Amiens, and Compiègne, French crowds voiced their relief at the end of Napoleon's extravagant tyranny, shouted for peace and for the Bourbons. But the King had no more liking for the crowd and no more confidence in its loyalty than did the Emperor whose throne he was now ascending. He had, if possible, even fewer illusions over what was needed to keep that throne: in the short run, the support of the allies whose armies held France in subjection; for the future, the acquiescence of French soldiers, the willing cooperation of Napoleon's formidable civil service, and the confidence of the bulk of those men whom the Revolution had raised to wealth and power.

Historians still question the feelings of Louis XVIII at the time. Whatever his inner preferences, he understood that his return could not be a restoration of the sort expected by many of his *émigré* followers.

He no doubt foresaw the disappointment of old and faithful companions of his exile; it was not long in coming. To their discomfort, Louis received a number of Napoleon's marshals at Compiègne and flattered them with familiarity. Next came a delegation from Napoleon's Corps Législatif, to be charmed in turn. But he held off the Senators, who had demanded, in exchange for their recognition, his acceptance of a constitution whose boldly stated object was to preserve their own positions and incomes. If the King of France could be no longer either feudal or absolute, he would at least be legitimate, the true successor of Louis XVII by divine right and not by the permission of a venal Senate. Nor would he, as he made clear to these two personages in subsequent interviews, be King by the favor of Monsieur de Talleyrand or the Tsar Alexander.

## THE BOURBON RESTORATION

Regardless of who had brought him back to France, the King himself would set the limits on kingly authority. From Saint-Ouen on May 2–3, 1814, he issued a declaration affirming that he was a Bourbon and proving that Bourbons could learn. "Louis, King of France and Navarre by the grace of God," recalled to the throne of his ancestors "by the love of the people," had been "enlightened by the sorrows of the nation," and his first thought was "to encourage that mutual confidence" so necessary to its well-being. The Senate's constitution, he went on to say, had good points but betrayed a certain haste. He was calling both houses for the 10th of June, to consider the draft of a "liberal constitution" which he and their representatives would by then have composed. Its principles would include representative government; liberty of the individual, the press, and religion; the inviolability of property—including that which had been confiscated by the revolutionary governments—the guarantee of all public debts; the maintenance of all existing pensions, ranks, and honors, of the "new nobility," the Legion of Honor, and equality of opportunity for public service. The declaration expresses the essential balance of the Bourbon restoration until nearly its last years, when that balance was destroyed by the folly of Charles X: the style of divine-right monarchy but the substance of moderate, bourgeois revolution and the frank recognition of vested interests created by that revolution. All would depend upon how well the Bourbons defended their compromise against the extremists of Right and Left, and, as it turned out, against their own misunderstandings of a country they had not seen for twenty-five years.

Before Louis entered Paris, the transfer of authority had been well prepared. The provisional government, emanating from the Senate and headed by Talleyrand, had succeeded, with Artois' somewhat reluctant help, in convincing the imperial officials and national landowners that their winnings would be respected. Not a single prefect or leading general resisted; no Jacobin disturbances arose; France obeyed, in effect, a government that was Napoleon's, without Napoleon. Even allowing for the presence of allied armies, it was a remarkable demonstration of public order—and apathy. Napoleon, on the road to Elba, had ample proof of the solidity of the administration he had given to France. If outward calm and unexpected shows of devotion to Louis XVIII meant anything, Frenchmen had repented and were ready to live in peace with Europe and with each other.

The allies, reassured, expressed their gratification in the Treaty of Paris, signed on May 30, 1814. To the envy of twentieth-century historians and diplomats, they could ignore the popular hatred of France which they and Napoleon had so recently aroused at home and make a generous peace with a government they wished Frenchmen to respect. This desire, together with their expectations of safer aggrandizements elsewhere, made Talleyrand's problem easier. France retained her frontiers of 1792, including Avignon, parts of Savoy, and border strongholds in the northeast she had taken from the Austrian Netherlands and the Holy Roman Empire. There was no indemnity, no occupation, and even the looted works of art remained in the Louvre. France renounced the conquests of the Directory and Empire, agreeing that a general European conference would decide the fate of her former satellites. As always, there were those who believed every defeat to be the fruit of treachery and any subsequent concessions to be appeasement. Talleyrand suffered attacks for "giving away" Napoleon's conquests, but such charges were not serious for the regime until other events widened the circle of discontent.

In September of 1814, Talleyrand went to Vienna, where he took and has been allowed to retain, too much credit for creating divisions among the allies that were already there, and for securing a place of honor for France that was already implied in the Treaty of Paris. England and Austria opposed Prussian designs on all of Saxony and Alexander's plans for a reconstituted Poland under Russian tutelage. By January of

1815, they were ready to sign a treaty of alliance with France against Prussia and Russia; its existence helped these two powers to be satisfied with somewhat less than their full demands. Talleyrand wrote to Louis in triumph that French isolation was at an end; impressive at the moment, it was the kind of surface victory cherished by lesser diplomats. France was nonetheless contained. Austria was reinstalled in Italy, Holland enlarged with Belgium as a buffer to the north. By supporting Austria and England in keeping Prussia from taking all of Saxony, Talleyrand had helped Castlereagh put Prussia on the Rhine instead. But Talleyrand deserves no more blame than credit; the real author of Vienna was Napoleon. The conqueror of Germany had helped to unite her, had stirred Prussian nationalism, and had brought Prussia to the Rhine. The self-appointed defender of Europe from the Slavs was in the end responsible for Russian gains hardly less spectacular, for that day, than those called forth by the Nazi saviors of Europe in 1941.

The nineteenth century is too complex for historians to conclude that the diplomats at Vienna prevented general war in Europe until 1914. But after twenty-five years of chaos, it was no small accomplishment to make war avoidable even for a time. In the short run, their success depended upon the ability of the Bourbons to hold the throne of France, to keep that still-powerful nation from starting on its travels again. Louis' pledge of Saint-Ouen was fulfilled on the 4th of June, hurried by the insistence of the allies. The Constitutional Charter he issued was to serve as the basis of French government until 1848. In it, the Declaration of the Rights of Man gave way to a list of simple laws for Frenchmen: judicial equality, common sharing of taxes, equality of public employment, freedom of religion and the press, the abolition of conscription, and the sanctity of private property. Here the authors were careful to include the property "called national," for this was no document spun out of abstract theory. Even more openly than most earthly constitutions, it was a contract, almost feudal in its itemization, among substantial powers that had to be reconciled. Article 11 ordered citizens to forget the past; Frenchmen were forbidden to concern themselves with votes or opinions prior to the restoration. Near the end, four articles guaranteed the special rights of soldiers, pensioners, creditors, the imperial nobility, and the members of Napoleon's Legion of Honor. To complete this pact with the recent past, Article 68 decreed that the Civil Code and other laws not in conflict with the Charter would remain in force.

The Charter's system of government was a constitutional but not a parliamentary monarchy. The King held all executive powers in his own hands; the ministers were responsible to him, not to the legislators; formally, he held the initiative even in legislation. The Chambers could also suggest laws, and yearly approval of direct taxes gave the lower, elected, Chamber some power of the purse. But on balance, the executive had the advantage. Article 14 gave him Napoleonic control over the armed forces, the judiciary, the administration, as well as the power of decree law to insure the security of the State. He could pack the Chamber of Peers with his own appointments. He could influence elections through his choice of the electoral college presidents. In sum, the Charter depended overmuch upon the character and aims of the King. The Deputies could sustain a serious quarrel with royal authority only if they were free to put their case before the people and were thereafter sure of honest elections. Hence the lively concern of politicians during the restoration—and the July Monarchy—with press laws and electoral practices.

The Charter set five-year terms for the Deputies, one-fifth to be renewed by annual elections. Property qualifications were high: direct taxes of 300 francs for suffrage allowed only 80,000 to 100,000 Frenchmen to vote, and only some 15,000, paying 1000 francs, were eligible to sit in the Chamber itself. Such restrictions naturally raised no objections from the upper middle class of landed and commercial wealth that shared active political citizenship with the aristocracy. Louis further eased the transition for them by accepting Napoleon's Corps Législatif as the first Chamber of Deputies and choosing most of the imperial Senators as peers of the new upper house. The Charter did much to satisfy the demands of the new political and social elite cast up by the Revolution, but there were other interests whose appeasement would inevitably reopen old quarrels. Louis, pressed by Artois and the court, was determined to restore the dignity of the Bourbon throne. The Charter opened with a long preamble celebrating it as a royal gift bestowed on the people from above and closed with a reminder that 1814 was the nineteenth year of Louis' reign. These touches suggested not only forgetfulness but rewriting of the past; the attacks they provoked, among them satirical cartoons, only diverted attention from the liberal points of the Charter and did less than nothing for the dignity of the monarch. This small matter was unfortunately typical of much in the restoration: a willfully Royalist surface, often meretricious and trivial, obscured real concessions to the new France and, at least in Louis XVIII, a genuine desire for reconciliation. The Royalists had learned much, but too few had learned to admit it.

A more serious portent of trouble was Article 6, which made Catholicism the State religion and restored the alliance of throne and altar that had done so much to discredit both in the past. Louis XVIII himself had little or no religious faith but valued the services of the clergy to the Bourbon cause during the years of exile and expected even more from its support in the future. Other members of the royal family, notably Artois, and many of the *émigré* nobles had shed the pose of enlightened skepticism so fashionable in the last years of the old regime and were now immersed in the militant Catholic revival which persecution had generated, and which was to be officially sponsored by the restoration. The government raised priests' pay, which even anticlericals admitted was too low for a decent living. But the readmittance of preaching and monastic orders, the breaking of the University's hold over religious schools, and the forced public observance of Sunday, religious holidays, and special processions (including a number of ostentatious memorial ceremonies for victims of the Revolution) met sharp protests, which were redoubled as *émigrés*, prelates, and parish priests publicly attacked the evils of confiscation and predicted the return of all the Church's property. By early 1815, the debate over religious affairs was so noisy that the government resorted to censorship of the press.

The demands of the budget, another old bane of the monarchy, forced more unpopular measures. To achieve economy, Baron Louis, Minister of Finance, cut over 12,000 positions from the administration. Thousands of Napoleon's officials repatriated from the liberated satellites, and other thousands of returning *émigrés* who had expected royal favors, were disappointed to find the doors closed. The King's refusal to dismiss imperial officers from the reduced bureaucracy earned him the enmity of Royalists, who showered "King Voltaire" with epithets. The monarchy had learned the danger of fiscal irresponsibility, perhaps too well. The budget of 1814–1815 called for austerity. Public works were sharply reduced, increasing the already high level of unemployment in the cities. Taxes, which Artois and others had promised to lower, remained high and the hated excises on tobacco and alcohol were kept in force. The financial community applauded, but the early popularity of the Bourbons faded quickly.

Not only the budget but the allies demanded reductions in the army. Many soldiers were already disgruntled over the substitution of the white flag of the Bourbon household—which had waved over enemy ranks for two decades—for their national colors. Talleyrand, whose renowned practicality did not allow for the practical force of symbols, managed the army's acceptance of the Bourbon flag, characteristically, by the childish ruse of telling one marshal that another had ordered it flown. In a nation beset with joblessness, demobilization would have been a serious problem at best. The Minister of War was General Dupont, remembered for the disgrace at Baylen, and hardly the most popular man to discharge 300,000 men, retire 12,000 of Napoleon's officers on half pay, and disperse the Imperial Guard in batches to remote provincial army posts. To make things worse, the King revived the old royal household guard, 6000 *émigrés*—most of whom had never fought— all officers on high pay, including 400 generals. Louis could probably have found no better way to appease job-hungry nobles, keeping them out of those active positions in which he sensibly retained experienced imperial officials. But to the veterans and other Frenchmen who were asked to pay for these new sinecures, the restored splendor of the court was an affront.

## THE HUNDRED DAYS

By the early spring of 1815, these apparently contradictory attempts to satisfy various demands had produced wide disenchantment. The cabinet was loosely organized under a mediocre royal favorite, the Comte de Blacas, and could neither explain its program—on which it was itself divided—nor silence the outcries of *émigrés* who expected nothing less than a reversion to the 1780's. Still, there were no serious disturbances; France was passive, more suspicious than angry or frightened over the Bourbon regime. The bureaucracy and prefects would serve any master, and revolt against none who seemed secure. The only force that might take advantage of the prevailing apathy to make a revolution was the army, but it required a leader to focus its energies.

On March 5, 1815, the news reached Paris that Napoleon had escaped and was marching to restore the Empire. He had heard of the soldiers' unrest and knew also that the allies were thinking of moving him away from convenient Elba. On March 1st he landed in France with a thousand men, most of whom the allies had imprudently allowed him for his court. The Hundred Days began in the best imperial style, with a promise that was kept: "The Eagle, bearing the national colors, will fly from steeple to steeple until it rests on the towers of Notre Dame." His procession northward was triumphant. At Grenoble, the soldiers refused their officers' orders to fire on their old commander; at Lyons, crowds of workers greeted him with cheers—and with nasty epithets for Bourbons, nobles, and priests; at Auxerre, Marshal Ney, who had sworn to bring Bonaparte to Louis XVIII in an iron cage, embraced him in tears. On the 19th of March, the King left his palace in a midnight rain for his flight to Ghent, and the next evening, Napoleon entered the Tuileries as tricolor flags waved over all of Paris.

In an effort to regain the confidence of the middle classes, Napoleon assumed the role of liberal, and proclaimed an additional act to the imperial constitution. The author was Benjamin Constant, his sworn fealty to Louis XVIII cast aside in the hope that even a Bonaparte could learn. A half-hearted plebiscite ratified the new regime, of British parliamentary style, which most have assumed Napoleon would have ignored had he survived the war. The new lower Chamber had a large majority of liberals, adorned by Lafayette. The new ministry was distinguished; Caulaincourt was Foreign Minister, Carnot Minister of the Interior, and Davout worked to revive the army as Minister of War. Fouché returned as Minister of Police; determined to play a leading role whichever way the Emperor's fortune turned, he corresponded with the Bourbons at Ghent and with Talleyrand, still at Vienna.

Napoleon's promise to respect the Treaty of Paris availed him nothing. The allies interrupted their quarrels over the rewards of victory and sent a million men to bring him down. The Emperor had overestimated France's eagerness for his return; only 150,000 soldiers were raised despite all the efforts of Carnot, Davout, and those prefects who chose to exert themselves. Some 30,000 had to be diverted to meet a Royalist revolt in the Vendée. The rest, under Ney and the new marshal Grouchy, followed Napoleon to Belgium where the English and the Prussians were advancing. On June 16th, Napoleon threw back Blücher's Prussians at Ligny, but Grouchy bungled the pursuit and Blücher was able to rejoin Wellington (whom Ney had barely held) late in the afternoon of Waterloo, June 18, 1815. The British lines had withstood for many hours Napoleon's uninspired tactic of repeated frontal assaults; Blücher's arrival turned numbers and spirit against the exhausted French and the stalemate became a rout. Napoleon fled to Paris, then to Malmaison after the Chambers demanded his abdication. For a moment the liberals, fearful of Bourbon revenge, thought of the King of Rome as his successor, but Fouché worked brilliantly, playing group against group, to make himself head of a new provisional government. Meanwhile, Louis XVIII sped to France and arrived too quickly for the allies to settle on any alternative to his restoration— and almost too soon for Fouché to carry off his role as savior of the throne.

Napoleon reached Rochefort in July, where a frigate waited to take him to America; but he hesitated and, as British warships closed in, wrote a letter of surrender to the Prince Regent, "like Themistocles, to claim hospitality at the hearth of the British people." On October 15th, HMS *Northumberland* put him ashore at Saint Helena, smaller than Elba and lost in the expanse of the South Atlantic. It was fortunate for the Napoleonic legend that he did not end his life submerged in bustling America but on a lonely isle, where he could cast himself as a Promethean martyr bound by the forces of reaction. After Waterloo, Lucien and Carnot had pleaded with him to call a *levée-en-masse* and revive the Jacobin fervor of '93, but only in the memoirs of Saint Helena did he finally become a democrat, the people's Napoleon. Not long after his death on May 5, 1821, the Bonapartist legend grew into a craze and by 1848 it was a political force.

Historians generally assume that Napoleon's defeat was inevitable, given the balance of forces, and would have come shortly after, on another field, even if Grouchy had beaten Blücher back to Waterloo. It is conceivable, of course, that a victory in Belgium might have roused the French to greater effort, enabling Napoleon to negotiate with wounded allies whose interests had already divided them at Vienna. But in earthly fact, the allies were united, victorious and exasperated over the Hundred Days. They held France, not their own criminal negligence at Elba, to blame for Napoleon's return. The second Treaty of Paris, November, 1815, was punitive; it restricted France to her boundaries of 1789, imposed an indemnity of 700 million francs and an army of occupation in the eastern departments. This time the Louvre lost its captured art and the irascible Blücher was barely restrained from blowing up the Pont d'Iéna.

## THE SECOND RESTORATION

The second restoration opened in an atmosphere of violent abuse and recrimination. Artois and his party clamored for a thorough purge of "traitors" in the army, the administration, and the courts. Furious at their humiliation in March, bands of Catholic Royalists struck out against liberals, Bonapartists, and Protestants in a White Terror of lynch law in the south of France, in some instances abetted by imperial officials trying to save themselves. There were about three hundred deaths, few compared with the great Jacobin Terror carried out by a central government facing foreign invasion. In 1815, the Paris government (and its allied mentors) opposed such violence and was able to end it within weeks. Royalists denounced the softness of the King and were doubly angry when, under Wellington's advice and his own inclination, he failed to name a single one of their number to the new cabinet. Talleyrand returned to Foreign Affairs, Baron Louis to Finance, Marshal Gouvion Saint-Cyr to the War Ministry, and the nimble Fouché collected his usual reward as Minister of Police—all had been imperial dignitaries. To appease the Ultra-Royalist party, and to ferret out the truly dangerous Bonapartists, Louis turned to an official purge. Fouché reluctantly composed a list of the officials and soldiers whose disloyalty had been most blatant or decisive, but forewarned many of the accused and provided passports and money for their escape.

The Hundred Days made necessary a new election for the Chamber of Deputies. Talleyrand and Fouché used every administrative influence to achieve a victory for moderates of their own sort. But the Ultra-Royalists overwhelmed the official candidates in August and dominated a Chamber which Louis XVIII inadvertently dubbed *Introuvable*, by which he meant unheard-of, and, before long, outlandish. In the Royalist strongholds of the south and west, the ballots were not always kept secret, and pressures upon the voters swelled the majority. But Royalists also did well in other areas. To many, a vote for them meant a lesson to those who had welcomed the Hundred Days, and the best way to hurry the departure of the allies, whose million soldiers were trampling the eastern provinces in vengeful occupation. And to honest liberals and Bonapartists, Fouché and Talleyrand were triple traitors, whose chosen candidates offered little inspiration. Fouché went into exile;

Talleyrand retired, for the moment, to display his wit at the expense of the Bourbons and their ministers.

The rightist majority of Ultra-Royalists was now more than ever determined that France should be set aright as a hierarchical and obedient society under a divine-right monarchy, less under the influence of parliament than under the tutelage of the Church and a restored nobility. There were many gradations in the party, from those who accepted the Charter to those who would abolish it, from those who asked only an indemnity to those who demanded the immediate return of all Church and *émigré* property, from those who were, as Louis put it, "more Royalist than the King" to those who were more feudal than the Frondeurs. To the most intransigent, the Comte d'Artois, the King's younger brother and heir to the throne, offered the greatest hope. He willingly took the head of the party from his quarters in the Pavillon Marsan, held court for its leaders, and applied what pressures he could on his brother and the government. Artois had charm, vigor, a kingly manner, a rather new but fulsome piety, intelligence without systematic knowledge, and impulsive judgment in matters of history and politics.

In the Chamber of Deputies, the Comte de Villèle acted as party leader until, in the 1820's, even he became too moderate for extremists like La Bourdonnaye, who would have made the White Terror a settled policy of government. In the Chamber of Peers sat Jules de Polignac and Mathieu de Montmorency, who had led a Royalist political organization called the Chevaliers de la Foi in 1814. Then, it had done invaluable work in preparing the return of Louis XVIII; now it helped to direct the party's strategy. The Ultras' theorists were Joseph de Maîstre and the Vicomte de Bonald; their literary polemicist, Chateaubriand. All preached the romantic conception of a happy France, quietly at work under benign priests and kings, untroubled by the selfish individualism and false equality of the Revolution, guided in its affairs by a disinterested aristocracy.

The *émigrés,* to whom these ideas were most appealing, never made up more than a fraction of the Royalist party, but it was they who most often determined its tone. For twenty-five years, they had lived in exile with their bitter memories of lost relatives and friends, cut off from developments in France. On their return, they found their lands gone or greatly reduced, their old paths to office closed, their places even in the rural districts taken often by men of no notable distinction who had profited by the persecution of Church and aristocracy and who now displayed no great attachment to the ideals of their own revolution, little interest in the land or its workers beyond the rate of return. The *émigrés'* contempt was boundless, partly justified, partly a matter of birth. But contempt was not enough to deal effectively with the new conditions in the countryside, in the growing cities, or in the new and subtle political balance which even the tiny electorate represented. They believed that twenty years of blood and chaos surely proved them right and their liberal opponents wrong, ignoring the twenty years of change that had raised a nation against their hopes of turning back the clock.

It was insufferable to such men, taking their seats in the Chambre Introuvable, to find a King who rejected their views of what had to be done. The Ultras' demands for the return of national property, the abolition of the University, the repudiation of the national debt (owed to their bourgeois enemies), the purge of the Chamber of Peers, a monopoly of prefectural offices, were all denied. Before long they found themselves using the liberal argument that the King and his ministers ought to be subject to the will of the parliamentary majority—while their liberal opponents defended the royal prerogative. Later the Ultras would ask for universal suffrage, which they believed would win the lower-class enemies of the bourgeoisie to their support, and finally (before they regained power after 1820) a decentralization of political functions from Paris to the local notables.

In 1815, the forces of moderation and reconciliation were too strong for the Ultras to break, despite the shocks of the Hundred Days—and also because of them. The allies feared that political reaction would excite popular revolt and urged Louis XVIII to staff his ministry with experienced, moderate men. No doubt the great majority of Frenchmen, the bourgeoisie, the imperial notables, and many liberal aristocrats also stood across the path of reaction. But the crucial role was the King's. At sixty, Louis was prematurely aged, fat, infirm, and indolent, but with a certain ponderous dignity lightened by a quick intelligence and a wit ironic and bawdy. Whether he was politically moderate out of intelligence, indifference, a selfish desire not to go on his travels again, or from lazy acquiescence in the wishes of the allies and his ministers, the result was the same: a policy he himself described (to Artois) as a fusion of "two peoples" into one.

In that spirit, he dissolved the Chambre Introuvable in the fall of 1816 and called for new elections. The Chamber which met in November was probably more representative of the electorate, despite official support of moderate candidates. In it the three political parties of the restoration emerged. On the Right were some 90 Ultra-Royalists, wrathful over the "crowned Jacobin's" destruction of their majority. On the Center and Left sat 146 Deputies who would soon divide into two parties, the constitutionals of the Center, who supported the Charter, and the independents of the Left. The Center, on which Louis XVIII's ministers based their parliamentary majorities until 1820, had at its core a distinguished group of political writers and orators known as the Doctrinaires. Among them were Camille Jordan, the Duc de Broglie, François Guizot, and Royer-Collard, their acknowledged leader. These men expounded government according to the Charter, equal political privileges for the propertied, regardless of social background. They were, for the moment, less ready than the Ultras to admit the lower classes to political life and believed fully as much in France's need for a strict social order.

The delegation of the Left—a very mild Left if compared with that of the Convention or even of the Directory—grew slowly after 1816 to embrace a loose alliance of Bonapartists, liberals, and republicans. The Charter was too conservative and too clerical a document for such men as Benjamin Constant, Paul-Louis Courier, Jacques Manuel, and General Foy, for wealthy bourgeois like Casimir-Périer and Jacques Laffitte. Lafayette was of the party, eminent enough to give it protection; and Béranger was one of the most gifted satirists and songwriters of the early nineteenth century. Their electoral strength lay among those discarded imperial officers and middle-class owners of national property who most despised or feared the Bourbons and the *émigrés*. As the only Left remaining, they also enjoyed a wide popular following in Paris and other cities.

From 1816 to 1830 French politics passed through three distinct phases. The first, lasting until 1820, saw relatively little interference with the press and elections; a moderate royal policy was sustained by the constitutional Center in the Chamber with the help of a few on Right and Left. But the party of the *juste milieu* could not hold; independent gains in the elections of 1818 and 1819 and the exasperation of the Royalists forced a choice and Louis chose a rightward path. From 1820 to 1828—Artois succeeded his brother as Charles X in 1824—a series of unpopular conservative measures and Ultra-Royalist proposals disturbed public opinion; the government resorted to censorship and the rigging of electoral laws to conserve its majority in the Chamber.

The third and last phase opened in 1828, when not even official inter-ference in elections could keep a majority for Charles X and he was, as Thiers put it, shut up in the Charter with only two alternatives: to submit to a parliamentary regime, with Center and Left majorities choosing his policies and his ministers, or to change the rules of the game and govern by decree. His choice of the second provoked the Revolution of 1830.

The Duc de Richelieu's first ministry began in 1815 and ended in 1818; between those years France regained her freedom and her stature as a European power. Richelieu, a disinterested, moderate man of un-mixed integrity, had won Tsar Alexander's admiration—and freedom from *émigré* quarrels—as the able governor of Odessa during the Empire years. He had little of Talleyrand's talents for debate and dissimulation, but his good judgment and sense of honor won him universal respect. With Russian and English help, he resisted the most extreme demands of the Prussians and Austrians, and in the second Treaty of Paris undid some of Napoleon's work at Waterloo, completed Talleyrand's at Vienna.

The financial reforms of Baron Louis restored French credit at home and abroad, enabling the Richelieu ministry to pay the allied indemnity and to settle the costs of occupation despite a business recession in 1816–1817. The last allied soldier left France in 1818. Two other works of the period illustrate the policies of the constitutional Center. The election laws of 1817 and 1818 rebuffed the Ultras' attempts to widen the suffrage by affirming the provisions of the Charter. Rather than *scrutin d'arrondissement,* which may be roughly equated with single-member constituencies and which the Ultras believed would give an advantage to rural, local and presumably conservative, notables, the law established *scrutin de liste,* a system whereby all electors for each de-partment met at the chief town to vote for a list of all the Deputies from that department. The latter offered advantages to the urban electors, to government agents who wished to exert their influence, and, later in the century, to party discipline. The *scrutin de liste,* however, has been the exception rather than the rule in French elections since.

In March, 1818, the Chambers reorganized the army under the law Gouvion Saint-Cyr. Over the Ultras' objections, the law revived conscription for up to 40,000 men a year chosen by lot, enough to main-tain an army of 240,000. Since the wealthy could buy substitutes and city boys were often unfit, the peasantry filled the ranks. The six-year

terms were expected to produce a near-professional corps; little attention was paid to the need for reserves. Especially repugnant to the
Ultras was the law's attack on the last privileges of the nobility; most
promotions were to be given on seniority and nobles no longer took
precedence over their fellows in any given rank. Louis went so far as to
invite the law's opponents on royal carriage rides during crucial debates. One historian has called it the final blow to the old regime,
completing the work of August 4–5, 1789. Part of Louis' active compromise, it was the reality underlying the gilded surface of his household
guard. The Ultras were not deceived.

When Richelieu resigned after the liberation of the territory, the
King's personal favorite, Élie Decazes, became the chief minister. As a
former imperial official and a liberal ally of the Doctrinaires, Decazes
was the Ultras' *bête noire*. He pursued a policy based on the Left
Center, which Louis seconded by appointing an added number of
Bonapartists to liberalize the Chamber of Peers. Decazes removed Ultras
from the administration, the army, the Council of State, and allowed
regicides to return to France. He capped his concessions to the moderate
Left in a liberal press law abolishing censorship. The Left, on some of
whose votes Decazes now depended, was not appeased and in the elections of 1819 it gained 30 seats at the expense of Center and Right.
Among the successful candidates was Grégoire, the former head of the
constitutional clergy, who had approved the execution of Louis XVI. In
a bid to defeat the government candidate and to discredit Decazes,
Ultras in Grenoble had helped elect this man they despised but whose
name they knew would reopen old wounds and expose the frailty of
reconciliation. A universal tactic, in France it is known as *la politique
du pire*. The Center was pulled apart, Richelieu and de Broglie for
turning Right, others for compromise with the Left. Louis XVIII was
incensed at Grégoire's election; Decazes decided to appease the Right
and introduced an electoral law favorable to the rural conservatives, but
he was too late to save himself.

On February 13, 1820, the Duc de Berry, Artois' younger son, was
assassinated by a madman, Louvel, and the Ultras quickly seized the
chance to blame Decazes' "Jacobin" leniency for the crime. As Louis
XVIII had no children and the Duchesse d'Angoulême, wife of Artois'
other son, was beyond the age of childbearing, Berry's death meant an
early end of the Bourbon line, and raised the hateful prospect of the
Duc d'Orléans and his several sons invading the Tuileries. The Ultras

stormed and Louis reluctantly dismissed his favorite, opening the way for a second Richelieu ministry based on the Right. The constitutional Center never regained its power; some of the Doctrinaires and their followers moved slowly toward a moderate, bourgeois, Orléanist Left.

## THE ULTRA-ROYALIST REVIVAL

The conservative phase of restoration politics began with the Right imposing censorship on the press and passing a new electoral law designed to insure itself a permanent majority. France returned to the *scrutin d'arrondissement* and a double set of elections, of which the second round was limited to 1000-franc taxpayers, voting for an added 172 Deputies. With full power in sight, the Ultras failed to press their earlier demands for universal suffrage, preferring to depend upon the wealthiest proprietors. The law passed amid riots and demonstrations in Paris, encouraged by Manuel and Constant's fiery speeches in the Chamber. Liberal and republican societies, despairing for the future of legal opposition, organized an insurrection under Lafayette's uncertain leadership, but the government quickly discovered the plot. Richelieu contented himself with frightening off the leaders, and the Chamber of Peers prudently avoided an investigation. In September, 1820, the Royalists celebrated the birth of the Duc de Bordeaux (later Chambord), posthumous son of the Duc de Berry and called *l'enfant du miracle*. The event, seven months after Berry's murder, was miraculous only in the political sense. The Royalist victory in the November elections seemed more immediately exploitable.

Through 1821, Richelieu managed to delay introducing the impatient Ultras' most cherished legislation. But his attempts at compromise were foiled by the refusal of Villèle and Chateaubriand to support him. Each considered himself the most able man in France and hungered for power, but it was Villèle who had the ear of the enfeebled King, through Louis' new favorite, Madame du Cayla. The Left willingly joined the Ultras in their attacks on the ministry and Richelieu resigned in disgust in 1822. Villèle, a vigorous but cold and prideful little man from the Midi, became chief minister and gave France five years of honest and efficient financial management. His keen sense of the possible made Villèle less of an Ultra in office than he had been in opposition. But certain issues were irrepressible and provided the Left with several causes for battle, in clerical legislation, in the indemnity for *émigrés* who had lost their lands, and in foreign affairs.

In the decade of the 1820's, the Left in France struggled to revive, as the Right, considering itself secure in office, proceeded to unravel some of the compromises of Louis XVIII. There was one more attempt at insurrection in 1821, a loosely organized French version of the Carbonari whose failure once more discredited the reluctant revolutionaries, like Lafayette, who led it. Four sergeants at La Rochelle died in silence after an abortive coup and were honored as martyrs, as much to the ineptitude of their leaders as to the severity of the Bourbon regime. The Left then turned its main efforts to the platform, the café, and what was left of the press—dozens of their journals appeared, were closed, and appeared again under different names. The first major controversy to occupy them was the French intervention in Spain.

In the widespread European unrest of 1820, revolt had failed in Greece, Naples, and Piedmont as it had in France. But a military and anti-clerical coup in Spain had imposed a moderately liberal constitution on the Bourbon Ferdinand VII. Some of the French rebels had invoked the Spanish example and in the early 1820's Spain appeared to European conservatives in the unaccustomed role of revolutionary agent. The Ultras demanded that France have the honor of restoring Ferdinand to his rightful powers and the Church to its dignity. Villèle resisted the war party, fearing for his budget and doubting the loyalty of the army in a reactionary crusade. But Chateaubriand, working partly on his own as Foreign Minister, won the tacit approval of the allies at the Congress of Verona in 1822 and turned the aging Louis XVIII to a policy of intervention. The Left confidently predicted a military disaster, remembering Napoleon's Peninsular Campaign (but not its circumstances); Manuel tartly reminded the Royalists that foreign intervention had once caused the execution of a king, Louis XVI. He was ejected bodily from the Chamber. The royal army under the Duc d'Angoulême had little more trouble with the Spanish liberals, entering Madrid on the 24th of May, 1823, and capturing the Trocadero fortress at Cadiz in August. The clerical countryside, through which the French were careful to pay their way, had offered no resistance to an intervention wholly different in purpose from Napoleon's. Angoulême was disgusted by Ferdinand's savage reprisals against the liberals and hurried home to a hero's welcome from Frenchmen who had not tasted victory in many years. The army had proved its discipline under the Bourbon flag; the Royalists, with new confidence and prestige, swept the December elections. Only 19 liberals kept their seats in the "Chambre Retrouvée."

Villèle had foreseen that a triumph too overwhelming would split the Ultras, but he speeded the event by dismissing his rival, Chateaubriand. The latter had glorified his own role in the Spanish affair too blatantly. Now he took the widely read *Journal des Débats* into the opposition, or counteropposition, of Ultra "impatients" against Villèle and proceeded to prove how inconvenient to any government is a disappointed prodigy in politics. In September, 1824, Louis XVIII died and the Comte d'Artois became Charles X. Villèle remained chief minister, with a Chamber dominated by the King's party and elected, under a recent change of law, for seven years without renewal. After their discredit and defeat over the Spanish campaign, the liberals expected the worst.

Villèle's proposal in late 1824 to indemnify the *émigrés* for their lost lands had had the blessing of Louis XVIII and was a fair and sensible solution to the vexing problem of the national property. But its financing involved a lowering of interest paid to government bondholders; bourgeois Paris, led by liberal politicians, exploded in righteous anger. Villèle was forced to float entirely new loans; the *émigrés* received far less than they expected; the smaller proprietors received substantially less than their share. The effects overflowed with paradox. Hitherto suspicious owners of national property could now rally to the Bourbon monarchy, but the Ultra *émigrés* were unhappy and blamed Villèle. The liberals were given a safe, dead issue to exhume at their convenience, while their leaders, opponents of the Bourbons and Villèle, carried off the largest indemnities (Lafayette and the Duc d'Orléans). The market place had no difficulty seeing through the agitated surface to the bourgeois reality; the value of the national lands, up to then unsteady because of *émigré* demands, rose to its natural level. The indemnity was one of the restoration's most vital contributions to the closing of revolutionary wounds.

The issue that came to overshadow all others in the reign of Charles X was the government's relation to a reviving Catholic Church. It meant more than incessant argument over detail and degree of clerical influence in education, politics, or daily life, more than a dependable alarm both sides could raise to gather their followers—or to obscure and avoid other issues, tax reform, suffrage, economic welfare, social services. To many on both sides it meant a decision for or against the eighteenth century, a dialogue between two concepts of man and society which was carried on at various levels. De Maistre and de Bonald sought to establish the union of King and Church as philosophical axiom. The eighteenth century, said the former, was "an insurrection against God" by wicked men who foolishly believed themselves capable of erecting alone, without and therefore in defiance of God, a society built on fallible human reason. The Revolution was the inevitable result. The natural law of God was that religion and absolutism should govern a nation united and happy in its faith. Whatever government could do for religion, and religion for government, would therefore help to restore the divine plan.

After their experiences under the Directory and Napoleon's later years, the great bulk of the French clergy and the most articulate Catholic laymen agreed that royal favor was essential to religious revival. Leadership came from the aristocracy, which had more than spiritual reasons for hating the anti-clerical bourgeoisie. Many members of the Chevaliers de la Foi also belonged to the Congregation, a society of priests and laymen dedicated to reviving the faith and Catholic social action. Chateaubriand's *Génie du Christianisme*, published in 1802, inspired these men, who believed that only in a Catholic revival could the French people find peace and justice. The vogue of romantic enthusiasm for the medieval, the mystical, and the religious cast an aura of lost—but recoverable—tranquillity over the old regime. Young poets like Victor Hugo, Lamartine, Musset, and Alfred de Vigny were Royalists, full of hope—though not for long—that Charles X would wear the mantle of Saint Louis. Many a country noble could believe, looking out over a corner of France outwardly unchanged for five hundred years, that the last three decades had been but a passing storm, that the people's hearts were sound and faith would win them back from the self-serving ideas of a few avaricious bourgeois. The mood of the restoration is a mystery unless this streak of honest optimism is added to the more familiar motives of revenge and material recovery. It was one of the better reasons for the Ultras' early demands for wider suffrage; it justified, in their eyes and the clergy's, many actions that others saw only as political or theocratic aggrandizement; and it made their ultimate failure all the more bitter and disheartening.

With the triumph of the Ultras and the accession of the ostentatiously pious Charles X, the monarchy and Church were openly, proudly, bound together. In 1821, the bishops had won control of secondary education and a vigorous priest, Msgr. Frayssinous, became Grand Master of the University and later Minister of Public Instruction and Ecclesiastical Affairs. Church supervision of teachers on all levels was extended, and made more objectionable to liberals by purges of laymen in favor of priests. Even the Sorbonne was not spared; Guizot and the liberal philosopher Victor Cousin were forbidden to lecture. The École Normale was closed, publishers of the Philosophes' works and of liberal newspapers were prosecuted under a new law forbidding criticism of King or religion. The climax was a law of 1825 making sacrilege a capital offense (there had been many thefts of sacred vessels). Royer-Collard, one of the few prominent Catholics who still argued for a reconciliation of religion and liberalism denounced it in vain as a misuse of civil authority in the cause of theology. Villèle himself regretted the law, which raised the most violent objections from anti-clericals, disquieted many who had hitherto remained neutral, provoked raids on churches, ugly disturbances of services—and, finally, was never enforced.

The coronation of Charles X at the end of May, 1825, allowed the monarchy's opponents to exploit the clerical question still further. In itself, the coronation was a natural bow to tradition and Charles carefully placed imperial officers at posts of honor, revised the coronation oath to include the Charter and omit any references to the "extinction of heresy." Reims and its great cathedral were brilliantly decorated as Charles received the sacred oil of Saint Remi and Clovis. That the King should lie prostrate before the Archbishop seemed natural enough to those who were there, like Hugo and Lamartine, caught up in the exalted spirit of the day. But most of France was not there and Béranger's biting satire on the *Sacre de Charles le Simple* set the tone for a rising anti-clerical campaign.

In a divided society, it was natural that the schools should become, and remain to this day, the main battleground. The liberals' chief worry was that a clergy antipathetic to the French Revolution and its ideas, given government support, would seize a monopoly over learning and thus, in time, over the intellectual life of the country. Their accusations fell most heavily on the Congregation, some of whose members were Ultra party leaders, on missionary priests whose zeal frequently outweighed both their taste and their theology, and on the Jesuits, whose name in the vocabulary of anti-clericals stood for all that was devious, bigoted, and reactionary. The French clergy of the restoration was in several ways vulnerable to attack. After thirty years of neglect, clerical recruitment and training were only beginning to recover lost ground; in 1815 the priesthood had barely half its numbers of 1789 and most were past middle age. With a greatly increased budget for seminaries, numbers had been made up by 1830 and the prelates and priests of the time were generally superior to those of the old regime in piety and devotion to duty. But their education prepared them badly for winning the minds of the young, or the respect of the intellectual world. The restoration's aristocratic bishops often lived apart from ordinary society and its needs; their priests, who came most often from peasant families, emerged from seminaries which were still poorly endowed in teachers and books and which deliberately insulated their charges from "new ideas," thus making it likely that they would henceforth be unable either to comprehend or to combat them.

The virulence of the clerical question abated somewhat in the late 1820's, partly because of quarrels within both the Ultra party and the religious community. A Gallican reaction against the influence of Rome, the Congregation, and the Jesuits (whose role the Left had successfully exaggerated) started in 1826 when the Royalist and Gallican Comte de Montlosier published a mordant pamphlet denouncing all three as dangers to "true religion," society, and monarchy. Several French bishops sympathized with this attack, some because they feared the growing influence of the most gifted clerical polemicist of the day, the Abbé Félicité de Lamennais. In books and articles widely read by the lower clergy, the once-Royalist Lamennais argued for complete papal supremacy in religious affairs and attacked the Gallicanism of the French hierarchy, its patron, the crown, and the tyranny both of them exercised over priests and laity alike. Under counterattack from the government and bishops, Lamennais gradually moved to a demand for separation of Church and monarchy, then of Church and State. As 1830 approached, more and more young Catholics agreed with him that religion could not perform its spiritual, or social, mission until it cut itself free of the vested interests of government and ruling classes.

The Royalist party in parliament also suffered from factional rivalries. A Villèle proposal to reintroduce a measure of primogeniture among the wealthy raised liberal protests in 1826 before it was rejected by the Peers. The Ultra-Ultras despised him both for the moderation of his project and for its failure. The violence of the press stirred him to present a law taxing all printed matter so heavily as to endanger the entire printing industry. Even the lower Chamber's majority was intimidated by the public outcry and several joined Chateaubriand in denouncing it. Again the government's proposal died in the Chamber of Peers and Paris rejoiced. In April of 1826, Villèle abruptly dissolved the National Guard after a few had shouted their hatred of the Ministry and the Jesuits at a review by the King. As his rivals within the Ultra party worked to remove him, Villèle risked his career on new elections in November of 1827, confident that official manipulation and the rising liberal threat would return a rightist majority loyal to himself. Instead the combined Left, Center, and Ultra-Ultra oppositions outnumbered his Deputies by some 70 seats and he was forced to resign.

The third and final phase of restoration politics began with the ministry of the Vicomte de Martignac. Charles X allowed it to follow a policy of appeasement toward the liberals, partly because there was no choice and perhaps also in the hope of proving to the country and his party the futility of such a policy and the need for an exclusively Ultra regime. Guizot and Cousin resumed their lectures; press censorship was once more abolished; the Ministries of Religion and Education were separated; seminaries were restricted in the number of students they could enroll; unauthorized religious orders lost their right to teach; bishops lost much of their power over primary schools. The liberal press announced its triumph over "the Inquisition." The Ultras mourned and raged over the weakness of the government. Martignac warned the King that the coming elections would return a Left-Center majority and that there would be no alternative to a continued policy of reconciliation. But Charles was already assembling a new cabinet, composed of the purest Ultras, which he thought would rejuvenate the only party that stood between Bourbon France and the Revolution, and would insure him an electoral triumph. Instead, the publication of the ministers' names on August 9, 1829, proved to be the first episode in the overthrow of the dynasty.

## THE REVOLUTION OF 1830

More than any before or since, the Revolution of 1830 was a Parisian affair. Its setting, its action, even its fate, were almost implausibly romantic and fixed a pattern for revolution in the minds of Frenchmen, especially among the workers and rebellious young, that was to become traditional, classical in its regularity of form. The "three glorious days" of July, 1830, were for many of the participants a self-conscious replaying of the great Revolution, a drama which they and their younger contemporaries were to play again in 1848 and 1870, though with altered issues and with more tragic effects. In the French revolutionary tradition of the nineteenth century, the line between history and literature, fact and legend, is irrevocably blurred. But the tradition itself is historical fact, a force for inspiration or fear that has exalted but also confused and embittered the struggle for liberty and equality.

There were few new social forces or ideas at work in Paris in 1830. The city and its industries had grown (the population was 800,000), but true proletarians were only slightly more numerous than in 1789; the mass misery of the Industrial Revolution had not yet infested Paris as much as it had the English manufacturing towns, or French cities like Lyons and Lille. The poverty and squalor that shocked visitors were as old as cities themselves. In 1830, the Paris crowd was much the same as it had been in 1789, composed of the poor, the unemployed, laborers, craftsmen, shopkeepers, and all the lower ranks of the middle and professional classes who were shut out of legal political activity by the Charter as they had been by earlier constitutions. Parisians had fewer leaders and less organization than in the early 1790's, when the clubs and *sections* provided both under a friendly Commune and a national government not yet armed with the disciplined soldiery and police who accompanied the Directory and were fixed in place by Napoleon.

Despite a decline in real wages since 1815 and a lingering depression in the late 1820's, the ordinary people of Paris were probably somewhat less poor than forty years earlier (though the disparity between them and the newly affluent was more obvious). They were also a good deal more literate. In the rapidly growing number of cafés, men read for themselves the political news of the day and argued questions a generation old. Only scattered groups of devotees were as yet impressed by the social doctrines of the Comte de Saint-Simon or Charles Fourier. Although Buonarotti had followers in France, *Babouvisme* was for the moment only a memory. The old faith was the strongest, Jacobin republicanism, now and then spiced with an elusive flavor of the new Bonapartist democracy. It stood against the old enemies, the Bourbons, the aristocrats, the priests and their collaborators, the *haute bourgeoisie*. But as long as these ruling elites confined their own quarrels to the Chambers and the polling place, the unfranchised had little chance of making any change in government.

Apart from the political refugees from eastern, Metternichian Europe, the most boisterous new arrivals in Paris under the restoration were the students, artists, and intellectuals who congregated on the Left Bank. They came to the city of revolution and opportunity by the hundreds, determined to make their marks in a society that no longer exalted military or clerical careers and was not yet so devoted to money-making as it would become in the next generation. They came to the schools of law, medicine, engineering, and science, to the theaters, cafés, salons, and galleries where art and wit and learning were prized above birth and riches—or so it seemed. Like the heroes and dupes of Stendhal and Balzac, they fled from the provinces to Bohemia, where they could freely live and work, or cluster about those who worked, in a city that never slept. And they came in the first, fresh flowering of romanticism when a play, a painting, or a symphony could in itself be an act of revolution.

For a time, romanticism had appeared to be the natural ally of the restored Church and monarchy, not so much, perhaps, as a revolt against the eighteenth century's rationalism or even against its Revolution as against the conformities both had ended in. To bind romanticism to any political platform is impossible, but its favored political attitude is clear: a rebellion against tyranny of any sort (except, later, its own) over men's minds and actions whether exercised by Church, society, or government. It was no contradiction, therefore, to idolize Chateaubriand as a victim of Napoleon and later to idolize Napoleon as the victim of reactionary powers. Nor was it inconsistent to idealize the Catholic Church—often without sharing the faith—while its ministers and cathedrals fell under the hammer of official anti-clericalism, and later, in the 1820's, to despise —often, for Catholics, without abjuring the faith—its restored power and pretension. Romanticism embraced the lost cause and glorified the underdog; not long after 1830 it was to grow a social conscience and make a cult of the working class, putting flesh and blood on the forbidding bones of socialist doctrine and deeply marking western intellectuals to this day.

The reaction against the cults of reason and classicism, or neoclassicism, had begun well back in the eighteenth century, and Rousseau's own complexity is indicative of romanticism's untidy definition. He by no means rejected reason in politics and education or all the standards of classicism in literature and art. Neither he nor those who followed discarded the idea of progress but insisted that in life and art men should not be bound by authority or the dictates of reason alone. The official canons of the revolutionary and Napoleonic governments, and of the established academies, theaters, and literary circles appeared to them crabbed and superficial. The rebels were younger men and, significantly, often emerged from classes and regions which did not share the values or amusements of established Parisian society. They saw themselves barred from recognition and rewards freely given to men of birth and of mere talent for imitation. As rebels, they found it easy to admire what their rivals seemed to despise: sentiment, imagination, and spontaneity; the medieval, the religious, and the exotic.

Too much can be made, however, of social and political forces, and of the familiar clash of generations. These may explain the number of romanticism's followers or, partly, why its spirit became a pose and its style a fad. But art and letters have their own inner history and influential figures. Of the last, Chateaubriand and Germaine de Staël were crucial in France. In his *Génie du Christianisme*, the former idealized the generous emotion and spontaneity of the old religion and its mystical insights. In *René* (1805), he offered uneasy youth a hero of impulsive heart, unabashed sentiment, a brother to Goethe's young Werther and Byron's Manfred. Chateaubriand's intensely personal style, his artful evocation of exotic lands and people endeared him to a generation that found Empire society stifling and the restoration dull. Madame de Staël's *De l'Allemagne* (1813) introduced to France the German romantics Schelling, Goethe, Herder, their theories and tastes, their insistence that true literature was natural and national. The tales of Sir Walter Scott reminded some Frenchmen of a medieval, hierarchical, and ordered society, but others, perhaps less comfortable, of the rightness and glamour of revolt against injustice. Byron's celebration of the generous, tortured, egoist soul, on paper and in life, made a deep impression in France, which turned to near worship upon his death in the cause of Greek independence at Missolonghi in 1824.

By then, leading French romantics were growing disillusioned with the restored monarchy, whose pretentious timidity hardly fulfilled their ideals of medieval kingship, and with the Church, whose militancy appeared more hysterical than mystical, graceless rather than spontaneous. Chateaubriand went into political opposition in 1824 and Lamennais, whose romantic view of religion had inspirited young Catholics, became progressively unhappy with the hierarchy's Gallican compromises.

The Napoleonic legend was growing and many Frenchmen who were neither romantic nor politically-minded resented the sermons from altar and throne belittling the accomplishments of the Revolution and Empire. To such men, the coronation of Charles X at Reims was an absurd pantomime, unrelated to the real France which they and the dead had forged in blood and fire.

A new generation of romantic artists had opened their struggle for recognition. In painting, Géricault's "Raft of the Medusa" had shocked the more literal followers of David at the Salon of 1819 and in 1824 Delacroix's "Massacre of Scio" drew even sharper attacks from the academicians. In drama, the established pundits stoutly resisted the playing of Shakespeare. Stendhal's defense of him and his simultaneous attack on Racine (*Racine et Shakespeare*, 1822) was a romantic manifesto, a plea for liberty of expression, lauding Shakespeare's lusty poetry and his happy ignorance of the classical unities. In 1827 a British troupe played Shakespeare in English to enthusiastic audiences, and to the dismay of entrenched critics, playwrights, and theater managers. Victor Hugo's *Preface to Cromwell* in the same year marked his revolt against the monarchy as well as against the classical rules of the stage. Calling for liberty in every sphere of life, Hugo was host to a romantic circle including Delacroix, Alexandre Dumas, Sainte-Beuve, de Musset, and de Vigny. In music, Beethoven too had conquered Parisian audiences in the late 1820's, partly through the remarkable performances of the young and willfully romantic Franz Liszt. Rossini's *William Tell* had florid music and a heroic tale to make it successful in 1829. Hector Berlioz was the foremost French composer; his extravagant orchestral effects and turbulent personal life made him an archetype of French romantic enthusiasm.

By 1830, these men were in that stage of rebellion at which the enemy has already partly given way and victory is in sight. Around them gathered a variegated crowd of followers and faddists, young people who had their uses as claques and shock troops against the forces recruited by the other side. Their cultivation of eccentric dress and behavior annoyed as much as it amused the leading artists themselves and led no few of them to reject the "romantic" label. But leaders and followers alike were conscious that theirs was a moment rare in history, conscious, for example, that their battles were being watched by the aging Goethe who had given them their heroes—ignoring, most of them, Goethe's retreat from unbridled romanticism. Delacroix sent the old man a set of lithographs for *Faust* and Berlioz sent his score for the *Damnation of Faust*. For all the ardent young men, 1830 was the year of triumph. It began with the successful performance of Hugo's romantic play *Hernani* on February 25, 1830, which the classicists had vowed to hoot off the stage. All day the romantic partisans occupied the theater, picnicking, then packed the balconies to shout down their opponents. Berlioz and Delacroix were there, to demonstrate their common interest in the liberation of the arts, together with Dumas, de Musset, de Vigny, Théophile Gautier, Gérard de Nerval, and, sitting apart, Balzac and Stendhal. Over a recurrent din, *Hernani* ran for several weeks and the older neoclassical playwrights irretrievably lost their monopoly over the Paris stage.

At the end of the year, on December 5th, Berlioz' *Symphonie Fantastique* finally received the acclaim of a Paris audience and of some of the critics. But four months before, Berlioz had joined his colleagues in another revolution which to them was no less romantic for being political; the Church and the Bourbons were part of the establishment and their overthrow would advance the cause of liberty in cultural as well as political affairs. From the moment that Charles X published the names of his Ultra cabinet, clearly in defiance of the Chamber majority, Paris talked of revolution. For the romantic young, it was a chance to act out again the glories of 1789, and to bring to power a government worthy of their triumphs in art and letters.

The great Revolution was much on the mind of the reading public in the 1820's. Already in 1818 Madame de Staël's *Considérations sur la Révolution française* had discomfitted the Royalists by its defense of the Revolution (up to 1792) as a natural reaction to the old regime's assault on ancient liberties. In 1824 Mignet published his short *Précis de la Révolution française* and by 1827 Adolphe Thiers had finished a ten-volume *Histoire de la Révolution française;* both accepted the Revolution, if not its excesses, as necessary and progressive. All three, together with Guizot's lectures at the Sorbonne, suggested that a truly liberal monarchy would be responsive to the opinions of enlightened citizens. Guizot in 1826 and Carrel in 1827 had also published histories of the English Revolution; few readers could miss the parallel between the fatal errors of the Stuart restoration and certain acts of Charles X. In August of 1829, the liberal press was ready to remind its readers of James II and of the ease with which he had been replaced by a relative who was more respectful of parliament.

Many believed that Charles X must already have planned a forceful *coup d'état*, so obviously distasteful were the men he had chosen to succeed the Martignac cabinet. Jules de Polignac, who became chief minister, was a leader of the Chevaliers de la Foi, an Ultra *émigré* who had been imprisoned by Napoleon and had originally refused to take the oath to the Charter of Louis XVIII. A self-righteous, egregiously pious man, he dreamed aloud of restoring royal prerogative and was accused by his enemies of taking reactionary instructions from visions of the saints. At the Ministries of War, Justice, and Interior were Marshal Bourmont, despised by patriots for having deserted Napoleon on the eve of Waterloo; Courvoisier, a Voltairian bigot turned zealous Catholic; and La Bourdonnaye, the most outspoken advocate of the White Terror. Wellington and Metternich expected a royal *coup d'état* followed by a popular revolution. For the moment there was neither. The government, preoccupied with foreign affairs, seemed oblivious of the gathering resentment.

The liberal *Globe* said that such a cabinet divided France into two parts, the court against the nation. The comic *Figaro* appeared bordered in black and suggested that Polignac might like to begin by rebuilding the Bastille. In January, 1830, appeared the new Orléanist *National*, financed by Talleyrand and the banker Lafitte, who managed the vast fortune of the Duke; its editors were Thiers, Mignet, and Carrel, dutifully pointing to the Glorious Revolution of 1688. Others thought of 1789 and 1792, among them a republican society recruited from students and young professionals, calling its paper *Jeune-France*. Lafayette led a revival of the society *Aide-toi, le ciel t'aidera*, organized a few years before by Guizot to press for fair elections; now it suggested that resistance to taxation would force the King to cooperate with the elected representatives of the people. The rightist press answered with declarations of royal prerogative and the King's powers of decree in the Charter's Article 14.

The first confrontation of the two sides took place in the Chamber's opening session on March 2, 1830. The King's speech warned that any opposition to his will would be met resolutely, that the love of his people would grant him the needed power. His supporters argued the letter of the Charter: Ministers were responsible to the crown. The Chamber, by a vote of 221–181, answered that the overall system of the Charter depended on a basic harmony between the King's ministers and the representatives of the nation, that such harmony did not exist, and that the

King could restore it by changing his ministers. Charles refused to give up his view of the Charter so easily and, rejecting advice to resort to bribery, dissolved the Chamber and called for new elections in July.

The King's confidence rested on a hazy view of French political realities in 1830. Forty years before, he had blamed his brother's fate on weakness and had never changed his mind. His recent tour of the provinces had drawn enthusiastic crowds. Given a vigorous campaign by King and Church—the bishops threw themselves into electioneering, much to the chagrin of more astute Royalists—his people would spurn the self-serving bourgeois radicals and return an Ultra Chamber. Charles' belief in his own unselfish devotion to France was undoubtedly sincere; and, in the midst of the protracted elections, news came of a foreign success which he expected would win him further popularity: the capture of Algiers.

After the triumphant intervention in Spain, French policy had gradually evolved toward intervention in favor of Greek independence. Both Left and Right, impelled by Christian, romantic, and humanitarian impulses, had assailed Villèle for his caution, which they said betrayed French honor. Men like Chateaubriand and Lafayette had joined hands with romantic philhellenists to launch a campaign of aid to the Greek insurgents. Charles X was won over, by sentiment and by the necessity to act before Russia and Great Britain reaped for themselves the rewards of intervention. In the battle of Navarino, October 20, 1827, a combined French-British-Russian naval force destroyed the Turkish-Egyptian fleet. A year later, a French expeditionary army forced an Egyptian evacuation of the Morea. The Bourbon government was able to take credit at home for Greek independence (London Protocols, 1829 and 1830) and almost immediately Polignac set out to win added laurels by humbling the Algerian pirates. Liberal opposition notwithstanding, the French invasion was well managed by Marshal Bourmont, and Algiers fell on July 5, 1830. French losses were small, the entire cost of the operation was made up by the Dey's captured treasury, and the liberals had been proved wrong again. Charles could believe that his foreign victories alone had won him the loyalty of his people.

The elections proved a sad disappointment but did not end his illusions. The opposition won 274 seats to the ministry's 143, but the King was still a prisoner of the Ultras' dogma that the Chamber majority represented only a troublesome coterie of bourgeois electors, that the country as a whole would applaud a vigorous assertion of royal authority.

On the 26th of July, the government published the Four Ordinances dissolving the Chamber, reducing the electorate to some 25,000 landowners, muzzling the press, and calling for new elections. In blind confidence, Charles failed to reinforce or even to alert the troops in Paris and went off, in the worst Bourbon tradition, to hunt at Rambouillet.

The events of the next three days unrolled on two very different levels: in the sun-baked streets of Paris, a popular, romantic uprising aglow with the democratic ideals of 1789; in the offices and salons of the moderate bourgeois notables, a quickly organized effort to convince Charles X of his folly and, failing that, to insure the accession of the Duc d'Orléans and the preservation of the Charter. The moderate Deputies wanted no revolution and no Republic, no appreciable widening of the suffrage; they were content merely to undo a royal action that threatened their political power. Although liberal newspaper editors immediately published and circulated a protest against the King's "violation of the laws" and suggested public resistance, a cluster of opposition Deputies met on the 27th at the home of the banker Casimir-Périer and decided to oppose such resistance. It was already too late. The printers, who were the best-organized and naturally the most articulate of workers, were in the streets with the students, urging others to join them in demonstrations; a few old members of the Carbonari hastened to rouse the *arrondissements* to insurrection. The King's contribution was to appoint Marshal Marmont, another hated betrayer of Napoleon, to command the royal troops in the capital.

On the 28th of July barricades rose at several points in the city, manned by armed republican workers and students, bourgeois National Guardsmen, and Bonapartist veterans. That night the tricolor flew atop the Hotel de Ville; excited crowds shouted "Down with the Bourbons!" and sang the Marseillaise along the boulevards. The alarmed moderates, among them Lafayette, Guizot, Laffitte, and Casimir-Périer, appealed in vain to Marmont and Polignac to force the King's withdrawal of the Ordinances, then hastened to offer power to the Duc d'Orléans. He had long been in the wings—since the allies had used his name to hurry along Louis XVIII's dissolution of the Chambre Introuvable in 1816.

The 29th of July was decisive. Students poured out of the Latin Quarter to join workers from Saint Antoine and well-dressed bourgeois to drive the soldiers out of Paris. Two regiments defected to the insurgents and Marmont abandoned the city, leaving behind 200 dead. Paris had lost nearly 2000 in the fighting, but there was little looting or reprisal. "The people," said Berlioz, "have been sublime," and the romantics celebrated the perfect revolution. Young republicans like Raspail and Cavaignac proclaimed the Commune and the Republic at the Hotel de Ville, hoping to make Lafayette President. But when he arrived, it was as commander of the reorganized National Guard and at his side were the Orléanist managers Laffitte and Casimir-Périer.

It is said that from Saint Cloud Charles X could see the tricolor on the towers of Notre Dame. Too late, he offered to withdraw the Ordinances and name a new ministry. His messengers were rebuffed and the real answer—to King and republicans alike—appeared the next morning, July 30th, plastered on the walls of Paris:

Charles X can never return to Paris; he has shed the blood of his people. The Republic would expose us to dangerous divisions; it would involve us in hostilities with Europe.

The Duc d'Orléans is a prince devoted to the cause of the Revolution.

The Duc d'Orléans has never fought against us.

The Duc d'Orléans was at Jemappes.

The Duc d'Orléans is a citizen-king.

The Duc d'Orléans has carried the tricolor under the enemy's fire; the Duc d'Orléans alone can carry it again. We will have no other flag.

The Duc d'Orléans does not commit himself. He awaits the expression of our wishes. Let us proclaim those wishes, and he will accept the Charter. . . . It is from the French people that he will hold his crown.

Unsigned, it was composed by Thiers and Mignet. The revolution, perfect or not, was to be that of 1688.

None other than Talleyrand persuaded the Duke to leave his retreat at Neuilly that night, to proceed to Paris and assume the Lieutenant-Generalcy of the realm, which was duly conferred by the Chamber on the 31st. As he rode to the Hotel de Ville, the crowds were sullen, but Lafayette was ready with a dramatic gesture; on a balcony draped with the tricolor, he embraced Orléans and the people massed in the square below shouted their approval. Charles X abdicated on the 2nd of August, hoping in vain that the dynasty would survive in the person of his grandson as Henri V, under an Orléanist regency. Philippe d'Orléans had done as much for the infant Louis XV in 1715 (not without seizing power for himself at the expense of the crown), but the Duke ignored his promises to Charles and accepted the throne for himself from the Chamber on August 9th. To loyal followers of the Bourbons, it was a second regicide, more brutal than the first because less dictated by the force of circumstance. Charles X, last of the Bourbon kings of France, crossed the Channel to exile on August 16, 1830.

The ambition of Orléans, added to the fatal illusions of Charles, thus prevented the establishment of a genuine parliamentary system under the legitimate dynasty, and exposed France to further division and abiding bitterness. The King's abandonment of his older brother's position as an active mediator, above the strife of parties, had made him a partisan ruler, a willing prisoner of men whose vision of the "true France" was distasteful to other Frenchmen. Worse, the hierarchy had confirmed the fears of Lamennais and the liberal Catholics in making Catholicism a party Church, which had kept silent even during the White Terror. In 1830, only religious houses suffered damage at the hands of the insurgents. By relying too much on political force to reconvert France, Church and monarchy had once again suffered a common disaster.

The fall of Charles X overshadowed for a century the solid achievements of the Bourbon restoration, which, if it failed to restore the Bourbons, did much to restore the nation. Its fifteen years had made a new start, never in serious danger of reversal until Charles dismissed Martignac. The political history of the restoration complicates the common view that it was a reactionary throwback after a generation of progress. More surely, the reaction against liberty began in 1792, against equality at Thermidor, in social and religious affairs under Napoleon. The restoration admittedly did nothing for economic equality and, if anything, social cleavages were deepened; in religion and education there was reaction. But until nearly the end, France enjoyed a measure of political liberty unmatched since the early 1790's and, within the narrow suffrage, a parliamentary experience unique in her history to that time. Despite press restrictions and official influence on elections, a losing or minority party did not have to fear repression, imprisonment, or deportation. Until 1828, the restoration held a better balance among the active forces of its day than did the regime which followed it.

The nation was liberated and revived, its place among the European powers regained, its economy restored, its public finances and credit managed with uncommon integrity. The Catholic Church paid dearly for its reconstruction but it was reconstructed nonetheless and drew to itself new men and new enthusiasm which were crucial in the difficult century ahead. Lay societies proliferated, notably for work in prisons, hospitals, poorhouses, and workingmen's shelters. The restoration saw the birth of social Catholicism, directed by a lay elite that was destined to transform the economic and social policies of the hierarchy itself. The defeat of 1830 forced many Catholics to reexamine their mission and freed them to pursue it along new and broader paths. For good and ill, the restoration founded a new colonial empire in North Africa and did much to rebuild French military power. It left to its successors a society which was, for the early nineteenth century, relatively prosperous. The throne still rested on Napoleon's blocks of granite. It had not collapsed; its occupant had climbed down. The man who clambered up had much to thank his cousins for. It was not the fault of the restoration that the Orléanist dynasty lasted only eighteen years.

## THE JULY MONARCHY

Well before Delacroix finished his famous painting it was evident that not Liberty but interests had led the people in 1830. Delacroix pictured the Revolution as classless and disinterested—workers, students, and bourgeois offering their lives together in the cause of freedom—but a single class emerged the winner, or a portion of a class, the upper bourgeoisie. Between the illusions of Charles X and the romance of the Paris crowds lay the reality; there had been no revolution, only the defeat of a Bourbon *coup d'état*. To the frustrated democrats, the July Monarchy was nothing more than the restoration by other means and a few, very few, other men. Republican disturbances continued in Paris and other cities, but the peasant army quickly recovered its discipline and snuffed out opposition. To the Left in France, the classic pattern of revolution has always ended in betrayal and reaction—in 1830, 1848, 1871, 1936, and 1944; the July Revolution was an oft-remembered lesson in the futility of cooperation with the classes above one's own, and the eighteen years of the July Monarchy seemed to prove that the lower middle and working classes could expect no hearing for their aspirations from a bourgeois regime. Without being a revolution, then, the events of 1830 revived and hardened the French revolutionary tradition, sharpened class suspicions, and prepared the propertyless for more radical solutions to their problems.

The notables' solution of 1830 was hardly radical. The last Chamber elected under Charles X, which he had tried to dissolve, remained as the first of the July Monarchy. On August 7, 1830, two days before Louis Philippe was named, it expunged Louis XVIII's legitimist preamble to the Charter as an affront to the nation, imposing the Charter on the new monarch as an expression of the people's will. Louis accepted the title King of the French, as had Louis XVI in 1791, another sign of submission to popular sovereignty. Catholicism lost its standing as the State religion; as in Napoleon's Concordat it was merely the religion "professed by the majority of the French." To the section on the press was added a promise that censorship would never be reestablished. The two Chambers explicitly received equal initiative in legislation; the Chamber of Peers' sessions were opened to the public. In 1831 the peerage lost its hereditary nature, the King winning the right to name the members of the upper house. On the other hand, he lost the right, granted in the Bourbon Charter's Article 14, to suspend the laws of the land, and the right to name the presiding officers of electoral colleges and the Chamber of Deputies. The National Guard was formally revived, charged with the defense of the Charter, and the tricolor became once again the national emblem. It was implied but never settled that the ministers would be responsible to the lower Chamber.

The reign of Louis Philippe is known as the bourgeois monarchy, with accent on the adjective. But even if the word is applied, as it most often was in nineteenth-century French literature and history, to the wealthier strata of the middle class, the July Monarchy was never tidily bourgeois in its electorate and political leaders or civil and military servants. Its bourgeois nature lay deeper, in its demeanor, its values, and in the interests it chose to defend. Thanks to its defects and the acerbic genius of such critics as Balzac and Daumier, the Orléanist regime did more than any other to make "bourgeois" an epithet, ready on the lips of Frenchmen of all classes, including the bourgeoisie itself.

By a law of April 19, 1831, the qualification for voting was lowered from 300 francs of direct tax payment to 200, whereby some 200,000 French were now eligible, about double the number before 1830. Making up less than 3 percent of the adult male population, the *pays légal* was still restricted largely to the wealthiest landowners. Not only were the great majority who had waged the Revolution of 1830 thus excluded but also wealthy professional men and bourgeois whose income was mainly commercial or industrial. At best, the electorate approached that of England before the Reform Bill of 1832. Whatever the source of their wealth, and whatever their main occupation, French electors were also landed proprietors and little more representative of the society as a whole than their restoration counterparts had been.

If the electorate was only slightly more representative, the elite governing France was slightly less. The Chambers were cleansed of Ultras. The Orléanist government proceeded to discharge thousands of legitimist officers from the civil and military services in a purge far more sweeping than any under the restoration. The old nobility now carried out an *émigration intérieure,* retiring to their estates in the country and to the urban fortress of the Quartier Saint Germain, to await what many of them believed would be the quick demise of a regime so foolish as to deprive itself of their services. The results were complex. Although the regime did not collapse, at least in the manner hoped for, and many of its new officials were no doubt readier to perform their duties in a liberal spirit, a standard of probity in office was lost, giving way to an often too obvious collusion between officialdom and plutocracy. In Paris society, the salons of the Bonapartist nobility and Orléanist *haute bourgeoisie* in the Chassée d'Antin and Faubourg Saint-Honoré enjoyed a certain revenge for the hurtful snubs of the restoration, but social life was duller all the same and invitations from across the river were no less prized for being infrequent. For social purposes, the forced brightness of M. Thiers or of earnest academicians had never equaled the irreverent lighter touch of the old regime and was even less likely to do so now that the better-behaved intellectuals enjoyed favors from the new government.

Apart from the loss of many legitimist nobles and clerics, and the addition of new men like Thiers, Guizot, and Victor Cousin, the main body of notables which had emerged from the Empire and early restoration continued to dominate French economic and political life: new landowners, imperial prefects and army officers, professional politicians and bureaucrats, several leading bankers and manufacturers. Except for a few nobles like the liberal Duc de Broglie and the sons of the King himself, the notables were the heirs, or the sons of the heirs, of the Revolution and Empire. Not a bourgeois class in the economic or social sense, they made a political class bound together by their varied positions of power and by a view of the good society that has been called Orléanism, the French version of nineteenth-century liberalism.

Orléanist liberalism was a creed for the comfortable few, a middle group in opposition to those on the Right who would undo the Revolution—or, as under the restoration, would demand the lion's share of office—and those on the Left who would make the Revolution democratic, or worse. After winning liberty and equality for themselves and their interests from Charles X and the Ultras, they in turn demanded order and patience from the inferior classes of society, whom they considered unfit to share in government. Between the principle of popular sovereignty in the Declaration of the Rights of Man and the actual exercise of political power they interposed the *pays légal,* a body of citizens whose material stake in society presumably made up the *pays sérieux.* One wing of Orléanists, called the party of "movement" and including men like Lafayette, Laffitte, and Alexis de Tocqueville, believed that economic progress and education would bring a gradual extension of the *pays légal.* The party of "resistance," including several of the former Doctrinaires and soon to be led by Guizot, considered the Revolution of 1830 a final step, achieving the essential balance in society for generations to come. They saw the *pays légal* not as a temporarily narrowed expression of the sovereign people but as an instrument of sovereign government, called forth from above to serve the State and to share in the blessings of liberty which it alone could understand. The practical working-out of this view began with the refusal to submit the revised Charter to popular vote or even to a Constituent Assembly and it ended in Guizot's system of government, which epitomized *immobilisme* and helped provoke the Revolution of 1848.

Distrusting abstract principles as much as they distrusted the common run of men, Orléanist liberals of the resistance party put no less faith in "given" laws and institutions than their conservative royalist enemies, but they read history differently. What was "given" or natural to France was not the old regime alone but the old regime followed and transformed by the remarkable sequence of events that seemed to parallel so closely the English revolution of the seventeenth century: a moderate parliamentary start, a royal reaction bringing the execution of a King, war and civil strife, a military strong man, a compromise restoration of the royal house uneasily maintained by the first brother, foolishly upset by the second, 1688 and 1830. Instead of Bossuet and Metternich, they read Montesquieu and Burke, whom they very sensibly considered more relevant to nineteenth-century France, and thus concluded that a reasonable system of law, parliament, and sober judiciary was proof against the tyranny of man or mob. But their system was far more static than the British arrangements they professed to admire and far from consistent with Montesquieu's ideas on decentralization of power and a multiplicity of private associations standing between the individual (even the worker) and superior authority. Guizot and his party appeared to end their reading of English history at 1688 or, at the latest, 1831. But their *immobilisme* was not only the product of distorted theory or bad comparative history; it grew also out of circumstances. Guizot bore the responsibility of power, as Tocqueville and the others did not, and led an Orléanist elite which was aware of its smallness, of the unpopularity of its interests, and which constantly feared attack from Left and Right. To their fears, the Orléanist notables joined a complacent confidence in the essential rightness of their cause and in their own political abilities to meet any emergency. No combination was more likely to close them to new ideas or ameliorative actions to meet the changing needs of French society.

Louis Philippe himself exemplified the party of resistance. At fifty-seven he came to the throne an enormously wealthy man, with much experience and travel, including sojourns in England and America. He considered himself expert in economic, political, and foreign affairs, much the superior of his Bourbon cousins and the aristocrats he had outplayed in 1830. Without denying his own dignity, he eschewed the pomp, but also the grace, of the Bourbon court and appeared among Parisians on foot, dressed in bourgeois style, speaking bourgeois wisdom, driving bourgeois bargains with his own government over his royal allowance and that of his five sons. One of the greatest landowners in France, he avoided turning his holdings over to the royal domain according to tradition by prudently transferring title to his family. Although bourgeois guests often appeared at the Tuileries, he had little faith in their competence outside the world of business, and some reason to doubt it even there. With the crowd, he was condescending at best and always determined to be firm, yet at the end he shrank from the bloodshed that might have saved his throne. Neither pious nor irreverent, neither cold nor sentimental, he was a man of the *juste milieu* and under other conditions, perhaps in his younger, less complacent years, he might have built an enduring dynasty.

The early events of his reign confirmed Louis Philippe in his policy of resistance. Together with several attempts on his life, there were revolts of Right and Left. In 1832, the indefatigable Duchesse de Berry tried to revive the Vendée in behalf of her son, Henry V. The feeble uprising was a pale imitation of the past, and easily dispersed. Her humiliation included imprisonment and the discovery that she was pregnant from a second, secret marriage to an obscure Italian count.

Legitimist hopes had never fallen lower than in the decade of the 1830's. The Left presented a greater challenge. July's hopes died slowly among the petty bourgeoisie, the workers and the poor, the republican intellectuals who felt they had made the Revolution. Paris and the larger cities that autumn brimmed with political agitation in clubs, cafés, liberal and republican newspapers, pamphlets, conferences, and street demonstrations. Louis Philippe appointed Laffitte his chief minister in November of 1830, as an assurance of further liberalization to come. For a time, the republicans seemed content to hate the past. They clamored, unsuccessfully, for the execution of Polignac and his associates. In February of 1831 an anti-clerical mob pillaged the palace of the Archbishop of Paris while the police looked the other way. But neither Polignac nor the Archbishop could be blamed for continued unemployment and low wages or the scarcity of bread. The Laffitte ministry came and went without any sign of popular reform in any sphere, without a gesture of aid to the much-heralded uprisings in Belgium, Italy, and Poland. Resentment quickly turned against the new regime, next headed by the party of resistance in the person of Casimir-Périer.

The first serious attack on Orléanist society came not in Paris but in Lyons, where the silk-workers' wages had been cut arbitrarily, contrary to custom. Their peaceful demonstrations of October, 1831, won agreement from the associated manufacturers and local officials on a scale of minimum wages arrived at by conferences of workers and employers. But a minority of masters repudiated the plan and the weavers struck in November, expelling the royal troops from the city with the help of friendly National Guardsmen. The Paris government replied with overwhelming military force, after denouncing collective bargaining and the minimum wage as unthinkable violations of economic freedom.

Lacking their own leaders, workingmen were drawn more and more into republican-led agitation. In April of 1834, amid continuing demonstrations, the government struck at the political clubs in a law prohibiting association. Workers and republicans again rose in Lyons, after the authorities broke their promises of immunity and arrested several strike leaders. Repression was complete and savage. In Paris, a much smaller rising met the same fate; the exasperated National Guard (wholly bourgeois since a reorganization in 1831) butchered guilty and innocent alike in the rue Transnonain. Daumier's stark drawing of the victims recalled David's "Marat Assassinated" and was revered by the lower-class enemies of the regime. In 1835, the press's freedom to criticize the King and the Charter was curtailed by threats of heavy fines and imprisonment. But as disturbances died down and a measure of prosperity softened class feeling, the repressive laws on republican newspapers and societies were enforced only sporadically.

In the first decade of the reign, official relations with the Church were relatively placid. The Catholic clergy, whose support no conservative regime would lightly forego, fared better than the anti-clerical posturing of the Orléanists had suggested it might. Although the funds allotted to the Ministry of Religion were cut in 1830—as was the King's own civil list—the government soon made peace with the hierarchy and with Rome. In September of 1830 Pius VIII called upon French Catholics to accept Louis Philippe. On its side, the government interpreted the laws concerning religious orders very generously. The Protestant Guizot's famous law on primary education of 1833 provided for Catholic religious instruction and gave priests an active role in teaching and administration. The law and its discussion reflected the bourgeois view that religion was needed to keep social peace; the *pays légal* might be *sérieux* enough to content itself with Voltaire, but women, children, and workers needed the stronger rein of Catholicism. It was one thing to let the mob of 1831 despoil the Archbishop of Paris, de Quélen (who had urged Charles X to crush his domestic enemies as though they were Algerians), but in the face of economic and political disturbances it was time to reunite the forces of order. The King had something of Napoleon's practical view of religion, though he set a better example in church attendance and sober family life.

In foreign policy, Louis Philippe was no less cautious. To establish his dynasty he wanted peace and the respect of Europe's monarchs; therefore he opposed the wishes of French republicans and some in the party of movement that France support the revolutionary attempts of 1830 in Belgium, Italy, Poland, and Germany. Metternich and Nicholas I of Russia had been alarmed by the second fall of the Bourbons; Europe's liberals had thought of 1792 and hoped for French aid. Both were nearly as wrong as the Paris crowds had been in July. France remained inactive until the Belgian revolt succeeded; then Louis moved to insure its survival. Talleyrand went to London as ambassador and won British cooperation in supporting the new independent kingdom of Belgium against the Dutch, and against the inclination of the eastern powers to intervene. The King, though a veteran of Jemappes, retained no illusions of retaking Belgium for France and, fearing British reaction, even denied himself the luxury of an Orléanist dynasty in Brussels. The Belgians' election of his son, the Duc de Nemours, was ignored and Prince Leopold of Coburg ascended the throne. There were consolations. Louis Philippe's daughter was Leopold's wife; England's good will seemed insured in 1831 when a British fleet supported French troops against the Dutch; most important, one of the sentinels placed over France in 1815 had been dismissed, its place taken by a small, friendly and (after 1839) neutral state.

Louis Philippe refused any aid to Polish and Italian patriots, despite the outcries and insults of republicans and Bonapartists. Polish exiles in Paris had won the fervent acclamation of French romantics; they watched together in helpless anger as Nicholas I sent Paskievich to crush Warsaw and abrogated the Polish constitution in 1831. In Italy, Austrian troops snuffed out insurrections in Parma and Modena; it was only when they entered the rebellious Papal States in 1832 that France sent troops to occupy Ancona, not to support rebellion but to insure Austria's departure once order was restored. All foreign troops retired in 1838.

Louis Philippe was only slightly readier to follow Napoleon's example in the eastern Mediterranean, where the French protégé, Mohammed Ali of Egypt, had taken Syria from the Sultan in 1832 and threatened to go on to Constantinople itself. England and Russia could not accept the prospect of a vigorous regime in Turkey, especially one allied to France. But Thiers, as first minister, persisted in abetting Mohammed Ali's ambitions. In 1840, England joined Russia, Prussia, and Austria in the Treaty of London, which forced Mohammed Ali to give up all of his conquests but southern Syria. Although French opinion was inflamed and the army placed in readiness, Louis Philippe ended by dismissing Thiers and accepting the Convention of Alexandria, which granted Mohammed hereditary rule of Egypt. Predictably, this sensible policy was denounced as appeasement by the King's opponents and much was made of the "shopkeeper" who traded French glory for stable trade relations. But the storm passed and Louis Philippe's caution has probably been taken too seriously as a cause of discontent with the regime.

More dangerous was the complacent immobility in all matters of the governments which followed Thiers'. From 1840 to 1848, the chief minister in fact if not in title was Guizot, a historian, a former Doctrinaire, a personally upright Protestant whose abilities and conservative tastes earned him a larger share of the King's confidence than any previous minister had enjoyed. Louis Philippe, determined to impose his own views, resented strong ministers like Casimir-Périer and the Duc de Broglie, distrusted the liberalism of Laffitte, the pugnacity of Thiers. In Guizot he found a man who agreed with him and who possessed the political skill to keep a sympathetic majority in the Chamber of Deputies. To this end, Guizot employed all the devices he had so bitterly complained of under the restoration: lists of voters were altered, appeals delayed, opposition candidacies hampered, the elections conducted under prefectural pressures, electors bribed and intimidated. Once elected, Deputies were persuaded to Guizot's policies with favors, purses, and lucrative government offices. These last, the "placemen," made up as much as one-third of the lower house in the 1840's. Despite the broader franchise, the Chambers of the July Monarchy were less representative than some during the restoration and much more tightly controlled by King and ministers. Guizot's aim was to conserve and solidify the gains of 1830 by insuring internal peace and prosperity; but he and Louis Philippe, confident of their political sagacity, grew progressively out of touch with French realities and permitted no opposition, even within the *pays légal,* to remind them of changes that were making French society more complex with every passing year. The Guizot system won easy political victories at the polls and in parliament but failed to account for economic, social, and intellectual forces building up outside the comfortable world of the Tuileries and the Palais Bourbon.

## A CHANGING SOCIETY

Since the great Revolution, the French population had grown roughly as fast as French productivity in industry and agriculture. In this respect, the first half of the nineteenth century was but a continuation of the eighteenth. Although the Revolution raised great expectations of prosperity, its effects tended to hide what was in fact a decline in real income for many Frenchmen. The partial distribution of Church and *émigré* wealth, the apparent profits of war, the unnatural trade pattern of the Continental System, the great human activity concentrated in Paris, the modest improvements in transport and communication, and the increased consumption of nourishing but hardly luxurious items such as the potato, all combined with the incessant political turmoil to cover the backwardness of the French economy. But the relative calm of the 1840's, which gratified the Orléanist elite, helped reveal to ordinary

Frenchmen, from bank office to peasant hut, the negligence or incompetence of their superiors in economic affairs. That the decade ended in depression and revolution was perhaps less significant than that it was also a time of unprecedented emigration of ordinary Frenchmen to foreign lands.

It is a commonplace that France remained primarily an agricultural country to 1848 and well beyond, that the rural population actually increased during the first half of the nineteenth century, that in 1870 over half of all Frenchmen still lived and worked on the land, and that according to one (though hardly conclusive) indicator, half of all French wealth was in land as late as 1900. Apart from keeping high tariffs on foodstuffs, demanded by the large landowners who dominated the Chambers, the Bourbon and Orléanist governments concerned themselves only marginally with agricultural problems. In techniques, productivity, and peasant standards of living, the differences among various regions of France were as evident under the restoration and July Monarchy as they had been to the English traveler Arthur Young in the eighteenth century. In the 1840's, peasants in some departments still subsisted mainly on coarse rye bread from grain raised on land which was potentially versatile but insufficiently fertilized, often left fallow, indifferently harrowed with primitive tools, and reaped with sickles. In other areas, rye had long since given way to wheat, potatoes, sugar beets, vineyards, orchards, and livestock raised by farmers employing crop rotation, cultivated pasture, and improved tools for every task; there meat appeared more often on the peasant's table, as did wine, fruits, and vegetables.

Such differences reflected variations in landholding patterns, in sources of capital and credit, in examples of local proprietors, and in transport facilities nearly as much as variations in soil and climate. In some regions, large proprietors as well as small left their lands in tiny scattered plots to be sharecropped. Even for those who desired it, capital was scarce; only under the Second Empire did the government make a serious attempt to provide farm credit on less than usurious terms. The July Monarchy sought to provide good examples through local agricultural committees and societies supported by the Ministry of Commerce and Agriculture, prize contests, and exhibitions. Also helpful were some of the Bourbon aristocrats who returned to their estates after the debacle of 1830 and devoted themselves to improving farm methods. The extension of canals and roads in the 1840's allowed area specialization; together with the advent of the railroad, they promised to end the threat of local famines. But in spite of these changes, French agriculture by 1848 had more in common with that of two hundred years before than that of fifty years afterward: primitive methods, low productivity, unstable prices, dismal living conditions. Although young Frenchmen were not forced off the land, as were Englishmen, they went into factories and cities because they expected a higher standard of living or at the least a change from the dreary and ill-rewarded round of life which critics of industrial dreariness have too often succeeded in idealizing.

The abundance of cheap labor found no abundance of industrial jobs. Although French industry made relatively more progress than French agriculture before 1848, at no time did it attain the rate of growth that was transforming England's land and people. Many factors contributed to retard French industrial development. Napoleon's Continental System not only distorted the economy, ruining some trades and falsely encouraging others, but led at the end of the war to a general clamor by French manufacturers for a continuation of high-tariff protection, against English goods in particular. The landowners who dominated the Chambers between 1815 and 1848 gladly acquiesced in high tariffs as a means of retaining the inflated prices on food that wartime shortages had granted them. With the sheltered markets of conquered Europe lost, the unnatural demands of wartime greatly reduced, and frugal governments in power, industrial production grew very slowly, employment and wages lagged, while the workers' food remained high in price, and the employers' taxes low. The French economic system was thus nearly as exclusive in its benefits as was the political system with its limited suffrage. The profits of the governing elite, which they tended to equate with the good of France, were secure, and they showed little more interest in rapid industrial expansion than they did in agricultural modernization.

France had led Europe for generations in making luxury goods, in small quantities, of individual style and beauty. Men of unusual skills often preferred to retain their quality trade, in clothing, furs, glassware, jewelry, and furniture, rather than to seek larger markets for less expensive versions of their products. Mass markets did not yet exist at home and foreign retaliation for high French tariffs restricted the export trade, notably in wines, silks, and woolens. Pride in the small family firm and in traditional local products further discouraged expansion. Many wealthy men who might have invested in industrial enterprises chose instead the older paths to recognition in France that were now open to them for the first time, in the Chamber, the higher reaches of the administration, and the salon. And the ultimate gauge of success in the new plutocracy as in the old was the acquisition of land, still regarded as the safest form of wealth, and the most aristocratic.

More tangible factors also slowed development. Coal, which was England's greatest asset, was scarce in France, difficult to mine and to transport; the tariff discouraged its importation. Iron ore lay in small, scattered deposits. France still possessed a fair supply of wood, numerous but minor sources of water power, cheap animal and human labor. As long as protected prices insured profits, it was easier to remain small in size and primitive in method. The result was that French iron and steel—the stuff of the Machine Age—were the most expensive in Europe, and machinery was costly to buy and maintain. The steam engine came only slowly into use; by 1848 there were perhaps 5000 in all of France. French roads were unevenly maintained, French rivers difficult and unpredictable for freight in bulk. Connections between one market and another, one resource and another, were long and slow to a degree almost incomprehensible to the twentieth century, when France appears deceptively small on map and timetable.

Given these disadvantages and the formidable opposition of vested interests in the parliament, the financial community, and the civil service, French industry nonetheless made impressive gains before 1848. The forces of movement sufficiently outweighed those of resistance to pave the way for rapid growth later, under the Second Empire. The economic reforms of the Revolution, codified in Napoleon's *Code de Commerce*, facilitated the organization of enterprise. The schools of science and engineering, led by the École Polytechnique, were models for the world, including England and America, and produced thousands of men who gave France the leading role in the spread of technology on the Continent. Ultimately, perhaps, it was the scientists, engineers, merchants, bankers, and ordinary, ingenious citizens who refused to be content with their own or their country's economic condition who made the difference. Often well acquainted with the men and methods of English industry, they slowly opened to themselves at home and abroad sources of capital which enabled them to build modern facilities for manufacture. Their success, despite frequent business crises that intimidated the money market, at least complicates the common assumption that French entrepreneurs lacked vigor in the nineteenth century and suggests, on the contrary, an extraordinary tenacity and ingenuity in the face of obstacles which most of their English, German, and American counterparts never had to meet.

The governments of the restoration and the July Monarchy made helpful contributions to economic progress despite their primary concern with balanced budgets, and the outcries of their supporters against any expenditures that might increase taxes. Roads that had badly deteriorated under Revolution and Empire were repaired; to the 1200 kilometers of canal extant on Napoleon's fall, the restoration added 900, the July Monarchy 1400. Many rivers were improved for navigation, including the Seine at Paris. By the mid-1840's some 200 steamers joined the thousands of freight barges on French rivers. But the waterways were hardly adequate and rates remained excessively high, so high at Saint-Étienne, for example, that they led to the construction of the first French railroad.

In 1832, the 58-kilometer railroad between Saint-Étienne and Lyons was built by a group of engineers headed by Marc Seguin, the inventor of the tubular steam boiler and admiring student of English rails. From this tiny start, the July Monarchy witnessed, and alternately aided and retarded, the construction of some 2000 kilometers by 1848, when England had three times that length and Prussia nearly double. Financiers of Paris, including James de Rothschild, were drawn into the building of a line to Saint-Germain in 1837. An immediate success, it started a railway boom which attracted English and French capital in large amounts. The railway law of 1842 provided a basic plan for future construction by private enterprise, on land and roadbeds acquired by the government; but its operation was hampered by the desire of the government to limit speculation, by the rivalry of canal, coach, and local interests in the Chamber, and by the Corps de Ponts et Chaussées, which hoped for state construction throughout. Nevertheless, Paris in 1848 was connected by rail to Orléans and Bourges, le Havre, Brussels, and Boulogne; and plans were ready for a network to cover all of France. What wise men like M. Thiers had pronounced a passing fad was to revolutionize the French economy before his own lifetime had passed.

Although the railroads were to come under the financial control of the great Paris banks, smaller money markets of various kinds and sizes sprang up before 1848. These were barely adequate to finance the most modest local enterprises and never equal to the larger investments required for the growing textile, machinery, and metals industries. The relative scarcity of ready capital (in which England's lead was a matter of centuries) encouraged a tight interpenetration of industry and the large private banks of Paris run by the oligarchy associated with the Bank of France. This *haute banque parisienne* included Laffitte, the Périers, Mallets, Delesserts, Foulds, Adolphe d'Eichthal, and the great house of Rothschild. From the other direction, established industrialists in mining, metallurgy, and textiles such as the de Wendels of Lorraine and the Schneider brothers of Le Creusot joined the financial oligarchy until, on the eve of the Revolution of 1848, there existed for the first time in France a closely related group of magnates whose interests lay in the development of large-scale enterprise. In time, they might have made the July Monarchy bourgeois in the ordinary, Marxist sense of the word, but the Revolution intervened and their economic and political power was fully established only under the Second Empire and the Third Republic.

In 1848, French industry was still small in scale. Although Paris was perhaps the world's largest manufacturing city, with over 400,000 workers out of a population of 1 million, not one-tenth of its enterprises employed more than a dozen men each. Out of a total French population of 35 million, about 1 million worked in middle-sized or large-scale factories and the "middle" usually had less than twenty employees. The largest agglomeration of men and machines was found in the textile industry (mainly in cotton, the newest and fastest growing) of Alsace, the iron and steel works of the Loire basin and Lorraine, coal mines in the north, silk in Lyons and Saint-Étienne, and in the machine shops of Paris. Since 1815, the cities of Rouen, Lille, Saint-Étienne, Roubaix, Amiens, and Mulhouse had doubled or tripled their working-class populations.

No French city was prepared for the influx of new proletarians in the nineteenth century. Housing, sanitation, and schools were nowhere adequate, social services were rare and primitive. Only in the newest industrial centers such as Mulhouse in Alsace were there systematic efforts to build new housing. In the older, larger cities of Paris, Lille, Rouen, and Lyons the newcomers crowded into the oldest tenements, attics, and cellar slums that were cold, damp, verminous, and airless. To these cheerless holes they returned after 13-15 hours of work a day; constant fatigue and undernourishment made them prey to every disease; cholera swept through the working-class districts periodically, tuberculosis ravaged constantly; infant mortality was as high as 50 per cent in the industrial regions, the statistics cruelly complicated by infanticide. Of the million who worked in large establishments, notably in textiles, at least half were women and children who worked at a fraction of men's wages, which were often set at bare subsistence and kept there by the relative abundance and utter disorganization of labor. Family life and education for the young were often impossible. Men avoided the ties of marriage, preferring concubinage, against which the right-thinking railed in vain. Women, married or not, supplemented their wages in prostitution. Families tried to lose their problems in alcohol. Illness, old age, or unemployment meant bottomless misery, unless one had relatives in the country. The suffering which men on the land had borne alone was compounded when crowded into cities, and doubly resented as the bourgeoisie, eager to prove itself equal to the old aristocracy, paraded its wealth before the poor. In the newly industrialized centers, company houses and company stores, familiar from the Rhine to the Mississippi, made added profits for the "new feudal lords."

The expression was used by Villeneuve-Bargemont, a conscientious prefect of the Nord whose report of 1828 on workers' conditions in the new industries had forced many of the comfortable to face the social question for the first time in an official document. As in England, concern for the health of urban army conscripts prompted the first and only factory legislation of the July Monarchy. In some cities, nine of ten men called up were physically unfit; the average was at least half in the industrial departments, as compared with one-quarter from agricultural areas. The law of 1841, passed over the direst warnings of the supporters of laissez-faire, prohibited the employment of children under 8, set eight hours of labor as the maximum for those between 8 and 12, twelve hours for those 12 to 16, prescribed rest periods and a guarantee of primary schooling. Any likelihood of the law's enforcement was reduced by leaving inspection to unsalaried retired manufacturers. The practice, if not the principle, of laissez-faire was safe and its violations remained, in employers' terms, constructive. Only a few purists, faithful disciples of Adam Smith such as J. B. Say, were ready to challenge tariffs, subsidies, employer associations, and the like as contrary to economic liberty.

Except for a few Protestant employers in Alsace and a few Catholic entrepreneurs and officials who thought it possible to apply Christianity to the working class, the ruling notables were little concerned with social problems. Followers of Smith, Ricardo, and Malthus like Say, Charles

Dunoyer, and Frédéric Bastiat described the workers' plight as largely inevitable and made worse by the worker's own ignorance, his intemperance in wine and women. Until they learned better, said Dunoyer, they would continue to afflict society with the ugly spectacle of their misery. Guizot opposed discussion of the social question; since their suffering was inevitable, why call their attention to it? As in England, in America, and, more recently, in the Soviet Union, more optimistic men argued that only one or two generations might have to be sacrificed for the ultimate progress of all. To many bourgeois Frenchmen, the workers were a race apart, hardened to a brutish life ordained by nature's law as the serf's had been by God's.

The full weight of government fell on workers who tried to engage in common action, or even discussion, to improve their conditions. The restoration and July Monarchy preserved the strictures of the Napoleonic Code, enforced the laws against workers' combinations, and ignored employers' combinations which frequently contrived to force wages downward. Vagrancy laws were sometimes invoked to limit freedom of movement. The fiction was maintained that economic freedom for all precluded collective bargaining, that a worker whose unfed family waited at home could negotiate on equal terms with the masters of Le Creusot or the Anzin mines. The 1840's witnessed many strikes, but few were successful; strikers were coerced by soldiers and police, their leaders were imprisoned, their places were eagerly taken by other men, women and children, at least in the less skilled trades.

Only in the older crafts were the workers organized in their own behalf. The *compagnonnages,* dating from the Middle Ages, were secret societies of bachelor craftsmen that offered aid and shelter to young workers who were perfecting their skills on the traditional *Tour de France.* There were probably no more than 100,000 men in these societies, which were naturally strongest in the building trades, and they rarely overcame their quarrels to engage in common action. More numerous, and usually tolerated by the government, were mutual aid societies which gathered funds for workers struck by illness, accident, or unemployment. Despite close police surveillance, some occasionally managed to turn themselves into societies of resistance, as in Lyons in the early 1830's, for collective pressure on the masters. In general, these were artisan rather than proletarian movements; they fought mainly to preserve the *status quo* against the machine and industrial bigness of any kind, and were usually hostile to the illiterate, untrained factory workers who streamed in from the countryside. Short-range interests divided the working class, as the rival craft and industrial unions were later to do in much of western Europe and America, but long-range interests hardly existed for men who lived from hand to mouth.

Only the collapse of the July Monarchy in 1848 allowed the workers and those social theorists who sought to reform French economic life to press their demands to any effect, and the republican societies to gain their ends. The July Monarchy could not have satisfied any of them short of abandoning the Orléanist compromise and reducing the privileges of the wealthy and well-connected men who made up the party of Order in France. That party fell because it was divided against itself, on lesser questions of religion, economics, and politics that a more vigorous King or ministry might have kept from growing fatal. The Legitimists, to be sure, continued to oppose the "usurper" but they did not constitute a political threat. Those who took an active part in politics gave themselves to a cause which appealed to Catholic Frenchmen of all classes: freedom for religious schools. This campaign was led by the Comte de Montalembert, a Catholic moderate who managed to hold a middle course between the small number of French Catholic democrats and the larger body of Catholic Legitimists.

Montalembert had himself been a democrat in 1830, when he joined the priests Lacordaire and Lamennais to found the newspaper called L'Avenir. In that year of great hopes, they had dreamed of liberalizing Catholicism, of Christianizing political democracy by separating Church and State, allowing Catholicism to compete freely in a pluralist society, able to appeal to all classes because attached to none. L'Avenir bravely took "God and Liberty" for its motto and demanded freedom of conscience and religion, freedom of association, assembly, press, education, and universal suffrage. The Revolution and its ideas, it said, were from God, who gave sovereignty to the people. In outspoken articles it called for social reforms to end the exploitation of the working masses and liberation of the oppressed nationalities. This first Catholic democratic movement, whose guiding spirit was Lamennais, scandalized all of conservative Europe, not least the French hierarchy and the new Orléanist regime. The bishops forbade the reading of L'Avenir, but Lamennais and his friends, supported by many young priests and laymen, naïvely hoped for Rome's support. Had they not been the foremost champions of ultra-montanism and papal infallibility in the difficult years before 1830? The new Pope, Gregory XVI, had no intention of alienating the

Church's most powerful and affluent supporters among the conservative states and comfortable classes of Europe. After a frigid interview with Lamennais, Lacordaire, and Montalembert at the Vatican, he issued in 1832 the encyclical *Mirari vos*. It was the first defeat of liberal Catholicism at the hands of Rome, condemning the "absurdity" of freedom of conscience and the separation of Church and State, whose alliance, said the Pope, had always had "such happy and saving effects" for both. For a time, Lamennais submitted with the rest, but in 1834 his *Paroles d'un croyant* marked an open revolt against Rome. Only a handful of democrats and romantics followed this impatient prophet to obscurity. His fate discouraged Catholics who hoped to reconcile the Church and the Revolution. Only generations later did they, with many of his ideas, win a measure of acceptance.

Lacordaire and Montalembert broke with Lamennais in the 1830's, the former to win fame and converts as a preacher at Notre Dame, the latter to organize a moderate Catholic party on the issue of liberty in education as promised in the revised Charter of 1830. Guizot's law of 1833 was generous to religious interests but applied only to primary schools. Montalembert and the hierarchy aimed at a system of Catholic secondary schools which would break the monopoly of the unreligious and sometimes anti-religious state education. At stake, as always, was the intellectual formation of the future leaders of France. Bourgeois fears of radicalism helped the campaign, and by raising the cry of "Liberty" the Catholic party won the sympathy of other opponents of the July Monarchy. But its stand was compromised almost from the start by the clamor of Legitimists and Catholic intransigents for whom liberty obviously meant only a means to a monopoly of their own. Louis Veuillot, a recent convert and editor of *L'Univers,* led the violent polemics of this all-or-nothing faction, which was to submerge liberal Catholicism after 1848, under the archconservative papacy of Pius IX. For the moment, at his accession in 1846, Pius was a liberal and nearly as scandalous to Metternich as Lamennais had been. For the moment, Montalembert's middle course was safe.

The government's apparent hostility to Catholic interests in the 1840's discredited it in the eyes of many who had no other reason to oppose Louis Philippe. On the other side were anti-clerical notables alienated by the government's concessions to the Catholic party. Opponents of Guizot, like his great rival Thiers, could cite Veuillot's provocations as proof of the folly of appeasement in religious questions. An anti-clerical campaign reminiscent of the 1820's flared up, with the Jesuits once more bearing its brunt. In an effort to quiet the debate, Guizot suspended Edgar Quinet and Jules Michelet, two outspoken critics of religious education, from their posts at the Collège de France. The government was caught in the middle, at a difficult moment. In the later 1840's Thiers and other moderates opened a campaign for political and parliamentary reform within the Orléanist system. Their attacks reached to the King, for by now he was clearly responsible for the policy of immobility, a party monarch in the fatal style of Charles X. The bourgeois National Guard grew increasingly restive over the exclusion of most of its members from political life, as did many thousands of substantial middle-class citizens, lawyers, journalists, and intellectuals who thought themselves fully as *sérieux* as those who sat in the Chambers and electoral colleges, and a good deal more articulate.

If the government had been a model of efficiency and probity, political agitation might have been less dangerous. But the presence of placemen in the parliament and the tight oligarchy of business and political interests which monopolized public affairs could boast of few accomplishments to balance its egregious corruption. While Guizot talked of the ideals of 1789 and the perfect "Christian" government, scandals multiplied and the regime stood idle at a time of gathering economic depression. The crisis which began with the bad harvests of 1846 involved a collapse of the railway boom and the sudden unemployment of thousands in many localities. That it deepened the workers' misery and the government's fear of movement in any direction was perhaps less important than the loss of confidence of businessmen and financiers in official economic policy.

Even in foreign affairs, where Louis Philippe considered his talents preeminent, the regime lost credit. Its one success was the subjugation of Algeria, in which his sons the Duc d'Aumale and the Prince de Joinville distinguished themselves. But many public men deplored the cruelty of the army in Algeria; the "Africans," Marshal Bugeaud, the generals Lamoricière and Pélissier, did not help by publicly despising their critics in turn. In Europe, Louis Philippe had destroyed the English entente by an ill-considered intervention in the Spanish royal marriages of 1846, when his son the Duc de Montpensier was wed to the Infanta in the vain hope that her older sister the Queen would remain childless. This puerile dynastic game left France isolated in Europe, except for Guizot's highly unpopular attempts to win Metternich to collaboration.

By 1847, many Frenchmen who believed in the Charter and had accepted the Orléanist compromise when it was still a compromise were ready to make their antagonism a public matter. Opposition Deputies helped organize political banquets of eminently respectable mien (republicans were frequently rebuffed and forced to organize on their own), at which toasts and orations demanded parliamentary reform and slight extensions of the suffrage. The Catholic Montalembert joined the anti-clerical Thiers to assail the government. De Tocqueville warned that the regime was sitting on a volcano, that its failure to satisfy the friends of order would loose great forces utterly opposed to the system, would bring not only political but social revolution. He "felt" this revolution coming (it was January, 1848) and its cause, he said, would be the same as that of 1789: the egotism, indifference, and vice of men made them unworthy of bearing power.

All warnings were in vain. After his well-managed election victory of 1846, Guizot was confirmed in immobility. He and the King refused all compromise and must bear a heavy responsibility for what followed. The revolution would be one not only of anger but, as Lamartine said, also of contempt. For Guizot persisted in adding sophistry to inaction, boasting that no special privileges existed, that no interests divided the classes, that the electors therefore represented all the people, that the system fully embodied the ideals of 1789. This newer, more sophisticated conservatism, exploiting sacred words and symbols to obscure their opposites, proved more maddening than honest reaction. Men who had detested Polignac came to despise Guizot. Louis Philippe ignored the pleas of his sons to give way; Guizot stayed.

On February 22, 1848, the government forbade a much-advertised political banquet in Paris. Crowds paraded the streets; barricades rose in the workers' quarters. Instead of restoring order, the National Guard petitioned the Chamber of Deputies for reform and shouted for Guizot's resignation. The King dismissed the hated minister and called on the Comte de Molé to form a cabinet, then on Adolphe Thiers as Paris grew more excited. The banquet campaign had won, but it was too late. On the 23rd, troops had fired into a crowd on the Boulevard des Capucines, killing several demonstrators (some say ten, others eighty or more). A torch-lit funeral wagon bore the victims' corpses through the city and Parisians rose in fury. The National Guard stood aside as the crowd stormed the Hôtel de Ville. Thiers fought to save his long-coveted post, urging Louis Philippe to surround the city with regular troops and beat down the insurrection, as he himself was to do in 1871. But the King did not count himself as indispensable as M. Thiers and on the 24th embarked on his exile to England, hoping that the Chambers could save the dynasty in the person of his grandson, the infant Comte de Paris. Without the incident on the boulevard, this last compromise might have worked. But Paris was ready for something grander than compromise; a mob invaded the Palais Bourbon, dispersed the Deputies and proclaimed the Republic.

# REVOLUTION, REPUBLIC, AND EMPIRE

In name, the Second Republic lasted nearly five years, to December, 1852, when its President, Louis Napoleon Bonaparte, proclaimed the Second Empire. In substance, it lasted four months, to the class war of the June Days in 1848, which smashed the center party of liberty and divided France once more between the haves and the have-nots, the party of Order against and triumphant over the socialists and social Republicans of Paris. The coalition that toppled Louis Philippe in February of 1848 was much the same as that which had opened his way in July of 1830: disaffected bourgeois and petty bourgeois, artisans and proletarians, unemployed (many from the countryside, seeking relief from the prolonged depression), and the urban poor, stiffened by National Guardsmen and activists of the republican societies. As in 1830, political control of Paris after the Revolution swung from Left to Right, but this time not so swiftly, for the balance of forces was heavier to the Left and both the Republicans and the socialists had zealous leaders who were not to be put off by a balcony scene in the style of Lafayette. This time there was no Louis Philippe as the obvious choice for a party of propertied notables, even had they not been scattered and shaken by a revolution whose momentum they could at first do nothing to allay.

## THE REVOLUTION OF 1848

Only in 1848, thirty-three years after Waterloo, was it finally clear how much Europe had been affected by the ideas and events of the French Revolution and Empire. The tide of revolt rose first in Italy, in January, but only when Paris expelled her King did men all over Europe feel, in the words of the young student Carl Schurz at Bonn, that "a great outbreak of elemental forces had begun." In nearly every capital and major city of Europe, men struck for one or more of three great desires: for the unity and independence of their nationalities, for individual freedoms and self-government within their nations, for economic reforms and social justice. The three revolutions came together, pressed each other forward, momentarily united against the established order, which was almost everywhere overthrown. But in different localities and among different classes there was little agreement on the priority of aims, on what should replace the old society. Nationalists, liberals, democrats, social democrats, socialists fought over the future; and while they fought, the past crept back to power, in Italy, the Germanies, the Austrian Empire, and France. Yet in France, it was not only the past that returned; the forces for change were too numerous and solidly based to conjure away, even temporarily. The dictatorship of the Second Empire was far from a copy of the First; it bore the marks of 1848 throughout its life.

Paris in the 1840's was animated by men and a host of ideas that had played little part in the Revolution of 1830. For tens of thousands of new lower-class residents (the population had grown to 1.25 million since 1830, more than half again as many) and refugees from the depressed provinces, grievances were sharper and hopes now higher than ever that the disappearance of Louis Philippe would mean fulfillment of republican ideals so long deferred, and that social reforms would follow quickly after. After 1870, cynics in the Third Republic were said to remind each other how lovely the republican idea had been under the Empire. It was, perhaps, even lovelier under the July Monarchy, when all things still seemed possible. Then the republican faith still claimed most of the working classes as well as the lower bourgeoisie, still called forth the romantic outpourings of a generation of artists and intellectuals who were deeply committed to social reform. After a time of disillusion and retreat from political affairs after 1830, they had returned to exalt the common people, to preach liberty, equality, and fraternity in all matters, including economic. "Liberty in art, liberty in society," Hugo's preface to *Hernani* had said; now he wrote of the "cellar hells" of Lille, putting art at the service of social change. To one degree or another, Vigny, Musset, Sainte-Beuve, Lamartine, Balzac, George Sand, the young Baudelaire, Lamennais, Michelet, popular novelists like Eugène Sue and Alexandre Dumas, indicted their society for its cruelty to the poor. Some, like Pierre Leroux and Flora Tristan, were artists and active socialists at once. All were read by thousands of young Frenchmen who, if decidedly less impressed by romantic tenets in art than they had been in 1830, were more convinced than 'ever that right hearts and generous acts could transform human life, could liberate the individual spirit from the tyranny of the State and of the private interests which the Orléanist oligarchy shielded with the power of the State.

Their hearts opened to the exiles of Europe, who had come to Paris as the city of liberation: Alexander and Nathalie Herzen, Adam Mickiewicz, Heinrich Heine, Bakunin, Liszt, Engels, Chopin, Turgenev, Marx. Socialists, poets, republicans, painters, anarchists, musicians, idealists, materialists arrived each year from Italy, Poland, Germany, Russia, Hungary, making an agitated, quarrelsome community of incandescent hopes, and stamping Paris for all time as the refuge of spirits too free or turbulent for other realms. Out of it grew an emotional and contradictory religion of oppressed humanity which was to make 1848 a "mad and holy year" unique in its aspirations as in its disillusion. Unique, too, in that social concerns appeared to have penetrated the comfortable and conservative classes of society. Thanks to the peculiarly negative character of the July Monarchy—but also to its toleration of dissident thought and writing—Frenchmen seemed united across class and religious lines in a vague social humanitarianism. Frédéric Ozanam, a saintly and romantic Catholic, had founded in 1833 the Society of Saint Vincent de Paul for missions and conferences among the workers and the poor. His was the best known of many such works, which were defended against the suspicions of the government and of other Catholics by Msgr. Affre, the Archbishop of Paris. If these conferences failed to convert the mass of workers who were already outside the Church and if, as after the Second World War, priests who appeared too zealous in fraternizing with radical workers were suspect in the eyes of their superiors, many young upper-class Catholics were nonetheless exposed to the realities of the Industrial Age. Catholic noblemen like Armand de Melun argued vigorously in the last Orléanist Chamber for government intervention in social welfare. Liberal and social Catholicism was encouraged by the advent of Pius IX in Rome, a suddenly liberal Pope who, from 1846 to 1848, inaugurated a series of unprecedented reforms. Unique to the Revolution of 1848 in France was the absence of anticlericalism; workers invoked Jesus Christ on their banners, priests blessed the liberty trees, and prelates the Republic.

Other social ideas at work in 1848, however, went much beyond humanitarianism, charity, or piecemeal legislation. The distress of the workers and the backwardness of the economy under Louis Philippe provoked numerous plans for a fundamental reordering of human society. Since before Napoleon's fall, a remarkable group of social theorists had offered remedies; after 1830 their ideas attracted troubled Frenchmen, particularly among the petty bourgeoisie and the more literate workers, who had hitherto put their faith in mainly political creeds.

First among these founders of European socialism was Henri, Comte de Saint-Simon, who believed that politics and its pretensions only obscured and hindered the real business of society, which was to organize its economic life on rational bases. After centuries of class struggle necessitated by scarcity, modern technology made prosperity possible for all, if men would put aside their empty political debates and concentrate on proper management of the economy. Saint-Simon preached a religion of brotherly love, in place of the old Christianity which allowed men to indulge in vicious competition and in oppression of their workers six days of each week (and sometimes seven), the very negation of brotherhood. The "new Christianity" enjoyed a short-lived popularity after his death in 1825, but Saint-Simon's greater legacy was his insistence on an objective study of history and his confidence that men could master their lives through a systematic application of social and economic law derived therefrom. His own selfless work inspired young historians like Augustin Thierry and Mignet, nearly every socialist theorist who came after him, including Karl Marx, and a number of the leading planners and promoters of the Second Empire, among them Michel Chevalier, who led France into free trade in the 1860's, and the Péreire brothers, who founded the Crédit Mobilier. Like his contemporary Sismondi, Saint-Simon accepted private property but insisted that strong government, preferably in the hands of scientists, engineers, and industrial managers, subordinate private competition to a central plan for full employment and the just distribution of goods.

Charles Fourier also believed that the unregulated race for private profit underlay society's evils. But his solution, like Étienne Cabet's and Robert Owen's, envisaged not mass industrialization centrally planned but self-contained communities, more appropriate to an earlier technological age. His *phalanstères*, which would transform society by the excellence of their example, were modern only in the sense that tasks and rewards were to be allocated according to subtle differences in human abilities and psychology. Pierre-Joseph Proudhon, like Fourier, distrusted centralized power in any form. His devastating critique of private exploitation made him the most admired and feared commentator of his generation, but the extremity of his axioms ("Property is theft") obscured far gentler and inchoate proposals for reform. Calling himself an anarchist, he pleaded for local associations of worker-entrepreneurs which would prevent economic power from coming to rest in any single class or authority. The greater influence of Proudhon's *mutualisme* lay in the future, with the syndicalist movement in French labor, with cooperatives and credit unions.

Of the men who were able to gather appreciable numbers of working-class followers under the July Monarchy, three stand out: Philippe Buchez, Louis Blanc, and Louis-Auguste Blanqui. Buchez was one of the very few Catholics who was accepted as a genuine leader of the artisans in Paris. A co-founder of the French Carbonari and a Saint-Simonist, he became a convert in the early 1830's and inspired the first coherent Catholic socialist group in France, associated with the worker-run newspaper *L'Atelier*. As an editor of a 40-volume documentary history, he saw the French Revolution, including the Terror, as opening to mankind the ultimate Christian era, to be marked by political democracy and social justice. He denounced upper-class Catholicism as pharisaical, and papal views on public affairs as an "Italian babble" that betrayed true Christianity by preaching patience and resignation to the hungry while flattering their oppressors. Most Catholic social action he dismissed as patronizing; charity insulted and degraded the workers; it was an auxiliary rather than an answer to slavery. To end capitalist exploitation he proposed workers' associations, owning the instruments of production in common; one such, founded in the jewelry trade, lasted some forty years. Buchez' election as president of the National Assembly in 1848 reflected the fleeting hope of some that Catholicism, republicanism, and social reform might be reconciled; others were rewarding his moderation and his usefulness against more militant social leaders.

Louis Blanc won the widest following of the three in the 1840's after the publication of his *Organisation du travail* in 1839. Work must be rationally organized, he said, and guaranteed to all. The brutish competition and monopolies that corrupted men's souls must be destroyed by government action, in setting up social workshops in every industry, under labor control, which would in time supplant the capitalist economy. A muckraking journalist with broad popular appeal, Blanc voiced the plaints of the workers but also the fears of the lower middle class in his constant attacks on big business combinations. Like Buchez, however, he failed to organize his followers into an effective party for action.

All these men hoped ultimately to revolutionize society, but none stressed violent revolution as the means. Saint-Simon and Fourier had relied on the most enlightened of the bourgeoisie, Proudhon and Buchez on the workers themselves, Blanc on intervention by a democratic government. Of the minority who combined socialist ends and revolutionary methods, Louis-Auguste Blanqui was the most prominent. His turbulent career spanned five regimes from the restoration to the Third Republic; of his seventy-six years, forty passed in prison. Revered by his followers as "L'Enfermé," Blanqui was the most faithful heir of the Hébertist and Babouviste traditions, scorning the romantic and Christian humanitarianism of his time, and the socialist theoreticians who debated while the people starved. He believed in a tight, disciplined party of revolutionaries who would, at the right moment, seize power and transform society through a dictatorship of the proletariat. Its first task would be to educate the people to the realities of political and economic life, so long hidden from them by a press, church, and school system perverted by capitalism. A properly socialist economy could follow only afterward. In the 1830's, Blanqui joined Armand Barbès and Martin Bernard in forming the secret republican Society of the Seasons. Imprisoned after an attempted rising in 1839, Blanqui was released by the revolutionary government of 1848, only to be rearrested the same year. Although his right moment never came, he remained a legend and an inspiration to militants of the Left, one of the few French socialists to earn the approval of Karl Marx.

During his stay in Paris in the mid-1840's, Marx had perceived the weaknesses of French socialism, its lack of unity and discipline, most of all its lack of plans for action. Except for Blanqui and, for a fleeting moment, Proudhon, Marx distrusted French leaders as bourgeois moralists who would divide, betray, or abandon the workers at the first sign of danger. There was in fact no socialist movement, only socialism in the air, popularized and confused by romantic authors as eclectic and wishful as the Utopian theorists themselves.

To the maelstrom of social ideas which were progressively alienating Frenchmen from their government, the Napoleonic tradition made its own peculiar contribution. Louis Napoleon, the nephew of the Emperor, had popularized the democratic Napoleon in his *Des idées napoléoniennes,* published in 1839. And he had added a social ingredient to Bonapartism in a pamphlet of 1844, *L'Extinction du pauperisme,* which advocated the resettlement of surplus labor in state-run agricultural communities. This and other articles in the Saint-Simonian spirit won him the approving attention of George Sand and Louis Blanc. On his part, as if to compensate for his own pacific policies, Louis Philippe did much to honor the Empire's memory, employing Marshals in high office, completing the Arc de Triomphe at the Étoile in 1836, sending his son Joinville to fetch Napoleon's remains at Saint Helena for a magnificent reburial in the Invalides in 1840. Meanwhile Hugo and the romantics continued their panegyric to the martyr; Adolphe Thiers published a history of the Consulate and Empire whose tone would have merited it the imprimatur of Napoleon himself.

As in 1830, Frenchmen were reading new histories of the great Revolution, decidedly more radical in tone than the earlier versions by Madame de Staël, Mignet, Thiers, or Guizot. Impatient patriots read Buchez, Lamartine, and Michelet (and Thiers on the Empire) to remind themselves that the business of France had not always been business and to convince themselves that even business had been better when France subordinated all to the liberation of mankind. The heroes of the new histories were no longer the moderate bourgeois constitutionalists of Guizot. Lamartine's *Histoire des Girondins* idealized the Republicans, not excluding Robespierre, to the delight of democrats who despised the Orléanist compromise. Jules Michelet's lectures at the Collège de France anticipated his great *Histoire de la Révolution française,* completed only under the Second Empire, which made the common people the heroes of an epic so dramatically retold that it remained a literary and historical influence for generations. In 1846 he published *Le Peuple,* in which he deplored the exploitation of the workers and envisaged the classes reconciled, without quite explaining how, in a democratic society faithful to the principles of 1789. No book is more typical of the spirit of 1848, or of certain leaders of the provisional government after the flight of Louis Philippe.

## THE SECOND REPUBLIC

As in 1830, the best-known critics of the regime had been associated with opposition newspapers; at the Palais Bourbon a number of them were chosen to act as a governing committee by the excited crowds which had dispersed the Orléanist Chamber. From the group around *Le National*, a moderate republican journal, came Lamartine, who acted as the leading spokesman for the Republic from the very first, Crémieux, Marie, Garnier-Pagès, Marrast, and the aged Dupont de l'Eure. A working-class demonstration at the Hôtel de Ville forced the addition of socialists, or social Republicans, Louis Blanc, Flocon, and a worker known as Albert, all associated with the radical *La Réforme,* as was Ledru-Rollin, a prominent radical Republican chosen by both groups. The balance of the provisional government thus stood at seven to four, in favor of moderates who saw the Revolution as mainly political, with Lamartine sometimes trying to mediate between the two tendencies. Had he succeeded and the eleven remained united, it is possible that a viable Republic could have emerged, even under the universal manhood suffrage they hurriedly proclaimed. Together they commanded, at first, the National Guard and many political activists in Paris and other cities. Together they might have appeased urban discontent and parried extremist demands which a frightened country was to find reminiscent of the Terror. But they were inexperienced, divided by temperament and personal ambition, diverted by the endless celebrations of the "perfect" Revolution, and worst of all, unprepared with plans or personnel for a new regime. The governing committee represented nearly every possible gradation of social belief, from conservative Republicans with Orléanist sympathies through those, like Ledru-Rollin and Lamartine, who would concede a measure of social legislation, to Louis Blanc and Albert, who desired a socialist society. No single man emerged who was strong enough to impose unity, no member was able to produce a compromise on which all would agree. As Marx had feared, Louis Blanc himself had no fixed plan by which to put his beliefs into practice, and no organized party to support him. Almost immediately they divided over the social question, which was envenomed by depression and complicated by the shortage of public funds, and were pulled apart, into the arms of Left and Right.

If 1830 was the last French Revolution directed mainly against the privileges of birth, 1848 was the first against the privileges of wealth. As Lamartine expressed it, the rich had climbed the ladder to political domination, then pulled the ladder after them to keep the people from following. But he and the moderate Republicans of the majority were concerned first with wiping out the political inequalities of the Orléanist years and thus prepared their own defeat by failing to appease in time the economic and social demands of the working classes, their indispensable allies. Their failure had many roots, chief among which was the republican dogma that political democracy alone would solve society's major problems. Natural to this faith was an exaggerated idea of their own popular following. They seriously underestimated the abiding influence of the conservative clergy, notables, and Monarchists on their Right—particularly over the peasantry—and overestimated their own ability to detach the workers and poor from more radical, socialist leaders on their Left. As republican orators, writers, and intellectuals, they believed themselves (as had Charles X) to be disinterested. They did not doubt their own sympathy for the poor, but it was an onlookers' sympathy, shallowly rooted in the romantic commiserations of George Sand and Victor Hugo, or in nostalgia for the common cause which had been beaten down in 1830.

In eighteen years, the Paris crowd had changed. The working class was larger, with ideas and leaders of its own. Depression and its continuing misery fed a grim determination that 1830 should not be repeated. And in the first days of March, the armed workers held a balance of power in the Paris streets. Under physical pressure at the Hôtel de Ville, the provisional government conceded to the "Social Republic" a declaration of the right to work and created an assembly of employers and workers under the presidency of Louis Blanc to discuss industrial problems amid the fading splendors of the Luxembourg Palace. The principle of laissez-faire was further breached by a decree limiting the working day to ten hours in Paris, eleven in the provinces. Although none of the long-standing laws against unions, strikes, and collective bargaining were disturbed, spokesmen assured the workers that changes would follow upon the election of a Constituent Assembly. Lacking close knowledge of economic affairs and unable to agree on any systematic alternative to the socialist innovations they distrusted, the moderates could only leave decisions to the future, when an assembly and revived armed forces would restore order.

In the meantime, their most fateful concession, given to relieve mass unemployment from the near-collapse of business activity (production in Paris had fallen to one-quarter its normal level), was the establishment of the National Workshops. The name was adapted from Louis Blanc's proposal for "social workshops" in his *Organisation du travail,* thereby suggesting to the workers a basic change in the economic life of France, while arousing the fears of the bourgeoisie. Beneath the high-sounding title was nothing more than the organization of relief under Marie, who was hostile to socialism in any form and who assembled gangs of unemployed to pass the time at trivial pick-and-shovel projects, repairing the city's fortifications or leveling the Champ de Mars. Skilled workers resented this pointless manual labor at a few francs a day, but the government had no intention of competing with private business. Louis Blanc was kept away from the Workshops, at his Luxembourg conferences; suggestions from social-minded Republicans that the work be applied to useful construction, especially housing, were ignored. As unemployed streamed in from the provinces, the Workshops became a scandal to the bourgeoisie and a burden on the anemic treasury. Some of the Republicans who supported them hoped that they would discredit Louis Blanc's too-popular ideas or divide and appease the working class until they could gather strength to defy it. The Workshops in fact did both. But others, like Lamartine, were caught up in the fraternal spirit of the hour, underestimated the seriousness of the step, and counted too much upon a revival of prosperity that would permit its easy reversal. Meanwhile, scores of radical newspapers and over 100 clubs, radical leaders like Barbès and Blanqui who were excluded from government, aroused a jealous vigilance among the crowds, ready to pounce upon any sign of impending betrayal.

To all factions, it was clear that the character of the Republic would be determined in elections to the Constituent Assembly. Not a month had passed since the King's departure before the socialists and social Republicans began to doubt the wisdom of entrusting their fate to universal suffrage. On March 5th, the provisional government had scheduled elections for April 9th, enfranchising all males over 21, making an electorate of 9 million, of which urban and working classes barely made up a quarter. What would be the response of peasants to Paris' radical leadership, in an election administered by officials of the previous regime?

Ledru-Rollin, as Minister of the Interior, exerted himself in the spirit of the Jacobins, replacing the prefects with a corps of Republican commissioners sent from Paris to educate the people in their choice of properly revolutionary candidates. Radical clubs sent their own emissaries, to organize branches in the provinces. But 1848 was not 1789; the masses in the countryside had had their revolution. The peasants and townspeople who owned property, or who expected to, had seen little reason to oppose the Orléanist regime; they had some reason, often religious, to suspect the Republic and every reason to fear the Social Republic. That many of them were illiterate was a secondary matter; so were most of the newly arrived workers in Paris, but their revolution was still in the making. Rural proprietors needed no erudition to see that the first act of the new government to affect them was an added 45 centimes to their direct tax.

Other news from Paris was educating the countryside and the reviving forces of order. The most radical leaders, Barbès and Blanqui among them, had led a march to the Hôtel de Ville on March 17th to demand a postponement of the elections. That the government gave way at all taught the Right that it was weak or radical, or both. That it allowed only two weeks for republican campaigning, to April 23rd, stirred some of the clubs to more demands, this time for decrees nationalizing banks, insurance companies, transport and mining (the provinces, of course, heard that all property would be taken), in order to present the assembly with a *fait accompli*. But the provisional government held its middle course. Ledru-Rollin, distrusting other leaders of the Left, Blanqui above all, and concerned lest the radicals undo his work in the provinces, took the lead in quieting the demonstrations. On April 16th, he earned the enmity of the Left by employing the National Guard to overawe still another crowd that gathered to demand further postponement of the elections. Thus, a week before elections, the social Republicans in the provisional government held a shrinking Center, the object of suspicion and rising fear on both Left and Right. A Catholic party, emboldened by the absence of anti-clerical feeling in February, saw impending success for its long struggle over the school question and campaigned energetically for candidates who would pledge themselves to support religious education. Such were not ordinarily to be found among devoted Republicans, as the provisional government perceived; it ordered its schoolteachers to campaign against the clericals.

The election results confirmed the worst fears of Ledru-Rollin and those to his Left. Despite a return to the *scrutin de liste,* which supposedly facilitated official pressure, the provinces elected local notables, men of tradition and property who took all but 100 of the 876 seats; 300 or more were self-styled moderate Republicans, 400 were Legitimists or Orléanists, and all were substantial taxpayers. Even in Paris, where some of the moderates in the provisional government had worked against their social Republican colleagues, Albert, Ledru-Rollin, Flocon, and Louis Blanc were returned near the tail of the list. Such an assembly could as well have peacefully emerged in 1847 under the Orléanist charter, if Guizot had given way to the Catholics and moderate bourgeois reformers. But in May of 1848 it gathered at the Palais Bourbon in a seething, divided capital, where the poorer classes saw only betrayal of yet another revolution. The Assembly replaced the provisional government with a new Executive Commission, excluding Albert, Flocon, and Louis Blanc. Only Lamartine's efforts kept Ledru-Rollin from the same fate; Lamartine thereby lost the confidence of many moderates; Ledru-Rollin, by accepting office from men now openly hostile to social change, lost still more of his credit with the Left. The Assembly, showing its narrowly political view of the Republic, next refused Louis Blanc's request for a Ministry of Labor and rejected a new proclamation of the right to work.

The Left's disappointment could be contained no longer. On the 15th of May, several of the radical clubs and units from the National Workshops attempted to repeat the great days of the Paris Commune in the first Revolution. They invaded the Palais Bourbon, declared the Assembly dissolved, and marched to the Hôtel de Ville, according to the traditional ritual, to form a new government. But it was to be the ritual of 1795: the National Guards (many from the Workshops, fighting fellow workers) and an armed Mobile Guard of young toughs scattered the crowd. Barbès and Albert were arrested, together with Blanqui, who had participated reluctantly, rightly judging the moment ill-chosen; other club orators and socialists fled, leaving the workers leaderless, but not—as too many in the Assembly believed—powerless. The Luxembourg commission ceased to exist. Over the protests of a handful of social Republicans who still hoped to reconcile the workers, the Assembly proceeded to close the National Workshops.

The debate expressed all the conservative fears that had been mounting since February; Workshop support of over 100,000 men was ruinous for the budget, deprived employers of ready labor, drew unstable elements to Paris, and presented hateful socialistic precedents. Business, the

Workshops' opponents added, would revive only when they were dissolved. The Legitimist Comte de Falloux, chief influence in the Assembly's committee on labor, pressed for an immediate end to the experiment; confident of the regular troops and of the National Guards' devotion to property interests, he ignored warnings of probable resistance, ignored Marie's plea for a gradual approach, which many of the moderate Republicans now endorsed. But this new Center, asking only for patience and unable to unite on any alternative, could not hold and the Assembly backed Falloux. The Republic was already in the hands of Monarchists and Republican conservatives, mainly from the provinces, that party of Order which for a generation had lacked even the urban Republicans' hazy understanding of social realities, and which hated Paris for its radical presumption.

Near the end of June, the government offered the workers a heartless choice: the army for the young; unemployment or provincial reclamation work for the old. Since business remained depressed, private employment offered no alternative to destitution or banishment. Some Deputies no doubt hoped to provoke the lower classes to resistance, then to crush by force of arms all remaining agitation for social change. But ignorance, hatred born of fear, and the kind of political stupidity that follows oversubtle calculation also played their parts, and the urge, always tempting to unimaginative men, to return by mere decree to tidier, thriftier days.

The workers, whose hungry families lived from day to day, bitterly denounced the Assembly's violation of the right to work, and in the waning days of June a volcano greater than even Tocqueville had foreseen erupted in Paris. Without leadership or plan, barricades went up throughout the poorer quarters. Although many men stayed with the Workshops (the government hurriedly assured their pay) and others obeyed the summons to the National Guard, there were enough insurgents to endanger the regime. The republican General Cavaignac rushed regular troops and provincial National Guards to the city. The latter were ferocious in reprisals against men and women they thought guilty of subverting propertied society. In this fratricidal struggle, Cavaignac used methods learned in the vicious warfare of Algeria, luring his enemies to flimsy barricades and houses, then blowing them to rubble with artillery. The eastern sections of Paris bled for days, while the rest of the city quaked and raged behind its shutters. At the end, the forces of order pulled 15,000 men and women out of ruined tenements to prison, execution, or deportation. Between 1500 and 3000 had died in the fighting; 4000 were deported (mainly to Algeria); hundreds were executed without trial; many died untended in hospitals and hovels, others in prisons so crowded and filthy that guards refused even to approach the cells. The Social Republic was dead; henceforth the Second Republic and, after 1871, the Third, were to be socially conservative, almost constantly fearful of the workers. The bright romantic and Utopian hopes of February lay in ashes; whether the "Age of Realism" and "scientific socialism" can neatly be dated from June of 1848 is debatable, but a chasm opened between French classes which to this day has been rarely bridged, never closed.

The reaction following the June Days was not limited to political repression or bourgeois entrenchment. To be sure, the Assembly made Cavaignac military dictator and suppressed radical clubs and newspapers. Predictably, working hours officially returned to twelve, thirteen, and more a day; most establishments had never shortened them. But reaction also gripped the republican leaders who had lost political control. They blamed the workers for the June rising; in London of the 1850's, Ledru-Rollin joined other losers, Mazzini and Kossuth, in deploring proletarian influence on republicanism and resolving to exclude it in the future. The romantic intellectuals and artists who had made a cult of the workers before 1848 were horror-struck by the bloodshed. Lamartine, Victor Hugo, George Sand, even Michelet, largely repudiated their earlier idealizations. Social and liberal Catholicism was discredited; symbolically, the liberal Archbishop Affre was shot to death on a barricade while trying to mediate. Veuillot and the intransigents appeared to be justified. So did Karl Marx, who was confirmed in his earlier view that French workingmen were ill-prepared, badly led, and too willing to cooperate with their enemies ever to make a revolution.

Through the summer and fall of 1848, the Assembly prepared its new constitution. Cavaignac kept order and won the gratitude of those who still believed in the Republic, however conservative. The constitution which emerged in November was, on its face, politically democratic. Universal suffrage would elect a unicameral legislature of 750 every three years and a President of the Republic every four. In the decision for a strong executive independent of the Assembly, the June Days were cited (so were the "crimes" of the Convention) as proving the need for executive vigor, quickly employed. Lamartine, arguing for the popular election of the President, said the nation was "incorruptible," but others offered the soberer premise that the nation had already shown itself in April to be conservative and could be trusted to be safe, corruptible or not, and, according to one's party, republican or not. Jules Grèvy and a few moderates, Ledru-Rollin and the democrats, warned of a popular dictator who might seize power, once elected. But even a reference to the Empire and the current pretender failed to move the delegates; after June, security seemed more precious than liberty. The Assembly, without quite knowing it, voted for the Empire before the people did.

The long, detailed document promised nearly all things to all men and asked from them even more: love, loyalty, service to the death, private charity, morality, work, taxes, and, lest the State be burdened, savings for their old age. In return, the Republic promised education, relief and public works (though not the right to work), freedom of association, peaceful assembly, and petition. The original purposes of the banquet campaign were not forgotten; Deputies were to be paid and could hold administrative posts only in special cases. The President enjoyed wide executive authority, and the Ministers were made responsible to him, but the constitution contained safeguards against his seizing power. He was ineligible to succeed himself, as were members of his family; he was forbidden to command the army in person, to dissolve the Assembly or to suspend the constitution, to make war or peace without the Deputies' approval, or to exercise a final veto. The familiar charge that the constitution failed to insure against a conflict between the legislative and executive powers is largely beside the point. Once having decided on the separation of power and an independently elected President, the delegates did all that could have been done on paper. Short of the three-quarters vote needed to amend the constitution, only a *coup d'état* could upset the equilibrium.

## THE RISE OF LOUIS NAPOLEON

Not a few members of the Constituent Assembly were counting on just such a coup. Legitimists and Orléanists, hoping to arrange a line of succession agreeable to both, expected to restore the monarchy. Meanwhile, in the presidential election of December, 1848, Louis Napoleon won much of their support. Cavaignac, Lamartine, and Ledru-Rollin were too solidly republican, Raspail vaguely a socialist. Louis Napoleon had taken his place in the Constituent Assembly only in the autumn, after having won seats from several districts in the supplementary elections of June and September. His awkward, somnolent figure, and slow, thick speech in a German accent seemed to confirm the evidence of his laughable attempts to seize power in 1836 and 1840; the clever and subtle dismissed him as a cipher. Thiers saw only a *crétin* who could be used to restore Thiers and, if possible, the monarchy as well.

Charles Louis Napoleon Bonaparte was born in 1808, the second son of King Louis of Holland and Josephine's daughter Hortense Beauharnais. At seven, he witnessed the grandiloquent pageant at the Champ de Mars in 1815, when Napoleon proclaimed his liberal Empire of the Hundred Days. His mother carefully nurtured his devotion to the Emperor's memory; the rest of his variegated education came from a Jacobin tutor, the German *gymnasium* at Augsburg, and from wandering the face of Europe. At twenty-three he was briefly embroiled in an anti-papal insurrection in the Romagna where he knew, and may have joined, the Carbonari. He became pretender at twenty-four, when Napoleon II, the Duke of Reichstadt according to the Austrians, died in July of 1832; Louis' older brother had died the year before, after the Italian adventure. In 1836 his first attempt to overthrow the government of Louis Philippe was foiled by the commander of the Strasbourg garrison, which he tried to subvert. The King sent him to America, where his inclination to emulate Tocqueville was ended by Hortense's death in Switzerland. There followed two years in London society, where he found time to compose *Des idées napoléoniennes* in 1839. Another attempted coup, at Boulogne in 1840, went utterly awry and earned him "perpetual imprisonment" in the fortress of Ham in Picardy.

The "university of Ham," as Louis called it, allowed him six years of self-education and correspondence (much of it published, like *L'Extinction du pauperisme*) by which to prepare himself and his audience for the next opportunity. His escape in 1846 permitted him two more years in London, before the fall of Louis Philippe seemed to open his way to France again. Prudence and luck kept him in London until after the June Days, for whose horrors no faction could blame him. In December of 1848, universal suffrage and his magic name won him 5.5 million votes for the presidency of the Second Republic. Cavaignac was nearest, with 1.5 million; Ledru-Rollin polled 370,000, Raspail 36,000, and Lamartine, the hero of February, only 17,000. From a seemingly futile and picaresque adventurer, Louis Napoleon rose overnight to chief of the executive power; and in the villages, where people had not read the constitution, he was already known, simply, as *l'Empereur*.

Louis Napoleon has been called a proto-fascist, the first modern dictator of the western world. The evidence of his twenty-two years in power complicates this verdict considerably; it is partly applicable to his election in 1848, more so to his *coup d'état* in 1851 and its aftermath. The French mood of reaction which followed the June Days may pardonably be called proto-fascist. All parties had been discredited, all groups shaken by the events of 1848—the rural, propertied, and conservative by the social Republic's threat to their interests; the lower, urban, and poorer by its failure to satisfy their desires. The June Days proved to the Right that a liberal Republic was incapable of preserving order, to the Left that it would butcher the workers to preserve property. If the economy had recovered, the many citizens of all classes who were committed to no party might have voted for the *status quo* and Cavaignac. If the two monarchist factions had agreed on another candidate, the vote might have been close enough to throw the election into the Assembly, as the law provided. If the clerical party had put French liberty ahead of privilege for its schools, it might not have campaigned so actively for a Bonaparte. If the workers had been united and better organized, if their leaders had not been discredited by failure, the Left might have won solidly in the towns. Instead, a figure who appealed to national pride and military glory, and who propagandized himself as all things to all men (including democrats), won overwhelming victory. Also in the familiar pattern, Louis Napoleon's hurriedly organized party and press received vital funds from a few (though very few) industrialists and financiers, and his campaign gained support from that faction of the Saint-Simonians who were most devoted to dramatic new construction under a managed economy. Finally, he also won large numbers of votes from the workers and the poor, who had welcomed his attacks on economic injustice and his pleas as a member of the Assembly for the right to work and an amnesty for the victims of June.

Louis Napoleon came to power, then, partly in the twentieth-century Italian or German style, as opposed to his uncle, who seized it in the manner of a victorious Roman proconsul. But mere mention of the first Napoleon upsets the fascist pattern. Louis Napoleon was more than a rootless political adventurer come from nowhere to fill a void left by the failure of Republicans and the hatreds of a frightened society. He represented a tradition which, however idealized by the legend, stood clearly enough for order without utter reaction, for much of the Revolution without social upheaval, yet promising social amelioration. A vote for him was no more a "leap in the dark" than a vote for any of the other candidates in 1848. The voters were neither coerced nor swindled. Other ingredients of the fascist mélange were missing; there was no mass party, no paramilitary troop, no terror, thuggery, or political assassination, and, in the next two decades, far less ambition to remake the map of Europe or the minds of Frenchmen than evidenced by the first Napoleon.

In the three years between 1848 and 1851, those of his legal presidency, Louis Napoleon took every opportunity to entrench himself in power, demonstrating a political skill undreamed of by the seasoned parliamentarians who had taken him so lightly. He began tactfully, appointing a ministry of the Assembly's favorites, headed by the Orléanist moderate, Odilon Barrot; affecting civilian dress and tastes, Louis Napoleon ingratiated himself with the republican hero, Victor Hugo, who hoped that in the Prince-President the two political passions of his life would find happy equilibrium. In several instances, Louis managed to turn the actions of the Assembly to its discredit and to his own advantage, without alienating any substantial number of Frenchmen. In this he was aided by the long unpopularity of the July Monarchy and its most prominent political figures, several of whom emerged once more as leaders of the Legislative Assembly elected in May of 1849. The Orléanist prefects had returned to their posts and did well in managing the new electorate. The party of Order—Legitimists, Orléanists, Bonapartists—won 500 of the 750 seats, the liberal Republicans only 80, one-fifth of their previous number. On the other hand, the radical Republicans revived strongly in the cities, in the army, and in certain southern departments, polling one-third of the national vote and doubling their delegation. Ledru-Rollin led a group of 180 into the Chamber, but whatever influence they might have had was dissipated by another uprising in Paris that June. Ostensibly in protest against the pro-papal policy of the government in attacking the Roman Republic, this undermanned attempt, reluctantly joined by Ledru-Rollin ("I have to follow them, I am their leader," he is supposed to have said), involved many Republican Deputies in its failure. The Second Republic was left in the hands of men who desired its death: in the Chamber, a heavy majority of Monarchists; at the Élysée, a Bonaparte.

Louis Napoleon's aim (just when he resolved upon it is not clear) was to restore the Empire before Legitimists and Orléanists could agree on a line of succession, before the Republicans who had shown such strength in the elections could make another bid for victory in 1852, when his term and the Assembly's would expire together. He willingly joined the conservative majority in further repressive acts against Republican clubs and newspapers after June, 1849, while managing to cast most of the blame for restrictions of liberty on the Assembly. Apart from political questions, three major issues occupied both branches of government: the persistent economic crisis, foreign affairs, and the place of religion. The President exploited each skillfully, using all the funds at his disposal for newspaper support and the organization of Bonapartist clubs and veterans' leagues (thuggery and threats crept in here). In a series of well-staged tours through the provinces, he expounded the economic doctrines of the Saint-Simonians, painting visions of prosperity insured by vigorous government initiative in canals, ports, railroads, credit and industrial expansion, housing and public works. He carefully left the impression that economic recovery would elude France until a strong, forward-looking regime somehow replaced the narrow interests and unsettling political ambitions of the politicians in the Chamber. To an increasing number of businessmen, the slowness of recovery seemed to prove him right; they were further edified by his denunciations of the "Reds" (the term was already familiar) whom he presented as the only other alternative.

In foreign affairs the Second Republic had early disappointed those Frenchmen who envisaged the tricolor once more leading a crusade for the liberation of Europe. Even before the June Days, the Republican leaders who might have desired to send French aid abroad were preoccupied with their own dangerous position at home. Lamartine as Foreign Minister showed little inclination to imitate his admired Girondins of 1792. By the end of 1849, the old order reigned in Prague, Vienna, Budapest, Milan, Venice, and Naples. Only in Rome had the revolutionaries managed to keep control. As in 1830, the French government dispatched troops to prevent Austria from advancing her power on the peninsula, but to French Catholics—and therefore to the ambitious man at the Élysée—Austria was the lesser half of the problem. The militantly anti-clerical Roman Republic of Mazzini had replaced the exiled Pius IX and nothing short of the Pope's restoration would satisfy the faithful. To this end, Oudinot's army captured Rome in July of 1849 and Louis Napoleon won a short-lived reputation as a loyal son of the Church, which he neither deserved nor particularly enjoyed, apart from its political utility. With one brief interval, French troops were to remain in Rome until 1870, protecting the temporal dignity of a Pope whose reactionary policies were a constant source of embarrassment to a French ruler who preferred to stand for progress.

Louis Napoleon was better pleased with another measure designed to win the applause of Catholics; the Falloux law of March, 1850, represented the triumph of the Catholic party's long struggle for freedom of church schools. Henceforth, any private person or authorized religious body was free to establish schools on any level of education. The University and the state schools lost their monopoly and were themselves submitted to councils under clerical influence. After the June Days, the bourgeois were readier than ever to accept religious training for the young; the local priest and notables gained revenge for the too active campaigning of lay schoolmasters for Republican candidates in 1848 and 1849. The Left denounced the Falloux law as a threat to the survival of liberal ideas; at the other extreme the firebrand Veuillot led Catholic zealots in attacking it as a weak compromise with the ungodly lay schools still supported by the government. His faction soon won the support of Pius IX. The Second Empire was to see the nadir of liberal Catholicism in France and, partly in direct consequence, the revival of republican anti-clericalism.

If Louis Napoleon succeeded as President in holding the allegiance of many liberals and democrats despite his acquiescence in pro-Catholic policies, it was partly because the July Monarchy had proved, in one historian's words, that it was possible to be reactionary without being clerical, or, positively put, because the recent prominence of Catholics like Montalembert, Lacordaire, Msgr. Affre, and Buchez had suggested that it was possible to be liberal without being anti-Catholic. More important, the Legislative Assembly provided Louis a notable opportunity to show an attachment to democracy. In May of 1850, after radical Republicans had taken 20 of 30 seats in special elections, the Assembly approved a law denying suffrage to Frenchmen who could not prove three years' continuous residence in one locality. Together with the disfranchisement of those caught in the wide net of laws against political agitation, it deprived some 3 million men, mostly of the lower and working classes, of the right to vote. The President loudly demanded the law's repeal, denouncing it as a violation of the constitution. The Assembly, as he probably hoped it would, refused to reconsider its action.

In February of 1851, the legislators denied an increase in the President's allowances; he called it retaliation for his devotion to the common people.

By mid-1851, even newspapers not financed by Bonapartist funds were drawing battle lines: on one side, an Assembly of vested interests; on the other, the Caesarian democrat. But one could not be Caesar on a four-year term. Louis Napoleon and his party, which now included a good number of prescient Deputies, opened a campaign for a constitutional amendment allowing the President to stand for reelection. Public pressure was so adroitly worked up, by an administration already well staffed with Bonapartists, that 446 Deputies voted for revision in July of 1851. But 278 refused, and thus the vote was short of the needed three-quarters majority.

Only the other, more historically fitting, road was left open to Caesar: Louis Napoleon prepared the army for a new and, as it turned out, a better managed Brumaire. From the moment of his election, he had found many agreeable ways to flatter soldiers whose greatest memories were bound to the name he bore. Sympathetic officers were put in strategic posts. General Saint-Arnaud became Minister of War, Magnan commander of the army in Paris. More than his uncle, Louis Napoleon took a personal part in the planning of the coup with his half-brother Morny (the son of Hortense by her lover the Comte de Flahaut, natural son of Talleyrand), assisted by old fellow adventurers like Persigny and private funds donated by a few carefully selected supporters, like the English actress-courtesan Miss Howard, who was a frequent companion since the days in London. More seemly appurtenances were not forgotten: the code name for the *coup d'état* was "Rubicon," and its date, December 2, 1851, was the 46th anniversary of Austerlitz, the 47th of Napoleon's coronation at Notre Dame.

## THE AUTHORITARIAN EMPIRE

The traditional manner of calling the citizen soldiers of the National Guard to the defense of their favored institutions was the *rappel,* that ominous rolling of drums which had echoed through Paris streets so often since 1789. But in the early morning of December 2nd, the drums which had smothered the last words of Louis XVI on the scaffold, sounded the knell of Charles X in July and of Louis Philippe in February, and had beaten a death march for the workers in June, lay silent, each one punctured by order of Vieyron, the commandant who was in league with Louis Napoleon. It was only a detail, like the damping of the gunpowder, but typical of Morny's fastidious preparation, which included making himself Minister of Interior. Regular soldiers guarded the belfries to prevent alarm, and Parisians awoke quietly to find troops at strategic corners and everywhere the official white poster of a presidential proclamation, which confided to Frenchmen that their Assembly had become a "center of conspiracy." To "maintain the Republic" the Assembly was dissolved, the Palais Bourbon closed, and, without the hurly-burly of Brumaire, the opposition leaders politely arrested in their beds. On the 14th and 21st of December, the posters said, the French people, restored to universal suffrage, would be called to approve or reject a new regime whose constitution imitated that of the Consulate, signifying the personal dictatorship of a second Bonaparte.

For a day Paris remained silent, except for moderate applause greeting the President as he rode from the Élysée and for scattered bursts of indignation that Victor Hugo and a handful of Republicans could stir (in person, for the print shops were shut down by troops) in a city that seemed indifferent. But on the next day a barricade went up in the Faubourg Saint-Antoine; a republican Deputy bravely mounted it and was shot to death by the soldiers. His name was Baudin and it would outlive the Second Empire. On the 4th, small bands of Republicans and workers manned new barricades in a section north of the Hôtel de Ville. The overzealous Magnan sent thousands of troops against this shadow of June and crushed it without mercy, again in the best Algerian style; between two and four hundred died. On the more fashionable Boulevard des Italiens, the troops fired wildly into a bourgeois crowd, killing fifty more. Morny's tidy operation, which Louis Napoleon had hoped would win Paris' applause, was soaked in blood. But the troops held the city too tightly for further resistance to develop, and the poorer quarters showed little desire to fight for a monarchist Assembly which had itself cynically mutilated the constitution in the matter of suffrage.

Having destroyed the institutions he had sworn to uphold, Louis Napoleon carried out a brutal purge of his opponents, potential opponents, even possible opponents. Some 27,000 French were arrested throughout the country; 1500 were expelled from France, 9500 deported to Algeria, 300 to Guiana. As in most scourings of such magnitude, thousands were torn from their homes and families as the result of local or personal feuds having little to do with politics, or by officials anxious to prove their loyalty to the third regime they had served within four years. The repression was out of all proportion to actual resistance to the coup, which was limited to a few southern departments where landless peasants were faithfully republican. Louis Napoleon could not plead the hysteria of the June Days, nor can his apologists properly compare it with the aftermath of the Commune of 1871; both were civil wars. The Terror of December weighed on the regime until its fall, despite the nearly complete amnesties that Napoleon granted during the 1850's.

That Louis Napoleon ordered or allowed these actions and also regretted and sought to reverse them is only the first of many contradictions in the Second Empire that have complicated the judgments of historians and offered ample material for both critics and admirers of the regime. If they have been unable to agree on the deeper intentions of the first Napoleon, historians have at least a record of fairly consistent action, aggressive and authoritarian. Those who defend the sincerity of his pacific and democratic protestations on Saint Helena have only the dubious gestures of the Hundred Days to comfort them. With Napoleon III the problem is strikingly different. Although his statements of intent are only refinements of his uncle's memoirs in exile—more exact on working-class problems—his record of action is far more complex and elusive. The high and low lights of the Second Empire cannot neatly be divided in years or decades, between domestic and foreign affairs, economic and political, between the work of Louis Napoleon himself and that of his ministers, or between actions forced by circumstance and those taken on his government's initiative.

Historians complain that Louis Napoleon, once in power, revealed himself very little in speech or writing. But his taste for intrigue and dissimulation (often less complained of in politicians who are more voluble) was only one of the traits that make close judgment of him difficult. His periodic loss of energy and interest, his illnesses, his shifting moods, his welter of unordered values are more important reasons for the vagaries of the regime and the various interpretations placed upon it. Customarily, Louis Napoleon is held more closely to account for his misdeeds than are other leaders of the century, not only because he has been a natural target of republican historians since 1870 but also because he so willfully sought full power and thus asked to be judged as the only responsible agent in France. Knowing the dangers and burdens of French government, and knowing as well his own infirmities, he coolly wagered the future of a nation on the chance that his personal rule would prove superior to that of the men he displaced. If he had been slightly mad, he might be less severely judged; the uncle, whose ambition knew no rational bounds, is "the great Napoleon" even in liberal and republican histories, but the nephew remains, in Victor Hugo's adhesive phrase, *"Napoléon le petit."*

The second constitution of the Second Republic was promulgated in 1852; it made Louis Napoleon chief executive for ten years, holding legislative power as well, nominally shared with a Senate and the legislative body. This was the essence and it appeared first, after an article guaranteeing the "great principles proclaimed in 1789." The President was responsible only to the people—the Bonapartist plebiscite—and held all powers of war, peace, alliances, and commercial treaties, as well as the initiative in legislation. Cabinet ministers were responsible to him, all public servants, including teachers, swore an oath of loyalty to him, and he could "recommend" his successor. He appointed the Senators who would join the admirals, marshals, and cardinals of France in an upper house whose sessions were secret and fixed in duration by the President. The Deputies were elected in single-member constituencies, *scrutin d'arrondissement,* for six years; the report of their sessions was to be edited before publication, their officers chosen by the President. The Council of State, which had suffered something of an eclipse since 1815 and was elected by the Assembly under the democratic constitution of the Second Republic, was to be named by the President and entrusted with the drafting of laws. Amendments to the constitution were to be submitted to plebiscite. Napoleon's coup had been approved by a vote of 7.4 million to 640,000 in December of 1851, in balloting that was apparently free and secret, but under the shadow of the recent proscriptions. The constitution was only a formality; the alteration of a few words would make the Empire. Louis moved into the Tuileries, the object of his dreams, on January 1, 1852, and on December 2nd, proclaimed the Second Empire, taking the title Napoleon III. After a second plebiscite, it was announced that only 240,000 had voted No.

Louis Napoleon's defenders have said that his usurpation of power did not kill a democratic Republic, which had already expired in June of 1848, but forestalled a monarchical restoration predestined by the Royalist majority in the Legislative Assembly. The Monarchists, however, were divided and had showed before (as they were to show again in the 1870's) a remarkable ability to snatch defeat from the jaws of victory. Whatever the possibilities of the situation in 1851, it was at the time of the coup neither desperately reactionary nor dangerously radical; Louis Napoleon destroyed a Republic which, however conservative, had allowed relatively free elections and enough political activity and discussion to sustain a republican revival in several localities, rural as well as urban.

If not precisely proto-fascist, the imperial system meant emphatic political reaction; France was put back in uniform, except for the National Guard, which was disbanded. The police, secret and otherwise, gained new powers, numbers, and rewards; the methods of Fouché were studiously revived. The army won new honors, higher pay, and splendid trappings designed to recall the First Empire. The remaining political clubs were closed, the political press silenced by a system of warnings and heavy fines, political education hampered by the suppression of courses in philosophy and contemporary history in the *lycées*. The government dismissed teachers likely to be critical; Quinet, Michelet, Mickiewicz, and Jules Simon were only the most prominent among many who lost their positions. Fortoul, the Minister of Education to 1856, interpreted the Falloux law in a manner favorable to the Church, increasing government aid to religious schools. The well-rounded man was judged to be inconvenient or less useful to society than the specialist; studies were either narrowly scientific or narrowly literary, though this is a view of education hardly limited to the Second Empire, or to France.

Official pressure on behalf of favored candidates had been common in France since the Directory, but the Second Empire went a step further in employing "official candidates," who alone had the right to employ the government's white posters, who openly received all possible aid from prefects who were screened, and generously paid, by the Emperor. The elections of March, 1852, returned 253 official candidates to the 260 seats in the new legislature. Napoleon had rightly guessed that 260 elections would be easier to manage than 700, and the electoral districts were artfully tailored to fit imperial candidates. The press was forbidden to comment on their opponents; no political rallies were allowed. On the surface, the dictatorship seemed complete, the legislature no more than a club for amiable discussion of the Emperor's projects.

In fact, Louis Napoleon never succeeded in assembling a Bonapartist party made up of men who agreed with his major proposals for France and who were at the same time notable enough to replace the older economic and social elite which had grown up since 1815. He necessarily relied on a conglomerate of Orléanists, Legitimists, and conservative Republicans willing to proclaim their loyalty, even to fill out his rosters of official candidates. Most prefects were carried over from the July Monarchy until the late 1850's. Of the men personally closest to him, Morny had been—and remained—part of the wealthy Orléanist social circle, more interested in a good piece of financial business than in Bonapartist principles; Louis' cousin Walewski, son of Napoleon I and the Polish Countess Marie Walewska, was a conservative Catholic; his other cousin, Prince Jerome, was an erratically liberal Republican. "There is only one Bonapartist," the Emperor is supposed to have muttered; "that is Persigny and he, alas, is mad!" However easily the wealthy notables and country gentry might agree (and some did not) to a curtailment of political liberties, or even to certain foreign adventures, their economic interests could not be ignored, at least without first winning broad popular support for his programs. So in tours and speeches, Louis sought to educate the mass of Frenchmen in the new Saint-Simonian Bonapartism. The Empire, he said, meant peace. Its conquests would be inward, the economic expansion and prosperity of all France. While avoiding any direct challenge to established wealth, he insisted on the need to develop new wealth, through the expansion of credit, railways, public works, freer trade, and a wider distribution of income.

## ECONOMIC EXPANSION

Ironically, the most effective opposition to Louis Napoleon in his first decade of power developed over these projects, which are in retrospect altogether the most praiseworthy of the regime. The comfortable plutocracy, mainly Orléanist in sentiment, which enjoyed its family businesses, its family banks, and its industrial enterprises well-cushioned by high tariffs from the shocks of competition, distrusted the Emperor from beginning to end. The new Napoleon, even more than the old, was determined not to leave business matters—and the laboring classes— in their hands alone. They were vexed at the very start by Louis' confiscation and sale, in January, 1852, of the rich estates of the Orléans family, which Louis Philippe had thought to leave outside the national domain. Even Morny, who valued his business connections, felt compelled to resign for a while. From part of the proceeds, the government financed workers' housing, hospitals, orphanages, mutual aid societies, and labor exchanges. Once more, there were the contradictions. Was it an act of petty revenge or of patriotic recovery? A bribe to the workers or genuine social concern? It may have been all four, but to the bourgeoisie it suggested the unpleasant thought that Louis Napoleon rated the sanctity of property somewhere below his own or the nation's needs.

Louis' own estimate of France's needs was perhaps best embodied in his favorite device: Order and Progress. Each was indispensable to the other; each required some attention to the working class beyond mere repression. For the first years of the regime, after the Terrors of June and December, repression alone might have sufficed to keep the demoralized workers in place; Thiers and the notables thought so, after crushing the Commune in 1871. But Louis Napoleon hoped to bring the workers back into society, to wean them from radicalism, whether republican or socialist. No socialist himself, despite his occasional claims, he nevertheless had read Blanc and Proudhon, and shared their disdain for the rule of laissez-faire, which endangered social order and retarded economic progress. He immediately undertook a series of paternalistic projects which had the double effect of improving the workers' general welfare and bringing working class activities under strict government control. The various mutual aid societies were multiplied, enlarged, and taken over by the administration, though a few were left to the Church. The *Conseils des prud'hommes,* boards of arbitration first instituted by Napoleon I, were reformed to include genuine workers (rather than foremen), but also more closely administered from Paris. There were starts on accident and old-age insurance, lending agencies, free legal aid, health and hospital services, but little firm legislation and little money spent beyond some of the Emperor's personal funds.

The main impetus to proletarian welfare, Louis and his Saint-Simonian advisers believed, was to come from a general expansion of economic activity and large-scale public works. From above, rewards to the worker would trickle down; at the very least there would be full employment and steadier mass purchasing power. If workers fared slightly better under the Second Empire than previously, especially in the larger industries and in the Paris region, it was mainly because they enjoyed more constant full-time work, for their slowly rising wages almost nowhere kept pace with the inflated costs of food and housing. Much of the Empire period was prosperous, and marked by the swiftest rate of industrial growth attained by France until after the Second World War. But most of the expanded national income went into increased profits, interest, and dividends for the upper middle class and, to a lesser extent, to the middle and lower bourgeoisie—in sum, to those Frenchmen who would share political domination of the Third Republic. In this sense, the Second Empire was more truly bourgeois than the July Monarchy, adding numbers, wealth, and confidence to the middle classes. Yet many even in the new business community steadily gravitated to the opposition, particularly in the later years of the Empire. Their dislike of Napoleon's politics, domestic and foreign, was perhaps less important than their distrust of the Saint-Simonian "new deal" which had helped to create the opportunities they seized to make their fortunes.

For his cherished object of economic progress, Napoleon III arrived at a propitious moment. From the depths of 1847 and 1848, some measure of recovery was inevitable. After a long and sheltered apprenticeship under the constitutional monarchies, France was ready for industrialization and the coup of December quieted fears of further social upheaval. But outside conditions also helped; under the Second Empire France was enmeshed in the international economy created by the nineteenth century. For good and ill, depression or prosperity in any major western nation now had its effect in the others, through the tightening net of financial and commercial ties. Discovery of gold in California and Australia at mid-century had stimulated business activity in what is now known as the Atlantic community. Yet too often the Second Empire's industrial vigor has been ascribed simply to favorable conditions outside the Emperor's control. French governments after his managed very well to avoid the possible benefits of equally favorable world conditions. Without such aid, the Empire might well have failed to achieve the degree of expansion that it did—in the teeth of several domestic recessions and bad harvests—but Napoleon and his advisers took their full opportunity to ride the wave rather than to stand pat and let it break over them.

The Saint-Simonian economists had long believed that expanded credit was the secret of large-scale industrial growth. The Second Empire led France into the era of finance capitalism and corporate ownership. Before 1848, the *Haute Banque* (that informal circle of powerful bankers associated with the Bank of France) was primarily concerned with floating government loans and advancing short-term credit, only incidentally with industrial and railroad finance. Its operations, like those of the Bourse, interested only a small, wealthy group of rentiers. The new banks, encouraged by the imperial government, not only broke the near-monopoly of the older houses but challenged them to expand their own operations into long-term loans to French (and foreign) industry. At the same time, new laws on business association facilitated the formation of limited-liability stock companies. By 1870, the banks and the Bourse were drawing on the funds of millions of Frenchmen for investment, and speculation, in hundreds of large enterprises throughout France and the world; French securities in 1870 had more than tripled in scale, French holdings in foreign shares quadrupled. The most daring of the new banks was Isaac and Émile Péreire's Crédit Mobilier, founded in 1852, patronized and protected until the mid 1860's by Persigny and the Emperor himself. The Péreires also founded the Compagnie Générale Transatlantique (French Line) as a counterpart to the Messageries Maritimes, reorganized by another combine in 1851, which served the Mediterranean and the East. But their main activity was in railroads, French and foreign. The Rothschilds organized a rival operation from among the established financiers, and the ensuing struggle between Péreires and Rothschilds in banking and railroads was fully worthy of the later oil and rail wars of the American robber barons. It ended in the victory of the Rothschilds and the near-collapse of the Crédit Mobilier in the late 1860's, but in the meantime a revolution had transformed French big business.

For financing foreign trade, the Emperor encouraged the expansion of the Comptoir d'Escompte, which dated from 1848, and became active in colonial enterprises. In mortgage banking, the government helped found the Crédit Foncier in 1852, which dealt mainly in urban real estate, and the Crédit Agricole in 1861 for farm mortgages and agricultural improvements. The latter, like the Crédit Foncier, ran into the hostility of the many local lenders, in some instances full-blown usurers, and failed to alleviate the capital shortage in the countryside, the more so since it was diverted into town and foreign ventures of doubtful value. Despite the increased application of modern technology to farming in certain areas, improved transport, and area specialization (the wine *pays* emerged much as they are today), French agriculture remained an affair of small properties and wide variations in productivity. Under the Empire, the continued decline of cottage industry and the parallel expansion of factory work contributed to a relative drop in the rural population, from 75 to 68 per cent; cities and towns absorbed all of the 3 million increase which brought France to some 38 million people in 1870.

The most spectacular work was railroad building. Under the July Monarchy and the Second Republic, some 3000 kilometers were built; under the Second Empire, nearly 15,000 more completed a well-integrated system that was nearly the equal of Germany's, and three-quarters that of Great Britain. Nothing better illustrates Louis Napoleon's belief that economic growth was too serious a business to be left to businessmen alone. His government's railroad policy embraced three methods contrary to the dogma of laissez-faire but beneficial to free enterprise: government initiative and planning, government building of certain facilities, and government partnership in new enterprises. Several railroad companies had succumbed to the economic and political crises of the late 1840's; after 1851 the government helped some to revive, awarded long-term contracts to others which included a guarantee of 4 per cent return on investments. State engineers aided in planning routes and standards of construction. The state also built a number of stations and later subsidized secondary lines into areas where no quick profit was expected but whose development was essential in the long run. As in most countries, railroad building was replete with costly mistakes and compromises. Political and personal favors siphoned off funds and distorted some of the better plans. But by 1870 the partnership of government and private companies had rounded out the network essentially as it is today and, as in nineteenth century America, the railroads were crucial in overall economic development, bringing life or death to various industries and localities.

For France as a whole, they meant life. They ended the threat of famine, stabilized prices, and brought city and country closer together. Critics already complained that the old France of the provinces was disappearing; with the end of local isolation and its disadvantages came the end of many admirable crafts, customs, and cultural nuances. The provinces were opened to all of France, but criticism redoubled when Napoleon III decided to open France to the world, by removing protective tariffs. Throughout the 1850's, he had urged consideration of lower tariffs, but had succeeded only in a few limited instances against the opposition of the supposedly powerless Senate and legislature, or the pleas of local interests; preoccupied with other matters, he did not press them. But free trade was an old idea to him—he had met Cobden in London before 1848—and it promised not only economic progress but international amity. He was urged on by Michel Chevalier, a Saint-Simonian economist whom he had appointed to the *Conseil d'État;* and in 1859, when his Italian victories had given him added prestige at home but potential trouble with England, he had Chevalier open negotiations in London. These ended in the Cobden-Chevalier Treaty of Commerce of January, 1860—presented as an imperial decree, over the legislators' heads. The treaty ended all outright prohibitions on imports and drastically reduced duties across the board. A storm of protest followed from French industrialists, but Napoleon rode it out and similar treaties were arranged with Italy, Belgium, and Prussia in the next two years. They raised enmity against the Empire among the very classes that had most welcomed the Man of Order in 1848. Commercial policy must partly explain why many Frenchmen hailed the coming of the Republic after 1870 not so much for the political liberties it promised as for a return of freedom from competition.

The results of freer trade are nearly impossible to determine, so numerous were the other factors at work in the French economy. Shipping was the most obvious casualty. Cotton textile manufacturers, long terrified of British competition, suffered also, but the American Civil War so disturbed the cotton industry that no accurate appraisal is possible. Woolens, silks, and wine prospered; then the latter two were struck by blights. In coal, iron, and steel, less efficient producers were forced out of business, others found their profits reduced, and even the largest were compelled to modernize their methods. But easier transport by rail and the process of industrial concentration, already begun before the reduction of tariffs, exerted similar pressures. In an effort to soften the blow, Napoleon allotted 40 million francs in easy loans for aid in plant renovation, but the amount fell short of the need and failed to placate the losers. In the 1860's, other factors slowed the pace of economic expansion; political uncertainties at home and abroad undermined confidence, funds for public works and private ventures were drawn off by foreign investment, by speculation in the very active Bourse, by the ordinary citizen's fear of speculation, by the troubles of such promotions as the Crédit Mobilier. But Thiers and other political opponents found it easier to blame free trade, and it is unlikely that tariffs would have remained low even had the regime survived.

In sum, although its Orléanist and republican opponents attacked its economic policies as "socialistic," the Empire provided France with one of its few bursts of vigorous free enterprise in the broadest sense of the term. The partly forced enlargement of the established business oligarchy opened the way to a remarkable group of entrepreneurs, bankers, merchants, and government planners whose large vision and daring methods stirred not a few of the old oligarchs themselves to new activity. The material results were impressive. Foreign commerce tripled in value, as did the production of coal. The number of machines in industry increased sixfold, their horsepower twentyfold. Overall, metallurgy tripled its output; newer products like steel shot upward in volume. At the same time that production expanded, manufacture and ownership (or management) were progressively concentrated. Although France remained a country of predominantly small industry and commerce even to the early twentieth century, large business was firmly established by 1870 as an economic and political power that no French government could ignore.

Of all the material accomplishments of his reign, Napoleon III was proudest of his public works. Like the Romans he admired so much (he wrote a *History of Julius Caesar,* who also had "replaced anarchy with enterprising power"), he devoted men and money to draining swamps, reclaiming land, improving roads and harbors. But the summit of his work, to which he gave a remarkable amount of his own time and energy, was the renovation of Paris. His chief instrument was Georges Haussmann, Prefect of the Seine, whom Napoleon defended against countless enemies until a few months before his own fall. It is ironic that the city so beloved by the free in spirit should have received much of its present style from an imperious, often ruthless, administrator during the most dictatorial years of the Second Empire. The paradox is more apparent than real and illustrates again Louis' Saint-Simonian, Bonapartist view of enterprise. A nation's economy, particularly those aspects of it which most directly affected its style, was not to be left to business interests alone but managed by a partnership—complex, precarious, even dangerous at times—among businessmen, political leaders, scientists, planners, engineers, and whatever intellectual and artistic elite the society could enlist.

His purposes in rebuilding Paris were many; the least of them, perhaps, was a quick and proper return on investment. National and dynastic pride—the first Napoleon, too, had grandiose plans, only partly fulfilled—social improvement, full employment, and public order were the most obvious. Wide avenues cut through the traditionally rebellious poorer districts; cavalry and artillery could overwhelm barricades; rebellion could be isolated more easily. But new streets, 85 miles of them, appeared in the wealthy quarters as well, and streets were only a part of Haussmann's work. The water and sewer systems had grown dangerously inadequate; together with the crowded, sunless slums they were blamed for the 40,000 deaths from cholera since the mid-1830's. At enormous expense, water was piped from the countryside, lessening Parisians' dependence on the malodorous Seine. Belgrand's storm sewers were planned in size and shape to permit easy cleaning from within, and, to the envy of New Yorkers and other city-dwellers of "modern" North America, ample space for installation and servicing, also from within, of sanitary sewers, water, gas, and other utilities to come. Hundreds of square miles of park were created, mostly on the Emperor's own initiative; the Bois de Boulogne was turned from a dreary waste, the Buttes-Chaumont from a quarry. New squares were added, as were new bridges across the Seine, and the Canal Saint Martin was covered with a double tree-lined boulevard. For the first time it became possible to cross Paris in most directions without encountering detours, cul-de-sacs, and traffic jams, which were notorious even under the old regime.

The overall results were mixed, with fewer blemishes than partisan Republicans have claimed, more than apologists for the Empire admit. Much of the housing behind Haussmann's prescribed façades was wretchedly built by profiteering landlords; housing in the new workers' districts, on the outskirts, was deplorable. As in modern urban renewal, the artistic ingredient in the partnership was weakest; needless monotony was only partially relieved by the planting of trees. Many exquisite old buildings and historic streets disappeared; the Île de la Cité was overloaded with ponderous official monoliths; the setting of Notre Dame curiously demeaned by the great clearing made before its portals (though the slums there were among the worst in Paris). In proportion to the vastness of the work, however, the errors fade before the whole. Most important, the city does not scream aloud, as so many cities formed since the Industrial Revolution do, of that drab and jumbled chaos produced by economic expediency, and the lust for quick profit. In this sense, Paris is relatively free from the tyranny of the practical, as were its tyrannical builders, from the first of its monarchs to the last. Its streets offer heartening proof of what men can do when they are free to respect the past, the future, and themselves. Of all the rights that Paris has declared, few are more revolutionary and none more constantly in peril than this: the right of man to beauty. The credit cannot go to the Second Empire alone; but its work is a very large part of the whole and it came at a crucial moment, when a too-practical bourgeois regime might have allowed irreparable damage.

More than ever, Paris became the center of economic, social, and cultural life in France. The railroad lines from every direction led straight to its new stations. Then as now, the great central markets of Les Halles (whose site and design were approved by Louis Napoleon himself) were more than symbolic of Paris' own peremptory, and wasteful, claims on the rest of the country. Nor did it help the provincials' temper that the city their money had rebuilt often appeared as a gas-lit carnival of frivolity and sin. The Emperor, after a publicly rakish bachelorhood, publicly settled down to marriage in 1853, with a Spanish countess, Eugénie de Montijo. But her egregious conservatism and piety did little to dim the glitter of a splendidly expensive court which her own beauty and love of high fashion notably enhanced. Outside the Tuileries, whose dress balls and décolletage grew legendary, spectacles even more daring enticed provincials from Yonville, London, or New York: the cancan (perfected under the July Monarchy), the carriage courtesans, and, in the late 1860's, Les Folies Bergères. For those who could stay longer, there were the plays of Scribe and Labiche, Offenbach's Orpheus, La Belle Hélène, and La Vie Parisienne, the new sidewalk cafés, the new department stores (Bon Marché, Samaritaine, Printemps) and, closest to the Emperor's heart, the first great Paris Exhibition of 1855, which attracted the attention of all Europe to the economic modernization promised by the new regime, and that of 1867, which showed how far the promise had been fulfilled.

## FOREIGN ENTANGLEMENTS

Between those two dates, the main constructive work of the Empire was done. But economic affairs, even when they included the adornment of a dazzling capital city, did not command the main attention of any but those who gained or suffered most. In the public eye, the highest and lowest points of Louis Napoleon's reign were reached in diplomacy and war. Between the *coup d'état* of December, 1851, and the proclamation of the Empire a year later, Louis strove to assure France and Europe that the Empire would mean peace. But Europe was not convinced by the nephew of one who had also promised peace and then subjected half a continent only to defend himself. Foreign diplomats could not be blamed for expecting the worst, from a man whose very name was a challenge to the Vienna settlement. It did not help that he had brusquely asserted himself while President on the side of the Polish, Rumanian, and Hungarian nationalities, and pressed the restored Pius IX to liberal reforms. He had raised the question of Rhenish frontiers with Prussia and, as if to defy every major European power, had defended Greece against the British in the Don Pacifico affair. From the moment of the coup, he had set on parade an army of the most dashing imperial style, the eagle once more perched atop its tricolor standards.

Whatever Europe thought, there was in Napoleon III little of the personal craving for conquest which marked Napoleon I. But he prided himself on his knowledge of military matters and on the regard of soldiers for his name. He would seek prestige for his dynasty and France in an active foreign policy, making Paris once more the world capital of diplomacy not through French aggrandizement but by French leadership in a Europe reorganized according to nationalities. Unlike his uncle's afterthoughts on Saint Helena, Louis' liberal nationalism was probably sincere, partly the result of his travels as a young outcast who had learned to put himself in others' places. Some said of him that he was too good a European to make a good Frenchman, that he failed to foresee the contradictions between French interests and those of a united Italy or, more serious, a united Germany. He also gave evidence of being too good a European to see that Italians and Germans would not be satisfied with the half measures he was willing to grant them once the march to national unification was under way. Throughout his reign, Louis Napoleon's diplomatic aims appeared to be devious, imprecise, constantly shifting; he failed to communicate his plans, or lack of plans, to his own ministers and diplomats. What foreign emissaries reported back as deep, inscrutable design was often little more than watchful indecision. Even in the pursuit of Belgium and the Rhine, which Europe most expected, Napoleon III never developed a settled policy; the first would risk estranging England, which he was anxious to make a friend, the second he merely fumbled for at moments that seemed opportune. On the question of the Rhine, most public men from the court to the Republican opposition were more Napoleonic than the Emperor. It is too much to say, as many have, that he was a man of peace. But for one entrapped in the Napoleonic legend he preferred, more than might be expected, to win glory by negotiation and parade. In the 1850's, when he had firm command of himself and the regime, he limited his aims and emerged relatively unscathed. Only in the 1860's, when ill health and political opposition impaired his power, did he, by drifting, lead France into a disaster more complete than any Napoleon I himself had incurred with all his aggressive design. Historians have found it easy to sympathize with Louis the man, whom a journalist once dubbed "Napoleon the Well-meaning"; their judgment of Louis the Emperor, particularly in foreign affairs, has been something quite different.

His first adventure was a partnership with England—his one settled design—in the Crimean War. The aging Tsar Nicholas threatened to intervene in defense of the rights of orthodox Christians in Turkish territories and of orthodox control over the holy places in Jerusalem, which was disputed by Latin churchmen. Behind this "quarrel of monks" the western powers saw a Russian aim to divide the remains of the ever-moribund Ottoman Empire to Russian advantage in the Balkans and the Straits. In 1853, Nicholas invaded the principalities of Moldavia and Wallachia; in response, the British sent a fleet with French support to the Dardenelles. But they hesitated, Napoleon allowing himself to be called an appeaser (by Victor Hugo, among many), until Turkey declared war and the Russians destroyed a Turkish fleet in the Black Sea. England deemed her Mediterranean interests endangered by this shift in the balance of power; Napoleon vacillated between mediation and his desires to enhance French prestige, to cement the English alliance, and to satisfy those at home who called it a Catholic crusade. Both sides obtusely bungled several chances to withdraw with honor. In March of 1854, Austria's support of the Anglo-French demand for Russian evacuation of the principalities, and Russia's refusal, pushed the nations into war.

The confusion of diplomacy was exceeded only by the barbarous incompetence with which the war was fought. If the blunders on the

French side were not so criminal as those of the British, their common lack of generalship, of supplies and medical services cost tens of thousands of lives. Against the heroic efforts of Florence Nightingale was arrayed every enemy of human life that war, disease, and official obstinacy could muster. Neither at home nor in the field were there military men who understood the logistical problems of a campaign on the remote Crimean Peninsula. Many of the general officers were not only old, but old and inexperienced. The siege of Sevastopol dragged on for a year, under divided command and with untold deprivation in every camp. In March of 1855, Nicholas I died and was succeeded by Alexander II, but attempts at negotiation failed. Louis Napoleon was dissuaded from taking active command, mainly by the British who had no taste for turning their soldiers over to a Bonaparte, particularly in a war that was losing the support of summer patriots. In September, 1855, obstinacy finally won; the French General MacMahon's command took the Malakoff Tower and the Russians abandoned Sevastopol.

In February and March of 1856, Napoleon III reaped glory from the Crimean tragedy in the Peace Congress of Paris, the first of two high-water marks of French prestige under the Second Empire. The Grand Army had been avenged; he had won the acclamation of French patriots, the gratitude of war suppliers, and the friendship of England. There had been an exchange of visits with Victoria and Albert in 1855, during which the two couples, outwardly so different, began a friendship which would outlive the Empire itself. The conference met under the presidency of Walewski, as Foreign Minister of France. Napoleon dreamed of turning the proceedings into an anti-Vienna, raising the questions of Poland and Italy. His good intentions for Poland were frustrated, partly by the conservative powers, partly by England, partly by his own eagerness to conciliate Alexander II. But the Italian problem was manifested by the presence of Camillo di Cavour, Sardinia's chief minister, who had contrived to send a contingent of troops to the Crimea on the side of Britain and France. Cavour won nothing concrete but elicited sympathy and informal promises of support against Austrian attack from both the English and French representatives. Only in the matter of Rumania were Louis' ideas for freedom of the nationalities advanced; an international commission to supervise elections in the principalities of Moldavia and Wallachia proved to be a first step to unification, achieved in 1862 (full independence from Turkey came in 1878). In other matters, the powers agreed to respect the integrity of the Ottoman Empire; the Black Sea and the Danube were opened to commerce, the latter under an international commission; international law on blockade was defined, the Straits Convention of 1841 reaffirmed.

The Bonaparte dynasty never seemed more secure than in 1856. Eugénie's contribution to her husband's hour of triumph was a son, the Prince Imperial, born on March 16th while the conference was in session. For two years, Napoleon III enjoyed his success, worked on the plans for the improvement of Paris, paraded the Prince, hunted at Compiègne, and on January 14, 1858, was reminded by a wrathful Italian patriot of his long-standing promises to aid Italian unification. Felix Orsini's bomb killed eight bystanders, narrowly missing the imperial couple as they alighted from their carriage before the Opera House. Louis' reaction increased his reputation for enigmatic depths. Instead of suppressing his concern for Italy, he used Orsini's trial, with Orsini's help, to dramatize the plight of Italy and raise French sentiment for its unification. Letters signed by the condemned man were dictated by Louis' agents and eloquently pleaded for Louis' intervention. These were published throughout Europe, a direct challenge to Austria, and, some Catholics thought, an affront to the Pope.

In July of 1858, Napoleon met secretly with Cavour at Plombières to consider how Austria could be maneuvered into declaring war on Sardinia, upon which event France would come to the latter's aid with 200,000 men. Louis' desire was a federation of Italian states—a Kingdom of Northern Italy under Sardinia, the central duchies, the Papal States, and Naples—under the presidency of the Pope. His reward would be Nice and Savoy, which he expected would freely vote to join themselves to France. By January, 1859, after an autumn of doubts over French opinion and the readiness of the army, Louis was ready to move. On the 1st, he complained to the world of unsatisfactory relations with Austria; on the 30th, Prince Jerome was married to Victor Emmanuel's daughter; in February, articles in the official press attacked Austrian rule in Italy and proposed an independent federation. English and Prussian opinion favored Austria, French Catholics were incensed over dangers to the Papacy in any change of the *status quo;* Eugénie joined most of the ministers in hostility to her husband's policy. Again Louis wavered, but on April 20th Austria declared war after letting herself be goaded into an ultimatum that Sardinia disarm. This "aggression" solidified Frenchmen behind the war on which Louis now embarked, in personal command of his army in the best tradition of the Bonapartes.

The war went well, partly through accident, partly because the Austrians, also faithful to tradition, made more mistakes than the French and were inexplicably slow to move in any direction. Louis worked hard and confidently; how much he knew about what was happening is perhaps beside the point, considering the history of generalship. On one occasion, he used the railroad to improve on his uncle's plan of Italian battle and in the confused encounter of Magenta (May 4, 1859) the French won precariously. On June 24th, a bloodier battle at Solferino also ended in an Austrian withdrawal. But now the Austrians retired to strong points in the Quadrilateral which the French army, reduced by casualties and disease, was ill-equipped to take. And from a relatively defenseless Paris came news of Prussians gathering along the Rhine. On July 10th, Napoleon III and the young Franz-Joseph met at Villafranca to conclude an armistice. Austria agreed to give Lombardy to France for cession to Sardinia; Venetia, which the French had been on the point of invading, remained Austrian. Thus Louis' promise to clear northern Italy "from sea to sea" was unfulfilled; patriotic Italians raged at this betrayal and Cavour resigned in anger for a time.

In August of 1859, Napoleon III led his armies in triumph through Paris, but his Italian problems had only begun. During the fighting, patriots in the central Italian states had revolted against their Austrian-supported rulers and the Pope, demanding annexation to Sardinia. Napoleon exploited the issue to gain the spoils of war which he had forfeited by his failure to deliver Venetia. In early 1860, he traded his permission for Sardinia's annexation of Parma, Modena, and Tuscany for the Treaty of Turin (March, 1860) which gave Nice and Savoy, by plebiscite, to France. Except for those who worried for the Pope, Frenchmen applauded once again, but the coup discredited Napoleon in Italy, England, and Austria. Still the game continued. In July, 1860, Garibaldi and his Red Shirts cleared Sicily of the Neapolitan Bourbons, then in early September took Naples itself. Cavour sent Sardinian troops southward, brushing aside the papal Zouaves (including many French Catholic volunteers) on the way. Naples and Sicily joined the union in October, Umbria and the Marches in November. On March 17, 1861, Victor Emmanuel was proclaimed King of Italy, independent and unified except for Venetia and Rome.

Italian patriots immediately raised demands for an attack on French-occupied Rome, which they considered the predestined capital of Italy. In Paris, Napoleon held a middle course, ignored Prince Jerome's plea to abandon Rome, refused the clericals' demands that he use the army outside of Rome on behalf of a Pope who would force Italians to choose between their country and the faith. He had, on the contrary, publicly advised Pius IX in 1859 to give up his hold on the Papal States and be content with Rome. "The smaller the Pope's territories," he said, "the greater will be their sovereign's prestige." The advice had been good for at least 500 years, but Pius IX characteristically turned it aside as "a paradox," and openly denounced Napoleon as a liar. The English, also characteristically, expressed their delight at Louis' show of independence from "popish" pressures in France, but the Roman question was not thereby made easier. Italians railed at the French presence in Rome, French clericals (Eugénie not least) were aghast at Louis' unfilial attitude toward the Pope. Louis may well have preferred to satisfy the former and withdraw French troops immediately, but all knew that Rome would fall to the Italian kingdom if left to papal forces alone, and French Catholics were too important to Napoleon's power, and peace of mind, at home. The tortuous policy went on. In 1866, Louis encouraged the alliance between Italy and Prussia, which ended in Austria's cession of Venetia after her defeat in the Austro-Prussian War. On Victor Emmanuel's assurance that Florence would remain his capital, Napoleon withdrew the army from Rome in December of 1866. But Garibaldi attacked in 1867 and the French returned, defeated him, and stayed on until the collapse of the Empire in 1870.

Napoleon III remained entangled in the Roman knot throughout his reign, managing to offend all sides yet giving each in turn an occasional sign that he might soon decide the question in its favor. His dilemma over Rome was the archetype of several others that clouded the second decade of the Empire and contributed to a progressive loss of respect for his regime among the most articulate groups in France. In domestic, colonial, and foreign affairs, Louis' personal preferences and better instincts were blunted by a host of pressures and temptations he was unable to withstand. The decade that ended at Sedan was laden with good intentions but hedged round with every weakness known to political man. Insofar as each was responsible for his fate, the first Napoleon succumbed to an all-encompassing pride; Napoleon III, as if to justify the scorn of Victor Hugo, fell by a multitude of little frailties.

## THE MODERATE EMPIRE

In the afterglow of victory in Italy, the Emperor granted a complete amnesty to political prisoners and exiles (except for Ledru-Rollin), as a token of his intention to liberalize the government. From 1859 to 1870 there followed a series of concessions to political liberty and working-class initiative that, if not unknown in the history of dictatorships, are indisputably rare. Historians often divide, though never neatly, along two lines in explaining Louis' motives. The first is that he intended from the start to develop liberal, even democratic, institutions as soon as he judged the situation right, that he believed in the Bonapartism of Saint Helena, in the Napoleon whom his mother had described many years before as the Messiah of the masses. In 1853, the Emperor had said that Liberty would crown his edifice once it was solidly built; after his Italian victory and another electoral sweep by his supporters in 1857, he carried out that promise. The other view leaves him still the autocrat at heart but forced by weakness to appease the opposition rising against him on all sides—resentful workers and Republicans, especially in Paris (to whose moods he was always sensitive), Catholic leaders angry over his treatment of the Papacy, businessmen in rebellion against free trade and government spending.

To take something from both views is not merely expedient, but it most accords with the otherwise contradictory facts and with Louis' character, also contradictory. At several points in his career before and after 1848, he dreamed of being the Napoleon of Austerlitz and Jena, of the autocratic Empire in 1812. But other, more frequent, moods revealed the gentler spirit of the liberal and pacific nationalist, more European than French. Both were part of him throughout, but after 1859 the balance appeared to shift. Before, his autocracy was tempered by recurring strains of self-doubt and human sympathy; afterward, his liberalism was compromised by a lingering taste for personal, paternal authority. Through all the reign, an eagerness to be liked joined other forms of self-indulgence—indolence, amorous adventures, rewriting history, imperial pageantry—to make him inconsistent, dilatory, and, in the eyes of many who might otherwise have supported him, an unreliable collaborator.

The Italian war may well have proved to him that he was incapable of sustaining the Napoleonic manner; he was sickened by the blood at Solferino, and he had the records of his chaotic orders burned. He distrusted the actions of some of his ministers and entourage. While relying on them too much to dismiss them and unable to supervise them in person, he may have expected a freer press and Chamber to keep them closer to public opinion, on which he himself was, or could be, well informed by the assiduous reports of his prefects, which are still invaluable sources for historians of the period. More certainly, he distrusted the mentality of conservative Catholics like Veuillot who demanded favors for the Pope and a clerical monopoly in education. He was deeply unsympathetic with those Orléanist businessmen who clamored for freedom from competition and from taxes while refusing all concessions to their workmen. His policies in Italy and free trade created this new opposition on the Right, from the party of Order which had welcomed him to power. On the other hand, the majority of anti-clericals were by now Republican, and the workers' spokesmen radical Republicans or worse. To satisfy the Right would have meant abandoning his own beliefs, his view of the nation's basic needs, and would have reopened the great wound he had sought to close. To satisfy the Left would have meant all of these and more, his own abdication. By pursuing a middle course, he might mollify the moderate opposition leaders, isolate the extremists, and, most of all, appeal to the mass of ordinary men in all camps on whose approval his authority, and the dynasty's, ultimately rested. Different motives may explain different acts, but the changes he made and those he did not make reflected Louis' desire to remain all things to all men.

This was especially true as it applied to his immediate entourage, which was sharply split over whether the regime should remain autocratic or evolve toward parliamentary responsibility. In general, Eugénie and Persigny opposed any relaxation; they were joined by Eugène Rouher, who was Napoleon's legislative leader during most of the 1860's. On the other side, the most influential figure was Morny, an Orléanist liberal at heart and anxious to win over a new generation of notables from any faith—Legitimist, Orléanist, Republican—to found a new, respectable, Bonapartist parliamentary group. And from Prince Jerome came a steady stream of liberal memoranda with advice far better and far worse than the Emperor could usually apply at any given moment. The relationships even within this small group illustrate the difficulties Louis had to face. Eugénie and Persigny, who agreed on autocracy, disliked each other heartily. Persigny was anti-clerical, pro-Italian, and favored free trade; the Empress was quite the opposite, at least on the first two questions. Morny, who stood for political liberalization, opposed much of the Italian policy, was an uncertain convert to free trade, and progressively anti-clerical. Walewski was clerical but cooperated with Morny against the Empress and Rouher, who preferred authority but was the best grass-roots politician of the lot. Not surprisingly, Napoleon III never finally chose one side over the other. If he is counted on the liberal side, it is because of his temperament and because he chose the liberal of alternative courses rather more often than circumstances seemed to compel. Charming and invariably kind (some say weak) with each of his advisers in turn and, perhaps because of his infidelities, especially indulgent of Eugénie's high-pitched demands, Louis seemed to make decisions at one moment, then to change or postpone them at the next. Naturally, those ministers who remained loyal to him were constantly under public attack as compromisers and careerists.

Louis Napoleon has been called an *arriviste* who had the misfortune to arrive, a man who sought the honors of power without the convictions or ideals to give it form. The accusation is plausible only in the 1860's, when his plans for Italy, for Paris, the economy, and free trade had been largely fulfilled. Even then, he clung to each of these when it would have been easier to give way. But they were not negotiable; and it is only in relation to these settled policies, and to the determined opposition they raised, that he pursued a middle course, and that it developed as a hesitant, contradictory attempt to reconcile Caesar and the open society. The wonder is that it almost succeeded. By 1870, the Second Empire was in form a parliamentary government, with a cabinet collectively responsible to the Deputies and an Emperor who seemed ready to retire to a relatively modest political role (as he already had, in practice, during several bouts of illness). When a plebiscite in 1870 approved the liberal Empire as overwhelmingly as another had approved the coup of December in 1851, the problem of domestic politics appeared to be solved. But the first test of the fledgling system was to avoid—or win—the Franco-Prussian War. Its failure not only destroyed it, but discredited the Emperor's liberal Bonapartism. Those who had opposed all liberal concessions attributed France's defeat to change itself rather than to the fatal delays and dilutions of change which left no time for the liberal Empire to set its house in order. Bonapartism became an affair of the Right, reverting to its authoritarian source in the First Empire.

The legend of Saint Helena faded with Louis Napoleon, perhaps the only public man who ever believed in it.

Following the final amnesty of 1859 for political offenders (twelve thousand of the fourteen uprooted by the December purges had been released in earlier years), the government relaxed its restrictions on political commentary in the press. In the following year, the Senate and the Corps Législatif were allowed to publish their debates and to discuss and vote a reply to the annual address from the throne. At the end of 1861, the lower Chamber won the right to debate and pass on an item budget, though the Emperor could later revise it with impunity. At the same time, 1859, Napoleon sought to reassure the business community by appointing to the Ministry of Finance Achille Fould, an associate of the Rothschilds who was said to oppose government spending. But Haussmann, their bête noire, stayed on, spending increased in the years immediately following, and in 1860 the advent of free trade permanently alienated a large segment of business and industry. The rising opposition, an economic slump in 1862, and the new freedoms in political life were reflected in the elections of 1863. Since 1857 and 1858, elections and by-elections had deposited in the Corps Législatif the famous Republican "Party of Five" (Henon, Darimon, Ernest Picard, Jules Favre, Émile Ollivier), who kept up a lively critique of the regime. In 1863, their number was tripled and another fifteen Rightist opponents entered the Chamber; 2 million of 7 million voting had opposed the official candidates (who were as divided as the Emperor's official family on his ill-defined schemes for broadening political liberties). Louis chose to regard the election results as a defeat for Persigny, who as Minister of the Interior had waged a singularly aggressive campaign for imperial candidates. He was retired, and more liberal Bonapartists, under Morny's leadership, took precedence. But Morny's death in 1865 and the advent of Rouher seriously delayed further liberalization.

Meanwhile it seemed that the time had come for concessions to the working classes, whose votes had helped elect eight Republicans from Paris. Since 1851, imperial policies had managed to destroy nearly all of the producer and consumer cooperatives that even the conservative Second Republic had tolerated after the June Days. The government's thinly disguised assertion of control over the aid societies and Louis' charitable works made few converts to the Empire, whose police mercilessly crushed strikes and persecuted their leaders. But the Italian war was popular among the working classes, the more so since it appeared to worsen relations between the Emperor and the Church. In 1861, Louis pardoned the leaders of a typographers' strike which had been broken by concerted action of employers. In 1862, he provided funds for a workers' delegation to the London Exposition led by the moderate Proudhonist Tolain. After the elections of 1863, the bourgeois Republicans whom the workers had supported responded only with familiar platitudes; but Louis Napoleon, aided by Ollivier, who now broke with his Republican colleagues, revised the Le Chapelier law of 1791 to allow strikes and whatever temporary coalitions were necessary to organize them (1864). Since permanent associations or unions remained illegal, the numerous strikes that followed were badly planned, underfinanced, and readily turned to violence, the more so as the police continued to deal harshly with their leaders. In 1868, the government took another step, permitting unions and revoking the hated Article 1781 in the Code which had imposed inequality before the law. The French trade-union movement was finally under way, but other events and ideas had already insured that its history would be turbulent and divisive.

Although workers were to give their votes overwhelmingly to bourgeois Republican candidates until the end of the century, the Second Empire marks a decisive step in proletarian class-consciousness. The lessons of 1848 confirmed those of 1830; to prevent betrayal, workers would have to think and act for themselves. Where Louis Blanc and the Utopians had failed, it was hardly likely that the polite social theorists of the Second Empire would succeed. Auguste Comte believed in employer benevolence to keep the workers respectful until positivism should set the world aright; the Catholic Le Play depended upon the return of employers to Christian principles; among the Republicans, only a minority had yet progressed to social legislation and the income tax. And whatever Louis Napoleon did, he remained the protector of businessmen (whatever businessmen thought), apparently unable even to enlighten his own police on the new benevolence. If the Emperor expected Parisian workers to be grateful for the renovation of the city, he was mistaken. The new parks, most of them well clear of the workers' quarters, did not compensate for the higher rents they had to pay and the higher living they saw about them. Thousands were forced by demolitions to move out to newer slums in what would be known as the "Red Belt" of industrial suburbs. Their increased class-consciousness is sometimes blamed on the physical separation of the classes resulting from Haussmann's work; in certain sections before the 1850's, all classes had resided together in the same building, in reverse order from bottom to top as one climbed the progressively narrowing stairs. But there had been workers' slums before, many of the mixed dwellings remained after Haussmann (new ones were built in his time), and it is difficult in any case to be sure what emotions familiarity bred. It is perhaps more important that prosperous Parisians saw less of the workers and that the Church was slow to build new parishes amid the factories and railroad yards of the outskirts.

The workers' delegations at the London Exposition of 1862 had been eager to counter employers' claims that wages would have to be lowered to meet the new competition forced upon them by free trade. If wages could be standardized by international action, the argument would disappear. It was on these grounds, and in the shadow of wide unemployment as a consequence of the American Civil War, that French and English workers founded the Workers' International in London two years later. In subsequent meetings at London, Geneva, and Lausanne, the French delegation led by Tolain suffered the lash of Karl Marx and his followers for their loyalty to Proudhon and his moderate ideas of workers' cooperatives, for their suspicion of state collectivism. In 1868, the imperial government forced the French section of the International underground, thereby discrediting the moderates, who had accepted official patronage, and raising more violent collectivist members to leadership. The influence of Blanqui encouraged young militants in the same direction, especially as Louis Napoleon's unsteady regime helped to break a series of strikes in 1869 and 1870. Karl Marx welcomed Prussian victory in the war of 1870 as insuring the ascendancy of his ideas (already dominant in German workers' circles) over the French and Proudhon. The following years were to prove that class-consciousness did not guarantee class solidarity; the French workers were to remain divided among several, usually conflicting, approaches to social betterment.

Perhaps the most lastingly beneficial of Louis Napoleon's reforms in the 1860's, for the workers and many other Frenchmen and Frenchwomen, was his appointment of Victor Duruy as Minister of Education in 1863. It was typical of the Emperor to choose this liberal, anti-clerical historian at a moment when his regime was under heavy fire from the conservative Catholics. It was also typical of him to give Duruy insufficient support, against conservative Bonapartists in the cabinet and both chambers, on several crucial issues, and typical of his Republican and Orléanist opponents in the Corps Législatif to refuse needed appropriations (for projects they approved *en principe*) on the grounds that Duruy served an unworthy regime. Despite innumerable obstacles, Duruy materially advanced the causes of free, obligatory primary education (which Guizot and some employers opposed as a violation of laissez-faire), adult education, vocational training, and equal education for girls. One of his first acts was to restore philosophy and contemporary history to the secondary curriculum. His pleas for increased teachers' pay and pensions, for modernization of France's long-neglected system of higher education, went largely unheard. In the Third Republic other men were to bring his dreams to fulfillment and, belatedly, his name to the honor it deserved.

Many of Duruy's difficulties arose from the continuing quarrel over the Church's role in education. The opposition of the French hierarchy all but destroyed his projected schools for girls. It was on this issue that *L'Osservatore Romano,* shortly after Napoleon's troops had rescued Rome from Garibaldi in 1867, argued that Catholics should refuse to support Napoleon until Duruy was dismissed. This intervention quite naturally had the opposite of its desired effect, and illustrates the growing estrangement between the Empire and Rome after the Italian war. The Papacy of Pius IX and the concurrent history of the Church in France were marked by the most startling contrasts. On the one hand, the Church as religious institution was immeasurably strengthened and centralized, the moral quality of its prelates and priests never higher, the work and self-sacrifice of its missionaries (French missionaries at the forefront) incontestably glorious. The vision of Bernadette at Lourdes in 1858 and its aftermath were only the most famous of several religious manifestations that made France appear to be the most Catholic of nations. In direct contrast, the same generation witnessed the rebirth and extension of a militant anti-clericalism which was also more anti-Catholic than at any time since the Terror and which was to become nearly synonymous with republicanism—and socialism—until the first World War.

The sources of anti-clericalism were many, most of them familiar since the old regime and the restoration. In the early 1850's the Church eagerly supported a dictatorial State which had overthrown a Republic, had deported and imprisoned Republicans. For men who represented the Church Eternal, some of the politically-minded bishops displayed a pathetic desire to run with the tide; having lavished praise on the Republic in 1848, they were ready to compare Louis Napoleon with Charlemagne and Saint Louis in 1852. The Church, said Victor Hugo, offered the criminal an altar cloth on which to wipe his hands. Only a few of the prominent Catholic laymen who had pleaded for liberty under the July Monarchy stood out against Louis Napoleon—Ozanam before the coup of 1851, Montalembert afterward. Liberty, it appeared, could be traded for favors to the Pope and a guarantee, which Napoleon gave to Montalembert, of support to Catholic education. And social amelioration seemed expendable as well, for after the June Days, Catholicism appeared indissolubly linked to the propertied bourgeoisie, its most prominent spokesmen combining conservatism in politics with liberalism in economics, laissez-faire except for charity. No combination could have been better calculated to alienate the working classes.

As under the restoration, the proliferation of religious orders and church schools, the unchallenged influence of churchmen in French education until 1863, provoked the fears of those who equated religion and counterrevolution. Once more, extreme begat extreme. And it was particularly unfortunate for the Catholic cause that its foremost champion under the Empire was Louis Veuillot, whose violent and vulgar attacks on unbelievers and Frenchmen of other faiths, among which he included liberal Catholicism, were read in *l'Univers* and repeated from pulpits all over France, by a clergy whose education in public affairs was rarely equal to its moral fervor. In the face of Veuillot's support from Rome, from the French hierarchy and government, the few liberal Catholics who rallied to Montalembert and his paper *Le Correspondant* in the mid-1850's—Falloux, Lacordaire, the young historian Albert de Broglie, the brilliant Msgr. Dupanloup—found almost no hearing among their co-religionists. After the Emperor's Italian war, which both Catholic factions deplored, the liberals believed their principles of separation of Church and State to be justified. At a Catholic Congress in Malines, Belgium, in 1863, Montalembert pleaded for separation, for freedom of conscience as the only way to reconcile Catholicism to a nineteenth-century society that was frankly pluralistic. Should the glory of Catholic martyrs, he asked, be tarnished by Catholic, and Catholic-supported, repression?

The answer which came from Rome was directed not only at Montalembert and his circle, but to liberal Catholics in Sardinia and other lands. On December 8, 1864, Pius IX published the encyclical *Quanta cura* and the *Syllabus of Errors,* eighty modern propositions to be condemned as contrary to Catholic teaching, including socialism, communism, Freemasonry, Gallicanism, rationalism (insofar as it denied revelation), materialism, doubts on the propriety of the Pope's temporal power, separation of Church and State, freedom of conscience. The most striking article was the eightieth, wherein the Pope denied that "the Roman Pontiff can and ought to reconcile himself to progress, liberalism, and modern civilization." Pius also denounced liberty of the press, lay teaching, and equality of sects before the law. Veuillot and the intransigents exulted, the *Correspondant* group was in despair. Napoleon III, who took the pronouncements as attacks on his own regime—which they were—forbade their publication in France. His orders had little effect; the French Catholic community was bitterly divided; the liberals were accused of heresy, the Pope in turn assailed as an enemy of mankind. At this point, Dupanloup performed an invaluable service in issuing an interpretation of the encyclical and *Syllabus* which considerably softened the most controversial points; the eightieth article, he said, referred only to the abuses of liberalism, to modern civilization as defined by the enemies of religion. Over 630 bishops from all the world immediately applauded Dupanloup's interpretation, as did Pius IX himself. But the damage to liberal Catholicism was irreparable. As the Pope prepared the Vatican Council of 1869–1870 which was to declare papal infallibility, the Vatican paper *Civiltà cattolica* not only implied that liberal Catholics were somehow a breed apart from "Catholics properly speaking" but rejected in advance the arguments against the doctrine that were being prepared by several influential French bishops and theologians. That the relative intransigence of a Pope under physical attack by Italian nationalism and liberalism should have been transmitted to many Frenchmen (and especially anticlericals) by the totally intransigent and theologically untutored Veuillot needlessly exacerbated a quarrel that was already reopening old wounds. Each extreme felt itself justified in its worst fears and accusations. Between clericalism and anti-clericalism, liberal Catholics and tolerant nonbelievers remained almost voiceless until the pontificate of Leo XIII, which began in 1878.

## THE IMPERIAL DEBACLE

Despite the growing hostility between Napoleon III and Rome, the Emperor never openly broke with the conservative Catholics and the two were naturally associated in the eyes of their common enemies. The colonial policies of the Empire further strengthened the impression that it was ready to employ—and risk—the nation's power in the cause of religion. That Napoleon overemphasized the religious motive in foreign ventures was proof of his continuing desire to keep the mass of French Catholics loyal to his dynasty, particularly in the 1860's when Rome was no longer friendly. In 1859 French forces took Saigon, ostensibly to protect Catholic missionaries; but the subsequent conquest of Cochin-China and the establishment of a protectorate over Cambodia were sustained, even over Napoleon's own doubts, by military and economic interests. In 1860, when the French landed in Syria to prevent further Turkish massacres of Christians, and joined the British in an attack on Peking (also to avenge missionaries), both acts also expressed Napoleon's determination to have French power taken seriously in those parts of the world. It was the same with his continuous, though not always enthusiastic, support of de Lesseps in the completion of the Suez Canal, finally opened by the Empress in 1869.

In Africa, Louis Philippe's trading posts on the west coast were expanded into the colony of Senegal by the enterprising Faidherbe, one of the shapers of a French colonial policy that was to be applied over a wide area by the Third Republic. The inchoate nature of Louis Napoleon's colonial attitudes is best illustrated in Algeria and shown at its worst in the Mexican disaster. In the former, he attempted to halt French colonization and form instead an autonomous Arab kingdom under its own rulers and customs. He feared, with many French businessmen who were forced to compete with its products, that Algeria would become a burden. His policy was reversed by the Third Republic. In the New World, his dream of building a Latin Catholic state under French protection was spoiled by the Mexican Republic, and doomed by the American. France, Spain, and England sent an expedition to collect Mexican debts in 1861 from the anti-clerical government of Juarez. When the others withdrew, the French stayed, captured Mexico City, and Napoleon placed the Austrian Archduke Maximilian on the throne of a Catholic Empire. The adventure appeared to combine many advantages, but its most enthusiastic supporter was the Empress Eugénie, who was willingly misinformed by conservative Mexican clericals on the true economic and spiritual desires of their people. Louis dreamed of regaining the foothold his uncle had sold to the Americans in 1803, of an interocean canal more spectacular than the Suez, of spreading French culture and Bonapartist democracy in Central and South America. Morny was interested in collecting on the Mexican bonds of his Swiss friend Jecker, who was conveniently made a French citizen. French Catholics were induced to regard it as a crusade, but like most crusades it was costly (of 40,000 soldiers, 6000 died) and its success depended on the inability of interested powers nearby to gather their forces in opposition; as Bazaine entered Mexico City in June of 1863, Lee was marching into Pennsylvania and Lincoln had not yet found a general. But the Mexican guerrillas refused to be beaten and the generous Maximilian failed to reconcile his new subjects. The Union victory in the American Civil War, however unexpected, left Napoleon no option but to withdraw his troops; the logic of Appomattox led to Queretaro, where Maximilian was shot by the Mexican Republicans in 1867.

This shattering defeat followed upon several rebuffs to Napoleon's diplomacy in Europe, each involving the rising power of Prussia and her new-found master, Otto von Bismarck. Each was also the result of a basic contradiction in French foreign policy. After 1860, neither the Emperor nor most of his articulate subjects wanted war in Europe; Louis Napoleon asked relatively little for military preparations apart from the needs of the Mexican campaign, and the increasingly difficult legislators gave him even less. On the other hand, few Frenchmen were ready to give up the European prestige they assumed had been regained after the Crimean and Italian wars, when Napoleon had successfully presented himself to his countrymen as the arbiter of European war and peace. So in 1863, when Alexander II crushed the Polish insurrection and abolished Poland's constitution, Napoleon appeased the consciences of French Catholics, Bonapartists, and Republicans by a vigorous protest to the Tsar. Since he was unwilling to act and England opposed his suggestion of a European congress to settle the matter, the end result was antagonism in Saint Petersburg and dismay among those Frenchmen and Polish exiles who had taken him seriously. Meanwhile, Bismarck had offered Prussian aid to Alexander in restoring order in Poland.

The next year Bismarck's campaign against Schleswig and Holstein tempted Napoleon to open his notorious campaign for compensation in Belgium or the Rhineland, in return for his "approval" of Prussian aggrandizement. When Austria was lured by Prussia into a joint seizure of the two provinces from Denmark, England sought French cooperation and was rebuffed on the sensible grounds that nothing could be done short of war, to which Louis frankly added that France would move only in the hope of compensation that England could not offer. He thought that Prussia could, or would be compelled to, make such an offer in her coming conflict with Austria. In two successive meetings, in 1864 and 1865, Bismarck suggested to Napoleon III that French neutrality might win Prussia's support for French aggrandizement in Belgium and the Rhine. His French host expected an Austrian victory or a protracted war; in either case, the Rhine would be left open to him. He assured Bismarck of French neutrality and urged an Italian-Prussian alliance against Austria; in the event of a Prussian victory Napoleon not only would have his own reward but could claim credit for completing Italian unification.

After Prussia's lightning victory in the Seven Weeks' War, against the Emperor's expectations, all that remained to him was the claiming of credit. Austria ceded Venetia to France, for transferral to the Italian Kingdom; and in September of 1866, Louis issued a memorandum in which he resumed the pose of arbiter of Europe, asserting that French diplomacy had successfully overthrown the Vienna settlement and selflessly advanced the causes of German and Italian nationalism. It was noted that for his part in this success the French Foreign Minister, Drouyn de Lhuys, was dismissed. The reality was that at the moment of Sadowa, where the Prussian army routed the Austrians, de Lhuys and the Empress had demanded a French troop concentration on the Rhine, to hold Bismarck to his promises. Louis had refused; ill, unsure of the army, concerned for the budget and public reaction, anxious to preserve what remained of England's good will, he preferred to depend upon Bismarck's word, which had never quite been given. But the Chancellor, victorious over Austria, the North German States, and his own domestic opposition in a single stroke, not only refused French demands for Luxembourg and for the left bank of the Rhine, but published them to all of Europe, through the Paris newspapers. Not content, Louis stepped further into the trap. He instructed the French Ambassador, Benedetti, to offer a secret treaty in which France would recognize the confederation of all the German states under Prussia in return for

Prussia's support of French absorption of Luxembourg and Belgium. Bismarck acquired Benedetti's draft, but only to publish it four years later for the edification of European opinion on the eve of his war with France.

Under the shadow of these setbacks and no doubt partly because of them, Napoleon III opened a new series of political concessions in 1867, beginning with the right of the Corps Législatif to question his ministers on their policies. In 1868, a new press law released a flood of new journals, many of them hostile to the regime. After the long silence, during which political opinions had to be carefully inserted in articles purporting to be philosophic or literary, it appeared that no attack on the government was too scurrilous to satisfy the public. Foreign defeats, the slowing of economic activity, corruption real and alleged, the personal lives of ministers and courtiers, all the topics reminiscent of the press campaigns against Louis Philippe in the late 1840's were revived. The conservative Bonapartists remembered 1848 and urged Louis to reverse his liberal policies, but he understood 1848 differently. When the elections of 1869 gave the opposition candidates three of every seven votes, he dismissed Rouher and in January, 1870, called Émile Ollivier to head a cabinet which would be responsible to the representatives of the people. Ollivier, a former Republican, had been chosen by Morny several years before to play just such a role. Despite Napoleon's delays and vacillations, Ollivier had remained loyal to the ideal of the liberal Empire and now was determined, as he put it, to "give the Emperor a happy old age." In the Chamber, he was actively supported by a "Third Party" made up largely of Orléanists but including a number of liberal Bonapartists and a fluctuating number of conservative Republicans. What this party, had it remained in control, would have made of the Second Empire is impossible to say. It was largely protectionist and clerical (in the political sense), and had consistently opposed government spending and easy credit. One of its leading members was the indestructible Adolphe Thiers.

A revised constitution formally proclaimed the liberal Empire in April, and in May—over the protests of some of the Orléanists—a plebiscite offered the new order to the French nation: "The People approves of the Liberal reforms made in the Constitution since 1860 by the Emperor in agreement with the official bodies and ratifies the *senatus-consulte* of April 20, 1870." The question was ambiguous, but the Republicans clarified the issue somewhat by campaigning vigorously for rejection. They won the cities and 1,570,000 No votes in all, but the Empire, or the liberal Empire, or both, polled 7,350,000, nearly as many as in 1852. It was clear that much of the earlier opposition had been aimed not at the destruction of the Empire but at its reform. In the summer of 1870, it thus appeared that the dynasty had turned a difficult corner without losing its balance; Republicans gloomily predicted a long reign for the Prince Imperial. The economy showed new life and quotations on the Bourse went up. But on July 19, 1870, France stumbled into war with Prussia and six weeks later the Second Empire was dead.

To Otto von Bismarck fell the role of exposing to the world the incapacity of French diplomacy and arms in 1870. Napoleon III had been rebuffed too often for Bismarck to suppose that the South German states could be absorbed into the new Germany without a major European crisis, quite possibly ending in a war with France. In such an event, France had to be cast as the aggressor, lest she find allies or enough diplomatic support to delay final German unification. The exiling of Spain's Queen Isabella in 1868 gave Bismarck an opening. In early July of 1870, Prince Leopold of Hohenzollern-Sigmaringen accepted a Spanish offer of the throne, an offer encouraged by Bismarck himself. As he expected, the French government and press were outraged at the prospect of a relative of King William of Prussia enthroned on their southern frontier. The Duc de Gramont, Napoleon's Foreign Minister, immediately took up the challenge, brusquely accused Prussia of attacking French interests and French honor. Diplomatic pressure from Paris induced Prince Leopold to withdraw his candidacy, and to Bismarck's dismay the crisis appeared to be dissolved in favor of France. But now the French added folly to pride. Gramont, Ollivier, and the Emperor, under chauvinist pressure from the Paris press, the Chamber, and imperial courtiers, ordered the French Ambassador Benedetti to extract King William's promise that the candidacy would never be renewed—an admission, in effect, that Prussia had acted wrongly and now repented.

This was not diplomacy but a meretricious appeal to French public opinion. The old King firmly but courteously refused to see Benedetti, then reported his action in a telegram from Ems to Bismarck in Berlin. The famous Ems dispatch, artfully abbreviated by Bismarck, aroused storms of patriotic protest in both Paris and Berlin. Each side felt itself insulted. The French Chamber ignored the warnings of Adolphe Thiers and voted war credits. Members of the imperial court (including the

Empress) and administration believed war would revive imperial prestige and allow the reversal of political concessions made since 1860. The Paris press of all political shades demanded vengeance, and street crowds shouted for a victory march through Berlin. Napoleon III was well aware of his army's defects and the doubtfulness of his cause, but he was too weak to resist the pressures born of his own government's decade of bluff, bluster, and misstep. On July 19th, France declared war, without allies and without friends. British and American opinion was already alienated when Bismarck published Napoleon's four-year-old demands for compensation at Belgian expense. The Italians gleefully occupied Rome as French troops marched northward and Gramont's airy promise of an Austrian alliance came to nothing.

What the French army lacked in numbers it failed to make up in quality of plans, organization, supply, transport, modern arms, or leadership. Its color, smartness of drill, its dash and horsemanship, its undeniable courage and skill at last-minute improvisation counted for little against a larger Prussian army better prepared in everything but small arms. Napoleon III, tired, ill, and pessimistic, took nominal command in the field. He achieved little coordination between the armies; and, as in 1940, the French kept few forces in reserve, sent most of their strength forward to an extended line from which they were unable to fall back in time to regroup. Marshal MacMahon was beaten at Worth in Alsace, Marshal Bazaine shut himself into Metz. On September 2nd Louis Napoleon, with MacMahon's army, was pinned at Sedan by superior Prussian artillery and forced to surrender. He was taken prisoner with 80,000 French soldiers—and the Napoleonic legend faded under the leaden skies of eastern France.

# ～Ⅴ～

# THE ADVENT
# OF THE THIRD
# REPUBLIC

What France remembers as *l'année terrible* was six weeks old when news of the debacle at Sedan reached Paris. There, as in most of the cities that had voted against the Empire in the May plebiscite, what remained of imperial authority collapsed in the face of popular demonstrations on September 4, 1870. According to historic precedent, Eugénie fled to England, the crowd flooded into the Palais Bourbon and put an end to the desperate attempts of the legislators to contrive a transitional government. Two of Napoleon's Republican opponents, Jules Favre and the fiery young lawyer, Léon Gambetta, led a mass of Parisians to the Hôtel de Ville, lest more radical leaders forestall them, and the Republic was proclaimed in language full of the bright hope of 1848, the patriotic defiance of 1792. Although the Prussian armies were advancing on Paris unopposed, the regime that was to last longer than any since the Revolution, and whose essential form was to survive another defeat and occupation seventy years later, opened in a burst of confidence and exaltation.

## WAR AND DEFEAT

Men who had cheered Napoleon's war policy, who had shouted for another Jena, another victory march through Berlin, the seizure of the Rhine frontier and beyond, now found it easy to believe that only the imperialists had wanted war and only the imperialists had lost it. Now all was changed—except the taste for historical allusion. Empire France reverted to Republican France, once again defending herself and the ideals of 1789 against German autocracy. As in 1793, Republican Paris would lead France in a *levée-en-masse,* for a cause purified by the fall of the usurper, strengthened by the substitution of a people's army for the jaded imperial mercenaries. Such was the language of the street, of Victor Hugo returned from exile, of the hotheaded journalist Henri Rochefort released from the prison of Sainte-Pélagie, of the newly appointed mayor of Montmartre, the 29-year-old surgeon, Georges Clemenceau.

Of the leading members of the Government of National Defense—made up, in haste, of Deputies well known to Paris—perhaps only Gambetta believed that the legend could be made real. As Minister of the Interior, he quickly replaced imperial prefects with men he thought capable of organizing resistance—and securing the Republic. In Paris, he worked to arm an expanded National Guard which, in the absence of normal employment, became the main source of support for over 350,000 men and their families. Jules Favre as Vice-President and Foreign Minister proclaimed to the world on September 6th that France would yield not an inch of her soil. But the President and military commander, General Trochu, had known better how to criticize the army of Napoleon III than to organize Paris for a proper defense, much less for a victory in which he probably did not believe. Apart from the amorphous mass of National Guards, he commanded some 75,000 regular soldiers and sailors, 100,000 reservist *mobiles;* but only the haziest plans for their use were ready when the Prussian armies closed around the twenty-mile perimeter of Louis-Philippe's obsolescent fortifications on September 19th. On the same day Bismarck refused Jules Favre's plea for an armistice to allow the election of a Constituent Assembly. Instead his demand for Alsace and Lorraine told Frenchmen that only a continuation of the war could save their country from mutilation.

Parisians settled down to siege, confident that their forces and those gathering outside would make salvation a matter of weeks.

As in 1793, the political leaders stayed in the capital and sent the old veteran of 1848, Crémieux, with a few little-known colleagues to Tours as delegates to organize the provinces. Without personal or legal stature, they were floundering ineffectually among quarreling generals, prefects, and provincial notables when Gambetta escaped from Paris in a balloon, joining them on October 10th. The energy and fervor of this son of an Italian immigrant were enough to move a bewildered country into the second phase of the Franco-Prussian War. "Gambetta's War" was to prove no more successful than Louis Napoleon's had been, and in the short run it brought down upon him and the radical Republicans the resentment of exhausted Frenchmen. But it redeemed the legend in part, it brightened the name of the French Republic, and when the immediate shock of defeat had passed, Frenchmen came to honor the man who had honored them with his faith.

In early October of 1870, there was reason to hope. Bazaine and 170,000 soldiers still held Metz, tying down more than that number of Prussians. The siege of Paris required over 250,000 others; their elongated lines of supply and the needs of occupation further drained Prussian strength. From the unoccupied departments, Gambetta (who made himself Minister of War) and his deputy, the civilian engineer Charles de Freycinet, were raising a new Army of the Loire, fairly well clothed and armed, fairly well generaled by d'Aurelle de Paladines, Chanzy, and Faidherbe. But junior officers and experienced men were few, training was indifferent, transport and shelter were rudimentary. Had Gambetta controlled all of France's assets, the deficiencies might have been made up with time, but time depended on Paris and Metz. Bazaine could have held out longer; to his lasting obloquy, he surrendered on October 27th, after trying to tempt Bismarck into restoring the Empire. At his trial in 1873, he was to plead that there had existed no legitimate authority for him to obey, to which the presiding officer replied, "Monsieur le maréchal, la France existait toujours." Unhappily for Gambetta, France then had two authorities, one at Tours, the other at Paris. And at the end of October—when the Army of the Loire might have beaten the Prussians released from Metz to the battle of Paris—there was added a third, Adolph Thiers, who did not believe in further resistance.

Thiers had refused membership in a Government of National Defense which he feared would soon be discredited by radicalism or defeat, preferring to serve France as roving solicitor of aid from the European powers. Arriving in Tours after failures in London, Vienna, Florence, and Saint Petersburg, he arranged a delay of the march on Paris so that he might press Bismarck into an armistice for elections and negotiations. But on his arrival at the besieged capital, radical and patriotic crowds rose against the Paris government to demand continuation of the war. On October 31st, a mob surrounded the Hôtel de Ville, shouting obscenities at "traitors" who would surrender France in order to save their property. It was a foretaste of the Commune which neither side forgot. Thiers blamed the "raving madmen" (among whom he named Gambetta) for preventing an early peace; Parisians blamed Thiers for delaying the advance of the Army of the Loire, the more so when news finally came that d'Aurelle de Paladines had defeated the Prussians at Coulmiers on November 9th, liberating Orléans, but had been unable to advance farther in the face of Prussian reinforcements.

Whatever chance remained of liberating Paris now depended upon more time for Gambetta to strengthen the new provincial armies. But Trochu and his colleagues neglected to organize supplies for the inhabitants of the capital. Since no one knew how many people had to be fed or how much food remained, no one knew that Paris would hold out until the end of January, 1871. In fearing an early capitulation, Gambetta wasted half-prepared armies in November and December in fruitless advances northward. The unrelieved series of defeats, the winter suffering of the troops and the population, wasted as well the prestige of the Republican warmakers throughout much of France. Of the several myths that died in "the frightful year," not the least was that of Republican military invincibility. By the end of December, the Prussians had cut the Army of the Loire in two and Gambetta's government retreated to Bordeaux. Chanzy and Faidherbe fought skillfully but vainly in the west and north; the demoralized Bourbaki accompanied more than led a ragged, freezing army to the east where Denfert-Rochereau, the *lion de Belfort,* still held that last fortress-city. But its German besiegers were too strong and in January the half-starved French straggled to internment in Switzerland.

Now Paris was alone with her hunger, disease, and bitter cold. Suffering bred hatred, as the poor watched the prosperous consume their hoarded food; the latter would have pretty stories to tell their grandchildren of eating elephant meat from the zoo, but for the masses not even bread was rationed until near the end. Several sorties had been incompetently, halfheartedly made; the regulars and National Guards remained suspicious of each other; discipline was sapped by idleness and drink; all muttered against the craven provincials who failed to come. But together with the folly, the cowardice, and self-seeking went heroism and self-sacrifice, lives given for comrades and for ideas well or vaguely known. As in most great sieges and plagues, some shriveled or broke, others found new courage, while the masses endured, buried their dead, and waited. The Prussian bombardment began early in January and killed several hundred; but disease and scarcity of food, fuel, and medicines proved more decisive, and the Paris government feared the rising combativeness of the Left. After the defeat of a sortie in mid-January and the bloody suppression of an attempt by radical National Guardsmen to seize power and continue resistance (January 22), Jules Favre accepted Bismarck's terms for an armistice and the city surrendered on the 28th. Ten days before, Bismarck had enjoyed his greatest hour, when William II was hailed as German Emperor in Versailles' Hall of Mirrors. *L'année terrible* was only half over and for Paris the worst was yet to come.

Gambetta resigned in fury, protesting that the Paris government had broken its promise to allow the rest of France to continue resistance under the Bordeaux delegation. But his prefects reported that much of the rest of France, the unoccupied half, was weary of war and even more weary of Republican hotheads who exhorted Frenchmen to fight against all reasonable hope. In rural areas, fear that the social Republic of 1848 would be reborn spread among conservative notables who had up to then given wholehearted support to Gambetta as war leader. But even such reports did not prepare the Republicans for the results of the election of February 8th. Of the more than 650 Deputies who hastened to Bordeaux, nearly 400 were forthright Monarchists, another 80 were conservatives whose feelings on the Republic were at best uncertain, 100 or more were moderate Republicans in the style of Favre. The Bonapartists and the Gambettist Republicans were discredited as responsible for making and losing the war; at most there were 20 of the former, 40 of the latter. The proportion of votes was not so overwhelming as that of seats—as in 1849, the departmental *scrutin de liste* was used, partly for its greater simplicity in the very short time allowed, partly to break down whatever remained of the Bonapartist-tailored constituencies— but even the general vote was solidly for peace and social order.

The prudent had triumphed and the most prudent won national acclaim; the septuagenarian Thiers, indefatigable critic of four regimes and now honored as the prophet of disaster, was elected in 26 departments. It was impossible not to recognize his mandate; on February 17th, the Assembly named him Chief of the Executive Power of the French Republic. France was to be governed by a man still assumed to be an Orléanist and an Assembly dominated by rural, royalist, Catholic notables. Historians, particularly of the republican faith, have often deplored the political illiteracy of the peasant masses in the nineteenth century, their docile obedience to whatever local authority was predominant at the moment; the same rural vote that had sustained Louis Napoleon against the enlightened cities, they say, turned blindly to local squires and priests in 1871, as it had done in 1849 against the Second Republic. But it is just as possible that the peasantry knew well what it wanted on all three occasions: internal and external peace, no social experiments or political revolutions likely to upset order or take their sons. That their wishes had coincided, more often than not since 1800, with those of the imperialist, royalist, or clerical officials and notables proved their subservience not to dynasties and priests (not even the Vendée had proved that) but to their own family and property interests. They were, in short, conservative; and if not long afterward they rallied to the Third Republic it was not because they had changed but because the Republic had turned nearly as conservative as they had always been.

In February of 1871, conservative candidates won generally except in the southeast, and in some of the forty occupied departments of the northeast. Cities like Paris, Marseilles, Bordeaux, Grenoble, Lyons, Toulouse, Lille, Dijon, and several others voted Republican, but their lists were in many cases overturned by rural majorities in the same department. As a result, most radical Republicans were converted back to the *scrutin d'arrondissement*. But it was not the machinery of voting that mattered to men like Thiers. "The Republic must be conservative," he said, "or it will not be"; and Gambetta, who preferred the practical opportunities of office to purity of doctrine, was soon to agree. At Bordeaux in February, Thiers was content to leave the question of Republic or monarchy to time, and in the so-called Pact of Bordeaux promised the royalist majority to do nothing to prejudice the future. To accept a Republican, Jules Grévy, as presiding officer and to allow the hated word to appear in Thiers' official title seemed minor gestures to solidarity (and Bordeaux, like other cities, was noisily Republican); the

Royalists were also not eager to make a monarchy responsible, as the restoration had been, for a peace which would surely be more onerous than that of 1814 and of 1815. Time was to show that for once they had been too prudent, but they had, in any case, little choice; half were Orléanist, half—the less experienced politicians—were Legitimist, and no agreement on the succession was in sight.

As long as a Republican electoral victory had seemed possible, Republican spokesmen had insisted that the Assembly have power to make a constitution as well as to decide the issue of war or peace. Now they regarded the results as disastrous in both respects and gladly supported Thiers in delaying the political issue. The peace could not be so easily put off. While the Assembly waited in apprehension, Thiers and Jules Favre went to face the victors at Versailles on February 21st. The Chancellor of the Second Reich met his "little friend Thiers" with Germany's demands: all of Alsace, a third of Lorraine, Metz, a triumphal march in Paris, a punitive indemnity of 6 billion francs (three times the cost of the war), an occupation that would be reduced in proportion as the indemnity was paid. It may have been an opening offer meant for bargaining, but Moltke and the generals did not see it thus. An exhausted Thiers emerged on the 26th, having cut the indemnity by one billion and excluded Belfort (which had not been taken by the enemy) from the cession of Alsace. It is said that in the carriage taking him to Paris, Thiers wept for the wars that would follow, over provinces that Frenchmen would never accept as permanently lost; the Deputies from Alsace and Lorraine had already protested the impending amputation. Across the Rhine, another historian, Heinrich von Treitschke, who had once disparaged blood and iron, brushed aside the argument that Alsatians and Lorrainers preferred French nationality: "Against their will we shall restore them to their true selves." There was no plebiscite. Like the first Napoleon's humiliation of Prussia, like most advantages seized in victory that ignore the human spirit, the taking of Alsace-Lorraine was tragedy for all concerned and nightmare to the victor.

By the preliminary peace of Versailles, confirmed at Frankfurt on May 10th, France lost 1.6 million inhabitants, great tracts of forest and farm, invaluable industrial works, notably in textiles and metallurgy, and most of her iron ore deposits. The war itself had cost 135,000 soldiers' lives, 140,000 wounded, heavy damage in the battle areas; the rigors of the Paris siege had added at least 25,000 premature deaths. In six months, France had fallen from a position of European leadership

200 years old, to find herself at the feet of a united Germany unquestionably her superior in numbers (41 million to 36 million), resources, industry, and military power. To the south lay a united Italy 27 million strong, whose troops had quickly occupied Rome in September of 1870. The guilt of the Second Empire appeared incontrovertible; few Frenchmen have ever expressed a desire to return the ashes of Napoleon III from Farnborough.

The National Assembly voted, by 546 to 107, to accept the Versailles *Diktat* on March 1st, quickly so as to hurry the parading Prussians out of Paris, where further humiliation could be dangerous. Gambetta, Louis Blanc, Clemenceau, Hugo, Quinet, Delescluze, Ledru-Rollin, Rochefort, Arthur Ranc, Felix Pyat, all the radical Republican and socialist Deputies of Paris, voted No with the Deputies from Lorraine and Alsace; one of the latter spoke for his colleagues in denying the validity of a treaty made against the people's will and pledged their return to France by every means the future might allow. The Assembly was sympathetic but helpless, and, unfortunately, impatient in its sorrow and shock. It had feared the worst; now, with Thiers, it was eager to begin the work of renewing the normal life of France, rebuilding her economy and government, closing her wounds. Instead, it opened the greatest self-inflicted wound of the nineteenth century.

## THE COMMUNE OF PARIS

The revolt of Paris called the Commune was at bottom a collision between that tortured city and an Assembly dominated by men who hated and feared its power to upset what they regarded as the good national life. Of the 400 Monarchists in the majority, nearly half were Legitimist, Catholic nobles and country squires mainly from west and southwest, men with little understanding of the feelings or problems of Parisian workers and petty bourgeois. The Orléanists, wealthier men, many of them prominent in urban society, business, or officialdom, were better acquainted with the effects of modern economic life but, because or in spite of it, were even less ready than the Legitimists to entertain the demands of social malcontents. On the Center Left—an indication of this Assembly's conservatism—sat 80 men, mostly upper-bourgeois liberal Monarchists or conservative Republicans, including Léon Say, the leading spokesman for laissez-faire. And on their Left sat the *Gauche répub-*

*licaine,* 112 moderate Republicans led by Jules Grévy, Jules Favre, Jules Ferry, and Jules Simon, all destined to lead the infant Republic in its first generation and, in 1871, deeply concerned lest Paris radicals and socialists repeat the follies that had killed the Second Republic. To these 600 Deputies, the 40 radical Republicans and workers of the extreme Left, most of whom represented Paris in the Assembly, were anathema, and several were so openly ostracized—or outraged by the acceptance of the German terms—that they resigned in disgust: Tolain, Benoît Malon, Felix Pyat, Ledru-Rollin, Arthur Ranc (but not his friend, Clemenceau), Rochefort, and Victor Hugo. Gambetta, who had chosen to sit for Alsace, also resigned after the peace vote. Only a handful of Deputies remained to speak for Paris, and, distrusted by all sides, they failed to effect a compromise; in this, Louis Blanc lost his final battle, Clemenceau his first. The Assembly blamed Paris for uselessly prolonging the war, making the peace terms harsher than Thiers said they might have been.

Most immediately, Paris lay across the Deputies' path to normalcy. As with the abrupt closing of the Workshops in 1848, it is impossible to unravel innocence from stupidity and malice in the measures hurriedly passed in early March. The state of siege was ended, but only in those matters that offended the business sense of the landed and wealthy; the wartime moratorium on unpaid notes and rents was repealed. The middle and lower classes of a city barely breathing again, whose economy was paralyzed, where most were unemployed, were asked to pay their bills at once or face bankruptcy and eviction. At the same time, the Assembly reduced or cut off the pay of National Guards, the only income for tens of thousands of men, women, and children. In economic affairs, then, the crisis was solemnly declared to be over, but in politics, the emergency measures were tightened. The regular troops in Paris were reinforced under General Vinoy, who had succeeded Trochu and was despised for having surrendered Paris to the Prussians; d'Aurelles de Paladines, the imperialist general dropped by Gambetta for failing to push through to Paris, was given command of the National Guard; the Assembly sentenced Flourens and Blanqui to death *in absentia,* for having led the patriotic uprising of October 31st against Thiers; radical newspapers were closed; no new political journals could publish until the lifting of martial law. Yet even these precautions were thought insufficient and the Assembly betrayed its fear of Paris by voting, on March 10th, to hold its meetings at Versailles. With this news Paris heard rumors: Thiers had declared the Republic "provisional"; Paris, rejected as the capital, was also to be denied self-government; the Monarchist majority was about to set up the throne and discard universal suffrage.

Under the best of conditions, Paris would have been provoked. But Parisians, who believed they had sacrificed themselves for the rest of France, had just endured that black March 1st on which victorious Prussians paraded the Champs-Élysées, and into empty streets of shuttered and silent houses. And there was more than humiliation, fatigue, and economic distress at work. Among the lower classes in particular, suspicions of betrayal had been growing since September 4th itself, when the moderate Republican Deputies had so swiftly seized control, excluding even such docile Jacobins and socialists as had won places in 1848. In petty bourgeois and workers' quarters, Committees of Vigilance sprang up, some of Blanquist inspiration, others of self-styled Jacobins, others Proudhonist, unionist, some affiliated with the French section of the Workers' International, and most connected with the less-prosperous battalions of the National Guard. As the Government of National Defense constantly hid the realities of the war behind optimistic propaganda, Parisians asked who but traitors could have been responsible for Trochu's inactivity, for the provincials' delay, for Thiers' and Favre's attempts to surrender, who but bourgeois profiteers behind the shortages and inequalities of food, fuel, and medical care? In October, the vigilant had barely saved the city from Thiers' defeatism; in January, Vinoy's provincial Mobile Guards shot down patriots so that Favre could deal with the Prussians to make France safe for property and political reaction.

The news from Bordeaux in March seemed to confirm all these suspicions. An Assembly of rural slackers, descendants of La Vendée, had made a coward's peace to save themselves the danger of a popular social Republic. Now, as Blanqui said, they wanted to put out the lights of Paris. It was to be the old, familiar betrayal, of 1848, of 1830, of 1815, of the Directory and Thermidor. Paris, mother of revolutions, was to be brought back to September of 1789, with her betters still at Versailles, before the women had fetched them to face the sovereign people. To the petty bourgeois and workers facing economic ruin, the prospects were intolerable. Both classes had been much enlarged under the Empire, had suffered its inflation and bad housing, had hated its bourgeois opulence. There were 500,000 workers, one-quarter of the city's population. The wretched quarters of Menilmontant, Belleville, La Villette, Montmartre, Clichy, Les Batignolles on the Right Bank, in Montrouge and behind Les Gobelins on the Left, had been swollen with ill-assimilated new arrivals in the decades since 1848; and in 1871, thousands of refugees from the eastern departments added to the *classes dangereuses* or, at least, *impatientes*.

February had seen popular protests against submission to Prussia, demonstrations and minor riots. But apart from the removal of some 200 National Guard cannon (which had been bought by public subscription) from the bourgeois west end to Montmartre and Belleville—so that they would not fall into Prussian hands, it was said—there was little coordinated activity. Even after the Assembly's folly, some chance of compromise remained; Parisian mayors and Deputies pleaded for a degree of municipal autonomy. But Thiers was determined to consolidate his authority by subduing Paris; on March 18th he precipitated the crisis by sending ill-prepared and ill-disciplined troops to seize the cannon. An outraged crowd on Montmartre brushed aside the halfhearted appeal to legality of Mayor Clemenceau and, with the sympathetic or frightened soldiers looking on, retook the cannon and murdered two generals, Lecomte and Thomas. As other government troops fell back or fraternized with the crowds, Thiers quickly adopted the strategy he had vainly urged on Louis Philippe in 1848. He evacuated Paris, taking the ministries and his remaining troops to Versailles, where in time enough force could be gathered to overwhelm the rebellious city. By the end of March, many prosperous residents had also fled—they were to prove as vindictive as *émigrés* had ever been—and Paris was left to its National Guard and a bewildered, divided populace.

The ten weeks that followed were, like the first siege of Paris, at once heroic and pathetic; the city's leaders never achieved a unified military command, much less a plan of offensive or defensive action, never built a united political authority or effective administration, or agreed upon a consistent program of social reform. The Communards were not communists, though they were later so described by Marxists eager to inspire the proletariat and by men of Order, to frighten the bourgeoisie. Of the 86 elected on March 26th to the municipal council, called the Commune as in 1792, nearly one-fifth were moderate Republicans who resigned almost at once. Some of them, with other middle-class residents, left the city at various moments, but others remained behind and acted throughout the crisis as advocates of compromise with Thiers and the Assembly.

The delegates elected from the poorer quarters included 25 workers, half of whom belonged to unions (*chambres syndicales* or *syndicats*) affiliated with the Workers' International, the French members of which were more often Proudhonists, or anarchist admirers of Bakunin, than Marxists. The other 45 members were petty bourgeois socialists of various persuasions, Jacobins or Blanquists, though of the latter several did not grasp Blanqui's own program and might better be termed latter-day Hébertists, fervent egalitarians and devout priest-eaters. Blanqui himself won election but was in the hands of the Versailles government (Thiers had arrested him on March 17, before moving against the guns), helpless at the moment he had given his life to bring about. Although supplementary elections in April returned several more Internationalists and socialists, including the Proudhonist Charles Longuet (who later became Marx's son-in-law), the Jacobins retained a majority throughout, notably on the Executive Commission which more and more dominated the Council. But the communal government was never alone in its authority. The Central Committee of the 200 National Guard battalions which had federated in February—hence the name *fédérés* usually applied to all of the Parisians who did the fighting at the end—remained in existence, exercising a divisive influence, especially in military matters. Less effective and clearly more moderate than the Jacobins and Hébertists were a few labor union and International leaders who pressed for social legislation.

The one aim upon which all agreed, partly because it was imposed by circumstances, was Parisian autonomy, the freedom of their patriotic, progressive, Republican Paris (and, it was hoped, other French cities) from the unlettered, clerical, reactionary provincials who had frustrated the city's initiative so often before. That Paris always led was axiomatic, but that the rest of France followed was clearly a myth even by 1848 (it should have been clear before that; Jacobin Deputies-on-mission had discovered it, painfully, in 1794). Under the Second Empire the theory of a nation made up of autonomous communities naturally appealed to many Frenchmen from moderate Republicans to Proudhonists, some (like Proudhon) because they believed in the advantages of decentralization, others (like Blanqui) only tactically, as the Jacobins momentarily had championed local rights while their rivals controlled the Assembly in 1792 or as the Ultras had in the early reign of Louis XVIII, until the rest of the country was ready for the correct sort of unitary government. The Communards proclaimed the right of Paris to organize her own police courts and public services, her own budget and taxation, laws on credit, labor, and business, her own schools—as opposed, said the declaration of April 19th, to the "despotic, unintelligent, arbitrary, and onerous" centralization of Empire, monarchy, or Assembly. The name Commune thus also brought to mind the often savage struggle of the medieval towns against the dictation of King, noble, or prelate.

The primarily Jacobin character of the Commune emerged in its other actions, closely paralleling the Belleville program of 1869 proclaimed by the radical Republicans and Gambetta: the separation of Church and State; free, compulsory lay education, freedom of assembly, association, and press; popular election of all officials; abolition of conscription and the standing army. Some churches were closed, others used by the innumerable political clubs that sprang up in imitation of the 1790's. The revolutionary calendar was revived, as was a Committee of Public Safety, in early May when the Versailles army approached. Patriotic proclamations abounded; but the need to conciliate the Prussians, who could easily cut off supplies from the northern and eastern approaches they guarded, was too obvious to allow anything but brave words. The government which was afterward to be execrated as a proletarian dictatorship found little time for social reforms; like the Belleville program itself, it was amiably vague on such matters and only in the last days did unions and workers' clubs coordinate their efforts to remind the Commune that there was more to be done than reenact the glories of '93. It abolished night work in the bakeries; it proclaimed—without having the time to put into effect—the seizure of shops abandoned by bourgeois employers and their transformation into workers' cooperatives; it toyed with a plan for petty credit to replace the onerous pawnbrokers; it merely extended the moratorium on bills and rents, without repudiation of either. Property was not disturbed, many bourgeois Parisians remained quietly in the west end, the Bank of France calmly financed both the Commune and the Versailles governments.

The horror inspired by the Commune among right-thinking people had little to do with its legislation, but arose in part from fear of what might have come in time, which is unknowable, and, far more, from the savagery of the final struggle. Although the Commune rightly refused any responsibility for the killing of the generals on March 18th, the Versaillais were not appeased. Thiers and the Assembly conservatives felt doubly humiliated in Prussian eyes by the city's defiance of their authority. No doubt some measure of the hatred on each side grew from its conviction that the other was subversive, traitorous to France, and thus undeserving of any mercy. When a badly planned National Guard march to Versailles was dispersed on April 3rd, its leaders were shot on capture, as other prisoners of the Versaillais had been on the preceding day. The Commune retaliated by taking hostages, including Archbishop Darboy and several priests, though they were not in danger until the very end, when the remnants of the Commune's authority broke down and the rabid Hébertist Raoul Rigault contrived their execution. A succession of military commanders—Cluseret, Roussel, the Polish refugee Dombrowski—tried and failed to build a fighting force out of the National Guards, of whom perhaps only 30,000 were trained combatants. After the first days, when Versailles had lacked troops, offensive strategy was probably hopeless, but not even the treasured guns or the Montmartre heights they rested upon were employed for defense. The forts and walls were often undermanned, especially in the western sector where the Versaillais would most certainly attack first and where bourgeois residents were least in sympathy with the Commune. There was no hope of aid from the outside; the ill-planned attempts to proclaim Communes in other cities met defeat; Thiers cynically dismissed them as the work of common criminals and Bonapartist traitors. Meanwhile, the Versailles army under MacMahon's command was speedily enlarged to nearly 130,000, thanks to Bismarck's release of imperial regulars from Prussian camps.

As this vengeful army pushed forward, its artillery blasting a path before it, the Commune's leaders debated, orated, deposed officers and ministers while small detachments of Federals gave their lives in futile, isolated combat at the city's approaches. The overall defense was criminally neglected, with the result that on Sunday night, May 21st, the Versaillais poured through a western gate (Porte Sainte-Cloud) opened by a turncoat and occupied the prosperous districts friendly to them before most of the Communard partisans realized their danger. Instead of uniting in what would have been a formidable redoubt behind the guns on Montmartre and the Buttes-Chaumont, the Communards, already deserted by the more prudent National Guards, chose to defend their own quarters in the old, familiar way. Centers of resistance were widely scattered, often isolated by broad avenues which had not existed in the pre-Haussmann Paris of 1848 or 1830. Had Thiers and MacMahon sent their troops rapidly along the main avenues, much of Paris might have been taken without bloodshed. Whether they hesitated through overestimating or underestimating the preparations of the Federals—or whether, as some believe, Thiers preferred a thorough bloodletting to cleanse Paris of its militants—the result was the same. Barricades manned by desperate men, women, and children with literally nothing to lose, sprang up on the 22nd and 23rd, and Paris was doomed to "Bloody Week" and the ferocity engendered by prolonged violence. The Versaillais, mostly country troops, with the ugly fervor of the once defeated, already wrathful against the perennial disturbers of property and moral order, were led by Parisian *émigrés* and anti-Communards to merciless reprisals. Prisoners were shot down as they surrendered. In answer, the most extreme Communards took authority into their own hands and executed the hostages; Msgr. Darboy and the priests died on May 24th at the prison of La Roquette in the east end (Thiers, ever prudent, had refused an offer of the Commune to exchange him for Blanqui). On the same day, retreating Federals set fire to the Tuileries, the Louvre, the Palais Royal, the Palais de Justice, the Hôtel de Ville. All but the first and the last were saved by fire brigades, as was the Cathedral of Notre Dame. Many other buildings were set afire by shells or to rout their defenders. On the 24th, the Versaillais overpowered barricades in the rues de Grenelle, de l'Université, Rennes, Cherche-Midi, Vieux Colombier, then, eastward, at the Boulevard St. Michel, rue St. Jacques, and Place du Panthéon until all the Left Bank was in Versailles' hands on the 25th. On the Right Bank, the old and painfully ill Delescluze, the most popular of the leaders, found death and Jacobin immortality by ascending a barricade at the Boulevard Voltaire, defiant in his top hat, frock coat, cane, and sash of office. On the 26th, only the traditional stronghold of the poor, the Faubourg Saint-Antoine, and the areas behind it still held out, and on the 27th the final battle was fought through the Cemetery of Père Lachaise. Some 200 Communards died with their backs to its far wall, which has ever since been a place of pilgrimage for the militant Left—*le mur des fédérés*.

Since it had used artillery to good effect, the Versailles army lost only 1000 men to its opponents' 4000 in actual fighting. But now that the fighting was over, the slaughter mounted to nearly 20,000. In the days following, any Parisian who could be suspected of armed resistance—man, woman, child—was condemned by military tribunal and shot. Thousands died at execution grounds in the Champ de Mars, Père Lachaise, Jardin du Luxembourg, Place de l'Italie, and elsewhere, their bodies dumped into common graves or burned in mounds. In the following weeks, countless Parisians were denounced as Communards by zealous citizens, 40,000 arrested and 30,000 prosecuted, 13,000 imprisoned or deported to Noumea in New Caledonia, to Guiana on the South American coast. Their sufferings en route equaled that of mass deportations in the twentieth century—the unspeakable degradations of human cattle-cars were first endured—and 3000 more perished. Except for the tens of thousands of families mutilated by death or deportation, except for the prisoners flagellated and rotting in Noumea and Guiana, apart from the leaden memories and class hatred no future well-being would entirely dissolve, *l'année terrible* was over.

The Commune, which began as a patriotic Republican and Parisian protest against national humiliation and conservative rule, ended in a working-class myth. Not without reason, for although it was neither begun nor led by proletarians, those who did most of the fighting and dying, and the most numerous victims of the subsequent proscriptions, were the workers of Paris. Their organizations were decapitated by the death or exile of all leaders who could be identified (there was no lack of informers to point them out), and for a decade the socialist movement languished. The Marxists, by honoring the aspirations and sacrifices of the losers, won favor, if not always obedience, from their descendants. Karl Marx's *The Civil War in France* (1871) presented the Commune to the workers of the world as the first struggle to establish the classless society, and many of the beaten found a measure of solace in believing it.

On their side the victors blamed the "Reds" of the Workers' International as a means (destined to world-wide imitation) of justifying their hysterical repression, and took credit for saving society, religion, and property. Once more, as after the June Days of 1848, much of the rest of France and the world was ready to applaud. The popular press vied with facile orators in excoriating the Communards, filling the heads of an avid public with magnified or invented stories of cruelty and degeneration. Amid this *bourrage de crâne* the sources of working-class miseries were left politely unexplored. Thiers could say, "We are rid of socialism," but the immediate result of the Commune was that the social question itself was obscured; Republicans could ignore it and thus win the confidence of Frenchmen who had always before—and as recently as February of 1871—feared the Republic as disrespectful of property. By repressing the Commune, Thiers had all but eliminated the socialist and social Republican Left from the political equation. The Third Republic, if it survived, promised to be conservative, at least in regard to what peasants and bourgeois thought were their best interests.

## THE REPUBLIC OF THIERS

According to the pact of Bordeaux and the dreams of the monarchists, the regime was still provisional. But Thiers had no intention of relinquishing power until French life returned to normal and, some historians believe, every hope of holding it as long as breath remained, under whatever constitutional façade circumstances would dictate. He considered himself indispensable, with somewhat better reason than political leaders often have, as the man who divided Frenchmen least—given the disappearance of the Left. Events soon led him to declare openly for the Republic. Supplementary elections to the Assembly were held in July of 1871, to fill over 100 seats left vacant by death, resignation, and the many multiple candidacies of February. Some monarchists, recalling the triumph of the party of Order after the June Days, confidently expected another landslide. But in many departments other monarchists omitted demands for a restoration from their platforms, so uncertain were they of the country's temper. They were not alone in seeing that a new party of Order had appeared. The moderate Republicans, having chosen respected candidates in long-prepared primaries, campaigned vigorously for the Republic. Their royalist opponents were often inexperienced and awkward country gentry who could easily be accused of wanting a return to feudal privilege and, as devoted Catholics, of preparing a French crusade against Italy (and Italy's ally, Bismarck!) to liberate the Pope. The heedless Veuillot and prominent bishops had already demanded as much, to the horror of wiser royalists. Legitimists and Orléanists wasted strength in denigrating each other, while Republicans calmly annexed all the principles that had defeated them in February: national unity, peace, order, and property. Prudence had changed sides, and so, it appeared from his hints and Republican appointees, had Thiers. Republicans won nearly 100 seats, some even in the rural west, to three Legitimists, nine Orléanists, and three Bonapartists.

After this stunning reversal, political activity at Versailles quickened along two lines: the daily task of liberating and restoring France, for which all sides desired credit, and a determined effort by the royalists to restore the throne before their majority could be further reduced. Thiers' success in the first and the failure of the royalist Right in the second brought about the definitive establishment of the Republic. The royalists insisted that the Assembly had constituent power; the Republicans, a minority awaiting future gains, denied it. But the compromise of August 31, 1871, was in effect another sign of the future. Thiers was named "President of the French Republic" with power to name a cabinet and address the Chamber. The office would end with the Assembly (or before, if the Assembly desired it), but Thiers had forced the issue by threatening to resign and the royalists again swallowed the word they so despised. Thiers' personal authority was still unshakable; the work of the next two years was the apogee of his career; when it was done, the people heaped honors on the "Liberator of the Land," and the Assembly dismissed him.

The "Republic of Monsieur Thiers" prefigured in several ways the essential compromise that would mark French government for seventy years. The royalist demands for decentralization were largely frustrated; under the local government law of August, 1871, only the mayors of small towns were popularly chosen, and they, like the elected councils, were nearly as subject to the Napoleonic prefectural system as were officials appointed by the central government. The Conseil d'État was revived in 1872 (its members appointed by the Assembly until 1875, afterward by the executive), and resumed its role in shaping laws and the effects of laws by supervising the administration and judging cases brought against it. Thiers' government was able to pay the war indemnity as early as 1873, by bond issues which were heavily oversubscribed. Evidently Frenchmen were solvent and, what was not always to be the case, sure of their governors. This success, partly attributable to the increase of private wealth under Napoleon III, allowed Thiers and the Orléanist-moderate Republican Center to avoid any serious discussion of taxes on capital or income suggested from extreme Left and Right in the Assembly. The budget was to be balanced by increased taxes on commerce and consumer goods, by the interest from certain stocks (a measure Thiers opposed), and by a slightly increased rate of tariffs, which began the erosion of that imperial free trade Thiers had long abhorred. The army was reorganized in 1872 on the principle of universal conscription in imitation of victorious Germany; but Thiers' preference for a professional army (as more politically dependable), the fiscal burden of drafting all young men, and the Assembly's regard for the sensitivity of the comfortable classes combined to weaken the principle considerably. All were liable to five years' service, but only half (chosen, as of old, by lot) would serve beyond the first year; young men prosperous enough to outfit themselves could meet the requirement by enlisting for one year. Like all other taxes, the "blood tax" was markedly lower for those best able to pay. But the inequalities were less flagrant than previously, and on this law was built a new army, superior in most respects to the rakish old careerists of the Second Empire.

Thiers' greatest triumph in office was his negotiation, in March of 1873, for the departure of German troops from French soil that September, eighteen months ahead of a schedule that had seemed impossible in 1871. France rejoiced and the Assembly voted an impressive accolade: "The President of the Republic has deserved well of his country." But the majority of the Assembly was royalist and, while it could hardly avoid paying Thiers this compliment, it had already determined to bring him down. On May 24th, a Rightist coalition engineered by the Orléanist Duc Albert de Broglie forced Thiers' resignation by 360 votes to 344. Since the supplementary elections of July, 1871, the monarchists had been progressively dismayed by events. As Thiers' prestige had risen, so had his frankness in espousing the Republic, in violation of the pact of Bordeaux. He had appointed Republican cabinet ministers, prefects, and mayors, had become publicly reconciled with Gambetta, and on November 13, 1872, lectured the Assembly; the Republic existed as the established government, he said, and to desire its overthrow was to risk revolution. Supplementary elections in 1872 and 1873 further reduced the royalist majority in the Chamber; radical, though hardly social, Republicans and Bonapartists were regaining numbers and confidence. Thiers, who had been thought a caretaker for the monarchy, was now an obstacle, unable or unwilling to use the official machinery to assure a royalist majority. Since the King's appearance was delayed, it was vital that a loyal caretaker, unafraid to break a few eggs, be put in the presidency. Their choice was the sober, honest, stubborn Catholic soldier, Marshal Patrice de MacMahon, victor in the Crimea, loser at Sedan, nemesis of the Commune.

## THE MORAL ORDER

The first part of MacMahon's presidency is known as *la République des ducs* in honor of the Orléanist Ducs de Broglie, d'Audriffet-Pasquier, and Decazes, who with their associates on the Right and Right Center dominated political life during four years. More evocative is the term "Moral Order" which de Broglie proclaimed to the Chamber in May of 1873 as the aim of the royalist coalition. The euphemism betrayed their inability to agree on a monarch who would accept the French throne on their terms. Since 1871, the Legitimists and Orléanists had painfully worked out a compromise which would place Charles X's grandson, the Comte de Chambord, the celebrated *enfant du miracle,* on the throne as Henry V, to be followed—since he was childless—by Louis Philippe's grandson, the Comte de Paris. For a moment in August, 1873, the mutual hatred of the royal branches seemed forgotten as the Orléanist heir visited Henry V at his home in Austria. Chesnelong, the emissary of the majority at Versailles, hurried back from an interview at Salzburg in the autumn to assure the expectant royalists that the King accepted the conditions of parliamentary government and the fundamental rights of Frenchmen. What he did not add was that Chambord still refused to accept the tricolor, insisting on the white Bourbon flag of his ancestors, Henry IV, Louis XIV, Charles X.

It is unclear how much his stand, no doubt sincere, also covered doubts that the kind of kingship he dreamed of was in him or in the situation. The common opinion of him notwithstanding, Henry V knew something of events in France since his birth, and if his explanation of facts was somewhat naïve (concerning 1830, in particular), he saw more clearly than did many of his warmest supporters. And in October, 1873, he ended their splendid preparations for his return by publicly repeating his refusal of the tricolor, which, even Legitimists knew, neither the Assembly nor the country would surrender. It was impossible for the Orléanists to put forward the Comte de Paris; the Legitimists' disappointment revived their hatred of the usurping branch, and Chambord refused to abdicate in favor of his younger cousin. In early November, Chambord appeared suddenly in Versailles, apparently hoping that MacMahon would impose him on the Assembly.

Loyal to the Assembly's authority, the Marshal-President refused and Henry V returned to permanent exile.

On November 20, 1873, the law of the Septennate made Mac-Mahon's term seven years; in that time Chambord might change his mind, or abdicate, or die, and the President make way for the monarchy. The Right was determined, in the meantime, to consolidate "the Moral Order," a restoration without the King. All the powers of the State would be exerted to impose conservatism and religion on an erring people, whose vagaries since 1847 (1829, said the Legitimists; 1789, said their right wing) had brought unrelieved disaster. The new restoration had all the aspirations of the old, many of them unquestionably high-minded, for the Right in 1873 possessed the considerable virtues as well as the flaws of its predecessors under Louis XVIII and Charles X: probity, industry, personal honor, patriotism, and, in the Legitimist ranks, a measure of social conscience which, for all its outdated rural and hierarchical bent, was otherwise absent in the early Assemblies of the Third Republic. All this was not enough; policies that were already controversial in the 1820's were now impossible. A series of electoral defeats was to prove that France no longer tolerated the exclusive rule of notables and priests. To the extent that both employed their temporary political ascendancy between 1873 and 1877 to humble their rivals and force them to obedience, both succeeded only in worsening old quarrels and preparing their own eclipse. In pursuing the chimera of the Catholic monarchy, they had overthrown Thiers, whose Republic would have left them a fair measure of influence, and who could have told them that their restoration would have to be liberal or it would not be.

In religious matters, the Legitimist Right insisted upon acting as though France were a Catholic society rather than a divided nation whose majority was nominally Catholic. The difference was great, as Montalembert had known, and even greater since Veuillot and the intransigents had discredited liberal Catholicism, since Pius IX had issued the Syllabus and proclaimed the unpopular doctrine of papal infallibility. As Montalembert had feared, the inevitable identification of a state Church with every sin and folly of the Empire further widened the schism between Catholicism and the proletarians, Republicans, and intellectuals. For the last two, the revival of Freemasonry under the Empire provided a meeting ground, as did the *Ligue de l'Enseignement*, founded in 1866, to press for compulsory lay schools which would replace the Catholic faith of Pius IX with the positivist faith of Comte and Littré. Thus the Republicans who after 1871 dared not be radical on social or economic questions were more vigilant than ever in politics, religion, and education. In their eyes, the honest faith of Legitimist notables was a greater threat to Science and Reason than the hypocrisies of a Louis Napoleon.

To temper their religion in the hope of placating such opponents was unthinkable to Catholics who followed Veuillot, still the loudest voice of the faith. For ninety years France had denied and offended God; her punishment was surely manifest. Only the obdurate could deny it. So there were great pilgrimages to Lourdes, La Salette, Mont Saint-Michel, and Chartres, the announcement of new miracles, the dedication of France to the Sacred Heart at Paray-le-Monial in June of 1873, and a vote by the Assembly in the same year to build the basilica of the Sacred Heart where the Commune's cannon had stood on Montmartre. That only a few zealots talked of Sacré-Cœur as expiating the sins of France (the fleshly sins of the Empire more than the political sins of the Commune) did not matter—all were ridiculed by the Republican press. The Right's plea for increased clerical control over education met even greater denunciation. All this was by now normal and to be expected. What was not normal, what many Orléanists who preferred a more liberal Catholicism feared most, was the growing coldness of Catholic rural voters toward Catholic candidates of the Right. Here skillful Republicans found it easy to accuse Catholic notables of prolonging an Assembly that had lost its mandate in order to impose a Bourbon despot and to make war on Italy to liberate the Pope. It was true that Catholics on pilgrimage, including scores of Deputies, publicly prayed to "save Rome and France in the name of the Sacred Heart" and it was not clear to many Catholic peasants and bourgeois why the Pope's temporal pretensions or the return of Henry V (and feudalism, added the Republicans) should be the first concern of God, or of Deputies who had promised them tranquillity. The Legitimists on their part believed as strongly as their fathers had in the 1820's that only a Catholic Bourbon Kingdom could bring real tranquillity.

The weakness of the Right was its division into intransigent Catholic Legitimists and a Center Right of Orléanists and moderate Legitimists like Falloux who could hardly disavow, or explain the nuances, of their allies' religious enthusiasm and political Ultracism. The Roman question which had plagued Napoleon III was more vexatious than ever, compromising the already controversial efforts of de Broglie and the moderate Right on the political side of the Moral Order. In May, 1874, a law gave the central government power to appoint village mayors. Republicans and moderates, elected by the people, were replaced by men of Order. The government carried out a purge of prefects, and the familiar electoral pressures of the authoritarian Empire (and many of its seasoned officials) were used to hold back the tide; Republican candidates were disqualified, newspapers closed, meetings forbidden. The Republican revival was slowed but not stopped and now men well to the Left of Gambetta were winning office. What was worse—in the eyes of every faction—Bonapartist candidates also showed alarming strength in several districts; Napoleon III had died at Chislehurst in 1873, the Prince Imperial was soon to come of age and was far more appealing a pretender than the Empress or the erratic Prince Jerome. Across the Rhine, Bismarck and German generals were speaking of the dangers posed by the reviving French army and the "threat" to Italy; some German patriots talked of preventive war. By the end of 1874, all these dangers convinced moderates, both Republican and monarchist, that France could no longer afford the uncertainties of a provisional government.

## THE FOUNDING OF
## THE REPUBLIC

The Third Republic was founded in 1875 on a series of constitutional laws agreed upon by men of the Center and Center Left who desired a conservative Republic, and by men of the Center and Center Right who desired a constitution which could legally be made the basis of a parliamentary monarchy, Chambord willing or dead. At crucial moments, they received the support of Léon Gambetta, who convinced enough Deputies of the Left that the same constitution could, with time and revision, incarnate the democratic Republic of their dreams. The fundamental laws of 1875—not a constitution in the formal sense—reflect these contradictory hopes. The place of the President was already partly settled. The Rivet law of August, 1871, gave him power to execute the laws of the Assembly, to appoint and dismiss ministers who were responsible to the Assembly. According to a law of March, 1873, passed by the Right to circumscribe Thiers, he could not address the

Assembly without its prior permission or take part in debate; this law, together with MacMahon's repugnance for the daily work of politics and de Broglie's vigor as spokesman for the cabinet, presaged the importance of those parliamentarians who were later to be called Premiers, first of the ministers chosen.

On January 30th of 1875, an amendment to regulate succession to the presidency was offered by Henri Wallon, Catholic monarchist turned conservative Republican; it became a constitutional law by one vote, 353–352: "The President of the Republic is elected by absolute majority vote of the Senate and the Chamber of Deputies, meeting as the National Assembly. He is named for seven years; he is reeligible." The simple words spoke volumes and showed that the monarchist and Republican Centers had succeeded, under pressure, in finding the needed compromise. Monarchists had insisted on a Senate well insulated from universal suffrage and with powers equal to the Chamber's, as a stronghold of local notables ready to vote for a restoration. An upper house so conceived violated the republican doctrine of popular sovereignty; a single Convention, a single Assembly in 1848–this was hallowed republican tradition. Bicameralism recalled the tainted Directory, the Empires, the constitutional monarchies. The Republican Left had denounced every proposal of a second chamber. On its side, the royalist Right had resisted as hotly any idea of accepting the word "Republic" in a constitutional law. These extremes, in fact, were not moved, but men from both sides drifted to the Center; the outstanding convert was Gambetta, whose confidence in the ultimate conversion of rural France to republicanism lessened his fear of a Senate, however indirectly it might be elected.

The compromise was eased by an agreement that the constitution could be revised on a majority vote of the two houses in joint session; each side could dream of something better on that day when the electorate, enlightened, gave it the majority. That the monarchists (excluding Bonapartists) had won only two dozen of some 160 contested seats since February of 1871 appeared to give every advantage to the republican dream. But the Right expected to dominate the Senate, already owned the presidency, and thereby, many thought, the administration—and persisted in believing that the local notables were still the natural leaders of opinion in "normal" times. But even if it were wrong in all three assumptions—as many Orléanists suspected—it was time to salvage whatever one could before the public pressure for dissolution of the four-year-old Assembly grew irresistible. With such factors at work, Wallon's dramatic one-vote victory was perhaps less a turning point than a sign of how slowly hope died at either end of the Assembly.

The other constitutional laws passed more quickly and with greater margins. Two days later, February 1st, a second Wallon amendment, giving power of dissolution of the Assembly to the President, but only with Senate approval, won by 425 to 243. By the end of February the Deputies had voted the basic laws, which pleased no one entirely, which were thought to be nearly as provisional as the Assembly itself, but which typified the political system of the French Republic to the spring of 1958. Legislative power was shared equally by a Chamber of Deputies renewed every four years by universal suffrage, and a Senate, most of whose 300 members served nine years, one-third to be renewed every three years. As a guarantee of conservatism, 75 would be appointed for life by the Assembly (and thereafter by the Senate itself) and the other 225 chosen by departmental electoral colleges of local, elected officials. Since each commune—whether village or metropolis—was to be represented equally, the Senate would greatly favor the rural voters at the expense of the urban. No Senator could be younger than forty, but, unlike the Directory's Ancients, he was permitted to be a bachelor. The Chamber's members, as determined by a law of November, 1875, were elected by *scrutin d'arrondissement;* the conservatives (and some urban Republicans of the Left) were by now, once more, convinced that well-known local notables would thereby hold an advantage over Republican candidates whose party organization (and more positive programs) might carry department-wide elections by *scrutin de liste.* The allotment of constituencies also heavily favored rural areas.

The Senate's veto over legislation and the President's power, with the Senate, of dissolution seemed to safeguard the conservative, the monarchist, aspirations of the majority. But there was a crucial limit. No presidential act was valid without the countersignature of a Minister, and Ministers (who could come from either house) were collectively and individually responsible to the Chambers. There was no provision for a possible clash between the President and one or both houses. Events of the next four years decided the issue in practice and secured the supremacy of parliament over the President. The first conservative bastion to be weakened was the Senate, by the old division between the Ultra-Right, fiercely loyal to Henry V, and the supple Orléanists, more concerned with political reality than dynastic dignity. Outraged over the constitution as the work of "treason" by Orléanists and moderate Legitimists, the extreme Right intrigued with the equally bitter extreme Left to elect over 50 Republicans out of 75 life Senators. This petty act of *la politique du pire* meant that after the elections of 1876 the Center Right's Senate majority would be thin at best. Thus only the presidency seemed solid for the "Moral Order" when, on December 31st, the Assembly disbanded and France prepared for the first elections of the Third Republic.

MacMahon and the conservatives employed varying degrees of administrative pressure in the elections of 1876, but all was in vain. In February and March, Republicans won 370 seats in the Chamber of Deputies, Bonapartists 75, Orléanists and Legitimists only 80. In the Senate, the royalists had a majority of 4. To the extent that the poll was a plebiscite on the republican constitution, the majority was clearly with the Republic, for the moment. But there were other issues, and the clerical question was foremost among them. In July of 1875, the late Assembly's Catholic majority had passed a law authorizing Catholic universities—forbidden since Napoleon I, but on the verge of passage in the last year of the Second Empire; the bishops hastened to set up faculties at Paris, Toulouse, Lyon, Angers, and Lille. In the electoral campaign the Left worked up a violent anti-clerical temper, which the Republican moderates felt bound to appease. The new Chamber immediately voted to withdraw the right of Catholic universities to grant degrees (the Senate reversed the action), then attacked the budget of the Ministry of Religion and restrictions on civil funerals. In early May of 1877, Jules Simon, the moderate Republican Premier, was compelled to prohibit the circulation of a Catholic petition calling for "all means" to achieve the Pope's independence from the Italian government, and soon afterward to reprove a bishop for having demanded the end of diplomatic relations with Italy. In an ensuing Chamber debate, Gambetta launched his famous version of an already well-worn cry: "Clericalism, that is the enemy!" and followed it by impugning the patriotism of French Catholics. The Chamber voted to condemn unpatriotic, ultramontane activities and demanded government action to halt them.

The Catholic soldier at the Élysée had already bristled at several attacks on the Moral Order: the Chamber's invalidation of certain Rightist elections, Simon's purge of Rightist officials and attempted removal of conservative army officers, the Chamber's critique of the established military and fiscal order, the Left's demand for an amnesty to the Communards. Now his enemies had passed from anti-clericalism to anti-Catholicism. MacMahon decided, with encouragement from Msgr. Dupanloup and Broglie—both more interested in guarding the political power of notables than encouraging ultra-montanism—to replace Simon with a man of Order. The famous crisis of May 16th opened with his dismissal of the Premier, ostensibly over the law that ended administrative control of the press. It was partly a pretext, for clericalism was thought even by ardent Catholics to be a dangerous issue for an election, but a controlled press was also one of the principal tenets of the Moral Order. Broglie formed a cabinet of royalists and Bonapartists, clearly unacceptable to the Chamber, which as expected voted him down, 363–158. The Senate authorized dissolution and the government called for a general election in October.

The campaign of 1877 was savagely fought, for here, unquestionably, was the decisive struggle between the Moral Order and the Republic of the Republicans. The Minister of Interior purged hundreds of Republican prefects and officials in favor of Bonapartists; every device of Villèle, Guizot, and Rouher was employed; teachers were dismissed, Masonic lodges closed, newspapers suppressed, bribes, threats, and favors generously sown; Gambetta himself was convicted and sentenced to jail for suggesting MacMahon's resignation. Some moderates were no doubt repelled by this reversion to despotism, and others by the public prayers of certain prelates on behalf of the official candidates. The Red bogy reappeared; the Republicans were reviled as accomplices of the Communards; with Thiers adorning the Republican campaign, the charge was more laughable than vicious. On the positive side, MacMahon stumped the country and was afterward derided by ungrateful Rightists for his clumsiness; the old soldier's gift for muddled clichés was heroic, but so was his good intent and on balance he probably won added support, especially in rural areas, for men less worthy than himself.

Republican unity and spirit were never higher. None of the 363 who had voted against Broglie were opposed by other Republican aspirants; Gambetta led the campaign a furious pace, seeming to be everywhere at once, pleading with peasants, reassuring bourgeois, haranguing workers, and even embracing Thiers, his old nemesis. For a moment old ideals rekindled a popular front. When Thiers died at the height of the campaign, the Republicans organized an immense funeral procession, and the workers of Paris solemnly accompanied the body to Père

Lachaise, where his troops had massacred their comrades only six years before. The campaign was nonetheless profoundly divisive for France. Once more, the clerical issue hardened the lines while confusing every other question. Catholic Republicans suffered defeat in nearly every case. In October, the party of Order won 46 per cent of the vote but only 200 seats against 320 for the Republicans. In November, Broglie resigned the premiership, and after a month of maneuver MacMahon surrendered, called the conservative Republican (and Catholic) Dufaure to form a cabinet which would have the Chamber's confidence.

The *Seize Mai* crisis, which Republicans sometimes insist was a monarchist *coup d'état*, broke the Right's main bulwark of the Moral Order, the powers of the presidency. But given the Republican Chamber majority of 1876, the clash could have been avoided only if the Right had voluntarily given up its hope. If the bulwark proved defective, the Right had itself to blame; the laws passed by a royalist Assembly in 1871 and 1873 to weaken Thiers had begun the shift of power to the parliament. MacMahon's dissolution of the Chamber was not a *coup d'état* but an attempt to define the constitutional laws in favor of the presidency. He and Broglie failed; but even had they won the election, some later President would have failed, for the laws were weighted in favor of parliamentary supremacy. The President could not act without a Minister's signature; in case of a conflict with the Chamber he could, of course, appoint a Minister willing to support dissolution (even then he would require Senate approval), but that Minister was in turn responsible for his actions to both houses, and unless the ensuing election overturned the Chamber majority, the Minister would be forced to resign. The power of dissolution in effect amounted only to a chance for the President (himself chosen by the parliament) to appeal to the electorate against a Chamber chosen by that same electorate never more than four years earlier. The *Seize Mai* not only discredited the President's power of dissolution, but also weakened the office of Premier by freeing the Deputies from fear that a cabinet chief, frustrated in his program, would force them to the trouble of an early election. Although the power remained on paper, it was never used again in the Third Republic, not only (perhaps hardly at all) because it was associated in 1877 with an un-republican, royalist assertion of personal authority, but because it had failed, owing to the timid careerism and jealousies of so many later Presidents (carefully chosen for timidity) or Premiers, and, most important, because the only circumstances in which it could succeed—a willing Senate, a state of public opinion and party discipline that would encourage an executive to foresee an upset of the Chamber majority—so rarely appeared in French political life.

The office of President henceforth would be largely honorific—or as honorific as the often mediocre men appointed to it could manage. Its main influence lay in the President's frequent choice among several candidates for Premier who might be acceptable to the Chamber; he could lessen or aggravate a cabinet crisis; he could bestow or withhold the prize of office within a limited circle of aspirants. His other role would be to exhibit a certain moral tone in his own person as Chief of State. The Presidents of the Third Republic failed, with few exceptions, to distinguish themselves in either role. In dignity and probity, MacMahon was one of the exceptions, but good Republicans do not count him. The Senate majority which had approved the dissolution was itself overturned in January of 1879, when partial elections gave the Republicans a margin of 50 seats. The victors proceeded to attack MacMahon by purging a number of senior army officers; rather than agree, the Marshal-President resigned. His successor, quickly chosen on January 30th by Chamber and Senate, was the aged, conservative Republican lawyer Jules Grévy, who in 1848 had argued that there should be no president at all. He immediately, self-righteously, pledged that he would never resist the "national will" by defying the Chamber. In practice, Grévy was fond of power and exercised it from behind the scenes. In the next two years, Republicans captured a solid majority in local offices and departmental councils; Gambetta had been right in expecting an overthrow of conservative notables in the countryside. So feeble was the Right's effort in the Chamber elections of 1881 that it gathered only 25 per cent of the vote, giving the Republicans more than 440 of the 541 seats. By then, the majority had voted a return of the parliament to Paris, the Chamber to the Palais Bourbon, the Senate to the Luxembourg, had made the 14th of July the national holiday and the rousing Marseillaise the national anthem. The symbols of the Republic were in place; its already ancient slogan—emblazoned on public buildings—promised liberty, equality, and fraternity. Frenchmen waited to see how beautiful the Republic would be, now that it was finally in Republican hands.

# THE TRIALS OF THE REPUBLIC

The great political crisis opened in 1789 was closed ninety years later; the solution to the French problem of government was to be Republican parliamentary democracy. By 1880, after three generations had watched, deplored, and entangled themselves in French affairs, good Anglo-Saxons assumed that a virulent political frivolity was in the French national character, although the time elapsed since the calling of the Estates-General was only slightly longer than that between the first stirrings of the English Revolution under James I and the accession of William and Mary in 1689 and exactly equal to the time it had taken the American Republic, 1775 to 1865, to decide the meaning of its own revolution. That they had also enjoyed many generations of parliamentary experience prior to their revolutions occurred to few of the English-speaking peoples (including survivors of Antietam and the Wilderness) who shared Tennyson's horror at the "red fool-fury of the Seine." But comparing the political good sense of nationalities has always been more popular than profitable, and whether a certain people possessed the spirit of compromise always less useful a question than what it had to compromise about. From this point of view, the political record of the Third Republic is more impressive than many, including French Republicans, have been ready to admit.

The Republic of 1880 had several advantages. By then it was more than what Thiers had modestly suggested, the regime which divided

Frenchmen least; it appeared to offer what the majority wanted most: internal and external peace, sound money, the protection of economic interests, a limit on the power of the Church and great landlords, and to some—their numbers unknowable, in any society—the joys of personal liberty. The failure of every other alternative through three generations of unrest and insecurity gave it some of the leverage of Henry IV after the Wars of Religion, of Louis XIV after the Fronde. But like them, the Republic carried the burdens of the past as much as its favors: a constitution formed partly by its opponents; a medley of factions hardened by old sectional, economic, social, and religious antagonisms; an aura of defeat and national humiliation; the urgent problems of growing cities, industry, and proletariat—all complicated by the inexperience, the jealousies, and the worldly temptations natural to a newly arrived political elite.

## THE REPUBLICAN SYSTEM

The constitution of 1875, as defined in 1877, gave the legislators decisive power over the executive, in accordance with the bowdlerized legend of the great Convention and the fears of a new December 2nd or May 16th. It is often said that France has never found a "balance" between liberty and authority, between the free expression of popular opinion and executive efficiency. Leaving aside the doubtful implications of such language, it is true that the French have usually avoided deadlock between Assembly and executive by rather drastically disarming one in favor of the other. In crisis, according to the needs of the moment, other nations have done as much, but without fixing the imbalance in their constitutions. Whether the tyranny of the Chambers under the Third Republic made any great difference in the Republic's destiny is difficult to say; men on all sides of every issue have deplored it, each assuming that a stronger executive would have furthered their own, healthier solutions. What they complain about is not absence of authority. The Napoleonic structure of administration and law remained; a strong civil service insured continuity in all departments, and no nation has been more thoroughly administered by central bureaucracy. But the elected government has lacked initiative, demonstrated an incapacity for change of basic policy when change has been needed.

One of the hardiest clichés on French politics is that bad constitution-making in the 1870's was responsible for the *immobilisme* which kept France from adjusting to a changed world inside and around her, that the constitution encouraged a multiplicity of ill-disciplined parties, making coalition cabinets unavoidable, and that to preserve coalitions French Premiers were forced into weak compromise, into drift rather than action. No doubt the manner of electing the President and the weakness of his office removed a source of national party cohesion that America's quadrennial rush for power provides, and the inability of Premiers to dissolve the Chamber of Deputies removed a penalty for indiscipline often invoked by the British Prime Minister. Likewise, the single-member constituency, tied to local interests and acquaintances, is perhaps less conducive to party unity, or the broad-mindedness of Deputies, than the *scrutin de liste,* for which candidates would need department-wide party support. But periodic experiments with departmental lists after 1880 failed to prove that electoral devices alone could appreciably alter the party system or the quality of those elected.

However much it was aggravated by the constitution, the multiplicity of parties rested at bottom on a multiplicity of factions thrown into mutual antagonism by a century of revolution. Unlike the British and American Revolutions, the French had failed to achieve in one generation a set of political institutions to which an overwhelming majority of citizens became reconciled or resigned. Frenchmen had quarreled for a century not only about the balance or purposes of their institutions but over the institutions themselves. Continuing political instability had bred hope in every faction that its own version of the true France would emerge triumphant. Hope forbade compromise, and encouraged action that elicited reaction, which in turn heated partisanship. Few French problems, whether economic, religious, military, or even cultural and intellectual, were considered apart from each faction's political ideal. Private, local, or apolitical efforts at solution were discouraged; French life was politicized to a degree unknown in Britain or America; most public questions were distorted by partisan feelings and the supposed necessities of partisan strategies.

Moreover, and beyond the divisive effects of foreign intervention and war in the first decades of the French Revolution, the Third Republic inherited two other problems which the Anglo-Saxon democracies largely avoided and which were by themselves enough to make a two-party system unlikely. The first, of course, was clerical—the confusion of religious faith and political partisanship which crossed all other issues and automatically doubled the number of points of view on each of them. Just as there had been liberal Catholics and liberal anti-clericals under the July Monarchy and the Second Empire, so there would develop before the Third Republic had run its course a separate Catholic party or faction sitting in every sector of the Chamber side by side with at least one anti-clerical party agreeing with it on all issues but those which touched religion—the whole complicated by many Frenchmen who were Catholics but anti-clerical, and others, a lesser number, who were not Catholic but welcomed clerical efforts (and expenditures) in education and social services.

The other great disturber of Republican life was the coincidence in France of the political and industrial revolutions. Again, English and American political forms were settled before the intrusion of industrial capitalism, modern technology, urban masses, and the factory proletariat. Even so, the struggle to reconcile seventeenth- and eighteenth-century politics with social justice has been difficult, more violent than Britons and Americans like to admit; and its ultimate outcome—in the age of automation—is at least uncertain. The Industrial Revolution came to France when political forms were far from settled, when confidence and cooperation between or within social classes were broken by the most ardent political and religious disputes. The lateness of the political revolution had brought, in 1848 and 1871, a tragic involvement with social revolution, raising new enemies (or, at best, jealous allies) on the Left for Republicans already beset by sufficient enemies on the Right. The social question was further complicated for the Third Republic by France's relatively slow industrial development which gathered a working class large enough to be dangerous but neither numerous nor united enough to impose a consistent program of reform upon the national powers. Here the constitution and electoral arrangements of the 1870's worsened the situation, for as in twentieth-century America rural interests were heavily overrepresented in both Chambers. As time passed, the Senate appeared the greater barrier to social reform. Gambetta had correctly foreseen that it would be Republican, but not the extent to which its members would adopt their un-Republican predecessors' respect for the interests of the propertied class, or their complacent ignorance of urban and industrial problems. The Senators were more than once, up to the late 1930's, to defeat social and economic measures enacted (sometimes in good faith, sometimes in happy confidence of Senate reversal) by the Chamber of Deputies.

Given its constitutional framework, the Third Republic took on much of its distinctive character, its private ways and public tone, in the years between 1879 and 1885. As heirs and victims of the revolutionary tradition, the Republicans who took command interpreted that tradition cautiously. Gambetta had warned his colleagues after the defeat of MacMahon in 1877 that there should be no "indiscretions" before the Senate elections of 1879, and even afterward he argued for Republican moderation. He still adhered to the Belleville program of 1869—universal suffrage for all offices of the Republic, equal constituencies according to population, civil liberties, freedom of the press, freedom of assembly and association, separation of Church and State, free compulsory primary education, free higher education for those of proven intellectual capacity, tax reform, the end of standing armies and of "privileges and monopolies." But these measures, he now believed, could not be hurried; they would await, each in turn, the opportune moment. On his Left, radical Republicans like Clemenceau and Floquet repudiated his leadership and denounced him as an "Opportunist," a name henceforth applied to (and accepted by) the majority of Center and middle Left Republicans who governed France until 1900.

Their Republic was not to be the Republic of Danton or Robespierre, or of Lamartine or Blanc. Nor, it soon appeared, even of Gambetta, for upon assuming the office of President in January of 1879, Jules Grévy passed over the obvious leader of the Republicans and chose as Premier the colorless, cautious Waddington. Although Gambetta had cultivated moderation since the furious days of 1871, had worked himself to exhaustion as the Republicans' leading campaigner in three critical elections, had even stepped aside for Grévy as titular leader on the death of Thiers—lest memories of 1871 hurt the party's cause among conservatives—the jealous old man was determined to keep him out of power. Gambetta was relegated to the presidency of the Chamber. The greatest of Republicans was already isolated, accepted by neither Opportunists nor Radicals as their leader; here was another blow to party discipline and to the prestige of the Premier's office. Henceforth any moderately well-known Deputy could aspire to the premiership—provided he had not offended too many through brilliance or initiative. After a futile attempt to organize a permanent Republican party on a national scale, after a short-lived Ministry of 1881 in which other prominent Deputies refused to join, Gambetta died in 1882 at the age of 44. The man who, with Thiers, was most responsible for the triumph of the Republic, who almost alone among Republican leaders could arouse national enthusiasm and—what was soon to appear more important—the respect of Frenchmen, had little effect in the formative years. The Republic was sufficiently virtuous, many Republicans thought, to have no need of heroes and victorious enough to do without party discipline.

## THE REPUBLICANS IN ACTION

Badgered and coaxed by the Radicals on their Left, determined to reduce the numbers on their Right, a succession of Opportunist cabinets proceeded to carry out a program designed to please the bourgeois, petty bourgeois, and peasants who made up the bulk of the electorate. Gambetta had spoken of "new social strata" taking control of national affairs once the Republic of dukes and notables had been defeated, and it is true that the elections of 1881 in particular showed the extent to which middle- and lower-middle-class men—doctors, lawyers, shopkeepers, teachers, clerks, and civil servants—were rising to local and national office. The prosperity of the Second Empire had provided the Third Republic with a new elite of petty bourgeois and professional men far surpassing in numbers and confidence those who had rallied to the Second in 1848. The Masonic lodges, progressively agnostic and democratic in spirit, provided them a national organization. But the change to new men was not nearly so complete as Republican oratory liked to claim, nor could a Republican program be built on the desires of the petty bourgeoisie, for Republican majorities depended on the peasant masses. And although the most prominent Orléanist dukes and magnates no longer headed cabinets, they and their *haute bourgeois* allies remained politically powerful, not a few joining conservative Republican factions in the style of M. Thiers. Neither they nor the peasants could be ignored; in practical matters, the Opportunist and moderate Republicans could and did ignore the interests of only two groups: the urban proletariat and the legitimist Right.

Even had all the new men demonstrated the Republican idealism Gambetta had expected of them—and many did not—there would have been few concessions to the Left, given the balance of forces in French society. Under Radical pressure, the Chamber voted in July of 1879 a partial amnesty for Communards still in prison or exile. A full amnesty, freedom of assembly, and wide liberty of the press followed in 1881. In vain some of the Radical electors and Deputies of Paris and other large cities clamored for graduated income and inheritance taxes, old-age and accident compensation, nationalization of rails, utilities, and mines, enforced limits on working hours, and the right to unionize. The general elections of 1881 returned a mere 45 Radicals (only a few of whom were "social") to over 400 Opportunist and conservative Republicans. The only social legislation of the first Republican decade was the law of March, 1884, on freedom of association; unions would be legal (many had been informally tolerated) provided they published their officers' names. Since there was no protection against dismissal of unionists, against black lists or lockouts, many preferred to continue outside the law. Yet even Republicans who called themselves Radicals felt no need for apologies; the Belleville manifesto itself had held the social problem "subordinate to political change"; social legislation would be meaningful only when the Republic had secured the two great bases of human progress: universal (manhood) suffrage, and free, compulsory, secular education for all French children.

In France, as in America and elsewhere, universal education was probably the nineteenth century's chief claim to the gratitude of common men (of those, at least, who saw beyond the marginal wages brought home by children kept out of school), and one of the chief causes to which young Republicans could give their hearts. But in France, it also became the central battleground between Church and Republic. The test of true Republicanism lay not in social matters but in how much a man was committed to *l'école unique et laïque,* the monopoly of secular schools; it is still a lively issue in the second half of the twentieth century, when Church and State have been separated for two generations, when French Catholicism is socially and politically the most liberal, intellectually the most intrepid, in the Roman confession.

In 1879, few French Republicans who had fought a decade of electoral campaigns against the zealots of the Moral Order could have believed Gambetta's oratory extravagant. Clericalism was the enemy of the Republic, of human betterment through Science and Reason. Each side, clerical and Republican, professed to believe—against good electoral and literary evidence—that a Catholic education produced Catholics subservient to bishops and priests in all matters including those political and intellectual. That there was a middle group, as there had been since 1792, ready to be both Republican and Catholic, or to allow others to be, was rarely taken into account. The leading spokesmen of reconciliation were dead or defeated with liberal Catholicism, and the new Pope Leo XIII, the successor of Pius IX in 1878, was not yet ready to speak openly. Before the 16th of May, it had appeared possible that a center coalition of conservative Republicans and Orléanists would temper the storm that was gathering over a Church dangerously compromised by its association with the Second Empire, with Chambord, with a crusade for the Vatican. But they had separated as the Chamber divided down the middle in 1877, when the campaign gave France her closest facsimile of a two-party system. However salutary such a system might have been on other issues, it fatally aggravated the clerical question.

The Republicans' revenge began in 1879, led by Jules Ferry, Waddington's Minister of Education and the strongest figure in the cabinet. To Catholics who attributed the disaster of 1870–1871 to impiety and moral decay, Ferry and the Republicans, the Masonic lodges, the *Ligue de l'Enseignement,* and societies of Freethinkers answered that illiteracy, ignorance of the modern world, of science and technology, had earned France defeat at the hands of enlightened, Protestant Prussia. France required not more basilicas but more schools. For national regeneration, Ferry said, Republicans must "liberate the souls of French youth" from the Jesuits and their allies. As Minister of Education and then Premier, the positivist Ferry gave his name to a series of laws, also called the Laic laws, reducing Catholic influence over education, which had grown steadily since the Falloux law of 1850. A law introduced in 1879, and passed in 1880, forbade the title *université* to private schools of higher learning, retroactively canceled their right to grant degrees, a cruel disappointment to many who had earned them since 1875. Another removed all ecclesiastical members from the High Council of Public Education. A series of laws made public primary education free and tax-supported—in itself a serious blow to Catholic schools in many localities —obligatory, between the ages of six and thirteen, and secular, by decreeing that "civic and moral" teaching must replace religious instruction (1882).

It was obvious to all, however, that in a nation whose primary schools depended heavily on tens of thousands of Catholic teaching brothers and nuns, such legislation would remain inoperative until a new corps of lay teachers could be trained. A system of departmental normal schools for women was set up, the training of male schoolmasters accelerated; these, said the *Ligue de l'Enseignement,* would be "lay missionaries," sent to the people of every village to teach Republican virtues, civic duties, and French patriotism. By a law of 1886, Catholic priests and brothers were to be replaced within five years, nuns on their retirement, from all public schools. These years extended to all of France that abrasive confrontation, which had appeared under the Directory, between the Republican school teacher and the Catholic pastor, nun, local Catholic noble or notable, and much of polite, especially female, society. As their miserable pay made them less than enthusiastic over Republican officials in Paris, the teachers tended to turn to the extreme Left for amelioration; rarely to the Right, for the snubs of their local enemies frequently made them, if possible, more anti-clerical and Republican than ever.

Secondary schools, though also subject to laicization from the top, were neither free nor compulsory; careers, as always, were to be more open to prosperous talent than to poor; the Belleville program still had far to go. Ferry attacked Catholic competition on the secondary level by creating secondary schools for girls, as Duruy had tried to do under the Second Empire. But a wider attack on burgeoning Catholic secondary schools emerged in the famous Article VII, inserted in a law of 1879, forbidding unauthorized religious orders to direct, or to teach in, public or private schools. This was to attack all that Catholics had won since Montalembert's great campaign under the July Monarchy. When a moderate coalition in the Senate defeated it in 1880, the Chamber pushed Ferry to enforce by decree the terms of the Concordat against unauthorized associations. This was open war, nearly as welcome to the extreme Right as to the Radicals on the Left. Through Cardinal Lavigerie, Leo XIII unsuccessfully tried to save the congregations by having them offer a pledge of political neutrality—in the spirit of the Abbé Emery under the Directory—but tempers were too high. Royalist journals denounced the compromise; the Protestant Freycinet, who had replaced Waddington as Premier, favored reconciliation but was forced to resign by Ferry, who took the office himself. The Jesuits, ever vulnerable as the "agents of Rome," were singled out and expelled in June of 1880. The other orders refused to apply for authorization; some barricaded themselves in their residences and regular troops had to be called up to besiege them. But once again the more combative clergy and their royalist allies, having mistaken the fervor of popular pilgrimages for popular support of their politics, had counted too much on public indignation. Except for a few skirmishes, the people did not interfere and the Republican sweep in the elections of 1881 showed how little the masses were inclined to punish anti-clericals. In all, about 5000 members of religious orders were expelled; most nuns were spared, as were some male teaching orders. Within a few years almost all—including Jesuits—had quietly returned, though in most cases to schools maintained by the secular clergy. With the main points of their school program enacted, Ferry and the Opportunists were content to bide their time. The expulsion had little practical effect; Catholic secondary schools continued to prosper. But it was an ugly precedent and hardened the lines of an irrepressible conflict.

Had the clerical question involved only partisan politics or differences over the proper degree of Catholic influence in French life, it might have been dissolved by compromise, or by the reemergence of liberal Catholicism, under Leo XIII's encouragement, in the 1890's. But Republican intellectuals and Radical polemicists like Clemenceau were not merely anti-clerical as a matter of politics but anti-Catholic as a matter of faith. Men whose grandfathers in 1830 and whose fathers in 1848 had most likely been Voltairian rationalists affected with social and literary romanticism—and thus ready to take a utilitarian or nostalgic view of the Catholic Church—were themselves, by 1880, determined to extirpate Catholicism from French life, and from French memory. Thus proper Republican geographies and student tours omitted the great medieval cathedral towns; Republican histories dismissed such inconvenient heroes as Saint Louis and Joan of Arc. Republican schoolteachers were trained from manuals as rigorously purged of bad thoughts as those of Catholic seminaries; historical obscurantism was taught in the interests of Reason and Republican Patriotism as fervently as in the interests of Faith. While more fortunate peoples were softening the memories of their revolutions in the interests of national respectability, Frenchmen were, if anything, teaching their children that the cleavages of the 1790's were deeper than they in fact had been.

Behind this zeal was the new religion of positivism and scientism, a faith in progress by the application of science to material improvement and of the principles of science (as understood, often, by nonscientists) to the study and organization of human life on earth. To millions of ordinary men throughout the western world, the products of science and invention presented undeniable, tangible proof of temporal progress. To disciples of Auguste Comte, Émile Littré, Herbert Spencer, Buchner, and Darwin, to fans of the chemist Marcelin Berthelot, the physiologist

Claude Bernard, the literary skeptics Renan and Taine, God had little place in the earthly scheme; and men who claimed to speak for God and, worse, to order society in His name, deserved none at all. The new rationalists were often less tolerant than the old, for they believed themselves to be more scientific, and generations wiser. Did they not trumpet their humility before the complexities science had yet to explain? The principal exponents of the system at the Sorbonne and l'École Normale Supérieure were men of indisputable learning and subtlety; but in its vulgar form—in the rodomontades of the Chamber, in provincial normal schools, in local societies of Freethinkers—scientific positivism seemed to its critics nothing more than bull-headed materialism, bereft of Voltairian wit and romantic generosity, appeared to Catholics, especially, as the negation of God, the human spirit, and moral society. It was true that many leaders of the movement shunned what they thought the easy optimism of the eighteenth-century Philosophes and scoffed at the dreams of the romantics. The failure of 1848, the experiences of the Second Empire, the Franco-Prussian War, and the Commune had intervened, the tides of blood and iron had engulfed the well-meaning. Faith in progress remained—and in work and education—but progress was no longer expected from constitutions, good will, or sudden mass conversions. Mankind struggled upward through stages of Darwinian conflict; the strong, the scientific, the objective men alone could ease the way for ordinary people. Progress had to be earned.

This set of beliefs played a large, though never the whole, part in the ideology of Republicans after 1870; Clemenceau was a dogged exponent of it, when he was not immersed in the lighter pleasures of political debates that made him famous. At its best, it inspired a new generation of young men and women, for whom the beauty of the Republic was only enhanced by her maturity, who devoted themselves to education, science, medicine, social reform, and usually radical or socialist politics. For others, often their elders, it did markedly less; certain political figures seem oddly shrunken by their efforts to be soberly pragmatic. At no time has the penchant of minor French politicians to affect literary and intellectual modernity been less attractive. To such men, the enthusiasm of a Gambetta was already anachronistic in 1879, the effusions of old Hugo embarrassing; the latter's great funeral procession in 1885 was for advanced minds a salute to the far past. In this sense, the cult of evolutionary politics also suited very well those conservatives who desired few changes in their world as it was. Had not Taine, as historian, told them that human events were the product of the milieu and the moment? Opportunism appeared doubly justified. The role of government was at most to destroy the obstacles to progress, not to force progress itself. Here again, the Catholic Church was the logical target; not only logical but politically safe—as the elections of 1877 and 1881 seemed to prove. And raging anti-clericalism would satisfy in part the enthusiasts of the Left, giving an impression of movement; better, some frankly admitted, to secularize society than to socialize it.

Honest intentions and tawdry merged in the series of lay laws enacted in the 1880's. Military chaplaincies were discontinued, seminarians made subject to military training (though in war they would be attached to the medical corps). In 1880, the Sunday rest law was repealed, limits were imposed on religious processions, soldiers were forbidden to take part in them or to enter churches as guards of honor. Public prayers were forbidden, civil marriage reinstated. Nuns were progressively dismissed from service in those hospitals and charitable works supported by public funds. In 1884, crucifixes were removed from courtrooms, divorce became legal once again. In 1885, the Church of Sainte-Geneviève reverted, once more, to a Republican Panthéon in time to shelter the remains of Victor Hugo. But Ferry and his immediate successors refused to go so far as separation of Church and State, preferring to retain the leverage that financial support gave the government in religious affairs; to prove the point, several outspoken priests were deprived of their salaries.

The Radicals remained unsatisfied with the Opportunists' half-measures against Catholicism and soon felt political and economic frustrations as well. They had long demanded a revision of the constitution according to Jacobin dogma, especially the end of the Senate. But an Opportunist-dominated National Assembly of the two houses in 1884 confined itself to minor adjustments. Life senatorships were abandoned, the vacancies left by death to be filled by regular election, and the Senate retained its powers; members of former reigning families were declared ineligible for the presidency; the Republican form of government was formally written into the constitution; any dissolution of the Chamber would have to be followed by elections within two months, the new Assembly to meet no later than ten days afterward. The only Jacobin gesture was to forbid formal prayers at the opening of sessions.

This was the middle of the road, as were most of the majority's political measures. A law of 1884 made the Senate slightly more representative by giving more votes to the electors of larger communes. Another law gave the election of all mayors (except for Paris) back to the people through their local councils. The office grew in importance, provided many a Republican schoolteacher an ally, became the breeding ground for future Deputies and Senators, and enlivened local politics—as fact and literature piquantly demonstrate. But the prefect kept the final word; in essence the old Napoleonic system of centralized administration, police, and courts was preserved. Rather than make judges elective, as the Left demanded, Ferry contented himself with another purge of some 600 conservative Catholics in 1883 (many had already resigned rather than uphold the decrees against religious orders). Nothing was done to weaken the military hierarchy or to shorten or equalize military service, except for the taking of seminarians. As a small step toward democratizing the diplomatic corps, the Council of State, and administrative bureaus, positions were opened to competitive examination. But as education beyond the primary level was costly, only the prosperous could afford the required training in such schools as l'École Libre des Sciences Politiques, founded in 1872, destined to furnish many leading civil servants, and an object of suspicion to the Left until its nationalization after World War II.

In economic affairs, the social Radicals soon repented of having joined in Gambetta's overthrow. His cabinet of 1881 had bruited an income tax, savings insurance, sickness and disability insurance, and the nationalization of rails. The banks and business interests which had kept bourgeois Republican Deputies out of his cabinet now held unshakable influence over the Opportunists. Far from nationalizing the railroads, the government in 1883 not only gave up its rights to buy them but gave the six large companies a guarantee of profits on the construction of new lines in underdeveloped areas of the country. These formed part of the Freycinet Plan, drawn up in 1877 and begun in 1878, to modernize rails, roads, rivers, canals, and ports on a grand scale, at a time of budget surpluses. As an answer to the despised Haussmann's concentration on Paris and a few other cities, the Republic made every effort to win provincial favor by a judicious distribution of appropriations. The political results were gratifying and the economic result helpful in the long run, but no less expensive than the public projects of the Second Empire; and by the early 1880's budget deficits were slowing the work.

## CRISES AND SCANDALS

As the elections of 1885 approached, several forces were working to endanger the moderate Republican majority. Recession had set in after 1881; as an earlier depression in the middle 1870's had probably hurt the conservative Moral Order and a boom in 1880 aided the Republicans, now the Opportunists were held responsible for the new decline. Farmers had long suffered from rising American wheat imports, from cattle and silk disease, from foreign competition in sugar and meats. But the most grievous loss was in wine, whose production had fallen more than half since 1875 from the ravages of phylloxera. Many growers and local dealers were ruined, and the distress of the countryside hurt consumer industries. Both the earlier boom and the later unemployment revived labor organizations and several socialist groups; among workers of some areas, Bonapartism revived and strikes multiplied in the early 1880's. Urban Radical politicians joined in denouncing the government's subservience to big business and the banks. In this they found support on the Right, for in 1882 the Union Générale, a Catholic bank, had collapsed, partly under its own imprudent management but also under pressure from its Protestant and Jewish rivals. As a repository for the savings of country people and a source of credit for them, its fall combined economic distress with religious feeling—and stirrings of anti-Semitism, shared by those workers, Radicals, and socialists who saw the Rothschilds behind every politician opposing social reform.

Not the least ingredient in Catholics' distaste for the Republic was the prominence of Jews and Protestants in its political leadership, as in the financial, social, and journalistic life of the capital. Adding to the Right's bitterness over political defeat and odious legislation was this intrusion of men considered alien, un-French. To many, even Clemenceau's atheism was preferable as somehow more familiar, almost traditional, and easier to combat. Religious and racial feeling was to reach its apogee on the Right only in the Dreyfus affair, but both grew rapidly under the first years of the Republicans' Republic. Its first Waddington cabinet of ten had included no Catholics but six Protestants, among them Waddington himself, Freycinet, who became the next Premier, and Léon Say, the conservative Republican exponent of laissez-faire who later helped to destroy Gambetta's social program. In the hierarchy of the new schools appeared many Protestant and Jewish teachers and administrators; Protestants and Jews replaced several Catholics in the universities. The sponsor of the hated divorce law was the Jew Naquet. In Catholic minds, all formed part of the conspiracy of Freemasonry against all that was best in French tradition.

Such feelings played a part in the elections of 1885 and were sometimes combined with outcries from both the Left and the Right that the governing Republicans were soft on Germany and willing to sacrifice French national interests—including Alsace and Lorraine—to their chase after profits. The Republic suffered to 1914 from having inherited defeat and dismemberment. Unless it made war or threats of war, it could be accused of cowardice, of slavish coexistence with an enemy whom only traitors would refuse to hate—publicly, on every occasion. Patriotism, in that raucous form that despises quiet love of country, had helped defeat Gambetta, suspected of hoping to reach an understanding with Bismarck. Now it attached to Jules Ferry, who not only maintained good relations with Berlin—and worse, was personally liked by Bismarck—but had plunged France into a colonial policy that promised to distract her attention and deploy her strength far from the Rhine and *revanche*.

Although the Second Empire had left a farflung if considerably mottled legacy of colonial enterprises, it was the Third Republic that brought France into the main stream of European imperialism. It was natural that Bismarck, while abstaining at first from colonial ventures himself, should encourage French activity outside Europe and, if possible, in a way that would keep her isolated within Europe. The French seizure of Tunis and the establishment there of a French protectorate in 1881 fulfilled his hopes admirably. The Italians, who had coveted it, were estranged; and the English, whose Foreign Secretary Salisbury had joined Bismarck in suggesting the action at the Congress of Berlin in 1878, showed their customary irritation at foreigners' taking an interest in the Mediterranean. Though Tunis had been under joint financial control of England, Italy, and France since 1869 and was long considered the next African step by many Frenchmen, military officers, diplomats, and Algerian settlers, the Radicals and the Right professed to believe that Ferry had been duped; his first cabinet was overthrown on the issue in 1881. But Tunis was not given up. Gambetta, who succeeded Ferry and who had supported the Tunisian initiative, then attempted to bring France into military cooperation with England against the Khedive of Egypt, whose ability to satisfy his French and British creditors was endangered by a revolt of Egyptian nationalists. But Freycinet, the next Premier, recoiled and Egypt was left to Great Britain.

Under Ferry's later cabinets, French activity resumed, impelled by the multifarious motives well known to students of imperialism: hopes for markets and materials, the salvaging of prior financial and missionary activity, the personal *élan* of military and colonial officers on the spot, the spiraling race for balance of power and prestige, and, perhaps not least, the preoccupation of the French parliament and public opinion with more immediate issues at home. So Savorgnan de Brazza's decade of exploration north of the Congo ended in the creation of the French Congo colony in 1885, joined by the July Monarchy's acquisitions (Gabon) three years later. In 1883, the French pushed northward from the coast of Dahomey, in 1885 northward from the Ivory Coast. From the older settlements in French Guinea and Senegal, French forces moved eastward through the region of the Upper Niger after 1883. In 1884, on the opposite side of Africa, the French established a protectorate over part of the Somali coast, behind Djibouti at the head of the Gulf of Aden. And between 1883 and 1885 they waged a war in Madagascar, which ended in French control of the Hova government's foreign affairs and the cession of a northern port. In the Pacific, the protectorate of Tahiti (taken under the July Monarchy) was annexed as a colony in 1880.

Most of these operations were carried on with no great expenditure of men or money and the French public was diverted from time to time by exotic tales and souvenirs brought back by a new breed of heroes. Many accepted the colonialists' claim that they were calling in the benighted world to redress the balance of Europe. Ferry himself was at first half-hearted toward colonial activity, but his tough spirit warmed to the task and he ended by writing defenses of colonialism on economic, humanitarian, and strategic grounds. His involvement in a costly war in Indo-China raised a political storm against him on the eve of the 1885 elections, overturning his cabinet and splitting the Radicals from the Opportunists at a critical moment. Cambodia (where Catholic missions had worked since the seventeenth century) and Cochin-China were occupied under the Second Empire, and in the late 1860's and early 1870's French merchants and explorers had pushed into Tonkin, to open south-central China for the trade which most Europeans (and Americans) assumed would be limitless. By the Treaty of Hué in 1883 the Annamite

Emperor accepted a French protectorate over Annam and Tonkin, but the Chinese and Chinese-supported guerrillas (the Black Flags) resisted and French losses mounted. In the wake of a minor defeat at Langson, in March of 1885, the Radicals in the French Chamber, a vituperative Clemenceau at their head, overthrew Ferry, to the accompaniment of shouts for his death from the mob outside. All the accumulated resentments of Left and Right had burst forth, over an event greatly inflated by them and the press, against a man whose political skills and strength of will had given him more power than any Republican leader since Thiers. Brisson, his successor, barely won the needed credits to continue the war; in June the Treaty of Tsientsin gave France China's approval of a protectorate over Tonkin. But the Republicans entered the elections of 1885 divided and on the defensive.

The Right had found temporary unity after the death of the Prince Imperial in 1879 and of Chambord in 1883. Although often without enthusiasm, Bonapartists and Legitimists accepted electoral alliances with the Orléanists, whose chief, the Comte de Paris, was now the legitimate pretender. The Right campaigned vigorously, avoided any demand for the restoration, built a network of local electoral committees to draw assorted conservatives to their side, and succeeded in reversing that mass abstention of their sympathizers which had been so disastrous in 1881. Under an electoral law passed in 1885 (which Gambetta had earlier demanded and been refused), France returned to a system of departmental *scrutin de liste,* which worked to the advantage of the largest party, or alliance of parties, over a department-wide area. On October 4, 1885, the united Right captured 177 seats to the Republicans' 127, and only a last-minute return to "Republican discipline"—common Republican support of a single list—allowed them to win 240 seats to the Right's 25 in the second ballot (October 18) held in those departments where no list had gained a majority in the first. The final results gave the Right 202 seats from 44 per cent of the vote, the Republicans 367 from 56 per cent. The voting balance had returned to that of 1877, despite Republican administrative pressure in many departments. The conservatives, organized in a Union of the Right in the new Chamber, took heart. But the Radical Republicans took a share of power, for the first time. With some 120 seats, their support was necessary to the embattled Opportunists in the formation of a cabinet.

Now the trials of the Republic began in earnest. Grévy won reelection to the presidency in December and in January of 1886 called

Freycinet as Premier. Amid continuing dissatisfaction over the economy, the schools, the colonies, and revelations of waste and corruption in public works, there appeared a new actor: General Georges Boulanger. Clemenceau and the Radicals forced this dashing, much-decorated officer into the Freycinet cabinet as Minister of War, under the impression that as a self-styled Radical he would cleanse the army of royalist and clerical influence. Instead, the ambitious general rode a tide of febrile nationalism and hero worship to within striking distance of dictatorship. He began by appealing to the Radicals who had sponsored him. As an answer to the Right's gains in 1885, the government had exiled the heads of former ruling houses, the Comte de Paris, in effect. Boulanger went further on his own, cashiering the pretender's uncle, the Duc d'Aumale, from his generalship. On a broader front, he prepared a reduction of army service to three years, demanding that seminarians serve the full time, to the delight of anti-clericals. At the same time, he took advantage of the natural lethargy of war departments to rush a series of reforms that had long been discussed: better barracks, better food, better clothing—any change was likely to be for the better—and a speedier adoption of modern weapons. The little people everywhere with sons subject to the draft were grateful, but Parisians were especially stirred by his revival of well-staged and clattering parades. In a Republic without heroes, a red-blond beard, brave words, and quick horsemanship won easy applause; at the Longchamps review of July 14, 1886, the crowds responded wildly and Boulanger was feted in songs, poems, and pictures as the symbol of French military revival. Rochefort, the incorrigible, released by the amnesty for Communards, filled *l'Intransigeant* with praise; the fiercely nationalist Republican Paul Déroulède brought his League of Patriots, founded in 1882, to the general's side, and preached the *revanche* which, he said, Opportunist politicians were too cowardly to mention.

Bismarck added the final touch. In an appeal to the Reichstag for increased military funds in January, 1887, he singled out Boulanger as a danger to German security. French patriots redoubled their acclaim. That Bismarck disliked their *général Revanche* was proof enough of Boulanger's worth, a method of judging public figures not unknown in other democracies. The newspapers of both countries lashed out in mutual hatred. In April, a French police official, Schnaebele, was arrested in German territory; Boulanger demanded an ultimatum and partial mobilization; Grévy, who had the virtue of immobility as well as its vices, refused, and Bismarck, who had won a majority in the Reichstag elections for his army program and needed no further tension, released Schnaebele. Frenchmen convinced themselves that Boulanger was responsible for the German retreat. His reputation was immense, but the Opportunists had seen the danger; to remove him, they overturned the cabinet and turned to an alliance—their first—with the Right. In July, 1887, the Rouvier cabinet banished the hero to a command at Clermont-Ferrand, over the frantic protest of Paris crowds who nearly blocked his departure from the Gare de Lyon.

For three months, Grévy and the Republicans of the Center breathed freely, though the agitation of Radicals and patriots continued. In the autumn a new crisis erupted over the discovery that Grévy's son-in-law, the Deputy Daniel Wilson, had used his residence at the Élysée to peddle decorations and favors to affluent clients. It was a sordid affair of average, ordinary greed, lacking the *grandeur* (and profit sharing) that marked American bossism of those days. Coming as it did after persistent rumors of jobbery in the implementation of the Freycinet Plan, after cynical Republican pressure in the elections of 1885 (followed by the unseating of 18 Rightists for "electoral malpractice"), after generous distribution of the spoils of office to Opportunist relatives and friends, the scandal encouraged the Right to hold the Republic utterly discredited. The habits of graft and favoritism, well developed under the July Monarchy and the Second Empire, rose to plague the Republicans who had so violently denounced them before. The Right knew itself to be pure, not only because it was out of power and temptation, but because the restoration and Moral Order had in fact been fundamentally honest, at least in money matters. On its part, the Radical and socialist Left dreamed still of the Republic of Virtue. The Opportunists had neither heroes nor issues left to them; but they held power and proposed to defend their Republic against all enemies.

Grévy bluffed, evaded, and clung to office against a storm of criticism; for a while, Rouvier and the Opportunists sought to cover their man, but upon the fall of the Ministry—Clemenceau led the attack, again—no politician would form another and Grévy tearfully resigned. Ferry would have been the natural successor, but Parisian rioting against "Ferry-Tonkin" and "Ferry-famine" (he had tried to organize food supplies in the Paris siege seventeen years before) encouraged Radicals and Catholics to block a strong man they disliked for what they thought were better reasons. On December 3rd, when the Deputies and Senators gathered at Versailles to elect a President, Clemenceau is supposed to have said, "Vote for the stupidist." He probably did not, though it would have been in character, and in many other minds. Frenchmen, Clemenceau not least, were later to regret this preference for weakness at the Élysée, but the choice of Sadi Carnot, a loyal, upright Republican engineer, the grandson of the great Lazare Carnot, was respectable, considering the tradition. He was not a hero, but no Republican was. For now Boulanger was turning to the salons and money of the Right to nourish his ambition. Although many Radical leaders repudiated him, the rank and file did not, and the crisis deepened because in 1888 most of the Opportunist Republic's enemies were united in the campaign of *Boulangisme.*

In 1888 the government imprudently retired Boulanger from the army and he was free to launch his political adventure. While a number of chauvinist Deputies and journalists acted openly, the Baron de Mackau, who led the Union of the Right, quietly enlisted Bonapartists, including Prince Jerome, Orléanists, including the Pretender (watchfully), and the Legitimists, among whom the ardent Duchesse d'Uzès provided heavy financial aid for an avalanche of American-style publicity and rallies. A Boulangist journal, *La Cocarde,* proclaimed an appropriately vague program; *Dissolution, Revision, Constituante* meant only that the system would be changed. Whether Boulanger would reward the workers, make war on Germany, restore the Empire, restore the monarchy, make himself a strong President or dictator, purify the Republic, rescue the Church or bury it, were questions best postponed in favor of general assurances that strong action would follow on all French problems—and it was by no means clear even to leading figures in the imbroglio how much Boulanger had promised to how many. After winning a series of by-elections with good majorities, Boulanger presented himself at a Paris election in January, 1889. Some Republicans were vaguely sure that radical Paris would halt the General's string of victories; others knew that Paris' Radicals retained a bitter patriotism and predictable disdain for whoever held power at whatever time, that petty bourgeois and workers had few reasons to be grateful to the Republic of Ferry, Grévy, and the "interests," that Catholics and conservatives were ready for revenge. Both sides poured money into this climactic campaign, the government fearing that a Boulangist victory would trigger another of Paris' "days"; the Republic was eighteen years old and no regime of the nineteenth century had survived its second decade. Would ordinary, colorless politicians succeed where two kings and two Napoleons had failed?

For one moment, on the night of January 27, 1889, dictatorship seemed near. Boulanger won by 80,000 votes and mobs demanded that he lead them to the Élysée; his manager pleaded for action. If the Republic was in danger—some believe that the police and soldiers would have obeyed him—it was Boulanger himself who spared it. Through fear, confusion, or regard for legality, he refused to move, professing to believe that the general elections in September would carry him to triumph at the head of lists in each department. In reality, it was the end, as some of his friends foresaw before the night had passed. The Tirard cabinet, with the resourceful Ernest Constans at the Ministry of Interior, now decided to break the Boulangist movement by any means it could employ. Believing Boulanger could be discredited through flight, Constans made known a plan to bring him to trial before the Senate for "treason." Constans was right; in April Boulanger fled to Belgium with a mistress to whom he was utterly devoted. For a while, his followers still hoped, but a movement built on an image of fearlessness was shattered. In the elections of 1889, only 40 declared Boulangists were elected. The despondent fugitive shot himself in 1891, on the grave of his mistress. His former patron, Clemenceau, observed that the man died as he had lived, "like a subaltern." Later subalterns, lifted to power by many of the same emotional forces in Italy and Germany, would be more fortunate but meet no better ends.

What the success of *Boulangisme* would have meant is impossible to say, since all men expected all things from one man, of mediocre mind and character, who scarcely knew what he wanted beyond the joys of notoriety. But that he appeared irresistible long enough to lure the Right into open alliance made his failure all the more disastrous. Monarchists who had begun to consider the advantages of a purely parliamentary opposition within the Republic had once more thrown away their prestige at the first temptation of success through anti-constitutional agitation. They had thought the Grèvy Republic contemptible but had employed against it a contemptible adventurer rather than responsible conservative opposition. More seriously, the Boulanger episode encouraged the Right's alliance with the forces of nationalism and militarism, hitherto the preserve of Bonapartists and Radicals. The Right lost 30 seats in September, 1889. To prevent a repetition of the Boulanger affair, the Republicans had returned to single-member constituencies and forbade multiple candidacies; they returned to the Chamber 360 strong. Two years of scandal and demagoguery had left the parliamentary balance unchanged; if anything, the Opportunists were more numerous, as certain Radicals compromised by *Boulangisme* met defeat.

It was a happy ending to a year that began with the disastrous Paris by-election. The centennial of the Revolution proved triumphant, crowned by the great Paris Exposition of 1889, so dazzling (it was the first to be lighted by electricity) that it probably had no little part in diverting the passions that nourished *Boulangisme*. M. Gustave Eiffel provided an unavoidable something to fight about. But his tower, like most of the Exposition, stirred national pride, and confidence in French ability to accomplish material wonders. As for colonial success, each overseas territory had its own exotic pavilion. Millions of visitors found their way to the gaily decorated buildings on the Champ de Mars, before the Invalides and the Trocadéro (which dated from the Exposition of 1878), and perhaps the majority of them went on to the gaudy sights and sounds of the Montmartre, where the unfinished Sacré-Cœur looked down on that quarter's first great age of gaiety. As in 1878, 1867, 1856, the Exposition seemed to generate of itself a Thermidorean atmosphere suitable to the celebration of so much material wealth and bodily pleasure. But another political scandal was developing behind the scenes that would far outdo the scabrous sideshows of the Exposition year.

Tens of thousands of ordinary Frenchmen had invested their savings in the bonds of the Panama Canal Company, on the strength of the name that had conquered Suez, Ferdinand de Lesseps. But the Isthmus of Panama, with its mud and jungle, its deep, unstable cuts and yellow fever, had devoured men and money for every yard of progress since 1881. Only after enormous waste did the engineers abandon the old man's dream of a sea-level canal and turn to locks. But it was too late; in 1889 the company went bankrupt after gathering and losing more than a billion francs, and the French public learned, three years later, that the company had managed to keep its precarious position secret since 1884 through lavish bribes to journalists and parliamentarians. These last, it was said, had approved legislation for an issue of lottery bonds in 1888 while fully aware of the danger that all might soon be lost. The coalition of discontent that had formed around Boulanger leaped to the attack, led this time by the anti-Semite Édouard Drumont, whose new paper *La Libre Parole* first broke the scandal in September of 1892. The anti-republican Right now added to its appeal for authority and militant patriotism a blanket indictment of the Jews in France, for the most prominent dispensers of bribes had been the Baron Jacques de Reinach and Cornelius Herz, both of Jewish origin and well connected in Jewish and Republican society.

The Republican politicians tried to avoid the inquiry demanded by Boulangist Deputies, but Reinach's suicide (he was being blackmailed by Herz) forced at least a show of government activity. The directors of the company—de Lesseps, father and son, Eiffel, and others—were found guilty of fraud and bribery; their sentences were reversed on a technicality by the highest court. Most of the accused politicians—many of them prominent Republicans, including Grèvy's brother—did not even stand trial. Five did and were acquitted. Only one official, the former Minister of Public Works Baihaut, was found guilty and given five years (he had confessed). Herz fled to England. The Right stormed at the Republic's comradely attitude toward its corruptors. These were the Republicans of virtue who had attacked Haussmann, the sons of men who excoriated Louis Philippe; now they were allies and protectors of thieves, blackmailers, and Jewish enemies of religion, patriotism, and the common man's right to his money. Paul Déroulède showed his bravery by going further than general denunciation and singled out the formidable Clemenceau as Herz's protector (receiving support in return for his newspaper La Justice), which was true, and accused him of being an English agent, which was not, but probably cost Clemenceau his seat in the elections of 1893.

The voters seemed little moved by the revelations of Republican corruption. The Right's decline was nowhere halted, for all its attacks on the "Republic of Pals"; from 210 seats gained from 45 per cent of the vote in 1889 it fell to 100 seats from 25 per cent (there were many abstentions), and over a quarter of its Deputies were Catholics who declared themselves loyal Republicans in response to pressure from Leo XIII. The moderates and Opportunists, by now calling themselves by the less suggestive name of Progressists, won 280 seats, the Radicals 140; but striking was the emergence of a socialist and social radical group of 50 on the extreme Left. How much Panama affected the results is unknown. There were, for example, sufficient other reasons for the success of socialism among the workers. More surely, Panama struck down many small investors; some henceforth would be wary of French enterprise and turn to safer investments, such as Russian bonds. It also ruined several political careers, interrupted others, like Clemenceau's. In a less tangible way, it shook again the myth of Republican virtue, encouraged a mood of watchful cynicism among Republican voters, even as they remained loyal to the party. Under attack, the Republicans had protected their rascals, arguing that the attackers were enemies not of corruption but of the Republic itself. It was more than an excuse. There were perhaps no fewer rascals elsewhere, but to throw them out—as in Washington, New York, or Boston—meant only a change of party. In France it could have meant a change of regime. The extreme Right was, if possible, more disdainful than ever of that Republic it commonly called *la gueuse*, the slut, but its leaders were now admitting that they could not replace it by legal means.

## CATHOLICISM AND SOCIALISM

Two other developments of the 1880's and early 1890's more clearly affected the balance of forces in the Republic: the growth of a socialist Left and the emergence of Republican and social Catholicism. Since 1878, the year of his accession, Pope Leo XIII had been increasingly concerned to loosen the knot that Veuillot and Pius IX had tied between French Catholicism and political reaction. Like his predecessor, he hated the abuses of the modern world, but to deny its existence or its generous side, to ignore the responsibility of Catholicism to apply the Christian spirit to democracy and social justice, was unthinkable. Upon the collapse of the Boulanger campaign he expected, with some reason, that prominent Catholics would be ready to give up the sterile royalist idea and honestly enter Republican politics, which was, he believed with even better reason, the only way to safeguard Catholic interests in education. In the encyclical *Libertas* (1888) Leo had said that democracy was as consistent with Catholic doctrine as any other form of government; its reception among French bishops and laymen was frigid. They were convinced, rightly, that many leading Republicans aimed at nothing less than a godless society through godless schools, but refused to admit that the issue hung on the attitude of the great middle group neutral enough in religious affairs but needlessly alienated by Catholic efforts to overturn a form of government that suited it. In 1890, Leo XIII acted through Cardinal Lavigerie, the venerated founder of the missionary White Fathers. At a banquet in Algiers, the Cardinal dramatically toasted the Republic and asked all Catholics to support it. The

Catholic Right and several bishops were adamant, launched repeated attacks on Lavigerie "the African," and the Pope found it necessary, in February, 1892, to speak directly in an encyclical (*Au milieu des sollicitudes*) recommending the *Ralliement* of Catholics to the Republic.

The Royalists persisted in opposition, rediscovered the principle, forgotten under Pius IX, that the Vatican had no right to interfere in political affairs, and tried with some success to organize a financial boycott of the Church and its missions. French bishops supported the *Ralliement* reluctantly; but in time a Catholic party gathered, including the Comte Albert de Mun, until then a Royalist (and a supporter of Boulanger) but concerned before all to make Catholicism a force for social reform. He, together with the Republican Étienne Lamy and the moderate Jacques Piou, also a former Royalist, led a hurriedly organized campaign for the elections of 1893. Only 27 *Ralliés* were elected, but their followers' second-round support of moderate Republicans rather than Royalists helped to bring the latter down to 58 Deputies. At this moment, the influx of socialists to the Chamber and the renewed interest of some Radicals in economic and social reforms impelled the opportunist Progressists to seek allies on the Right, which they found in the *Ralliés*. In 1896, Lamy organized a federation of Catholic groups that accepted the Republic, hoping to expand the base of a Catholic party. Although openly supported by the Pope, the effort was undermined by a majority of the French hierarchy and the leaders of the Assumptionist Order, through their paper *La Croix,* the most widely read Catholic organ in France. The royalist and anti-Semitic press, Drumont's *Libre Parole* at the head, fulminated against "Papal Republicans," and a new tax on the property of religious orders in 1895 helped discredit the policy of *Ralliement* among the laity and clergy alike. In the elections of 1898, the *Ralliés* won only 35 seats; the Dreyfus affair was to weaken their influence still further, as moderate Republicans were forced back to alliance with the anti-clerical Left and the great majority of Catholics in political life united on the other side.

If in its immediate aim, the creation of a conservative Republican Catholic party, the *Ralliement* failed, it nonetheless called Catholic votes away from the old monarchist Right and accustomed Catholics to supporting conservative Republican parties, and these, in turn, to relaxing their anti-clericalism on the eve of the great war. The *Ralliement* encouraged also the early progress of two other movements that were destined to fulfill many of the hopes of Lamennais: social Catholicism and

Catholic trade unionism. Both were encouraged at a crucial moment by Leo XIII's great social encyclical of 1891, *Rerum novarum*. Prior to that time, social Catholicism had been mainly the work of Legitimists led by Maurice Maignen, Albert de Mun, and the Marquis de la Tour du Pin. Their acute consciousness of the workers' misery led to a nation-wide organization of Catholic workers' discussion clubs and appeals for social legislation. Their paternalistic and hierarchical views of society did not, however, appeal to working-class activists and were abhorred by the politically dominant bourgeoisie, Catholic or not. Much of the clergy opposed any lay activity, and the nobility, whom de Mun considered the natural allies of the workers, remained largely indifferent. But the social Catholics' denunciation of laissez-faire capitalism awakened other consciences and, together with like-minded Catholics in Germany, Austria, and Belgium, they reached the ear of Rome. Particularly appealing to Leo XIII was the work of the selfless Léon Harmel, who had made his textile factory near Reims a model of social welfare while managing to leave the direction of workers' affairs in the workers' hands.

In *Rerum novarum*, Leo XIII confronted the Catholic world with the proposition that its moral precepts must be applied to social and economic questions, that it was no longer enough to preach Christian resignation to the workers while reaping profits from their misery. The workers enslaved to "the inhumanity of employers and the unbridled greed of competitors" must be restored to freedom and dignity. If employers would not do it, the state had a right to intervene to guarantee family security, a just wage, and proper hours by encouraging the workers' own societies and unions. Now taken for granted, Leo's words, together with his views on political democracy, were bitterly resented by a middle-class society accustomed to regarding the worker as a creature apart. But for other Catholics Leo offered liberation after decades of Church approval or silence in the face of caste privilege, economic injustice, and political reaction. Ardent young priests promoted a Christian democratic movement which held a series of national Catholic workers' congresses in the 1890's. But it was too hastily set afoot, without a definite program or discipline, was attacked from both within and without by conservative Catholics, exploited by political opportunists, and compromised by the anti-Semitism of several of its leaders. The movement failed to survive despite the great numbers its meetings attracted, but, like Lamy's moderate Republican federation, it left behind small groups of persistent men to prepare the future.

Beginnings made by Catholic aristocrats, politicians, and priests in the 1890's were matched by the independent action of Catholic workers. By then, several unions in the Paris area had freed themselves from the tutelage, useful at first, of priests and upper-class laymen associated with de Mun and others like him. The SECI (*Syndicat des Employés du Commerce et de l'Industrie*) was founded in 1887 and encouraged Catholic workers in other areas to oppose the efforts of most Catholic employers to keep them in mixed ("yellow") unions of employers and employees. In this they made very slow progress against well-meaning disciples of de Mun or industrialists who wanted no genuine unions at all. Local prelates were often suspicious and interfered with Catholic organizers, all of which aided the task of rival, anti-Catholic militants in the working class. Only in 1903 was the first congress of Catholic unions held, and it was not until after World War I that a national organization was established, with a total membership in 1919 of 140,000 in 500 unions. The fundamental weakness of the Catholic union movement was, of course, the de-Christianization of the working classes which had proceeded rapidly since before the Revolution of 1789. Neither the Church nor the Catholic bourgeoisie had faced the social question in the crucial years of industrialization and urbanization, much of which had occurred during the long pontificate of Pius IX. Lamennais and his successors had been driven out or silenced and the common French saying that "the Church is always one revolution behind" was, in the eyes of the working class, rather an understatement. Leo XIII came too late for France. By 1890, the majority of workers had long since turned away.

After the Commune, as during and before it, French labor and socialist groups remained divided on means and ends, not perhaps so much out of legendary French individualism or passion for ideology as out of complex circumstances and mixed experience. The artisans of Paris and other cities of small industry had less in common with the proletariat of the mining, textile, and metallurgical centers than the latter had with the rising number of landless agricultural day laborers, or with the new thousands of railway and dock workers. As factory industry grew up in the Paris suburbs, even working-class neighbors, one trudging inward to a small printing shop in town, the other outward to a modern foundry, saw their daily problems in very different lights. To some workers, furthermore, it appeared axiomatic that all genuine change in France had come through armed revolt and capture of political power, that the failure of the Commune proved only the need for better preparation and leadership in class warfare. Others read the past differently: revolution had brought only frustration and repression; parliament must be conquered by labor party organization and electoral struggle. Still others rejected all forms of political action; better, some said, to concentrate on worker cooperatives and mutual benefit societies, to which a fourth group preferred militant unionism and direct economic action against employers in strikes, boycott, or sabotage. A fifth began to dream of a nation-wide general strike, a sixth of turning capitalist society to anarchy by signal acts of terror and assassination. Each approach and mixtures of several had adherents enough to prevent the dominance of any one among them. But all could agree that the worker had served too long as the human sacrifice to the comfort of others.

Perhaps 400,000 unionists were organized by 1895 in the *Fédération des Bourses du Travail,* led by the valiant young Fernand Pelloutier, disciple of Proudhon, and like him suspicious of political parties and national collectivism. Each bourse served as a local clearinghouse for unions in all trades, providing mutual aid, training, and employment information. Differing widely in temper from city to city and often hostile to their own national organization, the bourses represented the old tradition of local action, aiming at autonomous cooperative societies. It was to take the name syndicalism and to dominate, while fragmenting, French unionism to the First World War. Beside it, founded in 1895, was the weaker *Confédération Générale du Travail* (CGT), mixing in socialist politics (despite its efforts to remain neutral), striving for a tighter national organization of labor unions in each craft or industry. Apart from such old and well-established national unions as the printers, however, wider organization than the local achieved solidity only after 1900. Local strikes were frequent in the 1880's and 1890's but often ill-financed, uncoordinated, and turned to violence by the inevitable appearance of strikebreakers, *agents provocateurs,* and private or public security forces. And even local unions were weakened by the rivalries of the several socialist parties whose members sought to turn the activity of their fellow unionists to party ends.

In the immediate aftermath of the Commune, the moderate, cooperatist (syndicalist) ideas of Proudhon were dominant among the few socialist workers' circles that remained above ground. The First International foundered in strife among Marxists, Bakuninists, and Blanquists in the early 1870's. But Marxism came to France with the publication of Marx's *Capital* in Paris between 1872 and 1875 and with the return of several militant exiles in the late 1870's and early 1880's: Benoît Malon, Paul Brousse, Paul Lafargue, and Jules Guesde, who most faithfully reflected Marx's own ideas—and temperament. They plunged into acrid quarrels with the Proudhonists on the one hand and the anarchist followers of Bakunin and Prince Kropotkin on the other, and with the Blanquists, soon to be disarrayed by the death of *le vieux* in 1881. But already in 1881, Malon and Brousse split from Guesde and won a majority of the Saint-Étienne workers' congress (1882) to a policy of coexistence with the Republican majority, to coax immediate, practical reforms out of parliament. Guesde and Lafargue, scornful of these possibilists, formed the *Parti Ouvrier* in 1883 on an orthodox Marxist program. Each socialist faction held its own congress on the occasion of the Paris Exposition of 1889, the possibilists winning the larger share of French union support, the Guesdists attracting foreign delegates to the organization of a Second International. In the following year, the possibilists themselves split between Broussistes and Allemanistes (after Jean Allemane) over questions of personalities, specific demands to be made on parliament, and rivalries in the Paris *Bourse du Travail*. To these quarreling socialist parties, the mass of artisans and proletarians were slow to give even their votes, much less their energies or contributions. The enthusiasm of several working-class areas for Boulanger showed how far they were in the 1880's from any settled allegiance to the organizations claiming to speak on their behalf.

The ultimate turn of the worker to Marxism or syndicalism appears to have been far from inevitable, but the Republicans in parliament, except for a handful of social Radicals, consistently refused to recognize, and press for, the workers' demands. While Great Britain and Bismarckian Germany introduced social legislation, the Chamber of Deputies did nothing beyond hoping that the law of 1884 would encourage docile unions; the Opportunists spoke for the employers; and Radicals often acquiesced, fought clerical rather than social battles, and compromised themselves with speculators in the Panama affair. By the early 1890's, the Republican Left had lost much of its chance to retain working-class loyalty. After the election of only 10 socialists or social Radicals in 1889, the appearance of nearly 50 in the Chamber of 1893 awakened many Frenchmen to a new challenge from the Left. At first, reaction was violent, with the socialists unjustly accused of complicity in a series of terrorist acts culminating with the assassination of President

Carnot in 1894. In vain socialist and social Radical leaders denounced both the anarchists and the security laws (*les lois scélérates*) passed in an atmosphere of national panic. But anarchism suffered a rapid eclipse and it seemed that social questions would now finally be considered.

In the Republican parties, new men who replaced the casualties of Panama felt less in common with each other than had their predecessors, who had fought the Moral Order, the clericals, and the Boulangists together. The distance between Radicals, who were coming to see the political necessity of moving toward the socialists, and the moderate Republicans now widened, as more Radicals advocated the income tax, inheritance tax, and social legislation. On their part, most of the Opportunists had moved to the Right, not only physically in the Chamber, but toward moderation in clerical affairs and the defense of property interests. It is typical of French political nomenclature that they should choose this moment to call themselves Progressists, when, in frank alliance with the *Ralliés* and some even further Right, they had finally given up the cherished fiction that a true Republic could have "no enemies to the Left." To succeed Carnot, they and their allies in the Chamber and Senate chose a millionaire mining entrepreneur of Orléanist heritage, Jean Casimir-Périer, the grandson of Louis Philippe's conservative Premier. But he resigned in frustration over his limited power—and prestige—in 1895. In his place, the moderates chose a bourgeois politician of no outstanding éclat, Félix Faure. In the same year, the first Radical cabinet came into office under Léon Bourgeois, on the votes of socialists, social Radicals, Radicals, and a few moderates still anxious to have "no enemies to the Left." Bourgeois announced a wide program of social reforms: income and inheritance taxes, insurance and social security, and arbitration of labor quarrels. Over the violent opposition of the Progressist and conservative Republicans, the Bourgeois cabinet won the adoption of a graduated income tax. This timid measure prescribed a maximum of only 5 per cent, but the idea of opening one's books to official scrutiny repelled great sections of French opinion, from industrial magnates to small growers. For the first time under the Republic, the Senate intervened to overthrow a Premier. The conservative Jules Méline formed a new cabinet that lasted two years, and the income tax was to await the irrepressible demands of 1914.

In the aftermath of this defeat, the socialist factions achieved a fleeting unity in 1896 when the independent socialist Deputy Alexandre Millerand succeeded in drawing the Marxist Guesde, the brilliant Normalien Jean Jaurès, and other leaders to the program of Saint-Mandé. At a banquet near this Paris suburb, Millerand proclaimed the socialist counterpart of the Belleville manifesto: socialism would come to power not by revolution but by "conquest of the State" through universal suffrage. Large industry would be nationalized, but small property—an appeal to peasants and lower bourgeois—would remain private. Socialists recognized the international solidarity of workers but would never abandon their own loyalty to France, mother of human progress for over a century—an appeal to Radicals and, admittedly, to the rank and file of workers whose patriotism was unquestionable. With socialists winning *mairies* and local councils in the 1890's (whereupon Republicans congratulated themselves on having left the prefects with wide powers), and a growing parliamentary delegation ready to support social Republican cabinets, the movement appeared on the verge of decisive new gains. In early 1898, even a Méline government felt obliged to pass a law fixing employer responsibility for compensation to victims of industrial accidents, and another subsidizing mutual aid societies in industry and agriculture. In the late 1890's it appeared that a new alignment of political parties debating modern economic questions might emerge at last. But the Dreyfus case intervened, to revive outworn issues, rekindle old hatreds, and postpone the reconciliation of Catholics to the Republic and the Republic to social reform.

## THE DREYFUS AFFAIR

France entered the twentieth century with her parliament, parties, press, and articulate public embroiled over early nineteenth-century issues. But the Dreyfus affair looked forward as well as back, revealing forces of ill omen to the twentieth century: racism, rabid nationalism, and the exploitation of both by demagogues and entrenched elites to divert popular unrest to their own ends. This fateful mixture of old and new developed out of the arrest in October, 1894, of Captain Alfred Dreyfus, the only Jewish officer attached to the general staff, on charges of selling secrets to the German military attaché in Paris. As in the Panama scandal, the French public was first given the news by Édouard Drumont's *La Libre Parole*, which hastened to demand that this time no mercy be given Jewish betrayers of the people's trust. Pressed by Rightist journals, and a Commandant Henry of the Army Intelligence who had kept Drumont informed, the Minister of War, General Mercier, in turn pressed a secret military court into convicting Dreyfus on evidence withheld from the defense, warning the judges that disclosure would risk war with Germany. The doubts of the court, Dreyfus' protests of innocence, and his lawyer's disgust notwithstanding, the wealthy young officer was publicly degraded and condemned to perpetual imprisonment on Devil's Island, whose brutal conditions had already silenced so many incorrigibles. The Republic, particularly the army which was its most Catholic and conservative agency, had proved it would not be bribed by Jewish gold. Some of the stain of Panama appeared to be washed away and Republicans were no less gratified at the outcome than the Right, especially those who were at the moment moving into an alliance with it to preserve society from socialism. Those patriots and socialists (like Jaurès) who grumbled were unhappy only because the man had not been shot.

For four years, Dreyfus slowly failed under heat and damp and an animal diet, while his family worked unsuccessfully to clear him. Meanwhile, a Colonel Picquart of Army Intelligence, aware that a spy was still at work, discovered that the one piece of evidence openly used at Dreyfus' trial—the *bordereau,* a list of secrets for sale, found in the German Embassy's trash—was in fact the work of a disreputable officer named Esterhazy. He next examined the secret dossier which had condemned Dreyfus and found it ambiguous enough to suggest that military justice had miscarried. The determination of his superiors, Chief of Staff Boisdeffre and General Gonse, to prevent a review of the case confirmed his suspicions, and their abrupt dispatch of him to a dangerous post in Tunisia at the end of 1896 impelled Picquart to share his evidence, which ultimately reached the vice-president of the Senate, Scheurer-Kestner.

Independently, Dreyfus' lawyer Demange discovered that his judges had based their verdict on secret evidence, contrary to legal procedure. The family appealed in vain for a retrial on this ground, was rebuffed, and made its case public in late 1896 through a courageous Jewish journalist, Bernard Lazare. Now the nationalists were rearoused, with press and Deputies deploring such attacks on French justice and the army's honor. The new Minister of War, General Billot, swore to the Chamber that Dreyfus had been legally judged, while the loyal Henry manufactured new documents for the secret dossier Picquart had already examined—only one example of the bizarre and fatuous habits of an intelligence agency operating independently of any higher authority than the indulgent chief of staff. After the affair, it was brought under civil authority, but in 1896 the political trimmers of the majority were no less anxious than the soldiers that the case remain closed. Faure, Méline, Billot all belittled Scheurer-Kestner's version of the facts; so the Senator, reacting as Picquart had before him, published his demands for a revision of the case in the *Temps*. Lazare published a facsimile of the *bordereau* and all Paris knew, or could have known, what Picquart had found, that it was in Esterhazy's hand. The Dreyfus family, supported now (November, 1897) by Clemenceau in his paper *l'Aurore*, demanded Esterhazy's trial and the liberation of the prisoner.

At this juncture, old forces and new turned the affair into a national struggle between Dreyfusards and anti-Dreyfusards which was to go far beyond the merits of the case itself—of which many on both sides were ignorant or indifferent—to a confrontation of what too many Frenchmen had learned to regard as "the two Frances." In the months that followed, to be a Dreyfusard, or revisionist, was to stand, or appear to stand, for the Republic, for justice to minorities and the individual, for democracy untrammeled by militarists, clericals, or chauvinists. To be against Dreyfus was to defend, or claim to defend, French national prestige, the honor of the army, and thereby the safety of the State against pacifists and cosmopolitans, the name of the Church and thereby the morality of French society unstained by atheism, Freemasonry, or Jewry. To see the quarrel as between Frenchmen who were for or against Dreyfus the man, or divided on his guilt or innocence, is to miss most of its significance and—since Dreyfus was innocent—to calumniate one side and to allow the other too much credit for devotion to individual justice. There were, nonetheless, several heroes, villains, and fools. The greater heroes were those who disregarded their own interests and prejudices in choosing their position. Picquart, a Catholic and anti-Semite, risked his career, as did the Dreyfus lawyers Demange, Leblois, and Labori; Lazare risked his personal safety in those lonely opening days to defend a man he little admired; and Scheurer-Kestner courted political ostracism. The greater villains, or fools, were the officers who knew the facts but hid them to save their places, which they equated with saving the honor of the army and national security, and the politicians who chose political quietude (so they thought) before all else.

The army's role was crucial, for upon discovering Esterhazy's guilt, it might have forestalled the crisis by revising its decision. But the few whose personal integrity seemed at stake chose to rely on evasion, on Henry's forgeries, and on hints of secrets too dangerous to divulge lest war with Germany result. And the mass of officers who did not know the facts naturally chose to defend the integrity of respected colleagues and superiors, especially against Frenchmen whose race, or religious and political views, they despised and whose honesty and patriotism they doubted. The officer corps by the 1890's was largely Catholic in faith and royalist, Bonapartist, or conservative in political sentiment. The army was the last honorable public career left fully open to such men, with the diplomatic, colonial, and judicial corps offering far fewer posts. For them, their families and sympathizers, the army appeared as the last repository of proper French tradition. Dreyfus was an intruder and his supporters the men who had overturned the Moral Order, attacked religion, amassed offices and fortunes while sending young men to die in Indo-China, Africa, and Madagascar, soldiers said, for lack of support from the Chamber.

Many Dreyfusards were equally certain that the army and the Monarchists and clericals who supported it were the last enemies of human liberty, whom the Republic had tolerated too long. Here was a chance to humble them forever. Only in a society in which all sides were already discredited could the Dreyfus crisis develop as it did. In it, the Right paid again for Boulanger, the 16th of May, the 2nd of December, even the Brunswick Manifesto (or the massacre of Saint Bartholomew); the Republicans and the Left paid for Panama, the expulsion decrees, the Commune, the June Days, the Terror. France— the third France, of Frenchmen more occupied with present problems and hopes than with recrimination—paid for all, and was afflicted as well with newer human follies: anti-Semitism and ultra-nationalism.

Both were revivals, in modern dress, of old European scourges. But they appeared now in their twentieth-century, proto-fascist form, attached to the political Right, the social and economic establishment— thereby to many churchmen—and finding their shock troops (later, their leaders) among the half-educated, insecure, and sullen crowd of men who thrive on hate, who prefer their answers simple, their amusements violent. Anti-Semitism's foremost spokesman, Édouard Drumont, had published in 1886 *La France Juive,* purporting to expose the Jews' conspiracy to control France, with their Protestant and Masonic allies. His lively style and clear-cut answers appealed to a wide audience—"from priests to Communards," someone said. Jewish involvement in the Panama scandal and Jewish prominence in the theater, literature, the professions, politics, and commerce helped the anti-Semites to exaggerate the power of France's mere 80,000 Jews. Anti-Semitism appeared widely, before the Dreyfus case, among socialists, Christian democrats, and writers (Zola was one) who attacked the power of banks and big business. Jewish society itself was divided by the influx of Alsatians like the Dreyfus family, then by poorer refugees from eastern Europe. The popularization of racial theories, perversions of Darwinism, had set many lesser intellectuals on a course of anti-Semitism and xenophobia.

The nationalist movement overlapped but was never identical with anti-Semitism. Nationalists, too, saw in the *affaire* a chance to seize power. Paul Déroulède and the *Ligue des Patriotes,* the novelist Maurice Barrès, first elected to the Chamber in 1889 as a Boulangist Deputy, other Boulangists, Bonapartists, and patriotic royalists were joined by a young Provençal poet, Charles Maurras, in defending the army as the main hope of *revanche* and the rehabilitation of French glory, not only to make France once more *la grande nation* of Europe but because they believed glory and military virtues to be the cement of French society. In the elections of 1898, an anti-Dreyfusard party entered the Chamber using the name Nationalist, and a new kind of Right was born, in which integral nationalism largely replaced clericalism as the last refuge of conservative opponents of the Republic, and as a vehicle for discontent on any issue. Religion had never been enough, even in the 1870's when practicing Catholics had been more numerous, and the *Ralliément* had spoiled its political unity; it was Maurras and his colleagues in the royalist society Action Française, founded in 1898, who were to exploit what seemed a stronger passion in a forty-year vendetta against the Republic and the Jews, Protestants, democrats, immigrants, internationalists, and liberal Catholics who degraded their idea of France.

These forces were gathering in the autumn of 1897 when Billot and the others decided to let Dreyfus stay where he was. The streets and most of the press supported them and made Esterhazy a hero when a secret court acquitted him in January, 1898. It was Picquart, the anti-Dreyfusards said, who was the villain or, like all those in France and outside who doubted Dreyfus' guilt, was duped and bought by the Jewish world syndicate. Now Émile Zola entered the case, with an open letter to Félix Faure excoriating the army leaders for forcing their judges to acquit the guilty Esterhazy after lying about Dreyfus. Clemenceau chose the resounding title *J'accuse* and printed it in *l'Aurore* on January 14, 1898. Some, perhaps too conscious of literary fashion, have lately minimized Zola's role, but it should be said that his letter, for all its pomposity, appeared well before it was safe to be a Dreyfusard, and it helped call to Dreyfus' side a majority of leading academics, artists, and intellectuals, among them Marcel Proust, Claude Monet, Charles Péguy, Lucien Herr, Daniel Halévy, Maeterlinck, André Gide, Léon Blum, and Anatole France. Not since the romantic days of 1830 and 1848 had a public question so gripped the intelligentsia.

On the other side the literary critic Jules Lemaître led the *Ligue de la Patrie Française;* he, with Bourget and Barrès, gathered a smaller group of literary lights, more familiar to society and readers of the popular press. Not always comfortably, they joined with Drumont, Déroulède, and Rochefort's *Lanterne* to defend the army's honor. Since the Dreyfus case, French intellectuals have assumed a reputation for objectivity and perception beyond the ordinary in political matters; most political parties pride themselves on having a number about on public occasions, and as regular contributors to party journals. Although their reputations have sometimes been ill-deserved, they have surely no worse record than public divinities elsewhere. They have enlivened French politics and consistently lifted the level of debate, if not the chances of compromise. Naturally they have been at their best in the darkest hours, notably in the early 1940's, when clandestine writers ennobled French self-consciousness in the face of occupation. Then, as in the early phases of the Dreyfus case, they struggled to defend the lonely individual's right to life and justice against the claims of insensate authority. Yet no man of letters was more eloquent than the journalist-politician Georges Clemenceau, whose writings were on other occasions almost unrelievedly turgid. This was his finest hour, when his faith in men and their ability to deserve the ideals of 1789 appeared still intact. In 1898, he helped revive the League for the Rights of Man, to which most of the Dreyfusards adhered. To deny justice to one, he said, was to endanger the freedom of all; and to those who insisted that the security of France demanded silence and respect for authority, he answered that freedom and justice were France's reason for being, that to sacrifice them was to rob France of her soul, the ultimate source of any nation's security.

By openly challenging the government, Zola and Clemenceau forced it to display in public the repressive judicial procedures that had condemned Dreyfus. Zola's trial was farcical, his defense hampered at every turn, and he was found guilty of defamation. The mob was violently against him—he was in physical danger, as was Clemenceau— but now the world, and Frenchmen who would, could see the nature of his enemies on bench and street. In Paris, Algiers, and other cities Jews were assaulted, their shops and synagogues pillaged and set afire. For a while more, the anti-Dreyfusard movement seemed all-powerful. Picquart was arrested, tried, and cashiered from the army. Dreyfusard teachers, officers, and civil officials were discharged and the Méline government prepared for the elections of 1898 by pretending there was no Dreyfus case. For much of the country outside Paris, there was not. Local issues predominated in the May elections. The Center, moderate Republicans, fell slightly, to 235; the socialists rose to 65, social Radicals and Radicals to 180; the Right and *Ralliés* remained at about 100. The veteran Radical Brisson headed a cabinet based on the Center Left, but General Godefroy Cavaignac, an ardent defender of the army, became Minister of War and immediately undertook to close the case by producing additional evidence against Dreyfus in the Chamber. It was an error. Picquart told Brisson that two documents were falsified and, confronted with this accusation, Henry committed suicide. Esterhazy fled to England and the case had to be reopened.

Although stunned by these developments, the anti-Dreyfusards redoubled their campaign, which now assumed the look of an attack on the Republic itself. When President Félix Faure died in February, 1899, and the moderate Senator Émile Loubet was elected over Méline, considered an anti-Dreyfusard, the excited Déroulède prepared a *coup d'état* on the occasion of Faure's funeral. For a moment, the more ambitious Orléanists and Bonapartists were tempted, but they withdrew and Déroulède was left with a feeble troop from his *Ligue des Patriotes,* without plans or the accomplices inside the army or government that a coup required, without even a Boulanger to draw attention. Apart from the public's growing doubts over the case against Dreyfus, a funeral was not the best setting for a patriotic revolution and Faure had not helped matters any by expiring in an amorous rendezvous. As the ceremony ended, Déroulède and his band tried to subvert a column of troops; Déroulède seized the bridle of General Roget's horse and shouted, "To the Élysée!" but the General and his horse returned to barracks and there Déroulède and a few straggling accomplices were arrested. Of no more danger to the Republic was Baron Christiani's sudden, and crushing, assault on President Loubet's top hat at the annual Auteuil steeple-chase, where for several hours Loubet and his wife had been loudly insulted by Rightist socialites. But more serious acts were possible; and in any case, repeated asininities did nothing for the dignity of the regime. Now the Left was fully committed to sweep the streets clear of anti-Dreyfusards. Jaurès had rallied to Dreyfus earlier, Guesde followed, and a great workers' demonstration at Longchamps in June alarmed the Chamber more than nationalist riots had. It was time to restore order.

Senator René Waldeck-Rousseau, a protégé of Gambetta and a lawyer of impeccable reputation, proceeded to form a Government of Republican Defense (June 22, 1899). The cabinet was based on Dreyfusard moderates but extended to the Right with the old but tough and dashing Marquis de Gallifet, a general remembered for his repression of the Commune, and to the Left with Alexandre Millerand, the first socialist to assume cabinet office. The socialists were split over Millerand's acceptance of office in a bourgeois government, but enough supported him to assure the cabinet's confirmation in the Chamber by a narrow vote; the Right, *Ralliés,* and most Progressists opposed it; the Radicals held the balance and were to keep it until 1914. Waldeck-Rousseau's aim was to close the Dreyfus crisis as quickly as possible. Several score Rightist agitators were arrested. Gallifet, as Minister of War, retired the most outspoken anti-Dreyfusard officers. The Court of Cassation had already ordered a retrial. Dreyfus returned from Devil's Island and faced a second military court at Rennes in August of 1899. Its verdict astonished the world and infuriated the Dreyfusards; by five to two, Dreyfus was found guilty, but with "extenuating circumstances," and received a ten-year sentence. This senseless equivocation was allowed to stand; the government, partly in fear of world opinion on the eve of the 1900 Exposition, allowed Loubet to pardon Dreyfus rather than risk the political troubles of forcing another trial. Over the protests of Clemenceau, Zola, and other leading Dreyfusards, Dreyfus accepted. In 1906, the Court of Cassation annulled the verdict. Thanks to the Radicals in the Chamber, Dreyfus returned to the army with a promotion and received the Legion of Honor; he later served as a lieutenant colonel in the First World War. The hero of the piece, Picquart, became a general and Minister of War in 1906, in the first cabinet formed by Clemenceau, whose political career the Dreyfus case restored.

# ~ vii ~

# THE REPUBLIC OF
# THE RADICALS

Captain Dreyfus returned to his family in 1899, but the crisis born of his misfortunes rolled on into the twentieth century. Its immediate political effects were manifest in the realignment of parties before the elections of 1902. For the first time under the Third Republic, most had some success in organizing themselves as permanent groups. The hitherto dominant Progressist Republicans were split over the issue of revising Dreyfus' conviction as well as over Waldeck-Rousseau's acceptance of socialist support; when most of them (under the name *Fédération Républicaine*) moved into loose cooperation with the *Ralliés* and other Republican conservatives, they bolstered a parliamentary Right loyal to Republican forms, but increasingly conservative on all other issues. Progressists who followed Waldeck-Rousseau, on the other hand, formed in 1901 the *Alliance Républicaine Démocratique*, a party mainly representative of middle-sized business, which was in its turn to be counted on the Republican Center Right after the First World War. In it were Waldeck-Rousseau himself and two rising young men, Raymond Poincaré and Louis Barthou. To their Left, the Radicals and many of the social Radicals founded in 1901 the *Parti Républicain Radical et Radical-Socialiste* (to be known as the Radical-Socialists or Radicals), which, with its lower-middle-class and increasingly rural clientele, was radical in a political and anti-clerical sense, only vaguely interested in social legislation. Impelled to strengthen their national organization by

264

the Dreyfus battle, they were closely identified with the more intransigent Masonic lodges and the League for the Rights of Man. The two main socialist groups were the *Parti Socialiste de France,* made up of Guesdists and Blanquists who opposed any socialist participation in bourgeois cabinets à la Millerand, and the *Parti Socialiste Français,* which, with Jaurès as its spokesman, defended the utility of alliances with progressive Radicals. Within and among all these parties there drifted a number of politicians whose ideas or local electoral interests encouraged them to remain aloof from party discipline, loose as it was, and who, either alone or with small coteries of friends, took seats in the Chamber according to their individual tastes.

The elections of 1902 were fought over many issues, making it impossible to judge the weight of the Dreyfus question, though it was vigorously, even viciously, debated in many constituencies. Counting the Republican conservatives, the Right came close to equaling the vote of the Left overall, but the *Alliance Démocratique* and Radical-Socialists profited by their common support of candidates in many areas. The former elected some 100, the latter 200. With the support of some 40 socialists, including Jaurès and Aristide Briand, the Chamber's *Bloc des Gauches* had a majority. The extreme Right elected 60 Nationalists, 80 Royalists and conservatives of various hues. About 20 *Ralliés* and 100 anti-Waldeck Progressists won election, many of whom might be counted upon in critical moments to preserve Republican solidarity (and property, should the socialists threaten it). For the first time, the Radicals held a clear balance of power in whatever Republican majority could be gathered; and the period 1902–1914 is often called that of the Radical Republic. When Waldeck-Rousseau retired as Premier because of ill health and the better-known radical leaders Bourgeois and Brisson declined, President Loubet chose the Radical Senator Émile Combes to head the cabinet and the way was clear for the most combative Dreyfusards to take revenge on their enemies.

As a sign of what the Republic of Radicals was to mean, the fiercely anti-clerical Combes (he had studied for the priesthood) took the Ministries of Interior and Religion for himself, and Millerand, though hardly a revolutionary and already repudiated by the socialists, was dropped. Jaurès and most socialists continued their support nonetheless, both as anti-clericals and in the hope of social reform to follow. To Waldeck-Rousseau's chagrin, Combes carried to a vengeful extreme those policies already undertaken against the army and the Catholic

Church, ignoring all other issues. The next three years saw the victory of the Dreyfusards degenerate, as Péguy said, from a triumph of the Republican *mystique* to political profit-taking at the expense of the defeated.

## THE SEPARATION OF CHURCH AND STATE

The first great struggle of the new century was religious and out of it came a revolution of the government's relations with Catholicism. The French Church itself had not, in fact, taken a public part in the anti-Dreyfusard campaign. Its bishops had maintained a prudent silence and the mass of secular priests followed their example. But the paper read by many of them, La Croix, and its brash Assumptionist publishers had imitated the worst attacks of Drumont's *La Libre Parole* and Rochefort's *Lanterne*. Some Jesuits had been close behind, their paper in Rome having said that the only judicial error in France had been the emancipation of the Jews in 1791. The monarchists, militarists, and anti-Semites were often prominent Catholic laymen. Worse, most of the *Ralliés* had ranged themselves against revision of Dreyfus' sentence, so that nearly all Catholic public figures were compromised by the affair. In such circumstances, the silence of the episcopate did nothing to save it; prudence appeared to both sides as abject trimming and to the Dreyfusards as abdication of a Christian duty to defend the innocent.

To men less violent than Combes, the events proved once more the danger to the Republic posed by Catholic education of so many influential French citizens. Not long after taking power, Waldeck-Rousseau had undertaken to satisfy the Left by suspending publication of *La Croix* and dissolving the Assumptionists as an unauthorized religious association (January, 1900). In accordance with his wish to submit all regular clergy to government control, as the French secular clergy had been by the Concordat, he denounced the increasing numbers, wealth, and influence of congregations never recognized as legal by the Republic. To his chagrin, he was forced to accept from the Chamber's anticlerical majority a general Law on Associations (July, 1901) which went much beyond his own desires, back to Jules Ferry's famous Article VII. After opening sections which liberalized the status of lay associations—to the delight of socialists and Radicals—it severely restricted religious associations as directed from abroad and thus requiring special treatment. These were given three months to apply for authorization, which would be granted by legislative action; no member of unauthorized orders would be allowed to teach. The harassed Premier assured the congregations and Leo XIII that he would secure authorization for most and see that the law was applied in a liberal spirit, particularly in the case of teaching nuns. But the electoral campaign of 1902, full of vitriolic exchanges between Catholics and anti-clericals, ended in victory for the latter, heavily concentrated in the Radical-Socialist party, and shortly thereafter Combes replaced Waldeck-Rousseau.

The most rabid anti-clericals desired nothing less than the final fulfillment of the Belleville manifesto: expulsion of all regular clergy, a monopoly for lay education, the separation of Church and State. To this end, 2500 Catholic schools were immediately closed, most of them primary, staffed by women's orders; in 1903 some 10,000 more institutions followed—hospitals, charities, and schools—and the Chamber majority refused authorization to 135 religious orders. Only a few missionary and contemplative orders were spared, among them the White Fathers, Cistercians, and Trappists. In July of 1904, the right to teach was denied to all members of congregations, authorized or not; this resulted in the closing of nearly 2000 more schools on the primary and secondary levels. Throughout 1903 and 1904, tens of thousands of priests, brothers, and nuns fled France for Belgium, England, Italy, and America. Marked by scattered resistance of Catholic laymen, especially in the west, this destruction of selfless works and uprooting of devoted Frenchmen, most of whom had taken no part in anti-republican agitation, was the darkest hour of French Catholicism.

The triumph of anti-clerical bigotry, or bigotry simulated for political gain, was even more the fruit of the exploitation of Catholicism by men more royalist, nationalist, or anti-Semite than Christian, and of the Catholic intransigents' long refusal to accept the need for compromise urged upon them by Leo XIII. Having preferred Veuillot to Montalembert, Drumont to Lamy, their reward was Émile Combes. Wiser Catholics were not to forget that Combes' policies were vigorously denounced in 1904 by Waldeck-Rousseau himself, by Jules Guesde, who decried Jaurès' support of the new "anti-clerical church" of bourgeois Masons, and by Clemenceau, who ridiculed the transfer of infallibility from Pope to State. Public indignation rose when it was found that the property confiscated from the orders (including the liqueur works of the Grande

Chartreuse, which had to be captured by force) went to favored private buyers at bargain prices, and that over half the revenues were siphoned off by middlemen (17 of 32 million francs). Combes had boasted that the fortune of the religious orders would go to charity. But before his government's remarkable definition of that word became fully clear, Combes had already fallen, partly on the question of his treatment of the army.

The Waldeck-Rousseau cabinet, with Gallifet and then General André at the War Ministry, had already by retirements and resignations improved the Republicanism of the high command, made promotions subject to the Ministry (an officers' commission had hitherto decided all), and brought the intelligence branch under closer supervision. Under Combes, however, the ambitious André went further, to organize a system of spies, linked with Freemasonry, to report on the suitability of officers for promotion and favors. Republican and anti-clerical officers could clear the way for themselves by reporting on their fellows who attended services, sent their children to Catholic schools, uttered anti-Republican sentiments, or on those, including sincere Republicans, who were merely inconvenient superiors or rivals. This sordid practice was discovered in 1904 and André compelled to resign before irreparable damage was done to army morale, though certain personal and factional rivalries persisted which even the great war did not dissolve. Upon the subsequent discovery that Combes had also organized secret surveillance of elected and civil officials through the Ministry of Interior, his government was branded shameful and "abject" not only by conservatives but by men of the Left, Clemenceau in the Senate, Millerand and Bourgeois in the Chamber. Obeying the decision of the Second International Congress at Amsterdam against participation in bourgeois governments, Jaurès also reluctantly withdrew his support. In January of 1905, Combes submitted his resignation to a hostile President Loubet, and the more moderate Rouvier formed a new cabinet.

Before its fall, the Combes Ministry had prepared the final act of its anti-clerical campaign, the separation of Church and State. The event was hastened by the accession of Pius X to the Papacy in August of 1903. The saintly former Cardinal Sarto of Venice had little of Leo XIII's knowledge of the modern political world and none of his desire to compromise with men found guilty of trespassing on Catholic rights. Pius' rigor was amplified in practice by his intransigent young Spanish Secretary of State, Merry del Val. The Vatican's resentment of Combes' policies and certain of his episcopal appointments prepared the way for a break in diplomatic relations in 1904, when Pius protested an official visit of President Loubet to Victor Emmanuel III as offensive to a Papacy despoiled by the Italian kingdom. A subsequent quarrel concerning each side's authority over bishops—an issue older than the Republic, as old as the Merovingians—further aggravated matters, to Combes' undisguised pleasure. By the autumn of 1904, Combes, the Grand Orient, the Radical party congress, the *Ligue de l'Enseignement*, all demanded the end of the Concordat. Rouvier was forced by the Chamber majority into accepting separation, by the law of December 9, 1905. All clerical salaries were abolished, Catholic, Protestant, and Jewish; duties and privileges of the State and all religious bodies as outlined in the Concordat of 1801 and subsequent laws were abolished; church buildings would remain state property but be loaned to local religious associations, with a lay majority, which would privately collect money for their maintenance and regulate their use.

The last provision, reminiscent of the Civil Constitution of the Clergy, opened the way to schism, or quarrels between laymen and priests, dangerous to the Church's hierarchical authority. Most French bishops were nonetheless inclined to accept it rather than risk the loss of invaluable property so soon after losing clerical salaries. The supple and diplomatic Aristide Briand, who designed the bill to please the anticlericals while keeping it palatable to the clergy, had no desire to prolong what he considered a sterile religious vendetta. His brilliant defense of it in the Chamber, with word and gesture luxuriously blended, was the first of many great performances in a career built upon remarkable knowledge of men and gifts of persuasion. The Rouvier government was no less anxious to apply the law of Separation in a conciliatory manner. But Pius X excommunicated all who voted it and condemned the legislation as contrary to Catholic doctrine (encyclical *Vehementer*, February, 1906). Considering anterior events and the feelings aroused by the expulsions, the reaction was perhaps inevitable. It was, in any case, encouraged by the unbending Merry del Val, the superiors of exiled orders, and other Vatican figures—some of whom were scarcely less hostile to the French Church than to its anti-clerical enemies. French prelates now faced the problem of finding a formula satisfactory to both government and Pope.

There ensued another of those debates between Catholic liberals and intransigents familiar in France since the 1790's. And, as so often before, an act of the government intervened in 1906 to raise tempers even higher and discredit the conciliatory. The law of Separation provided for an inventory of art works and precious objects in the churches, that a clergy hard pressed for funds might be discouraged from selling them at low prices to unscrupulous dealers or—as some already feared—to avid Yankee collectors. The language and manners of a few inventory-takers easily provoked the devout, and both anti-clericals and Catholic intransigents loudly, and falsely, proclaimed that the inventory was a prelude to seizure. Riots spread, young crusaders invaded Sainte-Clotilde in Paris over the pastor's protests, in order to "defend it from government agents"; elsewhere parishioners stood armed guard, fought police, or set animal traps around the altars. After a death in Flanders, Sarrien replaced Rouvier as Premier in March, 1906; Briand became Minister of Religion, and Clemenceau took his first cabinet post as Minister of the Interior. Both men deplored the effects of the inventories, were content to drop them, but to ardent Catholics their names were anathema. Once more, as elections approached, the Right tried to capitalize on religious feelings to return to power. Its loss of some 40 seats showed how little the expulsions and separation touched the masses, or, more likely, how little they trusted the Right on any issue, including religion. The victorious Radicals gave Clemenceau his first premiership and he was, with Briand, determined to bring the religious quarrel to an end.

An Assembly of French bishops in May, 1906, condemned the principle but accepted the practice of the Separation law, provided the religious associations would respect pastoral authority. Pius, concerned lest other governments take heart at a surrender of papal prerogative in France, replied by condemning any accommodation to the law, in the encyclical *Gravissimo*, in August, 1906. After prolonged public dispute in which Rome and the French anti-clericals did all possible to frustrate a compromise between the cabinet and the French hierarchy, the government ordered the evacuation of all seminaries and episcopal buildings. But through Briand's incessant efforts the clergy was left free to use the churches, without the formation of lay associations, by laws of January and March, 1907. The long struggle was over, leaving the Catholic Church in France poorer, and freer, than it had been for nearly a thousand years. The bishops, priests, and Catholic school directors were reduced to begging money from the faithful—not everywhere numerous, or open-handed—but were henceforth free to write, speak, and teach without fear of official pressure and, what was no doubt as important, without the aura of subservience to government about them.

That most Catholics, lay and cleric, thought the losses more weighty than the gains was natural. The calamities borne since 1900 appeared to crown two centuries of defeat and humiliation: the intellectual and moral decline of the upper clergy in the eighteenth century; the desertion of religion by worldly nobles; the seizure of church property in 1790; the persecution of its clergy in the Terror; its enslavement by Napoleon; the progressive de-Christianization of large segments of the urban middle classes, the intellectuals and artists, the workers; since 1870, even the peasantry of several regions; and declining practice among great numbers who stayed Catholic in name. Shackled by events, interests, and sentiment to a lost political cause, Catholicism shared in every retreat. The return of the upper bourgeoisie since the middle of the century, the nobility since the Revolution, did little to comfort priests who saw Christian zeal too often reborn as a social defense or as political expediency. Now the majority of Catholic schools were closed, many orders expelled, the seminaries seized as state property, priests left in poverty, and churches in physical decay. The great medieval cathedrals, half empty behind their broken windows and beheaded statues, were forlorn reminders of what had been, since Charlemagne, the proudest Church in Christendom.

How much of its revival sprang directly from the latest calamity and how much was already building beneath the surface is difficult to measure. The recruitment of priests declined markedly in numbers; but if intellect and energy accompany devotion more often than not, the new were superior to the old, as Pius X predicted they would be. Still, whole regions were to lack enough priests and do to this day, when France, which sent so many missionaries to the world, is herself a mission country, with several rural and industrial areas empty of parishes. Over these greatly reduced numbers, the sole remaining authority was the French episcopate, in its turn more completely subject than ever before in history to the authority of the Vatican, facing it as scattered individuals since Pius X forbade further episcopal assemblies and appointed conservative, politically intransigent priests to high French and Vatican posts.

Material revival was uneven. Wealthy Catholics donated houses or money for seminaries, schools, and residences; some confiscated property was bought back; the government agreed to help maintain those churches old and noted enough to be classed as national monuments, an agreement only partially fulfilled—as any traveler can see—according to the interest of Deputies and to local feeling. Many exiled priests and nuns returned to their teaching posts, in schools directed by secular clergy or by orders which, never having applied for authorization, had simply been left alone. By 1914 there were still a million students in Catholic primary and secondary schools, but state schools had three times as many and the proportion steadily increased in their favor.

Overall, the poverty and demonstrated political weakness of the Church appeased French anti-clericalism and the great war softened the old quarrel. The intellectual revival of French Catholicism, with its roots in the pontificate of Leo XIII, continued and was probably speeded by the separation, which attracted ardent French spirits to a faith now unencumbered by wealth and its corollary, political interference. In their eagerness to catch up to the latest intellectual currents, to recapture the long-lost respect of the French historical and scientific community for the Church, certain priests—the Abbé Alfred Loisy was the most prominent—appeared overquick to dilute Catholic doctrine in adapting it to the findings of biology, geology, archeology, and Biblical studies. Although the majority of scholar-priests were more prudent, and many of Loisy's own ideas have since been accepted, the Vatican forcibly condemned "Modernism" (encyclical *Pascendi*, September, 1907). The intransigents in Rome and France grossly misapplied it to all inquiring, or social and democratic, Catholics. But the reaction passed with time and the advent of a new Pope, Benedict XV, in 1914. By then, the main stream of Modernism and the vigorous neo-Thomist movement (whose leading figure was to be the convert Jacques Maritain), together with a flow of Catholic literary and scholarly works, lay and clerical, had gone far to prove Catholicism able to confront the intellectual problems of the nineteenth and twentieth centuries.

In facing up to social and political problems French Catholics were less successful, except for a promising group called *Le Sillon* (the furrow) inspired by Marc Sangnier. Even before the relative failure of Albert de Mun, Lamy, and the Christian democratic movement of the 1890's, Sangnier assembled a number of young men in 1894 pledged to ally Catholicism to social democracy, to bring young bourgeois intellectuals and workers together on the same footing for each other's education. In seeking to apply Christian ethics and charity to the betterment of man's life on earth, the *Sillon* faced the task of reconciling forces separated by a century of contention: Catholicism and Republicanism, Christianity and socialism, bourgeoisie and workers, spirituality and material progress. Sangnier's magnetic person and his followers' devotion spread the movement throughout France, assembling by 1914 some 10,000 young men and women of all classes, arousing their fervor by attacks on poverty, on profiteers, on repression of minorities (Jews in France, Jews in Russia), on militarism and chauvinism, on class exploitation, on materialism, whether capitalist or socialist. The workers, they said, must themselves enjoy an education fully equal to that of their oppressors and of their self-appointed leaders; then, with democratic Catholics of all classes they would form the vanguard of a new society free of the hatreds left by history. The Church, said Sangnier, would be refined by suffering and material losses, and Catholics would deserve the name only by defending all men who suffered poverty or injustice. The clergy who clung to class privilege, or to narrowly Catholic politics based on Rightist parties, only prepared new disasters for Christianity in France.

After 1907, Sangnier moved into broader political grounds, organizing the "greater *Sillon*" embracing non-Catholics who were willing to accept his premise that "democracy alone can bring the reign of perfect justice." In the superheated aftermath of the religious struggle, Sangnier was soon under attack from anti-clericals and from Catholic conservatives supported by the hierarchy and the Vatican which had earlier honored him. Priests were forbidden to take part in the *Sillon;* and in 1910, Pius X condemned the movement as wrongly desiring to level all classes, to upset the "natural and traditional" bases of Christian society. The *Sillon* was "a wretched tributary of organized apostasy"; its members should submit forthwith to diocesan organization under the bishops, around whom the Papacy in these years was vainly seeking to organize yet another conservative Catholic party. The royalist Action Française and Charles Maurras enjoyed favor at Rome and among French prelates, who denounced the *Sillon* for daring to associate Catholicism with a particular form of government, for subordinating religion to the interest of a political party. Despite this provocation and the one-sidedness of the papal condemnation, Sangnier and most of his followers submitted. The *Sillon* was dissolved, the small minority of Catholic social democrats was compelled to find other paths to the future. With the advent of a new spirit at the Vatican—and subsequently among French bishops— Sangnier and the Sillonists, together with the followers of de Mun, the

Christian democrats, and the Catholic trade unions, were to nourish Catholic social democracy between the wars.

## RADICAL CONSERVATISM

It remained to be seen whether Republicanism would be as refined by its victory as Catholicism had been by its defeat. After what most Republicans saw as forty years of battle against political and clerical reaction, the elections of 1906 seemed a final vindication of their ideas. The Right won only 180 seats in all, 30 for the nationalists, 80 for the various conservatives and *Ralliés* combined, 70 for the *Fédération Républicaine*. The socialists of different hues elected 70, Radical-Socialists 240, and other Republicans (including the Centrist *Alliance Démocratique*) 90. Senator Georges Clemenceau became Premier of France for the first time in October of 1906, a few months after an electoral campaign in which he and the Radicals had promised to enact long-delayed economic and social reforms: a graduated income tax, the eight-hour day, workers' insurance and compensation, the nationalization of monopolies, and old-age pensions. Clemenceau kept the Ministry of the Interior and chose a promising group of Ministers: Briand, who had left socialism behind, was Minister of Education and Religion; General Picquart, Minister of War; and Joseph Caillaux, the Radicals' most prominent economic expert and advocate of the income tax, Minister of Finance; a new Ministry of Labor was given to the socialist René Viviani. Although refusing a part in government, the socialists in the Chamber were ready to tolerate a cabinet which promised social justice to all Frenchmen.

Its performance was to be otherwise. As Minister of the Interior under Sarrien, Clemenceau had already used troops to choke a miners' strike in the Pas de Calais, which followed an underground explosion killing more than a thousand men (March, 1906). The company's notorious neglect of safety precautions notwithstanding, Clemenceau determined that property and public order must be preserved; strikers had a right to strike, but strikebreakers had a right to work. Under this benevolent social doctrine, soldiers protected the latter and several fatal clashes resulted. Clemenceau then arrested the leaders of the CGT who had called a mass protest demonstration in Paris for May 1st. In answer to Jaurès' attack in the Chamber, the Tiger who had lacerated so many Ministers as defenders of privileged interests calmly replied that he was now "on the other side of the barricades." It took months of new promises, a general amnesty for arrested strikers, and the creation of a Labor Ministry to assuage socialist resentment; but not long after Clemenceau had taken office as Premier another wave of labor troubles was met by another series of repressive measures.

Soldiers marched to the sound of strikes, union organizers were arrested, *agents provocateurs* and police spies derailed union action, giving employers excuses to avoid collective bargaining, pushing workers to violence, to disillusion, or into the hands of progressively more revolutionary leaders. When thousands of small winegrowers of the south requested official aid against phylloxera and falling prices from Italian and African competition, the government merely counseled patience. As mass demonstrations threatened to disturb the peace (some say 700,000 gathered at Montpellier in June of 1907), Clemenceau sent troops and arrested the leaders, which resulted in violence and a mutiny of peasant soldiers. The gentle rustic Marcellin Albert, whom the growers idolized as "king of the destitute," was coldly received by the Premier, who packed him off with a hundred francs and orders to send his followers back to their farms. Disciplined troops ended the affair. When Caillaux's income tax project passed the Chamber in 1907, Clemenceau fell silent when his help was needed in the Senate, which rejected it. Although the cabinet lasted nearly three years—the longest of the Third Republic —not a single major reform was enacted to deal with the condition of labor or of the poor. The one gesture was nationalization of the Western Railroad, at great profit to the owners, who were then allowed to neglect it until the government assumed control in 1910.

The retreat of the Radicals, after a generation of promises, after the vaunted solidarity of the Left in the Dreyfus crisis and in the assault on the Church, disillusioned many generous spirits, particularly among the young, who had expected the Radical Republic to do something more with its victory than defend established interests. To many who had believed in them, the Radicals appeared already old and congealed, their familiar battle cries laughable substitutes for ideas, proof that they were unable, or unwilling, to distinguish dead issues from live ones. The desertion of Republican parties by the educated, urban young and by working men after 1900 was a serious blow to Republican institutions and thus to the chances of social compromise. If the Third Republic lacked young leaders between the World Wars, desertion before 1914 was perhaps as responsible as the great loss of life in war itself. New intellectual currents supplanted the quasi-official Republican ideology of positivism. And new movements, Marxism and syndicalism on the Left, integral nationalism on the Right, also contributed to the drift of lively spirits out of Republican politics.

The sources of Radical *immobilisme* were many. Not the least were Clemenceau's misunderstanding of social issues much changed in the forty years since his difficult days at Montmartre, his preoccupation with other questions—the German threat and military preparedness first among them—his jealousy of colleagues like Caillaux, his sinking view of human nature in general, and his basic conservatism, so long hidden behind a fiery temperament. To those who had welcomed the *Ralliément,* Clemenceau had retorted that "the Revolution is a bloc," to be accepted wholeheartedly or not at all, something the Catholics would not do. But his revolution, like that of most Republicans, was radical only in politics and religion; Babeuf was not of his bloc, nor was Robespierre. Of the heroes, Clemenceau most resembled Danton. A decade later, France would need a new Danton, but in 1906 something more modern might have served her better.

Like all political systems, the Third Republic raised its own bars to timely reform: executive weakness; the cabinet's vulnerability to repeated debates provoked by Deputies unafraid of dissolution; the multiple parties pressing cabinets to compromise; the conservative force of civil servants who knew much better than Ministers could the workings of their bureaus and who stayed on to administer—or, with the Council of State's cooperation, to forget—legislation long after Ministers had departed; the growth of permanent parliamentary committees able to harry both Ministers and bureaucrats; the Deputies' appeasement of local interests, often at high cost to the nation; the jealous watch over them by local electors fearful of power's tendency to corrupt; and the corruption, petty or otherwise, which did appeal to career politicians with fortunes to make. Each helped to detour or negate vital legislative programs, to discredit Republican institutions and the parties in power. But other nations have had comparable defects and yet managed to deal in time with pressing issues. It is not at all certain that any political reform—as long as it left the government free and representative—would have insured swifter action.

More important, the parties in power were out of credit only among minorities in France, not with the mass of electors. Clemenceau's and later cabinets depended mainly on the Radical-Socialists and Republicans of the Center. By 1900, the Radicals represented markedly different segments of society than in the days of the Belleville manifesto. No longer the party of the urban poor and the workers, it drew its strength from small bourgeois, from small towns, from peasant proprietors, from men—in that familiar phrase—whose hearts were on the Left but whose pocketbooks were on the Right. An income tax touching only the wealthy might be acceptable, but not a tax that compelled them to reveal their own affairs. Laws that limited big business were welcome, but not a welfare program that threatened to raise their taxes. It was one thing to embrace the socialist Left in order to defend the Republic and laïcisme from the Right, but once defended, the Republic's duty was to protect their interests. If to do so, their leaders were forced to ally themselves with parties to the Right drawn from the bourgeoisie and higher realms of commerce, industry, and banking, it was a lesser evil. This alternation was to typify French politics to the Second World War, was the main impulse behind that frequent "drift to the Right" of Chambers elected on political issues and then forced to deal with economics. For forty years, the Radical Socialists determined the style of the Third Republic. Their popular spokesman, "Alain" (Émile Chartier), never ceased to defend the rights and individuality of the "little" against "the others": bureaucracy, big business, organized labor, the orthodoxies of religion or military life or conservative politics, and all those too eager for economic and political power to be honnêtes hommes. Small-minded and cautious as it was, this orthodoxy had honorable ancestry coming down from the great Revolution, appeared to be justified by a century's struggle against "the others," and, at its best, encouraged men to nurture their own individual spirits. It was probably both a source and an effect of France's failure to keep pace with other nations in modern industry, mass production and consumption, social legislation, and common civic action.

That the majority of Frenchmen felt little need for any of these novelties before 1914 meant that no political system sensitive to public opinion would exert itself to provide them, particularly one as representative of the countryside and small town as the parliament of the Third Republic. Chances for social reform were further lessened until shortly before 1914 by the factional rivalries and numerical weakness of workers' organizations. After the Amsterdam Congress of the Second International in 1904, where the Guesdists forced Jaurès and most of the socialist Deputies to end their alliance with the Republican parties, Guesde and Jaurès combined in 1905 to form a single socialist party, the Section Française de l'Internationale Ouvrière (SFIO). But unity was far from perfect; the active rank and file tended, with Guesde, to orthodox Marxism, while the parliamentary delegation, with Jaurès, kept the reformist tone set by Millerand at Saint-Mandé several years before. The party, outside parliament and inside, suffered from several other weaknesses. Nearly one-third of the 70 Socialists elected in 1906 preferred to call themselves independents and were on balance less militant than Jaurès. Socialist discipline and the confidence of the workers in bourgeois leadership were further broken by the desertion of prominent Deputies more anxious to make policy (or careers) than to keep the label of a party whose national structure was too weak to be a help or a threat to them; Millerand, Briand, and Viviani all accepted cabinet office. Many militants expected Jaurès to be next; in fact, he never broke his pledge of Amsterdam, but his moderation, his warm friendships outside the party, even his facile, florid oratory were held against him. Worse, he had held the party for years to a sterile alliance with Radicals who now repudiated social progress.

All this contributed to the party's fundamental weakness, its failure to command the financial and organizational help of the working masses. Events had provided the French worker with several institutions claiming his allegiance: a local benefit, credit, or insurance society, a local union, a local or regional bourse, a national union council (all or none might be affiliated with the CGT), and at least one socialist faction. His time and his few extra francs were most likely to be contributed in that order and, if he were a militant unionist, the Socialists might get nothing, perhaps not even his vote; for the union member, imbued with the idea (called ouvriérisme) that workers alone could be trusted, was likely to be suspicious of any political party in the years before World War I.

French unionism was as divided as the Socialist party itself. As the latter failed to mobilize the political strength of the working class, so the unions failed to enlist enough workers to make use of their potential economic strength. Strikes, slowdowns, boycotts petered out for lack of funds, trained leadership, and solidarity, or were broken by government action whenever workers in their weakness resorted to the only weapons left, sabotage and violence against employers and strikebreakers. Only in a few skilled trades did union action bring satisfactory results; again, the printers led the way. In many large and medium-sized plants, industrial labor was weak and, because weak, violent and susceptible to the creeds of anarchism and revolutionary syndicalism. When the CGT and the *Fédération des Bourses du Travail* merged in 1902, neither gained clear authority over the other or over the loosely affiliated local unions, which in turn counted not more than 500,000 members, one-tenth of French industrial workers. But the new organization took the name CGT; and its leaders, revolutionary syndicalists like Victor Griffuelhes, were long identified with the entire union movement in the public mind, an illusion which the bourgeois press was pleased to nurture.

The CGT Congress of Amiens in 1906 voted a charter that repeated its refusal to be bound to any political party or to a parliamentary program based on the doubtful premise that universal suffrage alone would ultimately create a socialist state. Instead the CGT declared the general strike to be the best way of overturning capitalist society. It would open the way to an economy of workers' syndicates, autonomous and collective societies of production foreseen by Proudhon and Bakunin. But the syndicalist movement suffered, as Marxists said, from several inner contradictions. It was strong in France because there the spirit of "federalism" or local autonomy dominated the unions, for reasons as diverse as the ideas of Proudhon and Alain, the tradition of the Commune, the primacy of local unions, and the habit of withholding union dues. But the way to a syndicalist society was the general strike—of all mass actions the one most dependent on unbroken national discipline. To stimulate class-consciousness and militancy, local strikes, sabotage, and, where anarchists persisted, even terrorism were encouraged, whether tied to specific economic demands or not. But such action appealed only to a doubtful kind of elite, repelled many other workers, aroused the employers and the state to brutal repression, and—the final contradiction—was in fact relatively scarce considering all the violent language and the hard conditions of French labor. As a substitute for numbers, strike funds, and discipline, the theory of violent action never sufficed and it is symbolic that its most famous exposition, Georges Sorel's *Reflections on Violence,* was the work of an outsider, an engineer-intellectual, and appeared only in 1908, when reformist ideas, always present, appeared to be gaining favor among union leaders.

## THE HESITANT ECONOMY

Even had Socialists and unionists found unity within and between their movements, and exerted all possible pressure on government and employers, it is doubtful that the working class could have won significant legislation. It was, first of all, still not large enough to hold a balance of power in society before the First World War. France was not an industrial country; her economic development since the Second Empire had not yet destroyed the preponderance of agricultural property and workers. Of some 40 million people in 1914, almost half still worked the land; few more than 10 million lived in towns of over 20,000; another 10 million in towns between 20,000 and 2000. Nearly as important, the proliferation of small retail outlets, with great numbers of people engaged in handling rather than producing goods, meant an unusually large lower middle class. Finally, industry itself remained strikingly small in scale compared with American, British, and German, preserving that familiar balance between artisans and proletarians which proved so divisive in the social struggle. Even at the beginning of the twentieth century only 150 industrial works had more than 1000 employees, the national average per establishment was 6, and only 40,000 of 575,000 workshops employed more than 10.

Although French national production rose steadily to 1914 (as did per capita income), industrial and agricultural labor's share in rising living standards was notably smaller than that of other classes. Even more unpromising for France's future social welfare—and national power—her rate of industrial growth and foreign trade fell seriously behind that of other advanced countries. In 1870, French trade was second in value only to Great Britain's; though it roughly doubled by 1914, it had slipped to fourth place, behind Germany and the United States. Coal production rose from 14 million tons in 1870 to 41 million in 1913, but Britain produced 292 million by then and Germany nearly as much; France was forced to import from both; of iron and steel, France's 5 million tons of 1913 was less than a third of Germany's output. These industries were, like textiles, reduced by the transfer of Alsace-Lorraine to Germany in 1871, but France's failure to keep pace in other fields showed that more complicated factors were working to slow her economic expansion. Among industries developed mainly since

1870 were chemicals, explosives, aluminum, rayon, electrical products, rubber, automobiles, and machine tools—in all of which Frenchmen had led in invention or early refinements, only to see other nations surpass them in production and distribution.

The most valuable export products of French industry were, as they long had been and were to remain until after the Second World War, textiles, luxury goods, and specialties. The Paris dressmaking industry, whose great era had opened with the Empress Eugénie's patronage of the House of Worth, increased its hegemony over the fashion world. Perfumes (almost alone among French industries to take full advantage of advances in chemistry), laces, silks, glass and chinaware, furniture and tapestries—all the items coveted by the prosperous American and English bourgeoisie, together with the tourist trade, were vital in maintaining the French balance of payments. Many were, at the same time, the most sweated of industries, in which women in particular were exploited with impunity. Agriculture increased its productivity, though the small farm remained typical and modernization was as uneven as always. As under the Second Empire, better transport encouraged area specialization. The Third Republic doubled the traffic on the canals, built an additional 30,000 kilometers of rails and thousands more of roads which for their day were the best in the world and should, but for the high cost of imported oil and gasoline, and even higher taxes, have speeded the automotive industry. But the trucking business languished (as the French army was to discover to its sorrow in the World Wars), and it was more often on rails and canals favored by the government that the best products of French fields, orchards, and pastures traveled to Les Halles, and thence, at notoriously high shipping and transfer costs, to the tables of those western Europeans who could afford them. The wine industry slowly revived from the phylloxera, with the aid of resistant American graftings. By 1914, climate, soil, and local genius had selected the great *pays* of wine: the Côte d'Or, Champagne, the Bordelais, corners along the Yonne, the Loire, the Saône, Rhône, and Tarn, in Roussillon and Languedoc. Clemenceau's abrupt treatment of the southern winegrowers was an exception to the generally favorable policy of the Republic toward the farmer; agricultural schools, testing stations, and touring experts were offered and, above all, a comfortably high tariff.

Her balance between agriculture and industry and her great variety of products made France highly self-sufficient and slower to be depressed by world economic conditions, though she rarely escaped their ultimate effects. But industrial lethargy, outmoded methods, inability to utilize her resources and skills, prepared her badly for the twentieth century, put heavy burdens on the lowest classes, bred disenchantment and weakness in the face of her old rivals, Germany and Great Britain. Historians continue to debate the reasons for France's failure to maintain the economic exuberance of the Second Empire. Some are so obvious as to be often overlooked. The Empire started from a far smaller base; even with limited resources and spirit, it would have been easier to achieve a high rate of growth; the Republic's effort was spread over several added industries; it had lost two productive departments to Germany; also, the rate of growth was uneven—slow in the first three decades of the period 1870–1914, faster after 1900. The two periods roughly coincided with outside trade conditions and also with inner changes: from the effects of defeat and Republican instability to domestic peace and higher colonial and military expenditures, from disease to cure in wine, from quiet invention and experiment to the building of new industries. Other reasons are more familiar, nearly as hard to measure, and can be described (though hardly separated) as economic, cultural, or political, and one which may be called all three: an aging population with falling birth rate.

France lacked materials vital to a modern economy: coal, oil, and iron ore, until 1900 when new smelting methods made the ore in French Lorraine profitable to mine. As in most of the nineteenth century, the high cost of power to run machines, already costly to make, slowed concentration and preserved the smaller shop. Capital for industrial expansion was also costly, especially for enterprises threatening to compete with those in favor with the banks; and capital was drawn out of France by investment in high-yield foreign government bonds, notably Russian, in colonial ventures (although not mainly French), in choice securities of other European states, and in the capital-hungry Americas. The returns on foreign investment no doubt were spent mostly on French goods, when they were spent at all. Still, home investment probably would have enlivened basic industries. Whether higher production would have found a home market very quickly is less certain; the marginal income of the masses kept demand low, and the distaste of higher classes for mass-produced goods is legendary. A stagnant population with fixed means and tastes promised no great reward for American-style enterprise. In short, French bankers and the investing public sent their money where returns were highest at the time, showing what economists call reasonable capitalist behavior.

Thrift and prudence, unfortunately, are only part of modern capitalism, and observers who see French cultural factors retarding economic progress find uncapitalist attitudes at work. Rather than taking advantage of their technical and financial superiority, large firms often (not always) allowed smaller, weaker rivals to survive. The high incidence of family firms content with limited profits, under little pressure from investors to expand, is often cited, as is a bourgeoisie preferring to devote its time—once enough money was assured—to pleasure and distinction in other fields. French workers often criticized their employers and managers for an unenterprising spirit. But the introduction of new machines, time studies, and scientific management was also resisted, especially in those factories (the majority) where the workers were denied a share in increased productivity. At the same time, tariffs kept inefficient small producers going, insuring wider profit margins for larger, modern firms already enjoying the lion's share of a limited market. Class cohesion and political cooperation between the higher and lower bourgeoisie may have played a part as well, especially in the face of dangers from the Left. Tradition, taste, family feeling, Republican political theory and tactics worked to benefit the small, varied, independent manufacturers, retailers, and farmers. The domination of American life and politics by a plutocratic few who forced cheap standardized goods on overworked helots was already a familiar tale in France before 1914. The French view of the good life, which was to be a lively source of suspicion between the two peoples after the First World War, involved less the owning of things than the enjoyment of individual human services: domestic help, the café and restaurant, the dressmaker and tailor, the special pleasures of a neighborhood market, and the half dozen shops independently owned that one American grocery store embraced. But other peoples, who surpassed the French in economic progress, had many of the same tastes; too much can be made of what the French preferred as opposed to what was offered. The lower classes, in particular, had very little choice. Once their clothing, rooms, and bread were paid, if anything at all remained in reach, it was likely to be meat or vegetables, the café, or the park, not the products of modern industry.

On this point turns the debate over the effect of the protective tariffs raised by Republican politicians since the 1880's, culminating in the Méline tariff of 1892. As high tariffs coincided with a period of relative prosperity, they were easily defended in the Chamber, but economic historians are much divided on the part protection played in discouraging innovation and enterprise. Falling prices in the 1880's had made them politically advisable; as Republicans sought to win the rural vote, farmers were rewarded with security, the small farm survived, and modernization could be put off. This, together with the reluctance of Frenchmen to leave their familiar *pays,* discouraged the mobility that, however doleful, seems necessary to a modern economy. But French foodstuffs remained among the most expensive in Europe, drawing an unnecessarily large part of labor and petty bourgeois income. Other French products were priced out of the world market or excluded in retaliation. Apart from tariffs, other essentially political factors appeared. Banks and citizens were urged to invest in Russian bonds, to bolster France's main ally, especially as the Tsardom reeled under the Japanese War and the Revolution of 1905.

Republican politicians who had fought their battles and built careers on legal, political, and religious issues found economic problems new and uncongenial, the more so as their class interests seemed secure enough as matters stood. Economics was the language of their class enemies, a subject usually omitted from the traditionally classical school curricula, as were science and technology. In the latter fields, the great schools dating from the old regime and the Revolution kept up their standards, but the numbers of graduates fell far below the needs of a modern industrial society. Before 1914, and despite all its oratory on progress through science, the Third Republic starved scientific research and technical facilities, did almost nothing to aid students. At the turn of the century, Pierre and Marie Curie worked in jumbled squalor; many students in science, who were neglected by Republicans and distrusted by political and religious conservatives, early displayed an affinity for socialism. Whether French schools, industry, or business actively sought them is questionable, for many went abroad to find work and distinction. How well the government understood their importance to a nation's power is revealed in the practice of commissioning graduates of the Écoles Normale and Polytechnique as combat second lieutenants; whole classes were slain in the first years of the great war. Many political leaders were not only ill-informed on economic matters, but allied in sentiment and financial interest with the business community. The government was rarely free, as the Second Empire had partly been, to encourage innovation that threatened the establishment, whether in taxation, tariff, regulation, or public enterprise. In short, a government too benevolent to business interests did much to hamper free enterprise.

Another aspect of France's relative lethargy was a steady decline in the birth rate. From 36 million in 1871, Frenchmen increased to only 39 million in 1914; unlike Britain, Germany, and especially America, France had no great new demand for the necessities of life to spur production. From the Napoleonic days when France had been literally *la Grande Nation* with 15 per cent of Europe's people, she had fallen to fourth place by 1914; Russia had 130 million excluding Finland, Germany 68 million (with 7.8 million men of military age to France's 4.5 million), and Great Britain 44 million. The French reproduction rate from 1870 to 1914 was under 1.0 and French population increased only because of greater longevity and immigration, particularly of young male workers from Spain, Italy, Belgium, and Poland. French emigrants after 1870 were numerous only to Algeria and Tunis; but they never equaled immigrants and the outward flow dwindled by 1900. The French birth rate, which fell to only 18 per thousand by 1914, was already attributed by foreign critics and by Frenchmen themselves to lack of confidence in the nation's future, or to that moral decadence so often reported by tourists returning from their favored Paris haunts. But the facts were less simple. Although worse than elsewhere, the decline of births in France only preceded comparable declines in other industrialized societies in the century after 1850. In much of the western world, families became smaller as living standards rose or, perhaps more exactly, as a rise in social or economic status appeared within reach of those prudent and knowledgeable enough to limit their families. With the advent of compulsory education and restrictions on child labor, even working-class families were smaller than in the first era of industrialization, when children could earn wages at ten or even younger. Now parents ambitious for their children calculated closely, to give them the expensive, protracted education needed for success, or to satisfy their own desires for the comforts and amusements of modern life.

In France, the demographic crisis was hastened and aggravated by the Napoleonic Code's stipulation that offspring share inheritances. Peasants who would otherwise have welcomed many hands restricted their families lest the division of their already small property return the heirs to penury (a calculation even more compelling for young fathers who did not yet own property but expected to). Two other conditions appear to have been worse in France than elsewhere by 1900:

housing and alcoholism. Haussmann's exertions under the Empire had not come close to housing the newcomers to Paris itself. Far less was done in the suburbs and other cities, and in workers' housing the Third Republic did almost nothing. The dirty gray façades of the Restoration or earlier, so picturesque to the few tourists who ventured into the poorer districts, hid dank, crowded, rat-infested, and noisome tenements without heat, toilets, or running water. Here disease cut short the lives of children deprived of food, sunlight, and exercise, and of young adults weakened by alcoholism, which cheap Algerian wine spread among the poorest classes. The per capita consumption of wine and spirits probably tripled in the two generations before 1914. The sunniest villages were often no more healthy, the poorer peasants and day laborers penned in huts as grimy as the shanties along Paris' walls and farther from medicine of any sort. The great scourge of tuberculosis touched all classes, rural and urban, to haunt the life and literature of Pasteur's country until after the Second World War. The rate of stillbirths and infant mortality remained scandalously high, to decimate the families of many who desired more children.

## LA BELLE ÉPOQUE

The years before 1914 are often called "La Belle Époque," but the term hardly applied to society in general and means, in part, that what followed brought added misery to most and insecurity to many who had been comfortable. The Paris Exposition of 1900 is remembered with nostalgia; but among its darker spots are two that illustrate French problems. The exhibits of other nations showed that France had slipped in industry and technology, and the crowds of prostitutes were swollen by working girls whose salaries were derisory. Each was symptomatic of an economy sunk in privileged laissez-faire. All industrial nations had evils enough for the day—English cities had their fetid slums, New York its great Triangle fire of 1911, killing 150 helpless sweatshop workers—but the Third Republic was last in enterprise and, with the United States, in social legislation. There were a few laws, loosely drawn and indifferently enforced. In 1898, the employers' responsibility for accidents on the job was recognized in principle; in 1903, a law on sanitation in factories; in 1906, a law obliging employers to grant one day of rest in seven; in 1910, the beginnings of an optional pension system; various laws purporting to limit hours of work, the most meaningful being a general ten-hour day in 1900 and an eight-hour day for miners (1905). Nearly 3 million agricultural day laborers had not even these in their favor, and in practice the majority of industrial or commercial employees worked more than ten hours a day, at least six days a week without vacation, with few reserves or aid in case of illness, accident, unemployment, or old age. On them and on the petty bourgeoisie rested the main burden of taxation.

The happier side of France—some, of course, experienced something of both sides—has more often been told. A gradual rise in real wages developed after 1900. Meat, sugar, coffee, vegetables appeared on most family tables. The flow of immigration from southern and eastern Europe, as from the countryside, suggests that even the lower classes in France were (or appeared to be) better rewarded than the mass of Europeans. And as the great war would show, even the poorest districts bred men of vigor, tenacity, and pride. La Belle Époque nonetheless offered far more to that broad band of middle-class Frenchmen, from all but the poorest farmers and shopkeepers to business magnates, who gathered much the largest share of the nation's growing wealth. The nobility survived in great numbers and a minority retained substantial wealth in land alone. Others intermarried with bourgeois dynasties in industry and banking, some entered business for themselves. But the bourgeoisie dominated most of the nation's life, from bank to Chamber bench to communal councils. As the franc had kept its value since the Restoration, life itself appeared predictable. A certain number of bonds, of acres, of children, a certain level of sales, of extra work, of yearly savings, assured a certain kind of future. The government they controlled thus satisfied, for them, the temporal aims of the French Revolution, no small reason for confidence and loyalty among those who possessed or seemed about to. After a war which struck down family, franc, and certainty, the good years were likely to be recalled as better than they were, as more innocent, more amusing than any era is.

Like their fathers who had sighed for the gas-lit Empire, or as Americans would for the Gay Nineties, many Frenchmen were to remember La Belle Époque for its novelties, its celebrities and entertainments. The automobile, the airplane, the moving picture, the first craze for sports, impassioned the young well before 1914. Louis Blériot flew the English Channel in 1909; two other Louis, Renault and Chevrolet, turned from auto-racing to auto-making, one at home, the other in America, where he was, prophetically, bought out by men who turned his varied models into one for mass production. The bicycle finally came within the purchasing power of the masses, giving them new mobility, and new heroes, as the annual Tour de France began in 1903. Football and boxing had their heroes, too, and gentler games like tennis, though the frenetic age of spectator sports in France, as in America, lay ahead in the 1920's, with that of the moving pictures. Older Frenchmen preferred to remember La Belle Époque as starting with the Exposition and Centennial of 1889; it was doubtless more spirited and original than the garish Exposition of 1900, which left to Paris, as its most subdued creations, the Pont Alexandre III, the Grand and Petit Palais. In 1900 visitors saw the opening, in July, of the first Métro line (Porte de Vincennes–Maillot); they could watch Sarah Bernhardt at 56 in Rostand's *L'Aiglon,* though his *Cyrano* of 1897 was still more popular, or hear, in quite a different key, Yvette Guilbert sing of Paris' cruelty to lovers. On Montmartre, the Moulin Rouge was by then startling only to tourists, like that intrepid proper American, Richard Harding Davis, whose illustrator, Charles Dana Gibson, gave the dancers a softer mien than did Toulouse-Lautrec. Farther up the hill, the little café Lapin Agile had just begun to attract the writers and artists whose later fame would make it celebrated. Their work and that of their fellow painters, musicians, poets, novelists, and sculptors made the good years an epoch of beauty and intellectual distinction, shedding luster on the Third Republic, despite the near-impossibility of relating a period's creativity to its politics.

Since Gustave Courbet had signaled the end of the Empire and, he hoped, all privileged society by pulling down the Vendôme column in 1871, French painting had wrought revolutions of its own, more astounding than any political or social overturn could have been. By 1914, the language of painting, which had been immediately comprehensible to all men since the paleolithic artists of Lascaux, had broken into abstract tongues each viewer had to learn for himself. Before the turn of the century, conventional artists continued to dominate the academies and to sell their works to government and public. Many, like Moreau, Puvis de Chavannes, and Bouguereau, were deservedly honored in their day. But the future, as far as the intelligentsia was concerned, belonged to men who moved further from the public than the romantics had ever done. Their quarrels with society were not mainly political or social, no matter how subversive the establishment considered them, but aesthetic. Painting, like poetry, was for art's sake, or for friends and fellow artists; if some considered mankind, it was to deepen its perception of the world, not to guide its actions. Even under the Empire, Daumier and Courbet were exceptions in their social concern; both died in the first decade of the Republic, as did the gentler Corot and Millet. If they were honored, it was as men, and craftsmen who had painted contemporary folk and landscapes, had turned from the shaded studio to bright open air, or, with Delacroix, Boudin, and the Englishmen Constable and Turner, had suggested new ways of capturing the subtleties (and "distortions") of outdoor light and color. The innovations of the Empire had been mainly in subject matter and its candid treatment, as in the realism of Courbet's "Stone-Breakers" (1850) and Manet's "Luncheon on the Grass" (1863).

In 1874, an independent show announced a new school, impressionism, derisively named for Claude Monet's "Impression, Sunrise." The impressionists—Monet, Sisley, Pissarro, Berthe Morisot, Bazille, Renoir, for a time Degas and Manet himself—diffused form and design in lights and shadows. Some painted in multiple detached strokes of color which broke light, shadow, and reflection down for the eye of the viewer to reassemble. As scientists had known, light was color and color, light; the fusion of divided colors in the eye gave livelier hues than colors mixed on the palette. The painter sought to capture what he saw in his first moments at a scene, the essential impression, rather than photographic reproduction. Monet especially pursued the technique to delightful ends in his many studies of Rouen Cathedral and Waterloo Bridge at different times of day. By 1886, when they held their last common exhibition, the impressionists themselves, and others who had shared their discoveries, returned to an interest in design and composition. Thus Degas, Manet, Renoir were also post-impressionists, with Seurat, Van Gogh, Gauguin, and Cézanne. At the exhibition of 1886 appeared Seurat's "Sunday Afternoon on the Island of Grande Jatte," done with precisely placed points of color (*divisionisme* or *pointillisme*) and sharply outlined forms in studied composition. In Van Gogh, Gauguin, and Toulouse-Lautrec appeared the influence of Japanese prints and the vivid color of various primitive arts; each was estranged from society, and their unhappy lives did much to set the stereotype of the artist as victim of society, which others would take on as a pose. Van Gogh and Gauguin presented their own emotions and visions on canvas, exaggerating colors and distorting shapes to force the viewer into recognition of the good and evil that lay beneath, or outside, his normal, lazy observations of a world grown ugly. Van Gogh approached abstraction, as in his "Wheatfield with Blackbirds" (1890). With Cézanne, at first glance more conventional, another step was taken toward abstraction. More than essential atmosphere, or essential symbol or mood, he sought essential forms of objects, treating nature, as he advised a younger man, "in terms of cylinder, sphere and cone," and using planes of color to portray shape and perspective, sometimes under several lights or points of view at once. On even the most literal-minded (perhaps on them especially) the impressionists and post-impressionists imposed unshakable ways of seeing, or recalling, the French countryside, villages and people, *la vie parisienne*. No other country has been so vividly painted into man's imagination.

The Salon d'Automne in 1905 first brought the *Fauves* to public view, and critical derision. Together with the German expressionists, they continued and exaggerated the subjective freedom with form and color of Van Gogh and Gauguin, the unconventional perspectives of Cézanne. Retrospective exhibitions of the three helped inspire Derain, Dufy, Rouault, Vlaminck, and Henri Matisse, as did their growing interest in primitive and Oriental arts, and the vogue of a contemporary French "primitive," the self-taught Henri Rousseau (*le Douanier*). Their often starkly simple lines and clashing colors earned them the epithet *Fauves* (wild beasts); but they, with Bonnard, Utrillo, Chagall, Modigliani, Rousseau, and Jacques Villon, differed too widely in their signatures to be considered under any single school. Then, as if to fix irrevocably the new pluralism of painting styles, Pablo Picasso came from Spain to epitomize several schools in a succession of "periods." In 1910, he and Georges Braque founded the unfortunately named style of cubism. In Picasso's "Young Ladies of Avignon" (1907) and Braque's "Road near l'Estaque" (1908), Cézanne's techniques were carried to the verge of abstraction; and in the years before the war, as Picasso's "Accordionist" (1911) illustrates, cubism portrayed objects as seen from different vantage points, at different times, in geometrical patterns. The various adaptations of abstractionism and cubism opened to painters and their publics new worlds of form and idea which, as science was finding, as mystics and philosophers had always said, existed in time and memory as well as in the daily three-dimensional world.

French poetry in the same period traveled partly along the same paths. After the Parnassians, whose severe, objective verse paralleled the realist and positivist revolt against romanticism, new poets appeared, well acquainted with their counterparts in painting, who sought to express similar new perceptions of reality through symbols and tones of word and rhythm, to suggest emotion or idea rather than to name it. Charles Baudelaire (1821–1867), who as a youth had followed the romantics in the social dreams of 1848, had championed the rejected painters of his time, was also the precursor of symbolism in poetry, seeking his imagery in dream and fantasy. Verlaine, Rimbaud, Mallarmé, Jules Laforgue, then Valéry and Apollinaire followed in the years from 1870 to 1914 to fasten the various modes of symbolism on much of the western world's contemporary poetry and, less widely, on the novel and theater after the First World War. More intentionally than painters, the poets—Parnassian and symbolist alike—wrote for the few who could be expected to learn their dialects, partly subjective, partly common to the erudite. In sculpture, Auguste Rodin dominated the scene, his prolific work ranging through all modes from polished classicism and romanticism through realism to impressionism, annoying cultists, moving and delighting men of all ages and sensibilities. Relatively few of these artists were engaged in political or social causes. Delacroix and Hugo, if not ignored, were heroes of aesthetic, not popular, emancipation. But the romantics' *panache*, their cultivated sensibility, their disdain of the respectable and established, clung to the new men and made them part, willy-nilly, of the intelligentsia of opposition, all the more so as industrial society seemed to be submerging taste and individuality, with machine and money breaking man from man, and from nature.

## NEW CURRENTS OF THOUGHT AND ACTION

The novelists were more likely to mount a frontal attack, partly by design, partly by the nature of their medium. Whatever Flaubert's intent, his realism had convicted bourgeois society. Zola assaulted it in his Rougon-Macquart series (1871–1893) which purported to explain objectively, by the methods of social science, how human traits were formed, handed down, and what their consequences were—a purpose somewhat obscured by Zola's forcing Third Republic economic and social life into a setting of the Second Empire. Literary naturalism, in Zola, the Goncourts, Alphonse Daudet, and Maupassant, was the counterpart of scientific positivism, but it carried a more pessimistic, sardonic tone, traceable no doubt to their reading of Taine and Renan, but also to their own personalities and their disillusion with society around them. In the same tradition was Anatole France, whose humane and polished style hardly veiled a profound skepticism regarding man and his illusions, fully worthy of Taine's own dark account of the French Revolution. That France committed himself as a Dreyfusard was proof as much of what he hated as of faith in Republican ideals. It was enough, however, to mark him, with Zola, as a man of the Left, as did his subsequent dalliance with socialism. The Right assailed them as cosmopolitans without attachment to country or religion, and, characteristically, said their writings were responsible for the ills they only pretended to deplore. The controversialists of the Right were, naturally, no less critical of contemporary society than their rivals were, but found their creed in other novels. Paul Bourget's *Le Disciple* (1889) pilloried the school of scientific positivism and called for a return to the traditional values of the family, of social, political, and religious authority; Maurice Barrès' *Les Déracinés* (1897) pictured young Frenchmen as uprooted, demoralized, and turned to ineffectual skeptics by positivist Republican teachers and the tyranny of sophist Paris. Only a reverence for one's native soil, its traditions and its patriotic dead, said Barrès, could nurture individual self-respect and a revival of national energy.

Although a Boulangist and a nationalist Deputy who demanded strong political authority, Barrès, like Déroulède, remained loyal to the Republic and to social reform of a paternalistic sort. To full-blooded Rightists, this was inexplicable—or explicable only as weakness (to use their softest word) as bad as that of liberal and social Catholics. From the other direction, the intransigent Left attacked Jaurès as too prodigal in reference to patriotic and spiritual values, too ready to compromise with class enemies. Jaurès and Barrès were very far from being allies, but their common fate at the hands of extremists suggests that there was before 1914 a broad middle ground of loyalty to an ideal of Republican society of all classes and all creeds, and, more important, that the revolt against the cult of positivism was not only a political affair but intentellectual and spiritual, affecting men in every camp. That cult, in the hands of men like Renan and Taine, reflected in the novelists and academicians who followed them, was far less optimistic than Comte had been. Imbued as it was with the gloomy determinism of the social Darwinists, it left no room for progress, at least as the Philosophes had seen it, through man's own rational action, or for that human or national dignity which, as Catholics and patriots believed, man could build by force of will and spirit. Few, if any, Frenchmen were thoroughgoing determinists, ready only to resign themselves to events; not Zola, for all his scientific jargon, not France, for all his irony, not even Taine and Renan had been, despite the charges against them. But the language was widespread, used against other propositions, and the pose was easy to take up against enthusiasts of any kind. It was, in short, an intellectual style, in keeping with the aftermath of *l'année terrible* and with the absurdities and injustices of industrial society in the late nineteenth century. Why it should grow vulnerable and out of date by the turn of the century—when artists and prophets saw human life as more uncontrollable and absurd than ever—is difficult to say exactly. All styles grow tiresome to the young; defeat had receded into the past; many Frenchmen had tasted success and much preferred to attribute it to strength of will and virtue; religious men had never accepted its brand of pessimism; patriots refused to leave past glories to chance or impersonal forces; now they begged for human energy and courage against the German threat; on the Left, reformist socialists and revolutionary syndicalists both relied on the human will for change (distrusting Marxism as another form of resignation); the Dreyfus case had focused men's attention on the drama of the individual and he had won, or seemed to. Not least, new and persuasive leaders of thought appeared who insisted on the power of other forces than heredity and environment.

Their names suggest the impossibility of assigning the new intellectual styles to any single prior school of thought or politics: Lucien Herr, Henri Bergson, Georges Sorel, Charles Péguy, and Charles Maurras. They varied greatly in their concerns, their depth or subtlety of mind, their long-range influence, but each in his own way affirmed the power of personal and moral forces to change the world. The step from scientific positivism to socialism was the shortest for young men of the 1890's, and the brilliant Lucien Herr had installed himself as librarian at the École Normale Supèrieure in 1886 purposely to help them take it. Many Normaliens responded to this powerful, devoted personality; Herr and his friend Jaurès became the heroes of a youthful elite, which included Léon Blum and Charles Péguy, united by the Dreyfus affair for a rare moment of combat. When the Dreyfusard victory turned to political exploitation, Jaurès backing Combes, and

Herr insisting on conformity to Socialist party doctrine, many young men fell away, Péguy among them. *Mystiques,* he said, degenerated into politics.

One that promised not to was Henri Bergson's. His *Creative Evolution* (1907) and immensely popular lectures as professor of philosophy at the Collège de France liberated, as his disciples said, Frenchmen from materialism and mechanism by asserting the primacy of spirit, sentiment, and individual intuition in arriving at truth and action. The force driving men and nations on was their *élan vital,* an unconscious motivation, not to be scientifically measured in space, weight, or number, but perceived, by intuition come to the aid of reason, as the expression of creative energy; to what science could tell or create, man's spirit added the difference between quantity and quality. Bergsonism by its nature was less a school than a general influence, exerted in many directions, several of which the humane, democratic Bergson was to deplore. *Élan vital* furnished racists a conveniently indefinable trait to ascribe to peoples they deemed superior; it encouraged the integral nationalists who read Barrès and gathered about Charles Maurras' Action Française; it gave army officers who believed in the superiority of the offensive a phrase to describe the ferocious spirit which could overcome Germany's greater numbers; it gave Georges Sorel and other theorists of syndicalism a justification for saying that numbers and organization were less important to labor than the militancy of a few; it helped turn Jacques Maritain, Péguy, and others toward Catholicism (Bergson, a Jew, approached Catholicism himself at the end of his life). In each case, other, earlier influences worked in the same direction; Bergsonism's special contribution was to provide an alternative to the official philosophy taught in state schools and to give each new movement a philosophical argument expressed in modern terms. Now Frenchmen could love their country and their religion while keeping their intellectual respectability. But contradictions abounded. The Maritains went on to Thomism, less mystical, more rational than Bergsonism; Maurras denied it altogether, claiming that objective political science alone proved that monarchy was the only rational government for France; Bergson, who opened a way back to Catholicism for so many, saw his works placed on the Index in 1912; against his warning that intuition only followed upon and perfected reason, many of his auditors rushed into cults of action, irrationalism, or instinct; in place of Bergson's ideal of refining man's life within democracy, they sought to submerge it in revolutionary, authoritarian movements.

To the cult of violence as a means of exalting man's spirit, Georges Sorel came late in life, after retirement as a provincial engineer. A disciple of Bergson and friend of Péguy, Sorel despised the wordy cleverness of Paris, believing it empty of those heroic virtues he found in more barbaric ages. The remnants of such vigor he saw in the working classes and applied *élan vital* to syndicalism in his *Reflections on Violence* in 1908. The general strike was a *mystique* fit to rally heroes; its practical accomplishments were less important than its value as a myth to stir enthusiasm, the main attribute that raised men to dignity. Sorel threw over Bergson for failing to apply his intuition to the social question, then abandoned the syndicalists, who never fully understood him, in favor of Maurras and l'Action Française. Next Mussolini, as a new, national socialist, won his admiration and before the war had ended, Sorel turned to Lenin as the embodiment of his hopes. In each, he saw heroes who hated with him the dull utilitarianism of bourgeois society, which made vegetables of men.

Péguy, too, was sickened by his age and its mandarins, but while Sorel searched for new myths, Péguy found, reconciled, and personified in himself those already old in France: Catholicism, French patriotism, democracy, and socialism. Of peasant stock, the son of Orléans artisans, baptized a Catholic, he came to his faiths naturally, seeing at the heart of each a *mystique* related to all the others in its appeal to courage, charity, social justice, and personal dignity. But Péguy was no gentle eclectic. He was endowed with a stubborn, thorny integrity, a scourge to his enemies, a constant trial to his friends. He could not abide the cultists or established pundits of any of his faiths; they were all too overbearing and ambitious, too lazy or too proud to stop and listen to common men, or afraid that common men would demand of them an integrity that no establishment could endure. Péguy celebrated Joan of Arc and made a pilgrimage on foot to Chartres, but he also denounced clerical reaction, avidity for money, eagerness to be approved by the privileged of the earth while the workers and their children lived in misery. He fought for Dreyfus, the Republic, and socialism but disdained the party men who sought profit, fame, or power, denounced the anti-clerical exploitation of the affair while distrusting many of its victims. He opposed the chauvinists, colonialists, and militarists of his day but cherished the soil of France and glorified the individual soldier who freely chose to give his life, especially in the war he saw coming, which would be fought to end wars and achieve disarmament. In poetry and essays which appeared in his own *Cahiers de la Quinzaine* (he often wrote, set type, printed, and delivered the journal himself), Péguy argued tirelessly for the *mystiques* that made France great, against the degradation of each by politics, materialism, and bigotry. For a decade before the war, he begged Frenchmen to prepare themselves to meet the German threat. By 1914 he was exhausted, ill, and penniless; as a reserve lieutenant he died leading his men on the first day of the battle of the Marne, September 5, 1914. As a prophet and exemplar of France's abiding ideals, he has been remembered and at no time more honored than after 1940, when German occupation silenced lesser debates and forced the better men of all contending factions to join in the defense of those ideals.

In seeking to reconcile the Republican and socialist *mystiques* with those of patriotism and religion, Péguy was in his own day nearly alone. Most of the angry men of his generation and younger plunged, as usual, into bitterly partisan attacks on their opponents, attributing all evil to one side, forgiving all on the other. Between 1900 and 1914, a new Right arose in France, with its main strength in Paris and its extreme expression in Charles Maurras' Action Française. The old-fashioned monarchist and Bonapartist Right had suffered from the Boulangist fiasco and the *Ralliément,* and met another defeat in the Dreyfus affair; the electoral victories of the Left in 1902 and 1906, the Republic's action against the army command and the Church confirmed the worst fears of the anti-Dreyfusards. But out of the affair the scattered forces of monarchy, Bonapartism, Boulangism, and anti-Semitism learned a new combativeness, found new leaders and a doctrine in the Action Française.

Maurras himself had come to Paris as a loyal Provençal, determined to defend his local culture—as the most purely Latin and classical in all France—against the corruption of half-breeds in Paris. At first content to brandish Provençal poetry and literary criticism, Maurras was drawn into politics by the Dreyfus case. But classicism remained central to his message: order, authority, and through them national prowess, could be attained only by restoring a Catholic monarchy, though Maurras himself was not a Catholic and believed only in the political and social utility of religion. To him, the Church was a fortress, but Christianity was an incitement to weakness, anarchy, or pious socialism. In 1908, *l'Action Française* became a daily newspaper, in which Maurras' icy contempt for the Republic and its leaders, expressed in flawless classical prose, appealed to one kind of discontent, Léon Daudet's vulgar incitement to hatred and thuggery stirred up another.

Despite the royalist protestations of Maurras, the Action Française was more attached to militant nationalism than to the person of the King, was frankly elitist and authoritarian. Purporting to hold itself aloof from the "rotten political game," it styled itself a movement of national purification and revival, attracting exalted spirits and sullen, pious and violent, in the manner later to be known as proto-fascist. It enjoyed the sympathy of those who considered themselves defeated by the Dreyfus affair, the moral support of much of the Catholic hierarchy and of Pius X, the financial support of many wealthy Frenchmen. Its notoriety sprang from its enrollment of bourgeois youth in the *Camelots du Roi* (newsvendors of the King) and their attacks on teachers, bookshops, meetings, and even theatricals that could be called un-French. But its success in winning adherents and wide respectability by 1914 was due less to these brutal inanities than to other circumstances.

The new extreme Right fed upon the social fears of the new Republican Right and Center. Despite Clemenceau's, and after him Briand's, forcible repression of strikes, their frustration of teachers' and civil servants' unions, despite the increasing hostility between the Socialists and the Radical cabinets of 1906–1912, propertied conservatives remained uneasy. Strikes and syndicalist agitation continued and in the elections of 1910 the united Socialists rose from 53 to 75 Deputies, the independents to 25. The Rightist and bourgeois press voiced its fear of social revolution. At the same time, the German threats over the Moroccan crises of 1905 and 1911, the Balkan troubles of 1908 and 1912, and the burgeoning armaments race prepared the French public for a revival of patriotism and military power. Since much of the socialist and syndicalist Left and some of the Radicals were engaged in an antimilitarist, anti-patriotic campaign of their own, the Republican Right was ready to approve the activities of the Action Française as contributions to national feeling and political conservatism. Thus it was, as one historian has said, that a national cult of Joan of Arc was sponsored by many of the same forces that had betrayed her five centuries before.

In 1912, the conservative and patriotic Lorrainer Raymond Poincaré became Premier and, with the former Socialist Millerand as Minister of War, opened a campaign for increased military preparedness, which included a revival of public parades and reviews. The major political issue of the next year was conscription, the length of military service. The *bloc des gauches* in 1905 had succeeded in reducing compulsory service to two years and applying it, for the first time, to all citizens of military age. The expansion of the German and Austrian armies in 1912 and 1913 led the French high command, Premier Barthou, and the Minister of War, Étienne, to sponsor a bill in 1913 reinstating three years' service. Its passage only intensified debate as the Socialists and most Radicals, aware of its wide unpopularity, made reversal their major pledge in the electoral campaign of 1914.

The military and its supporters argued that three years would insure a larger army-in-being to meet German numerical superiority and allow the complex training needed to carry out the offensive tactics then in favor. The opponents—apart from pacifists and advocates of complete disarmament, led by the violently anti-patriotic Gustave Hervé—argued that the reserves would not thereby be enlarged, that the cost would be prohibitive, that the old Republican concept of short-term training of a people's militia, the nation in arms, was better suited to a democracy than a standing army of such size. As in 1905, they also warned of authoritarian indoctrination of youth, by un-Republican officers. But the Radicals were divided on the issue and the Left's victory in the elections of 1914 proved only that the nation was far from being swept by the nationalist enthusiasms, and fear of Germany, that were gripping Paris and some sections of the east, and, perhaps more important, was not wholly repelled by the income tax, again proposed by Jaurès and the Radical leader Joseph Caillaux. The Socialists polled nearly 1.5 million votes, winning 103 seats; 27 independent Socialists were elected and some 230 Radicals. But Poincaré, elected President in 1913, held out against demands for immediate repeal of the three-year law. In René Viviani he found another independent Socialist willing to forget the Left's campaign promises; Viviani became Premier in June. The income tax passed the Senate a month later. The Left warned Poincaré of the dangers in defying its majority on the conscription law, but the First World War cut short what might have been a serious constitutional crisis.

It cut short many other things, foremost among which was the cause of gradual social reform. Failure of the more aggressive union tactics and the discredit earned by syndicalists in calling for a general strike against military service had brought more moderate leaders to the CGT, notably its general secretary Léon Jouhaux. Cooperation between the CGT and the SFIO seemed imminent in 1914. But the first casualty of the war was Jean Jaurès. This eloquent, able, and appealing man had first united and then led the Socialist party into a Fabian path of gradual, humanitarian socialism. Its steady growth in the Chamber promised much for the future, on condition that the radical Left accepted, as some wished to, a program of social legislation and tax reform. Jaurès, like Guesde and most of the Socialist party leaders, was an ardent patriot, though he worked to the very end for two-year military service, for Franco-German reconciliation, and believed it possible for the working classes to restrain their respective governments. The integral nationalists of the Action Française and the Right-wing press reviled him incessantly in the years before 1914 as a paid revolutionary agent of Germany. On July 31st, the evening before French mobilization, one of their fanatic readers shot the "traitor" to death. French socialism lost the most formidable leader it ever knew; France lost what was very rare in the Third Republic and would be missed after the war—a man who combined political power with a social doctrine and, rarest of all, the courage to use both in moderation.

# THE GREAT
# WAR

According to the atlas, the Third Republic in August, 1914, ruled the second greatest empire on earth, embracing 4.5 million square miles of territory and 55 million souls, not counting metropolitan France. Since the overthrow of Jules Ferry in 1885 on the question of Indo-China, the French government had managed to keep pace with Great Britain in the race for empire without fear of significant opposition to colonialism at home. As the idea of *revanche* and recovery of Alsace-Lorraine died down after Boulanger, the idea of empire gained respectability and, at times, when the exotic colonial displays at the Expositions stirred their curiosity or English rivalry their pride, the press and public showed positive enthusiasm. In 1894, the Ministry of Colonies was established and various private, patriotic, and colonialist societies helped found in 1895 the *Union Coloniale*, financed by traders, bankers, and many ordinary Frenchmen who wished to promote French power, glory, or good works in backward areas. Of the old colonies acquired before the Revolution, there remained in the western hemisphere the little islands of Saint-Pierre and Miquelon off Newfoundland, Guadeloupe and Martinique in the Caribbean, Guiana on the Atlantic coast of South America; in India, five trading posts, chief among which was Pondichéry, and in the Indian Ocean, the island of Réunion, east of Madagascar. The new empire, started by Charles X in Algeria in 1830, hesitatingly pursued by the July Monarchy and Napoleon III, was mainly the work of the Third Republic, led by energetic Frenchmen in the field and a few colonialist leaders at home, like the Algerian-born Eugène Étienne who became an Undersecretary of the Navy for Colonial Affairs in 1887. Étienne founded the French Colonial School in 1889 to train administrators, clarified the missions and authority of French explorers and officers, helped organize private pressure groups for colonial activity, and later, as a Deputy, led a colonialist parliamentary faction.

## FRENCH IMPERIALISM

At Ferry's fall, France was entrenched in Indo-China, with China's reluctant consent in the Treaty of Tientsin (June, 1885). But over a decade was needed to break local resistance. Here the young officers Lyautey and Gallieni first distinguished themselves by the famous "stain of oil" method: as an area was conquered, it was made a haven of peace and stability, to win over the natives and draw others from the still-rebellious regions. By the mid-1890's only small forces were required to govern Indo-China. Laos too became a protectorate; in 1896 Siam escaped conquest, and the British and French a possible war, by an agreement to respect Siam's independence and neutrality as a buffer between British Burma and France's protectorates of Laos (Luang-Prabang) and Cambodia. But France had little success, either politically or economically, in Southeast Asia until shortly before the First World War. To govern an area divided between Chinese and Indic cultures, both in decay, and between an outright colony in Cochin-China and the protectorates, all in poverty and social oppression, would have required an effort well financed, intelligent, generous, and consistent. Instead, the Republic managed to export more of its faults than its virtues, and what happened in Indo-China was repeated, *mutatis mutandis,* elsewhere in the Empire. Residents-general and their principal assistants came and went with each cabinet in Paris. To the disgust of those Frenchmen who had grown close to the people, French policy on the treatment of natives changed nearly as often. A Resident like the ardent Republican Paul Bert (1886–1887), who allowed natives to keep their cultural and political institutions, but hoped to educate them for full participation in French administration, would be replaced by a man who reversed both policies, and he in his turn replaced by another who might retain one and reverse the other. The whole was complicated by an official policy of "assimilation," ostensibly applied to colonies and not protectorates, but actually applied, in part, to both. Carried over from French practice in the old colonies and Algeria, it envisioned natives made French in culture and, ultimately, in citizenship as each area gained its own representatives in the French parliament, with laws indistinguishable from those of the home departments. Much was made of France's *mission civilatrice*. But even when ministers in Paris consistently supported it—and they rarely did—assimilation broke on innumerable difficulties.

The most generous and most presumptuous of colonial ideas, assimilation should also have been the most expensive and the best staffed. But imperialism was never so popular, or regarded as so necessary, in France as in Great Britain, Holland, or Belgium. The colonies were starved for funds; schools, housing, and medical facilities were utterly inadequate. Frenchmen did not emigrate in large numbers, even to Algeria, and did not seek careers in empire building as often as the English or Dutch. More than most, the French Empire was made by those Shaw said made revolutions, men too good for their society and men not good enough. The former were usually missionaries, doctors, teachers, and a few young officers like Lyautey, not often in positions of power. Between well-intentioned ministers in Paris (or governors on the scene) and daily practice lay the difficulties. Those minor bureaucrats who stayed were sometimes the dregs of the civil service, as corrupt or indifferent as the local oligarchs and hangers-on through whom they dealt with natives whose language they did not bother to learn. Since frugal Deputies insisted that the colonies pay for themselves, the colonial administrators were as much occupied with immediate revenue as with development. Without one, there would be none of the other. Taxes were rigorously collected; in Indo-China the French established and promoted official monopolies of salt, opium, and alcohol, which were harmful and odious to the native population.

French private enterprise was no more farsighted than the Dutch in Indonesia or the American in the Philippines; and perhaps, by its nature, somewhat less. Investors who could reap large, safe dividends at home from foreign bonds were not disposed to take the long view of returns in colonies whose business conditions they could dictate as they liked, and businessmen who had not yet learned the language of French workers at home did not exert themselves abroad on behalf of defenseless native labor. Even had it been financially and culturally possible, assimilation did not appeal to officials and entrepreneurs on the spot who knew that keeping order and proper labor relations could only be complicated by turning natives into Frenchmen. Preparing them for self-government, was, of course, as contrary to the ideal of assimilation as to the vested interests involved. So only an elite, thought to be submissive, was Gallicized and even this was smaller in the French colonial administration than in that of other nations. Thus native cultures and political forms were disrupted, but French culture and French institutions were provided for only a few. Liberty was no more exported than fraternity and equality; individual rights, though protected from native encroachments, were little considered by French officials and police. Yet all three were preached and, what was more significant, instilled in the native students who went to school in France.

That many Frenchmen devoted their lives to sharing the benefits of Frenchness, and others to the even more generous ideal of improving native life in a revived native culture, is the other side of imperialism, the side presented to the public at home. According to their numbers and their means, the French provided—particularly through missionary works—oases of medical care, sanitation, and education in hinterlands where none had been available before; French soldiers ended local warfare and banditry. After ten years of stagnation, Indo-China received Paul Doumer as Governor-General (1897–1902) and he began a vigorous program of public works. But the construction (on native taxes) of roads, harbors, communications, and urban facilities served mainly the comfort and interests of the conqueror—as a look at Saigon will show—and the new agricultural methods were introduced on French-owned plantations which took much of the best land. Native agriculture was, for obvious reasons, left depressed, and industrialization was discouraged. The colonies were regarded as sources of raw materials and markets, subordinate in all ways to France, cut off from other trade by tariffs and prohibitions, even, as in Indo-China, economically partitioned within themselves. The Third Republic was, outside of France, an autocracy; and when the Chamber occasionally tried to soften its rule, colonialists in Paris and abroad successfully resisted it. Only with the arrival in Hanoi of the Radical Albert Sarraut as Governor-General was there a slight increase in native participation in the civil service, in native justice and local politics. But it was already 1911, the year of the birth of the Chinese Republic.

The press and Chamber paid more attention to the drama of Africa's subjugation to Europe. There events moved quickly, on many stages, and national rivalries appeared to involve the European balance of power and prestige. In Madagascar, Great Britain accepted a French protectorate in 1890, in return for recognition of her own authority in Zanzibar. But it required several years for the French to break native resistance, to upset the Hova dynasty and its English missionary and commercial allies. One campaign in 1894–1895 cost 5000 French lives, enough to cause protests in Paris, but Madagascar was annexed outright in 1896, Gallieni installed at Tananarive as Resident-General. His *taches d'huile,* coupled with recognition of ethnic and tribal rights, pacified the island by 1901, whereupon a rigorous program of taxation and economic development was set afoot. The greater clash with England developed in the 1890's on the Upper Nile. After humiliating the Italians (whom the British considered allies) at Adowa in 1896, the Ethopian government was ready to press its own claims to the headlands of the Nile. The French, then in favor at Addis Ababa, sent a mission westward in 1898 with the Ethopians in the hope of meeting another marching eastward from French Africa. Some dreamed of a great railway linking the Atlantic to the French Red Sea port of Djibouti. The British regarded any such linkage as a threat to their interests in the Sudan and their own dream of a Cape-to-Cairo railroad. Lord Kitchener was no dreamer; and as he marched in 1896 to reconquer the Sudan from the Dervishes, he built a rail line southward, insuring British presence in force. In the next year, a much smaller French expedition of the Anglophobe Captain Marchand started out from Brazzaville to the gap between British Uganda and Khartoum, at Fashoda on the Upper Nile. After one of imperialism's high adventures, in which he dragged a dismantled steamer (the *Faidherbe*) through long stretches of jungle, Marchand reached Fashoda first, in July of 1898. But Kitchener routed the Dervishes at Omdurman (young Lieutenant Churchill was there) and arrived in September with a river fleet, artillery, and infantry many times the number of Marchand's Senegalese. The two flags flew together and the leaders waited for London and Paris to give them orders.

Behind this impasse lay many years of Franco-British rivalry in Oceania, Siam, Madagascar, Ethiopia, Egypt, and on the Niger, as well as a clear British warning in 1895 that an attempt like Marchand's would be an "unfriendly act." Behind it also lay a developing European alliance system that seemed to give France, with her Russian ally, an advantage over isolated Britain, estranged even from Germany by her threats against the Boers. But the practical situation by 1898 reflected only too well the disparity of forces at Fashoda. The British could reinforce Kitchener at will; Marchand was alone, the Ethiopian mission having failed to arrive. The French navy was obsolete and demoralized, Russia was unwilling to support France diplomatically. At home, the Dreyfus affair raged, and the government feared a British turn toward Germany. As tempers rose in London, the new Foreign Minister, Théophile Delcassé, had no choice; Marchand was recalled and in 1899 France renounced all claims to lands along the Nile. The nationalist Right had one more reason to belabor the cowardice of republics.

In retrospect, the Fashoda crisis settled two matters. It limited French activity in Africa and, by concentrating it, probably made it more effective; it also cleared the way for an entente with England, as Delcassé hoped it would. France's expansion into West Africa had proceeded rapidly since 1885, her explorers, soldiers, and merchants pushing inland from several footholds on the coast. In 1893, the French advanced down the Niger to Timbuctu, made colonies of Guinea and the Ivory Coast, and of Dahomey in 1894. After another near-clash with the British over the lower Niger in early 1898, French missions from Algeria, Senegal, and the Niger met at Lake Chad. Political forms followed the explorers; in 1904, French West Africa, embracing Mauretania (not conquered until 1909), Senegal, Guinea, the Ivory Coast, Dahomey, and Niger, was organized under a Governor-General at the capital of Dakar. It was ten times the size of France, and some officers believed its conscripts could counter Germany's numerical advantage. But except for the Senegalese, its men were wasted by slavery (the trade was ended, the condition persisted), disease, and tribal war. To the south, in the French Congo, companies enjoying official concessions added vicious labor practices, nearly as bad as in Leopold's Congo Free State. Throughout West and Equatorial Africa, the policy of assimilation was announced, with better promise of success than in the more sophisticated cultures of Indo-China and North Africa. But funds were scarce, French political control was heavy, and very few Africans became French citizens. Although the army, missionaries, and French schools spread the language and technical skills to a few more, colonial progress in Africa was to await the end of the war, when political controls were somewhat relaxed, economic improvements began to benefit the natives, and an educational compromise was struck between French and indigenous culture.

Overall, French imperial activity before 1914 was more extensive than intensive. Only 10 per cent of French private overseas investment went to French territories, about 4.5 million francs or roughly 900 million McKinley dollars; Great Britain's colonial investment was ten times as large, as was her Empire's trade. When French funds sought underdeveloped areas, they more often went to the United States, Latin America, or Australia and other British areas. The illimitable markets portrayed by Ferry (Europe's power to consume was "saturated," he said in 1890) proved illusory, and the harvest of raw materials disappointing; all of West Africa's annual trade amounted to less than $50 million by 1914, the French Congo's to less than 5 million. Despite French near-monopoly of trade in Madagascar, it remained a negligible part of France's commerce; and since only a fifth of Indo-China's trade was with France, profits went mainly to enterprises on the spot and to the shareholders of the Bank of Indo-China. As Hobson might have said, any French government keeping close accounts would have abandoned its empire. But long-range economic hope persisted as a motive—or justification—for imperialism, and in the short run a few prospered, the French fleet had stations in every ocean, and before the great war ended, half a million native troops had fought for France on European fronts. The Third Republic could take pride in having outdistanced every continental state in empire building, but the thinness of activity and results suggested that France needed imperial outlets for money, goods, and men even less than most of her neighbors did. The human effects of French imperialism were mixed; there were far fewer conversions to Christianity than had been expected, more conversions to western ideas of democracy and nationalism than westerners thought appropriate to the moment, and very uneven results in living standards, health, and education. After 1919, activity increased, but so did native resistance; only after 1945 did the ultimate effects of Europe's intervention in Asia and Africa begin to emerge—and its cost to both parties. One great price paid before 1914 was a heightening of national tensions in Europe herself.

The last African land to be subjugated was Morocco, and more than all the rest its fate was bound up in the network of alliances that divided Europe before 1914. After 1871 Bismarck bent his great talent to the task of isolating France from allies whose aid might make *revanche* seem possible to her. The loosely articulated Three Emperors' League of 1873, which Victor Emmanuel II also approved as a guarantee against French rescue of the Papacy, gave way in 1879 to a close Austro-German alliance directed mainly against Russia, and in 1882 to the Triple Alliance of Germany, Austria, and Italy. While Bismarck held power, he nonetheless worked to keep Russia neutral in case of French attack, as in the secret Reinsurance Treaty of 1887. Upon Bismarck's fall in 1890, young William II allowed the treaty to lapse and reduced German financial and commercial ties to Saint Petersburg. French loans very soon replaced German and prepared the way for a Franco-Russian alliance, which was finally concluded in 1894, as a tight military agreement to last as long as the Triple Alliance itself. France thereby escaped her isolation, but was henceforth to be involved in whatever quarrel arose between Russia and Austria in the Balkans, between Russia and Germany in the Near East. Not only for this reason was the Russian alliance long unpopular among Frenchmen of the Left, who thought their government's support of Tsarist despotism one more betrayal of Republican ideals. That the despoilers of Poland and perennial agents of counter-revolution were rewarded with French arms and gold was to patriots, however, a small matter compared with French security. An enthusiastic welcome of a Russian naval squadron in 1893 suggested that the public agreed, and French bankers and journalists benefited from Russian willingness to pay well for services rendered. To 1914, 12 billion francs were exchanged for Russian bonds, one-quarter of all French investments abroad and over twice as much private capital as Frenchmen sent to all their colonies together. But the government that encouraged this investment did not think the Russian alliance sufficient to France's security, especially as Saint Petersburg refused to side with France in colonial crises. The choice was an approach to Berlin or London. Gabriel Hanotaux, Foreign Minister from 1894 to 1898, inclined to the former, Delcassé to the latter, though neither seems to have excluded the other.

The Fashoda settlement was only one of the circumstances which allowed Delcassé, who was Foreign Minister for seven years, 1898 to 1905, to achieve a *rapprochement* with London. The Kaiser's liking for the Boers and his naval plans had upset hesitant approaches by the English for an entente with Berlin; on their side, the successful colonial powers had no inclination to allow Germany her "place in the sun." Least of all was Britain ready to concede the presence in Morocco of a nation which threatened her naval and commercial supremacy. In 1904, the Anglo-French entente was signed, not at first an alliance but a world-wide truce between two prosperous old rivals who feared that any further quarrels would only weaken them against the German challenger. France recognized British primacy in Egypt in exchange for freedom of action in Morocco; remaining differences in Atlantic fishing grounds, Siam, Madagascar, and the Pacific were liquidated. In 1907, Britain and Russia composed their problems in the Straits, Persia, Afghanistan, and Tibet, and the Triple Entente confronted the Triple Alliance. For the first time since the defeat of Napoleon, each major European power was bound to one of two armed camps.

## THE COMING OF THE WAR

The war that changed the world, and blackened the body and mind of Europe, opened in August of 1914. No adjective suffices to describe its obvious effects; no doubt others are not yet revealed or are still to come. Historians and social scientists have explored its causes nearly as far as known evidence and methods permit; poets and philosophers have joined them in pondering the causes of war in general, the nature of historical causation and the nature of man. Many have attempted to measure the relative responsibility of each combatant for the immediate outbreak. In this exercise, France has usually fared best next to Great Britain. Austria and Serbia, or individual Austrian and Serbian leaders, have led the infamous list, followed by Russia and Germany or Germany and Russia. If such ranking is misleading even for the summer of 1914, its application to the long-range preparation of circumstances is only an intricate game, in which the errors of the medieval German Emperors can have as much importance, or as little, as the wrong turn of the famous chauffeur at Sarajevo. What remains to a national history of France is to suggest (without ranking) what part the French people and their leaders played in the developments scholars have blamed for general war in 1914: imperialism, the system of alliances, nationalism, economic rivalries, military doctrines and the armaments race, and those domestic leaders and circumstances that made war as easy to choose as peace.

The succession of Franco-German crises over Morocco was one of imperialism's major contributions to prewar tension. Economic impulses appear negligible in the race for Morocco. The few who expected to profit could hardly have drawn their governments along if the latter had not already believed in the strategic importance of the site, and in its significance as a sign of national prowess and honor. To Frenchmen who believed in their *mission civilatrice*, their special qualification for dealing with all Africans, it seemed only logical that Morocco should be next. Its position on the Atlantic and Mediterranean made it appear important to French interests on both coasts, and its pacification imperative to Algerian settlers who needed security for lands on their side of the border and coveted more land on the Moroccan side. Like Egypt and Tunis before her, Morocco's economic and political turbulence invited intervention by the powers. Delcassé first arranged for Italy's agreement; in 1900 France gave in return her approval to Italian "influence" in the other Ottoman lands of Tripoli and Cyrenaica. Spain's approval of French tutelage over the Sultan of Morocco followed the Anglo-French entente of 1904. London and Madrid joined Paris in publicly declaring their support of the territorial integrity of Morocco and of the Sultan's sovereignty; both signed secret articles agreeing to eventual partition, with Spain to keep a narrow coastal strip opposite Gibraltar. Delcassé's omission of Germany amounted to a provocation; Germany's Moroccan interests were well known, as was her hypersensitivity as a colonial late comer. But to consult Berlin was to risk all, since Germany desired equal rights in Morocco and the prospect of buying her off was slim. Having won England, Delcassé decided to upset the Moroccan *status quo*, which the powers had respected for a generation precisely to avoid the crises that would surely follow any change.

The Kaiser now discovered how solid was the Anglo-French entente. Debarking at Tangier in 1905, he upheld Morocco's independence and the equal rights of the powers to trade there, then demanded an international conference to settle the question. The German Chancellor von Bülow bluntly warned Paris that the continued presence of Delcassé was an affront to Germany. Delcassé opposed any compromise, but over the howls of the nationalist press was forced to resign by Premier Rouvier and other French leaders who wanted no war in 1905; Russia was occupied in her disastrous war with Japan, France's army was wracked with dissension over the religious quarrel, and her cause, in any case, was hardly pure. At the Algeciras Conference of 1906, France enjoyed British support and emerged with *de facto* control of Moroccan police, though financial and commercial affairs were ostensibly left to international, including German, supervision. The French proceeded with their plans of penetration, more sure than ever of British support, for during the conference naval and military conversations began between Paris and London to prepare for the eventuality of war.

The episode proved unhappily typical. A French initiative had drawn a German response that was largely justified but violent and clumsy, using open threats in an attempt to break the Dual Entente. Britain, already disturbed over Germany's diplomatic, naval and commercial assertiveness, reacted by supporting France, which led France to pay even less attention to German feelings. Despite a French occupation of Casablanca and Rabat in 1907 (rebellious tribesmen had attacked the former) and an incident of 1908 in which French police manhandled German consular officials for harboring deserters from the Foreign Legion, the German and Clemenceau governments came to an agreement in 1909 which recognized France's political interests in Morocco in exchange for "economic equality," that is, a number of Franco-German mining, rail, and financial combines in Morocco and other parts of Africa. Neither Rouvier nor Clemenceau had admired Delcassé's policy of rigid alliance with Russia and England, coupled with open defiance of Germany. Both hoped for an accommodation with Berlin, but did not believe enough in its possibility to sacrifice any public or private French interest to it, or risk their own political reputations with nationalists and the more chauvinist French newspapers. The day had not come (nor has it yet) when democratic governments were able to compel influential citizens on the scene to observe the niceties of international agreements. The French military, police, and private entrepreneurs would brook no interference from German rivals; the agreement of 1909 was being widely ignored when the Radical leader Joseph Caillaux became Premier in July of 1911.

Caillaux was one of the few French politicians ready to court unpopularity in seeking *rapprochement* with Germany, but he was fated to exhaust his credit merely in liquidating the final Moroccan crisis, which developed in the same week he came to power. Two months before, a French army had occupied the Moroccan capital of Fez, to protect the Sultan and European residents from an anti-foreign rebellion. Once again, Germany demanded compensation for what amounted to a French protectorate in violation of the Algeciras settlement, backed up her protest by sending the gunboat *Panther* to Agadir, then suggested that France cede the major part of the French Congo to the German Empire. Once again, Berlin's overreaction threw Britain and France together. The press and jingoists on all sides demanded no retreat, but Caillaux and the German Foreign Minister Kiderlen-Wächter achieved a compromise: France would have her protectorate in Morocco and cede a strip of the Congo to Germany in compensation. Caillaux hoped to proceed to a broader settlement and arrange Franco-German business cooperation in several lands, from Turkey to the Far East. But the Chamber, after approving his Moroccan-Congo agreement, overthrew him in early 1912 to the accompaniment of a nationalist uproar in Paris and the press.

Caillaux's failure was perhaps inevitable; he was detested by conservatives for his appeasement of Berlin, for his support of the income tax, distrusted by the Socialists for his connections with high international finance, and for his failure to appease Germany further. Also, perhaps most important, French leaders were reluctant to endanger France's hard-won alliances with Britain and Russia on the chance of finding a stable agreement with an erratic and aggressive German government, whose object was assumed to be the renewed isolation of France, and whose officials refused to discuss the oldest question of all, that of Alsace-Lorraine. In 1912, many Frenchmen believed war inevitable; the new Premier, Raymond Poincaré, was probably among them. But even to those who thought differently, the anarchic world of national rivalries presented hard alternatives: full alliance with an England engaged in a bitter naval and commercial race with Germany which was exacerbating tempers on both sides, and with a decrepit Russian Empire whose ambitions in the Balkans and the Straits clearly threatened Austrian and German interests, or—and there is little evidence that Caillaux himself would have chosen it—a gamble that France's hereditary enemy, far more powerful than she, would accept any agreement that stopped short of military and diplomatic hegemony in Europe, naval parity with Britain, and at least a share in most French colonial interests. In this sense, Jaurès' claim that the German workers would never allow their government to go to war was—even if it had been true—beside the point; given a France separated from her allies, Germany would not need war to impose her will. Jaurès was even more vulnerable than Caillaux; as a Socialist, he was automatically opposed by most political and economic powers in France. His heroic efforts at Franco-German understanding seemed fruitless to all who considered the German government impervious to German public opinion and were denounced as treasonous by nationalists; his patriotism, denied by the Right, was denounced by the extreme anti-patriots and anti-militarists of the Left. Hervé's outrageous attacks on the flag served only to compromise Jaurès, Caillaux, and all proponents of *détente*.

The year 1912 marked a turning point in France's international position. Although the Moroccan crisis ended without war, it narrowed Europe's room for maneuver; nowhere is imperialism's preparatory effect so clear. Both Germans and Frenchmen considered Agadir a defeat and resolved not to let it happen again; both sought to bolster their alliances. France and England came to a naval agreement by which the French navy was to guard their common Mediterranean interests and the British navy to guard France's Channel and Atlantic coasts. Though London refused a final commitment to declare war if France were attacked, plans were made for British army landings, and a moral obligation, reinforced by Britain's unwavering support on Morocco, was implicit. Russia had not chosen to support France in 1911; there, too, the alliance needed strengthening. Poincaré went to Saint Petersburg in 1912 and assured Russia of France's support in the Balkans and naval cooperation at the Straits. Almost immediately, the first promise was tested and France found wanting. The tremors of the Moroccan crisis had raced eastward. Italy collected on her bargain of 1900 by attacking the Ottoman Empire in Tripoli; Bulgaria, Serbia, and Greece took the opportunity to attack it in the Balkan Peninsula in 1912. After an easy victory, Bulgaria claimed lands disputed by the others and was defeated in a second Balkan War by a coalition of Serbs, Greeks, Rumanians, and Turks. Russia's victorious protégé, Serbia, demanded an outlet to the sea; Austria protested, and the European powers, including France, allowed the creation in 1913 of the independent state of Albania, blocking Serbia from the Adriatic.

For the second time in five years, Serbia and Russia were humiliated by an Austrian government determined to prevent the unification of the south Slavs in a greater Serbia. By 1914, Pan-Slavist leaders in Russia and Serbia were bent on revenge; Vienna was awaiting an opportunity to destroy Serbia's rising power. The Balkan confrontation involved French interests so marginally that the French government refused its support of Serbia in 1913, but the alliance was shaken, for France had also held back in 1908 when Austria had seized Bosnia, to the dismay of Serbia and Russia. Poincaré, now President, and Premier Viviani sailed to Saint Petersburg in July of 1914, to assure the Russians once again of French fidelity to their interests in the Balkans. Franz Ferdinand was already dead at Sarajevo, Germany had already given Austria her "blank check" and urged quick action against Serbia. Thus the fortunes of two great modern states were tied to two decaying empires ruled by mediocrities and martinets who preferred war to social and political reform, who preferred a local war, to be sure, but expected enough support to risk a general war. To the extent that Poincaré realized this danger, he and France bear responsibility for encouraging a forward Russian policy. That he wanted war is doubtful; that he saw it as inevitable and thus risked everything to make sure of Russian aid is more likely.

The system of alliances that made a general war probable once any two powers decided on a local war was no doubt hardened by the European race for commercial, naval, and colonial power, in which France's Moroccan ambitions played a fateful part. But the system itself, and France's dependence on Russia, grew out of events far back in the nineteenth century. In escaping the thrall of Bismarckian diplomacy, France had only entangled herself in Russia's doubtful schemes for the Balkans and the Straits. Bismarckian diplomacy, the attempted isolation of France in Europe, was in turn imposed upon Germany by her fear that France would seek revenge for the seizure of Alsace-Lorraine. The amputated provinces barred the way to any lasting agreement between the two countries. German fear and French resentment might seem almost to disappear from time to time, but both were too easily revived— by other Franco-German quarrels or by one domestic faction or other for partisan advantage. German nationalists felt bound to demand their retention, French nationalists to prevent their abandonment. The initial error—perhaps the greatest in nineteenth-century diplomacy—was Germany's. With Bismarck's urging, an aggressive German nationalism, abetted by the familiar insistence of military men (and industrial leaders) on every possible advantage, dictated the seizure. But behind 1871 lay the equally myopic nationalism of Frenchmen unwilling to admit the force of German sentiment for unity and thus perpetually astonished to be considered the enemies of that unity, and partly responsible, since Napoleon I, for the explosive nature of German nationalism.

The wider role of nationalism in aggravating international anarchy has often been described. As a general idea, in its liberal form, nationalism should have helped each people see the legitimate national aspirations of others. In practice, it proved no more sensitive to the limits of aggrandizement than the much-abused diplomacy of seventeenth- and eighteenth-century dynasts. Each nation knew (and knows) its interests to be righteous and pursued them without regard for others' to the brink of war. At that point, a compromise would emerge—sometimes with the mediation of outside powers—provided one or both antagonists feared war or defeat, and provided one government or both felt free enough from foreign or domestic pressures to alter its course. Even among people of minimal national pride, a succession of such crises, in which their government gave up demands long considered justified, would build a mood of impatience, in its turn exploitable by public or private interests desiring a more aggressive policy. For many reasons, French and German national sensitivity was very far from minimal by 1914. When a crisis developed in which leaders on all sides felt themselves tolerably well prepared for a war they thought inevitable, whether they desired or feared war was no longer important, especially if at that moment both foreign and domestic pressures made war as easy to choose as postponement. Such a crisis engulfed Europe in 1914.

French leaders were pressed by Russia; the alliance, like most alliances, seemed at once to endanger and to safeguard the peace. When so much else endangered peace, the alliance appeared the least of evils and a guarantee of victory. Domestic circumstances helped. The long and acrid French debate over the three-year law raised tempers of both sides, not only against each other but against Germany for making debate necessary. That Germany could justly claim a need for larger armies in her encirclement was ignored by the same popular press that had ignored or obfuscated William II's periodic gestures of reconciliation—as the German press had Caillaux's. Jaurès himself contributed to popular discussion of military questions; his book *L'Armée Nouvelle*, though opposed to three-year service and its cost, proclaimed the right of self-defense by a nation in arms. Military men and tools attracted admiration among the middle classes which had until recently preserved a jealously civilian bias. The patriotism of the working classes was taken for granted by most French leaders whether they welcomed or deplored it. Newspapers gladly magnified French strength, as they had masked Russian weaknesses even in the Russo-Japanese debacle. The dominant military doctrines of Europe, built on mass armies and the advantage of the offensive, were heartily accepted by the French high command (which took credit ˊ r itself and its predecessors back to Napoleon and Jomini for inspiring them), and worked to discourage political leaders in all capitals from endangering national security by prolonged discussions at the moment of crisis.

There were doubts and minority currents, of course. Some wondered why, if war were imminent, so many champions of the three-year law opposed the income tax. A popular pamphlet (the Socialist Marcel Sembat's *Faites un Roi, sinon faites la paix*) argued that the Republic could not organize a war; Maurras and his friends agreed; pacifists and anti-patriots listened to Hervé; there were some who believed German arms unbeatable; to conservatives who argued that war would end the socialist danger, others answered that it would assure socialist victory. All and many more were to be repeated in 1939, far more plausibly, to a people torn by competing ideologies. But 1914 was not a time of international civil war, of mutual fear of class betrayal of the nation to one totalitarian state or other. On the whole, Frenchmen entered the crisis of 1914 united in national feeling, persuaded that responsibility for war, should it come, lay elsewhere. As the weeks following Sarajevo moved by, no great debate arose to force or stay the hands of leaders. French democracy exhibited that most necessary, yet often dangerous, faith that those in charge knew what they were doing and had the power to do it. Such faith was to be derided in years to come, but given the generally low level of political and military leadership that plagued all Europe in 1914, it was perhaps the least misplaced of any people's. Not all Frenchmen went to war, as Scott Fitzgerald later said, upheld by "tremendous sureties," but most seemed to believe in the Republic and in each other's loyalty to France.

In the last few days of peace, France's role was mainly passive: no dramatic initiatives for peace, which might have alienated Russia; no aggressive acts, which would have risked British opinion. Poincaré and Viviani were sailing home from Saint Petersburg on the *France* when they heard by wireless of Austria's ultimatum to Serbia on July 23rd. By word and attitude, Poincaré had heartened the Pan-Slavists in Russia; but it is doubtful that their pressure on the Tsar and Sazonov, the Foreign Minister, for full mobilization (as opposed to Sazonov's dangerous enough plan for mobilization directed only against Austria) would have been any the less had the visit never occurred. Only an outright French refusal of support could have daunted them and in 1914 such a refusal was far from Poincaré's mind, and from the French Ambassador Paléologue's, who encouraged Sazonov's policy of bluff toward Austria. The bluff did not work. Although Serbia's response was so adroit as to convince the Kaiser peace was safe, Austria attacked Belgrade on the 28th of July. Poincaré and Viviani did not arrive in Paris until noon of the next day. At the fatal moment (July 29–30) when Nicholas II vacillated between a partial mobilization against Austria and a general mobilization, which would push Germany to that immediate response all military men considered automatic, the French leaders asked only that Russia's military preparations be made in such a way as not to alarm Berlin. The warning was too late and too weak to matter; on the 30th Nicholas II ordered general mobilization.

Poincaré's main concern was to obtain an immediate declaration of British support in case of general war, which Grey, uncertain of the cabinet, Commons, and public, refused to give. He also feared that British support would only encourage French and Russian intransigence —again the dilemma of alliances. Paris did all she could to win British confidence. The errors of 1870 were not to be repeated; when war came, it must be first declared and set afoot by Germany. In ordering a state of readiness, the French were careful to keep all troops far enough from the frontier to avoid incidents; it was a last, slim gesture for peace that might rally world opinion to France's side. So close were the calculations of the military that France and Germany ordered general mobilization simultaneously on the afternoon of August 1st. The German plan of campaign did the rest. To survive a two-front war required a quick defeat of France before the ponderous Russian forces could move westward through Poland and East Prussia. Accordingly, Germany declared war on France on August 3rd and the German army's march into neutral Belgium helped bring the British in on August 4th. As Grey said, the lamps went out all over Europe. Of the leading actors in 1914, Churchill alone lived to see them regain their full brilliance—and then only in the west—nearly a half century later.

## CATASTROPHE

Among the several initiatives and errors of the Central Powers that have led historians to assign them a large share of war responsibility, some were traceable to underestimation of their enemies. The extent of British efforts on land and the speed of Russia's mobilization were surprises. Fully as unexpected was France's *union sacrée*. Poincaré's appeal for unity was answered by dramatic reconciliations between men who only weeks before had attacked each other without restraint—or so it seemed, until the 1930's uncovered new depths of hatred and invective.

The government's care to remain on the defensive, its restraint of chauvinist demonstrations in the last few days of the crisis, Germany's rape of Belgium after years of tactless diplomacy, gave Frenchmen and Englishmen one of the few luxuries open to men at war, the certainty of fighting for a just cause after making honest efforts to keep the peace. The government acted wisely to encourage unity. Viviani broadened his cabinet to include representatives of all factions: Jules Guesde from the Left, Émile Combes from the Radicals, the conservative Catholic Denys Cochin from the Right, Delcassé to the Foreign Ministry, Briand to Justice, Millerand to War, the popular young Radical Malvy to Interior. Jaurès was already a national martyr, his spirit invoked by men who had detested him in life. The laws against religious associations were suspended; French priests returned from Canada, the United States, the colonies, and every corner of Europe and the world to serve in the army. The Ministry of Interior's *Carnet B,* a list of Leftist and pacifist extremists who were to be arrested to safeguard national security in an emergency, was forgotten. Gustave Hervé reverted to the militant patriotism he had discarded years before; he and Déroulède were reconciled; so were Blum and Barrès, and many other old adversaries of the Dreyfus case. Strikes died away; reservists reported to their regiments in a swiftly completed mobilization. Men expected a quick war, an 1870 which ended in victory, for this time Russia and England would add their weight to France's. Some shouted, "À Berlin!" to the soldiers swinging through the Place de la République on their way to the Gare de l'Est, but there and in the press and music halls, chauvinist theatrics were superfluous and embarrassing. Not imperial glory but Republican defense of French soil was the cause, and Alsace-Lorraine was destination enough.

Four years and 1,350,000 French lives were spent in covering the 245 miles from the Gare de l'Est to Strasbourg. For nearly the whole time, the armies engaged on the western front were evenly matched in men, material, and generalship, yet in the opening weeks it appeared possible that one side or the other would strike an unanswerable blow. The so-called "war of movement" began with the German march on Belgium on August 4th and ended in the middle of November with the German armies occupying all but a corner of Belgium and most of ten French departments on a line running from Switzerland by Nancy, Verdun, Reims, Arras, and Ypres to the sea between Dunkirk and Ostend, with all but the last in Allied hands. It was a time of lost opportunities for both sides. In general, the French command made as many errors as in 1870 and 1940—often the same ones—and the Germans made more, but unlike 1870 and 1940 the rough equality of forces prevented quick exploitation of error, as did the sluggish pace of mass armies not yet motorized. For all the slowness of movement, both sides were often ignorant of the enemy's deployment, and sometimes of their own. Reconnaissance failed at critical moments; cavalry's two last months of usefulness in western Europe were wasted, the first months of aircraft clumsily employed.

The French Plan of War XVII called for a massive attack east and northeastward against German Lorraine. In underestimating the weight and breadth of the German sweep through Belgium, it nearly brought disaster by leaving only a weak French left to guard Paris and the rear of the main armies. This misreading, or disdain, of intelligence had a familiar source: the untidy facts did not fit an already decided plan that was politically and psychologically appealing, that was in accordance with French promises to Russia for a quick attack, as well as dictated by the military dogma of the offensive then ascendant in the high command. General Michel, who feared a German thrust through Belgium and believed defensive operations best-suited to a conscript army, had been replaced as Commander-in-Chief in 1911 by General Joffre. Under him, Plan XVII was developed by officers impressed by Colonel de Grandmaison's belief that in modern war an army trained and equipped for constant attack would gain a moral, then a military, advantage over the enemy. The "will to conquer," the *élan vital* or *furia francese,* would make numbers less important than spirit and momentum. The doctrine was invoked to support the three-year law, as necessary to train men in the more complex field maneuvers of attack, and caused the French army to value the rifle, bayonet, and light field gun (the famous .75) over the machine gun, entrenching tools and training, and heavy artillery. In the same spirit, men were sent to combat in close ranks, with martial music and bright uniforms, their officers, for quick recognition, in different colors. So armed, Joffre's main force struck the waiting Germans in Lorraine and southeast Belgium and were soon thrown back to their own line of fortifications. In only two weeks of August, the blind folly of this Battle of the Frontiers cost France 300,000 dead, wounded, and captured. But had Plan XVII taken longer to collapse, had the French actually penetrated into Lorraine or beyond, they might not have been able to turn in time to meet the German tide that now poured over northern France.

The German plan, worked out by the former chief of staff, Count Schlieffen, was more impressive, so practical that it almost succeeded, but so realistic in its disdain of Belgium's neutrality that it stirred the British to quick action. By August 14th, when Joffre was attacking Lorraine, Sir John French's five divisions of tough British regulars had joined the 5th French Army on the left flank near Mons and Charleroi in south-central Belgium. Together these fourteen divisions, intended by Joffre to outflank the Germans, were forced instead to fall back under the pressure of three full German armies of 34 divisions, the heavy right wing that formed the hammer of the Schlieffen plan. By it, an overwhelming German force was to sweep west and south through Belgium, then swing eastward to roll the French against the Alsatian and Swiss frontiers. For two weeks, the German advance was inexorable and on September 2nd the French government abandoned Paris for Bordeaux. A newly formed 6th French Army was called to the capital's defense by its military governor, the illustrious colonial officer Gallieni. But 1870 was not to be repeated; already on September 4th, this army rumbled out of Paris, some of its soldiers riding the famous, high-slung Renault taxis, to strike the first blow in the battle of the Marne.

This turning point of twentieth-century history was the product of innumerable factors, not least the tenacity of France's much despised reservists in making a ten-day, hundred-mile retreat from Belgium without breaking order, and the ability of Joffre to keep his head despite the failure of all his plans. On the 4th of September, five German armies pressed upon a French line that sagged below the Marne between the fortresses of Verdun and Paris. But they were weaker than the forces Schlieffen is reputed to have begged for on his deathbed in 1913. Their supreme commander von Moltke, nephew of the victor in 1870, was compelled by the Belgians around Antwerp to leave strength behind; his supplies were partly choked by Belgian destruction of rails and bridges on the Meuse, his advancing soldiers were underfed and prey to fatigue. At this moment, the Russian alliance returned the full value of French loans. With unexpected speed, two Russian armies converged on East Prussia (which Schlieffen had insisted was expendable) and von Moltke hastily detached two army corps from the right wing's reserve on August 25th for service on the eastern front. Joffre's defeat in Lorraine (where Schlieffen also meant to allow a French advance) had pushed his troops back to prepared positions from which large-numbers could be spared to march westward, so that in early September the numbers along the Marne slightly favored the French. Still Joffre was inclined to retreat further and await fresh troops before starting a counterattack. But Gallieni intervened and on September 4th persuaded his former subordinate to turn about. What Gallieni saw was von Kluck's 1st Army on the German right presenting an open flank to Paris as it swung southeastward to cross the Marne and crush French armies in the field before risking an assault on Paris' immense perimeter.

On the 5th, Gallieni sent Maunoury's 6th Army against this German flank. Von Kluck turned to meet it and left a thirty-mile gap between himself and von Bülow's 2nd Army. That day the British and French retreat stopped; the next morning a million men turned northward and started back. The British entered the gap on the 9th. To their right the 5th French Army of Franchet d'Espery, to his right the 4th Army of Ferdinand Foch, broke von Bülow's front, and the great German right wing fell back. This, if any, was the moment for de Grandmaison's vaunted *élan*, but it had choked in blood a month before. Haig and Joffre failed to pursue closely enough to exploit their victory; the Germans had time to dig in along the Aisne. Now the line of armies stepped sideways to the northwest, each hoping to outflank the other, but both were too faded and neither was confident (or well informed) enough to take the quick long step required. This so-called "race to the sea" ended above Dunkirk at the end of October. Meanwhile Antwerp had fallen, its forts crushed by siege guns of unprecedented destructiveness. The Belgians retreated along the coast to the Yser, where they stopped the Germans by opening the dikes, and kept a tiny part of their kingdom at Furnes. Von Falkenhayn, who had replaced the disconsolate von Moltke, turned southward to shatter the unstable Franco-British line and seize the Channel ports, Dunkirk, Calais, and Boulogne. In a month of fighting, the British Regular Army was all but consumed at Ypres, but the Germans failed to break through there, or at Dixmude against the French, and the ports were saved. The Marne had prevented the quick victory Germany needed; Ypres ended the war of movement and opened the greater slaughter of stalemate.

The war now changed its character, though most authorities were slow to see it. The outcome would depend less on sudden turns of military fortune in the field than on the moral and material stamina of entire societies whose fighting fronts ground incessantly against each other along 350 miles of trenches. The mass war of soldiers became a total war of peoples; offensive war was contained by defensive war. At first, neither lesson was learned. Then, with time, each became a dogma with the French. Unhappily for later years, the second, the superiority of the defense, was temporary and brought about by a combination of weapons and transport that would be obsolete even before the end of 1918. Moreover, it operated mainly in the western theater, between massed antagonists of fairly equal weight, and then only after the initial momentum of the German attack was slowed by circumstances much more complex than mere defensive fire power. In the agonizing years that followed, it was hard to remember that the universal expectation of a short war was very nearly justified in 1914; men caught up in the first great industrial war forgot that but for the Marne they would have had no second chance.

For such a war the Entente appeared far stronger than the Central Powers in men, money, resources, industrial potential, and the ships to bring them together. In contrast to 1870, French military mobilization had been rapid and efficient; within a month, nearly 3 million men had joined the already active army of 900,000. But none of the belligerents had prepared for economic mobilization; it took time, fumbling, and waste, and a degree of government intervention in economic life unknown to western nations in that day. In France, the idea of wartime controls had been familiar since the Terror and Napoleon, and the peacetime actions of government to foster the national economic interest had multiplied since the Second Empire; export and import controls, subsidies, aid to communications and transport, protective tariffs and colonial policies—all had interfered with free trade to the assumed benefit of domestic industry, commerce, and agriculture. Wartime intervention, then, was not so abrupt a departure as it is sometimes described. The French government had prepared detailed economic plans for war, the military had power, dating from a law of 1877, to requisition anything it needed, from farm animals to entire industries. But all plans were tailored to a short war, fought by every able-bodied man on existing stocks of food, equipment, and munitions. Thus normal economic activity halted in August of 1914. The Bourse closed, banking was disrupted, credit dried up, moratoria on rents and debts were declared, railroads carried only military traffic, and even a number of munitions contracts were allowed to lapse in the belief that the war would be over before they could be fulfilled. Mobilization stripped industry and agriculture of workers; over half of all French enterprises simply closed down and production fell by the same proportion. German capture of France's major iron and coal fields, of steel and textile centers in the north and east, posed serious problems to which little thought had been given before the war. For months, upward of 2 million unemployed joined nearly a million refugees from Belgium and the occupied departments in economic deprivation relieved only by charity and a public dole. In all these respects, Norman Angell had been right: modern war wreaked havoc with advanced, complex economies. But the great illusion, shared by pacifists and militarists alike, had been to think that this alone would force nations somehow to shorten their conflicts.

From the early winter of 1914, the government struck out in many unaccustomed and sometimes conflicting directions, first to restore and then to expand production of food, clothing, and war materials. Orders for guns, shells, tools, and trucks were hurriedly placed, old factories converted and enlarged. New industries grew up to replace those captured. Refugees and unemployed were put to work, over 500,000 skilled workers were demobilized, women drawn into unprecedented tasks, foreign and colonial labor imported, especially for farm work. Food exports were forbidden, import duties dropped; the government requisitioned grain, and as it grew clear that domestic production would not suffice, took most foreign purchasing of food and material into its own hands. Shortages of manpower, capital, and resources hampered production, and innumerable official and semi-official boards, bureaus and commissions crisscrossed each other's work. Central direction remained loose and inconsistent until nearly the end, when Clemenceau took decree power over economic affairs and the Allied nations finally agreed to economic cooperation among themselves. But at no time did France's habitual Système D (for débrouillage, or improvisation) break down seriously enough to endanger the overall war effort. Not the least of heroes were those officials, industrialists, engineers, and workers who shortened their lives by unceasing labor behind the lines.

The heaviest burdens of the home front were borne by the families of soldiers, the petty bourgeois, and some of the workers, whose income was more rigorously controlled than the prices they were forced to pay for life's necessities. Only bread prices were controlled early. Rationing was generally applied only in 1917, maximum prices in 1918. Long working hours, reductions in fuel, clothing, and nutrition sapped resistance to disease; the incidence of tuberculosis rose sharply and medical facilities were less adequate than ever. On the other hand, some made fortunes. Profiteering on war goods was rife, so was shoddy manufacture; too few contractors were delicate enough to regard such practices as a form of treason and politicians feared to limit the freedom of wealthy and influential citizens. Not even Clemenceau was Tiger enough for that when he took near-dictatorial powers in 1917. Besides, there was the American example. Before the war was two years old, the Entente found that the price of steel in Pittsburgh had nearly tripled; American war suppliers had doubled their dividends by the end of 1915; American food suddenly was worth its weight in the French and British gold that poured into New York. In France, not only munitions and uniform makers found that war had its consolations; so did certain skilled laborers, suburban farmers, and strategically placed handlers of goods and money. The sight of their prosperity embittered those whose wages were frozen, and soldiers home on furlough. Had the favored been more numerous, bad feeling could have threatened national unity—as it did in the Second World War—but most Frenchmen knew well that those who suffered far outnumbered those who profited and that even the latter had sons and brothers among the half-million French soldiers already dead or missing by Christmas of 1914.

As stalemate persisted, it was not economic inequality so much as the fear of France's literally bleeding to death that undermined public morale and broke the *union sacrée* in politics. Through 1915, 1916, and 1917, the French high command was obsessed by a massive breakthrough on the western front as the only means to victory. No more than Haig did it tolerate "side shows" in the Balkans and the Near East, or believe in the importance of naval blockade. Thus the Serbs were allowed to collapse, the Dardanelles expedition was eviscerated, and Russia left to falter in isolation. Yet no more quickly than the British did the French experiment with new weapons and field tactics to deal with trench deadlock: the tank, the mortar, the airplane, the smokescreen, loose-order assaults, night infiltration, even the machine gun, were dismissed, delayed, or used halfheartedly. Massed attack with rifle and bayonet, after routine artillery bombardment (which rarely dislocated well-set defenses and always warned the defenders), remained the favored tactic until near the end. "Confronted with this deadlock," said Churchill, "military art remained dumb." Again and again, generals hurled masses of men against murderous defensive fire to no avail, seizing a few hundred yards of blasted earth only to lose it again, answering critics with the patent lie that the defenders lost more lives than the attackers. Joffre called it "nibbling," others the war of attrition. Behind the phrases, the fact was that as long as the Germans remained on the defensive in the west, they were free to help the Austrians and Bulgarians crush the Serbs in 1915 and the Rumanians in 1916, and batter the munitions-starved Russians into demoralization and ultimate revolt against a corrupt and incompetent Tsarist regime. Meanwhile, French families endured an avalanche of telegrams that made gibberish of official optimism and censored casualty reports. Over a million were killed, missing, prisoners, or wounded by the end of 1914. Joffre's assaults of 1915 in Artois and Champagne cost another million casualties, 1916's offensives half a million—added to the half million from Verdun's defense, where 200,000 Frenchmen died with 200,000 Germans, partly fulfilling von Falkenhayn's satanic dream that France would commit suicide rather than lose the fortresses. Pétain's role in the defense and the stoic "They shall not pass" won him fame, but the carnage helped convince him and many Frenchmen that a military victory over Germany was not to be expected without far greater outside help.

Joffre's authority as Commander-in-Chief was finally shaken at the end of 1916, partly by parliamentarians increasingly assertive of their rights to direct the war. After the Viviani cabinet and the general staff had held power alone in 1914, the Chambers reassembled in January of 1915 (the government had returned to Paris in early December). Any close estimate of parliament's effect founders on half-known detail and might-have-beens. Its war committees and the individual work of Deputies and Senators no doubt combined help with hindrance, as did political pressures in the choice and treatment of military commanders. But its meetings provided almost the only forum for questioning the wisdom of war leaders, civil and military—many needed questioning— and its presence belied the prophecies that a Republican system would not survive a war. Its failure to raise taxes proved to be costly, but it was generally patient with the executive. The latter, with its civil and military bureaucrats, must bear the major onus for administrative confusion, for the crudities of censorship, the propaganda and the lies familiar to all states in wartime, and the corruption and delays in arms provision, though parliament's failure to limit all these was disappointing. Perhaps its most unhappy political intervention was in the choice of the popular Republican General Nivelle as Commander-in-Chief in late 1916, but

President Poincaré was as bent upon it as were the Deputies and he, with Premier Ribot, was guilty of retaining Nivelle beyond the danger point.

Nivelle's choice was also and above all a result of many men's exasperation with stalemate. Although he had nothing better to offer and much that was worse, his faith in one overpowering offensive buoyed his associates and admirers, who expected 1917 to be the year of victory. It was in fact the nadir. In March, Alexandre Ribot had replaced Briand as Premier of a repatched *union sacrée* cabinet, as Briand had replaced Viviani in August of 1915. Both changes reflected the Deputies' discontent with the War Ministry or the military, or both; War Minister Millerand's unquestioning support of Joffre helped undermine Viviani in 1915, Lyautey's opposition to Nivelle had shaken Briand's majority. In turn, Ribot's Minister of War, Paul Painlevé, was suspicious of Nivelle but unable to remove him until the worst was obvious to Poincaré, the Chambers, and the public. On April 16th, Nivelle launched his offensive in Champagne despite French knowledge that the German defenders knew his plans, had pulled backward to prepared positions, and quintupled their numbers. Over 50,000 died to gain a few hundred yards. A month later, Nivelle was succeeded by Pétain. At last French morale was cracking; mutinies spread through several army units and Pétain spent the next few weeks in personal tours of the front, in reforms of furlough and supply, in directing punishment of the leaders, many of whom were executed. Pétain's relative moderation and well-known preference for the defensive were no doubt more salutary than the wholesale reprisals other military and civilian leaders would have had him take. The United States entered the war in April and Pétain wished to await her massive human and material reinforcements. Sir Douglas Haig disagreed and in the autumn proved himself fully the equal of other western front commanders by sending 130,000 Englishmen to die (400,000 casualties in all) under long-prepared German crossfire in the rain and slime of Passchendaele. He gained four miles in three months of obstinacy. At the end of October the Italians collapsed at Caporetto; in December the Bolsheviks took Russia out of the war by an armistice, allowing the German high command to shift its masses westward for an offensive to end the war.

Ribot's cabinet survived until September, when it was succeeded by Painlevé's. By then, the *union sacrée* was dead, as Socialists and pacifists openly campaigned for a compromise peace. In retrospect, the chances for such a peace appear infinitesimal, given the temper of rival governments, peoples, and powerful military leaders. The governments had sent out several peace feelers by mid-1917, but neither side was ready to concede on major points, such as Alsace-Lorraine, and as one side felt itself ready for talks, the other would turn to dreams of total victory. So the peace offensive became an affair of Leftist opponents of the governments in power. The French Socialists withdrew from the government upon its refusal to grant passports for a conference at Stockholm in 1917 with their counterparts from Britain and Germany. With the rise to prominence, and then to power, of Lenin in Petrograd, it was easy for conservatives and patriots to associate those who desired a negotiated peace with defeatists, revolutionaries, and traitors in common discredit. This Clemenceau did, upon becoming Premier in November of 1917. Since 1914, he had stood for *guerre à l'outrance*, goading cabinets, Ministries, and soldiers to greater efforts. During the darkest hours of 1917 he poured venom on defeatists, pacifists, and strike leaders, on Minister of Interior Malvy, who had ignored the *Carnet B,* who now allowed the Leftist press to talk of negotiation and to attack Poincaré and the war effort. Caillaux had returned to prominence; he and Briand also spoke of a negotiated peace. Clemenceau was not much less ready than *l'Action Française* to accuse them all of treachery and associate them with enemy agents like the sordid Mata Hari.

When Painlevé fell, Poincaré turned his hated rival Clemenceau loose on the Socialists and pacifist Radicals. Socialists and syndicalists were muzzled, Caillaux and Malvy arrested and tried, the former imprisoned and the latter banished. Briand was hounded out of politics for a time. Clemenceau's single-minded drive to victory recalled the Jacobin tradition; he was called France's one-man Committee of Public Safety. But Clemenceau was no longer a Jacobin, in social affairs he never had been, and much else had changed since 1793. Now it was the Right that clamored for war to the end, the Left that was for peace. His indulgence toward financiers, industrialists, and profiteers was at least Dantonesque. This species of anti-patriot, to be sure, was silent—or chauvinist—and there was no time for nuance in 1917, no other source of production. But his one-sided prosecutions were remembered, fouled the memory of his victory and helped divide the notions of equality and patriotism, long after the Tiger's own concern for the ordinary soldier and his family was forgotten.

In rallying the French for a final effort, Clemenceau probably spoke for a great majority, in whom propaganda and personal bereavement produced a mood of intransigence. To give up war aims, especially Alsace-Lorraine, for which so many had died was unthinkable. The more so as America was arming; between Lenin, who released Germans to the western front, and Wilson, who sent Americans, the choice was easy for all but a minority on the Left. The appeal of Wilson's "new diplomacy" to most Socialists and Radicals made Clemenceau's task easier. So great was his prestige and formidable his temper that he was able to rule dictatorially without openly suppressing the parliament. At seventy-six he drove himself mercilessly to meet the inevitable spring offensive of the Germans. His first aim was to bring the British, American, and French leaders into a Supreme War Council with full powers of decision on the western front, as well as economic cooperation. But only after a German offensive in March, 1918, approached Amiens and Haig threatened to fall back on the Channel ports did Clemenceau succeed in imposing Foch as Generalissimo of all Allied armies.

Foch had painfully learned the need of remaining on the defensive until the enemy attack was spent—and until the Americans arrived in force—but Ludendorff's offensive nearly swept all calculations away. With German manpower near depletion, German masses hungry and restive behind Allied blockade, the military took its final gamble, rejecting the idea of negotiation. The Belgian gamble had brought in the British; the submarine gamble, the Americans. Now Ludendorff introduced methods that were later studied too little in the Allied war colleges: quick-moving shock troops, specially trained to disrupt the enemy's rear; simultaneous air raids on headquarters, transport and communications centers; the bombardment of Paris (by "Big Bertha") to demoralize civilians. In May, the Germans broke through the supposedly impregnable French line of the Chemin des Dames (the French were completely surprised and in their haste failed to blow their bridges), took Soissons, and reached the Marne, forty miles from Paris, on the 30th of May. After four years of sacrifice, Frenchmen faced defeat again, as they had before Gallieni and Joffre stopped von Moltke. But Clemenceau ignored his critics, defended Foch, and relied on German exhaustion to slow Ludendorff's advance.

While the latter called up his last reserves, the first American units went into action at Montdidier and Château-Thierry. By the middle of July, Foch was ready to assume the offensive he had waited for, and behind him pushed the far greater industrial and human power of a coalition finally mobilized to the full. The second battle of the Marne began the German rollback; a nearly constant series of Allied offensives, now bolstered by tanks, smoke, and aircraft, kept Ludendorff from consolidating positions he might have held three months before. By August 1st, over a million American troops had landed in France; by November they were nearly two million, half along the firing line. In September Franchet d'Espery advanced from Salonika to wring an armistice from the Bulgarians; Ludendorff lost control for a moment, ordered Prince Max of Baden to beg for an armistice. Allenby and Lawrence forced the Turks to capitulate at the end of October; the Austrian and Hungarian armies' collapse ended in surrender on November 4th.

## PYRRHIC VICTORY AND PEACE

Two days later, the German delegates left Berlin and on November 11, 1918, they sat in Foch's railway car in the Forest of Compiègne to sign an armistice. That night and for two days after, churches were as crowded as cafés, and squares in every city and village were alight with celebration. Among the terms of armistice was the immediate German evacuation of Alsace-Lorraine. The Chambers had already acclaimed the tough old man who reminded them of his protest against the cession of 1871; now he was Père la Victoire. A few days later the young General Julien Dufieux led his troops through the cheering crowds of Strasbourg; the black crepe had fallen from her statue in the Concorde and for months little knots of visitors gathered before it to remind themselves of victory. But France's triumph was darkened by widows' weeds and endless memorial services. The known costs of war bore upon the peace negotiations; the hidden and unmeasurable, upon the life of France for decades, though they were probably less determinative of the future than commonly assumed. One million, three hundred and fifty thousand Frenchmen had died on the battlefield, at surgical stations, and in hospitals (in proportion to population, comparable American losses would have been at least 4 million; there were in fact 115,000, over half from disease in camps). A quarter of all Frenchmen between the ages of 18 and 30 were dead. Six hundred thousand were disabled in body or mind or both. Counting civilian deaths and those unborn because of war, France lost 3 million people. Only the return of Alsace-Lorraine (1.8 million) and immigration enabled her to return to 40 million by 1930, but it was an older population than in 1914 and the birth rate was still declining.

Frenchmen were also appalled by their first impressions of material losses, as soldiers, then refugees, officials, newsmen, and tourists moved across a 300-mile-long zone of devastation left by the fighting and by the German policy of scorched earth. Some 250,000 buildings were wholly, 350,000 partially, destroyed—factories, warehouses, churches, stores, and homes in what had been one of the most productive industrial areas of France. Half the merchant fleet was lost; 3600 miles of railroad, 31,000 miles of road torn up; coal mines flooded; bridges and canal machinery shattered. Peasants returned to crumpled villages and farmsteads, their livestock gone, diseased or dead, orchards cut down, wells and ponds polluted, over 7 million acres of land ravaged by blast and fire. In Champagne, the retreating Germans had consumed or dumped the stored wines, then destroyed the vineyards. The severed vines, like one's dead or broken sons, bespoke a sterile future; the shell of Reims Cathedral, a past beyond reviving. Frenchmen who saw needed no propaganda to convince them of German guilt. The harvest of 1918 was sorrow and wrath, and determination that it should never happen again.

In this atmosphere, the peace conference opened at the Quai d'Orsay on January 18, 1919. The conflicts among the Big Four—Clemenceau, Lloyd George, Orlando, and Wilson—and after Orlando's departure, the Big Three, have often been told, and the Versailles Treaty as often condemned, usually by Anglo-Saxons (and Germans, of course), or defended, usually by the French. Less often have the detractors admitted the intolerable pressures of those few months, the painful difficulties weighing on the French delegation, or the extent to which the effects of the war limited the freedom of all participants. It is commonplace to note that the Big Four, as elected leaders, were captives of public hatreds their governments had promoted by wartime propaganda, that they were thus unable to treat a German democracy, which they had every reason to support, as generously as Bourbon France was treated by the autocrats at Vienna in 1815. Leaving aside the question of whether Germany was as ready for a republic in 1918 as France was for a Bourbon restoration in 1814–1815, the two conferences dealt with vastly different worlds. Even before the great war, Europe in the early twentieth century was incomparably more crowded, faster-moving, less tractable in her economic, social, political, and intellectual realms than Europe in the early nineteenth century; and the World War further jumbled all at least as much as had all of Napoleon's campaigns.

In 1919 eastern Europe was in chaos, the Austro-Hungarian Empire broken into several excited and impoverished nationalities, the Russian Empire dead and in its place a Bolshevik regime which appeared to threaten half of Europe, including prostrate Germany and new Poland, with Marxist revolution. Hunger and disease tormented most of Europe, economic dislocation and financial uncertainty plagued governments under pressure from their people to return the world to normal so they might enjoy what their newspapers still called the fruits of victory. But what the war had done, the Paris conference could not reverse. Three great empires had perished; the German was the victim of Wilsonian diplomacy, not of France's doing. When Frenchmen looked eastward they saw not this or that form of government but simply Germany, still nearly twice as populous as France, heavy with industrial plants and skills. If her revolution proved abortive, the old danger would remain; on the other hand, a genuine revolution—as Frenchmen had good reason to know—was not likely to be docile. In removing France's eastern ally, the Russian Revolution had narrowed her choice of paths to security. An alliance with Lenin's Russia was out of the question for the moment. Clemenceau and his supporters thought it abhorrent and even the French Left was divided over Bolshevism, the majority in early 1919 still reformist in domestic affairs and Wilsonian in foreign. No Russian delegation appeared at the conference; and before it was over the Big Three entangled themselves in the Russian counterrevolution, half-heartedly, in part because they half feared a victorious White government would come to a separate agreement with Germany over Poland. That problem was to recur, in other circumstances.

Two paths remained to French security. The Socialists, and some on the Radical Left, out of power, their press and spokesmen still partly muffled by censorship, acclaimed Wilson's new diplomacy and more: a peace without annexations or transfers unless consented to by the populations involved, self-determination (even in colonial areas, some said), removal of economic barriers, disarmament and nationalization of what arms-making should remain, public control of foreign policy, and reliance on international organization rather than national arms and allies to keep the peace. Wilson arrived in Paris to find himself acclaimed loudest by the opponents of the governments he negotiated with: the British Labour Party, and in France, the SFIO, the CGT, and the

Radical *Ligue des droits de l'homme*. It was an unhappy parallel to Wilson's position at home, where the elections of 1918 had returned Republican majorities to the Senate and House. Theodore Roosevelt told Europeans that Wilson no longer spoke for America; but even had he won a Democratic Congress and Republican silence it is unlikely that Wilson could have satisfied the expectations of the European Left. He had already, in the prearmistice negotiations, given way to Britain on freedom of the seas and to Clemenceau on reparations. At the conference, he felt obliged to agree to secret sessions and big-power dominance, to avoid discussion of racial equality in immigration, and to insist on the privilege of the Monroe Doctrine against League authority. The chances for American reduction of tariffs, for naval disarmament, or nationalization of war manufactures were obviously remote. These limits on the new diplomacy suggested that America no less than France was concerned first with her own security, and would sacrifice little for the sake of a new, untried world order. Marcel Cachin, the Socialist editor of *l'Humanité,* moved quickly from adulation of Wilson to disillusion. And even those French moderates like Léon Bourgeois who had hopes for a League with inspection and police powers quickly found that the Americans in Paris were nearly as wary of an active League as were the British, who wanted only a forum for discussion. Wilson's version of the new diplomacy, then, defeated itself in the eyes of both French factions; too conservative and hardheadedly American for the internationalists, it had never been accepted by conservatives and patriots like Clemenceau as nearly hardheaded enough for France.

To the French Right and Center, the conference presented not "the policies of realism and idealism come to grips," but the needs of a nation in danger versus the indifference of nations already secure and satisfied, well able to suggest concessions provided it was France who made them. But France could not afford to concede. Her path to security, the Right believed, lay in physical guarantees against German resurgence: a permanent military superiority for France through German disarmament, the detachment of the left bank of the Rhine from Germany (most envisaged an autonomous Rhine republic, not direct annexation), and the maintenance and extension of those wartime alliances which had made victory possible. Wilson and Lloyd George utterly opposed any permanent separation of German territory in the west; there should be no new Alsace-Lorraines to kindle German resentment.

The debate was long and acrid, suggesting the attitudes that were to divide the Allies in years to come. The British preached the need for reconciling Germany to her defeat, avoiding any unnecessary affronts to German pride. Clemenceau reasonably pointed out that Britain's conscience had awakened only after she herself had deprived Germany of a navy, merchant fleet, and colonies, placing Germans at great commercial disadvantage—all sources of German resentment before the war. The French thought this an unpromising way to reconciliation, and unjust as well, since Germany was to be appeased only at French expense. England, safely across the Channel, won everything she had fought for in 1914; America, behind the Atlantic, enjoyed unparalleled new wealth from a war in which France made the greatest sacrifices of men and property. French security, Clemenceau argued, was not so easily attained; France alone was exposed to German invasion; she required safeguards which were surely no more onerous to German pride than Britain's winnings, none of which was as essential to British survival as a defensible frontier was to France's. Clemenceau also doubted that any concessions would assuage a defeated Germany; only a policy of strength could prevent her taking revenge at the first opportunity. Brest-Litovsk, he said, showed what Germany would have demanded had she been victorious, showed how foolish it was to hope that Germans would be satisfied by mere equality in Europe.

Lloyd George and Wilson remained adamant; Germany must lose no territory in the west. Foch and Poincaré pressed Clemenceau to hold out, and behind them were some who wished to dismember all of Germany to her pre-Bismarckian condition. But France had won only with outside help and Clemenceau judged it necessary to choose the Allies over the separatists and annexationists. In return for an American and British Treaty of Guarantee to aid France in case of German aggression, he agreed to limit Allied occupation of the Rhine's left bank—and bridgeheads on the right bank—to fifteen years, the time to be shortened or prolonged according to Germany's fulfillment of the reparations clauses of the peace treaty. In addition, the Rhineland was to be permanently demilitarized to a line running 50 kilometers east of the river. Short of annexation or dismemberment, this was the best guarantee that the opening battle of the next war would be fought on German soil and that whatever its result, the British would have time to land more than General French's five divisions. To Frenchmen who believed neither in the League nor in disarmament—even on the Left there was more hope than belief—the demilitarization of the Rhineland and the Anglo-

American Treaty of Guarantee were the guardians of French security.

The Treaty of Versailles was signed on June 28, 1919, in the Hall of Mirrors. Alsace-Lorraine was restored to France. In compensation for her damaged mines, France obtained the coal mines of the Saar and administration of the Saarland for fifteen years, after which a plebiscite would say whether its people wished to be governed by Germany, France, or themselves. Germany was disarmed, allowed no capital ships, no submarines, no air force, no general staff or conscription, only a 100,000-man service force lightly armed to keep internal order. Germany's colonies were distributed among the victors, but as mandates under the League; France received most of Togoland and the Cameroons as well as that portion of the French Congo ceded by Caillaux in 1911. There were no annexations in the west, except for the tiny areas of Moresnet, Eupen, and Malmédy given to Belgium. The political settlement in the east was less respectful of German nationality; the lands given to Poland and Czechoslovakia were justified in various ways, though to Clemenceau they meant a bolstering of allies. In sum, the new political lines of Europe followed the lines of nationality more closely than they ever had, though this was little consolation to German nationalists.

The economic decisions, or lack of them, at the Paris conference proved to be more questionable than the political, and were almost immediately denounced by economists and statesmen in several countries. The imposition of unrealistic reparations, and the historical lie of exclusive German war guilt by which they were justified, grew out of many circumstances: national emotions, political expediency, economic insouciance. Germans themselves admitted the justice of payment for physical damage in Belgium and France. Clemenceau's agreement to Lloyd George's claim to war costs including pensions was disastrous, but here again Clemenceau was motivated not only by the hope of solving French financial problems but by the need to keep the British close, with their own stake in Germany's obedience to the treaty terms. The tragedy had deeper sources; Frenchmen recalled that fifty years earlier Germany had forced payment of an indemnity twice the amount of war costs, this after the seizure of Alsace-Lorraine. However false the idea that Germany alone was guilty in 1914, the fact remained that by 1915 Germans alone were occupying and destroying Belgium and large tracts of France. It could be argued that most of this was inevitable, given Germany's problem of self-defense, but the claim of self-defense was shaken by Brest-Litovsk and by the gratuitous acts of soldiers in the west. Rarely has a nation suffered greater obloquy as a result of its civil leaders' abdication in favor of military men. It was Germany's fate to lose after nearly having won, and after politicians had given way to generals with contempt for any factors not prescribed in military manuals. In an age when public emotions weighed on statesmen, revenge was perhaps inevitable.

The delay in settling final amounts of reparations to 1921 might have allowed the victors to think again, but domestic politics intervened and by then France had lost the Anglo-American guarantee and was ready to employ reparations for political ends. Even so, the French were ready to accept major reductions only a few years later. Of all the nations involved, the United States took longest to admit the economic facts of postwar life. The other failures of Versailles in economic matters were not so much errors of the moment as prolongations of nineteenth-century ways of looking, or not looking, at problems already present before the war and exacerbated by it: the interdependence of national economies, and the rising expectations of the masses at home and in the colonies. Most of what were called the economic consequences of the peace were more the consequences of heedless national capitalism and of the war that it, among other forces, had brought about.

When Clemenceau presented the Versailles Treaty to the Chambers in the autumn of 1919, the Left denounced it as too harsh, the Right as not harsh enough, for French security. It was, in fact, a compromise between those who believed in peace through reconciliation and those who insisted on repression. Hindsight now suggests that one or the other, consistently applied, might have better kept the peace. But French domestic politics lent themselves to consistency abroad no more than those of any other state between the wars. Had France been stronger, or if she could have been made to feel secure, one or the other line might have been more determinedly pursued. But the United States Senate, in a flurry of idealism, isolationism, partisanship, and confusion, repudiated Wilson's word on the Treaty of Guarantee, did not even bring it to a vote. The British seized the chance to escape their own commitment. Clemenceau may not have been surprised; most Frenchmen were, and it was a betrayal they did not forget. The Russian alliance was dead, the Entente dismantled. There remained the League. In March, 1920, the Senate refused the Treaty of Versailles and America turned her back on wicked Europe. When France, conscious of the

League's inability to serve a wider purpose, went on to use it for her own immediate advantage, she was most often denounced by Americans who had abandoned it, by Britons who had eviscerated it. Anglo-Saxons have rarely admitted to themselves how these actions looked or what they meant to a shaken continent. France entered the 1920's exhausted and without allies, less secure in victory than she had been in 1914. Wilson and Clemenceau knew Versailles to be a first, imperfect instrument for peace; to refine it required the closest collaboration of the victors. This lacking, France took it up as a weapon of desperation.

# ~ix~

# THE POSTWAR REPUBLIC

The history of France during the twenty-year armistice moved swiftly through three short eras: the immediate postwar, 1919–1925, beset with economic and social difficulties at home and the failure of an aggressive policy toward Germany; a few years of economic stability and diplomatic reconciliation, 1926 to 1932, which many Frenchmen and their visitors could believe was a new Belle Époque; finally, the years of crisis and decline, opening with depression and the rise of Hitler, to close upon another *année terrible*, the collapse of 1940, the death of the Third Republic, and German occupation through the Second World War. Such a division suggests that the good years of the late 1920's witnessed a full recovery from war's effects and at least the possibility of progress toward prosperity and lasting peace for French and European society in the years following. No one can prove the inevitability of Hitler or depression, at least depression as abysmal as it turned out to be. Nor can one prove the inevitability of France's failure to meet those threats once they arose. But in retrospect the odds seem very long indeed and the failure hardly to be blamed on the French governments of the 1930's alone. The prosperity and confidence of the late 1920's were shallowly rooted in a society that had failed to meet economic and social problems two generations old, problems which the war and its aftereffects made at once more pressing and more difficult to solve. Worse, and deeply disturbing to Frenchmen who saw it, France lay exposed to outside forces over which the most vigorous national government could have little control.

## THE RETURN TO ROUTINE

Until 1914, Frenchmen, like Americans, lived in a world which allowed them to believe that their destiny lay in their own hands. Foreign power had of course intruded in the nineteenth century, sometimes brutally, as in the defeat of the two Napoleons, at other times more stealthily, as international economic advances or declines reached into the Bourse, the factory town or wheat market. But the first had been blamed on imperial errors and the second obscured, as most economic questions are, by factional debate, by the noise or silence of special interests, and by a general failure, common to all nations, to comprehend the growing interdependence of modern economies. But the coming of the war showed how far France's will was bound to Allies she needed to contain Germany's military power, and the fighting proved how indispensable was outside help so dearly paid for. The war also proved that the French economy was not by itself equal to a direct challenge from Germany, that massive Allied loans and matériel were needed to equip her armies and to keep the franc from collapse. France in 1919 reached that painful time to which all great nations come, when dreams of overweening power and national self-sufficiency begin to fade and national sovereignty itself is diminished, in fact if not in law, by alien forces the nation cannot do without. The Paris conference demonstrated the new facts of foreign relations to all who would see, and in seeing them (on the diplomatic and military plane more than on the economic) the great antagonists Wilson and Clemenceau had more in common with each other than with Lloyd George, or Wilson's Congress, or Clemenceau's xenophobic critics. Their conviction that isolationism was out of date made their battles all the sharper, as they sought different ways to collective security, Clemenceau by alliances, Wilson by the League. Both were overthrown by men willing to promise that America and France could manage their own destinies, and by men who knew better but hated them or their compromises at Paris.

Many articulate Frenchmen, from the poet Paul Valéry to the hard and brilliant politician André Tardieu, were shaken by what the war had done to France and Europe, and begged for new departures to meet the revolution which had altered all the old relations between class and class, nation and nation, hemisphere and hemisphere. France and Europe were shrunken and impoverished in the face of two giants loosed upon the earth: the United States and the Soviet Union. Some already insisted that France and her sister nations would shortly have to choose one of the two, unless a new, united Europe rose to stand between, or others said, unless France herself contrived to harness every resource at home and in her empire to build a greater France, of wholly new dimensions, whose sheer quantity of men and machines could compete in a world of superpowers. At home, Socialists and union leaders demanded sweeping legislation to right the wrongs of half a century; some businessmen urged renewal of French scientific and technical education and a turn to modern mass production, distribution, and consumption; some politicians of the Right and Center saw a powerful, efficient executive as the only hope for national greatness. All the changes, in short, which the Fourth and Fifth Republics have brought to France in some degree or other were sought by a prescient minority after the First World War.

The contrast between French responses to the two postwar worlds was striking. To begin with, the appearance of victory in the first war hid from many Frenchmen the need for hard action in any sphere but reconstruction of the invaded areas, and something, whatever it might be, to halt the inflation of the franc in 1919. Devastating as the war was, its effects were not devastating enough to break the illusion that France could return to normal and by normal means, an illusion also prevalent in London, Washington, and even in Berlin. Those who thought differently were nowhere united or politically powerful enough to challenge the practical men who now took power and who, for the most part, believed in and toiled to restore the world of their youth. The elections of November, 1919, returned a conservative Chamber of Deputies, seating many war veterans new to politics; hence the name "Horizon Blue Chamber," after the color of French army uniforms. As in the Chambre Introuvable of Louis XVIII and the Bordeaux-Versailles Assembly of 1871, the majority tended to look backward rather than ahead for their ideas of the good France. No more than Harding or his Congress were they ready, for example, to deal with economic and social questions in that new spirit so often promised to the men in the trenches by so many effulgent orators.

The elections took place in the midst of social unrest. Although the

Chamber and Senate in early 1919 had hastened to pass laws for an eight-hour day and official recognition of the results of collective bargaining, several events stirred bad feeling that was vented in strikes and demonstrations. Many employers refused to honor the labor laws and the government failed to press them, to the dismay of other businessmen, perhaps a majority, who were eager to start afresh in labor relations. Such division among employers was long familiar and destined to play an especially vicious role in France to 1940; the intransigents, who were often the largest, and closer to financial and bureaucratic powers, could threaten those who tried to cooperate with responsible trade unions. On their side, labor leaders who preferred moderation, led by Léon Jouhaux of the CGT, were discredited among their followers for failing to take a stronger line to force compliance. The Bolshevik Revolution and the founding in March, 1919, of the Third International widened the split within the Socialist party and the unions between reformers and revolutionaries. In March also, a French court acquitted the assassin of Jean Jaurès. Nothing could have been better calculated to exasperate the working class. The immense May Day demonstration in Paris turned violent and police wounded several participants; strikes followed in many industries, coal, metallurgy, textiles, the Métro and buses of Paris. Before the year ended, a million workers had taken part in hundreds of stoppages. Behind this agitation lay also the spiraling cost of living; the franc, which had held firm during the war, lost ground as American and British support was withdrawn and the government, allowing itself to believe that German reparations would soon rescue it, borrowed freely from the Bank of France.

In these circumstances, it was easy for conservatives to blame inflation on labor troubles which, by halting production at a time of high demand, were no doubt contributory (as were delays in demobilization of workers from the army). The famous election poster of the Bolshevik with a knife in his teeth was generously displayed by conservative parties subsidized from the business community. Many Radicals refused to make electoral alliances with the divided Socialists, who on their part were reluctant to resume a practice so sparse of results before the war, the more so as the militants looking to Moscow derided it. Other Radicals turned to the *Bloc National,* an alliance made up of nearly all the Right and Right Center parties. The final blow to the Left was the new electoral law based on departmental lists, giving all seats in each department to the party or bloc with a majority of votes. Although the Socialists increased their popular vote of 1914 by 300,000, to 1,730,000 or 23 per cent of the total, they sank from 103 seats to 68, or 11 per cent of the Chamber. The Radical-Socialists and other Left Republicans who ran alone won only 67.

The various parties of the *Bloc National* won 437 seats and no fewer than 350 members of the wartime Chamber failed to reappear. The overturn misled conservatives on the state of opinion; many voters had abstained and subsequent local elections returned a higher proportion of Socialists and Radicals. But departures from the prewar pattern were unmistakable in the new Chamber, whose balance lay on the Right Center. The nationalist revival which had stirred up Paris before 1914 was prolonged by war; but most Rightists, except for the followers of Maurras in Action Française, now seemed loyal to a Republic which had proved its strength and conservatism; anti-clericalism, already declining before the war, was further dissipated by *l'union sacrée* and the wartime record of Catholic priests and laymen; the French Catholics had protested the compromise peace attempts of Benedict XV and the fiercest priest-eater of all had chosen the rigid Catholic Foch as Commander-in-Chief; more Catholics were elected than at any time since 1871. For a while, the press and spokesmen of the Right talked of a new political era, the old system transformed by new men imbued with the selfless spirit of the trenches. But given so many inexperienced members and the pressing fiscal crisis, familiar names and habits reemerged. The Center Right parties of business, the *Alliance Républicaine Démocratique* and the *Fédération Républicaine* (heirs of the Opportunists and Progressists who had dominated the Chamber in the 1890's), joined with assorted Republicans and Radicals of the Center Left to support a cabinet headed, after Clemenceau's departure, by Alexandre Millerand. This moderate Right Center coalition was to dominate French politics between the wars; the recurring pattern was to see the Left win every election but those of 1919 and 1928, only to lose its coherence in the Chamber as Radicals drifted back to Center on economic questions that divided them from the Socialists they had campaigned with on ideological and foreign issues.

Whatever the new Assembly thought of wartime heroes, there was one it hurried to retire. Although Clemenceau refused to make himself a candidate to succeed Poincaré as President, the world, the French public which had heard his name so often from the candidates it had just made Deputies, and the old man himself, expected his election.

But he had wounded too many; Briand led those who now could take revenge. Catholics suspected the old-fashioned atheist, Republicans the authoritarian, Socialists the breaker of strikes and jailer of pacifists, patriots the peacemaker who had given up the Rhine to salve the Anglo-Saxons' consciences in exchange for a treaty their consciences allowed them to forget. On January 17th, the moderate, inoffensive Paul Deschanel, president of the Chamber, was elected President of France. Clemenceau retired, at seventy-nine, to his cottage on the ocean shore of the Vendée, defiant and embittered, to watch his successors' struggles to keep the complicated peace he had left them. Millerand, who had led the *Bloc National,* succeeded him as Premier. But in the autumn, the unfortunate Deschanel suffered a mental breakdown and Millerand became President of the Republic, hoping to increase the powers of the office and of the executive arm in general whenever an opportunity should present itself. Aristide Briand returned to political life as Premier and Foreign Minister in January, 1921, with Louis Barthou as War Minister, Albert Sarraut as Minister of Colonies, Paul Doumer as Minister of Finance, and several other veterans, or veterans-to-be, of the ministerial round. Politics, at least, had returned to normal, familiar channels.

Economic and social life had not. Real wages continued to decline through 1920, and a short, sharp world-wide depression succeeded the brief postwar prosperity. Now the deeper effects of war on the French economy emerged. The human losses were most serious for agriculture, although the disproportionately high rate of deaths among graduates of *Normale, Polytechnique,* and other schools for scientists, engineers, economists, and administrators deprived the whole economy of badly needed talent. Farm production, which had fallen during the war to less than two-thirds of its 1913 level, revived slowly; and with the abrupt end of price controls (except for wheat) in 1919, food costs increased, though without returning enough profits to the farmers to halt a drift of young men to the cities. Much arable land, abandoned during the war, was not reclaimed and large proprietors were still slow to invest in modern means of cultivation. Farm housing and village services remained antiquated, even in some of the rebuilt areas, which were restored rather than modernized. Urban housing, inadequate even before the great wartime growth of industry around Paris and other cities, also languished as rent controls discouraged landlords from new building or repairs, and a state burdened with reconstruction costs undertook no renewal program. The effects of bad housing on the health and spirit of the working and lower middle classes grievously demoralized them between the wars, serving as a daily reminder of underprivilege and the inability of the system to respond to a primary human need. Men who had expected that after four years of agony a grateful nation would offer them homes and jobs fit for heroes returned to prewar conditions of life and labor, made worse by inflation. Tens of thousands joined unions affiliated with the CGT, already swollen with masses of war industry workers new to unionism and, especially in the Paris area, drawn to the Leninist example.

The strikes of 1919, some economic and others wildcat or revolutionary, most of them defeated, were followed in February, 1920, by a rail strike, in which both government and private employers failed to keep the agreement reached. The union's moderate leaders gave way to militants, and a second strike, demanding nationalization of the badly deteriorated railroads, failed utterly as the government jailed its leaders and ran trains with blacklegs and soldiers. The CGT's reformist leaders, Jouhaux and Alphonse Merrheim, had just beaten back an attempt of revolutionaries to wrest control of the national organization. Now they had to move or be accused of complicity with reaction. The general strike they called in May, 1920, broke down upon their own hesitance, the quarrel within many unions between moderates and extremists, lack of discipline, planning or strike funds, and the refusal of non-union workers to cooperate. But the Red Scare in France nearly equaled that in America; the press, bourgeois public, and Chamber cried for repression and the ex-Socialist Millerand obliged them with arrests, police and army intervention. The railroads threw 20,000 men out of work and industry conducted a purge of active union members. In the six months following defeat, CGT membership fell from nearly 2 million to under 600,000; Leninists, anarchists, and syndicalists inveighed against the treachery of leaders who had failed the working class after having kept it in a bourgeois war with promises of reform. In 1921, the Paris unions led a number of others in forming the CGTU (*Confédération Générale du Travail Unitaire*) which was captured by the Communists in 1924. Since the Catholic unions, strongest among northern textile and white-collar workers, had organized the CFTC (*Confédération Française des Travailleurs Chrétiens*) in 1919, the French labor movement was split into three major and several minor fragments.

The year 1920 also saw the division of the Socialist party. At the Congress of Tours, a heavy majority revolted against Léon Blum and voted to accept the conditions imposed by Lenin and the Third International: obedience to Moscow, war on bourgeois "reformists," the class struggle, secret and illegal action, anti-militarism and anti-colonialism, assistance to the Soviet Union, strict party discipline, and regular purges of deviationists. Blum and the minority, pledged to parliamentary action and the Second International, withdrew, leaving the party treasury, offices, and Jean Jaurès' famous daily l'Humanité in the hands of a new French Communist party. Its majority did not last long. Like the CGTU, it suffered from over-rigidity, inner dissension, and the often obtuse and contradictory intervention of Moscow. Blum founded Le Populaire and skillfully rebuilt the Socialist party, to which 56 of the 68 Deputies remained attached. By the mid-1920's both the Socialists and the CGT had regained a majority of the rank and file. But the Sacred Union which moderate labor and Socialist leaders had loyally maintained throughout the war—even under Clemenceau's provocation —had been smashed by intransigence of government and employers on the Right, by extremists on the Left. The working class had once more been shut out of the nation's life, its interests ignored by those officials and employers shortsighted enough to rejoice at Communist success in fragmenting the power of gradualists like Jouhaux and Blum. The eight-hour day was forgotten in many industries, collective bargaining and the rights of unionization and strike were violated with impunity.

In an era of full employment and union debility, social strife subsided. Now another threat ocupied the Chamber: the decline of the franc, which if it persisted would undermine the confidence of Frenchmen in their government. Like so many others, inflation was a new problem to the French; the franc had been stable for over a century. It was easy to believe that its fall was due to speculation and that it must shortly right itself. But in fact, the effects of war were largely to blame. French production had fallen off in every area but the wasteful industries of arms; the government was forced to purchase food, raw materials, and manufactured goods at inflated prices from allies and neutrals; French holdings abroad were wiped out; trade and tourism had come to a standstill. Government policy was also partly responsible: all war costs were borrowed, internally or abroad; the government had allowed enormous profits and taxed them very gently if at all; the Right had balked at a genuine income tax, the Left at raising the old indirect taxes. The debt, which stood at 33 billion francs in 1914, had risen to 141 billion in 1919. Only a program of national austerity and forced disgorgement of wartime profits could have begun, only begun, to close the gap. The Chamber deemed neither politically feasible. The budget was "balanced" by placing the costs of reconstruction and pensions in special accounts for which "the Germans would pay." Reparations, then, was the magic answer for those whose fiscal irresponsibility, or honest ignorance, added to the pressures on the franc created by the great expense and destruction of war.

## FORCE AND DIPLOMACY

In 1921 the Inter-Allied Commission on Reparations fixed the sum of German payments at $33 billion, of which some 50 per cent would come to France. The British, partly under the influence of John Maynard Keynes' brilliant, intolerant book, *The Economic Consequences of the Peace* (1919), thought the figure too high. Apart from their desire to see Germany revive as a trading partner, they believed that France's object in pressing for full payment was the permanent weakening and perhaps dismemberment of Germany. With great reluctance, Lloyd George had agreed to an occupation of east-bank Rhenish cities until Germany agreed to the terms of 1921. At the Cannes Conference in January of 1922, he sought Briand's agreement to the German government's request for a moratorium until its economy and currency regained their equilibrium. Briand was pressing Lloyd George for a treaty of alliance in return when Millerand brought about the Premier's resignation. Determined to pursue a hard policy toward Germany and doubtful in any case of the chances of British agreement to a military convention embracing the Rhineland, Millerand called on Poincaré to form a government whose main object would be to make the Germans pay in full, by any means, regardless of British or American opinion.

French disenchantment with London and Washington had reached a critical point; Harding's Washington Conference in 1921–1922 saw the representatives of both belabor France, for maintaining large land forces, in those lofty moral tones reserved, as Frenchmen said, for the unconverted heathen. That British and American naval reductions not only saved them money but still left them masters of the seas made the sermons less than edifying to Frenchmen who believed, rightly, that

Germany was already planning her rearmament on land. In 1922, Harding demanded that France begin to pay the 40 billion francs she owed in debts; on her part, France believed that since she had paid in blood and devastation for what Americans had called the common cause, and since most of the money had gone to enrich American producers, it was incumbent upon Washington to be patient and, in justice, to link the settlement of Allied debts to that of German reparations. Washington's refusal and France's inability to pay (except in goods, which American protectionism forbade) poisoned Franco-American relations for a decade and more. Britain's offer in 1922 to collect in reparations from Germany only what she paid America further exasperated the French, as this was to turn the question of reparations and debts in the wrong direction, to benefit the nations which had suffered no physical damage while weakening the entire case for reparations to the nations, Belgium and France, who were most entitled to them. Finally, Britain and France were disputing each other's interests in the Near East and backing opposite sides in the Greco-Turkish War.

In May of 1922, the reparations commission allowed Germany a moratorium to the end of the year, to save the mark from further inflation. The French Right and Center, probably most of the public as well, were convinced that Germany, abetted by a business-minded British government, was purposely evading reparations. The Rapallo Treaty of alliance between Germany and Soviet Russia in April had already aroused French patriots. After unsuccessfully asking of Britain a policy of "productive guarantees," including the appropriation of certain German capital, in return for a moratorium, Poincaré decided to act on his own. When Germany partly defaulted on coal and timber deliveries, French and Belgian troops invaded the Ruhr in January of 1923, accompanied by a mission to supervise production in mines and factories and the transfer of goods to France and Belgium. The British protested sharply; the German government ordered passive resistance. With its industrial heartland idle, the German economy stood still and Berlin's massive support to the resistance (by reckless printing of bills) totally undermined the currency. By autumn, the mark, which had suffered even more than the franc from loose wartime and postwar fiscal policies, was worthless. Owners of real property and foreign paper prospered and industrialists rid themselves of indebtedness at home, as they had partly done by encouraging the earlier inflation. But for ordinary men, an entire life's savings would not buy a meal, and a generation of thrifty

German bourgeois was bankrupted. Passive resistance ceased, but the franc was also falling, the costs of occupation weighing heavily on Paris. A Rhineland separatist movement encouraged by French officers failed; an embarrassment to Poincaré, who disavowed it, it seemed to justify British fears of French designs on German unity. Germany promised to resume payments; and Poincaré, fearing to alienate Great Britain further and facing rising protests at home on the eve of an election, gladly seized the occasion to agree to an Anglo-American plan to review the entire question of reparations. The Dawes Plan, accepted by Germany in April of 1924, stabilized the mark, provided foreign loans to Germany, and arranged a scaled-down series of reparations payments. Under it, Germany paid reparations regularly until 1931.

Although Poincaré could argue that his toughness had forced the issue and proved France's ability to impose her will, the long-range effects of *la politique de la Ruhr* were debilitating to French foreign policy. Whatever the provocation, French defiance of Great Britain was recognized even by Poincaré to be incompatible with French security. The Right's hard policy toward Germany had, in a limited sense, succeeded, but only at great expense, against a defenseless German Republic. Short of dismembering Germany, which only a few extremists thought possible, France could find security only in containing her, or reconciling her, or both. As Clemenceau had insisted, the first was impossible without British cooperation, which in turn could be achieved only by attempting reconciliation, which was Britain's German policy. From 1924 to the rise of Nazism in Berlin, French diplomacy sought to combine containment, that is, the preservation of the Versailles Treaty's limits on Germany's frontiers and armaments, with Franco-German reconciliation. Whether, with time, even a prosperous, democratic Weimar Republic would have accepted such conditions is questionable. The depression-ridden Nazi Germany of 1933 could not and when a new hard policy might have been justified and effective, Frenchmen held back partly because they believed the Ruhr to have been an error. To whatever extent that France's seizure of the Ruhr was responsible for German inflation (considering earlier German policies, it was an occasion more than a cause) she helped open the way for the Nazi regime. Although Hitler came to power only later, in the depths of depression, the German middle classes had already been demoralized and were unable to withstand the second economic disaster as they might have, had their confidence and self-respect been spared in 1923.

In the short run, Poincaré's Ruhr adventure helped to bring the Left to power in the French election of May, 1924. That he had kept the franc from falling lower by a number of adroit moves in the money market appeared less important to many Frenchmen than the 20 per cent increase on indirect taxes he imposed to meet the expense of the Ruhr campaign. Although the popular vote was not notably different from that of 1919, the Left parties now enjoyed the stronger electoral alliances, in the Cartel des Gauches, led by the Socialists under Blum and the Radicals under Édouard Herriot, the bluff, versatile, and politically gifted mayor of Lyon. Both had opposed the Ruhr invasion; now they made capital of its difficulties in a campaign against "Poincaré the war-maker." Denouncing the tax increases, which allowed the wealthy to escape again, and the Right's refusal to allow unionization of civil servants, the Left added to these and other social questions the old issue of anti-clericalism, reopened partly by the Right's proposal to grant tax money to church schools and by the resumption of diplomatic relations with the Vatican, arranged by Briand in 1921. Under a slightly modified version of the electoral law of 1919, the Cartel des Gauches proper won 38 per cent of the vote, 47 per cent of the seats, or 266 including 103 Socialists and 142 Radicals; the Communists polled a surprising 875,000 votes, or 10 per cent, to win 26 places in the new Chamber; the Right won 229, the Center 47, many of whom were at first allied with the Cartel on anti-clerical grounds. President Millerand was associated with the Ruhr and had too openly campaigned for the conservatives. The new majority forced him out of the Élysée, by refusing to form a ministry until he resigned; but it had to be content with the moderate Gaston Doumergue when the Senate majority and the Chamber Center joined to oppose its vaguely socialist candidate Paul Painlevé. It was a sign of things to come and, like the election, proof that the Center Republicans and independent Radicals had kept the power to preserve or destroy a majority, whether of Left or Right. On the Cartel's left, the Socialists pledged their support to an Herriot cabinet but refused to take part in it, a return to the prewar practice made more urgent by the presence on their own left of Communists ready to exploit every sign of compromise with bourgeois interests.

The Cartel governments managed to introduce far more of their foreign program than their domestic, inaugurating that hybrid policy of containment and conciliation that was to be called *Briandisme,* after the great tactician who was Foreign Minister from 1925 to 1932. Herriot was his own Foreign Minister in the first Cartel cabinet and immediately undertook to mollify England, then under her first Labour government. In August, 1924, he promised complete withdrawal from the Ruhr; in September, the Dawes Plan went into effect; in October, he recognized the Soviet Union. With Ramsay MacDonald, Herriot agreed to the Geneva Protocol which might have fortified the League's system of sanctions by making international arbitration of disputes mandatory and identifying as aggression any nation's refusal to submit to arbitration. But the Protocol was refused (1925) by the succeeding Conservative government of Stanley Baldwin, on the excuse that the Dominions objected to entanglements. On the fall of the Herriot cabinet in April, 1925, Aristide Briand began his long tenure at the Quai d'Orsay.

After the advent of Hitler in 1933 and the rapid series of Anglo-French retreats called appeasement, Briand was accused by the Right of having given way too much to Germany and Great Britain, by the Left of not having gone far enough to bolster the Weimar Republic. Apart from illustrating the familiar confusions implicit in blaming an administration for the problems it inherits and the problems it cannot foresee, the accusations suggest Briand's dilemma and the nature of his policy. In effect he did not, could not, follow consistently the entire diplomatic line of either Right or Left, for neither was consistent with itself. The Right demanded that France insure her security by keeping military supremacy in Europe, a ring of alliances in eastern Europe as protection against both Germany and Communist Russia (the famous *cordon sanitaire*), by using the League only when it advanced immediate French interests, especially in preserving the Versailles settlement, and, whenever necessary, by unilateral French action against any German infringement of that settlement. The Right believed that Germany, whatever her form of government, was vengeful and would stop at nothing less than European hegemony. But unilateral action in the Ruhr had already broken down over French determination, shared by all but a few on the Right, to keep Great Britain close. However impressive her continental ascendancy appeared to visiting journalists, France was not strong enough to act alone for very long and her eastern allies were never considered equal to the British. The Left on its part demanded thoroughgoing internationalism in principle, dependence on the League, friendship with Britain, reconciliation with a democratic Germany, and progressive disarmament. But the Left itself did not welcome the prospect of revising Versailles' provisions on German boundaries in the east or of abandoning French alliances with the new nations which guarded those boundaries. And in its much-repeated claim that there were "two Germanies," that the democratic Germans must be bolstered by every means at France's disposal, the Left admitted the continuing presence of a nationalist, militarist German party against which France must ever be on guard.

Briand's policy was a brilliant improvisation, designed, as must be all foreign policies whose success depends on steadiness over a long period, to win broad approval at home. That the consensus outlived him (he died in March, 1932) and, worse, outlived the Germany it was meant to deal with, was not mainly his responsibility. Briand retained intact the eastern alliances already concluded: the military alliance of 1921 with Poland, which a team of French army advisers under General Weygand had helped to save from Russian invasion a year before; the treaty of mutual assistance with Czechoslovakia of 1924. To these he added defensive treaties with Rumania in 1926, with Yugoslavia in 1927, completing France's links to the Little Entente, of which Czechoslovakia was the third member. The mutual suspicions of the French and Soviet governments flowing from Allied intervention in the Russian civil war, from Moscow's refusal to assume responsibility for the Tsarist bonds, and from the disruptive tactics of the French Communist party, precluded any revival of the Russian alliance. The small states of eastern Europe were poor substitutes. The economic and military aid supplied from Paris between the wars was never enough to insure either their prosperity or their security. The Czechs and Poles, whose frontiers the Germans most resented, persisted in quarrels with each other. Germany, not France, exercised natural economic power in the area. This contradictory situation prevented many Frenchmen, especially in the army, from taking such allies very seriously.

The main object of French diplomacy was the restoration of British guarantees against German revenge. In the Locarno Treaties of 1925, Briand appeared to have combined this object with German reconciliation. Their ultimate failure should not detract from the possibilities they presented—as long as Weimar survived—for ultimate success. On the initiative of the conciliatory, though patriotic, Stresemann of Germany and Austen Chamberlain of Britain, Briand arranged a series of pacts guaranteeing the Versailles frontiers of Belgium, Germany, and France. Britain and Italy agreed to come to the aid of any of the three should it be subject to unprovoked attack; France and Belgium signed arbitration treaties with Germany, which in turn, on French insistence, signed similar treaties with Poland and Czechoslovakia. France then added treaties of mutual assistance with the latter two in case of German aggression. In the five years that followed, years of relative prosperity and political stability in Europe, the "spirit of Locarno" appeared to have set the nations on the road to peace. In 1926 Germany joined the League as a permanent member of the Council and a disarmament commission opened talks in Geneva. In 1927, the victors' military control commission withdrew from Germany, the League assuming responsibility—though not inspection—of Versailles' disarmament provisions. In 1928, France reduced her military service to one year and the Kellogg-Briand Pact collected the signatures of most world powers on a promise never to resort to offensive war. In 1929, the Young Plan scaled down and fixed a final schedule of German reparations payments, and in 1930 France withdrew the last of her troops from the Rhineland, five years ahead of schedule.

Beneath the placid surface of international relations, however, were uncertainties and contradictions that worried many Frenchmen and provoked attacks from Right and Left on Briandism. Most important, Locarno failed to provide a firm British guarantee. It was not an alliance, involved no military arrangements, and the close escape of August, 1914, haunted French imaginations. Moreover, it was vague on what the British would do should the demilitarized Rhineland be occupied by German troops; the key article was interpreted by the British as allowing French action (and British support) only if the occupation were clearly preparatory to invasion of French soil. Nor would the British respond to Briand's pleading that they join to guarantee the eastern frontiers of Germany against revision. In short, what made Locarno appealing to the British—its lack of commitment—made it unsatisfactory to the French. Vocal groups in Germany continued to demand revision of the eastern boundaries, which the German government professed to believe the French, quieted by Locarno, might accept in time. Evidence accumulated of German rearmament, of the rebuilding of the general staff, with the approval of President Hindenburg, who had stoutly denied Germany's responsibility for the war. Briand himself was increasingly uncertain; in September of 1929 he proposed a European federation, but his political support at home was dwindling. Three weeks later Stresemann died and less than a year later—in September, 1930, three months after the last French troops left the Rhineland—Adolf Hitler's National Socialist party won 107 seats in the Reichstag, and the time of troubles opened for the two Republics.

## DOMESTIC AFFAIRS

The Cartel des Gauches, whose electoral triumph in 1924 permitted a reorientation of French foreign policy, failed in nearly all it tried to do at home. The Herriot government rested on a coalition of Radicals and Socialists in the style of Combes' and other prewar cabinets, but there was a difference. The old issue of anti-clericalism was no longer lively enough to hold together two parties of opposing views on the most lively issues of the day: finance and economic reform. The cabinet tried to remove the French ambassador to the Vatican and failed, tried to impose the lay laws in Alsace-Lorraine, where the Concordat was still in force and primary education was largely Catholic or Protestant. This gratuitous violation of promises made upon reannexation in 1918 also failed, in the face of local indignation and a nation-wide Catholic reaction. The cabinet's threat to apply the association laws to religious orders whose members had returned during the war was likewise dropped. These sallies did nothing but needlessly anger Catholic Republicans; they failed to impress Socialists who were now under greater pressure than ever, from the Communists and their own militants, to force the Radicals to meaningful reforms in the economic sphere. But apart from reinforcing rent controls and tolerating the unionization of civil servants, the Radicals could not agree on economic and fiscal questions, the most pressing of which was the relentless decline of the franc.

At first they refused Socialist demands for a capital levy to balance the budget and pay for reconstruction, public works, and social services, but not decisively enough to stop a flight of capital which further depressed the franc. Bondholders rushed to redeem their holdings and the Bank of France resisted advances to the government, the financial community setting the press against Herriot's cabinet in a campaign to destroy public confidence in it. In 1925, after denouncing "the wall of moneybags," Herriot led the majority to vote a tax on capital. The Senate refused it and Herriot resigned. A Painlevé cabinet slipped to the Center; the anti-clerical program was dropped and Joseph Caillaux returned to the Finance Ministry to pursue an orthodox policy of government economy and indirect taxation. Still capital fled. Painlevé became Finance Minister and swung back to a capital levy; he failed and was overturned. By July of 1926, Caillaux was back, to ask decree-law power for a program of austerity; both Left and Right refused. The franc, which had been 18 to the dollar in 1924, fell to 50 and the French public feared a repetition of the German debacle.

Amid popular demonstrations and an ominous gathering of Rightist forces, Doumergue called Poincaré back to power and a Government of National Union was formed, including Herriot, Briand, Painlevé, Barthou, and Tardieu. The Cartel was dead, the business community immediately took heart, and the franc rose to 40 to the dollar before Poincaré had taken a single step. His reputation as a national leader, his probity and solid republicanism served him well in crisis. The Chamber granted him the decree power it had refused Caillaux. By a series of new taxes, mostly indirect, a reduction of government expenses, an inviolate fund to meet bond payments, and a rise in interest rates, he achieved a budget surplus and returned the franc to 25 to the dollar. The "savior of the franc" might have allowed it to go higher, but French exports would have been priced out of foreign markets. There was nothing to do but stabilize it, at one-fifth its prewar value, though this was not officially done until after the 1928 elections. Thus were the great war and reconstruction finally paid for, by a devaluation which took four-fifths of the 1914 value of all French savings, pensions, and bonds—and a rise in taxes which struck hardest at consumers and small property owners. So serious was devaluation, however clearly it might have been foreseen, that politicians were sure it could never be done again. Inflation remained a dreaded word to all the middle class and small proprietors who had always placed such hope for themselves and their children on the value of money they saved in a lifetime of prudence and self-denial.

Tens of thousands of small businessmen, bondholders, peasants, middle-rank civil servants, and pensioners redoubled their resolve to preserve what remained of the *status quo*. In an economy which, while prosperous enough, was relatively static, new careers and opportunities were scarce in every field. It did not pay to move, expand, or experiment; son—there was, so often, only one—followed father and the economic habit of *gagne-petit* was reinforced, to the detriment of enterprise, and civic spirit. If one missed his footing, he fell very far indeed, in a country with little social legislation. But social legislation meant government spending, higher taxes, perhaps more inflation. The rank and file of the Radical-Socialists and of parties to their right was even less likely to accept it now than in the days before the war, and their Deputies, increasingly subsidized by business interests, were not at all likely to force them to it. The working classes, on their part, felt betrayed once more by a Chamber which had been elected on a platform of social progress but had moved to the right and then done little but raise their taxes. But they remained a minority within French society, and as divided as ever, between Communist and Socialist parties, among several union organizations, or attached to none. For half a decade, general prosperity covered over social fears and class antagonisms, but depression was to see them reemerge, at a moment when the life of France was threatened again by the old enemy across the Rhine.

The elections of April, 1928, were held according to *scrutin d'arrondissement*, single-member constituencies, both Left and Right having once more lost their faith in *scrutin de liste*. As usual, the boundaries of voting districts were so drawn as to overrepresent the countryside. The Right and Right Center enjoyed an effective electoral alliance in *l'Union Nationale*, led by Poincaré, who could boast of presiding over financial stability, a balanced budget, and full employment. The Radicals, as in 1919, were divided between supporters of Poincaré and those drifting back to the Left, but even the latter were wary of social promises and fell back on the anti-clerical refrain. The Communist party refused to withdraw its candidates in the second round in favor of Socialists or Radicals, and its voters, to their rivals' dismay, stood fast. Communist candidates polled a million votes but won only 14 seats; the Socialists took 106 from 1.75 million, the Radical-Socialists 113, and the Socialist Republicans (a newly formed union of un-affiliated former Radicals and independent Socialists) won 40. Had the Communists adopted "Republican discipline" and dropped their minority candidates, the Left could have won 60 more seats. The National Union won 320 seats, though some on the far Right could not be counted on for cooperation in the Chamber. Without a serious displacement of the popular vote, the Poincaré government (and Briand) had nonetheless been reinforced, on a Right Center concentration that resembled those of the 1890's, when the *Ralliément* had first made possible the alliance of Catholic Republicans and non-Catholic Republican conservatives.

In the late 1920's the clerical question was barely alive as a national issue, though the village rivalry between priest and schoolmaster could be as piquant as ever. The reign of Pius XI at the Vatican (1922–1939) brought several new shocks to French Catholic intransigents. In 1924 the new Pope approved the organization of lay diocesan associations to take custody of church buildings according to a modified version of the Separation Law of 1905, over the objections of the Left, the extreme Right, and a few intransigent bishops. Pius XI was in fact determined on a second *Ralliement,* to which the main obstacle was the great influence of Charles Maurras' virulently anti-Republican *l'Action Française* among the French clergy, upper-class Catholics, and well-to-do students in law, administration, and commerce. For a quarter of a century Maurras, Léon Daudet, and the Action Française had done all in their power to harness French Catholicism to political reaction and integral nationalism. The scurrilous nature of their polemics against all who disagreed, especially liberal Catholics, was offensive to Pius XI and the more liberal prelates he had installed in Rome and in whatever vacancies occurred in France. Concerned over the Communist threat, Pius XI sought an answer in the spirit of Leo XIII; in France this meant Catholic social democracy, the encouragement of forces Maurras had fought, successfully, before the war. It meant also the Vatican's warm approval of M. Briand and his policies, over which Action Française could hardly contain its disgust. In 1926 the Vatican denounced it for "atheism, paganism, and amoralism," and followed by placing Maurras' books and its daily paper on the Index, forbidding Catholics to read it on pain of exclusion from the sacraments. The Catholic Right remonstrated in vain; Pius forced the retirement of the Jesuit Cardinal Billot, forced recalcitrant members of the hierarchy to support his condemnation in public. Maurras' newspaper reacted violently; the Vatican, it said, was reverting to the days of Alexander VI and his Borgia brood, and plotting with Germany to destroy France. In numbers, support, and prestige, the Action Française suffered from the events of 1926–1927, but the 1930's found its litany of hatred, if not its dogma, more popular than ever with conservatives.

In 1929 Pius XI defended Catholic unions against a northern employers' consortium and its charges that they were Marxist and revolutionary for demanding family allowances. Two years later, he issued his encyclical on labor, *Quadragesimo Anno,* to commemorate and reinforce Leo XIII's *Rerum Novarum.* While condemning communism and socialism, Pius also condemned unregulated capitalism as an "economic dictatorship of the privileged" and warned those who would deny to labor its right to organize action for a just share of the fruits of production. Rejecting both collectivism and individualism, he repeated that the State was responsible for furthering the health, housing, insurance for sickness and old age, wages and working conditions of labor, while leaving to subordinate bodies all social action they were capable of initiating for themselves. The head of the family's wages alone should suffice for all needs of life, for savings, and for the acquisition of property; the workers should progressively be admitted to a share in ownership, management, and profits of industry. Pius' social doctrine encouraged in France between the wars a number of Catholic action movements of social and democratic character: the national labor union (CFTC), the *Jeunesse Ouvrière Chrétienne*, Marc Sangnier's *Ligue de la Jeune République,* the small Popular Democratic party, all of which were to support the Popular Front governments of Léon Blum in 1936 and 1938, and to reemerge after the Second World War as part of the *Mouvement Républicain Populaire* (MRP), the first Republican Catholic party in French history to rival in numbers the major parties founded under the Third Republic. Concurrent with the advance of Catholic democracy in France was the decline of Freemasonry's anticlerical character. Despite the accusations of the Catholic Right that they cherished their "plot" against Christianity, the lodges concerned themselves relatively little with clerical questions between the wars; and as the threat of fascism increased, the Radical-Socialist and Catholic Left found it possible to cooperate in defense of the Republic. What Lamennais had asked a century before came to fruition between the wars. Catholicism was no longer chained to a single view of politics and society; Catholics could, and did, choose more freely among French parties from Left to Right; whatever the enthusiasts of either extreme believed, France was a pluralistic society, and in accepting that fact the French Church after a century and a half became once more French.

Religious peace was only one side of French domestic stability in the late 1920's. The economy had made an impressive recovery from its postwar fluctuations, a recovery more solid than either Great Britain or Germany attained. Reconstruction of the devastated regions stimulated the entire economy, particularly the always crucial building trades. By 1926, almost all of the ruined factories had been rebuilt and, unlike the villages, consolidated and modernized. Nearly all 200 damaged coal mines were working again, more efficiently than before, as were textile and metallurgical works. The return of Alsace-Lorraine and control of the Saar basin gave France a valuable complex of well-developed iron and coal industries and a new potash industry; French wool and cotton production rose by one-quarter. The newer industries of rayon, chemicals, rubber, and automobiles also prospered; the State rebuilt canals, bridges, and roads, and public buildings; with heavy government aid, the railways restored their operating efficiency, surrendering in return the State guarantee of interest given in the 1880's and submitting to State control of rate schedules and financial operations. Hydroelectric facilities offered alternative power sources to many industries and widened the market for new electrical goods. Together with the new wartime construction of heavy manufacture around Paris, reconstruction and repair accelerated the spread of mass production and concentration of ownership and management in France, though the "modern sector" of the French economy was still proportionately smaller than that of Britain, Germany, and the United States. From an index of industrial production of 100 in 1913, France had fallen to 60 in 1919 but attained 125 in 1926; exports (by weight) rose from 25 in 1919 to 166 in 1927, imports from 87 to 117. The devaluation of the franc in relation to other currencies promoted the tourist trade and a healthy balance of exports between 1924 and 1928. More broadly, inflation followed by stabilization and business confidence—that is, controlled inflation—facilitated reconstruction and business expansion by enabling the State and business houses to pay interest and older debts in depreciated francs. Heavy postwar borrowing and new issues of currency stimulated new enterprises, wages, and profits. In 1928, there were probably no more than 50,000 unemployed; nearly 2 million foreign laborers were absorbed, primarily in construction, mining, and agriculture.

## NEW FORCES ABROAD

There were other victories to celebrate in the second half of the decade. In 1925, the able Riff leader Abd-el-Krim, after penning Spanish troops into a narrow coastal strip, attacked the French forces in Morocco. Marshal Pétain, the hero of Verdun, led 150,000 men against the Riffs in their rugged mountain country; and after a deadly campaign, Abd-el-Krim surrendered in May of 1926. That the rest of the protectorate remained quiet was, in part, a tribute to the man who had ruled it for France since 1912. But the great colonizer, Marshal Lyautey, aging and ill, had already been forced by the Cartel des Gauches to resign as Resident-General. His long and tactful work had transformed the Moroccan protectorate into a model of European enterprise in Africa. Roads, railways, mines, and other French enterprises were protected as much by Lyautey's encouragement of medical care, sanitation, native crafts, and agriculture as by French bullets. Lyautey scrupulously respected the dignity of the Sultan and the Moslem faith, employed as many Moroccans in the administration as Paris would allow. Moorish culture was preserved, and furthered by the founding of Moorish schools and colleges. Casablanca and Rabat became modern cities, with markedly less contrast between European and native quarters than obtained elsewhere in Africa and Asia. Nowhere did France's vaunted *mission civilatrice* come closer to justifying itself than in Morocco. That it was the work of a Catholic general who was as strict with French entrepreneurs as with native Moroccans and left much fertile land to the latter, pleased neither the Left nor that breed of colonialists who preferred free rein. But Lyautey's example, and the relative failure of his civilian successors to keep Moroccan good will, imbued French army officers attached to North Africa with a sense of mission or, at least, of special competence in its affairs that was to affect events long afterward. The old Marshal presided over the great Colonial Exposition of 1931 at Vincennes; it was a moving personal triumph for "Lyautey Africanus," marked the apogee of France's imperial adventure, and encouraged many to believe in that "greater France" of 100 million souls.

Deeper currents were running the other way, carrying more souls with them every year. The Lyautey tradition had come late; his success in Morocco grew partly out of circumstances, partly out of his long experience—and mistakes, his and others—in Indo-China and Madagascar. Even had Paris discovered several Lyauteys and, what is even less likely, been willing to use them, the future of "greater France" would have been doubtful. In 1931, depression, drought, and locusts prepared Morocco herself for unrest, and the excitement of a Pan-Islamic Congress in Jerusalem was spreading westward, through Egypt, to Tunis and Algeria. In neither had young nationalists waited for this to begin their campaigns against French rule; to many of them, the revival of united Islam appealed far less than the nationalist-liberal heritage of 1789 they imbibed in Paris. Graduates of French schools, they had been stirred by the war, by the Chinese and Russian revolutions, by Wilsonianism, by acquaintances and emissaries from the French Left, to demand varying degrees of political participation, economic reform, and ultimate independence.

In Tunisia, the moderate *Destour,* or constitution, movement had petitioned Wilson in Paris for reforms under the protectorate; the more radical *Néo-Destour* asked full independence and drew upon itself and its publications severe French repression in the early 1930's. In Paris, Algerian dissidents joined others from Tunisia and Morocco to found in 1926 the Étoile Nord Africaine, out of which would grow the Algerian People's Party of Messali Hadj. Unrest in Indo-China was more serious; agitation and violence developed in several areas. As in North Africa, leadership was to come from the young men who gathered in Paris during and after World War I. Well acquainted with the North African nationalists, the young Ho Chi Minh appeared at the Socialist party congress at Tours in 1920 to vote with the majority against Léon Blum, later studied in Moscow, and with many other Indo-Chinese sojourned in China to consult the teachings of Sun Yat-sen. In 1930 he brought a number of rival factions together in the Indo-Chinese Communist party. Another group, the Viet Nam Nationalist party, was founded in 1927, taking as its model the Kuomintang. It was nearly destroyed after a revolt of native soldiers in Tonkin in 1930. Famine, drought, and flood led to a peasant uprising in 1930–1931, in which the Communist party took part. Only the most harsh, and indiscriminate, French reprisals managed to pacify Tonkin and Annam. Ho dropped out of sight for several years. Saigon, capital of Cochin China, became the new center of revolutionary activity shared among Stalinists, Trotskyites, and nationalists. The most serious trouble of the decade arose in Syria, which had been assigned to France as a mandate in 1920, after a Syrian national congress had demanded independence. In 1925, the Druses rebelled against an oppressive administration and the tactless rule of General Sarrail. The French were twice forced to withdraw from Damascus, then bombard it. A costly campaign ended resistance in 1927, but a Syrian Nationalist party rapidly gathered strength in the following years.

Vexing as political opposition within the empire proved to be, it was easily contained before the Second World War, though the methods employed only built up opposition for the future, no political authority in France being ready to admit the possibility of autonomy or future independence for the colonies. In the economic sphere the hopes for "greater France" were disappointed, at least in the short run. Much impressed by the colonies' contributions of men and materials to the war effort, the French government bravely announced a program of investment (*mise en valeur*), but what a wealthy financial community would not do before the war, a poorer one could not afterward. Considering the needs and budgetary condition of the homeland, the government's building of railways, roads, docks, public buildings, schools, and hospitals, was impressive, though more for leaving colonial tax revenues on the spot than for expenditures from France herself. Private investment in commerce and industry lagged, with a few exceptions. Small local businesses did well in the major cities of each colony; Morocco and Indo-China achieved high rates of industrial growth partly because they were freer of French protectionism. World competition and outside trade were shut out of others; in manufactured products the colonies, except for Algeria, were all but shut out of France herself. They remained primarily sources of food and raw materials; but even here, as in the case of North African wheat and wine and West African oils, they competed directly with French growers who had to be subsidized. In the 1920's, all French colonial trade still amounted to about one-tenth that of the British Empire, from an area (4.5 million square miles) one-third as large, with a population (60 million) one-seventh as large. Although her colonies, again excepting Indo-China, bought the larger part of their imports from France (Algeria, Tunisia, and Morocco, about 65 per cent), Belgium alone was a greater market for French goods than was the whole empire—until the advent of world depression, when colonial markets absorbed nearly a third of France's much restricted exports. This circumstance, added to the threat of a new European war, inspired the first French Imperial Conference in 1934–1935, which worked out a fifteen-year plan for the empire's economic unity and development on a budget of nearly 13 billion francs. Promising as it was, it was also an admission that the empire had failed to play the economic role many had expected of it, to enliven and enlarge the home economy in a decisive way.

A few Frenchmen had put their faith in another way of transforming economic life; they recommended *l'Américanisme*. French journalists, economists, businessmen, and a few labor leaders and Socialists crossed the Atlantic to see how Henry Ford and his contemporaries had applied

Science and Reason to industrial production. Most returned to France impressed by the sheer output of rationalized mass production through time studies, assembly lines, and standardization of parts, and by the material results of mass consumption based on high wages, easy credit, and intense advertisement of standardized products. America had developed a neocapitalism, replacing the old capitalism which garnered its profits from low wages and the cornering, or sharing, of existing markets. But even the most enthusiastic doubted that the American system could quickly be transplanted to a much smaller land without America's resources, without her immense and growing population or her fortunate history, free of a feudal past, free of invasion, military burdens, and social hatreds—or that the system could survive in a French economy dominated by producers, small and large, who preferred the *status quo* and who had the political and financial power to preserve it against innovators, whether neocapitalist or proletarian. Others were disturbed by the American waste of resources, the danger of overproduction, and the technical joblessness that machines might create. The publicists and businessmen who persevered were discredited by the American depression and entrenched interests at home. The disaster of 1929 proved to most Europeans that *l'Américanisme* should be rejected on economic grounds alone. But even at the height of American prosperity, when American products and tourists were flooding Paris, the American way was suspect on several other grounds.

Quite apart from the incessant recriminations of French and American newspapers over Versailles, the Treaty of Guarantee, the Washington Conference, the Ruhr, French debts, and German reparations, even apart from the tedious sermonizing of Coolidge, Mellon, Borah, and Hoover, which rarely, if at all, applied to the facts of European life, articulate French reaction to Americanism was usually unfriendly. Americans who sought approval had to face, as Donald McKay put it, the most difficult of psychological adjustments, that of the unrequited lover. On social and political grounds, the Left denounced what it called the capitalist dictatorship of Washington. The government of, by, and for big business that appealed to French economists and new-style entrepreneurs degraded itself, said the Left, by overworking and regimenting labor, breaking its unions, holding back social legislation, imposing prohibition, and entangling ordinary men in a whirl of installment buying and petty speculation. The Catholic trade-union leader, Hyacinthe Dubreuil, who agreed, remonstrated in vain that efficient production and higher living standards need not imply the rest and that both French labor and French management could learn from methods (and attitudes) he had observed in nearly two years of travel and work in the United States. The Socialist André Philip, who had also seen America firsthand, insisted that many of her economic techniques should be adopted as soon as, but not before, the working class assured itself of a role in ownership and management. Both were disregarded as America slipped into depression.

Not only the Left but most sectors of opinion believed that America's preoccupation with the needs, and rewards, of mass industrial society endangered her traditional ideals, submerged the individual, and degraded American culture. The repression of the Negroes remained a scandal; the French had seen the fate of American Negro troops in Paris and at the front and compared it, with pardonable satisfaction, to their own treatment of French African soldiers. The Sacco-Vanzetti execution caused more shock in France than the Dreyfus case had in America. The sudden rejection of immigrants and the endless, insulting scrutiny of French tourists confirmed André Siegfried's verdict: "In its pursuit of wealth and power, America has abandoned the ideal of liberty to follow that of prosperity." Nothing should stand in the way of public order and efficiency; America's "practical collectivism," he said, traded individuality for material success through mass cooperation. The most popular French book on the United States was Georges Duhamel's series of acid sketches, *America the Menace*. Much like Aldous Huxley's later novel, *Brave New World*, Duhamel's caricatured account of his visit to America warned Europeans that to adopt American economic methods and material compulsions would mean the death of European humanism and the devotion to nature, art, and the individual personality that was the glory of French civilization, not to mention the daily pleasures of conversation and gastronomy, both unknown across the sea.

Against this chorus of criticism, there were, of course, others who disagreed. What the general public thought remains unknown, though its warm reception of American visitors, war veterans, and fads, from jazz to moving pictures, suggested that sympathy and common tastes flourished on all levels of society. It was perhaps unfortunate for both sides that the twentieth century's first great burst of French interest in America occurred at a time when neither side appeared at its best, particularly in the eyes of its own intelligentsia. What was written, and taught, partook of the intellectual and literary atmosphere of the 1920's.

Frenchmen read Mencken, Dreiser, Dos Passos, Waldo Frank, and, most of all, Sinclair Lewis. The American expatriates who gathered at Left Bank cafés, at Gertrude Stein's, and at Sylvia Beach's bookstore on the rue de l'Odéon met their British and French counterparts, and most were repelled by bourgeois society, which they held responsible for war, for poverty, and for cultural degradation. America appeared as the most bourgeois of all, and the crowds of affluent tourists who arrived on the new *Île de France* were, admittedly, not always impressive in their moral sense or their understanding of European life, languages, and history. But the many who were, and the French public itself, found that the leading artists and writers of the day were more disdainful, or oblivious, of ordinary society and its problems than ever before.

## POSTWAR IDEAS AT HOME

At the beginning of the decade, Parisians were shocked, amused, or depressed by the cult of Dada, founded by the Rumanian Tristan Tzara in Zurich during the war. "Dada" is French baby talk for hobbyhorse; to adults it suggested a child's idea; to Tzara and his friends, who claimed to have chosen it at random, it signified nonsense, fit to describe anything at all in a world bereft of sense, whose political, moral, and aesthetic values were meaningless and had led only to insane destruction. From stages and table tops, Dadaist artists and poets expressed their individual revolt, singing and reciting, drowning even nonsense in shouts and music—Dada equaled Clemenceau equaled crumpled newspaper equaled God equaled paving block equaled oneself equaled don't know. Extreme skepticism, negativism, the cultivation of disorder and momentary impulse were to many artists a liberation from standards outworn and styles worked out by their predecessors, as well as the only reasonable response to a world mad enough to kill 10 million men. In it, too, reappeared the romantic pose a century old, the anti-bourgeois bias, the prewar intellectual styles of irrationalism and instinct, the revolt against positivism and nineteenth-century optimism, and the aesthetic implications of Freudianism. Truth and integrity—some values were assumed—lay in the gratuitous act or, in poetry and painting, in the recording of whatever entered the mind, however disjointed or bizarre in the light of ordinary reason. The attitudes of the Dadaists attracted many talented young men who were not of the cult itself, or left it early when its forced absurdities and hangers-on became distasteful.

The poets André Breton, Paul Éluard, Louis Aragon moved into surrealism, a word coined by Guillaume Apollinaire, whose prewar works, with Max Jacob's and Alfred Jarry's, they admired as models of intuition, free technique, and wild humor in parading the absurdities of life. The surrealists claimed to have found a deeper reality in Freudianism, to be expressed in "automatic writing," a flow of words and images put down without the intercession of reason or rule. In painting, too, Breton and others attempted the same; Salvador Dali's better-known "dream photographs" were, on the other hand, studied compositions, a conservative version of surrealism. Picasso also did surrealist work in his influential perambulations through twentieth-century styles—fittingly, for surrealist art like surrealist poetry owed much to prewar innovation, expressionism, Fauvism, cubism, to his and Bracque's *collages*. The Swiss Paul Klee, the Spaniard Joan Miró, the Russian Marc Chagall, Fernand Léger, and Marcel Duchamp shared to one degree or other in the surrealist movement, though they can hardly be classified under that single term. Other, older painters went their own ways between the wars. Matisse, with Picasso, perhaps had the most influence on younger painters; Bracque, Bonnard, Jacques Villon, Rouault, Dufy, and Utrillo won public recognition denied them before the war.

In the 1920's the romantic tradition of commitment to political or social causes had faded once again, after the Dreyfus case and war. The young artist or writer exposed to the war, to Dada and surrealism, was more often to be found exploring the exotic, the barbaric, the primitive, and, partly with their help, his own personality and its plight in modern society, which in turn revealed itself exotic if one burrowed beneath the surface. Here too the postwar generation looked to earlier figures for inspiration, to Rimbaud and Lautréamont in poetry, Gauguin and Van Gogh in painting, most of all to Marcel Proust and André Gide, both of whose careers dated from before the war, but whose reputations were made in the 1920's. Proust's many-volumed *Remembrance of Things Past* (written between 1913 and 1922) offered a detailed, untiring analysis of human personality and motivation behind the conventions of a fading aristocratic society. By following, in the light of psychology and intuition, every hint and sensation evoked by memory, he sought to vanquish time and to recapture a past more truly than it could have been perceived by participants distracted by daily action—as some of the non-objective painters (Mondrian, Kandinsky) held their creations to be all the more "concrete" for avoiding direct reference to the external world.

Gide's stories, novels, and *Journals* revealed a man of driving, and to society, scandalous, appetites which were checked, examined, and indulged against a Calvinist conscience, and described with an uncompromising devotion to truth. To reveal man, and man's plight, again with all the help psychology, intuition, and art could give, free of convention and a priori notions, was his purpose in writing. Yet reason, traditional learning, and severely classical expression marked his thought and work. Gide denounced public morals for denying man access to his darker side, thus hiding man from himself, forcing him and society to constant duplicity; he sought instead a moral that would accept yet dignify man as he was. Gide's presence helped make the *Nouvelle Revue Française* (NRF) and the publishing house of Gallimard dominant in the French literary world between the wars; his example liberated and disciplined young writers of two generations. In the mid-1920's, when most of his contemporaries were occupied with literary experiments and self-study, he journeyed to Chad and returned to denounce the cruelties practiced on the natives by French colonialism; a decade later, when the fashion was Marxism, he renounced his adherence to it after a visit to the Soviet Union.

Leaving aside the literature of entertainment in which the period excelled, the French novel, essay, and drama between the wars was dominated first by exploration in the 1920's, then by growing political commitment in the 1930's. Most authors and their works, of course, moved through or back and forth among all three and no label is accurate or inclusive enough to describe them fairly. Nonetheless, postwar prose, like poetry and art, pursued the quest for new forms and a better understanding of man in a world disturbed and threatening. All the revolts and disillusions that moved the Dadaists affected imaginative literature, as they do today. The war revealed a world of explosive power and mass violence that only a minority—often painters or poets—had discerned before 1914. Science, too, upset familiar views and in a new, more puzzling way, for even a primitive version of Freudianism and the new physics and genetics was more difficult to apply to man and his affairs than simplifications of Newton or Darwin had been. There was much else to be absorbed; men for whom Kant or Durkheim had been law and Bergson a revelation were likely to be reading Hegel,

Schopenhauer, and Nietzsche. The Russian novel, Scandinavian drama, Joyce, Pirandello, Brecht, and Rilke offered startling, stirring contrasts to French writers. Political refugees fled to Paris from Russia and Italy; students arrived from every continent in greater numbers than ever. As in economic and political affairs, France lay open to a wider world. America and the Soviet Union, Africa, India, and China presented civilizations to be explored not in the old, leisurely, and condescending way, but as forces on the verge of revolutionizing the earth. All this, too, had been perceived before the war; Valéry recalled that America's defeat of Spain in 1898 had been like a body blow to him. But now the reading public understood what he meant by saying that Europe might soon reap a bitter harvest from having sown her scientific and technical knowledge across the earth. Brute size would now determine a nation's power: "We have been fools enough to make forces proportional to masses."

French authors scattered over the globe, to discover it for themselves, or confirm ideas conceived at home. The bourgeois radical Duhamel, who much preferred his own garden or at most a hike around the Italian lakes, took himself off to New York, Chicago, and Moscow, Gide to equatorial Africa, André Malraux to China and Indo-China; the Dadaist and diplomat Paul Morand appropriately colored his frenetic *New York* (1930) with surrealism, tried psychological analysis of Orientals, Africans, and college-bred American amazons. An entire literature of globe-trotting grew up. Of the hundreds of novels and essays, some were escapist, others playfully exotic, most betrayed the author's own restlessness and his failure to find societies at peace with themselves or with the world of speed and violence made by modern weapons, electricity and oil, the automobile and airplane. Others explored their own society in more traditional ways, placing Frenchmen in the midst of new, impersonal forces; Jules Romains, Georges Duhamel, Roger Martin du Gard prepared their multi-volumed social novels. Some turned to the cult of speed itself, others to sports; of many who sought poetry and adventure in flying, Antoine de Saint-Exupéry found both in opening airways across the Sahara and the Andes, expressed both in works of striking beauty. A new generation of Catholic writers explored the modern complexities of sin and the new conditions of salvation; François Mauriac, Gabriel Marcel, and Georges Bernanos emerged in the mid-1920's to join the already honored Paul Claudel.

French life in the postwar decade, for all its shocks and novelties, per-

mitted writers the luxury of detachment, or of concentration on wider—
or more personal—themes than politics. In 1928 Julien Benda's famous
essay *The Betrayal of the Intellectuals* found a ready audience. Intellectuals, he said, betrayed their high calling by taking sides in political
and nationalist controversies; their proper role was to look ahead, or
within, to reason, and to know, and thus preserve, the values of western
civilization. These had been endangered by use as propaganda for
momentary struggles, and by the cults of irrationalism and intuition too
many intellectuals had adopted in order to appeal to popular passions, in
a vain effort to direct them. Barrès, Maurras, Péguy, Sorel, and especially Bergson he attacked as traitors to reason and objectivity. They had
not stood above common strife, and made what was inevitable even worse
by lending it the force of ideology. But Benda himself had not stood
apart in the Dreyfus case and in the end would commit himself again
in a struggle far more divisive. As the 1930's opened, depression and the
advent of Nazism in Germany set off a new conflict between Left and
Right, and another, not always the same, between the values of the
Enlightenment Benda cherished and several forms of modern tyranny.
The Dreyfus case had torn France from within; the coming battle would
be all the more terrible for the forces pulling France apart from without.

A minority of artists and intellectuals had engaged themselves already
to the foreign establishments of Left and Right. Maurras found Mussolini an authentic, though not a model, exemplar of integral nationalism. Before his death in 1924, Anatole France had declared his faith
in Soviet Russia; Sorel had preceded him. Romain Rolland, after holding himself neutral in the great war (he lived in Switzerland), followed
in the late 1920's. Of the younger generation, the surrealists Éluard and
Aragon had also accepted Communism. But the economic and political
crises arising in the early 1930's bore in upon the majority and called
most of them back to public affairs. The older, established figures of the
literary world usually applied themselves to awakening civic spirit and
to modest reforms of existing society; among them were Valéry,
Duhamel, Romains, André Maurois, Jean Giraudoux. Of those who demanded a fundamental recasting of society, often the younger men,
only a minority turned to the extreme Right. Out of the cult of action
or nihilism, out of disgust over bourgeois values, out of despair over any
other future for Europe, a few chose fascism even before its triumph in
1940. But most younger men turned, in varying degrees, to the Left. A
group of social Catholics, inspired by Péguy, led by Emmanuel Mounier,

founded the leftist Catholic journal *Esprit* in 1932. Jean Guéhenno, in *Journal d'un homme de quarante ans* (1934), assailed the bourgeoisie for dehumanizing the worker, shutting him off from society, and closing the world of culture around itself. His was the radical Republicanism of Michelet. The Marxist Left was represented at the Paris Congress of Revolutionary Writers in 1935, presided over by André Gide before his visit to the Soviet Union. Éluard, Aragon, Henri Barbusse, and many others condemned the earlier preoccupation of writers with Proustian analysis, with metaphysics or stylistic contrivances suited only to entertain the idle classes; they called instead for a literature of the proletariat in its struggle for dignity and social justice. Many of these writers adhered to Russian Communism only with reservations; but as western democracy seemed unable to bar the way to fascism, they chose Stalin over Hitler. For all the unhappy news coming out of Russia, its expressed ideals were true to the western tradition of the Left: equality, fraternity, peace, the liberation of man's spirit from material cares. Fascism rejected all; it was the ultimate in anti-Dreyfusism. The Spanish Civil War pulled many more into the anti-fascist coalition which accompanied the Popular Front and prefigured the Resistance. André Malraux, whose belief in the ennobling virtue of revolutionary action had already drawn him to the Far East, flew for the Loyalist Air Force. Pablo Picasso's great mural of 1937, *Guernica,* captured the horror of bombs falling into a defenseless Spanish town; it was a call to commitment more compelling than Delacroix's *Massacre of Scio.* By then the good feeling of the late 1920's had been forgotten, French public life was a bedlam of contending factions, and disaster was only three years away.

## THE END OF CONFIDENCE

As the elections of 1932 approached, much of France's political, diplomatic, and economic environment had changed. Less than a year after the electoral victory of Poincaré's *Union Nationale* in 1928, the Radical-Socialist Congress, in a burst of anti-clerical zeal, forced the withdrawal of Herriot, Sarraut, and Henri Queuille from Poincaré's cabinet, which had approved the establishment of certain schools for foreign mission priests. The franc having been stabilized and their constituents appeased, the Radicals thus signalized their return to the doctrinal Left. Poincaré formed a new government based on the Center Right, with

André Tardieu as Minister of the Interior, Briand remaining at the Quai d'Orsay. Ill-health forced Poincaré's retirement in July of 1929 and Briand became Premier for the eleventh time. Under attack by the Right for his foreign policy of conciliation, Briand fell in October when the Left refused him its support. Doumergue called Tardieu, who formed a young but conservative Right Center cabinet, including André Maginot as War Minister, and a rising leader of the *Alliance Démocratique,* Pierre-Étienne Flandin, as Minister of Commerce. Briand's national and world prestige kept him at the Foreign Ministry. A second Tardieu ministry in early 1930 saw two other rising men, Paul Reynaud and Pierre Laval, take the portfolios of Finance and Labor. Tardieu now presented a program of public spending that surprised the Left and dismayed the Right. In the social realm, the government abolished the fees for secondary education, and set afoot the modest system of social insurance voted in April, 1928, which protected workers and their families against old age, sickness, disability, and death. This law, debated since 1920, was designed to generalize the German system already established in Alsace-Lorraine and preserved by the French government after Versailles. In addition, a system of modest pensions to war veterans was voted. Tardieu had long admired the *élan* of the American economy and capped his proposals with an ambitious program of expansion and modernization, in which the State would lead the way by building roads and port facilities, by reforestation and conservation, by developing hydroelectric power and transmission lines, to continue and direct, in short, the economic recovery that dated from the war.

This brilliant, impatient, and intolerant man came to power at the wrong moment. The American depression appeared to discredit economic adventuring (though Tardieu's proposals hardly reflected the policies then current in Washington) and the drop in world trade had already begun to affect the French economy. A decline in government revenue wiped out the surplus before the end of 1930, even though Tardieu's projects were severely whittled down. Two years earlier, the French economy might well have supported such enterprise. And twenty years later, after depression and defeat had shaken orthodox economic theories, the French were to embark on a path very like Tardieu's. But in 1930 government spending, to say nothing of deficit spending, was anathema to much of the Right, Center, and Radical-Socialist Left. Most of the business and financial community also distrusted his espousal of a truly competitive economy, of rationalized production, mass distribution, and his willingness to see the demise of small, inefficient units of industry, commerce, and agriculture. The entire Left feared his propensities for a strong executive and the majority of his contemporaries in the Chamber were put off by his hauteur. In December 1930, a financial scandal touching one of his associates encouraged the Radical-dominated Senate to overturn Tardieu's cabinet.

Pierre Laval formed a cabinet of the Right Center in January of 1931. Having drifted steadily to the Right after a debut as an extreme Socialist and pacifist before the war, Laval was a self-educated Auvergnat with a rough personal charm and a capacity for making, and keeping, friends in all parties and corners of society. He was attached to no parliamentary group (and, it was said, to no political principles) but was so skilled a tactician that his presence was sought in several cabinets between the wars. The Laval government lasted a full year, taken up mainly with a deteriorating foreign situation. The Senate overthrew it in February of 1932 and a Tardieu cabinet held office until the elections of May, which resulted in a new Left majority.

By then both the symbol and the substance of the Locarno era of international good feeling had passed away. Upon Poincaré's retirement in 1929, Aristide Briand, called "the Apostle of Peace," had taken the premiership as well as the Foreign Ministry. His first task had been to carry out the negotiations at The Hague which resulted in the adoption of the Young Plan and the subsequent withdrawal of French troops from the Rhineland in June of 1930. At the same moment, work began on the great system of fortifications conceived by Pétain and the mathematician-War Minister Painlevé and named for the latter's successor, Maginot. Designed to make up in part for the reduced classes of conscripts that would appear in the mid-1930's as a result of the enormous losses of 1914–1918, it was also a sign of France's lasting distrust of any German government. And although its function need not have been purely defensive, it was discussed only on this ground by a Chamber which, significantly, made no mention of France's eastern alliances and the offensive obligations these might entail. Thus was added to the contradictions already inherent in Briand's policy of appeasement and containment a military doctrine that plainly put containment in question—at the very moment when the rise of German nationalists and Nazis made appeasement unpromising.

At the same time, Briand's renewed appeal for a European Federal Union in 1930 was considered by the other major powers to be a last

French attempt at European hegemony, by his enemies in France an admission of failure. As with Tardieu's call for new economic departures at home, Briand's lonely plea for closer political and economic ties among European states was ahead of its time. Only after another catastrophe and under the shadow of a third would practical men be brought to accept its practicality. Even those, like Herriot, who said they agreed, did not take Briand's initiative seriously enough to support him against his enemies in the Chamber. Given the strident demands of German nationalist newspapers and mass meetings for armaments, for the seizure of Danzig and Silesia, for the remilitarization of the Rhineland, for unity with Austria, given the election of 107 Nazis to the Reichstag in September of 1930 (they had been 12) and growing proof of German rearmament, Briand was kept in office only because the public at large still appeared to think him indispensable. In the last two years of his life he suffered a constant series of disappointments, the decline of German democracy foremost among them. In March of 1931 he was forced to oppose the projected customs union of Germany and Austria, which the press, the public, and the politicians professed to regard as a first step to *Anschluss* and thus a violation of the Versailles Treaty. Under heavy French financial pressure, Chancellor Brüning and the Austrians withdrew the project even before the Hague Court declared it a violation of postwar agreements. In May, the collapse of the *Kreditanstalt* in Vienna set off a widening circle of bankruptcies, bank closings, and industrial shutdowns which greatly increased the already serious (6 million) unemployment in Austria and Germany. Nationalists in both countries blamed French intervention and Brüning's weakness for an event largely occasioned by American withdrawals of funds from central Europe.

Also in May of 1931, Briand, attacked by the Right since before the war for softness on Germany, was beaten for the presidency of the Republic by the austere and notably patriotic Senate president Paul Doumer, who had lost four sons to German fire. The symbolism escaped few commentators, though Briand's physical decline made him an unpromising candidate. He remained at the Quai d'Orsay, but as barely more than an ornament; Laval, Premier since January, took effective control of foreign affairs. It was appropriate that this adroit promoter, who had made a personal fortune in that indeterminate zone where politics and business meet, should now attempt to use France's financial ascendancy as a diplomatic weapon. The world depression had reached the banking centers of Vienna, Berlin, New York, and London; but in

1931 France, with her heavy stocks of gold, appeared to be impervious. In early June, Brüning declared that the German economic and financial position (and, between the lines, his own political position) made it impossible to carry on even the restricted payments of the Young Plan. President Hoover, without consulting Paris, followed with his proposal of a year's moratorium on all intergovernmental debts. To Frenchmen who were owed more than they owed in turn, Laval's grudging acceptance was another surrender to American banking interests, whose frantic withdrawals from Germany were more serious for German stability than reparations payments would have been. Laval's voyage to Washington in the hope of gaining America's recognition of a link between German reparations and French war debts was a failure, and the French image of "Uncle Shylock," more concerned with tomorrow's bank balance than with international morality and responsibility, was complete. On their side, the Americans, British, and Germans believed that France's delay in accepting the moratorium had decisively worsened its chances of saving the international financial situation.

Germany desperately needed French help. Indeed, the Berlin crowds had shouted "Save us!" to Laval and Briand upon their visit in September. But Laval's earlier offer to Brüning of a French loan in return for a promise to halt rearmament and conclude a nonaggression pact came to nothing; Brüning was in no position to challenge German nationalism and it is doubtful in any case that French wealth or French opinion would have allowed enough support to make a difference. German banks and industries were closing their doors and Brüning had already been forced to declare a bank holiday. Only a French offer to end reparations and to allow Germany equal right to armaments would have satisfied Berlin and no party in France was ready to concede so much in 1931. Fear and hope were too high—fear of Germany's continuing demands for a total reversal of Versailles, hope that France's economic strength could be used both to stifle these demands and to cement the eastern alliances. That Brüning's fall would open the way to Nazism—or Nazism's meaning—was not yet clear and it was best to cling to whatever advantages one had in hand. That Americans, who in their insularity refused to give way even on the debt, should denounce France as hard of heart, only aggravated tempers in Paris.

In February, 1932, the long-planned Disarmament Conference opened in Geneva, with André Tardieu leading the French delegation. His position as Premier of a government expected to disappear at the general elections in May lessened his effectiveness, but the immediate international situation and the long-standing policies of the major powers promised little in any case. Germany demanded equality of armaments (or disarmament, as the Treaty of Versailles had promised); France insisted on the prior construction of a system of security. Tardieu's proposal tried to satisfy both: the institution of an international police force under the League to guarantee the peace in a world of nations disarmed except for internal security forces, without offensive, especially aerial, weapons. Whether Tardieu believed in the possibility of its acceptance, either in France or in Geneva, is a question. It was, if anything, even more ahead of its time than his plans for French economic rejuvenation. Only a few small nations approved; the refusal of London and Washington to consider such obligations must have been foreseen. The Conference dragged on with little hope. As if to signify the end of an era, Briand died that March, worn out and disillusioned.

Even the consolations of prosperity and financial primacy disappeared in 1932. The French economy was finally struck by the world depression. From a figure of 140 in 1930, the general index of production fell to 124 in 1931, then to 96 in 1932, or under the volume of 1913. Wholesale prices declined by nearly a third, and agricultural prices fell lowest of all, after a particularly good harvest in 1931. From 1929 to 1932, the value of French exports was cut more than half while other countries' sales to France, aided by their depreciated currencies (England had left the gold standard in 1931), declined somewhat less. Frenchmen would now have welcomed tourists, whose spending had been so helpful to the balance of payments, but these too had decreased from nearly 2 million in 1929 to under a million in 1932; the *Ile de France* no longer disgorged her crowds of dollar-laden Americans, and more than a few names which had headed the "Arrivals" column of the Paris *Herald* had long since appeared in the dreaded reports of bankruptcies (or suicides) in New York. Even the intellectual exiles were going home again, to a country in their eyes more humble and more human for its distress. A more doleful exodus was that of foreign laborers, encouraged to leave by the French government and labor unions, for unemployment, hitherto almost unknown, was rising. It was not yet so serious as elsewhere, nor would it be. The much-touted balance of the French economy between industry and agriculture, if it had not prevented depression from reaching France, at least afforded a village refuge for many workers who had left the farms for the factories and could return. But the numbers on unemployment relief, only a few thousand in 1930, reached 200,000 in 1932 and many who needed it most were ignored by the inadequate social system. The government's surplus had disappeared, the budget deficit for 1931–1932 threatened to reach 6 billion francs, and fear of devaluation was reborn. Another Belle Époque was at an end.

# ~✕~

# THE REPUBLIC
# IN DOUBT

The French cabinets that were called upon to meet the first assaults of economic depression and Nazi Germany emerged from the Chamber elected in 1932. It had, as in 1924, a solid Left majority, with the Socialists under Blum increasing from 106 seats to 129, the Radical-Socialists under Herriot from 113 to 155. Between these two parties, the Socialist Republicans slipped from 40 to 36; on the extreme Left the Communists fell from 14 to 11, with 11 other collectivists who accepted neither Socialist nor Communist discipline. The Right and Right Center had fallen from 47 per cent of the popular vote and 320 seats, to 45 per cent and 253 seats. Again, only a slight shift of voter sentiment was magnified by the tighter electoral alliance of Radicals and Socialists, aided also by the willingness of Communist voters to abandon their candidates in favor of other Left parties in the second ballot. The decisive change from 1928, however, was the Radical voters' readiness to support Socialists rather than turn to the Right Center. Several factors were at work. The financial debacle of the *Cartel des Gauches* in 1926 had faded as depression appeared and was blamed on the incumbents; the reassuring figure of Poincaré had disappeared from the Right Center, his place taken by more abrasive men like André Tardieu, whose demands for a stronger executive repelled Republicans faithful to Alain. Tardieu had also joined Premier Laval in supporting a bill in January, 1932, which would have limited general elections to a single ballot. Introduced by Clemenceau's former secretary and disciple Georges Mandel, it was designed to favor the Right and Right Center by making impossible the familiar between-ballot alliances of Radicals and Socialists. Ultimately, conservatives hoped, this would bring about a two-party system split along economic issues, with most Radicals deserting the collectivist Left for good. But the Radicals cherished their freedom of action and their stance as a party of the Left. The Radical-dominated Senate foiled the project by bringing Laval down, and many Radical voters followed by voting as conservatives feared they would.

## ECONOMIC AND DIPLOMATIC DEPRESSION

Once more, then, as in 1924, the Left came to power at a time of financial crisis, but in the much less hopeful circumstances of economic stagnation and diplomatic disarray. President Albert Lebrun, who had replaced Doumer (assassinated by a madman in May, 1932), called Herriot as Premier. Once more Herriot found himself forced to gather a cabinet of Radicals without Socialist participation but with Blum's promise of Socialist support in the Chamber. The Communists remained outside all parliamentary arrangements, their party newspaper l'Humanité pouring invective on the entire system and upon the Socialists in particular for associating themselves with it. Herriot chose for his Finance Minister the orthodox economist Germain-Martin, who had already served in a Right Center cabinet under Tardieu. There would be no innovations to disquiet the business community as in 1924–1926, so the abiding contradiction of the alliance between Socialists and Radicals emerged at once. To the Socialist demands for disarmament and recovery through increased purchasing power, government spending, and a general rise in wages, Herriot and his cabinet answered that the German threat necessitated armed strength and proposed a budget-balancing program of reduced spending, including salary cuts for civil servants and higher taxation in all categories. But civil servants made up an important part of SFIO membership and the core of the CGT. The Right and Center opposed increased income taxes. Between them, Herriot fell in December, 1932, opening an eighteen-month period of governmental crises rooted in the old problem of Radical and Socialist disaccord on defense and economic matters. The Republican Socialist

Joseph Paul-Boncour succeeded him, but with another conservative, Henri Chéron, as Finance Minister, who immediately proposed another austerity program, raising taxes, cutting salaries and pensions. Paul-Boncour fell in January and the budget deficit rose to 12 billion francs. The Radical Édouard Daladier became Premier, with another Radical, Georges Bonnet, at the Finance Ministry. Again the Socialists approved the new cabinet, enabling it to take office. This time Bonnet moderated both the proposed taxes and the economies and a number of Socialists led by Pierre Renaudel and Marcel Déat split from the SFIO to support him. A budget with a 4-billion-franc deficit was finally voted in June of 1933 after weeks of wrangling, as the Rightist press excoriated the parliamentary system for cowardice and jobbery.

In October Daladier fell when the Socialists refused yet another round of government wage cuts. Albert Sarraut, a prominent Radical, rearranged the Daladier cabinet only slightly; he was overturned in November by Left and Right. Next came the turn of Camille Chautemps, like Daladier a protégé of Herriot's. He succeeded in passing a budget for 1934 only because Blum led the Socialists out of the Chamber rather than topple the fifth government in less than two years. The Right and Center newspapers ridiculed the maneuver, *l'Humanité* pilloried the "social traitors," and all denounced the parliamentary game of musical chairs in which the same names had appeared again and again in barely different combinations. But Blum's dilemma was nonetheless real; a socialist party could neither support a policy of deflation urged (forced, Blum said) upon the government by the great banks, nor risk the onus of throwing the Radicals into the arms of the Right. Meanwhile, the Chautemps government was safe, or so it seemed.

If its problems had been merely budgetary or financial, it might have been. But the root of the treasury's problem was not inflation, as in the 1920's, but a steady fall in government revenue as all economic activity declined. The recession had become a rout. Agricultural prices continued their precipitous slide and unemployed industrial workers returned to villages already deep in hardship. Yet prices remained high as the antiquated but well-intrenched commercial interests were protected by a wall of tariffs—and when tariffs failed, by a barrier of import quotas —from the outside world. France's response to depression followed that of other nations: economic autarchy, deflation, and piecemeal legislation to subsidize favored interests. But others had soon resorted to devaluation, to enable their goods to compete in world markets and, hopefully, to stimulate buying at home by tempting savers to put their wealth in goods. In France the memories of 1924–1926 were too real and, perhaps more important, those who had suffered from devaluation were more powerful politically than elsewhere. Even the Socialists, who asked for government spending to prime the pump as Mr. Roosevelt was doing, opposed inflation of the franc. So succeeding governments thought only of what was done before by the well-remembered M. Poincaré, except, of course, for his most crucial act, acceptance of inflation, which had stimulated French foreign trade. But then a decisive spurt of trade had been possible in a bustling world, and perhaps too much is made of France's failure to devaluate in the early 1930's. Hindsight suggests that no nation's single act, however dramatic, could have reversed the downward spiral in a world of fearful, autarchic economies. And behind the political stalemates and parliamentary games that are blamed for French inaction was the fact that Frenchmen did not suffer catastrophe on the German, British, or American scale. The unemployed never made up a major portion of the population; millions of workers, peasants, shopkeepers, and civil servants made personal economies to match the government's; widespread deprivation there was, but no mass misery or despair to ready a whole people for drastic steps—all of which, paradoxically, engendered lack of confidence in a government which, not pushed from below, failed to lead.

The impression of official lassitude and impotence was reinforced by what patriots considered a diplomatic rout. The illusion of French hegemony was further dissipated by events of these two years. Herriot went to the Lausanne Conference in June of 1932, where the moratorium on German reparations was extended another three years; in December the American Congress solemnly resolved against cancellation or reduction of the money hired by foreign powers (Herriot chose this issue on which to be overthrown, by asking that France pay the current installment on her debt). In February of 1933, the Lytton Report on Japan's aggression in Manchuria was accepted by the League of Nations; the Japanese withdrew from the League and the first blow to collective security had been struck with impunity. But Japan was far away. In Berlin, Adolf Hitler had become German Chancellor at the end of January and after the Reichstag fire the Nazi terror began in earnest. In March Hitler received dictatorial powers; in October, Germany withdrew from the Geneva Disarmament Conference and from the League of Nations. And Frenchmen pondered bitterly the fact that

Britain and America blamed not Hitler and the German menace for the collapse of Geneva but France's "obsession" with security. The signing (it was never ratified) of Mussolini's Four-Power Pact in July of 1933 gained nothing. Germany, Italy, Britain, and France promised only to observe their Locarno, Kellogg, and League obligations; and it further shook the confidence of France's eastern allies. Concurrently, the London Economic Conference, called in hopes of restoring currency exchange and lower tariffs, foundered on American opposition. By the beginning of 1934, Frenchmen felt more isolated than ever, in a jungle world beyond the power of the quarreling politicians at the Palais Bourbon.

Defenders of the parliamentary system, as usual, were hardpressed to explain why it should not be wholly blamed for economic and diplomatic reverses so complex, and in large part attributable to outside forces. As ever, the defenders and explainers were few, especially in the popular press. It was easier, and more profitable, to be clever and cynical—without, of course, being candid—about politics in France. In some ways, the frankly political press was more honest and usually predictable; for obvious reasons the Socialist *Populaire,* the Catholic democratic *Aube,* the radical *Œuvre* were among the more restrained political papers. On the Communist Left *l'Humanité,* and on the Right *l'Action Française,* fulminated against the system and repeated the grossest accusations of cowardice, greed, and immorality against individual members of the center, Radical, and Socialist parties. Of the two, *l'Action Française* was the more sadistic, its personal attacks on ministers combining outright filth with incitement to violence. Behind it trooped the Rightist weeklies *Candide, Gringoire,* and *Je suis partout.* All busied themselves in manufacturing political scandals to discredit the government. But in January of 1934, *l'Action Française* and the nationalist daily *l'Echo de Paris* hit upon the Stavisky case, which was real, and in which all enemies of the shaky Left coalition, all popular journalists and cartoonists could revel with some justification.

## THE CRISIS OF FEBRUARY, 1934

Serge Stavisky was an indefatigable confidence man with a long record of graft and embezzlement but no convictions. The collapse of a bond swindle based on the Bayonne municipal pawnshop ended in his suicide, at the moment of his arrest by the police in Chamonix. That his trials on other charges had somehow been postponed since 1927 suggested that he had bought protection in high places; the Mayor of Bayonne, a Radical Deputy, was implicated; so too was one of Premier Chautemps' ministers, and the Premier's brother-in-law headed the office in charge of prosecutions. The Rightist press and its readers jumped to the conclusion that the police had been ordered to engineer the suicide to silence Stavisky; Paris and especially the streets around the Palais Bourbon echoed that winter to the old cry "À bas les voleurs!" and, as in the Panama scandal, the Right labored to convince the world that the Republic and corruption were one and the same. Chautemps made the old mistake; like Grévy with Wilson, Loubet with Panama, Méline with Dreyfus, he denied that there was a Stavisky case and refused a parliamentary inquiry. He could hardly have foreseen the danger that the affair would present to Republican institutions, which he and most Republican politicians complacently assumed had outgrown those early troubled years. In fact, the immediate danger was greater, for in 1934 several anti-Republican currents converged under circumstances that won at least the temporary sympathy of crowds of ordinary folk in all classes who did not hate the Republic but distrusted its leaders of the moment.

Added to the Panama-like atmosphere of scandal was the fear of patriots that a series of French governments had allowed victory to become defeat in only fifteen years and, as in 1924–1926, that the same dreary procession of cabinets had brought a prosperous nation to the verge of economic ruin. The Chambers' casual overthrow of cabinets and casual acceptance of the same men mouthing the same slogans was no longer a joke. Many came to believe, partly on the facts, partly from nostalgia, and always with the help of clever journalists and intellectuals, that these were little men compared with the leaders who had disappeared. Few now commanded respect outside their own party. Instead of Jaurès, there was Blum; instead of Clemenceau, Herriot; instead of Briand, Laval; instead of Poincaré, there was Tardieu or Flandin or Reynaud. None possessed the simple force, much less the charisma, of his predecessor; each appeared more narrowly partisan. Could such men make the world safe for democracy or France safe at all when the others had failed? By 1934, the democratic Europe of Versailles had disappeared; Mussolini ruled in Italy, Pilsudski in Poland, King Alexander was dictator in Yugoslavia, Salazar in Portugal, Hitler in Germany. Most of the press reported on them too little, the Rightist press too glowingly (except for Hitler, who was still the enemy of France). Strong leaders with strong ideas had emerged: Russia had Stalin, America Roosevelt, even China had her Chiang Kai-shek. Of all the major powers, some Frenchmen bitterly reflected, only the British, their uncertain allies, were also content with mediocre men.

By 1934, the French Right was itself equipped, for the first time, with a number of fascist leagues and paramilitary groups. Maurras' *Camelots du Roi* dated from before the war. Others, like Pierre Taittinger's *Jeunesses Patriotes*, François Coty's *Solidarité Française* took their inspiration from Mussolini's Black Shirts (and their money from champagne and perfume, respectively). The most prominent in the middle 1930's was the *Croix de Feu* led by Colonel de la Rocque. He had turned it from a veterans' organization into a mass movement whose membership ran to perhaps 100,000 by 1934, though far fewer were active. De la Rocque preached anti-communism, national renewal and purification, and authoritative government. Neither he nor the largely bourgeois rank and file of the *Croix de Feu* was fascist, as the later desertion of its activists proved; but the uniforms, the arms and "lightning mobilizations" by automobile and even airplane, the "maneuvers" held on comfortable rural estates were hardly normal in a Republic. Like several other veterans' groups, it was more patriotic than fascist, looking to the French past for a regime fit for right-thinking people, expressing nostalgia more than doctrine, seeking a permanent Poincaré or more sober Boulanger rather than a Mussolini or Hitler. De la Rocque himself lacked personal dynamism; his speeches, calling for "moral pressure" and selfless example, were hardly to be compared with the diatribes of *l'Action Française* but they suited well the anti-parliamentary temper of 1934.

As January wore on, that temper rose ominously. Nightly demonstrations or riots by the *Camelots* and assorted allies kept Paris, and the Deputies, on edge; the police restrained themselves too easily to reassure the Left, which recalled that police and *Camelots* had joined in the past to quell Leftist demonstrations much more harshly. What was worse, the public seemed to approve of the rioters, who drew sympathetic crowds. On January 25th, Chautemps resigned and Lebrun called Daladier, who formed another Radical cabinet when the Socialists and the Right refused his bid for a national government of all parties. The blunt, rough-featured Daladier had a reputation as a strongman. Unhappily he chose to be clever instead, in that cynical way too typical of the parliamentary game, and utterly misread the public mood. Instead of opening an inquiry, he promoted Chautemps' brother-in-law out of his office to a higher one, and, to show his Republican vigilance, fired the head of the *Comédie-Française,* ostensibly for producing the undemocratic *Coriolanus,* and replaced him with the chief of the Sûreté. To bolster his majority, he then dismissed the Prefect of Police, M. Chiappe, who was hated by the Left and suspect to Radicals as sympathetic to the rioters. If Daladier was removing a Rightist plotter, as he later claimed, it was senseless to offer him the Governor-Generalship of Morocco. No faction was pleased and all but the Socialist and Radical Deputies were enraged by Daladier's apparent contempt for public intelligence.

When he presented his new cabinet to the Chamber on February 6th, the Right and the Communists howled him down repeatedly. Across the Seine a great crowd gathered in the Place de la Concorde, later to be joined by cohesive formations of Rightist leagues (and a group of Communist war veterans) which had converged from various parts of the city. A cordon of police and mounted guards held the Pont de Concorde, which leads to the Chamber; and other, lighter, cordons cut off streets leading to the rear and sides of the Palais Bourbon. By late afternoon the police were being pelted with stones, iron fragments from tree guards, and Tuileries garden chairs as a younger element in the crowd surged toward the bridge with sticks, iron bars, and a few pistols. Repeated charges by mounted police caused injuries on both sides; riders fell into the crowd and were beaten as their horses slipped on the marbles strewn before them or were slashed by razor-tipped canes. Buses were overturned and set aflame, casting a pall of smoke and rubber stench over the scene. Excitement rose to fury, perhaps in part because the rioters had expected the police to turn aside. An attack led by the *Solidarité Française* reached the bridge at 7:30, a policeman was shot, and his overwrought companions fired back; six rioters died and several rioters and police were badly wounded. Attacks and counterattacks wearied the outnumbered defenders and thousands of new demonstrators marched up. At 10:00 a veterans' group charged the bridge; at 11:30 another charge ended in gunfire. Not until the small hours of February 7th did the crowd disperse. In all 14 of them were killed, 650 injured; the police had one death and 700 injuries. Hours before, Daladier had won his majority and the Deputies had slipped away.

The Left later alleged that February 6th was a carefully prepared fascist coup to invade the Chamber, disperse it, and proclaim a revolution. It pointed to the simultaneous, prearranged arrival of the leagues at various approaches to the Chamber, to the names bandied about by some of the rioters before and after: Chiappe, General Weygand, Marshal Pétain, ex-President Doumergue, and Tardieu. Neither proves very much. February 6th was the day of Daladier's first encounter with the Chamber, the natural time to protest his investiture; Chiappe was popular, but no activity on his part was uncovered; the military were known to decry the Left's economies on defense; conservative politicians had called for increased executive power. In the rear of the Palais Bourbon a large *Croix de Feu* column meekly allowed itself to be turned away by a few police; the violence had started at the Concorde well before the leagues arrived in force and seems to have been stirred in part by hotheads and toughs with a technical fascination for the tools and tricks of rioting. That some of the leaguers were fascist and would have welcomed a revolution is unquestionable, as was their desire for martyrs, which was satisfied by several impressionable young men. But there was little cooperation on the spot, few firearms, no attempts to seize strategic transport, power, or communications centers. The Left's insistence that a Parisian crowd exasperated by the antics of Daladier was really a fascist mob seeking a Right-wing dictatorship on the style of Berlin or Rome did nothing for French unity (or political sanity) in the months that followed. After the Second World War, the Left pointed to a number of ideas and men associated with February 6th and also associated with Vichy, but this proves only a continuance of anti-parliamentarism and not a fixed design.

The 6th of February was nonetheless one of Paris' memorable days, more violent than any since the Commune. To doubt the plot theory is not to minimize the danger, for the greater French upheavals had grown as often out of unplanned outbursts as otherwise. Had the Chamber been dispersed, the Paris Deputies and Municipal Council—many of whom had denounced Chiappe's dismissal—might conceivably have called for a new regime. But the police obeyed their new superiors, the Chamber was saved, and there is no evidence that the army would have lent itself to a *Putsch* against the Third Republic at the time. De la Rocque's claim that his only desire was to press the Chamber into rejecting Daladier in favor of a new, conservative Premier was probably sincere and it was consistent with his later acts. At any rate, the riots succeeded in this; Daladier resigned on February 7th under the threat of new riots for that night, President Lebrun called ex-President Doumergue to form a government of national union, and the anti-parliamentary fever disappeared, although the Rightist and Communist press exploded in denunciation of the "assassins of defenseless citizens."

The parallel with 1926 occurred to many. Then also Rightist demonstrations had toppled a Radical cabinet, and a national government based on the Center Right had broken the Leftist majority won two years before. Then it was Doumergue as President who had called Poincaré, and the Radicals had welcomed places in the new Ministry, relieved to escape the major responsibility for dealing with the crisis. On February 9th, Sarraut and Herriot took posts in Doumergue's cabinet, the former at Interior, the latter without portfolio, beside André Tardieu. The orthodox Germain-Martin returned to the Ministry of Finance, Laval to Colonies, Louis Barthou to Foreign Affairs, and the prestigious Marshal Pétain became War Minister at the age of 78. The array met wide approval, relief, and great expectations from all but Socialists and Communists on the Left, the Action Française on the Right. That "Papa" Doumergue, an old Republican politician, a Protestant and a Mason, at the head of a moderate cabinet should satisfy the Paris crowds suggests how feeble was their fascist appetite in 1934. If fascists and other Rightists expected to use him as an usher to dictatorship, they were disappointed. But so too were most Frenchmen who welcomed the national government, for the analogy to 1926 soon broke down.

Doumergue had neither the strength nor the intelligence of Poincaré, and the economic, political, and diplomatic problems he faced were far more serious. His main remedy was Tardieu's, increased executive prerogative. Not satisfied with the decree powers handed him by a frightened Chamber, Doumergue took to the radio in a series of condescending sermons to the nation, urging that the French Premier be given the power, with the President's consent but not the Senate's, to dissolve the Chamber. He also asked that individual Deputies be deprived of their right to initiate appropriations, a right much exercised to reward an endless range of private interests, with disastrous effects on the budget. The latter was granted him, with helpful results for the future. His use of decree powers to reduce government expenditures and raise taxes, together with the confidence of the banks in his governmen, enabled Doumergue and Germain-Martin to reduce the budget deficit. But it was not eliminated and a modest program of public works did little to improve the economy; unemployment continued to rise and government revenue to drop. In the autumn parliament returned and the Radicals who had earlier favored some measure of constitutional reform turned against Doumergue's proposal for easier dissolution. In November Herriot resigned from the cabinet and Doumergue was forced out. The threats of the *Croix de Feu* and Rightist newspapers came to nothing. Paris remained quiet and Pierre-Étienne Flandin formed a second national government, abandoning the constitutional project. Herriot returned, Tardieu departed—to mount an increasingly strident press campaign in *Gringoire* against the "spineless Republic." Pétain retired, but most of the others remained. On the surface, political life returned to normal.

The consequences of the bloody 6th of February far outran the Doumergue interlude. If one of the purposes of the extra-parliamentary Right had been to prove its virility and attract recruits, respect, and funds, it had succeeded. Blum had warned Daladier on February 7th that resignation would only encourage the Republic's enemies. He was probably right; but the resignation of a French Premier under pressure from the street, and the advent of a national government of social conservatives armed with decree powers, also awakened the Left as nothing else might have. That its leaders really believed February 6th to be a full-blown fascist *Putsch* is questionable. But the German example was before them; the Nazi revolution had early fed upon events no more dramatic or bloody than those Paris had just seen. After Hindenburg-Doumergue, who would follow? The fascist leagues had succeeded in sending Frenchmen to die rather than accept legal Republican authority; this in itself was tragic, and impressive. The Left reacted vigorously. On the 7th, the CGT called a general strike for February 12th, in its own name and that of the Socialist party and of the *Ligue des Droits de l'Homme*. On the same day the Communists called a protest rally at the Place de la République for the 9th, which was to be anti-fascist but also against "the killers" Daladier and Frot (the ex-Socialist Minister of the Interior), and for dissolution of the Chamber as well as the leagues. The demonstrators of February 9th were a mixed workers' group, for the rank and file of the Left progressively ignored the attempts of their leaders to segregate them neatly into Communist or Socialist, CGTU or CGT factions. Six were killed by the police, who had orders to cordon off the Place, and February 9th became a martyrs' day for the Left as the 6th did for the Right. The Communists and CGTU then joined the general strike and on the 12th all but essential services came to a halt for twenty-four hours; 100,000 Socialists and Communists marched together in Vincennes and, although the leaders still held back, the Popular Front was forming from below.

The building of the Popular Front was the most significant political work of the next two years and, in retrospect, of the entire interwar period. By the elections of 1936, Communists, Socialists, and Radicals had joined in a coalition that promised to achieve the social democracy frustrated for so long by their rivalries. Its emergence was not only a reaction to February 6th, to Doumergue, and to the rise of fascist leagues in France. Outside forces were, of course, crucial, the Nazi triumph in Germany first among them. By 1934 Moscow had recognized what ordinary Communists in China and Germany had learned in blood and torture, that the twentieth-century Right was something more formidable than the ramshackle Tsarist apparatus which had helped Lenin to destroy his liberal and socialist rivals. In May, 1934, the Communist leader Maurice Thorez returned from Moscow with orders to cooperate with anti-fascist parties, notably the Socialists, who had been the main target of Communist invective since 1919. Behind this reversal lay the preparations by both governments for the Franco-Soviet pact of alliance against Nazi Germany.

Now it was the Socialist leaders who were understandably reluctant to rush into common action with men who had so viciously attacked them only months before and who could be expected to turn all events to their ambition of capturing the entire French working class. But Blum was hurried toward a common front by several forces. In 1932, the novelists Henri Barbusse and Romain Rolland had drawn a large number of Socialists, CGT members, and pacifist Republicans of various parties into a world peace movement which met in Amsterdam and the next year in Paris. In 1933 the maverick Radical Gaston Bergery had launched an appeal for a "common front" against fascism which also attracted a wide range of leftist intellectuals. Many of the same people formed a "Committee of Anti-Fascist Vigilance" in March, 1934, and left-wing Socialists like Marceau Pivert were supported by an increasing number of party militants in urging cooperation with the Communists. Behind all was the foreign and domestic prosperity of fascism. On July 27, 1934, the Socialist party joined the Communist in a pact for "united action" against fascism, to "mobilize the entire working population" against the Rightist leagues, which should be disarmed and dissolved, to oppose war, to reverse the deflationary policies of the government at the expense of workers, to refrain from attacking each other's leaders and doctrines. Had the Socialists not agreed, Léon Blum later admitted, "the people would not have understood, and they would have come to dislike us."

Negotiations among the various Left groups continued into 1935, under the shadow of depression, which hit bottom that year, and of Nazi-fascist threats to the peace of Europe. The CGT, with about 750,000 members, reunited with the Communist CGTU's 250,000; the latter accepted a minority role on the executive board and the moderate CGT program of reforms within a "mixed" capitalist-regulated economy: unemployment insurance, the forty-hour week, public works, national economic planning, and the nationalization of some large industries and the Bank of France. But the new union still embraced only one-tenth of the industrial, commercial, and government employees of France and the CGT had henceforth to face the vigorous proselytizing efforts of Communist cells in the factories. The SFIO and Communist parties never seriously considered a merger, but the great popular demonstration of July 14, 1935, sealed their alliance in a moment of high drama. The *Croix de Feu* had staged several paramilitary rallies that spring. Meanwhile the younger Radicals—Daladier, Yvon Delbos, and Pierre Cot among them—had responded to Communist appeals for a wider Popular Front embracing all democratic bourgeois parties. On June 28th, Daladier spoke at a rally with Blum and Thorez, claiming to represent the petty bourgeoisie and pledging its common struggle with the workers against "the financial oligarchy." On July 14th, nearly half a million paraded under anti-fascist banners in the historic Saint-Antoine quarter to the Bastille. Although Herriot was still a member of Laval's national government (Laval had succeeded Flandin in June), many Radicals took part, bearing their tricolors alongside the red flags of Leftist militants.

Several more months were needed to conclude the alliance, but the ultimate adherence of the Radicals gave the Popular Front sufficient strength to make its triumph likely in the elections of 1936. Once more, then, this mobile Center party, still the largest in France, swung to the Left at a critical moment. Economic issues had divided it from the Socialists often before, in Clemenceau's day, in 1924–1926, in 1932–1934. Its political ideas and its electoral interests had brought it back each time. Herriot, a financial conservative since his ordeal of the 1920's, was reluctant to break with a national government enjoying the confidence of the banks and much of the business community. Although he foiled the Tardieu-Doumergue project for strengthening the executive, he afterward rallied the party's Deputies to the governments of Flandin and Laval. As the elections of 1936 approached and after a conservative budget was safely passed, the Radicals finally revolted, Herriot resigned again, and Laval fell in January. By then, the Radicals were thoroughly alarmed over the course of foreign affairs. On this ground, too, they now seemed prepared to take their stand with the Left.

## DIPLOMACY AND DOMESTIC SCHISM

The years 1934 and 1935 presented French diplomacy with a number of dilemmas unresolved by early 1936. The foreign policy of the Doumergue government in 1934 was designed to meet the Nazi threat in a traditional manner. At the Quai d'Orsay the vigorous old Louis Barthou undertook to strengthen France's alliances in eastern Europe and to promote an eastern Locarno with both Britain and the Soviet Union as guarantors, then to draw Russia into the League and a French alliance. A new approach was imperative, for Poland had signed a non-intervention pact with Germany in January. Barthou's trip to Warsaw was fruitless; the Poles utterly refused any arrangement which would bring Soviet Russia into their affairs. Reassured by Hitler's silencing of Nazi agitation over Danzig and far too confident of their own military strength, Polish leaders had begun to believe in their ability to play a lone hand. Not so with the Little Entente. Barthou was greeted warmly in Prague, Bucharest, and Belgrade, where he apparently lessened fears of a Franco-German deal over eastern Europe. In the same month of June, 1934, Germany underwent the "night of the long knives." Hitler rid himself of the Nazi "socialist" wing and assorted other rivals by murder. In August, Hindenburg died and Hitler buried with him the corpse of the Weimar constitution. A plebiscite approved Hitler's assumption of full personal power. A few days later, Russia was accepted into the League and all French parliamentary groups from Left to Right appeared willing to press negotiations for a Franco-Soviet pact, despite the fact that without an eastern Locarno, the alliance would conflict with France's Polish treaty. Barthou's policy also envisaged a closer tie to Italy, which would conflict with French support of Yugoslavia. Before Barthou could proceed to unravel these contradictions, he and King Alexander of the Yugoslavs were assassinated in Marseilles by a Croatian terrorist (October 9, 1934). At once France lost a spirited ally and a Foreign Minister who was devoted to rebuilding the alliance system France had enjoyed in his youth, and who was free of illusions regarding Germany.

Doumergue called Pierre Laval to succeed Barthou. It proved to be an unfortunate choice, not, as Laval's enemies have asserted, because he was already bent upon accommodating France to a German hegemony, but because this long-time pacifist believed himself capable of playing any man to his own and France's advantage under any circumstance. It was perhaps his only illusion; but, added to a surprising ignorance of the world outside France, and of the power of ideas, it was ultimately to lead him to obloquy and death. Laval reversed none of Barthou's initiatives; the negotiations with Russia went on, but at a slower pace. Whatever his inner thoughts of the Russian alliance, he meant to use its negotiation as one element in arriving at an accommodation with Germany. Doumergue, Tardieu, and subsequently Barthou had rejected Hitler's offer of an arms limitation accord in April, to the annoyance of the British government. Laval had opposed the rejection, considering it useless to continue insisting on the letter of Versailles, and a lost opportunity to curry British favor and to draw Germany back to the League. French rejection had in fact hastened the end of the Geneva Disarmament Conference in June, and the second half of 1934 saw a quickening of rearmament throughout Europe.

In November of 1934 Flandin became Premier, Laval remaining at the Quai d'Orsay. He now applied himself to bringing Italy to France's side. Mussolini's concentration of troops at the Brenner Pass in July, on the occasion of Dollfuss's murder by Austrian Nazis, had indicated a determination to keep Austria independent, between himself and Hitler. However different in their political styles, the "Latin Sisters" had a common interest in containing German power in Europe. The admiration of French conservatives and Rightists for the vaunted efficiency of Mussolini's regime helped Laval's Italian policy as it had Barthou's. Even the longstanding French contempt for Italian military prowess (to fight Italy, France needed two divisions; to watch a neutral Italy, four; to rescue an Italian ally, eight, one of many sayings went) was shaken by Mussolini's showmanship. Laval went to Rome in 1935 to assure him of France's aid in preserving Austria, but he also exerted himself to turn Italy from a "revisionist" to a "satisfied" power in colonial affairs. Mussolini received a desert area south of Libya, a strip of French Somaliland, a share in the Djibouti-Addis Ababa railway, and—most fateful—the impression (many say Laval's promise) that France would take no interest in the fate of Ethiopia.

Laval's policy toward Italy soon appeared justified. After his overwhelming victory in the Saar plebiscite of January 13, 1935 (90 per cent voted for reunion with Germany), Hitler openly repudiated the military clauses of Versailles and announced German conscription in March. The French response was shock, protests to Berlin and Geneva, but few signs in any quarter of a will to act forcibly. Having refused Hitler's offer to negotiate arms control on the ground that any rearmament violated the letter of Versailles, France now failed to enforce that letter, not least because Frenchmen had accepted—or knew that much of the world accepted—the principle of German equality. To mobilize, to strain already exhausted finances and endanger the franc, to risk war in the face of British disapproval (the Ruhr was remembered, not for the last time) was not seriously considered. Instead Laval and Premier Flandin met Mussolini in April at Stresa with MacDonald and Sir John Simon, the British Foreign Secretary. The "Stresa Front" spoke bravely of Austrian independence, of united vigilance against any further German moves, but it was silent on Ethiopia, against which Mussolini's preparations were well publicized. For a while the drama of the meeting hid its emptiness. In May Laval signed the Franco-Soviet Alliance pledging assistance in case of unprovoked aggression; he then journeyed to Moscow, receiving Stalin's and thereby the French Communists' approval of France's armament program. But no military conversations ensued; and Laval, apparently still hopeful of an accord with Hitler, delayed submission of the pact to the Chambers for ratification. It was Hitler, not Laval, who was to benefit from the maneuver.

To this point, all French parties generally supported the quest for alliances with both Communist Russia and Fascist Italy, though with varying degrees of enthusiasm. But in the latter half of 1935, three events combined to plunge foreign policy inextricably into the morass of partisan politics, on the eve of general elections each side was to treat as a matter of life or death for France. Hitler skillfully exploited each event in turn. The first was a wave of anti-British feeling which followed upon the abrupt signature, on June 18th, of the Anglo-German naval agreement which purported to limit German surface strength to 35 per cent of British. What the British saw as a logical accommodation to the demise of the Versailles military clauses the French saw as treacherous folly. London had broken the Stresa front, condoned Hitler's violation of Versailles without seeking French or League approval. After fifteen years of denouncing French armaments and consistently refusing to offer a military guarantee to facilitate French acceptance of German equality, Britain had struck a bargain to save herself expense. That the agreement, moreover, allowed Germany to match British Commonwealth numbers in submarines suggested that the British were ready to ignore not only French interests but their own as well. If this were true of France's closest associate, the need for other allies was doubly imperative.

The second event was the Communist party's sudden espousal of French armament and the military implementation of the Franco-Soviet pact. Though the Socialists were disquieted by this abandonment of pacifist internationalism and disarmament, the Radicals welcomed it and the broad Popular Front was now assured for the coming elections. To the Right, the Communists' new-found patriotism (they adopted Joan of Arc, "the girl of the people murdered by aristocrats and prelates") was cynical opportunism, akin to the torpid Radicals' embracing of a revolutionary party for electoral advantage. The Franco-Soviet pact was associated with the political and social enemy at home; the pact and the Popular Front appeared to reinforce, even to depend upon, each other. In the long interval before ratification, the Right discovered new arguments against a Russian alliance, not all of them without force. It conflicted with the Polish treaty; Poland would move closer to Germany than she already had. Poland, not Russia, had a German border and Russia could fight Hitler only over Poland's body; it would be unthinkable to sacrifice conservative, Catholic Poland to Russian ambitions in eastern Europe. The British disliked the Russian alliance; they had refused a military guarantee to France and were driven to the naval agreement with Hitler, because they feared being dragged into war over quarrels in the east, as in 1914. Most serious of all, and no doubt most worrisome to Frenchmen, was the Right's charge that the Soviet and the French Communist party urged defiance of Hitler in order to embroil France and the other bulwarks of western society, England, Italy, and—some now began to add—Germany, in a war which would open the Continent to Stalin's conquest. Adding weight to these objections was the obviously defensive nature of French military thought and preparations. In 1935, Colonel Charles de Gaulle's plea, seconded by Paul Reynaud, for armored divisions to make up a striking force was opposed by the Minister of War, General Maurin, who spoke for Pétain and leading strategists with astonishing candor in the Chamber debate; after spending fortunes on the Maginot Line, he said, "Would we be fools enough to advance beyond this barrier to who knows what folly?" There is no record that this admission of utter dissociation between France's military stance and her diplomatic commitments stirred any protest among his hearers. Frenchmen were profoundly pacific; the possibility of a new bloodletting like that of 1914–1918 was inadmissible.

The Right played upon French pacifism in its opposition to the Franco-Soviet pact. So did Hitler; in the second half of 1935 he repeatedly denounced "encirclement" of Germany, threatened to repudiate Locarno, which he said a Russian alliance would violate, and repeatedly offered a general settlement of all outstanding issues. The third event which played into his hands and inflamed French quarrels over foreign policy was Mussolini's attack on Ethiopia in the autumn. To the Left's faith in the Soviet alliance the Right had opposed its faith in rapprochement with Italy, which, if France persevered in a defensive posture, appeared more logical. Now France was forced to choose between preserving the League of Nations as an instrument of collective security and her nascent friendship with Rome. Laval hoped to do both, but Italy and England upset the chances for compromise. Mussolini wanted not a gradual penetration like France's in Morocco, but a resounding military triumph. Even more unexpected, England suddenly evinced a devotion to the League and to the duty of nations to band together against a lawbreaker. A national election was imminent and the so-called Peace Ballot, whose results were announced in June, 1935, had shown a wide pro-League feeling among the British people; a large majority of respondents had approved even the use of military sanctions against an aggressor. In September, the new British Foreign Secretary, Sir Samuel Hoare, stirred Geneva by announcing Britain's determination to uphold collective security. On October 3rd, the long-expected Italian attack began and on the 11th the League Assembly called for sanctions against Italy. Laval unhappily voted with England and the majority. Although doubting the sincerity of Baldwin and Hoare, Frenchmen thought that in a choice between Italy and the English the latter were clearly preferable, even though their vigor might reflect more worry over home politics, or over the Sudan and their Red Sea hegemony, than any eagerness to commit themselves permanently to the League.

Laval was determined to avoid the alienation of Italy and did all he could to minimize sanctions, for which the English public and some—far from all—of the French Left justly blamed him. But after the electoral victory of Baldwin's Conservatives in November, their brave slogan "All sanctions short of war" became all sanctions short of what provoked Mussolini to mention war, and Britain was ready to compromise. In December the Hoare-Laval plan to dismember Ethiopia was leaked to the Paris press. The uproar in Britain compelled Baldwin to sacrifice Hoare—and blame the French for holding back on sanctions. Laval's government barely survived a vote of confidence on December 28th. The entire Left attacked his policy as endangering the League; but no more than the British Left did it press for military preparedness in case sanctions should lead to war. Since the conservative governments in power on both sides of the Channel professed to believe Mussolini's threats, no oil embargo was imposed, the Suez Canal remained open to Mussolini's supply ships, and his troops made rapid progress. In May, 1936, they entered Addis Ababa; in July Great Britain moved in Geneva that sanctions be lifted. The prolonged and solemn farce had ended; so had confidence in the system of the League.

The Ethiopian affair had disastrous effects on French diplomacy and its domestic roots. The Right-wing press had denounced the League and its defenders in the vilest terms; *l'Action Française* had called for the murder of 140 pro-League Deputies if it came to war with Italy. The "loss" of Italian friendship was ascribed to a plot which would deliver France into Soviet bondage, and the parliamentary Right was nearly solid in its opposition to ratification of the Franco-Soviet pact in February, 1936, (it passed, 353–164). Italy was indeed lost, though whether she had ever been won is questionable. More important, Mussolini's triumph tempted him to Caesarian dreams that were hardly compatible with deference to "satisfied" powers he had bluffed so easily. The League was shattered, the eastern allies dismayed, and British opinion aroused against France at a critical moment. For these reverses the Left and the Radicals blamed Laval and the Right, though again, especially in the case of the Socialists, without admitting the risks and military requirements of a stronger policy. Despite the bad feeling between Paris and London, most French statesmen were determined to win back

British cooperation at all costs. It was Hitler who set the price: the German remilitarization of the Rhineland.

## SURRENDER AND APPEASEMENT

Attacking the French Chamber's approval of the Franco-Soviet pact as a violation of Locarno, Hitler sent his troops into long-prepared positions on the left bank of the Rhine in the morning of March 7th. The time was well chosen. France appeared to be alone and convulsed by the electoral campaign. The Laval cabinet had fallen in January, to be replaced by a hybrid caretaker government until the elections of May. The veteran Radical Albert Sarraut was Premier, with Flandin at the Foreign Ministry and General Maurin at the Ministry of War. Flandin, as did most informed Frenchmen, expected a denunciation of Locarno and was groping for British support. The general staff had long known of military preparations in the Rhineland; it too was preparing a plan of action, though in a leisurely manner, for it expected a move only later in 1936. That the providential political situation (which would spoil if the Flandin-Eden talks succeeded) might tempt Hitler to strike before he was militarily prepared was not taken into account. When a shocked French cabinet met in the morning of March 7th, Flandin, Sarraut, Paul-Boncour, the French delegate to Geneva, and Georges Mandel at first favored immediate military action. But Flandin admitted he could not say what the British would do; and General Gamelin, the Chief of Staff, admitted he had no plan for a local operation and insisted that no military action should be taken unless the cabinet were prepared to order a general mobilization. With the probable exception of Mandel, all feared public reaction to mobilization, which had always signified war, and feared also the expense, which would endanger the franc they had pledged themselves to save. In sum, the cabinet did not ask for an offensive movement to drive the Germans out nor, significantly, did the generals press for any action. It was decided to consult the British and public opinion, both of whose reactions most of those present must have been able to predict. Meanwhile, the Maginot Line was manned, Flandin notified the League and the Locarno powers that the Versailles and Locarno treaties had been violated.

Opposition quickly developed against unilateral French action. In a performance that was to be typical of him, Hitler had spoken reassuringly at the very moment of his coup. He deprecated its significance, described the occupation as merely "symbolic," and offered Europe a new Locarno in which Germany would accept a demilitarized zone on *both* sides of the Franco-German frontier (meaning destruction of the Maginot Line), a twenty-five-year nonaggression pact with France and Belgium, an air treaty to bar attacks on cities, nonaggression pacts in eastern Europe, and a return to the League. The British and Belgians urged France to do nothing before the Locarno powers met; both accepted the *fait accompli;* from Mussolini nothing was expected. Sarraut made a bid to arouse public opinion, and to set a strong French position in the negotiations with the Locarno powers; in a tough Sunday evening radio speech he called for national unity to resist the lawbreakers: "We are not resigned to leave Strasbourg under the menace of German guns!"

National unity was expressed by the newspapers of the next morning: France must not act alone or, most said, at all. The semi-official *Le Temps* approved the appeal to the League, hoped all would be "calm." The conservative and Rightist press blamed the Franco-Soviet pact, *Le Matin* applauding Hitler's eloquence in showing "the Communist peril," *Le Jour* charging that a government protected by "Russian revolutionaries" was pushing France to war with Germany. *L'Action Française* and the weeklies *Gringoire* and *Candide* opposed sanctions of any kind. In the following days, a Rightist pacifist campaign sprang up, replete with rallies and parades. On the Left, *l'Humanité* denounced Hitler, and also the idea of French military action as a fascist-capitalist provocation. The Socialist *Populaire* criticized Sarraut's belligerence and admitted the justice of Germany's claim to full sovereignty over her own territory. The British press reacted similarly and Eden assured the Commons that Britain would go to the aid of Belgium and France only in case of an "actual attack."

By Tuesday, March 10th, Gamelin had his plan for counteroccupation ready; far less complex than he and Maurin had insisted three days before, the plan was now too late. France was committed to whatever the League and the Locarno powers decided. Proposals and counterproposals went to and from Berlin; Hitler refused all compromise and nothing was done. German fortifications were already rising. Hitler had torn up Locarno and what remained of Versailles with impunity; his prestige was higher than ever, not least among the German generals who had opposed his gamble. The Sarraut government has often been blamed for losing a chance to halt German advances and perhaps to bring Hitler down with relative ease. Whether an immediate response on March 7th would have had such excellent results is unknowable; more surely, inaction gave Hitler and all Europe proof of French passivity. In this first of several acts of "appeasement," however, the French government was responding to pressures that even a Poincaré might not have resisted. The first was a profound pacifism born of the holocaust of only seventeen years before. Another was domestic political strife, coming to a head in an election campaign. The Chamber paid almost no attention to the Rhineland crisis, so occupied were the Deputies with local affairs; Left and Right blamed each other for the crisis as much as they blamed Hitler. The cabinet enjoyed little prestige and no internal cohesion. The business community was preoccupied with the stability of the franc and the economic consequences of disrupting the Franco-German industrial combines. The military in its defensive predilections no longer considered the Rhineland worth fighting for. That it was also routine-minded, which in military as in other affairs is to say incompetent, precluded a quick reaction. Most important of all, perhaps, was the popular acceptance in France, as in the other western democracies, of the attitudes of the new Wilsonian diplomacy. By the 1930's many Frenchmen, like Englishmen, had come to see the injustices of the Versailles Treaty, to agree that the Rhineland was not a proper cause for war because it belonged to Germany, that only when all legitimate German national rights were restored could other nations oppose German ambitions in good conscience, that only then, in fact, could the democratic leaders expect their people to fight at all.

The loss of the demilitarized Rhineland was not so much the source as the symptom of France's passive view of the eastern alliances. If these meant anything by the middle of 1936, they were merely added diversions for German strength, added "numbers" on the French side, should war come. That such additions were not believable without offensive preparations in the west and close military arrangements with Russia, Poland (both if possible, one at least), and the Little Entente was argued by too few. That they would subtract from French believability at the first sign of France's hesitation to act on behalf of a threatened ally was admitted by too few—until 1938. The loss of the Rhineland advantage might have been balanced by an immediate consummation of the eastern, particularly the Soviet, pacts. But they were not taken seriously enough even by the Popular Front government of Léon Blum to brave domestic opposition on the Center and Right. Crossing and obscuring all foreign issues from 1935 on were innumerable, conflicting notions popular in all the democracies: the Russian army was too weak to matter; the Russian army was about to engulf all eastern Europe; the French army was the most powerful in Europe; it was too feeble to have stopped Hitler in 1936 without British help; Britain would never help, thanks to the Left and its Soviet pact, or thanks to the Right and its refusal of sanctions against Italy; Britain would help, provided this or that compromise were agreed to; German rearmament was slow and bungled; Germany's arms were already unbeatable; her air force could obliterate Paris at any moment; there was time for contradictory policies to be worked out, for Hitler to fall, for America to awaken, for the Italian alliance to be salvaged, for Stalin and the Poles to fall into each other's arms.

Other ideas were systematically promulgated in the press, on public platforms, or in quiet talk. Liberals and much of the Left clung to the League, to disarmament, to pacifism, in which they were joined by men of the Right who had been the fire-eaters of 1914–1918. Conservatives and much of the Right saw Communism as the greater danger, at home and abroad. Not a few became frankly defeatist or pro-German and hoped above all that Hitler could be encouraged to strike eastward against Russia. Others preferred to disbelieve Hitler's aims or to believe that modern weapons were too horrible, that mankind, however reckless in Asia and Africa, was too civilized actually to fight again in Europe. Many failed to grasp the nature of totalitarianism and most were pre-occupied with domestic problems, with depression, with a search for economy, lower taxes, less effort. Amid these confusions, it was difficult for relatively democratic governments to build coherent foreign policies. In any case, none did. The British government and press were dominated by eminently practical men, sure of Hitler's practicality, or of their ability to make him so. They were devoted to peace, but insular, badly schooled in European matters, narrowly professional, and businessmen apparently not conversant even with British diplomatic and military history, often suspicious of those who were. In the agony of the next three years their leadership of the Anglo-French entente was to prove disastrous. In the same years, America's great power was to count for nothing. She was if possible more isolationist than in the 1920's, standing aloof from her two recent allies, with whom she had the closest ties of blood, language, culture, and political traditions. A later American

Secretary of State would call neutralism immoral, even when adopted by peoples having no such ties; in the 1930's it was called preservation of American national interests. In 1936 London and Washington were still wary of "French hegemony," against all the evidence of numbers, industry, and resources, still complaining of France's "obsession with security," without offering her guarantees, or any alternative but wishful thinking. But America was across the Atlantic and Britain behind the Channel; the errors and omissions of the French were to appear worse for being punished so terribly.

Apart from encouraging defeatism and further partisan strife at home, the loss of the Rhineland had serious diplomatic repercussions. The cautious Leopold III of Belgium renounced the French alliance in October, reverting to neutrality and a forlorn hope of avoiding invasion should war break out. Given the events of the First World War and the German strategic problem posed by the Maginot Line, it was a senseless gesture. But now the Line itself made much less sense, unless it could be extended to the sea. The Poles, who had offered armed support on March 7th in a fleeting moment of decision, settled back to their double game; the Czechs had not even this illusion to sustain them, but they were rearming, and fortifying the German frontier. Mussolini's contempt became explicit; in October the Rome-Berlin Axis was formed, though it had other sources including the Spanish Civil War. The single consolation was Britain's agreement to military conversations on plans to meet war in the west, something Paris had sought since Versailles. But the gain was questionable. The British agreed only because the Rhineland was removed as an "aggravation" to Berlin and, more surely, because they assumed French involvement in the east could now be only nominal. As full of suspicion over Russia as of illusion about Germany, the Conservatives in London were only half-ready, if that, to take military conversations seriously. Added to the secretiveness and vacuity of both commands, this promised little forward progress in military security. And it added to diplomatic weakness, for the common front between London and Paris was riddled with distrust. Instead of pooling strength, it added the weakness of each to the other; since each considered itself dependent on the other's agreement, it was henceforth likely that in crisis both would follow the desires of the one determined to do less. Until near the end, this was Britain, and France was all the more subservient for the simple geographic fact of being closer to danger and more in need of aid.

## THE POPULAR FRONT

France was also weakened by internal strife, as old as the Commune, as new as the Rhineland fright. The triumph of the Popular Front in the elections of April-May, 1936, was full of contradictions. The incandescent hope it inspired among the working classes and petty bourgeoisie contrasted ominously with fear and disgust among conservatives and the Right, and with the lowering darkness of the European scene. The electoral campaign of the Communists, Socialists, and Radicals in 1936 concentrated on domestic issues. The national governments of Flandin and Laval in 1935 had continued the deflationary economic policies of their predecessors. Government expenses were cut, salaries reduced again, taxes remained high, some rose, but the deficit persisted and the economy remained stalled. Flandin asked for an experiment with lower taxes and easier credit. The financial community, led by the Bank of France, refused, and the Chamber overturned him when he asked for decree powers in economic affairs. The gold standard was sacrosanct; Paul Reynaud was almost alone in pleading for devaluation, that French goods might compete again. In June, 1935, Laval returned, pledged to an even more drastic program of deflation; this time the Chamber voted decree powers and the Left was given additional proof that the 200 regents of the Bank of France could prescribe the nation's economic policies. That the regents were closely associated with big business, rails, coal, steel, armament, machinery, and hard goods—all maintaining, or even raising, their profits in the midst of depression— helped bring small businessmen and white-collar employees into the Popular Front's campaign against the "200 families running France for their own profit."

Laval's aim was to stimulate exports by lowering prices inside France; government salaries were cut another 10 per cent, private employers urged to do the same. But as other costs, and profits, held steady, prices did not fall to the same extent as wages, and France shared only marginally in the slow upturn of world production at the end of 1935. There were nearly 1 million unemployed at the beginning of 1936 despite the departure of 400,000 foreign workers. Agricultural discontent also favored the Popular Front. An earlier attempt to placate the farmers by fixing wheat prices foundered on the government's unwillingness either to buy the surplus or to prevent dealers from illegally driving the price down at the farm and, legally, maintaining the higher prices at the market. Corrective measures came too late, and the Leftist vote was to rise sharply in several rural districts. In addition to foreign and economic issues there was the continuing menace of the Rightist leagues. Their support of Laval, their pro-Italian agitation, their "mobilizations," at which speakers threatened violence to any Popular Front government, aroused the Left, especially the Radicals who had been their victims in February, 1934. To save his government, Laval in December accepted laws allowing the government to dissolve paramilitary organizations, to confiscate their insignia and weapons, to prosecute newspapers which incited their readers to violence. But enforcement did not follow swiftly enough to satisfy the Left and it became an issue in the campaign.

In January, 1936, the *Rassemblement Populaire* agreed on a program of "freedom, work, bread, and peace," which effectively compromised the differences among the three parties of the Popular Front. The press was to be purified by forced disclosures of its subsidies, action was to be taken against the leagues, committees were to investigate colonial exploitation. Peace was to be insured by a League fortified with automatic sanctions against aggressors, by progressive disarmament, by the nationalization of war industries, and by an end to secret diplomacy. Economic recovery would follow a restoration of purchasing power, reduction of the work week without reduction of pay, higher pensions, public works, and the abolition of Laval's economy decrees. The farmer was to be given better prices and protection against speculators and middlemen by the establishment of a Wheat Office, and marketing through cooperatives. Against "economic feudalism" the government would reform the tax system to tap higher incomes and to compel payment; it would control the export of capital, reopen the question of war profits, and, above all, break the power of the "200 families" over the Bank of France by submitting it to parliamentary control. It was, in short, a French New Deal, a series of moderate reforms well within the capitalist system and, significantly, it made no mention of devaluation.

That such a program, designed to appeal to workers, farmers, and the lower middle class, failed to win a landslide for the Popular Front was also significant, though generally overlooked in the elation of victory. The popular vote of the Right and Right Center (the national front) fell only from 45 per cent in 1932 to 43 per cent in 1936, but the Popular Front won 65 per cent of the seats, thanks to electoral alliances.

The Communists gained the most, from 800,000 votes and 12 seats in 1932 to 1.5 million and 72 seats, while the Radicals declined from 1.8 million and 155 seats to 1.4 million and 109 seats. That the results of their electoral pacts still worked to the Radicals' advantage, giving them a higher percentage of seats than votes (and the Communists a lower) was small consolation to men who saw the Socialists displace them as the single largest party in the Chamber, with 147 seats (25 per cent) from nearly 2 million votes (20 per cent). President Lebrun called Léon Blum as France's first Socialist Premier. The Communists adopted the earlier Socialist tactic, promising their support in the Chamber but refusing to take places in the government. The Communist party had what it wanted, or what Moscow wanted: assurance that France would not turn fascist, and, with Communist help, a good chance that she would step up her armaments and complete the Franco-Soviet pact by military arrangements. Free of responsibility for decisions and results, the Communists were free to pose as the guardians of working-class interests. Having pressed the Socialists to moderate their economic program in order to win the Radicals, they could now denounce it for not going far enough, and apply themselves to attracting the rank and file of labor and of the Socialist party as well. Blum's cabinet, announced on June 5th, was almost equally divided between the two other parties of the front. The Socialists Roger Salengro and Vincent Auriol became Ministers of Interior and Finance, respectively; Paul Faure, the Socialist party secretary, was Minister of State alongside the Radical Chautemps. The Radicals Daladier, Pierre Cot, Yvon Delbos, and Jean Zay became, respectively, Ministers of National Defense, Air, Foreign Affairs, and Education.

The great expectations of new beginnings that swept the French lower classes surpassed anything since 1848 and, in Paris, since the euphoria of the Commune's opening weeks. Hope centered on the sixty-four-year-old intellectual, Léon Blum, who had made his political debut in the Dreyfus affair, whose tenacity and clarity of mind made him successor to the assassinated Jaurès. He lacked the warmth, the common touch, the oratorical power of the Socialist martyr; but his integrity, high intelligence, and devotion to party principle won him wide respect among its members. As a journalist and party leader he had pressed for disarmament, for the League, excoriated the privileged, the banks, the capitalist press, the Rightist leagues and Mussolini; as a Jew he was all the more hated by the Right, whose newspapers descended to new depths whenever his name appeared. Several had openly wished for his murder. Their near-success in February, 1936, when he was savagely beaten by an Action Française mob, made Blum too a martyr to the Left and earned him a personal devotion he had not enjoyed before. Never a demagogue, he was a moderate, a Republican, and an evolutionary socialist. Of great personal courage, Blum was not naturally combative and longed for peace at home as much as abroad.

Before his cabinet could take office, events proved how difficult it would be to keep domestic harmony. The conservative and Rightist press redoubled its predictions of disaster, devaluation, depression, Bolshevism, war, and national shame. The Right gave not a hint of good will toward France's elected government or of any desire to maintain national unity in the face of crisis. Anti-Semitism appeared blatantly in several sheets; L'Ami du Peuple predicted that France's "nausea" would sweep Blum back to the ghetto, and Maurras renewed his incitement to murder. In early May the flight of capital brought the Bank of France's gold reserve to a new low and Blum had to reassure the banks and the Bourse that there would be no devaluation. Then pressure built up on the Left. In late May, there began the most spectacular series of strikes in French history. Largely spontaneous, led by individual militants, some of Communist, syndicalist, or anarchist persuasion, supported by exhilaration, expectation, and a resolve that expectation should this time not be deceived, the workers in the largest industrial plants staged sit-down strikes, occupying aircraft, automobile, machinery, and armaments works of the Paris region. After opening nights of somewhat untidy, though not destructive, hilarity, the workers settled down to a remarkably peaceful vigil beside their tools. The strikes spread to builders, printers, truckers, news vendors, and to the department stores whose help was the poorest paid of all. By early June, 2 million were on strike throughout France, confident for once that the government would not use force against them and so refraining from violence or sabotage themselves.

Blum took office when the strikes were still spreading. The CGT represented only a minority of the workers and was helpless to stop them, as were the Communists who later took credit for their success. Blum's intention had been to move more slowly, but he could not think of inaugurating the Popular Front by breaking strikes. The CGT's ability to keep public services and railroads moving assuaged public opinion, and the moderation of the workers' demands enabled Blum to find a solution in the Matignon Agreements (named for the Premier's residence) of June 7th. He met with delegates of the CGT and the CGPF, the General Confederation of French Production, an employers' group sponsored mainly by large industry. Neither was very representative of the contending forces, but there was no choice. Under Blum's arbitration, the workers won recognition of collective bargaining results (won and then ignored in 1919), the right to organize, guarantees against reprisals for strikes or other union activity, the election by workers of their own shop stewards to treat with management, and a general increase in wages ranging from 7 to 15 per cent. In the same month, parliament passed laws confirming collective bargaining, the forty-hour week without reductions in wages, and annual two-week paid vacations. The Senate agreed reluctantly; but it, with Blum, the Chamber, and the employers, grasped the significance of the fact that the workers had not evacuated the plants on the Matignon Agreement; after a century of broken promises they knew better. And upon finally returning to their jobs they joined the CGT in such droves that its membership was quintupled, to over 5 million within a year. Léon Jouhaux proclaimed "the greatest victory" in labor's history.

The celebrations of July 14, 1936, were the most joyful since the Revolution itself. Hundreds of thousands lined the streets of eastern Paris or marched, twenty abreast—workers, clerks, students, intellectuals, housewives, retired men, children, shopkeepers, entire neighborhoods together—sang the Marseillaise and the Internationale, danced the Carmagnole, waved red flags and tricolors, cheered the orators who told them that they were democracy's answer to fascism, depression, the privileged, and the war makers. More legislation followed. In August the Wheat Office was added to the Ministry of Agriculture, to fix the price and amount of wheat to be sold. Watered down by the Senate, the legislation nonetheless favored cooperative marketing and stabilized prices for farmers who had suffered from overproduction and speculation. Attacked as communistic, the regulations vexed a good many and the Popular Front lost support in the countryside among those who felt it went too far, or not far enough, and, as always, from those who now were satisfied and saw no more use for Blum's experiments elsewhere. The "200 families" lost their control of the Bank of France; its General Council was to be appointed by the government from all economic groups, its Governor was henceforth a civil servant.

One of the most popular acts of the Blum government was its nationalization of the armaments industries. That a few should reap immense profit from wars fought by the many was a moral outrage to Frenchmen not only on the Left. The Republic had found it possible to send ordinary men to their death by tens of thousands, but not politic to limit, or tax, the profits of munitions makers. The cabinet undertook the highly technical task of isolating and expropriating the armament sections of complex industries like Renault and of buying aircraft companies while leaving them autonomous. Although the program omitted many arms plants (increased efficiency would make them superfluous, it was thought) and was only half-complete at Blum's fall, it had set a precedent which, as the British journalist Alexander Werth said, seemed to put France once more at the head of human progress. In another direction, the Popular Front renewed the identification of the Left with scientific progress. Under the leadership of Blum's Under-Secretary for Scientific Research, Madame Irène Joliot-Curie, daughter of Marie Curie and wife of the brilliant nuclear physicist Frédéric Joliot, and with the help of Blum's friend Jean Perrin, another outstanding physicist, the government raised its support for laboratories, equipment, and scientists. The impetus was maintained after Blum's fall, through the Vichy years and into the postwar period, when the CNRS (*Centre Nationale de la Recherche Scientifique*) succeeded in returning France to the front ranks in pure and applied science. Not least of the Popular Front's works was its response to the complaints of Jean Guéhenno and many others that the lower classes were shut off from nature, travel, and French culture. The government arranged reduced rates for railroad travel, for resorts and tours; it expanded the hiking and hostel program, camping and winter sports. Socialist, Catholic, and Communist groups organized popular study clubs in art, literature, theater, radio, and films, sponsored special performances and exhibitions at low cost or none. The Popular Front's aim of liberating the worker and his family from the stifling routine of workshop, tenement, and corner café—hitherto an ideal identified with social Catholicism and for that reason restricted to a small minority of workers—lived on, under the bondage of German occupation, to emerge as one of the liveliest *mystiques* of the postwar Left.

## THE FAILURE OF REFORMISM

It was mainly as memory and *mystique* that the Popular Front left its mark, for the Blum government fell after only a year and most of its economic efforts failed or were reversed. The first great retreat, however, was diplomatic: the failure of the Blum government to aid the Spanish Republic in its fight against Franco's nationalists supported by Hitler and Mussolini. The public at first assumed that one Popular Front government would hardly fail to aid another, especially as it was the legal government of a neighboring state. The Spanish War, which opened on July 18, 1936, was for Leftists and democrats the world over a classic struggle between the fascist International and human liberty. Despite the intrigues of the Communists and the anti-clerical atrocities—neither was so easily condoned by Loyalist supporters as later critics were to allege—the Spanish Republic stood for western democracy. That the struggle was murderous and compromised by internal divisions was in large part attributable to the squalor and mindless repression Spaniards had borne too long. It nonetheless divided Frenchmen more deeply than Ethiopia had. The Right and most Catholics accepted Franco's pronouncement of a "holy war"; they were scandalized by other Catholics who rejected it: Mounier's *Esprit*, Bidault in *l'Aube*, Bernanos, Mauriac, and Maritain. Once more, the "peace" campaign erupted in the Rightist press, and to the surprise of his supporters, Blum acceded to it.

Under severe pressure from London and apparently believing that French aid would lead to war with Italy, and perhaps Germany as well, Delbos and Blum forbade even the sale of munitions and airplanes to the Spanish government. The second farce in two years, this time called nonintervention, was solemnly played out by London and Paris. Blum's policy was from the beginning to tighten the British alliance; he had abandoned sanctions against Italy in June on London's initiative and made no advances to Russia that might alarm the Baldwin government. Determined to avoid offense to Hitler, and indifferent or hostile to the Spanish Republic, the British took full advantage of French dependence to denounce even the trickle of volunteers and private aid that entered Spain, and Frenchmen were allowed to believe that Britain would refuse her support if France were to become involved with Germany over the Spanish question. The Communists, the CGT, many Socialists and urban Radicals begged for action, demonstrated, denounced the Blum government for cowardice, especially after the fall of Irun on the French border. Two days later on September 6th Blum faced a hostile Socialist audience at his famous Luna Park speech but won it over by appealing to the fear of European war—and denying the active intervention of Italy.

The Radicals, notably Delbos and Chautemps, refused to aid the Spanish Republic through fear of the cost, of their rural constituents, or out of sheer lassitude as much as worry over the English. The Rightists and much of the popular press had succeeded in equating aid and war. French journalists paid from Rome peddled the myth of Italian power and "endless resources." Blum in turn feared for his coalition. He also feared to worsen the divisions in French society that aid to Madrid—or a policy so dependent on Communist votes—might bring. It now appears that a modest amount of war material, aircraft in particular, might have saved the Loyalist cause and that no amount of appeasement of fearful Radicals, conservatives, and Rightists would have saved the Popular Front as long as it made any serious effort at domestic reform. Blum's dilemma seemed real enough at the moment, but he was later to regret his inaction and plead, unsuccessfully, for aid in 1938 when it was too late. The Spanish Republic died as western statesmen sat deploring the rising influence of Moscow and the Spanish Communists, doing nothing to balance that influence with aid of their own. The bell that tolled over Madrid tolled also for the Popular Front in France. For all its caution, its enemies naturally went on accusing it of Bolshevism and many of its friends who were not Communists lost faith in its courage to face the enemy at home or abroad.

The Spanish War emasculated the Popular Front not three months after its accession, although it was not until 1937 that the Radicals and the Radical-dominated Senate brought it down. The issues, as always, were financial and economic. The forty-hour week and higher wages were very slowly applied (in some areas not at all), but they raised the costs of production, which were passed on in higher prices. French exports continued to lag and real wages fell. The business community invested less than ever in new facilities or methods, preferred to wait until "discipline" was restored. Refusing to admit labor's gains as either justified or permanent, employers refused to turn to double shifts. Increased demand met no increased production. Profits were maintained simply by raising prices. Capital continued to flow abroad, government loans were undersubscribed, and government deficits mounted as did the cost of rearmament. The much-heralded program of tax reform came to nothing; the electors of the Popular Front continued to bear the main burden its wealthier enemies successfully evaded. The government finally accepted devaluation of the franc in September, but by then French prices were too high to compete in world markets and without exchange controls it achieved little beyond fulfilling the gloomy predictions of the financiers. The Rightist press fulminated against "the thieves." The Communists condemned the government for choosing to attack "the people's savings" rather than tax the rich.

The Popular Front's policy, to achieve recovery by expanding purchasing power, foundered on what was essentially a strike on the part of business and the investor. "Better Hitler than Blum" was not nearly so serious or widespread an attitude as "better stagnation" than the uncertainties of economic and social change. In February, 1937, Blum announced a "pause" in the Popular Front program, abandoned his plans for public works, for a sliding wage scale tied to living costs, for higher social insurance and pensions; promised a balanced budget, higher taxes, and withdrawal of penalties for dealing in gold. This surrender did nothing to revive business confidence, especially as in March disaffected Socialists and Communists vented their anger by attacking a *Croix de Feu* meeting in Clichy, where five were killed by the police. Blum was denounced by Communist, Socialist, and labor militants, who demanded that he press on to socialism. Strikes resumed shortly afterward. Capital fled abroad once more and leading bankers boasted of "breaking" the Popular Front. Blum was pressed by economic experts to return to a full policy of deflation. Belatedly he stiffened, determined to impose exchange controls, a tax on capital, and nationalization of key industries. The Chamber gave him decree powers in June, but the conservative Radicals of the Senate refused and the exhausted Blum resigned without a struggle. The "wall of money" stood firm; the Popular Front was mortally wounded.

In retrospect, Blum's failure to devalue the franc and control capital exports at the very start, when the Radicals and the Senate were amenable, or cowed by the stay-in strikes, was a fatal error. His policy, like the Popular Front's program, was a mixed economy, neither socialism nor economic liberalism. But a mixed economy would have required stringent controls over those able to sabotage it. Concerned before all to heal French differences, Blum ignored the fact that the very advent of the Popular Front made them worse and that to accomplish meaningful change he had no choice but to brave, perhaps in the short run even to aggravate, those differences. The malady of France was drift and the absence of strong leadership. A Jaurès might have provided it; Blum did not, despite a majority in the Chamber that made him nearly independent of the Radicals. In allowing them to share power, he had thought to rally the widest possible front against the fascist threat, but the resulting compromises only confused all sides, angered both labor and business. The Popular Front failed not from its extremism, but from indecision and the inchoate nature of its plans. No more than most French entrepreneurs did the Left consider production, rather than distribution, of wealth the primary problem. As so often before, the moderates proved too weak (and economically incompetent) to survive. Blum's authority and nerve had been shaken by rivals to his Left and by a hysterical Rightist campaign of slander, one instance of which (originated by the Communists) had driven his Minister of the Interior, Roger Salengro, to suicide under false accusations of desertion in the World War. The Popular Front's dissolution of the fascist leagues and its attempts to restrain the extremities of a venal press had changed nothing. Although by 1937 de la Rocque's *Croix de Feu* had meekly turned itself into the *Parti Social Français*, his tougher activists had deserted, some to the armed and conspiratorial *Cagoulards* (hooded men) who were financed in part from Rome. Others joined the ex-Communist Jacques Doriot's *Parti Populaire Français*, an increasingly fascist group laced with roughs from the Corsican and Marseilles underworld. Action Française prospered, as did several smaller but more up-to-date fascist cliques, anti-Semitic, pro-Nazi, and preaching a totalitarian wave of the future. The wheel appeared to have made a full turn, for Blum's successor was the opportunist Radical Chautemps, whose previous reign had stirred the riots of February, 1934.

For a while, the Socialist-Radical majority (the Communists withdrew) feigned a continuation of the Popular Front, Blum loyally accepting a place, without portfolio, in the new cabinet. But the return to dead center, then to economic and social conservatism, was inexorable. Blum had given indecisive leadership; Chautemps, a parliamentary gamesman, gave none at all, for neither he nor most of his party wanted movement in any direction. For the third time since the war, the Radicals proved how much they were a party of immobility, interested in defense of the political, economic, and social *status quo*. Republican defense (and an eye to electoral advantage) led them into the Popular Front, but many were hostile even to the modest reforms projected during the campaign, and afterward worried by their loss of votes and seats to the economic and social Left. That the dangers to their Republican ideals might require something more than passive defense occurred to only a minority. Apart from watching the fascist leagues, the only Popular Front program they believed in was increased rearmament—under Daladier, who remained Defense Minister—but even here neither they nor the Socialists showed a sense of urgency. The next war would resemble the last, except that the Maginot Line would spare France an occupation. Passivity ruled; military debates were rare; Daladier relied on the defensive presuppositions of the general staff; Reynaud's second attempt to win a hearing for de Gaulle's professional armored striking force was buried in early 1937. All sides clung to the Republican tradition of defense by the nation in arms; the Socialists especially were opposed to a professional, therefore "reactionary and aggressive," army.

Content with routine in defending the Republic from without, the Radicals were merely following the mood of the Chamber, in which only a handful of nationalist Rightists—Reynaud, Mandel, Louis Marin —joined the Communists in pressing for crash programs. In economic affairs, they followed the Center and Right, which meant reversing the gains of labor. Once again employers who would have preferred to move forward in social matters were isolated. Many politicians and the newspaper-reading public may sincerely have believed, against the evidence of sixty years, that French industry lagged mainly because of labor's unreasonableness. No doubt strikes, stay-ins, slowdowns and tedious disputes over work rules and labor's rights seriously impeded production. Violent talk and threats of action to match it, coupled with the government's vacillation, understandably frightened property owners and employers into waiting for better days. But at bottom 1936 was the price both sides paid for past refusals to compromise. And it was not the workers but the businessmen who had for two generations refused investment, modernization, multiple shifts, mass production, and lower prices, who had ignored the legislation of 1919, who restricted output by cartel arrangements, by forbidding imports and foreign competition, who eliminated domestic competition by manipulating credit, subsidizing obsolescence, outlawing chain stores, and combining against the rare entrepreneur who sought innovation. Nor was it the workers who could drain the treasury by setting inflated prices on government contracts, shipping capital abroad, and evading lawful taxes.

Insofar as the defeat of France was attributable to economic debility, the responsibility of the business community, from the largest bankers and industrialists to the smallest retailer or farmer, and their protectors in parliament, was overwhelming. The power of labor to affect events was minimal and indirect, however spectacular its acts. Compared with the sit-down of business and parliament (or with the contemporary action of American labor), the stay-in strikes were feeble gestures of temporary significance. But they and the Popular Front, whose aim it was to conquer France's economic weakness, occurred at a crucial moment, further lessening the confidence and enterprise of the established system, when every week of delay in arms production was perilous for the future. For having failed to solve her social problems in earlier, safer, years, France in 1936 found herself needing rearmament and social reform at the same moment. Each alone would have required a levy on national wealth. The Popular Front tried to accomplish both, without resorting to coercion of the holders of wealth, who as yet recognized the first need only grudgingly, the second hardly at all.

Chautemps feared that too much support for the Popular Front remained in 1937 for him to move quickly to an orthodox economic policy, and he needed Socialist votes to stay in office. But his choice of the conservative Radical Georges Bonnet as Finance Minister reassured the business community. Under quickly granted plenary powers, Chautemps and Bonnet carried out in June, 1937, a second devaluation, cut expenses, raised taxes slightly. After a dreary July 14th, which appeared to prove the despondency and division of the working classes, the flight of capital slowed, government bonds regained some of their value. But in the autumn strikes resumed, partly over the government's continued embargo on arms for Spain; and from the Right the *Cagoulard* terrorists bombed the offices of business associations in a clumsy attempt to provoke an anti-Left reaction. In December a stay-in strike at the Goodrich Tire plant in suburban Colombes, then strikes of truckers, bus drivers, and the Métro unsettled Paris. Chautemps gave way still further to business pressure. In January, 1938, he attacked the Communists so harshly that the Socialists resigned and after a decent interval Chautemps reconstituted his cabinet entirely with Radicals. It hung together for only a few weeks; Chautemps resigned again in early March, in time to escape the need for action over Hitler's seizure of Austria.

Lebrun called Blum to form a second cabinet. The latter first attempted to form a national government in the face of the foreign crisis, but the Center and Right preferred to wait for the final defeat of the Popular Front and a chance to govern without the Left. Blum turned to a Left combination resembling his first cabinet, but with the substitution of the Republican-Socialist Joseph Paul-Boncour for Delbos as Foreign Minister. Paul-Boncour was devoted to collective security, regretted French inaction over Austria, which clearly imperiled the Czechoslovak Republic. To the chagrin of the Right, he sounded out the intentions of France's eastern allies, including Russia, in the event of a German threat to Prague. He also relaxed the embargo on munitions to Spain. London's anger was manifest. But it was only a brief flurry of French independence, for in less than a month the Senate overthrew Blum upon a request for plenary powers to carry out his program for a planned economy. On April 10, 1938, Édouard Daladier succeeded him with a cabinet made up of Radicals, assorted moderates, and conservatives apparently united on a program of national defense. Paul Reynaud became Minister of Justice, the veteran Albert Sarraut returned to Interior, Georges Mandel to Colonies, Georges Bonnet to Foreign Affairs. Daladier kept the Defense Ministry for himself. Only the extreme Right refused its support to Daladier's request for decree powers.

In the brief respite between the *Anschluss* and the Munich crisis, Daladier carried out a third devaluation of the franc. In spite of and because of it, business confidence revived and Daladier decided to modify the forty-hour week in a bid to increase production. After Reynaud became Minister of Finance, the government authorized overtime work, made severe cuts in nondefense spending, and decreed a flat 2 per cent surtax on all incomes, small and large. In late November the workers occupied the great Renault plant; Daladier cleared it by force. Communist militants pressed Jouhaux to call a general strike; Jouhaux resisted, then argued, then tried to avoid it by negotiating with Daladier, but the Premier was determined to prove his return to a policy of "order." The general strike of November 30th was a nearly complete failure. Daladier had requisitioned the workers of railways and public services. Workers in most other industries were divided among themselves. Many needed overtime to support their families; some were strongly pacifist, distrustful of comrades who favored intervention in Spain; most, perhaps, had long since lost faith in leaders who had lost the Popular Front victory. After the defeat of the strikes, workers quit the CGT by tens of thousands as triumphant employers took revenge for 1936, purged union activists, and repudiated collective bargaining agreements; the government imprisoned 300 Renault strikers. In this atmosphere, Reynaud's rigorously orthodox economic policies revived the long-courted confidence of business; capital flowed back and production rose steadily as strikes subsided.

Little now remained of the 1936 alliance. The CGT had sunk to less than 2 million members; Socialists and Communists blamed each other for the Front's collapse, Radicals blamed both, and many, including Daladier, regretted their association with the collectivist parties. The effects of the Popular Front were, like its composition and program, contradictory. The Communist party had gained in numbers and respectability among the workers and, for the first time, in a few rural areas of the south. Its enemies made much of its subservience to Moscow, but between 1935 and the Nazi-Soviet pact of August, 1939, its patriotism and consistent anti-fascist foreign policy, the accuracy of its warnings on domestic affairs appealed to men (on both sides of the Atlantic) who had seen free economies crumble, democracy fail to block aggression, and the possessors scurry to appease or join the new Right. It doubly appealed to Frenchmen whose families were still wretchedly housed, badly nourished, and ill-clothed, whose children lacked proper medical care, recreation, and books, and were barred from most higher education. The so-called "Popular Front mentality" was to be called naïve after the outbreak of the Cold War in the late 1940's; but for a few brief years of the 1930's, the only sane voices seemed to come from the Left and one did not have to dismiss the Soviet threat to think that, for the moment, Nazism was the greater danger. From these circumstances, the Communist party drew lasting strength. Despite the temporary disgrace of the Hitler-Stalin accord, the party was to play a leading role in the Resistance, emerging more powerful than ever in 1944. Part of its success came from the sudden growth of the CGT in 1936, which enabled Communists to win control of unions in several basic industries and in the Paris area. Both the creation and the failure of the Popular Front thus strengthened those Frenchmen who believed that progress required revolutionary change. Paradoxically, the experience suggested to others that, with slightly altered methods and in a healthier international climate, a mixed program like Blum's could well succeed. The last two years had seen labor and management gain their first widespread experience in collective bargaining. That both sides often refused concessions and depended too much on government arbitration, provided for by a law of 1936, was natural after generations of mutual hostility and inexperience. But a beginning was made and some employers refused to take advantage of the workers' defeat in 1938. The more moderate CGT unions were, here and there, able to maintain their gains. These successes were to be remembered, even overestimated, after the war.

Other novel departures were taken in the late 1930's. Numbers of younger employers, and some of those who had been impressed by the American example, organized to discuss new approaches to labor-management problems. The thousands of new collective bargaining agreements uncovered many knowledgeable union officers, who had also learned the crucial importance of raising productivity. That they, along with some economists and civil servants, sometimes appeared more concerned with technocracy than democracy was perhaps inevitable. After the war, this modernizing current would be sustained by engineers, scientists, managers, the ubiquitous "expert"— and would present its own problems to Frenchmen determined to retain democratic control of national decisions. That one effect of the Popular Front's sudden increase in wages was to force many small industrial and commercial enterprises out of business was to technocrats a sign of progress, the first break in a static society. But to the small manufacturer, the individual shopkeeper, the political disciples of Alain, the cultural disciples of Duhamel, and other critics of bigness, it presaged a loss of precious variety and personal independence. Before the war, the debate was hardly audible; afterward, it would split the Radical party and turn many of its rural and small business supporters against the Fourth Republic's attempt to modernize the economy at their expense.

## THE MUNICH ERA

That a more immediate effect of the Popular Front was to push much of the bourgeoisie into the arms of the Right is by now a commonplace. More exactly, it accelerated what had happened many times before Blum's arrival. The difference now was the changed character of the Right, and the illusion that Mussolini and Hitler's New Order, despite all its nastiness at home, represented order as such, a defense of that *status quo* under attack from the working classes. Fear of what fellow Frenchmen would do to France (would the Left not prevail again in the election of 1940?) overshadowed fear of fascist hegemony in Europe, which, moreover, a cooperative France shielded by the Maginot Line might well survive. Many persuaded themselves that the only alternative was ultimate Soviet hegemony to which, on the contrary, a Leftist France might well succumb. Better Hitler than Stalin; and if the price of containing Communism should be surrender of democracy at home, was it so great a loss now that democracy had ceased to work in their class interest? Time and the German occupation would show that there were relatively few fascists in France but many who prized property and order at least as much as political and national freedom, who feared that democracy could not protect all of these, or any, and accommodated themselves to superior power in the hope that order at least would be saved. Prudence and apathy more than treason or fascist fervor led to collaboration after 1940 and appeasement before.

Neither trait was confined to the bourgeoisie; apathy and withdrawal are universal; prudence motivated pacifists on the Left as on the Right. Unions and fragments of unions, perhaps a majority of Socialists, thousands of provincial teachers as well as Parisian intellectuals were pacifist, persuading themselves that nothing was worth a repetition of the great war's slaughter. Not only pacifists believed that another such loss of her young men would destroy France's society and civilization; the toughest advocates of firmness agreed, as did the military leaders who planned a bloodless, defensive war. Defeatism was another, related source of appeasement. After his absorption of Austria, Hitler led a nation of 76 million; France had little more than 41 million, with a much lower proportion of young men to old. Industrially, Germany held a long lead, with (the Right never tired of adding) no interruptions of production. German discipline and efficiency were legendary, and magnified in the late 1930's by the defeatist and pro-German press, exaggerating French "anarchy," technical backwardness, faulty workmanship, and bureaucratization of army and industry. The long campaign of the daily *l'Action Française,* and its fascist imitators to destroy Frenchmen's faith in the integrity and competence of their leaders was increasingly successful in the face of the government's undisguised indecision. The minority who wished to strangle the Republic and the few who gladly envisaged Hitler doing it for them masked their intent with the anti-Communist crusade: repression at home, a Holy Alliance against Russia in Europe. For the latter, Germany and Italy must be kept strong; the sacrifice of small nations would be a small price to pay for European order.

As Hitler moved against Austria, Czechoslovakia, and Poland, this view was lent respectability by those who still believed that European peace depended upon the satisfaction of legitimate national demands. If Austrians, who after all were Germans, desired union under Hitler, why should France deter them? The advocates of the old balance-of-power diplomacy at Versailles had sinned against self-determination by placing Germans under Czech and Polish flags. When Hitler moved into Austria in March of 1938, there was shock over his methods but little demand for action. Soon after, the Nazi campaign against outflanked Czechoslovakia began. The British were weaker than ever. Eden, who was considered a strong advocate of collective security, had resigned in February; two days later Chamberlain told the British that they "must not delude small weak nations into thinking they will be protected by the League against aggression," that the big four—Germany, Italy, France, and England—would have to settle their differences among themselves. The defeatist Flandin made himself the French spokesman of the Chamberlain-*Times* group, loudly seconded by the pacifists, most of the popular and Rightist press, and in the Daladier cabinet by Foreign Minister Bonnet.

From Blum's fall in April, 1938, to March, 1939, when Hitler repudiated Munich and swallowed the rest of Czechoslovakia, the Daladier government was for the most part dominated by the appeasers. Whatever Daladier believed in foreign policy—and he seems to have changed his mind several times—he also believed in his cabinet's survival, if only to press rearmament without pause. The crosscurrents of opinion in France were now at their most bewildering stage. Still attacking each other violently over domestic issues, pacifists and defeatists on the Left were in accord on appeasement with defeatists and pro-Axis publicists on the Right. The Socialists and trade unions were divided on foreign policy, the Radicals on foreign and domestic issues alike. The resisters on the moderate Left—Blum, Jouhaux, and their followers—found the Communists, who were undercutting them at home, agreeing with them on diplomacy, and both tended to support Daladier on preparedness, though he in turn was trying to break their domestic influence. Finally, some of the Left's severest critics among conservatives—Reynaud, Henri de Kerillis, and Mandel—joined the Communists in pleading for firmness over Czechoslovakia, on which the cabinet itself was divided.

Daladier deemed it impossible to appease all of these factions and at the same time to keep the British alliance without acceding to Chamberlain's plan for transferring the Sudetenland to Germany. Hitler's threat of war did the rest. Even many who preferred resistance were persuaded that the French and British forces were still too weak to win, particularly in the air, that they must buy time to build armaments. Offers of support from Soviet Russia, the Right's *bête noire* and ally of the Popular Front, were ignored. Daladier allowed Bonnet to leave the initiative to London, although France was Czechoslovakia's ally and Britain was not. British pressure on Prague was relentless. In September, Hitler's rejection of a generous compromise, forced on the Czechs by the British and French, provoked the Chamberlain and Daladier governments to preliminary mobilizations. For several days, Paris was prepared for war. Mussolini intervened, to suggest a Four-Power conference; and at Munich on September 29th, Chamberlain and Daladier granted most of Hitler's demands. In Britain and France public approval, though doubtless exaggerated by the press, was widespread. Daladier, not sharing Chamberlain's illusions and ashamed of having deserted an ally, returned to Paris to be greeted by ovations. For a few months more, the appeasers were dominant; only the Communists (and two other Deputies) voted against the Munich agreement, which unleashed a Rightist campaign against them as warmongers. Prudence vanquished pride; the government cautioned the press against making too much of the vicious Nazi pogroms of November, lest Hitler be offended. In December, Foreign Minister Ribbentrop arrived to sign a pact of Franco-German friendship with Bonnet; the Jewish members of the cabinet, Mandel and Zay, were not invited. At the end of February, France recognized Franco Spain; crowds of ill and hungry Loyalist refugees were unconscionably neglected by the authorities in southern France. To diplomatic debility, the Daladier government added betrayal of human rights.

Some Frenchmen did not need the Nazi rape of Prague in March of 1939 to tell them that Munich was a blunder as well as a crime, a moral defeat in which the western democracies had bullied a sister democracy, had cowered before the dictators. Justified in a hundred ways, it was nonetheless a craven· act, and proved to Hitler the emptiness of the Franco-Soviet pact, the weakness of the Franco-British entente. After Prague more and more Frenchmen were convinced that war could not be far away. All the half-measures, the half-prepared safeguards were now exposed. As Jean Paulhan said in the *NRF* of March, 1939, France had had no foreign policy, only a too-clever mélange of ingredients from several, designed to satisfy all points of view, in which, of course, it had also failed even in the short run. A consistent Poincarist policy, a consistent League policy, even a consistent policy of appeasement and pacifism would have been better, he went on, but not all three. Paulhan's view is, of course, debatable. There were great difficulties and dangers in each course. Most observers have rejected the last as suicidal in a world of dictators and the first as unworkable by democratic governments responsive to popular demands that national policy be just before it dare be forceful. The middle course, collective security either through alliances or the League (or both, if they were compatible), has been judged the most promising by historians of the period—and adopted by western statesmen since. But the great difficulty of collective security was (and remains) the need for collective agreement on the justice and intelligence of each response to every crisis. The interests of one nation had to concern all its allies, however remote these interests appeared, and the one, in turn, had to order, or alter, its interests to win the cooperation of all. The First World War proved what had been true for many years, that France could not preserve her security alone; but public acceptance, especially in Britain, of the Wilsonian ideal made it doubly difficult for France to find support for her view of security as it was expressed at Versailles. In this sense, the first step to appeasement was not the Ruhr invasion but the advantages taken at Versailles and seen even then as contrary to the principle of self-determination. Only when the "inequalities" of Versailles were removed, the British said, was collective security possible; but the French replied that the guarantees of Versailles could be removed only after security had been won by other means. Over this point France and England carried on a dialogue of the deaf. Their incomprehension of each other, of the world about them, and of the strenuous requirements of collective security invited disaster. The limits on national ambition and action that collective security must impose went unacknowledged, as did the most delicate operation demanded by the system—the constant choice between the kind of appeasement that would strengthen the collective will and the kind that would undermine it, all the while preserving justice and building sufficient power to deter blackmail or aggression.

Events moved swiftly in the spring and summer of 1939. After absorbing Czechoslovakia, Hitler wrested Memel from Lithuania in March, then opened his campaign of threats to Poland over Danzig and the Corridor. The British were finally aroused and in headlong fashion gave guarantees of support to Poland, Rumania, and, after Mussolini attacked Albania in April, to Greece, then to Turkey in May. The Daladier government followed suit, somewhat cheered by Britain's unprecedented launching of peacetime conscription. In May Mussolini and Hitler completed their military alliance in the "Pact of Steel." Military preparations were hurried forward on both sides of the Channel, though well within the limits of routine and with predictable insufficiency of coordination. The Anglo-French negotiations in Moscow for military cooperation with Soviet Russia were a cut below routine, carried on by junior officers sent leisurely by sea in August. The main political negotiations had broken down over Soviet insistence on mutual guarantees for the Baltic states, Poland and Rumania. All these opposed Russian intervention. After having sacrificed Czechoslovakia to Hitler, Britain's scruples over the rights of small states exasperated Russia, already suspicious over Munich. The British, they held, were asking them to wait until Nazi troops had overrun all the buffer areas between the Baltic and the Black Sea before undertaking Russia's defense. The French were more eager than the British to revive the Triple Entente; they vainly sought to force Poland's acceptance of Russian aid or, failing in that, to ignore her. Some feared that Stalin must come to an accord with Germany rather than see all Poland and the Baltic states devoured up to his frontier. London dismissed the possibility; mixed with repugnance for Communist Russia, with the old disdain for Russian arms (no longer shared by the French), was confidence that Stalin had nowhere else to turn. Not only conservatives believed in Hitler's pose as Europe's savior from Communism. French Republicans, who had closer knowledge of rabid anti-Communists, were not so sure. On August 23rd, it was announced that Nazi Germany and Communist Russia had signed a non-aggression pact. Stalin had bought space and time, Hitler immunity from a two-front war against major powers. War now appeared inevitable. Last-minute pressures on Poland, appeals to Hitler, proposals for direct German-Polish talks, availed France and Britain nothing. On the morning of September 1st, German armies marched into Poland and the Luftwaffe bombed Warsaw. The next day London and Paris sent an ultimatum to Hitler to withdraw, and upon receiving no answer, declared war on September 3rd.

# ~ XI ~

# DEFEAT AND
# REVIVAL OF
# THE REPUBLIC

Once again, as twenty-five years before, French reservists inundated the great Paris railway stations. A common remark of soldiers and their families, observers said, was *"Il faut en finir."* After years of crisis, a partial mobilization before Munich, then another year of Nazi threats and invasions, there had to be an end of it, one way or another. The mobilization went as smoothly as democracies can expect, at least as well as in 1914. But the mood was more grim. In 1914, the previous war had been half a century past and though a defeat it had seen no such slaughter as the World War would be. Many of the young men of 1939 were sons of the victors of 1918 (many of the older were the victors themselves) whose victory had been lost, whose promised rewards had been forgotten. Whatever young Germans thought in 1939, few Frenchmen could pretend that war was anything but senseless waste. The uniforms —rough, ill-fitting khaki instead of the bright colors and smart horizon-blue of 1914–1918—suggested the dreariness that lay ahead for soldiers underpaid, undertrained, indifferently fed and housed by too-practical leaders separated from their men, and from the confusions of the field, by a sedentary, overorganized, paper-clogged system of command. It was probably no more bureaucratized than the American forces were to be, but behind it pushed no such flow of men, modern arms, and supplies as the United States would employ to beat down enemies smaller than herself. The French air force and anti-aircraft defenses were notoriously weak. Despite the busy optimism of official spokesmen, soldiers and civilians looked to the sky for the waves of German planes they feared could not be stopped. But Hitler's air power was occupied in Poland, the German divisions facing France and Belgium sat passively behind their fortifications, and the Second World War opened with seven months of inactivity.

## THE FALSE WAR

The "phony war" presented France with unforeseen opportunities and problems. The former were largely neglected, the latter unsolved when the Battle of France began in May of 1940. A forced production and purchase schedule might have narrowed the gap in modern armaments between France and Germany, even in aircraft. But Daladier and Reynaud, his Finance Minister, chose to spread foreign purchasing over three years and to prefer raw materials to finished tools, weapons, or supplies, in order to limit the financial drain while favoring domestic producers. The network of industrial regulations, committees, boards, regional organizations for war material, manufacture, and procurement was far more refined—that is, more complex and often less effective—than in the First World War. Once more, production was at first crippled by the mobilization of skilled workers; nearly a million out of 6 million were soon reassigned to factories and farms; women were again drawn into industry, colonial labor again recruited. The work day rose to 11 or 12 hours, the week to 60 or 72. But neither employers nor labor developed a Jacobin spirit of production. Part of the reason, as in Reynaud's leisurely purchasing plans, lay in the general expectation of a long war, encouraged by Hitler's failure to attack. If few Frenchmen expected a quick victory, few expected a quick defeat. The lesson of 1914–1918 had been learned; Germany would be worn down, by blockade and the Allies' superiority in resources, shipping, and manufacture. For the sustained effort required, crash programs could be unsettling. The armies were well equipped for defensive war, most authorities said, and the official press multiplied their boasts. The major worry was aircraft, though its importance was not quite grasped. French industry would, as in 1914–1918, help replace transport, arms, and munitions expended, help equip the British masses and keep the home front as well supplied as possible for the siege ahead.

It would, of course, be a siege. The doctrine of defensive war was unchallenged. But here too opportunities were lost. Little was done to extend the Maginot Line. Beyond its northern end, the Meuse and the Ardennes Forest offered natural barriers which Pétain himself had said would stop or fatally retard an invading army. Along the Belgian border lay much of French industry; to fortify it would invite destruction, so the battle would be joined behind it or preferably in front, on Belgian soil. The decision was taken to move into Belgium as soon as Hitler's attack was launched, to establish an unbroken defensive line sheltered by Belgium's own considerable fortifications. But no detailed planning was possible; Leopold's government clung to neutrality and refused even to exchange information on armies, roads, transport, communications, or defensive obstacles, and Belgian soldiers manned the French frontier as well as the German. Defense, then, would have to be planned at the last moment while armies were marching. And only scattered fortifications and tank traps were set up in northern France from Sedan to the Channel.

The offensive opportunities opened by Hitler's Polish campaign were also ignored, despite expectations in early September that the Poles would hold out for some time. The implications of the Rhineland surrender were now dismally fulfilled. Apart from a raid into the Saarland, the French did nothing. To conserve strength and in fear of retaliation, neither French nor British air attacks were launched on the industries or transport of western Germany. Poland collapsed unaided in less than a month, the Soviet armies moved to a prearranged Russian-German line after the middle of September. As at Munich, French and British passivity could be and was fulsomely explained, but the utter abandonment of a second ally did nothing to convince the world, Hitler, or the Allies themselves that they could summon a fighting spirit. The only action undertaken by the British and French turned to failure. The defeat and abandonment of a combined operation against the Nazi occupiers of Norway in April of 1940 was disheartening, the more so as Hitler had succeeded in convincing some that his invasions of Denmark and Norway were forced upon him by British mining of Norwegian waters.

Undertaken too late with too little imagination, too few men, machines, and aircraft, the Norwegian sideshow boded ill for the battle to come.

Many argue that the French fighting spirit would have been stronger had Hitler opened his offensive in the autumn of 1939, when the worst was expected and Frenchmen were apparently determined to make war. Difficult as it is to recapture a national mood, it is likely that the "phony" war drained morale both at and behind the front, and it is certain that prolonged inactivity aggravated the already serious divisions in French society. Hitler's forbearance even from air attack allowed wishful thinking on all sides and helped the defeatist and pro-Nazi argument that France should withdraw from the war, now that Poland had disappeared. The variegated "Munich party" became the "peace party". Socialist pacifists behind Paul Faure; neo-Socialists behind Marcel Déat, who had urged Frenchmen to refuse to "die for Danzig"; defeatists like Flandin, Laval, and Bonnet; assorted pacifists and pro-Germans; full-blooded fascists behind Marcel Bucard and the ex-Communist Jacques Doriot; nearly the whole Rightist press, were now joined by those Communist leaders who chose to follow the Moscow line denouncing the "capitalist-imperialist war against progress."

Frenchmen learned again, as they had learned often before (and as even Americans were to learn), that in troubled times patriotism meant love of one's own version of country more than love of countrymen, indeed that the two were likely to be in inverse proportion, and that the twentieth-century's international civil war between Left and Right was more damaging to national unity than the French Revolution itself had been. The peace campaign sowed confusion and more wishful thinking, all the more damaging in the light of Daladier's failure to form even a limited *union sacrée* and the unmitigated hostility of his government toward the workers and the Left. The Hitler-Stalin agreement served the French social conservatives admirably. After tolerating the anti-Republican tirades of the Rightist press and factions for half a decade —and while continuing to do so—the government closed the Communist press, expelled the Deputies from the Chamber, dissolved the party, and imprisoned Communist union officials, even though several repudiated the Nazi-Soviet pact. Thorez fled to Moscow, from the army to which he, together with other Communist leaders, had reported on mobilization. To those workers already lukewarm toward the war, the Communists became martyrs and the closing of *l'Humanité* relieved it of the need to explain why the proletarian party of Joan of Arc should now ally itself with the assassin of the workers. In several important war industries the Communists who followed party doctrine carried on a campaign of slowdown and obstruction.

Instead of offering the workers a patriotic alternative, the employers and the Daladier government used anti-Communism as a cover for destroying what remained of the Popular Front's labor reforms. The CGT and member unions expelled their Communists in vain; the confederation was now hopelessly split and fell to less than 800,000 members by early 1940. Government and management refused the offers of voluntary collaboration made by union moderates. Collective bargaining and compulsory arbitration were suspended, strikers were tried by military courts and imprisoned. Overtime pay was not higher but lower than regular pay—to prevent inflation, the government said, though wages were frozen and prices were not. Rationing and price controls did not appear until May, 1940. Protesting workers were often discharged, then immediately drafted for service in the front lines. This, like frozen wages and low overtime, was justified on the ground that soldiers recalled to industry labored at soldiers' pay, twenty centimes a day. That these practices, contrasted to the routinism of the rest of society, undermined morale in both factory and front line is hardly surprising. Naturally such Draconian measures were not applied to farmers, merchants, and manufacturers. So at France's most perilous hour the working class was once more shut out of national life, one of the main reasons it so quickly forgave the Communist party its anti-patriotism. Alongside the disloyalty of Rightists and the softness of the government's own war policy, the slavishness of the Communist leaders to Moscow appeared less disgraceful than it was in fact. Only at the end of May, when the Germans were everywhere victorious, did the employers' federation accept cooperation with the CGT and CFTC, having belatedly discovered that, in the words of their joint statement, there was "no room for selfish interests and class action." Two weeks later, Paris fell.

To worsen matters, the government suppressed civil liberties, muzzled its Jacobin critics, and interned, in brutal conditions, all suspected aliens, many of whom were anti-fascist refugees from Spain, Italy, and Germany. In place of truth or appeals to national effort, Daladier's government contented itself with puerile optimism, in the best twentieth-century fashion of government-by-press-agentry. Meanwhile the Rightist press was allowed to indulge in defeatism and to blame the Popular

Front, the liberals, and the Republic itself for stirring up a war they had made France "unfit" to fight. Having harried the patriotic as well as the pacifist and Communist Left out of public affairs, Daladier felt it politically dangerous to discriminate between the patriotic Right and those who doubted, opposed, or undermined the war effort, for among all but the last were industrialists, financiers, diplomats, civil servants, and military men on whose support his cabinet rested. Daladier was hated by the Left for destroying the Popular Front and by the Right for having helped create it in 1935. But so incoherent was political opinion and so scarce were politicians with executive ability that he remained. Daladier was at least well known and still kept some aura of the strong, simple man bravely attending to duty. He lasted until March, 1940, when he was overthrown, in part for having refused to send a military expedition to rescue Finland from Soviet attack. The Russo-Finnish War stirred much sympathy in France; on the Right, war on Russia found more support than war on Hitler. The peace party hoped to replace Daladier with one of their own, but to their chagrin the combative and pro-English Paul Reynaud became Premier, pledged to invigorate the war effort.

Under him, the ill-fated Norwegian expedition took shape. Its failure brought to a climax another plague of the alliance: Anglophobia, especially in the Right and Center parties, the popular press. As old as Versailles and nourished on every issue from reparations to Munich, French distrust of England fed on new quarrels that inevitably sprang up between two badly prepared allies. The British contribution was admittedly feeble; by May, 1940, only 10 divisions made up the BEF, against twice that number after a comparable period in World War I, and against 94 French divisions in 1940. British armor, transport, and artillery were also deficient, and London's reluctance to commit her air force to the offensive during the Polish campaign worried many Frenchmen. Despite unprecedented economic and financial cooperation and the British agreement to place their forces under the single command of the French General Gamelin, liaison between the two armies was unsatisfactory from beginning to end. The French public was told by the war's opponents to expect the worst: the British would fight to the last Frenchman, holding back their men, aircraft, and fleet to defend the island or come to an agreement with Hitler. The peace party regretted Reynaud's pledge of March 28th that the French would never make a separate treaty. Although the advent of Churchill in May, after the defeat in Norway, encouraged many Frenchmen, he like Reynaud was branded a warmonger by the defeatists.

The Reynaud cabinet was shaky from the start and he made only minor efforts, like the calling of two little-known Socialists, toward a *union sacrée*. Whether greater effort would have succeeded any better than Daladier's in a Chamber from which the Communists had been expelled, in which each party sheltered pacifists or defeatists, and some of the Right was pro-German, is questionable. And when, as the Germans advanced, he tried to appeal to all sectors of opinion he succeeded only too well in adding men to his cabinet who were to hurry the end of the war and of the Republic as well. When the Chamber, like the country, lacked the united spirit of 1914, it was dangerous to pretend that unity was possible. A better alternative would have been a cabinet of die-hards; but Reynaud judged, probably correctly, that his own popularity in the Chamber was too meager to support a government of such men, most of whom had been, by the nature of things in the 1930's, mavericks and Cassandras like himself. His policies, like his cabinet, were compromises. To keep Radical support he had to retain his jealous rival Daladier as Defense Minister; the latter sulked, refused even to accompany Reynaud to a London meeting (as he had refused to join him at the cabinet's first appearance in the Chamber), and protected Gamelin against Reynaud's halfhearted attempt to replace him with a more aggressive commander. Georges Mandel was the best-known Jacobin in the cabinet, like his master Clemenceau a Jacobin of the Right. But he held a minor post (Colonies) and was handicapped as a rough-spoken independent and a Jew.

In effect Reynaud chose to do what he could with a team of mediocre men, loosely disciplined if at all. It is a measure of the Third Republic's inability, and unwillingness, to produce strong leadership that Paul Reynaud was largely justified in considering himself indispensable in 1940. Many patriotic men sat in the Chamber or Senate but they were either not national figures or disqualified by temperament, experience, or political circumstances. Herriot, President of the Chamber, was already more an ornament than a leader; Blum lacked force and was in any case anathema to conservatives; Chautemps and Queuille, members of the cabinet, were politicians of a lesser order; Bonnet, Laval, and Flandin already accepted defeat; Daladier was tired and depressed. Reynaud had been prophetic in financial matters, had been energetic and ready to serve in Blum's abortive national government in 1938, had helped restore the economy under Daladier, had pressed for modernization of the army. But each initiative had made enduring enemies, and far less than Churchill did he retain their grudging admiration. He had little of Churchill's physical and moral strength, staying power, and oratorical skill, none of his experience of war command and administration. Bright but nervous and unsteady, Reynaud had few partisans to sustain him and an egregiously untidy personal life which, despite the myth, is no help to a French politician. In the last weeks he was distracted by a mistress who was hysterically defeatist.

## THE LIGHTNING WAR

France found no Clemenceau for the Second World War, yet Clemenceau himself had been put off until the dark hours of 1917, and the darker hours of 1940 were too brief to turn the tide even had a Clemenceau appeared. The Nazi blitzkrieg struck Holland, Belgium, and Luxembourg on May 10th. The French and British, expecting a second Schlieffen plan, left their indifferently prepared positions in northern France and advanced into Belgium to defend the line of the river Dyle. Later denounced as foolhardy, the advance was thought politically necessary to defend the Belgians and the Dutch, militarily necessary to prevent the ports facing England from falling into German hands. The German forces let the northern advance proceed unharried by air attack until the bulk of French and British armor and motorized cavalry was committed, then struck to their south at the weakest point, through the sector where the Maginot Line stopped short, behind the Ardennes Forest and hills which had been thought impassable. Here, well behind the Meuse, stood the French General Corap's 9th Army, nine low-quality divisions spread over a front of 65 miles, ill-equipped and with only rudimentary defensive works. On the 10th of May, seven Panzer divisions began rolling through the Ardennes, their tanks supported by dive bombers instead of the artillery whose slower movement the French had counted on. Sedan, where the Second Empire died, was taken on the 13th and the Germans held the entire right bank of the Meuse northward to Namur in Belgium—and much of Corap's army had not even reached its left bank. The enemy crossed immediately, held up in only a few places by artillery and pillboxes which, once taken, left only French reserve troops in the open, short of tanks and transport, without air cover. On the next day the Germans began their march to the sea.

In the north, Holland sued for an armistice on the 15th, after the Luftwaffe and artillery had incinerated Rotterdam as a "lesson" to those who thought they could hold Dutch cities. The same day, the Meuse breakthrough compelled Gamelin to order a retreat in Belgium, where the French mechanized divisions had shown themselves equal to the German in a two-day battle. The withdrawal was not quick enough to allow regrouping on a stable line or to transfer battle-ready units to the crumbling southern flank. Liaison with the British was careless, French communications failed the test of rapid movement under air harassment, the transport of men, munitions, and fuel was already breaking down on refugee-clogged roads. Units and command posts were separated as plans were discarded and new ones improvised. The familiar confusions of any battlefield were turned to chaos by the unprecedented speed of events and German control of the air. The enemy, as innumerable witnesses later testified, seemed always to be where he was not expected. The situation behind the Meuse was even worse. Giraud had replaced Corap, Brigadier General de Gaulle had delayed a German division on the Aisne, but the 9th Army was beyond repair. Gamelin had inexplicably left divisions concentrated as far south as Lyon, and behind the Maginot Line, as if its purpose were not precisely to liberate forces for maneuver. Now they marched up too slowly, trailing supplies behind them, under incessant air attack, and arrived in driblets only to be engulfed or bypassed. On the 17th the Germans crossed the river Sambre, the next day they reached Amiens, on the 20th they took Abbéville at the mouth of the Somme, and the best French armies, together with the BEF, were trapped with the Belgians in the north.

In Paris, a distraught Reynaud dismissed Gamelin and called Foch's lieutenant, Maxime Weygand, from Syria to take command. The armies left in the center and south were strung along the Aisne and the Somme, a weak line the Germans could have shattered had they not turned northward to close the trap. On neither side of the German corridor were there forces ready to cut through, though some feeble efforts were made from both sides, never at the same time for lack of Franco-British agreement and the delays attendant on Weygand's take-over. On the 28th of May, Leopold capitulated and the Belgian army ceased fire. There followed the epic of Dunkerque, where 200,000 British and 120,000 French were taken off the beaches, leaving most of their equipment behind. On June 5th, the German armies turned southward and five days later Mussolini thought it safe to join the attack on what remained of France. On the 10th, the government abandoned Paris, declaring it an open city. Its defense would have slowed the Germans considerably, but the leaders refused to contemplate its destruction; besides, there was the lesson of 1871: the German armies had prevailed despite Parisian resistance and, worse, there had followed the Commune. As they took the road to Tours, the exhausted Ministers were further demoralized by the crowds of refugees pushing southward in tumultuous confusion, terrified of air attack. Weygand was already pressing for an armistice. This time there was no Gambetta to defy the inevitable.

Reynaud had struck out in every direction to strengthen his position, and failed. On May 18th, he called Marshal Pétain as Vice-Premier; the choice no doubt heartened public opinion, for Pétain, who had always been careful of his soldiers' lives, was not only respected but genuinely popular, as few generals were. Unfortunately, he believed the war already lost and expected to act as peacemaker with Hitler. At the other extreme, Reynaud promoted Mandel to the Ministry of Interior. In early June he made de Gaulle Undersecretary for War but chose the pessimistic Paul Baudouin as Undersecretary for Foreign Affairs in place of Alexis Léger. As the cabinet moved from Paris to Tours and then on the 16th to Bordeaux, an angry debate between those in favor of carrying on the war and those who demanded an armistice turned in favor of the latter. By then, the Nazis were in Paris, the Maginot Line surrounded, and the French army falling away in disorder. The French air force was disorganized and Churchill had sensibly refused to throw precious British fighters into the deteriorating Battle of France. Reynaud's (and de Gaulle's) idea for a redoubt in Brittany was not taken seriously. The choice lay between moving the government to North Africa to carry on the war from the empire or concluding peace at once. Although there was probably a cabinet majority for the former, Reynaud's strength and nerve were exhausted and he allowed Weygand, supported by Pétain, to lead the way to armistice. After futile appeals to Roosevelt and the cabinet's rejection of Churchill's last-minute suggesgestion of a Franco-British union, Reynaud resigned and advised President Lebrun to appoint Pétain. On the 18th of June, resistance ended (except in the Maginot Line) after the Marshal's vaguely worded radio appeal to "stop fighting." In the early evening of the 22nd, General

Huntziger signed the armistice at Rethondes, aboard the famous railway carriage in which Foch had met the beaten Germans in 1918. Now France was beaten and in bondage, after the most stunning military reversal in her history.

When all is said about divisions and weaknesses in the French public and government, it remains that the defeat of 1940 was a military defeat, resulting primarily from a doubtful military doctrine made worse by faulty execution in the field, unrescued by the improvisations that Joffre and Gallieni had found time for at the Marne. No doubt there were instances of treachery, and some units were badly disciplined (wrongly or too little, it amounted to the same), weakened by desertion, defeatism, or passivity among officers and men. But too many units fought well, held (most doggedly, perhaps, at the Dunkerque perimeter) and even pushed back the invader in scattered areas to justify the popular condemnation of French soldiers that followed the defeat. Before May of 1940, Frenchmen, Englishmen, and Americans considered the French army the greatest on earth; afterward they hurried to disparage it. Neither view was realistic, though each made admirable headlines. An army is rarely greater than its equipment, commanders, and doctrine, but neither does it lose 100,000 dead in six weeks by running away.

Much is made of the defensive theory, the so-called "Maginot Line mentality" gripping French officers between the wars, taught and raised to dogma by the most illustrious veterans of the First World War, Marshal Henri-Philippe Pétain at their head. But defensive war has a respectable history and rarely has it appeared more suitable than to France between the wars. It had worn down the German Empire in 1914–1918; the victors were not likely to abandon it for an offensive doctrine which had failed hideously in 1914 or which proposed invasion of an enemy twice the size of France by 1939. In a nation still mourning 1.4 million dead, not many would discard a doctrine promising to be "sparing of French blood," as Daladier and many others put it, in favor of Colonel de Gaulle's one-sided theory of attack, which (like Hitler's) took little heed of what would happen if the attackers bogged down, outnumbered in a hostile land. The tragedy was not that the politicians and military chiefs dismissed de Gaulle's strategy but that they ignored his and others' warnings on the new tempo of war, the problems that aircraft, tank columns, and motorized armies would present to defensive tactics. French plans called for holding unbroken lines of fire; as in the First World War, mobile reserves would move up to support a sector under pressure or to reseal holes that might be opened. This assumed that rear-area communications would be clear, transport swift and adequate to insure at least equal fire power at crucial points, and that, should a major breakthrough occur, there would be time to fall back upon a succession of prepared defensive lines. None of these conditions were to be fulfilled in 1940.

It was inevitable that recriminations would arise well before the final surrender, and continue to this day. Indeed, the argument between politicians and soldiers over which were to blame was part of the argument over armistice or resistance from abroad. Weygand and Pétain refused a simple military capitulation partly because they denied its implication that the army had failed the Republic. It was their contention, and to be that of Vichy, that the Republic's political leaders had failed the army by denying it modern equipment, then provoking a war it could not win—all this apart from the broader accusations by many soldiers and anti-Republicans that the politicians, especially those of the Popular Front, had debilitated the French economy and ruined the spirit of the people. The politicians differed in their answers to such charges, but most agreed that they had provided all the military equipment asked by the generals, and that it was the generals' misuse of men and equipment that brought defeat. In retrospect the debate may appear unreal; a nation of 40 million without its great Russian ally of 1914 should have expected to be overwhelmed by one of 80 million, wholly geared to war, able to concentrate most of its superior weight on a single front. But questions persist; the armies actually engaged were not so unequal in number and the collapse was too sudden to be so simply explained. It was, as the great historian Marc Bloch called it, a strange defeat.

The facts now known about French equipment go far to exonerate the Third Republic's civilian heads and the economy, except in the case of aircraft. Including the British, each side had approximately the same number of tanks (about 4000) in 1940. The difference lay in design, and in manner of employment, which in turn largely determined design. According to the defensive doctrine of continuous fire, most French tanks were parceled out to support infantry units along the front, and designed accordingly; too heavy and slow, or too light with moderate fuel capacity and short-range communications. Only in a few divisions were they concentrated into mobile, offensive forces capable of independent operation, though more were coming, thanks to observations of the Polish campaign. When so organized, they did well, as long as fuel held up and the skies were relatively neutral. But the crucial Meuse sector had few tanks and elsewhere the French air force often failed to coordinate with ground units or, more often, was outnumbered, not only overall but at points of combat the Germans chose. The ratio in fighters was perhaps 1000 German to 700 French and, at first, enough British to make it nearly even. But the Germans also had 400 Stuka dive bombers working closely with the ground attack. In other bombers the Luftwaffe was far superior, though these had less direct effect. The fighters contested the battlefields and the French lost by being slower, too often used in driblets, dispersed over too wide a front (some remained in Africa), and caught on the ground or in repair shops. As a reconnaissance pilot, Antoine de Saint-Exupéry found that his controls froze at high altitudes and that his comrades in the fighter squadrons often were resigned to defeat by better German machines. In addition, French anti-aircraft artillery was hopelessly meager. Even so, the losses inflicted on the Luftwaffe by fighters and ground fire in the Battle of France decisively weakened it, especially in pilots, for the Battle of Britain. By June, the first shocks of German air tactics had been absorbed, French and British air power was growing at a faster rate. But there was no time.

The evidence supports the politicians. Defeat stemmed mainly from command failures: failure to see the new role of tanks and planes, whether in offense or defense; belated and confused use of what it had of each; failure to concentrate men and fire power at the unfortified points; failure to prepare lines of retreat or to retreat quickly enough, which was partly due to shortages of transport and signal equipment, in turn traceable to underestimating the new velocity of war. The last compounded confusion, in which men and officers trained to a slower pace lost confidence in their orders and superiors, nowhere more disastrously than at the Meuse, where the military planners suffered a complete surprise. Confusion turned to decomposition of whole armies, whose chiefs, said Saint-Exupéry, had control only over their messengers —when they had not run off to find a post that no longer existed. But it is too easy to condemn the military alone. Nearly all political leaders, when they thought of military problems at all, had agreed with the interwar commanders. And the few who disagreed presented no coherent alternatives, rashly allowed themselves to appear as advocates of offensive war and a professional army. Once the First World War was under way, civilian leaders in Paris and London had applied themselves to army problems to good effect, especially in pressing the use of new weapons of that day. Their abdication of this duty between the wars—the Americans and British did little better—made disaster all the more likely. The politicians were guilty not so much of failing to provide what the army asked (again, excepting aircraft) as of sharing and encouraging its complacency. Behind all this was the natural inability of free, peaceful nations to prepare for war as devotedly as others can, whose thought and emotions are committed. France gave far more of her peacetime budget to defense than Britain or America did, but spending and even overspending for military tools was not a substitute for militarism. To deplore the Republic's military failings is, in part, to deplore its virtues.

# END OF A REPUBLIC

The defeated Republic was soon afterward to die by its own hand. Reynaud was unequal to defying the minority in his cabinet who chose armistice rather than resistance from the colonies, even though he also had the sympathy of President Lebrun, of Herriot and Jeanneny, the presidents of the Chamber and the Senate. Hitler would hardly allow a government remaining on French soil to be free. But the alternative, to leave metropolitan France without a government of her own, involved hideous risk: the entire civilian population at the mercy of military occupation or Nazi Gauleiters, the 1.5 million prisoners of war abandoned in Germany, France plundered and laboring for German profit. Weygand and others warned of anarchy or the outbreak of a new Paris Commune should the army be destroyed, or sent to the colonies. The terrifying example of Poland was a weighty argument for preserving a French government and seeking by whatever means to lessen the weight of Nazi occupation. In June of 1940 not only Anglophobes believed that England would soon be beaten, or forced to make peace, and that Germany's hold on Europe would be unchallenged. The war over, occupation and direct rule would be withdrawn and France would be left a satellite's autonomy. Such was the least dismal of all the dismal prospects Frenchmen saw before them. Few men even in Reynaud's entourage had been unmoved by the eighty-four-year-old Marshal's simple declaration that he would never leave the soil of France, would stay and share the people's suffering, while serving as their shield.

However simple postwar partisans were to make it appear, rarely in French history was it more difficult to see in which course honor lay.

For a moment it appeared that Pétain's government would take both courses. While the terms of armistice were being explored (June 18–21), most of the fleet and air force fled to North Africa, and munitions were gathered at Bordeaux for the crossing. Marshal Pétain reluctantly agreed to divide the government, with Chautemps as Vice-Premier in Algiers, with a majority of the cabinet and all the Deputies and Senators who wished to go. At this point (June 21) the enemies of the Republic took a hand. Pierre Laval, joined by Mayor Marquet of Bordeaux and others, bullied Lebrun into delaying his departure, which would have put the Chief of State out of their reach. Meanwhile, some of the most determined resisters had sailed for Africa on the *Massilia*, Mandel, Daladier, Jean Zay, and Pierre Mendès-France among them. Late the same day, the armistice terms arrived and were considered so moderate in light of France's helplessness that Pétain was able to discourage any further departures. Laval entered the cabinet as Vice-Premier, Marquet as Minister of the Interior on the 23rd; both immediately denounced the *Massilia* passengers as traitors and ordered their internment on arrival in Casablanca. The character of the new regime was taking shape.

Pushed out of Bordeaux by the Germans, who were to occupy the Atlantic coast to the Spanish border, the government trailed to Vichy on the 1st of July. There the final scenes of the Third Republic were played. Pétain had been hostile to it for years; now he held it responsible for France's humiliation and determined to replace it with an authoritarian regime which would, in the words of his broadcast announcing the armistice on June 25th, bring about "an intellectual and moral regeneration" of France. Always patient, he at first opposed Laval's plan to call parliament and have it vote him power to promulgate a new constitution. But Laval's hour had come, and of the 600 Deputies and Senators who gathered at Vichy by the 10th of July, not one was equal to the task of leading a Republican resistance. The *Massilia* had taken away some of the most combative; Blum, Herriot, and Reynaud were silent or ineffectual; Flandin surrendered to Laval, as did Lebrun. For six days Laval charmed, cajoled, harangued, and threatened the representatives, alone, in small groups, and in full assembly. His ultimate argument was that their refusal to rally behind Pétain and a "French" solution would force Hitler to impose a Nazi constitution. Between denunciations of the Republic and the English, he pleaded devotion to

France, helpless now but capable of taking her place in the New Order. Doriot's followers paraded the streets, a growing number of "realist" Deputies worked the lobbies and hotel corridors. On the 10th, the two houses met together and, by a vote of 569 to 80, gave Pétain power "to promulgate by one or more acts the new Constitution of the French State." Most of the nays came from Socialists and Radicals, but even these parties gave a majority of their votes to Laval's proposal. No doubt the results reflected apathy and fear, guilt, confusion, and fatigue; but there was also somber hope of salvaging something of France from the debacle and a widespread trust in Pétain's honor and his ability, as the only hero left, to repeat in diplomacy the miracle of Verdun. In the national disarray of 1940, his national prestige was unquestionable.

If the Third Republic went largely unmourned in France, its defeat and disappearance caused a hideous shock in Britain and America, teaching an entire generation the meaning of mortality. Only then did the English-speaking world awaken to the threat and go to work. After shock came recrimination; Britons and Americans complacently repeated Pétain's own moral condemnation of the French and their Republic, its inability to "adjust" to the twentieth century, its anachronistic military, political, and economic ways—as though their own follies and anachronisms had been somehow of a different order. The passage of time has helpfully complicated such matters. Since the triumph of 1945, which brought the victors new foreign and domestic problems—many akin to those of France after Versailles—or left old ones unsolved, complacency has faded and the verdict on the Third Republic has been less easily rendered. Anachronism remains the central charge, but it is now recognized as a problem in all societies and the twentieth century's greatest challenge to the viability of democracy everywhere.

In this sense, French political life and public opinion in the 1930's were not nearly so chaotic as they seemed. Concerning the four great problems the Third Republic had to face, there were majority views that were readily expressed in the parliament. On economic questions, the majority was conservative, fearful of government control and spending, high taxation and inflation. In European affairs, the general attitudes of the new diplomacy prevailed: international reconciliation, the right of self-determination, a measure of disarmament, open diplomacy, and moral suasion—all coupled with increasing dependence on Great Britain. In military matters, the defensive stance. In political affairs, a refusal to risk the enlargement of executive power. All were most consistently championed by the Radical-Socialists, whose leaders repeatedly frustrated contrary initiatives. All seemed justified by experience. Strong executives had made, or seemed about to make, dictatorships. The military experts were trusted since they had, after all, won history's greatest war against heavy odds. A tough nationalist foreign policy had drawn world censure and British opposition; the Ruhr adventure (blamed on the Right) should not be repeated. Government spending, mainly on war and social experiments, had inflated the currency (blamed on the Left), which also should not be allowed to happen again. These were "lessons of history" and in the absence of forceful leaders willing to risk political eclipse by teaching otherwise, they were applied in the 1930's to problems they could not answer: world depression, Nazi expansionism, and lightning war. The trouble with such lessons, as Marc Bloch said in *Strange Defeat,* was that they neglected the essence of history, which was change.

Abetting all the political sins commonly attributed to the Third Republic—a parliament alternating between tyranny and evasion of responsibility, weak and divided parties, a tired and mediocre political class, vulnerable to personal and local pressures—was a national set of mind nourished on simplified, or false, memories of notable events in the past, from Louis Napoleon's seizure of power to the loss of family savings in the 1920's. Despite all the raucous controversy and endless points of view associated with French life, perhaps in part because of them, the terms of public debate on central issues were out of date. The press did little to coin new terms, French education was not directed to contemporary questions, French scholars and teachers (another complaint of Bloch's) rarely ventured into them on their own. The very moderation of the French depression, though it helped to spare France a large fascist movement, encouraged too many to assume that nothing need be changed. Under a turbulent surface, largely responsible for that turbulence, though fundamentally untouched by it, was what the political historian Stanley Hoffmann has called a stalemate society. Its external signs were a low birth rate; antiquated housing; rudimentary health, social, and civic services; and an economy which was regional or even local in its workings; backward, fragmented agriculture and commerce; a stagnant, protected industrial plant; a business community spurning risk in favor of fixed returns from an acquired sector of a market it assumed to be fixed in size.

That this society preserved family security, personal independence, and undeniable charms for so many Frenchmen made it politically invulnerable in normal times. Its political philosophy was Alain's, a jealous watchfulness of government but a readiness to evade local or private action in civic affairs by appeals to Paris for political or bureaucratic decision. Its political partisans at Paris ranged from conservative Socialists through its main defenders, the Radicals, to groups on the Center and moderate Right. Its Republican government was neither socialist nor laissez-faire, neither a planning nor a neutral, remote authority, but inconsistently interventionist, alternately obtuse and solicitous toward its main clientele, the farmers, the upper and middle bourgeoisie. And left outside (except when it came to paying taxes) were the industrial workers, agricultural laborers, the lowest commercial employees, and, not least important, the military, in all ranks but the very top. The stalemate was first shaken by the depression, first attacked, in a gradual way, by the Popular Front. It was attacked in a different way, and for very different ends, for a second time by the so-called National Revolution of the Vichy regime, after defeat had thrown it into turmoil and swept away its political defenses. Both attacks left impressions and beginnings of something new, but both failed and largely for the same reasons: a shortage of leaders with ideas and experience equal to their tasks, profound divisions within the ruling group, and the ultimately fatal intervention of forces from outside France.

## THE VICHY REVOLUTION

The defeat of 1940 opened a new era for France, pulling her ruthlessly into the twentieth-century maelstrom of mass politics, of industrial and military superpowers, of social and colonial revolution, of technocracy and science, whether beneficent or perverse. The Vichy years, 1940–1944, were among the most dolorous in any nation's history, at once shameful and heroic, darkened by intellectual confusion, bodily and spiritual torture. In the early weeks, Marshal Pétain's government at Vichy probably enjoyed greater popular acceptance, ranging from enthusiasm to watchful neutrality, than any since Clemenceau's in 1918. Amid defeat and total uncertainty, France's greatest soldier offered himself as a buffer against the invader and a promise that order would be restored under French, not German, authority. In essence, Vichy's chosen aims were three and each in time produced doubt, opposition, or revulsion in large segments of French society: the attempt to create an authoritarian new order; the attempt to limit the effects of German conquest, and—what was far more serious—the attempt to guarantee a favored place for France in Hitler's new Europe, by collaborating in Hitler's designs. However slight the chances that Vichy's National Revolution would have been accepted by Frenchmen once the shock of defeat subsided, they were utterly ruined by Vichy's appeasement of an enemy growing daily more brutal and rapacious.

To paint Vichy entirely black, to deny the presence there of selfless, patriotic, and idealistic Frenchmen is, however, part of the mythology of the Liberation, indulged in by publicists and political leaders who knew better but were quite as willing to exploit public feeling in 1944–1945 as their victims had been in 1940. Like so many "political necessities," it was to cause needless suffering and also to compromise several of the reforms they most desired to make in the postwar Republic. For to blacken Vichy was often to whitewash the Third Republic, and much of Vichy's critique of the Republic was only too well founded, many of its remedies not so wild or dismal as Vichy's enemies felt bound to insist. Several were taken up by the Liberation movements whose idea of the future was to create a new France *pure et dure*. Since some of the men at Vichy aimed at nothing less, it was no accident that both sides invoked the spirit of Charles Péguy or, later, when the Fourth Republic disappointed their hopes, that some of the more generous spirits in the Gaullist opposition came from Vichy as well as from the Resistance.

The generous spirits who rallied to Vichy in response to Pétain's appeal for national regeneration soon discovered, however, that the German conquest which made it possible to dream of revolution also made revolution impossible to achieve, first by occupying France, second by creating what can only be called a counterrevolutionary situation, granting the levers of power to Frenchmen of the old Right who were divided among themselves and, for the most part, dreaming of a France more anachronistic than the one they had inherited by default. For a while, the armistice terms gave some hope that France would retain a certain freedom of action. There was to be a French government and an unoccupied zone embracing about two-fifths of the country south of a line running from the Swiss border near Geneva through Bourges nearly to Tours, and east of a line running from there southward by Angoulême to the Spanish frontier. Moreover, the Germans promised to evacuate most of the Atlantic coast once England was beaten, and to allow the government to return to Paris, thence to administer all of France. The French were allowed a lightly armed 100,000-man army to maintain order in the unoccupied zone. The fleet also remained intact, to be disarmed under German and Italian control, not to be used for war on Great Britain. The armistice implied full French sovereignty over the empire and stipulated that French ground, sea, and air forces would be left for its protection.

Compared with the fate of the Czechs and Poles, all this appeared unexpectedly generous. But the initial price was heavy, and to be made much heavier by subsequent German interpretations of the armistice. Apart from the expected surrender of all modern arms, tanks, and aircraft in France proper, the French were to bear all occupation costs (soon to be set at 400 million francs a day, several times the actual cost and later raised), to leave all prisoners of war, about 1.5 million men, in German hands until conclusion of the peace, to safeguard all property which might be "put at the disposition" of Germany in the peace treaty, to hand over on demand all "Germans" (clearly, Jews and political refugees) anywhere in France or the empire. In addition, the interzonal line was to be a closed border, shutting off passage of travelers and goods except at German pleasure. Since most factories and coal deposits were in the northern, occupied zone and agriculture was divided between the two (wine and oil in the south; wheat, sugar, potatoes in the north), the Germans could threaten economic strangulation. Together with the retention of war prisoners, control of occupation "costs," and all the local pressures open to an occupying power, Hitler could blackmail any French authority at will. The main hope of alleviation was, of course, a quick German victory over Britain and a generous, or careless, German supervision of a French satellite. Frenchmen remembered Prussia's recovery after Jena, Germany's after Versailles. Again, doubtful lessons of history served only to confuse.

The political shape of the Vichy regime was decided almost immediately. Under the power granted him by the National Assembly on July 10th, Marshal Pétain abolished the Presidency of the Republic and made himself "Chief of the French State." The second constitutional act gave Pétain complete executive power and all legislative power except the declaration of war. The third adjourned the Chamber and Senate until the Chief should call them. Others were to follow, one designating Laval, then Admiral Darlan, then Laval again, as Pétain's successor, another requiring an oath of fidelity to the Chief from all civil servants and soldiers. No other constitution was promulgated, so Vichy remained a personal dictatorship exercised by, or in the name of, Marshal Pétain, whose policies were influenced by a succession of Rightist factions, carried out by a bureaucracy inherited from the Third Republic, enforced by a police and court system progressively more authoritarian in methods and leadership.

The first task of the government was to restore order and as normal an economic life as foreign occupation allowed. This it did, with an efficiency and speed that encouraged the population. Before the end of the year all but 300,000 of the nearly 4 million refugees from the north had returned to their homes; despite the shutdown of arms plants and the crippling of business in general, less than a million were unemployed by 1941, thanks to a vigorous program of public works and repair of roads, bridges, canals, harbors, and railways. There were moratoria on debts, loans to business, rationing, price and wage controls, increased unemployment benefits, and special efforts to step up imports from the colonies. Since the interzonal border was all but sealed, the Vichy ministers had uncertain contact with French officialdom in the north and west, which relied mainly on its own initiative, with little interference from the German military commanders, to fill in the broad outlines of policy established at Vichy. In the autumn, the harvest was brought in, schools reopened, and France enjoyed the least abnormal months of her ordeal, with relatively little deprivation. To a people who had found the victory of 1918 meaningless, Hitler was not yet ready to teach the meaning of defeat.

In this atmosphere, the National Revolution was launched, its aim nothing less than the cure of every weakness that the men of Vichy held responsible for defeat. Quite naturally, they agreed neither on French ills nor on their remedies, so that the ideas and policies of the National Revolution were nearly as heterogeneous as the crowd of malcontents, reformers, ideologues, technicians, and politicians who sought control at Vichy. These included every faction which had thought itself frustrated by the Third Republic: monarchists, clericals, civil and military officers, industrialists and technocrats, moral uplifters and opportunists, neo-Socialists, ex-Communists, and fascists. These last, most prominent among whom were Déat and Doriot, who demanded a thoroughgoing fascist state, lost out at once and retired to occupied Paris, where they hoped to win German support for their schemes. Meanwhile, with German encouragement, they launched vulgar denunciations of the Vichy "conservatives," and provided the Germans another piece of blackmail, the oft-repeated threat to replace the Vichy regime with a totalitarian substitute. To dub the Vichyites "conservative" was in some senses an understatement. The dominant school of thought at first was Maurrassian, though old Maurras himself was an infrequent visitor and took no direct part. Vichy has been called "the revenge of the anti-Dreyfusards," but in practice its early mien was closer to that Moral Order presided over by another Marshal, Mac-Mahon, in the 1870's. The militants of Action Française at Vichy, like Pétain's political adviser and Justice Minister, Raphaël Alibert, were outnumbered by mere sympathizers: General Weygand, a Catholic conservative; the banker Paul Baudouin; the gifted civil servant Yves Bouthillier who was Minister of Finance until 1942. Pétain had no more knowledge of politics and little more interest in political philosophy than MacMahon had shown, but he took himself much more seriously as a moralist, a paternal guide for an erring people. Disdainful of what the Republic had become, he gladly accepted the demise of parliament and the substitution of *Famille, Travail, Patrie* for *Liberté, Égalité, Fraternité*. And although he had not been a practicing Catholic and avoided Weygand's idea of adding *Dieu* to the official slogan of the French State, he conceived of it as a Christian corporate society, hierarchical, socially paternal, and politically authoritarian.

To fulfill this promise, the Vichy regime embarked on a great number of programs to transform family life, labor, and industry, to promote "national purity" and French patriotism. They ranged from reforms long overdue and almost universally applauded, to attacks on human rights and social democracy that stirred resistance from the start. Of the three realms, Vichy's family legislation was the most moderate and enduring, its handling of labor and economic issues decidedly mixed, and its nationalistic offensive a nearly total betrayal of all that was most generous in the ideals of 1789, not to mention the greater moments of the monarchy, as under Henry IV.

The Church's influence was strongest in family, youth, and educational matters, most of the French hierarchy being sympathetic to Pétain's aim of reviving traditional morality. For a while, liberal and even Leftist Catholics too were hopeful that ideals of social responsibility and community life would replace the exaggerated individualism of Alain's Republic, the obtuse materialism of the capitalist order. Vichy substantially raised family allowances (which the Third Republic had originated), to encourage larger families and to discourage working mothers. Although under Vichy the gains were more than wiped away by inflation and women were sent back to work as males were drafted for German industry, family allowances were to be retained as the heart of the Fourth Republic's social program. Divorce was made more difficult, adoption easier, abortion severely punished, and a campaign against alcoholism set afoot. Vichy set up a number of youth camps where moral and patriotic instruction (Péguy and Joan of Arc emerged again, in their more conservative stances), manual arts and agricultural skills were to supplant what Vichy regarded as Republican youth's unhealthy concentration on classical studies, Leftist politics, and city amusements. Larger camps for young men were compulsory, filled by conscription as a substitute for military service, and undertook strenuous rural labor projects. In the schools as in the camps, a new spirit of docility was sought; outspoken Republican teachers were purged, the teacher's union dissolved, textbooks were revised to suit the new ideology, free secondary education was dropped; the great École Normale lost its function and teachers' standards were lowered not only to replace those purged, or lost at war, but in accordance with the shift to physical, vocational, and domestic instruction, particularly for girls. For a time, Vichy tried to reintroduce compulsory religious instruction in public schools, but the clergy was wary of stirring up new trouble and Vichy dropped it as opposition rose. State scholarships and subsidies went to Catholic schools and have persisted in one form or other through the Fourth and Fifth Republics. For obvious reasons, Vichy's programs for new housing and schools were impossible to fulfill. As the war and occupation continued, shortages of books, equipment, food, and fuel caused great hardships to French students, who by 1944 were as badly ravaged by tuberculosis as they had been a century before.

The National Revolution in economic affairs followed a vaguely corporatist path; the quarrels at Vichy, the resistance of workers, and the exigencies of occupation prevented any coherent development. Agriculture was favored for ideological as well as practical reasons. France needed food but she would be both politically and physically healthier with a higher proportion of families living on the soil. Within the Agricultural Corporation instituted in December of 1940, various peasant organizations—cooperatives, credit and insurance societies— enjoyed limited autonomy, though anything resembling a union was suppressed, all leaders were chosen from Vichy, and affairs were dominated by the wealthier landowners. Industry was to be reorganized, said Pétain, so as to break the power of trusts and the capitalist obsession with immediate profit at the expense of the nation. The CGPF, the *Comité des Forges*, and other employer associations were dissolved in November of 1940, their places taken by *Comités d'Organisation* in each industry, staffed by experts from government and industry, with broad powers to regulate production, allocate material, and control prices. These new trusts were, in effect, dominated by big business even more obviously than the CGPF had been, though Vichy's intervention was necessary in defending French industry from German demands and government regulations proliferated. The experience of planning and the discovery of many businessmen that the cooperation of a right-thinking government could be even more profitable than its neutrality (it had, of course, been a good deal more than neutral under the Republic) were to prepare a new era of government-business technocracy after the war. All this harked back to Saint-Simon, and forward to the Monnet Plan of the early Fourth Republic. Engineers and administrators with what Americans call "a mentality of production" also enjoyed their freedom from the demands of organized labor. The losers in 1936 were determined to destroy labor's independence.

Together with the CGPF, the CGT and the CFTC were also dissolved in November of 1940. The "class struggle," said Vichy, must end. Shut out of the *Comités d'Organisation*, which decided all important questions, the workers were to be enrolled in single docile unions within each industry (except in the civil service and transport, in which there were none), without the right to strike or choose shop stewards and admitted only to "social committees" made up of workers, employers, and managers (all to be approved by the employer), to discuss social questions of a local nature. Under the Charter of Labor, promulgated only in October of 1941, the social committees were to be organized in a pyramid to the national level, but this was never done and its provision for a minimum wage remained a dead letter. Pétain's Minister of Labor was René Belin, formerly deputy secretary of the CGT, who had fought the Communist merger in 1935. Belin and others, some of them syndicalists like himself or old pacifist rivals of Jouhaux, struggled fruitlessly to make Vichy's labor organizations meaningful, and acceptable to workers. They failed in both; and the great majority of CGT and CFTC leaders repudiated them and denounced all state intervention as promoting enslavement to the employers. Even trade unionists loyal to

Vichy protested and frequently refused to take part in the social committees. Belin resigned in 1942 and Vichy soon afterward gave up its attempt to domesticate French labor, which was as forlorn a hope as that of regimenting French youth and their teachers. Students, intellectuals, teachers, and workers united in the vanguard of the Resistance and were to create together a vision of social democracy that not even the disappointments (and creeping prosperity) of two decades have entirely erased.

The doctrine of Action Française and the revenge of the anti-Dreyfusards appeared most strikingly in attempts to purify *la patrie*. The schools, camps, the censored press and radio of Vichy endlessly preached French nationalism, pride in one's ancestors and traditions, attachment to the soil and customs not only of France but of one's province or *pays*. French patriotism, as nationalists since Barrès had taught, needed to shake off its obsession with the febrile dramas of Paris. Not many even among the true believers of Maurras and Daudet expected a restoration of the monarchy. The Comte de Paris, pretender since the death of his father the Duc de Guise in 1940, was too little known, was already too suspect to pious Monarchists (as Orléanists had usually been) to be taken seriously, even had they believed that Hitler would stand for such a thing. Pétain had not the slightest intention of stepping aside in any case. His fame, his martyr's role, his vanity, all forbade it; a cult of Marshal-worship replete with songs, pictures, vows of fidelity, and special prayers grew up around Vichy to reinforce the image of paternal authority associated with kingship. The Rightist clergy, a dwindling group since Pius XI's attack on Action Française, outdid itself in paeans to the "successor of Saint Louis." Pétain appeared to enjoy the role, but his more sensible supporters feared, rightly, that such extravagance would stir more ridicule than respect. The old man was always more impressive in person; his dignity and simplicity of dress and manner, his occasional eloquence, were better propaganda than silly pieties could fabricate. At any rate, the Pétain cult retained far more the flavor of Charles X or Henry V than of the Führer or the Duce. Fascists in Paris, and politicians like Laval, were as contemptuous of it as the most rabid Republicans were.

National "purification" was something more serious. Maurras' politics of hate had, for forty years, prepared revenge on the enemies of "true France"; Jews, foreigners, socialists, democrats, and Masons were to be segregated from national life. In August, 1940, all secret associations were outlawed, known Masons purged from government employ, all civil servants forced to take an oath that they were not members. Even naturalized Frenchmen were excluded from certain professions and public service, and all naturalizations since 1927 were reviewed for "irregularities." Foreigners or sons of foreigners were also discharged; foreign males were liable to service in labor camps, their families receiving only a pittance for support and deprived of equal access to rationed food and fuel. These measures added greatly to the suffering already imposed on Spanish refugees by the Daladier regime. The camps and internment centers were dirty, cold, and damp, the food and clothing wretched; disease and death rates soared, as they would for urban Frenchmen in the last two years of war.

France, the traditional haven of refugees, was debased most of all by the treatment of Jews. The Statutes of the Jews of 1940 and early 1941, and their enforcement by the anti-Semite Xavier Vallat, expressed a French version of anti-Semitism as old as Drumont, the Panama and Dreyfus cases. For all its rigor, it was denounced as too mild by the Paris fascists and the Germans. Jews were excluded from public employ, including teaching, from the press, broadcasting, and moving-picture industries, from banking and real estate, from owning or managing industrial and commercial enterprises employing "Aryans." Jews were to make up only 2 per cent of lawyers and doctors, 3 per cent of university students. Later, partly under German pressure, partly by the tougher line of Vallat's successor, Darquier de Pellepoix, the Jews were to suffer dreadfully. But these first measures were undertaken voluntarily at Vichy, where anti-Semites were supported by others eager to court Hitler's favor and some who believed they were thereby forestalling his imposition of something worse. More than any of its early acts, the Jewish policy aroused French and world opinion and seemed to prove the Vichy government's subservience to Nazi Germany.

Vichy's repudiation of Republican principles naturally extended to those it recognized as real Frenchmen. Anyone considered "dangerous" was liable to arbitrary arrest and imprisonment. Retroactive laws made subversive opinions and associations criminal offenses. Any civil or military servant could be dismissed without appeal. The courts were wholly subjugated to Vichy's authority, as was local government. Elected councils of departments, cities, and the larger towns were abolished, the prefects henceforth placed in total control. The traditional demand of the conservative Right for decentralization was, of course, ignored once it gained power; the new device of regional prefects, while it sensibly recognized the inability of the departments to deal with regional problems, only tightened central control. Napoleon's *Conseil d'État* took on added powers and completely overshadowed a hand-picked *Conseil National,* to which Pétain at first gave the task of preparing reform decrees and a new constitution. Lest it take itself seriously, the *Conseil National* met only in committees and was later disbanded.

The anti-parliamentarism of the Vichy conservatives grew out of disdain of professional politicians, who had usurped the direction of society from its "natural" leaders, the most worthy men in each profession, trade, industry, or branch of agriculture. Ideally, they saw government restricted to police power in the narrow sense while a true elite ran society, coordinating its policies through institutions representing functions rather than arbitrarily-drawn political constituencies. Men were not citizens first (or at all, in any but an abstract sense) but members of family and economic communities, whose health underlay national greatness. This mixture of medieval, conservative Catholic, Saint-Simonian, and fascist corporative ideas appealed to men who admired Salazar's Portugal or Franco's plans for Spain more than the rabid, aggressive modernism of Nazi Germany or Mussolini's version of fascism. It failed, indeed it was never tried, in France for several reasons. France was not Spain or Portugal but the homeland of eighteenth-century revolution, of all the ideas most antagonistic to a docile, hierarchical society. She was a modern, urban, middle- and working-class nation which, for better or worse, was politicized, her people accustomed to direct and incessant participation in political affairs. The Paris fascists argued, plausibly, that the only alternative to the Republic was a regime upheld by a mass totalitarian party. France had, moreover, a Napoleonic armature of centralized administration, a bureaucracy accustomed to control and to constant intervention. For that seemingly eternal type of bureaucrat, policeman, soldier, or industrialist who believes that authority rather than liberty is the source of national greatness (or of his own), the end of the Republic was a gift from heaven, not to be given up for some medieval view of decentralization and provincial autonomy. The type, by caste and training disdainful of ordinary men, was legion at Vichy, and indispensable to the regime. Also opposed to functionalism were the politicians Vichy inherited from the Third Republic, Laval first among them. But above all, political centralization was imposed by the German presence. Whether to fulfill German demands or to oppose them and later to put down French resistance, Vichy exercised unprecedented interference in every facet of national life.

## COLLABORATION AND DISHONOR

The regime passed through several distinct phases, of which each turning point had more to do with foreign than with domestic affairs. From July to December, 1940, was the hopeful period of the National Revolution. Pétain's chief minister was Pierre Laval, who derided most of the projected domestic reforms but confined himself mainly to diplomacy. Believing Hitler's triumph inevitable, he worked to bring Vichy to full economic, and at least a show of political and military, collaboration, in order to win for France the second rank in Europe's New Order. Whatever his other motives—personal ambition, hatred of the Republicans and the English who had defeated him in 1935—Laval had an overweening confidence in his judgment of affairs, his ability to outplay Hitler or, at least, to deal with him more successfully than could any other personage at Vichy. To this task he brought a long and successful if not very broad experience of manipulating politicians, magistrates, and businessmen, a remarkably agile mind, personal charm, and physical courage well above the ordinary. Deeply attached to his family, to his peasant roots in Auvergne, and to the material blessings of peace, Laval had regarded France's acceptance of war "for Poland" as folly but now believed that together with Germany, and Italy as a junior partner, a sensible France could insure Europe's future against Bolshevism. He was nonetheless disliked by Pétain's conservative entourage as a "politician" who did not trouble to consult the Ministers or to disguise his contempt for the pieties and anachronisms of the National Revolution, or his lack of respect for the Marshal. Heedless of their views, he carried on a personal diplomacy through Otto Abetz, Hitler's representative at Paris.

For a while, it appeared that under Laval's influence, France would reverse her alliances and reenter the war on Germany's side. Anglophobia at Vichy worked for him in July. The French Right had long despised "perfidious Albion," had denounced Britain's hesitant war efforts, the evacuation at Dunkerque, the refusal to commit army or air force to the final Battle of France. Now Vichy was incensed by the

British navy's sudden attack on a French fleet at the Algerian base of Oran-Mers-el-Kébir on July 3rd, which left 1200 French sailors dead and several vessels destroyed. Despite Admiral Darlan's assurances to London that Vichy would insist on the letter of the armistice and never allow the French fleet to sail against England, Churchill had felt unable to leave so dangerous an instrument in the hands of a prominent Anglophobe who might not, in any case, be able to resist German seizure, particularly if it were accompanied by promises, or threats, regarding the French prisoners and homeland, helpless in Hitler's grasp. In British ports and at Alexandria, French sailors had turned over their vessels on demand; but at Mers-el-Kébir, needless haste and obtuseness on both sides led to tragedy. Even to Frenchmen who wished England well, it was a brutal shock and no doubt helped Laval convince the parliamentarians on the 10th that France was justified in cutting her ties with the past. Darlan, who had issued precise orders for scuttling should the Axis attempt to seize his ships, heatedly demanded an attack on Gibraltar. Laval supported him, but Baudouin and others found the Marshal ready to resist, and the crisis passed. Before the end of 1940, secret negotiations were opened with London which achieved a *de facto* understanding limiting the British Mediterranean blockade of food and fuel in return for a renewed pledge to guard the French empire and fleet from Axis seizure.

In the early months of Vichy, Laval's willing collaboration contrasted with Weygand's policy of resisting all German demands beyond the terms of the armistice. Pétain, whose powers of concentration were sapped by old age, hovered between, often agreeing (or seeming to, for he was devious) with whichever adviser saw him last. The combination of British blockade, German threats, German promises, and the prospects of a quick German victory helped Laval until December. While remaining determinedly polite and multiplying friendly appeals to a conquered people, the Germans also showed what occupation could become should cooperation be refused. Selective pillage of raw materials, machines, and French currency began at once; the indemnity and other "costs" were in fact confiscatory; and by setting the exchange rate of the mark at twenty francs, the occupiers bought out French goods at derisory prices. The demarcation line was sealed tight, making travel, communications, and the transfer of food, fuel, and goods a constant struggle, using up French energy, dividing families and friends, stirring resentment between Frenchmen of the two zones. The Nord and Pas de Calais were subjected to German rule from Belgium. Alsace and Lorraine were annexed to the Reich; 200,000 were expelled to Vichy France, forced to leave all property behind; another 200,000, many of them Jews, were deported to Germany. Vichy protested in September but not publicly; and as Weygand and Baudouin warned, silence made Pétain appear as an accomplice. He was frightened of German reprisals for even an appearance of resistance; in his mind were the prisoners and the hope of relaxing German pressure. It was the first step on a path that took his regime to disrepute and worse. Soon Vichy would go further, satisfying German wishes not yet uttered in order to win favors not yet offered. Weygand's removal from the cabinet to the proconsulship of North Africa eliminated the leading advocate of public resistance.

Pétain had chosen bargaining as the best defense. Laval won him to a conference with Hitler at Montoire on October 24th, at which Pétain agreed to the "principle" of collaboration. Public dismay was evident—photographs of the Marshal and the Corporal shaking hands were published all over France—and Montoire marked a sharp decline in Pétain's prestige at home. Several of his early adherents left Vichy in disgust. Luckily, Hitler's plan for marching through Spain to Gibraltar, thence across North Africa to Suez, had been derailed by Franco on the 23rd. Hitler contented himself with Pétain's public appeal for collaboration —in return for "studying" the questions of the prisoners and the inter-zonal line. Laval and Hitler took Montoire as opening the way to a reversal of alliances, Pétain as a play for time and German concessions. All three were deluded. German demands increased, the expulsions from Alsace-Lorraine were stepped up. Laval pushed Vichy to one concession after another, planned Franco-German military cooperation in Africa, tried to press Pétain into a ceremonial trip to Paris, there to receive the ashes of Napoleon's son, which the Nazis were returning from Vienna with pompous piety. Pétain refused and, together with Darlan, Baudouin, Bouthillier, and other Vichy conservatives who hated Laval, or his policy, forced his resignation and house arrest (December 13, 1940).

The first phase of Vichy ended with the advocates of the National Revolution and of diplomatic "wait and see" fully in control. By then, the RAF had broken German air power in the Battle of Britain and postponed the easy invasion so many Frenchmen had expected. The war might not, then, be so short. Nor would it necessarily end in German victory, for the American Congress had voted conscription and a great rearmament program, Roosevelt had made the destroyer deal with

Britain, and Frenchmen believed (more surely, perhaps, than Americans did) that the United States was on the verge of war. From December, 1940, to early February, 1941, Pierre-Étienne Flandin was Foreign Minister, sharing power with Darlan, which meant competing with him for Pétain's favor, and Germany's; his policy was Weygand's, open resistance on all but the armistice terms. But as a politician of the Third Republic, he was suspect at Vichy. His inclusion of former parliamentarians in Pétain's *Conseil National* was an affront to enthusiasts of the National Revolution; Pétain's preference for accommodation and the Germans' fury at Laval's departure made Flandin's position impossible. Abetz, Ribbentrop, and Hitler demanded Laval's return, redoubled familiar threats: Abetz would sponsor a French government of Paris fascists; the zonal border was resealed; negotiations over the prisoners were broken off. Pétain gave in, Flandin resigned, and Darlan, advocate of collaboration, became Vice-Premier and Pétain's designated heir on February 10, 1941.

The Darlan phase of Vichy lasted from then to April of 1942. Implicit from the very start was Pétain's policy of *attentisme* while collaborating to a point somewhere short of all-out war with England. But Pétain's strength was failing and he progressively lost control of daily policy. At home, Darlan left power to bureaucrats, technocrats, industrialists, and bankers who were pro-German. A tough and able sailor who had much improved the navy, Darlan mistook himself for an able politician and diplomat. Narrowly patriotic, imperious, avid for power and prestige, he led Vichy ever more quickly down the slope of collaboration with Nazi Germany during the very months when Hitler's attack on Soviet Russia revived the international civil war between Left and Right, and America's entry offered Frenchmen hope of early rescue. Vichy slipped silently into surrender after surrender, amid rising enmity among Frenchmen of all persuasions. Resistance to German occupation, in defiance of Vichy, steadily grew, especially as the party best equipped for underground life, the Communist, rejoined the anti-fascist struggle. Sabotage and armed attacks on German soldiers began. German reprisals were merciless; innocent hostages were taken and shot in several times the number of German victims. Now Vichy made a choice that was to divide Frenchmen as bitterly as ever in their history: it would itself denounce, hunt down, and punish French resisters. An added motive for this kind of collaboration was anti-Communism. A German defeat, Vichyites argued, would mean the Bolshevization of Europe; to unearth and liquidate French Communists was to defend western civilization. But to Frenchmen in the occupied zone, "western civilization" was represented at the moment by Nazism and the German army. The more Vichy denounced anti-German "terrorists" as Communists and named as Communists all those caught, the more prestige the Communist party recovered from the depths of 1939.

In August, 1941, the Germans took 100 hostages after the killing of a junior officer in Paris, and threatened to execute them unless French authorities, under a new, retroactive law, condemned 6 Communists who had been in prison since before the killing took place. Vichy protested and delayed but finally succumbed to the logic of arithmetic: 6 lives for 100. Here was the crux of Vichy's dilemma, the ground on which its justification and its condemnation were to meet. Its defenders argued that by collaboration it saved French lives and material resources; France did not suffer Polonization. Its enemies answered that it thereby abandoned French honor, debased French justice, and divided the nation against itself in the face of its mortal enemy. Saint-Exupéry believed in 1940 that the Third Republic perished because it had forgotten that a free community must be founded upon recognition of God's man in every individual, that if the community in need required a man to sacrifice himself, the community in turn must be responsible for every man, accepting it as equitable that a thousand should die to deliver one unjustly imprisoned. Vichy had talked much of restoring a Christian community, but no more than any government had it meant this, in any but its institutional and, being Vichy, hierarchical sense. Like most governments and armies it followed the arithmetical rule of means and ends: six to save a hundred, a hundred foreign Jews to save a thousand French Jews, a thousand French resisters to save ten thousand hostages. But Vichy was more severely judged for many reasons: the frequency and magnitude of such acts; its apparent lack of qualms or regret, or, worse, the positive enthusiasm of its more brutish servants; its readiness to serve the purpose of Nazism; its obvious singling out, for sacrifice, of Frenchmen who were its political, religious, or racial enemies. This last added a partisan fury to the postwar trials of Vichy's leaders.

While Bouthillier and other Ministers labored to resist German economic demands, the self-confident Darlan allowed himself to come perilously close to military collaboration. Still believing in, or desiring, a German victory and swinging from fears of annihilation to hopes of a full Franco-German partnership, Darlan agreed in May of 1941 to cooperate in Syria with German forces aiming at Iraq, to grant free passage through Tunisia, and facilities in other parts of North and West Africa. In return, 80,000 older French prisoners were to be released, the interzonal controls relaxed, the occupation costs reduced to 300 million francs a day. Aided by Germany's delay in fulfilling these promises and Hitler's refusal to settle postwar questions, Weygand stiffened Pétain, Darlan changed his mind, and collaboration was limited to opening Syrian airfields. When British and anti-Vichy French forces invaded Syria, the Vichy General Dentz fought back but, on agreement with his superiors in France, ultimately surrendered rather than call for German help. Hitler was by then absorbed in his attack on Russia and failed either to threaten or to tempt Vichy into co-belligerency in other theaters. To placate the Germans, Pétain and Darlan made collaborationist speeches, refrained from protest at the German execution of fifty hostages, and forced Weygand's retirement. Then, after America's entry into the war, Pétain and Darlan turned to open protests of German practices and refused Hitler's demands for French workers. In April, 1942, the angry Germans forced Pétain to take Laval back in Darlan's place; once again, they had threatened to appoint a Gauleiter and turn the Gestapo loose on France.

The second Laval phase lasted from April, 1942, to the end of the Vichy regime in August, 1944. In it Pétain was no more than Head of State, a Third Republic President in all but name; Laval became Chief of Government with power of decree and choice of Ministers. The National Revolution was over; many of its adherents resigned and left Vichy; Laval at first appointed obscure Third Republic hangers-on to their places. His main concern was to make the best of the altered balance of world forces. Ideally, he hoped for a German victory over Russia followed by a compromise peace—arranged by himself—in the west, leaving France and Germany at the head of a new Europe secure from Bolshevism and also from the economic and diplomatic tutelage of Britain and America. His notorious speech of June, 1942, in which he "hoped for a German victory" was an appeal for such a Europe, without which Bolshevism would "be dominant everywhere." Although it was clearly meant to gain German trust, it was also directed to the British and Americans, who surely could not mean all the nonsense they talked about their great Russian ally. Laval prided himself on his utter realism, regarded righteous anger and wartime ideology as dangerous luxuries, so ignored their real power to affect events. While underestimating the political idealism of Britons and Americans (he had made a similar error in 1935), Laval overestimated the political cynicism of the French. Knowing very well the secret ways of governments, from diplomatic blackmail to police interrogation rooms, he appeared unable to distinguish between what governments did and what they had to appear to be doing. The "realism" of collaboration, of arithmetical decisions, would surely be understood; and if it were successful in rescuing France without another round of war on her soil, he would be acclaimed as a national hero. That Nazism was abhorrent to most Frenchmen, Laval knew perfectly well; but he could not take seriously their readiness to choose reprisals, even annihilation, or war and European chaos simply to hurry its departure, when finesse (and lower human and material losses) could ultimately achieve the same. He had never accepted, moreover, the prospect of making war to overthrow Nazism inside Germany. Satiated in the east, German Nazism would ultimately settle down to coexistence in Europe as he, Laval, would surely do were he in Hitler's place. The Atlantic Charter was all very well for the moment, but an outcome so perfectly in accord with British, American, French, and German self-interest would hardly be ignored when it was time for decision.

As 1942 and 1943 wore on and German victory even in the east grew doubtful, as 1944 brought Germany near defeat, Laval fell back to a second line: to limit the damage to France that Nazi death throes might inflict and to keep himself in power as the man best able to revive something like the Third Republic—all the while guarding himself against the possibility of a last-minute German victory or compromise peace. To expect Frenchmen to understand the "necessities" of such a personal policy was asking too much. As Laval himself admitted, he would probably be shot, without even the aura of martyrdom that Pétain would enjoy. The alternative would have been to retire from power. Whatever the motives behind Laval's choice to remain—patriotism, ambition, pride in sheer political craftsmanship, a belief that he was, in any case, already marked as Hitler's man—they led him to a succession of surrenders to German and French Nazism, no different in kind from those of Pétain and Darlan but more odious in degree, in seeming to prolong Germany's war effort while punishing Frenchmen who were fighting to cut it short.

The Germans, increasingly exasperated at Vichy's tergiversations, conceded nothing for Laval's return. On the other hand, they lost interest in further attempts to win French military collaboration. Their exertions in Russia were draining manpower and material. What they wanted most from Vichy was French repression of resisters in both zones, French workers for German factories, and massive transfers of food and industrial goods. To make their point, they shot over 200 hostages in the month Laval resumed power, took reprisals against French prisoners of war, and sent the noxious "Hangman" Heydrich from Czechoslovakia to demand that Vichy recruit a corps of French Nazi-style police. Laval complied. As a rival to Doriot's *Parti Populaire Français* and Déat's *Rassemblement National Populaire,* and to give itself something of a mass base without creating a political party as such, Vichy had set up the *Légion des Combattants Français* in August, 1940, a moderate veterans' organization resembling the early *Croix de Feu.* In Darlan's time, a tough minority of activists formed the *Service d'Ordre Légionnaire* (SOL) to combat opponents of the regime. Out of the SOL and worse elements, the *Milice* (militia) was recruited by Laval in early 1943. Commanded by the fascist adventurer Joseph Darnand, the *Milice* was a well-paid mercenary army; together with carefully purged branches of the regular police and assorted storm troopers led by Paris fascists, they were ruthlessly effective in trapping fellow Frenchmen who had eluded German hands. In their ranks, as in such bands the world over, were simple-minded zealots, thugs, and bullies raised to power; their plunder, beatings, murder, and torture of French citizens guilty only of being unprotected disgusted the German military authorities. Of the Paris fascists, Frenchmen expected as much, but Vichy's creation and complaisant supervision of such units was its single most hated act. More than any other it discredited Pétain's and Laval's later claims that they had been playing "a double game," pretending to collaborate while secretly aiding resistance. No doubt they and most Vichy authorities sought to delay or limit response to German demands, but there is little evidence that they aided the "unofficial" resistance, which they regarded not only as a threat to their policy of salvation by collaboration but as inspired by political rivals for the future allegiance of the French people. Their plea of ignorance of the *Milice*'s character was damning, whether true or false.

Hardly less reprehensible was Vichy's acquiescence in persecution of foreign, and finally French, Jews. It had from the start countenanced the most hateful anti-Semitic propaganda. In June, 1942, the German rulers of the occupied zone demanded that Vichy deliver to them all foreign Jews in the unoccupied zone. Once more came the arithmetical decision; to avoid the deportation of French Jews, Laval ordered French police to turn over foreign Jews in both zones. Tens of thousands were carried off in unspeakable condition, herded into trucks and boxcars, left without food, water, sanitary or medical facilities, in pens like the *Vélodrome d'Hiver* in Paris; then, with families deliberately separated (children were locked up without adults), sent to the concentration camp of Drancy to await deportation to the death factories of Germany. The sharp protests of Protestant and Catholic Church leaders had little immediate effect, but probably encouraged Vichy to resist demands that French Jews be delivered as well. Meanwhile, individual Frenchmen inside government and out falsified papers and hid Jewish friends, and an underground ring succeeded in saving hundreds of children. But in the occupied zone and where the *Milice* held sway, all Jews remained in mortal danger.

A better case can be made for Vichy's resistance to German requisition of goods and workers. In both cases bureaucrats and local authorities deserve most of the credit, but in the latter case, Laval's talent for duplicity helped delay the inevitable. In June, 1942, the German labor agent Sauckel demanded 350,000 French workers; Laval, who wished to bolster Hitler's anti-Soviet war while appeasing French opinion, responded with the idea of the *Relève*, by which one French prisoner would be returned for every three workers volunteering to go to Germany. Some 50,000 had departed by September, when Sauckel threatened to conscript all the workers Germany needed. Although the Germans had set free only a few thousand disabled prisoners, proving the *Relève* a fraud, Vichy yielded again, decreed its own mobilization of labor, including regulations that made evasion easier. This *Service du Travail Obligatoire* furnished Germany 700,000 French workers by the end of 1943. Sauckel's demands for a million more were simply ignored and workers were henceforth seized directly by German authorities. At the war's end, some 1.7 million Frenchmen were laboring for Germany, over half of them prisoners of war. On the other hand, only a few thousand fascist enthusiasts joined the *Légion des Volontaires Français* and the *Légion Tricolore*, to join the anti-Communist crusade on the eastern front. Their military value was negligible, but they did lessen the number of ruffians roaming France herself.

In early November, 1942, the Anglo-American invasion of Morocco and Algeria resulted in the German occupation of all France. What remained of Vichy's autonomy disappeared, along with the rest of the fleet, which scuttled itself at Toulon, the armistice army, which the

Germans disbanded, and the North African empire. Although many local German military commanders preserved their courteous ways, the pretense of Franco-German solidarity was dropped. History's clumsiest courtship ended in the brutal confrontation of conqueror and conquered. Pétain lost a final chance to reunite Frenchmen; rejecting all entreaties to resist or flee, he held to his martyr's role, still convinced he could alleviate French suffering, could finally emerge with his authority intact whichever way the war turned out. Laval successfully defeated those who would have opposed German landings in Tunisia; instead, French troops were ordered to resist any Allied advance from Algeria. The American command, by excessive secrecy and tardiness, bungled its halfhearted alliance with anti-Vichy Frenchmen in Algeria and Morocco. But for Darlan's fortuitous presence in Algiers, French soldiers would have more strongly opposed the landings (as it was, many thousands were killed on both sides). As Commander-in-Chief of Vichy forces, Darlan was given a free hand by Pétain—who had little choice—and ordered a cease-fire in return for American recognition of his authority as High Commissioner in North Africa. Now France's Tunisian forces cooperated with the Axis, its Algerian and Moroccan forces with the Allies. *Attentisme* had reached its logical end. At Vichy, Laval failed to achieve Pétain's abdication, but he received full powers and was again designated as the Marshal's heir. When 1943 opened, French resistance at home and abroad made Laval in effect the leader of one side in a French civil war.

## RESISTANCE AND LIBERATION

Resistance to the Axis and Vichy from outside of France was proclaimed by General Charles de Gaulle in a series of radio broadcasts from London beginning on June 18, 1940. In that first memorable, though little-heard, address he denounced the senior military leaders who, having prepared defeat by their own incompetence, would now dishonor France by accepting an armistice. The war, he said, was a world war, and France had lost only a battle: "The flame of French resistance must not and will not go out." In what was a flagrant act of revolt, de Gaulle declared himself the true representative of France and called to his side all Frenchmen who would continue the fight. A month later, he was condemned to death *in absentia* by a Vichy military tribunal. Only a few thousand Frenchmen sought him out in the next few months, while the nation as a whole rallied to Pétain. From this obscure beginning, a brigadier general unknown to most Frenchmen, without a shadow of legal authority and upheld mainly by modest British funds, built a political career more spectacular and controversial than any in modern French history since Bonaparte's return from Egypt. He had, it is true, been a junior member of Reynaud's cabinet and since the early 1920's a lonely critic of French military theory—and of the debilitating effect of political parties on the nation's life. A professional soldier, a graduate of Saint-Cyr, de Gaulle's first post (his brilliance won him the right to choose) was in Colonel Henri-Philippe Pétain's 33rd Infantry Regiment. He later fought at Verdun, and in the early 1920's Pétain so approved of de Gaulle's unorthodox military ideas that he made him an instructor at *l'École de Guerre* and a member of his entourage on the *Conseil Supérieur*. His book *Edge of the Sword* (1931) was dedicated to Pétain. Their mutual regard made it appropriate at the time (they drifted apart soon afterward), and the book's exaltation of the authoritarian leader's role in national crisis was a prophecy for both men. The leader, de Gaulle said, would be prideful and wily, withdrawn and even mysterious, drawing men to himself by force of character and prestige. Since childhood, the devout Catholic and student of French heroes from Saint Louis to Joan of Arc to Napoleon had felt himself destined for such leadership. One day France would call him to restore the vigor of her army and society; for this he ceaselessly prepared.

His hour, like Napoleon's, came almost too soon. But in the years 1940–1944 de Gaulle succeeded precisely as he had foretold, by creating about himself a *mystique*. Long before he marched down the Champs Élysées in August, 1944, he had become the symbol of French authority to most of his countrymen. His mixture of egotism and patriotism, mission and ambition, made him a constant trial to Churchill and distasteful to the American government, whose representatives saw in him at once a dictator, an imperialist, and even a dangerous social innovator. Britons and Americans, accustomed to judging politicians by their practicality, their programs, or their personalities, saw little in de Gaulle to please them. Washington was in any case committed to a policy of wringing advantages from Vichy. But even Allied coolness became his asset; he was clearly nobody's man. His other assets enabled him, as Vichy's credit declined, to win national acclaim. To silent, occupied France the BBC sent his voice, full of defiance and dignity, recalling his prewar advice, narrating the war's events, promising liberation, in prose nearly as inspiriting as Churchill's. Frenchmen knew nothing of the mainly Rightist courtiers who surrounded him in London, their intrigues and rivalries, their attacks on French Radical or Socialist exiles, their merciless interrogations of Frenchmen they considered Vichyites, or of his tolerance of them, his intolerance and abusive treatment of loyal men who fell from his favor.

Churchill saw both sides but grasped the importance of de Gaulle's image to ordinary Frenchmen. He allowed de Gaulle to recruit followers and to form the Free French movement, to which the British contributed funds and equipment. Slowly his forces grew. De Gaulle was not to forget that the first overseas territory to rally to him was Chad, under the direction of its Negro Governor-General, Félix Éboué. By the end of 1940, the Cameroons, Togoland, the New Hebrides, and New Caledonia, the French enclaves in India joined French Equatorial Africa in recognizing de Gaulle's authority. The other colonies held to Vichy, the more so after the defeat of a badly planned Anglo-Gaullist attack on Dakar in September, 1940. A year later, de Gaulle set up a French National Committee in London; but only in 1942, as resistance developed in France herself, did he proclaim a clearly democratic and social program. Having hoped that an entirely new political pattern might develop after the war, perhaps a one- or two-party system, de Gaulle had little choice but to invite leaders of the prewar parties and unions to London, to support his claim to speak for all of France. By the end of 1942, the French National Committee had become a representative shadow cabinet, including the Socialist André Philip as Minister of the Interior; another Socialist, Félix Gouin, headed a committee to form a shadow parliament to study programs and a constitution for what was already being called the Fourth Republic.

The Allied capture of North Africa without de Gaulle's participation was only a temporary setback, though de Gaulle was to resent it long afterward, as he did Roosevelt's Vichy policy. Darlan was assassinated shortly afterward and the American choice for his successor, the conservative General Giraud, soon found that it was easier to escape the German prisons of two world wars than to survive the political onslaughts of de Gaulle and his entourage. As 1943 passed, Giraud was pushed aside and de Gaulle ruled alone over the French Committee of National Liberation with its capital at Algiers. A Consultative Assembly emerged in September of 1943, comprising delegates appointed by all

Resistance groups and parties including the Communists and leaders of the CGT and CFTC. As the invasion of France was preparing in England, the men of Algiers labored amid rising excitement and intrigue to prepare a Gaullist-Resistance government to assume power at Liberation.

The French Resistance at home passed through several stages, as did Vichy itself. Contrary to legend, the majority of Frenchmen were never directly involved, though they were doubtless anti-German from the start. Quite naturally, the ranks swelled with opportunists as Germany's defeat approached, including many who had rushed to Vichy in 1940 and thus had special reason to appear intransigent in 1944. Likewise many acts of "resistance" like many acts of "collaboration" were inspired by private vengeance, greed, or common brutality, and by political ambitions among rival Resistance leaders and factions. All this said, the internal Resistance remains the most glorious page in modern French history. The resisters were no insignificant minority; including hostages, over 30,000 French men, women, and children were executed, another 25,000 killed in fighting German or Vichy forces. One-third of the 200,000 French deportees who died in Germany were political prisoners. The practical effect of French opposition on Nazi power before 1944 is arguable, and the chances of any conquered people to liberate itself from a modern army and totalitarian police are no doubt very small. French underground fighters in 1944, however, greatly facilitated the Allied landings and advance; Eisenhower estimated their contribution as equivalent to that of several divisions. Their political organizations on every level greatly limited the chaos most outsiders expected would follow the collapse of German and Vichy authority. Above all, as so many have said, the Resistance saved the soul of France, restoring self-respect and dignity to Frenchmen who had profoundly doubted themselves since Munich or before.

Greater honor belongs to the resisters of the early hours, who fought less from hope of victory than from a desire to bear witness to the ideas of 1789, to a tradition of intellectual and religious freedom even older, to a working-class ideal developed since. Later, and until 1944, when the *mystique* of the Resistance turned to revenge and politics, they were sustained by visions of a just society to come, better than the Third Republic and very different from Vichy's National Revolution. It was natural, then, that the Resistance was, especially in the beginning, more likely to draw what right-thinking people called malcontents of the

Left, men and women who remembered the 14th of July, 1936, as the greatest day of their lives: the propertyless workers, their families, and those students, intellectuals, artists, teachers, civil servants, soldiers, and priests who had emerged from, or identified themselves with, the working class. It was, of course, a matter of relative participation, for in all classes were patriots who fought first and mainly to drive the Boches from France, especially in the northern, occupied zone. Still, the Leftist flavor of the Resistance persisted in all areas for several reasons. In ideas and personnel Vichy at first represented the Catholic hierarchy, military and civil officials, employers, property owners rural and urban, and much of the bourgeoisie. Even for members of these groups who chose the Resistance, the choice was not easy, for it meant risking one's material stake in society as well as almost certain ostracism, if not betrayal, by associates who demanded prudence, if not enthusiasm, for Vichy or the New Order. For those without property or office, choice and action were easier; they rarely suffered delusions over the New Order; workers and their allies knew that it meant wage slavery, scholars and writers expected slavery of the mind, Jews could await only degradation and death. All had reasons beyond patriotism to join the Resistance. As Vichy's hold on patriots loosened, the Resistance might have developed a closer balance of classes except for two events: the Communist party's wholehearted adherence upon Hitler's invasion of Russia in 1941 and the flight of workers into the hills and brush (the *maquis*) to avoid forced labor in Germany after 1942.

As one historian of the Resistance, Henri Michel, described it, participation ranged from merely keeping secret one's knowledge of another's work, to sabotage or armed attack on German soldiers. Many men and women moved from one through several stages to the other: keeping papers, passing messages, hiding arms and then resisters, finally taking the places of those arrested, leaving home, friends, and family behind or, what was worse, operating near and endangering them all, as the railroad and factory workers who engaged in sabotage, the priests and doctors who tended them, had to do. To the minority of Frenchmen who lived this way, the Resistance brought a unity of spirit that crossed all the older class, political, and religious lines. Keeping faith under torture, or giving way, was not a matter of Catholicism or Communism, aristocracy or shopkeeping, but of qualities all men had or had not. Marc Bloch, the middle-aged historian who joined the Resistance, to be tortured and executed by the Nazis, once said that French history could be understood only by men who felt the pull of both Jacobinism and Catholicism. In this the Jewish scholar and patriot was one with the Catholic poet and socialist Charles Péguy. Many Frenchmen who had heard of neither man discovered a fraternity under occupation that was to survive even victory. This was the great legacy of the Resistance. Its great failure was that many more missed or forgot it as victory loosened the tongues of parties, dogmas, and interests.

The turn of French Resistance from a *mystique* for which men died to the politics by which they lived (as Péguy had said) was probably inevitable. For a while, activists dreamed of a new mass party of the Resistance which would build and guard a new system run by new men. Apart from flying in the face of all historical experience, the idea had everything against it. Those who took it seriously were a minority within a minority and even they quite naturally associated in the Resistance with men they had agreed with before the war. The earliest groups to be formed in the free zone all had prewar affinities; and out of them, as out of the smaller and numerous resistant units in the more dangerous north, were to come several political leaders of the Fourth Republic. Soldiers, engineers, civil servants, and Christian democratic intellectuals formed the group *Combat* at Lyon, which included Georges Bidault, Paul Coste-Floret, and Pierre-Henri Teitgen, all leaders of the postwar Catholic *Mouvement Républicain Populaire*. The group *Libération-Sud* embraced many of the younger leaders of the CGT and the CFTC. *Franc-Tireur* (Marc Bloch's group) had a Socialist character, as did a Toulouse group including Vincent Auriol and Jules Moch, a Marseilles unit with Félix Gouin and Gaston Defferre, all to be prominent in the postwar Socialist party. In the north, *Libération-Nord* was also mainly Socialist, CGT, and CFTC. Most of the other groups in the north, where resistance tended to be localized and fiercely anti-German, were socially and politically mixed.

The Communist-dominated *Front National* operated in both zones, aiming to bring all groups under its leadership. Its directing committees were broadly based, from patriotic Rightists like Louis Marin through Catholic democrats like Bidault to its own organizers, who always commanded. The *Front*, like the Communist party itself, successfully combined violent resistance with mass organization, setting up units according to interests and professions. Vichy's endless anti-Communist tirade and the conspicuous suffering of Communists at the hands of the Germans and French fascists helped Frenchmen forget the party's belated conversion to resistance. To some who were not Communists, the *Front National* was the start of that new movement which would make France *pure et dure*. But the dream broke upon the Communists' too-obvious bid for control and the resentment of the Gaullists, members of other parties, and resisters of the first hour. The old parties were swiftly reconstituted; all (including the Communist) sent representatives to de Gaulle's headquarters in London and then Algiers. De Gaulle in turn sent the former prefect of Chartres, Jean Moulin, to coordinate the work of all Resistance groups under Free French direction, a task facilitated by his power to allocate money and arms provided by the British and Americans. Moulin succeeded in creating and presiding over the *Conseil National de la Résistance* (CNR), to which all groups sent delegates beginning in the summer of 1943, though the Communists kept their *Front National* as autonomous as possible. When Moulin was betrayed, tortured, and killed, the non-Communists who were also wary of de Gaulle put Georges Bidault in Moulin's place as president of the CNR. Although the uneasy, three-cornered coalition held together until Liberation, it foretold the shape of French postwar politics, with Bidault already at the head of the "Third Force" in which his MRP, the Socialists, and the Radicals were to dominate the Fourth Republic, to the chagrin of Communists on the Left, Gaullists on the Right.

All this was of secondary concern to the rank and file who, as in the days of the Popular Front, often deplored their leaders' quarrels. There was still a war to be fought. Even the anti-Communists in the CNR were forced to acknowledge their rivals' skill in clandestine operations by giving the Communists control of the Military Action Committee. From Britain and then North Africa, secret agents, arms, explosives and money, radios and their brave operators (over half of them met death) were parachuted into France by Gaullist, British, and American teams. They never furnished nearly enough, partly through reluctance to arm "radical" groups or set off premature operations; the proportion of funds and aircraft employed was tiny compared with the famous bombing missions which in France were far less efficient than sabotage from the ground. But by the end of 1943, tens of thousands of native Frenchmen were engaged in gathering and transmitting information, in rescuing downed fliers, in sabotage and counterespionage. Most of their exploits can never be known, though statistics and a few outstanding examples prove that they were far more grim and heroic than wartime tales (or Hollywood) made them seem. Over 10,000 underground agents died, among them Bloch, Moulin, and the valiant Pierre Brossolette. An equal number were deported after indescribable tortures. Those who escaped, like the intrepid British Parisian Yeo-Thomas (code-named Shelley and later dubbed "the White Rabbit"), bore early witness to Nazi death camps in which normal men on the outside could only half believe.

To those who might fail to see, or imagine, what was happening and what it meant, thousands of clandestine newspapers, pamphlets, and books were printed and distributed. The underground press showed French audacity, *débrouillage,* and, most of all, power of self-analysis at their best. Resistance poetry reverted to an ancient role, the fortification of men and women for struggle; Éluard, Aragon, and countless younger poets spoke directly to masses waiting in the dark. Poetry, novels, and essays were printed by Jean Bruller's press *Editions de Minuit;* as "Vercors," he wrote the moving *Silence de la Mer.* In *Combat,* Albert Camus emerged as the most searching political essayist of the era. *Résistance, L'Humanité, Franc-Tireur, Défense de la France* (published by Parisian students), *Libération,* and many other newspapers reported acts of resistance, repression, and reprisal, painted visions of the new world that would follow liberation. All this bore witness, for Frenchmen and their allies, to the ubiquitous Resistance and turned a war which had begun in resigned obscurantism into an ideological crusade.

As D-Day approached, the tempo of violence increased. Sabotage and attacks on Germans and collaborators were now answered by full-fledged massacres. The secret armies of the *maquis,* of various Resistance groups, of the disbanded armistice force of Vichy and other regular soldiers, loosely united in the FFI (*Forces Françaises de l'Intérieure*), were exposed to terrible risk as the Allies failed to supply them adequately. In several pitched battles with the *Milice,* the Gestapo, and regular German units in early 1944, their losses ran into the hundreds; in a few, into thousands. After D-Day, the FFI disorganized German forces in Brittany, Burgundy, the Loire region, and several pockets in south and central France. These actions greatly eased the Anglo-American sweep through the north and up from the Riviera, though they also drew down murderous reprisals such as the German massacre at Oradour-sur-Glane (June 10, 1944), where 600 villagers were burned alive in their church or machine-gunned as they fled.

The liberation of Paris was begun by its own citizens in late August, 1944; barricades appeared again as they had risen in 1871 and in most of the same places, for it was largely a worker and petty bourgeois uprising ordered by the Communists and other Resistance militants to face the Allies and the Gaullists with the *fait accompli* of a "People's Government." Had it not been for the Allies' rapid advance and the German commander's disregard of orders to destroy the city, Paris might have suffered the fate of Warsaw. In retrospect, the orders to revolt were foolhardy and dictated by political ambition, but it is likely that an uprising would have occurred in any case. Three thousand died in the fighting before Leclerc's Free French division entered the city on the 25th. The people had earned what de Gaulle proclaimed "a moment of greatness." By and large, it was the same people who had had no choice but to stay behind on that black June 14, 1940, when all the more prosperous sections had been emptied by flight, and also the same people who had suffered most from Allied bombings of industrial suburbs. But for an instant all differences were forgotten. On the 26th, immense throngs cheered de Gaulle as he walked from the Étoile to the Hôtel de Ville to Notre Dame with the leaders of the home Resistance, many of whom he soon appointed to his "Provisional Government of the French Republic." Snipers' bullets whined about them all the way, but they only added to the high drama of the hour.

The Fourth Republic was born in bright hopes but also in hunger, disease, cold, economic chaos, and great anger. As invasion threatened in early 1944, Pétain and Laval had been forced to accept Déat, Darnand, and other fascists in the Vichy cabinet. Even then, the fascist cliques had been unable to unite in a single party or on any common program but vicious attacks on their enemies. Extremists murdered Jean Zay and George Mandel, who were left unguarded by regular Vichy authorities, and the *Milice* redoubled its cruelties as defeat approached. As German armies fell back, four years of pent-up anger exploded; local Resistance groups, the FFI, and the inevitable opportunists dispensed vigilante justice to traitors, collaborators, or victims who could be called such. Between ten and twenty thousand died or disappeared in the Liberation Terror, the consequence of immense hatreds and suspicions left by war, occupation, and collaboration. Unlike the British, whose unity was enhanced by common suffering, the French were all the more bitterly divided by suffering inflicted in part by other Frenchmen. For this Vichy was not forgiven. Pétain was condemned to death, his sentence commuted to life imprisonment; Laval was shot after a farcical trial which dishonored Republican justice. In all, some 50,000 were arrested in the Provisional Government's official purge, of whom

800 were executed, 20,000 imprisoned. By 1950, nearly all of these had been set free.

In most sections of France, order returned quickly in the summer of 1944. The discipline of the people, their loyalty to de Gaulle, and the Communist party's readiness to obey his authority surprised Anglo-Americans who had expected protracted political unrest or radicalism. Resistance unity held as France entered another war, against human suffering. Allied bombing and invasion had been more devastating than the losing battles of 1940. Industrial production had fallen from a 1938 base of 100 to 43, wages stood at 165, official prices at 285, and the black market was six times as high. Agricultural production had declined over a third from 1939 and transport breakdowns nearly starved the cities. Housing and heat were everywhere deficient. The general mortality rate was up 12 per cent from 1938, as high as 35 per cent in urban areas; after years of malnutrition, tuberculosis and infant mortality rates were tragic, resistance to all disease was dangerously low. At the same time, France mourned 600,000 military and civilian war dead since 1939. Despite and because of all this, great hopes survived for a year and more, fed by the now free press of the Resistance, party meetings and manifestoes, the endless talk of cafés, clubs, and union halls. De Gaulle's Provisional Government decreed elections for October, 1945, after the conscripted workers, the political and military prisoners returned from Germany. The woman's vote was recognized, finally making French suffrage universal. So eager were Frenchmen to bury a dead past that 96 per cent voted against a return to the Third Republic and for the creation of a Fourth. The Constituent Assembly elected on the same day appeared to insure the triumph of a new, much larger Popular Front. The Communist party emerged the winner, with 26 per cent of the vote and 152 seats; the new Catholic *Mouvement Républicain Populaire* won 25 per cent and 151 seats, the Socialists 24 per cent and 132 seats. The Radicals, the party of the Third Republic, elected only 25 candidates, and the Center and Right did no better. In November, de Gaulle was again acclaimed President of the Provisional Government, heading a cabinet made up of leaders of the three major parties, all of them pledged to fulfilling the promise of political, economic, and social democracy made in the Resistance Charter of March, 1944. At the height of the Paris insurrection, Albert Camus had written in *Combat* that the people were in arms that night because they hoped for "justice tomorrow." Of the Fourth Republic, everything was expected.

## ∞◁ XII ▷∞

# THE FOURTH
# REPUBLIC

The great hopes of 1944–1945, like those of 1848, 1871, and 1936, were to be disappointed and the Fourth Republic accordingly condemned for failing to be *pure et dure*, for being instead as impure and unstable, as indulgent toward the privileged, as the Third had been. At Liberation it seemed that nothing could resist an economic and social democracy well to the Left of the Popular Front's compromise program of 1936. But from then to its death in 1958, the Fourth Republic moved by stages toward the Right according to a pattern established in the early twentieth century, when economic and social issues first took precedence over politics and religion. The Provisional Government of General de Gaulle and the Consultative Assembly, and (after his resignation) the so-called Tripartite government of Communists, Socialists, and Catholic Republicans in the Constituent Assembly, only half-fulfilled the promises of the Resistance Charter. In 1947, the Communists left the governing coalition, a new Right grew up around de Gaulle's RPF (*Rassemblement du Peuple Français*), and the Republic rested on a "Third Force" made up of Socialists, MRP, a reviving Radical party, and Republican moderates. This embattled, quarrelsome Center did little more in its four years than ward off assaults from the Communist Left and the Gaullist Right. With the elections of 1951, the balance of power moved still further to the Right as the Socialists left the cabinet, to be replaced by Republican conservatives hostile to state direction of the economy, and to the extension of social services. From 1947 to its demise, with one brief interruption, the Fourth Republic was progressively weakened by its own political *immobilisme*. Although the French economy made unprecedented gains in the late 1950's, social and political problems persisted, and the government's inability to meet the perils of the Cold War and colonial revolution led to debacle in Indo-China and to the ultimately fatal struggle over Algeria. In May of 1958, with France on the verge of civil strife, Charles de Gaulle returned, ostensibly as Premier of the Fourth Republic, in fact as the author of a presidential regime which replaced it as the Fifth.

## POSTWAR PROBLEMS AND PARTIES

Frenchmen and foreigners who shared the peculiar excitement of Liberation year have indicted the Fourth Republic as sharply as the disillusioned romantics did the Second after it stumbled into class war and the guardianship of General Cavaignac. But in relation to the problems it faced, rather than to the wishes attending its birth, the Fourth Republic and its work were not so mean as they have been painted. Some of its problems were only too familiar, but new in scale and simultaneity. War damage was worse and wider spread than in 1918. The industrial and transport equipment not taken off to Germany or destroyed in Allied air and ground attack was either unusable, in all stages of disrepair, or outdated and inefficient. The paucity of prewar investment in French industry and mining meant that normal production could not be resumed as quickly as after 1918. Agricultural production was lower than in 1918 and the wreckage of French transport kept much of what was produced from reaching the cities. French governments had suffered inflation before, in the mid-1920's, but inflationary pressures were far greater in the mid-1940's. All goods were scarcer, demand was heavier, an enormous black market defied regulation of prices. The occupying Germans had spent billions of confiscated francs, which now re-emerged from the hoards of newly rich farmers, middlemen, and black marketeers to bid up prices, tempting other Frenchmen to illicit trade, to furnishing amusement, personal services, or luxury goods rather than to the production of necessities for the majority.

Social unrest fed by deprivation was, for half a decade, worse than in the years of depression and the Popular Front; now it was exploited by a Communist party in command of the majority of industrial workers. The divisive memories, the *incivisme* and debilitating political habits of the Third Republic survived and were all the worse for the self-seeking and "patriotic lawlessness" that German occupation had encouraged. Over these problems hung an aura of defeat and national self-doubt unknown since the 1870's. Frenchmen knew that they were but nominal victors of the Second World War; their determination once again to be respected as a world power prepared them badly for two great problems that were not familiar: the bipolar struggle between the United States and the Soviet Union, and the national revolutions of the French colonial peoples. The effects of the First World War had merely narrowed France's freedom of choice in diplomacy and complicated old domestic problems. The aftermath of the Second imprisoned French leaders in a maze of contradictory world developments, all but a few of which were beyond their control, many of which aggravated France's own economic, social, and political difficulties.

In other ways, the second postwar era was more hopeful than the first. In 1944–1945, many fewer Frenchmen believed that they could revert to prewar routine, or that they should, for the 1930's had been no Belle Époque. The Third Republic stood condemned not so much for its military failure in 1940—no form of government was proof against such odds—as for the economic debility and social congealment which had prepared defeat, and denied to the mass of Frenchmen a decent living and the hope of something better for their children. Significantly, such complaints no longer came only from the doctrinal Left. The zonal demarcation had uncovered the regional as well as the national problems of the French economy; the demands of occupation had convinced Vichyites no less than resisters that state planning and intervention in the economy were necessary for the best use of resources and talent. The scale of German, then of American and Soviet, power obliged French patriots to consider the national need for international, European, cooperation. Whether to promote domestic prosperity and social justice or to restore France as a great power, the need for fundamental change was accepted.

Not so was the need for new political instruments to carry out that change. The constitution of the Fourth Republic revived the parliamentary system of the Third, which would have mattered less had there arisen a new system of political parties, fewer in number, free of old dogmatisms, aligned on issues of the present and future. Many resisters had dreamed of a great new party of the Left, of social democratic patriots, enlisting masses of former Communists, Socialists, and Radicals, crossing religious lines to embrace Catholics, crossing class and regional lines, and, what was particularly prized, drawing thousands of "new men" hitherto alienated from politics (or too young) who had proved themselves in the Resistance. Whatever chance such a party might have had—no doubt very slim—it was thwarted by the two powers claiming to be most scornful of the old party system, the Communists and Charles de Gaulle.

To improve his standing with the Allies, the General had called representatives of the prewar parties to London and Algiers and made much of their support, and of their right to speak for silent France. Similarly, from the hour that Hitler's attack on Russia revived the French Communist movement, a new, broadly based Resistance party of the Left became unlikely. By 1944 the Communists had won the bulk of the industrial working class, which refused to believe—with ample historical reason—that any other party could be trusted to defend proletarian interests. The Communist leaders never considered a merger with Socialists, Radicals, or the Catholic Left except on their own terms of total control. In each of these parties were some who wished to join the Communists at any risk, others who wished to unite in a new Resistance party without the Communists. Both factions were overborne by men who had always preferred to revive the old party system. At the moment of its greatest electoral triumph and the nearly total eclipse of the Right, the French Left was thus once more divided against itself. The "revolution by law" promised in the Resistance Charter was to depend on the willingness of Communists, Socialists, and the MRP to cooperate in a new Popular Front.

The Charter had promised (in March, 1944) state economic planning; the nationalization of "monopolies in the means of production," of energy sources, mineral wealth, insurance companies, and the large banks; the encouragement of industrial and agricultural cooperatives, and "the participation of workers in the direction of economic life." This "eviction of the great economic and financial feudalities" was to be prefaced by punishment of traitors, confiscation of their property and that of black-market operators, and punitive taxation of all who had profited from the occupation. Frenchmen were to have the right to work, and to leisure, a minimum wage, and family security. The free trade unions were to exercise "extensive powers" in French economic and social affairs. Reforms were also promised to small farmers and agricultural labor. All Resistance groups and parties had sworn to remain united until French life was renovated, and the determination of their rank and file to do so forced the leaders of the three big parties to endure a galling political partnership until 1947.

The Communists saw the Charter as only a first step toward a Soviet society. But by most loudly demanding its fulfillment, they expected to keep their title as "the first party of the Resistance," to dominate the labor movement and the nationalized industries. By adding vital cabinet posts, preferably Defense or Interior, or both, the Communists would then enjoy the "commanding heights" of postwar France, preparatory to the seizure of power, which had been patently impossible at Liberation because of the presence of Allied armies. Between 1944 and 1948, the party was at the peak of its numbers and wealth, a society within a society, with army-like discipline, led by proven officers, mostly of working-class origin, who had followed every twist of policy since the 1920's. Its largest membership and voter following lay in the industrial and mining region from Paris to Belgium, and in certain rural areas in the center and south, habitually Jacobin since 1870 and before. Its peasant following had increased fourfold from the late 1930's, thanks to its work in the *maquis,* to its tactful silence on peasant profits from the black market, and to its intense organizing efforts among farm laborers and tenants. The Communists were also stronger than ever in organized labor. By the end of 1945, they had gained control of the CGT and most of its component unions in mining, metals, rails, and chemicals.

The Communist Resistance record and the postwar prestige of the Soviet Union were incalculable assets, backed by an immense party treasury gathered in "patriotic theft" from the Germans, by the seizure of currency shipments in the disarray of Liberation, from levies on the salaries of Communist officials and Deputies, and from blackmail of collaborators and employers. The party spent lavishly for the elections of 1945 and 1946, as in its publication of newspapers, magazines, and books designed to appeal to every interest group in France and to insulate its own members from bourgeois society. In the afterglow of Liberation, most Frenchmen saw no reason to question its patriotic integrity and those who did often kept silent, so well defended was the party by wishful or highly paid apologists—and by the conspicuous wartime bravery of ordinary Communists. Claiming to have lost "75,000 martyrs" to German repression, the Communists took credit for most acts of Resistance heroism, while blackening the names of non-Communist underground fighters, discrediting rival groups by false charges of collaboration, undermining Socialist and Catholic organizations by demands that they purge members accused of insufficient anti-German zeal. De Gaulle's desire for Moscow's support of his German policy and his need for Communist cooperation to restore production led him to appoint Communists to his cabinet, to welcome Thorez home from Moscow—to pardon, in short, the party's betrayal of France in 1939 and its hysterical abuse of him and all resisters until June of 1941. De Gaulle's conclusion in Moscow of a new twenty-year Franco-Soviet pact in December of 1944 also discouraged critics, and even Léon Blum was belabored by the hopeful for having called the Communists a party of "foreign nationalists."

Blum's experience suggests the plight of the Socialists in the Fourth Republic, under which they declined in numbers, confidence, coherence of doctrine, and quality of leadership. Although many Socialists had brilliant Resistance records, they had not fought as a party in the Communist manner. Divided by Munich, by the coming of the war, and by the vote of full powers to Pétain, they owed their *élan* and electoral success in 1945 mainly to the Leftist mood of Liberation among the lower middle classes, civil servants, teachers, and clerks who made up for the loss of so many industrial workers to Communism. The party kept a labor following only in the Nord and Pas de Calais and in some sections of Paris, Marseilles, and other cities. It gained former Radicals in rural areas but failed to recruit youth and women as successfully as did the Communists and the MRP.

Léon Blum remained its greatest figure, honored for his successful defiance of the Vichy judges at Riom in 1941. There he and Daladier had turned what was to have been a show trial of the Third Republic's leaders into an indictment of the military (including Pétain) and he had eloquently defended the social democracy of the Popular Front. But even his prestige as the "first Resister of the Occupation," as a Jew who had purposely stayed behind while others fled, and as a prisoner of the Germans, was not enough to overcome the doctrinal and tactical quarrels of the SFIO. His plan for a reformist labor party of the non-Communist Left, including Catholics and the CFTC, was opposed by Marxist and anti-clerical militants still numerous enough to imprison party congresses in outworn slogans and in vain attempts to outbid the Communists for the industrial worker's vote. Reluctant to oppose the Communists, but afraid of anything like a merger, the Socialists produced only compromises between "Marxists" led by Guy Mollet and moderates around Blum, Vincent Auriol, and Daniel Mayer, between party theorists or recent recruits and trade-union veterans who knew Communist tactics from hard experience. The parliamentary delegation was also divided according to the nature of the Deputies' constituencies. Given these quarrels, it was to be expected that the hoary battle cry of anti-clericalism would be revived in late 1944, to defeat a party resolution that would have ignored the question of state aid to church schools—granted under Vichy—and that the SFIO would all but close the door to cooperation with the Leftist social wing of the MRP, with which most Socialists agreed on larger issues.

The MRP was also weakened by factions despite the efforts of parliamentary leaders like Georges Bidault to pretend that such did not exist. Even under the occupation it was clear that some Catholic democrats placed political, economic, and social reform before Catholic unity and that others turned the priority about. In the elections of October, 1945, the MRP vote was swollen by conservatives and ex-Vichyites temporarily without parties of their own, who thought the MRP a bulwark against Communism. Thus the small core of Catholic social democrats who were the heirs of Lamennais, Péguy, or Marc Sangnier's *Sillon* were outnumbered by conservatives and opportunists. And all was complicated by the desire of many MRP leaders to stand as de Gaulle's men despite the General's own desire to stay "above parties." Although the MRP Left, associated with the Catholic trade unions of the CFTC, wanted to work with the Socialists, it was suspicious of Marxist and anti-clerical rhetoric, however empty or ceremonial. In this situation, the Communists could disconcert both rival parties simply by eliciting more such rhetoric from those Socialists who prided themselves on having "no enemies to the Left."

## THE CONSTITUTION

The Constituent Assembly, ruled by the three parties, faced two tasks: to write a constitution for the Fourth Republic and to finish the work of the Resistance Charter already begun by de Gaulle and his Consultative Assembly. Much had been done by November 6, 1945, when the Constituent Assembly first met at the Palais Bourbon. Transport and communications were restored, the worst war damage to mines and industry was swept aside and rebuilding begun. All parties had approved a new Commission on Modernization and Renovation headed by Jean Monnet, whose task it was to prepare a heavy investment program in consultation with industrialists, labor leaders, economists, engineers, and technicians. No longer was France to rely on the moods of private investors, which had served her so badly in the past. Another of France's economic weaknesses had been her scant and costly energy sources; expansion of hydroelectric power was begun, and in October of 1945, Frédéric Joliot-Curie headed a Commission on Atomic Energy. To the same end the outmoded coal mines of the north were nationalized. More obviously political was the nationalization of certain aviation plants and of the Renault automobile company, whose chief, Louis Renault, was accused of collaboration. All this, with the spectacular trials of Vichy politicians and journalists, the last battles of the war, the endless public discussions, ceremonies, theatricals, and concerts (of Jewish works, especially), and the private joys of home and family, had prolonged the Liberation mood for a time.

French optimism was waning in late 1945, as a second winter of low fuel, crumbling housing, and shortages of every kind loomed. Had Frenchmen expected all to suffer hardship in rough equality, disillusion might have been put off. But most could verify what Resistance newspapers like *Combat* were saying, that a new class of bourgeois had grown wealthy on collaboration and the black market, and was still feeding on the misery of others. Returning prisoners of war were struck by plump and brassy prosperity amid mass deprivation. Rationing, price and wage controls decreed austerity—for all but the monied, who bought whatever they pleased on a black market so immense that it may have captured a third of the national income in 1945, all of it untaxed. De Gaulle's Minister of the National Economy, Pierre Mendès-France, had begged in 1944 and early 1945 for a concerted attack on the black market, to halt inflation and to restore government finance: the freezing of bank accounts, an exchange of the entire currency issue, general austerity, a census of property, and the confiscation of illicit profits. De Gaulle was preoccupied with foreign affairs, knew and cared little for economic matters, and failed to support Mendès-France against a host of enemies: the Bank of France, much of the business community, the farmers, who had accumulated currency under the occupation (and whose reactions the other Ministers professed to fear), and the Communists, concerned for their own secret funds and eager to court the peasantry and shopkeepers. Mendès-France resigned in April, 1945. Inflation went unchecked, ruining the French export trade, draining the treasury, encouraging speculation rather than investment or production, and catching up the worker in a spiral of price and wage increases, with prices ever out of reach. For those on fixed incomes, life had been easier under the Germans than in the first two years of the Fourth Republic. Later Ministers resorted to palliatives and concessions to all sides, which only canceled each other out; inflation hampered economic recovery until 1949, long after the dreams of Liberation had faded.

By late 1945, the trials of wartime offenders were also in bad odor. As in the Allied denazification program in Germany, the small and poor were tried early, and drew heavier penalties than those who could afford to have their trials postponed. Economic collaborators and profiteers escaped, while politicians, teachers, minor bureaucrats, and journalists were pilloried. Scandals linking Fourth Republic politicians and officials with the black market also erupted in late 1945 and 1946, suggesting why government "assaults" on illicit traffic so often netted innocent purchasers or minor go-betweens rather than the great sharks whose names were public knowledge. It appeared that the Fourth Republic was already at Thermidor, with its constitution not yet written.

The Constituent Assembly began its work in November of 1945 by unanimously electing de Gaulle President-Premier of the Provisional Republic. Unanimity lay only on the surface. The three major parties had campaigned on constitutional platforms asking different degrees of parliamentary supremacy. The Communists demanded a single chamber with unlimited power over an executive supervised by the chamber's committees; the Socialists, a single chamber dissolvable only by itself, on the occasion of its overthrowing the Premier and his cabinet; the MRP, a bicameral legislature resembling the Third Republic's but with a weaker Senate and a stronger Premier who, with the President, could dissolve the Chamber. De Gaulle clearly preferred a strong executive power residing in the President or President-Premier, and hoped that his own vigorous leadership of the Provisional Republic would show the virtue of such a system. Instead, de Gaulle was a prisoner of his office. The interim arrangement did not define his powers, and attempts to assert himself only aroused the parties, already resentful of his authoritarian manner. He had no choice but to parcel out cabinet posts equally among them, though he refused the Communists' demand for one of the crucial Ministries of Defense, Interior, or Foreign Affairs. Lacking direct authority, he used repeated threats of resignation to press the Assembly and cabinet. In January of 1946, his hope of a Socialist-MRP coalition broke upon the Socialists' decision to support the Communists on the constitutional draft and upon their attempts to cut his military budget. On January 20th, de Gaulle abruptly resigned in exasperation.

Having considered and rejected a *coup d'état,* he also gave up a radio appeal to the nation against the party regime and for his own idea of a strong executive. Instead he left behind only a letter justifying his retirement on the patently absurd ground that France had now solved her most serious problems. De Gaulle probably expected that the parties would demonstrate their inability to govern, that French problems could only grow worse, that fear of Communism at home and the incipient Russo-American clash would force his recall to power on his own terms. But many Frenchmen, including admirers of his constitutional ideas, thought him a deserter who failed either to warn the nation of its troubles or to offer his solution for them. De Gaulle's action blighted whatever hopes remained that the resisters of all factions who had joined to oppose Nazism and Vichy could agree on what kind of France they wished to build. From the symbol of French unity, de Gaulle lowered himself to that partisan role he had so often denounced. Although his conservatism was more personal and constitutional than economic or social, his quarrels with and defiance of a Leftist Assembly made him, willy-nilly, the rallying point for a new Right, including men of Vichy, opposing most of the reforms promised in the Resistance Charter.

The three parties compromised on Félix Gouin, a veteran Socialist and President of the Constituent Assembly, as de Gaulle's successor. The Assembly's draft constitution was offered to the voters in the referendum of May 5, 1946. A Communist-Socialist compromise, it provided a single chamber electing and dominating the Premier and cabinet, with a figurehead President of the Republic, all faithful to the Left's tradition of unchecked popular sovereignty. The Right, the Radicals, and the MRP campaigned against it as vulnerable to Communist control and ultimate dictatorship. The Communists mistakenly assumed victory (no referendum question in French history had been negatively answered) and played into the MRP's hands by clamoring for Thorez to succeed Gouin. The Socialist vote was split and the constitution rejected; 10,585,-

ooo voted No, 9,454,000 Yes, and some 5 million did not vote. The elections to the second Constituent Assembly in early June saw the MRP, widely considered to be de Gaulle's party, supplant the Communists as the largest delegation, with 160 seats from 5,590,000 voters, 800,000 more than in October, 1945. Accordingly Georges Bidault replaced Gouin as head of another tripartite cabinet. The Communists won 146 seats from 5,200,000 votes; the divided Socialists slipped from 132 to 115 seats, from 4,560,000 votes to 4,180,000. The Radicals and various Rightist parties held steady, the former winning 39 seats, the latter 62.

The second constitutional draft was a three-way compromise, with the chastened Socialists accepting some of the MRP's demands for limits on the chamber's powers: a second house, the Council of the Republic; a return of the President's power to name the Premier. The Communists accepted the draft after de Gaulle's return to politics. In June at Bayeux he proposed a semi-presidential system of government under which the President, chosen by an electoral college of elected local officials, selected the Premier, who was responsible to a parliament in its turn dissolvable by the President in case of dispute. The MRP was sharply divided between those who agreed with de Gaulle or feared to lose votes by opposing him, and those, led by Georges Bidault, who urged a Center Left coalition with the Socialists. In the end the MRP held to the tripartite draft, but in return Bidault forced the other parties to tighter controls over the colonies.

The first constitutional draft had set up the French Union on a vaguely generous basis, with membership on "free consent," with elective territorial assemblies, considerable local autonomy, the right to elect representatives to the unicameral French parliament and to an advisory Council of the French Union. The Gaullists, conservatives, MRP and Radical leaders, French nationalists, and colonists had attacked it as giving up the empire. Bidault's provisions returned all effective power to Paris, eliminated "free consent," specified that natives would be citizens of the Union rather than citizens of France, and imposed federalism from the top through an Assembly of the French Union, half of whose members represented metropolitan France. Rather than risk a crisis or prolong political uncertainty in the face of de Gaulle's challenge, the Socialists and Communists agreed. And in spite of de Gaulle's outspoken opposition and the equivocal attitude of some MRP leaders toward the new constitution, the voters accepted it in October, 9,279,000 for, 8,165,000 against. That another 9 million failed to vote at all no doubt reflected apathy and confusion as much as hostility, but de Gaulle and the Right could claim that nearly two-thirds of the electorate had refused the constitution of the Fourth Republic.

After six years of turmoil, Frenchmen had returned in nearly all but name to the political system of prewar days. The Council of the Republic, indirectly elected, had less of the old Senate's power; it could not overthrow a cabinet and could delay for only two months a law passed by the National Assembly. The Assembly's power to overturn cabinets was somewhat limited on paper; a one-day delay was imposed before final overthrow, which had to be voted by absolute majority. Immune from dissolution for its first eighteen months, the Assembly was liable to dissolution thereafter if it overthrew two cabinets within any subsequent eighteen-month period. But in practice the life of cabinets was as short under the Fourth as under the Third Republic; they were not overthrown but simply withdrew in the face of hostile majorities, avoiding a formal vote of no confidence or motion of censure. The President of the Republic, who was elected, as before, by the two houses for a seven-year term, designated the candidate for Premier (called President of the Council of Ministers), who then had to be approved by an absolute majority of the Assembly before taking office. The constitution removed the senatorial check on the Assembly, which was elected by a system of party lists and proportional representation according to the electoral laws of 1945 and 1946. In theory the popular will was untrammeled. Proportional representation, the example and challenge of the Communists, and the assumed lessons of French political history since Gambetta, all worked for greater party cohesion. But France was not Great Britain, and the constitution's workability depended no less than had the Third Republic's on several parties combining to act on urgent issues as they arose.

## TRIPARTITE REFORMS

The election of the Fourth Republic's first five-year Assembly in November, 1946, again returned an overwhelming majority for the three parties. Although the Socialists again lost ground, with 90 seats from 3,430,000 votes, they remained the key party, indispensable to the Communists on their left, with 166 seats and 5,490,000 votes, and the MRP on their right, with 158 seats and 5,050,000 votes. The Radicals had formed the *Rassemblement des Gauches Républicaines* (RGR) with the *Union Démocratique et Socialiste de la Résistance* (UDSR), the remnant of a Resistance party of moderates and mavericks; the RGR and its allies seated 60 deputies, and the Right seated 70. First Thorez and then Bidault failed to win approval as Premier; the post went to Léon Blum, as caretaker until January, 1947, when the President of the Republic would be elected. Quarrels between the Communists and the MRP blocked a tripartite cabinet and Blum was allowed to staff it entirely with Socialists for the one-month interim. In January, the veteran Socialist Vincent Auriol became President of the Republic and named a moderate fellow Socialist, Paul Ramadier, as Premier. The new cabinet modified the tripartite formula; Thorez, Gouin, and the MRP's Teitgen were joined by the old Radical Yvon Delbos as Vice-Premiers and the other Ministries were divided among the three leading parties, the Radicals, and the UDSR.

The coalition lasted only until May, 1947, when the Communists were expelled from the Ramadier government. The Resistance alliance, barely maintained since Liberation, was dead; but its accomplishments and failures in those three years largely determined the character of the Fourth Republic until its own death in 1958. The first Constituent Assembly had completed the work begun by the Consultative on an all-inclusive social security system. Health, maternity, and old-age benefits were sharply increased under a system in which, as in the nationalized industries, the CGT exercised wide administrative powers. Family allowances were also raised, so that they made up a significant part of a married worker's earnings. In April, 1946, a law required all enterprises employing more than 10 to recognize shop stewards elected by the workers to negotiate on grievances. In February, 1945, and May, 1946, laws established workers' councils (*comité d'entreprise*) in all factories employing 50 or more. These dealt with social matters, working conditions, welfare, mutual assistance, training, and housing; in theory they were also to share in management but in practice most did not. Militant Communist domination made some councils suspect to employers and non-Communist workers; other employers successfully ignored the councils; in either case the experiment was denied a fair trial. Workers trained and willing to take part were scarce and the councils had no voice on wages, which were, naturally, left to the trade unions. Only where workers' training programs were arranged and some satisfactory plant experience ensued—most often where the traditionally "associationist"

CFTC held sway—did the workers' councils begin to fulfill their purpose.

More spectacular were the nationalizations of key industries, which had formed part of the CGT's program in 1919, and again in 1934–1936. After de Gaulle's resignation in January, 1946, the first Constituent Assembly had nationalized the remaining coal mines, gas and electricity, the largest insurance companies and deposit banks, and the Bank of France. Later governments added the Métro and buses of Paris, Air France, the French Line, and other shipping. Together with the railways, united in 1937 under the *Société Nationale des Chemins de Fer* (SNCF), and the arms and aircraft industries nationalized by the Popular Front, the national enterprises and civil service employed nearly a quarter of all non-agricultural workers in France. They were managed by public corporations with representatives of government, consumers, and employees of various ranks. Most were vital to the national economic renovation planned by the Monnet Commission, and their own renovation required huge outlays by the State, in sums hardly to be expected from private ownership. The State's decision to keep transport, coal, gas, and electricity prices below cost, to spur other enterprises, and to lower living expenses, added large deficits. Political interference was troublesome at first; coal mining and aircraft production suffered from Communist and CGT control, and then, after the strikes of 1948, from a too-rigorous purge of Communists from all positions.

Although their job security and fringe benefits were generally better than in private industry and commerce, government employees and their unions were little more satisfied. The rivalries of tripartism were partly responsible. Each of the major parties regarded the national enterprises and the related Ministries as strong points to be conquered and defended from their rivals, often without regard to employees, to wider economic problems, or to the future of the enterprises themselves. Worse, the failure to stop inflation undermined wages, and made production or renovation costs nearly prohibitive, so that even less than in England was nationalization tried at a favorable moment. Nevertheless, the 1950's found French national industries operating successfully—conspicuously so in the case of electricity, gas, and the French railroads, the envy of American travelers.

The nationalization program was not so extensive as implied in the Charter, but others of the Charter's promises were hardly fulfilled at all. The MRP, less enthusiastic than the Communists and Socialists over economic revolution, cherished a number of reforms to purify political life. The venal press of the Third Republic was discredited; to prevent its return, the MRP and Socialists favored a law requiring publication of each paper's source of income, including foreign funds. The Communists blocked it. The MRP also proposed publication of all campaign income and expenses, and state support of equal campaign publicity. Again the affluent Communists were opposed, as were the Deputies of parties expecting business subsidies. Later American support of Socialist and MRP newspapers and campaigns buried the issue. More hopeful were efforts at educational reforms. The old, expensive École Libre des Sciences Politiques was nationalized and enlarged; a new École Nationale d'Administration was opened to train high-level civil servants. But the social backgrounds of students in higher education changed very slowly. Greater social mobility and the democratization of the bureaucracy, judicial system, and diplomatic corps awaited a decisive change in petty bourgeois, farmer, and working-class income, better primary and more secondary schools, and a broad expansion of the French economy to create new jobs at all levels of private and public employ. Here, as with most of the Resistance Charter's promises, everything depended on economic recovery and the continuing unity of the Left. The former was to be delayed, the latter lost.

The repeal of Vichy's labor laws and the revival of trade unions did not at first include collective bargaining, since in the postwar economic crisis the government kept control of wages. As long as the Communists remained in cabinets whose economic policies they could hope to direct, they and the CGT preached patience, discipline, and self-sacrifice to the workers. Thorez proclaimed the "battle for production" and supported the Monnet Plan for capital investment before consumer goods. Through the end of 1946 almost no strikes occurred; by then coal production surpassed that of 1938, as did rail traffic, and production in general had nearly tripled since the end of 1944 (from 32 to 88 per cent of the 1938 level). But inflation drained real wages; workers spent between one-half and two-thirds of their income on family diets that were barely sufficient and always drab. For the single month that Blum was Premier, he froze wages and prices. Most prices held steady and some declined, but succeeding governments did little to hinder the black market, or to insure food supplies for the official market whose prices were controlled. By early 1947, it was clear that the workers' efforts to raise production were not being rewarded; real wages were lower than in 1946. Revolts against the CGT broke out in several industries and Thorez' "Stakhanovism" was denounced by labor militants. In April, 1947, a wildcat strike stopped the large Renault plant; the Communists tried to break the strike and expel its leaders but they failed. Rather than risk their control of labor, the Communist Deputies then voted against Ramadier's continuance of the wage freeze and he dismissed their Ministers from his cabinet in May.

## SCHISM AND THE "THIRD FORCE"

All sides had long expected the break. The party's failure to take power peacefully and its inability to wrest it from the Socialist-MRP alliance which held the premiership, the presidency, the police and armed forces, left it with no alternative to resignation except to help administer, and to be considered responsible for, a system detested by its rank and file. To lose control of the CGT would have been to lose its seats on factory councils and social security boards and its offices in nationalized industries, to abandon the positions of strength on which any later coup would have to be based. Foreign events also were breaking up the wartime alliance. The Communists in eastern Europe were smothering the non-Communist Left and taking total control; Churchill had given the Iron Curtain its name in March of 1946. One year later Truman responded to pressure on Greece and Turkey by promising American aid to peoples resisting Communism. France needed American money and food, as well as American support for a greater share of German coal. In April of 1947 at Moscow, Bidault failed to win Soviet backing of France's demand for the Saar; his and de Gaulle's policy of subjecting Germany by mediation between East and West broke upon Soviet-American quarrels over Germany, Austria, and eastern Europe. At home the Communist party was ready to denounce the government's policy in Indo-China, where it had blundered into war while Blum and his all-Socialist cabinet fretted over economic and financial disorder. The MRP and Socialists had hoped for some time that Thorez would leave the cabinet—as the Belgian and Italian Communists already had done. And many who neither hated nor feared the Communists regretfully decided that the Cold War made a choice unavoidable.

On several grounds, it was time to choose the West—and American aid. But choosing the West abroad meant turning to the Center and Right parties for support in the Assembly at home, parties wanting an end, perhaps a reversal, of economic and social reforms. It was all a very old story, worsened by the feeling that Frenchmen had finally found a rough consensus on the moderate Left only to be pulled apart again from the outside, by the totalitarian drive of world Communism on the one hand and the fears and ambitions of world capitalism, led by the United States, on the other. The dilemma of the non-Communist Left was particularly cruel, and as old as the Resistance, the Popular Front, or the Russian Revolution. Given the balance of forces in France, Communist cooperation was needed for economic and social change, but the Communists offered not cooperation but conquest. Socialists, unionists, and Left Catholics had suffered Communist assaults since the First World War, had seen the Communists seize and exploit every advantage offered by the Resistance and tripartite governments, only to block fiscal, economic, and political reforms for partisan advantage, and for favor in the most backward economic regions and classes. They believed that Communist action perverted and discredited social experiments and pushed the undecided into the arms of reactionaries, and so chose to risk a defensive, Republican alliance with the MRP, the Radicals, and even Right moderates—at least until conditions should allow a resumption of forward movement.

Others, a smaller number, refused to admit the need for a halt and, under such labels as *Progressiste* (as in America, there was a Progressive party, led by the Popular Front Radical Pierre Cot), declared themselves with—or, more often, not against—the Communists at home or abroad. Most assumed, on solid historical grounds, that a governmental alliance with the Center and Center Right meant the final abandonment of the "revolution by law," that French capitalism, sustained by American aid, would nullify the gains achieved since 1944 and carry out an economic and social "counterrevolution by law." Some refused to believe that French Communists would, or could, sovietize France or that Soviet Russia desired to subjugate western Europe. Some who did believe both were eager (or resigned) to make the best of a Communist society. Still others saw it as the lesser of two evils, as a painful but necessary step toward a better world far in the future.

Events in the spring and summer of 1947 widened the schism in France and in the world. A frigid winter had exhausted coal supplies and killed the winter wheat; bread rations were down, the black market up; France's exports were anemic, her dollar holdings nearly gone. In June at Harvard Yard the American Secretary of State offered massive aid for a cooperative European plan for economic recovery. Bidault and the British Foreign Secretary Bevin immediately welcomed the idea. In July at Paris, Molotov refused the Marshall Plan—and speeded its passage by the United States Congress. In September the Cominform was organized to coordinate the world's Communist parties. At home, strikes for higher pay and food rations, combined with a business campaign against price controls, forced Ramadier in July to relax the anti-inflation program. The Socialists and MRP Left had hoped that American help would allow them to complete the Resistance program of economic reform without the Communists. But by the summer and autumn of 1947, it had become all but impossible to find support in the parties to their right for further structural change and the much-abused planned economy (*dirigisme*), which had not, in fact, been tried.

In mid-April, before the Communist departure, Charles de Gaulle had called for a *Rassemblement du Peuple Français* (RPF), above parties, to which all Frenchmen who "placed France's needs over partisanship" should rally, to promote a revision of the constitution in favor of executive authority. The Socialist and MRP leaders forbade their partisans to join the RPF, which they denounced as a danger to the Republic. But the Radicals, the UDSR, the peasant and independent groups, and the conservative PRL (*Parti Républicain de la Liberté*) left their members and Deputies free to join or not. After dropping the Communists, the Socialist-MRP coalition had to compete against de Gaulle's RPF for the support of enough Radicals and moderates to hold a majority. In August an RPF "intergroup" was organized in the Assembly and joined by much of the Right and Right Center, many Radicals, and even some rebel MRP Deputies. In October, the RPF led a similar coalition to overwhelming victory in the municipal elections, capturing 40 per cent of the vote. The MRP suffered a mass desertion to the RPF, winning only 9 per cent, against its 26 per cent of only a year before. Whatever the causes of defeat, the MRP leadership—as opposed to its Left and CFTC clientele—now took a more conservative stance in economic, social, and colonial affairs. De Gaulle demanded the dissolution of an Assembly "the nation no longer supported," but on the Republican system the MRP refused to give way; their alliance with the Socialists in opposition to Gaullism and Communism held firm.

The two parties made up the core of what Léon Blum called a "Third

Force," destined to govern France for the remaining years of the Fourth Republic. Robert Schuman of the MRP became Premier in late November of 1947, his party having replaced the Socialists as the pivot of governmental coalitions. The MRP was a third force within the Third Force; on economic and social issues it stood between the Socialists on its left and the Radicals and moderates on its right (although the Radicals sat to its left in the Assembly on the excuse of anti-clericalism). Schuman's cabinet stretched from the Socialist Daniel Mayer as Minister of Labor to the conservative Radical René Mayer as, appropriately, Minister of Finance and Economic Affairs. The latter's appointment was a sign that economic innovation was at an end, but the man who had to prove it to labor and the Communists was the Socialist Minister of the Interior, Jules Moch.

That the Communists led the hundreds of strikes which nearly paralyzed the French economy in late 1947 and turned them to political ends is undeniable, but they were not as much responsible for their origins or amplitude as was labor's economic distress and the death of its hopes. Another bad harvest sent food prices upward again, more than canceling the wage rises of May and August; the bread ration was lower (200 grams) than during the war. But all the while, production and profits rose and the prosperous flaunted their American limousines. Nearly 2 million workers walked out (or stayed in) during November. A man died in a Communist-Gaullist fight in Marseilles; violence and sabotage broke out in several industries; 23 died in the derailment of the Paris-Tourcoing express; non-Communist workers were forcibly kept from their jobs in the Nord. Communist-led columns marched in several places to seize prefectures, town halls, rail and power stations, and other strategic points. Moch feared for a moment that his security forces, even if augumented by troops, could hold only the largest cities and ports. He and Schuman apparently were ready to bring de Gaulle into the government should the insurrectionary strikes persist. But the Communists never employed the scale of violence they were capable of, and when they failed to cut off power and transportation in Paris, masses of workers pressed for an end to the strikes. The government's grant of a general pay increase helped the CGT's national committee to order a return to work. The aftermath critically weakened French labor; the wage rise was soon overtaken by prices and the CGT's membership drained away. In December, Léon Jouhaux led a minority of reformists into a splinter group, the CGT-FO (*Force Ouvrière*), but even with

Socialist (and later, American) support, the FO failed to attract a large working-class following. As in 1919 and 1938, CGT defectors simply joined the unorganized majority of French workers.

## IMMOBILITY

Communist and Gaullist attacks only stiffened the Third Force. Socialist, Radical, and MRP leaders formed a coordinating committee in January of 1948, but the parties were too much divided in their economic, financial, and religious views to do more than defend the *status quo*. The 5 million constituents of the Communist party henceforth counted for little in the political balance of a Republic which was ready enough to resist the party's demands, but unable or unwilling to attack the conditions underlying the party's strength. Mayer's program of 1948 was designed to end inflation by increasing production and exports, raising taxes, and cutting government spending. Income taxes were raised and the franc devalued to encourage exports and the tourist trade; the civil service was cut (many Communists lost their posts), as were subsidies to nationalized industries, made up in part by higher prices. A minor gesture against hoarders and black-market magnates was the recall of all 5000-franc notes, supposedly their favorite denomination; but more innocent Frenchmen were inconvenienced than culprits caught, and Mayer granted a partial amnesty to holders of gold and foreign securities, in order "to restore investor confidence." The black market, said the Left, was being made respectable.

Mayer's policies succeeded only in disturbing all factions; the inflationary spiral continued. In July Schuman's cabinet fell and was replaced by one based well to its right, with the conservative Radical André Marie as Premier. The 1930's seemed to have come again, for Schuman was overthrown by a Socialist vote for arms cuts and against dismissals from the civil service, only to have none other than Paul Reynaud become Finance Minister. As in earlier days, Reynaud's demands for thoroughgoing economic liberalism, for the curtailment of nationalized industries and social services were only half-accepted and Marie's cabinet fell in a month. A second Schuman cabinet failed of approval, prices were soaring, rationing was breaking down, and several strikes erupted. De Gaulle was saying that he would soon be called back to power. But then an old-time Radical, Henri Queuille, succeeded against all expectations in organizing a government that lasted over a year, from September, 1948, to October of 1949.

Queuille's success, proof of the Radicals' striking comeback, proceeded from a policy as typical of the prewar Radicals as of the postwar Third Force in general: to do as little as possible in any matter that divided the fragile coalition. Queuille was at first his own Finance Minister; Robert Schuman retained the Foreign Ministry; the Socialists Lacoste, Ramadier, and Moch were the Industry, Defense, and Interior Ministers respectively. By agreeing to postpone local elections, in which the Socialists and the MRP feared another Gaullist sweep, and to revise the method of electing the Council of the Republic (also in such a way as to handicap the Communists and Gaullists), Queuille won approval for a conservative financial and economic program. The Gaullist advance was stalled. But in early October the Communists launched their second great strike wave, again sustained by wage and price grievances, and by numerous dismissals of workers and officials from the national industries, particularly the coal mines. Again the unions of the CFTC and *Force Ouvrière* refused participation or followed reluctantly, as the CGT leader, Benoît Frachon, called for disruption of the Marshall Plan. Dockers, railwaymen, and seamen were ordered to block the delivery of goods from America. Strikers fought police and troops at several points; and in the mining areas of the north, there was near civil war when security forces entered the mines to prevent flooding and sabotage. The CGT's withdrawal of safety and maintenance workers was unprecedented—they had stayed even under the German occupation—and, together with its attacks on American aid, no doubt cost it popular support, as did Moscow's clear intent to wreck French (and European) economic recovery. The strikes ended in late November, with the labor movement still more weakened and divided. Together with the earlier Communist coup in Prague, the CGT's attack on the French economy completed the isolation of the Communist Left.

Although 1949 was a year of industrial peace, price stability and business confidence, French problems of production, trade, and dollar balances, housing and investment, budget deficits and tax evasion remained. It was doubtless true, as M. Reynaud said, that France was producing too little and consuming too much, but no consensus on a remedy could be found among the parties of the Third Force. To balance the budget implied collecting taxes from businessmen and farmers, or cutting social services, the bureaucracy, subsidies to the nationalized industries, and the government's crucial investment program. To increase exports implied lowering prices on French goods, by cutting labor costs or cutting profits, by an expensive program of modernization requiring heavy investment, or by devaluing the franc once more. In fact, something of each policy was adopted in turn, to the extent that the party whose constituents were offended could be persuaded to accept it in return for concession elsewhere. As the burden of both indirect and income taxes fell heaviest on the lower classes, whose major party could be ignored in the Assembly's game of coalitions, it was they who could most easily be made to produce more and consume less. Rationing by the pocketbook hit the proletariat and artisans, the white-collar workers in commerce and government, as well as all retired persons, widows, and pensioners. Given the ruling parties' failure to redistribute the rewards of production, hope for betterment lay only in increased production for home and foreign markets, under a stable currency and price level.

It was here that the Fourth Republic, with the help of American aid, improved upon the Third. The social legislation of the tripartite era provided at least a minimum of social security until the Monnet Plan and similar efforts to produce new wealth could offer rewards to all without unduly disturbing any vested interest in the ruling coalition. In this sense, the social and political *immobilisme* of the Third Force did not bar the way to progress as long as it was also able to maintain a high rate of investment and production. This was far from the ideal of the Resistance Charter, but it opened better prospects for the long run than the interwar period had seen.

## FOREIGN THREATS AND NEUTRALISM

The nemesis of the Fourth Republic, as of the Third, was war. Bidault succeeded Queuille in October of 1949 and lasted until June of 1950. By then French industrial production had passed the level of 1938, prices were stable, consumption was higher, and France's balance of payments was improving. But convalescence was slowed by the rising cost of war in Indo-China, and the outbreak of the Korean War in June of 1950 set off a new inflationary spiral world-wide in effect. The American demand for quick European rearmament, and then the rearmament of Germany, brought the Cold War forcibly into French political life, seriously delayed French economic recovery, and opened a series of debates over French foreign and colonial policy that divided the Fourth Republic until its death.

Together with other dreams of the Resistance, that of permanent controls over Germany had already fled. The three major occupying powers rejected from the start French demands for the separation of the Ruhr and the Rhineland, and for complete decentralization of Germany. Next the Russian demand for four-power control had ruined any chance of internationalization of Ruhr industry. The Anglo-American eagerness to rebuild West Germany as a bulwark against Soviet power in Europe had then defeated French attempts to postpone a centralized West German government. By 1948 the best hope of French security from Germany appeared to be European union, which also attracted Frenchmen of all parties who dreamed of building a Third Force in the world, to hold apart the American and Russian powers and recapture a measure of European independence. The Communist coup in Prague of February, 1948, was followed by the Brussels Treaty of March, in which France, Great Britain, Belgium, the Netherlands, and Luxembourg pledged each other military aid and closer economic and political ties. Although Churchill, many prominent Englishmen, and the Labour Party then in power had earlier called for European unity, the British refused to integrate in any but military affairs. Thus the main role of the Western European Union conceived at Brussels was as military predecessor and later as part of the North Atlantic Treaty Organization. The NATO pact was signed in Washington in April of 1949 and ratified by the French Assembly in July—after Foreign Minister Schuman assured it that Germany would never be allowed to rearm or to become a member.

French leaders were nonetheless eager to enmesh Germany in political and economic arrangements within a European community led from Paris. In early 1950, Germany was admitted to the Consultative Assembly of the Council of Europe at Strasbourg, set up in 1949 by the Brussels powers and ultimately including most European states. Since the Council had nothing to do with military affairs and was less a parliament than a permanent meeting of representatives of member governments, Germany's admission was neither dangerous nor very significant. It was a polite accompaniment to the separate admission of the Saar, which France hoped would remain autonomous, with economic ties to herself. The next step was the Schuman Plan, advanced by the French

Foreign Minister in early 1950 for the pooling of European coal and steel production under a supranational authority. Frenchmen hoped it would contain rising German competition within a partial economic union and, in Schuman's words, make war between France and Germany "materially impossible." Negotiations among "the Six"—West Germany, Italy, France, and the Benelux countries—began in Paris in June of 1950. Only in August, 1952, was the High Authority, comprised of several extremely complex committees and councils, finally established at Strasbourg.

In the meantime, the reverberations of the Korean War had upset European recovery and endangered the "European idea" by suddenly associating it with German rearmament barely six years after Liberation. The hurried American call for general rearmament and the substitution of military for economic aid was unpopular, but the demand for a German army raised a storm of French protest. For the sake of a few German divisions which could not possibly be ready in time to affect the current crisis, the Truman-Acheson administration seemed ready to invite Soviet retaliation, to throw eastern Europeans into Moscow's arms, to scuttle European union by offering Germans a quicker way to equality, and to endanger German democracy by reviving the same militarism which the Allies had labored so righteously to extirpate since 1945. Hitler would be proved right; the menace lay to the east and any means must be employed to counter it. Either Washington was still in shock over Korea—or it meant to create a German army large enough to merit such risks. In October of 1950, Premier René Pleven tried to satisfy Frenchmen and placate Americans by proposing a European army including small units of Germans to be integrated under a European political authority. The Pleven Plan was designed to prevent any German rearmament until Europe's political unity was achieved, with Britain as a counterweight to Germany—even though the Labour government was refusing even to join the Schuman Plan or to approve British participation in the European army. At home, the Pleven government lengthened military service from twelve to eighteen months and passed a military budget of 740 billion francs late in 1950. The casualty lists from Indo-China were growing longer; instead of the easy pacification the public had been led to expect, France was now engaged in a major conflict.

The events of the early 1950's deepened the mood of pessimism and disillusion that had settled over much of the Left, the Resistance press, and the intellectual, academic, and literary community since the mid-1940's. Not only were their dreams of Liberation blasted, but Cold War in the Atomic Age threatened human life itself. In this bleak Thermidor, the now conservative Fourth Republic, the American economic and military presence, the sleek prosperity of the minority amid the ill-fed, ill-clothed, and wretchedly housed majority were daily reminders of failure. Marshall Aid, which Americans were being told was a wholly unselfish act of charity, appeared to many Frenchmen as part subsidy to American exports, part reward to those prosperous Frenchmen who were most anti-Communist (and who had been least anti-Nazi during the war). Instead of forwarding the Resistance program of economic reform, it was allowing French business to escape it. What the western nations had done with their victory seemed obvious. What the Soviet Union had done was not, and many still judged it by its own word. In France, the Communist party did not share the onus of power; its own responsibility for the Republic's conservatism was not yet clear, nor was Moscow's for the Atlantic Pact, rearmament, and the revival of German power. The Communists were almost alone in denouncing the Indo-China war, the American "occupation" and "cultural imperialism" by automobile, Coca-Cola, and Hollywood films, in demanding liberation of colonial peoples, the outlawing of atomic weapons and of war itself.

For a moment at the very start of the Korean War, the American-United Nations response met wide approval. But as the dreaded Soviet move into Europe failed to come, the onus for world tensions fell back upon the United States, especially as Frenchmen, like most outside America, believed MacArthur's bellicosity responsible for the Chinese Communist march across the Yalu. From that moment, the war lost its aura of international resistance to aggression and assumed that of an American anti-Communist crusade, carried on over the dead bodies and charred villages of inferior peoples. In the early 1950's, America was pictured in most of the French press as engulfed by anti-Communist hysteria, her foreign policy frozen by McCarthyites and would-be wielders of the atom bomb. It was not difficult for the Communists to argue that only Soviet nuclear weapons were maintaining the balance of terror. In this atmosphere, the Communist peace offensive, based on the Stockholm petition and the Partisans of Peace, found a ready audience, and the movement called neutralism captured the non-Communist Left and many Frenchmen of all political persuasions.

Neutralism had many sources, ranging from French nationalism to pro-Communism, from abhorrence of spending for arms to militant pacifism, from distrust of American competence to virulent hatred of all America seemed to stand for. Its expression varied from the daily *Le Monde,* which called down a plague on both houses and grieved that the fate of mankind should now depend upon the vagaries of two adolescent giants, to the *progressiste* weekly *l'Observateur,* in which neutralism was often indistinguishable from the Communist party line. Since American forces were in France and France belonged to NATO, active neutralism was in any case bound to take an anti-American stance. But it did not usually involve, as its American critics claimed, a naïve trust in the intentions of the Soviet Union. Some adopted it because they expected a Soviet march westward and chose a Communist peace over nuclear war, which they assumed would wreak its worst destruction in western Europe. Others simply doubted that America would fight for Europe at all, despite her bluster, and instead would fight only from and for the "periphery" (Spain and the British Isles), or for the western hemisphere itself.

## DRIFT TO THE RIGHT

The general election of 1951 demonstrated that for most Frenchmen neutralism was only a nuance within older party allegiances. The few candidates who ran on neutralist platforms were left far behind by the regular party men. In an effort to reduce the effect of Communist and Gaullist voting strength, the Third Force revised the electoral law, designed in 1946 to favor large parties. The laws of May, 1951, favored instead the smaller parties of the Third Force, for alliances (*apparentements*) of parties were to be treated as single parties had been in 1946; an absolute majority gave an alliance all seats in the department, to be distributed according to each member party's share of votes. In the Paris region where Communists and Gaullists were strongest, a different system was employed. The tortuous new rigging of the laws evoked a good deal of public cynicism, and the results only partly met the hopes of the Third Force. Although *apparentement* was purely an electoral device and implied no common program in the parliament, the parties were too divided even to form negative alliances in all departments. The Socialists won 94 seats, or 17 per cent from 14 per cent of the vote; the

MRP 82, or 15 per cent from 12 per cent of the vote; the RGR (and "pure" Radical-Socialists who rejected the new label) 77, or 14 per cent from 10 per cent of the vote. The Communists remained the largest party, winning 26 per cent of the national vote (4.9 million) but elected only 97 Deputies, or 18 per cent of the Assembly. The RPF became the largest Assembly party, with 107 seats (19.5 per cent), from 4,125,000 votes (21.7 per cent).

The Third Force now needed the support of conservatives more than ever. Socialist, MRP, Radical, and RGR Deputies were 253 against a combined Communist-RPF opposition of 204. Thus the 87 Deputies elected by independents, peasants, the PRL, and other conservative factions could ease or block the formation of any cabinet. Overall, the election showed a swing to the Right in voter opinion. The combined Communist and Socialist vote was 30 per cent of all registered voters, down from nearly 36 per cent in 1946, while the MRP lost more than half its supporters. De Gaulle's RPF had receded from its astonishing vote in the municipal elections of 1947, and its relative success in 1951 was not so surprising as the revival of a Republican Center and Right, which had nearly disappeared in the first postwar elections. But for the massive Communist vote and the presence of de Gaulle's group, the Fourth Republic more and more resembled the Third; and since the Center parties simply excluded both extremes from the political round, the second Assembly of the Fourth Republic was in essence a Third Republic chamber with even less room to maneuver between Left and Right.

The most significant political change between the elections of 1951 and 1956 was the dissolution of the RPF. It had failed to repeat its triumph of 1947, perhaps in part because the Communist menace was reduced by 1951, and in part because neither de Gaulle nor his associates had announced any precise aims beyond increased executive authority by revision of the constitution. In 1951, the RPF appeared to be even more a party of the Right than it had seemed in 1947. Some of its militants engaged in demonstrations, processions, and brawls reminiscent of the old *Croix de Feu*; in 1949 de Gaulle himself softened his references to Pétain and Vichy, to the dismay of some Radical and MRP voters who had turned to the RPF in 1947. The success of M. Queuille and the clericalism of the RPF accelerated the Radicals' withdrawal from it, though a few, including Jacques Chaban-Delmas and Michel Debré, stayed behind. De Gaulle's pronouncements on economic and social issues recalled the early, ideal Vichy program of corporatism, hostile to labor unions and employers' associations as "politicized" and un-French; he denounced the parties as mere vehicles for political careers exploiting outworn issues, blocking the way to new men of talent, and devotion to wider interests. Once in the Palais Bourbon, the RPF Deputies at first refused to take seats on the right of the hemicycle; the other parties ultimately forced them to it. The attempt and its failure were symbolic. The Gaullists were too few either to dominate or disrupt the Assembly's work; since the majority of them were conservatives, it was as regular Rightist Deputies that they would be admitted to parliamentary life, not as members of a self-styled "rally above parties." During 1952 over 30 of them broke RPF discipline, then seceded altogether, to support the independent Premier Antoine Pinay's soberly conservative policies. An RPF "Left" of mainly urban Deputies also emerged, so the movement was split in three. In 1953, de Gaulle again withdrew from political life and his rally all but collapsed, leaving a small coterie of loyal followers to claim Gaullist orthodoxy in the Assembly.

The RPF, nourished by opposition and crisis, was undone by the movement of French governments toward a Republican Right after 1951 and the apparent stability of the regime. The Socialists refused to take offices but supported a Pleven cabinet organized after the elections. In September the RPF joined the MRP and the Center Right in voting the Barangé law, to rescue the impoverished Catholic schools by giving subsidies to parents of pupils. In essence this compromise of the church schools question—the last significant issue of the clerical struggle—has survived despite the efforts of intransigents on both sides to upset it. When the Socialists unsuccessfully opposed it and then overthrew Pleven in January of 1952, on the budget, the Gaullist leaders were confident of imposing their own terms on any cabinet, for no majority could be won without them. Instead the independent conservative Antoine Pinay built a majority without either the Socialists or the RPF by luring the latter's less disciplined Deputies to his support. Now the MRP was the most leftward government party on economic and social affairs, but it was shrunken and dispirited, to be torn (as the Socialists had been) between its militants and a parliamentary leadership willing to cooperate with conservatives on religious and colonial policies.

The defeat and disillusion of the Catholic Left were the worse for the great hopes it had raised. The second World War, even more than the first, had helped heal the French religious schism. The prominence of Catholics in the Resistance, the heroism of the clergy at home, in prisoner or forced labor camps in Germany, and the emergence of a lively Catholic Left at Liberation formed new bonds between Frenchmen who had hitherto regarded each other with suspicion. The Left wing of the MRP included leaders of the Catholic labor unions (CFTC) and of Catholic youth organizations, as well as members of the prewar *Jeune République,* a small democratic party which had supported the Popular Front. Among and to the left of these groups were the readers of such Catholic journals as Emmanuel Mounier's *Esprit* and the *Témoignage Chrétien,* founded in the Resistance. Both were neutralist, anti-colonialist, and, at times, *progressiste* in their politics. All these and thousands of younger priests had dreamed of a Christian social democracy.

Among the clergy there had also arisen, before and during the war, a missionary zeal to re-Christianize French society, particularly certain rural departments and the industrial working class. In 1942 Cardinal Suhard of Paris founded the *Mission de France* to furnish priests for dioceses that had too few, and, in 1944, the *Mission de Paris,* out of which developed the worker-priest movement. The ideal of these young priests, many recently ordained and of working-class origin, was to take Catholicism back to the factory, the mine, and the dock, not so much to convert workers long lost to the Church as simply to bear witness to the faith by sharing wholly the wretched lot of the worker and his family. They labored full time, ate, dressed, and lived as workers, and discussed in their evening meetings, open to any who came, the fundamentals of Christianity and its meaning in modern society. By 1952, several had grown close to, and some held offices in, the CGT and the Partisans of Peace. Their association with Communists and *progressistes* was inevitable, given the conditions and aspirations of the French proletariat, but it was unhappily brought to world attention in May of 1952 when two worker-priests taking part in an anti-American demonstration were arrested and beaten by the Paris police. In spite of their defense by Archbishop Feltin of Paris and the defense of the movement in general by the French hierarchy, the Vatican (which had long been suspicious) condemned the experiment in 1953, and so severely restricted the conditions of work (three hours a day) and life among the workers that the movement was all but abandoned. The worker-priests had nonetheless awakened great sympathy and a certain national, Gallican, pride. On the Left, their suppression was taken as part of the general

French and European reaction, another defeat of Resistance hopes. Several of the priests refused to submit, expecting that they would ultimately be justified, as Lamennais had been, by the Vatican's adoption of their ideas.

Fom March, 1952, to June, 1954, the governments of Antoine Pinay, René Mayer, and the conservative Joseph Laniel held to policies of social and economic conservatism in domestic affairs, of delay on German rearmament and the European Defense Community, and on colonialist war in Indo-China. Pinay's investiture was something of a scandal in itself, to those who still divided Vichy and the Resistance between black and white. The proprietor of a small-town tannery, Pinay had been chosen as one of Marshal Pétain's National Councilors in 1940. A small, dark, dapper man of eminently sensible mien, he symbolized for many the return to a prewar era of financial prudence, protection for the small entrepreneur, and general business confidence. By 1952, the inflation set off by the Korean War had run its course and a drop in world prices enabled Pinay to stabilize the franc. He nearly balanced the budget by an economic contraction worthy of the 1930's, reducing government investments, housing projects, and subsidies to public, though not to private, enterprises. To encourage confidence among the monied, Pinay's government granted a sweeping amnesty for tax frauds, avoided new taxes, and floated a loan guaranteeing investors a return tied to gold rather than to the franc. His one innovation was a sliding wage scale tied to the cost of living, passed in July, 1952. But so far above the actual cost of living was the "parity" line pegged that the Left opposed the law, the MRP and RPF were divided. Its supporters were on the Center and Right, conservatives and business interests, some of whom expected long-term price stability, others who were alarmed by signs of a recession and declining profits, and who wished to hold purchasing power within reach of prices they wanted to raise.

The press and spokesmen of the Left, Communists, Socialists, the urban MRP and RPF denounced the "betrayal of Liberation hopes," the "return of the money power," the "reaction of monopoly and the 200 families," but to little avail. Pinay's majority and, after him, Mayer's and Laniel's, were relatively solid. Divided labor had lost the leverage it had enjoyed in the mid-1940's. The reinstitution of collective bargaining in 1950 had been followed by a series of strikes that had failed to break the wage policy of employers, themselves more strongly organized in the CNPF (*Conseil National du Patronat Français*) than they had been before the war. In this they typified most pressure groups, which were far more numerous and better financed than in the Third Republic. Thus they partly offset the greater discipline of the political parties, which otherwise tended to protect the individual Deputy from outside pressure. Together with the CNPF, which subsidized newspapers and political campaigns, there was the confederation of small and medium businesses (CGPME, *Petites et Moyennes Entreprises*), with a clientele so numerous that all parties including the Communists were careful not to offend it openly. It successfully threatened shop closings and tax strikes to speed the end of rationing and price controls, to block new taxes as well as the collection of existing taxes. In agriculture, the CGA (*Confédération Générale de l'Agriculture*) contained within itself several powerful lobbies. The most notorious pressure group was that of the sugar beet growers, whose state subsidies and guaranteed prices encouraged overproduction of alcohol, a weight on the budget (which M. Pinay dared not remove), and an added menace to the nation's health. In an Assembly governed by coalitions delicately balanced, with few votes to spare, outside pressures could not be ignored. Even Pinay was overthrown upon his proposal to raise alcohol taxes.

The most egregious example of the Fourth Republic's congealment was housing. Dramatized to Frenchmen and the western world by the Abbé Pierre and his famous "ragpickers of Emmaus," the housing shortage undermined health, morals, and family life. Since rents had been more or less frozen since the 1920's, almost no new building was done except at government expense or at luxury prices. Government investment was barely able to restore housing damaged or destroyed during the war; France fell far behind much poorer countries in new housing, the more so as contractors and the building trade unions persisted in backward methods and complex regulation, making all construction slow and expensive. The scandal of bad housing weighed heaviest on students, on the working and lower middle classes, on the retired, and on the newly married, who saw no end to discomforts and frustrations they could escape only temporarily at the café, on the street, or in the park. Real wages might creep slowly upward, but only the well-to-do could afford the prices demanded by gouging subletters.

# DEFEAT IN INDO-CHINA

By 1954, Frenchmen of all factions despaired of the Republic's ability to make decisions in any sphere. Armament costs were soaring, the treasury was kept afloat only by manipulation of American aid, France's balance of payments in Europe and with the outside world remained unfavorable, the treaty for the European army still awaited ratification, nationalist tempers were rising in North Africa. Worst of all, the unpopular war in Indo-China was draining French blood and resources, giving no promise of successful conclusion, or of conclusion of any sort. Above the routine lamentations of press and Third Force politicians, three kinds of critics offered three kinds of solution. The Communists, their *progressiste* allies, and the neutralists blamed France's internal reaction and stagnation on America's anti-Communist obsession; attacked NATO, French armament, and the German military revival; urged withdrawal from the Cold War in Europe and from colonial war in the Far East. The Gaullists repeated their demands for constitutional revision, insisting that only strong executive authority would enable France to regain her greatness as a nation, independent of, though associated with, the United States, enable her to retain her empire, and to exploit her resources to the full.

The third critic excoriated *immobilisme* while remaining loyal to the Republic's constitution. Anti-Communist and anti-Gaullist, the veteran Radical Pierre Mendès-France demanded that French leaders find the courage to choose, to establish priorities, among their announced aims. France was living beyond her means, on the charity of others, and at the expense of her least comfortable citizens, delaying that economic recovery and expansion upon which any long-range security depended. With a series of astringent Chamber addresses since 1951, Mendès-France had built an enthusiastic public following among young Radicals and on the non-Communist Left, by calling for an end to the war in Indo-China, for political concessions and economic aid to North Africa, for reforms in taxation and administration, for higher productivity and more capital investment. His attacks on Third Force leaders and on the lobbies earned him the hatred of many powerful persons. As a Jew and one of the Deputies who had "deserted" to North Africa on the *Massilia* in 1940, he was despised by Vichyites. Even though hostile toward French subservience to America and to German rearmament, he was distrusted by Gaullists as insufficiently critical of EDC and too ready to relinquish French colonial power. On the last, many MRP deputies also opposed him—enough in 1953 to deny him the votes to become Premier. The Communists ridiculed his promises to break out of *immobilisme;* Socialist leaders and some of his Radical rivals resented his growing popularity among their followers. Only the military disaster of Dien Bien Phu in May of 1954 and the need for a rapid settlement in Indo-China opened his way to the premiership.

Before the Fourth Republic died in Algeria, it was grievously weakened in Indo-China. Hostilities there began in December of 1946, when Blum's one-month caretaker cabinet was struggling with a still shattered economy of shortages, inflation, profiteering, and corruption. French national pride had hardly begun to recover when it was shaken again by a number of setbacks. The Big Three frustrated French policy in Germany; in December, 1946, the Anglo-American economic plan to merge zones foretold political recentralization of Germany, which the Soviet Union had already demanded in July. In December also the Blum government had to announce the final evacuation of French forces from Syria and Lebanon, after surrendering to Arab and American pressure, and to a particularly threatening British note. In disastrous financial circumstances, Blum had also been forced to arrange an American loan on terms (including the opening of French markets to American films) that many Frenchmen found humiliating. Few public figures were eager to be associated with yet another "surrender," particularly to an uprising of backward people.

As serious, perhaps, was the unreadiness of the Resistance parties to deal with colonial affairs. As in their economic policies, so reminiscent of the Popular Front, their colonial views were optimistic and imprecise. Men of the Left were hardly less convinced of the grandeur to be regained by holding the empire than were men of the Right, though they foresaw political and economic concessions, to match those cultural gifts to colonials in which the French took such pride. The old design of 100 million Frenchmen had been revived, ambiguously, by de Gaulle's imperial conference at Brazzaville in January, 1944. The colonial peoples were to have a "larger share" in French life; autonomy was not an issue. Equally ambiguous was the constitution of the French Union, a statement of high principles and paper concessions which preserved the authority of the Paris government, and local domination by white settlers and colonial administrators, civil and military. Few Frenchmen at home knew how deeply the defeat of 1940, followed by Axis and then Allied occupation, had shaken French prestige in the empire, or how determined were native leaders to win those liberties promised by Allied propaganda and the United Nations Charter—liberties that many of the same Frenchmen had held dearer than life until 1944.

Even had the governments in Paris been less occupied with mountainous domestic problems or less sure of the political loyalties and economic rewards to be expected from the colonies, they would have had trouble in imposing new policies on French administrators in colonial capitals. At least as old as the Third Republic was the latter's belief, shared by soldiers, settlers, and businessmen, that the elected representatives of the French people were irresponsible or incompetent in colonial affairs and not to be taken seriously. Again and again, men on the spot who knew better were to ignore or reverse orders from Paris, in Indo-China, Madagascar, Tunisia, Morocco, and Algeria. Increasingly serious was the alienation of certain army officers and fighting units from their civilian superiors in Paris and from civilian society in general. Military men who had taken the blame for defeat in 1940, who had obeyed Pétain's orders only to find themselves demoted or outranked by Gaullists or Resistance fighters after 1944, who passed dreary months in German occupation, undersupported by weak governments in Paris, or in retreat from the Near East to crumbling barracks in France and North Africa, lamented France's decline as a world power. Popular anti-militarism, resistance to conscription and training, the paucity of talented young men choosing army careers made them aware also of their own loss of prestige in society. From 1945 to 1958, these men were thrown into savage colonial wars whose aims were never defined by governments drifting from one compromise to another, unable either to negotiate or to fight their way to settlement.

All of these problems brought tragedy to Indo-China from 1945 to 1954. The veteran revolutionary Ho Chi Minh reemerged after Japan's defeat as President of "Free Vietnam," supported by the People's National Liberation Committee and at first by Emperor Bao Dai, who abdicated in favor of the Democratic Republic of Vietnam, with its capital in the northern city of Hanoi. French troops based on Saigon reoccupied the south (below the 16th parallel) by the end of 1945. In a treaty of March, 1946, France recognized Ho's Republic and it in turn entered the "Indo-Chinese Federation" and the French Union. But the French had already snuffed out independence movements in Cambodia and Laos, and were landing troops at Haiphong, on the road to Hanoi. De Gaulle's zealous High Commissioner for Indo-China, the monk-Admiral Thierry d'Argenlieu, ignored Vietnamese appeals for implementation of the treaty; in September he obtained Premier Bidault's permission to clear Haiphong of Vietnamese troops. The French bombardment of Haiphong, without warning, killed 6000 Vietnamese and destroyed the native quarter. When Blum became Premier, Ho sent urgent appeals to Paris, but his messages were held up by French authorities on the scene until French troops entered Hanoi in December; on the 19th, the Vietnamese attacked them, were beaten, and withdrew to the countryside. The war had begun without the Blum cabinet or the Assembly having discussed Indo-China in any serious manner. Neither Socialists nor Communists—who still clung to the tripartite formula—were yet prepared to extend their principles to the Far East, and the MRP followed colonialist leadership.

The war became "civil war" in March of 1949, when the French purchased Bao Dai's cooperation by recognizing him as Emperor of an ostensibly autonomous Vietnam, in fact preserved and ruled by the French army. In 1950 it became a part of the Cold War, after the Chinese Communists had routed Chiang Kai-shek and marched to the Vietnam frontier. Ho's Vietminh regime was recognized by Moscow and Peking; the United States in turn recognized Bao Dai, and the Korean War loosed the flow of American military aid to the French in Europe and Indo-China. During four long years, French casualties mounted; French forces in Europe were depleted; the corps of young officers was decimated. France spent more than the equivalent of all Marshall Plan aid in the Indo-China struggle. When the Korean War ended in 1953, the Chinese and Americans each increased their support to the contending forces. Meanwhile, the war grew unpopular in France as the playboy puppet Bao Dai dallied on the Riviera and well-founded rumors of massive corruption and currency manipulation circulated in Paris. This last, the traffic in Vietnamese *piastres,* enriched the French dealers at both ends, as well as Bao Dai and his hangers-on, and even Ho's Vietminh, who purchased arms with the dollars given them for *piastres* by their "enemies" in Saigon. By 1954, many Frenchmen, including military leaders, regarded the war as hopeless; the Vietminh *maquis* made all but the cities and main roads untenable; French businesses had deserted for safer places. Still the Laniel government, with

Bidault as Foreign Minister, held on, encouraged by Washington, where Eisenhower said that all Southeast Asia would fall if Vietnam were to turn Communist.

The debacle at Dien Bien Phu forced Paris and Washington to a decision. Against this valley fortress, where General Navarre had committed French troops to block a Vietminh advance into Laos, the Chinese sent artillery in early 1954. As at Sedan in 1870, the French were pounded from the hills surrounding their self-made trap. Unlike Sedan, air drops enabled the defenders to stage a bloody, futile defense. In April, Bidault pleaded for an American air strike at the Vietminh. At first tempted, the Eisenhower-Dulles administration backed down, partly on the British government's refusal to take part. The powers had already agreed to a peace conference at Geneva and all but Bidault feared that Chinese intervention would wreck the conference and risk global war. Dien Bien Phu fell to the Vietminh's "human sea" attacks on May 7th. The Laniel-Bidault government was overthrown and Pierre Mendès-France became Premier, with a promise to end the Indo-Chinese war in thirty days. The American government and press were alarmed by his advent to power, but having refused to commit its forces, Washington could do little but complain that at Geneva Mendès-France gave away too much. Given the balance of forces, he did well to preserve the southern half of Vietnam—not for France, or for Bao Dai, who was later forced to abdicate, but for the troubled and arbitrary regime of Ngo Dinh Diem, who became an American charge.

## FAILURE OF MENDÈS-FRANCE

For the moment Mendès-France enjoyed wide popularity, despite the anger of nationalists, colonialists, military officers, and the displaced Bidault, soon to claim that he could have struck a better bargain at Geneva. Had Mendès-France been able to concentrate on domestic reforms, the Assembly might not have resisted him. But foreign problems gave him no rest. Tunisia was next. There, also, earlier governments had prepared disaster. In 1950, Foreign Minister Schuman had promised the neo-Destour leader Habib Bourguiba that France would negotiate Tunisian autonomy. But wealthy French settlers and the colonialists in Paris, some of whom directed his own MRP, forced Schuman to break his promise. In 1951, the Resident-General de Hautecloque ordered the Foreign Legion to put down riots protesting his demand that the Bey dismiss the nationalist ministers at Tunis. The Legion's calculated brutality, de Hautecloque's arrest and deportation of Bourguiba, and the arbitrary imprisonment of thousands of Tunisians in degrading conditions were followed by the murder of the popular Tunisian labor leader Ferhat Hashed in December, 1952, by French colonial terrorists of the Red Hand. Violence was endemic throughout 1953; and no sooner was the Geneva Conference of 1954 over than Mendès-France flew to Tunisia to assure the Bey that Schuman's original promise would be honored. Although he thereby defeated the colonialist lobby, negotiations dragged on until after Mendès-France's defeat in February, 1955; Tunisia gained autonomy under his successor, Edgar Faure.

Mendès-France's *coup de théâtre* in Tunisia, like his promised deadline on Indo-China, announced a new style of executive action, popular with the public but resented by political leaders even in his own party. So it was with his "Saturday chats" on the radio, appeals over parliament's head unheard since the days of Doumergue in 1934. Like de Gaulle, Mendès-France was cool, remote, or brusque in his personal relations, but paternal, intimate, sometimes exalted in speaking to large audiences. The Premier's vigor raised hopes in a people accustomed to trimmers and procrastinators. But his plan for sweeping economic and fiscal reforms added the forces of *immobilisme* to the colonialists already opposed to him. Now a third foreign issue, EDC and German rearmament, proved fatal to the impetus he had gained in his first few weeks of office—and to his greatest asset, his reputation for decisiveness.

A succession of French governments had avoided submitting the treaty of the European Defense Community to parliament for ratification. The idea of any German rearmament was increasingly unpopular, especially as the Korean crisis was past and Stalin's death had appeared to soften the Soviet regime. Even the Anglo-American bullying of Laniel and Bidault at Bermuda in December of 1953 had produced no results. The refusal of London and Washington to provide guarantees against German misbehavior in the future reminded Frenchmen of their abandonment after the First World War, an incident easily forgotten by British and American politicians and publicists, who were once again prematurely impressed by the stability of German democracy. Among those who accepted the inevitability of German rearmament were some, Gaullists in particular, who feared the French army's disappearance as a national force should EDC be adopted. Mendès-

France had promised to bring the issue before the Assembly and, after failing to secure the approval of the other five signers to a series of revisions which severely reduced the powers of the supranational authority, he presented the bill in late August without taking a position on it himself. The American government had made the familiar error of equating EDC with international morality. Dulles' threat of an "agonizing reappraisal" should the Assembly reject it was quite naturally ignored. EDC was defeated, on a technical motion, 319 to 264. In not choosing, Mendès-France had succumbed to the tactics he had so much decried in others; but the parties he depended upon were split and the emotions engendered by EDC worsened relations among all factions on every other issue. Now Washington demanded full German rearmament inside NATO, and Dulles bypassed Paris for direct negotiations with Adenauer in Bonn. To avoid French isolation, Mendès-France grasped Eden's plan for German rearmament in NATO, with assurances of continued British presence on the Continent. The Paris Agreements embodying this bargain were narrowly ratified by the French Assembly (under heavy Allied pressure) late in December, 1954.

Mendès-France was once again a hero in Washington, but in France his position was shaken. Added to his enemies were the enthusiasts of European union, in the MRP and among the Socialists. His quick acceptance of German rearmament disturbed many sectors of opinion; not only the Communists attacked him as more subservient to America than even Bidault had been. The alcohol lobby fought his taxes on liquors and his decrees reducing the number of tax-free distillers; his campaign against alcoholism and in favor of milk and soft drinks was ridiculed (though continued by governments after him). The outbreak of the Algerian rebellion in the Aurès Mountains in late October of 1954 was widely attributed to his concessions to the Tunisians. Although he promised to repress Algerian "criminals" and declared that Algeria was irrevocably part of France, his enemies on all issues united against him on the North African question. In February, before Mendès-France could set afoot his cherished reorganization of the French economy, he was overthrown by the Assembly in a debate over the still-dragging Tunisian negotiations.

Ironically, Mendès-France's quick resolution of the Indo-Chinese and EDC affairs made him expendable and also enabled the Fourth Republic to continue for a time the *immobiliste* domestic policies he so much deplored. His successor was Edgar Faure, a fellow Radical whose aims were not notably different, but whose methods were evasion, compromise, and postponement. Faure's main accomplishments were the grant of home rule to Tunisia, the settlement of the Moroccan imbroglio, and the defeat of Mendès-France's attempt to make the Radical party the nucleus of a new non-Communist Left. In June of 1955, the Assembly ratified the agreement for Tunisian autonomy. The other protectorate, Morocco, was a thornier problem, for the colonialists, the military, and French extremists there had enjoyed a free hand for several years. Morocco was a haven for French capital deserting Indo-China or the homeland itself; resistance to change was well financed. It was also rooted in nostalgia for the days of Lyautey, in French pride of ownership, development, and paternalism, and in the belief that France had to hold her North African territories to protect native as well as French interests from the machinations of Russian Communism and American capitalism.

To discourage Sultan Mohammed ben Youssef from supporting the nationalist (*Istiqlal*) party's demands for autonomy, the French employed El Glaoui, the old Pasha of Marrakech and leader of the Berber tribesmen, to threaten his Arab rival. In 1953, El Glaoui was pressed by French colonists and the Resident-General, Marshal Juin, to depose the Sultan in favor of a puppet, Mohammed ben Arafa. Through 1954 and 1955, Moroccan nationalists and French extremists fought a duel of terror, culminating in the latter's murder of a liberal French businessman and publisher of the conciliatory *Maroc-Presse*, Jacques Lemaigre-Dubreuil, in June of 1955. The role of the French police in this and other matters bespoke collusion with colonialist die-hards. Faure was forced to act; he sent the liberal Gaullist Gilbert Grandval to Rabat as the new Resident-General, with instructions to replace ben Arafa by a Regency Council including Moroccan nationalists. Grandval met the open hostility of French colonialists, the police, administration, and army; in Paris, Faure surrendered to the opposition and withdrew his plan. In August some forty French villagers were massacred by a Berber hill tribe. Faure reversed himself again, sent for ben Youssef from his forced exile in Madagascar, and was saved from his own colonialist opposition in Paris by the sudden and emotional submission of El Glaoui to the rightful Sultan. In October, France recognized Moroccan autonomy and ben Youssef took the title Mohammed V as King of Morocco. Not Faure but the addled old El Glaoui had foiled the North African lobby and its clients in Morocco. Both the Tunisian and Moroccan protectorates were formally ended in 1956.

During Faure's year in office, Mendès-France tightened his hold on the machinery of the Radical-Socialist party, with the blessing of the party patriarch, Édouard Herriot. His aim was as old as Gambetta's: to impose party discipline and a party platform on all major issues, to elect a parliamentary delegation obedient to the organized rank and file. Concurrently, he demanded a return to *scrutin d'arrondissement* to reduce the Rightist and Communist blocs in the Assembly by allying Radicals with Socialists and others who would accept a program of Republican forward movement. In this Premier Faure opposed him; and when he was overthrown on the issue in late November, he dissolved the Assembly, whose interminable wrangles had wearied the press. In so doing, he forced quick elections according to the law of 1951 and cut short Mendès-France's efforts to form a Left Republican alliance. Faure was expelled from the Radical party along with a group of conservatives including René Mayer, who had helped overthrow Mendès-France in February. These turned back to the RGR, from which the majority of Radicals had seceded earlier, and the party was split less than a month from elections.

The campaign was short and bitter, and drew more voters to the polls in January, 1956, than in any prior French election. The Center parties were divided between Faure's group, the RGR, the MRP, assorted conservatives, and former Gaullists, and the Mendès-France–Mollet alliance of Radicals and Socialists (and a few Gaullists headed by Chaban-Delmas) in the Republican Front. The Communists gained 48 seats, for a total of 145, or 27 per cent from 26 per cent of the vote (5.5 million). On the far Right, a new formation led by the small-town demagogue, Pierre Poujade, polled a surprising 2.6 million votes to win 52 seats. Poujade's personal crusade against taxes and bureaucracy had rallied small shopkeepers, small farmers, those who detested economic modernization, technocracy, central planning, the power of labor and of big business. *Poujadisme* was proof of the economic change going on under the surface of political stalemate in the Fourth Republic. Another side of *Poujadisme* was xenophobic, imperialist, anti-Semitic, and anti-intellectual. Its activists included Rightists with links to de la Rocque's *Croix de Feu,* to Vichy or fascist formations, to peasant, independent or Gaullist groups. But in its appeal for a new "Estates General" and its lively egalitarianism, it also had a Jacobin flavor and no doubt captured for a time many former Radical, MRP, and other votes from those "small people" whose defense Alain had made a Radical creed but whose interests a Mendès-France would subordinate to national economic renovation. The *Poujadiste* group in the Assembly failed to hold together and had little effect beyond adding to the troubles of the divided center parties, whose delegations its success had reduced.

The *Mendèsiste* Radicals won only 57 seats in the Assembly, while the RGR and UDSR were electing about 35 between them, the MRP 71; assorted moderates and conservatives numbered 95. The Socialists made up the largest non-Communist delegation, with 90 Deputies; and their leader, Guy Mollet, became Premier. The MRP and others vital to Mollet's majority vetoed Mendès-France's appointment as Foreign Minister; he became instead a Minister of State without portfolio. Under Mollet, with whose party he had fought an electoral campaign, Mendès-France could influence policy only from within, and as head of a group numerically less important to Mollet than others (especially the MRP) and much less obedient to his direction than he had hoped. One issue—Algeria—was to lose Mendès-France many of his remaining followers, to hasten his resignation from the Mollet government, and to end all chances for the new domestic programs Frenchmen expected from a Mendès–Mollet government based on the Left Center.

## TRAGEDY IN ALGERIA

Many observers noted a revival of aggressive nationalism in French politics, the press and public in 1956, a taste for military force after so many retreats and compromises. As the Algerian rebellion turned into guerrilla war, Frenchmen faced the prospect of losing their most cherished possession, long considered part of France herself. The initial reaction was shock and anger, especially as the rebels resorted to assassination not only of Frenchmen but of Moslems (in Paris as in Algeria) who hesitated to join them. The Algerian question divided Frenchmen along some of the same lines as in the 1930's, among some of the same political "families" active then as in the Dreyfus era and before, between conservative patriots who insisted that French greatness lay in preserving French authority and acquired interests, and liberal patriots who said it lay in fulfilling the promises of liberty, equality, and fraternity whatever the initial cost. In each camp were opportunists and men of principle. In each were many who believed their solution to be the most practicable, who based their demands that France hold on or give up on honestly differing views of the facts and thereby of the possibilities in Algeria herself, or on differing estimates of how war or concessions in Algeria would affect France's position in the world, and French problems at home. Had these been the only factors involved, the successes of the Algerian nationalists and the inability of nearly a half million French soldiers to pacify Algeria might of themselves have allowed the Fourth Republic to make peace as in Tunisia and Morocco. Indeed by late 1957 and early 1958 the French public seemed weary of a war so costly in blood (conscripts were sent to Algeria, as they had not been to Indo-China), and in money and materials sorely needed at home.

In the evolution of French opinion away from the belligerence of 1956, the religious, intellectual, and literary community played a major part. It was to be expected that certain Communist and other Leftist journals would denounce the Algerian war. On any but the already convinced, they produced little effect, except to make it easier for conservatives, the military, and the government to label all criticism as Communist. More influential were questions raised by Catholic and Protestant clergymen over the brutality of French settlers and certain units of the army. Well-known writers joined the debate. François Mauriac hotly denounced French colonialism in *l'Express*; Albert Camus, himself Algerian-born, asked for a "truce of civilians," to spare innocent Arabs and Europeans caught between the insensate terror of the rebels and the obtuse repression of the French. In 1957 appeared *Lieutenant en Algérie* by Jean-Jacques Servan-Schreiber, founder and editor of *l'Express*; the brilliant *l'Algérie en 1957* by Germaine Tillion, an anthropologist at the Sorbonne; *Le Socialisme trahi* by Mollet's party rival, André Philip; and *La tragédie de l'Algérie* by Raymond Aron, professor at l'Ecole des Sciences Politiques, and Gaullist sympathizer. All these, and the reports home of French soldiers, officers, and conscripts, complicated the simple versions of the war provided by the government and popular press; it was possible by early 1958 to discuss alternatives to simple repression and the imposition of a unilateral French solution.

Algeria, however, was very different from Tunisia and Morocco. Regardless of the support that a more conciliatory policy might have enjoyed at home, the governments of Mollet, Bourgès-Maunoury, and Félix Gaillard were too weak to defy two forces that were determined to keep Algeria French: the European settlers and the army officers in charge of pacification. Whereas there were only 200,000 of the former in Tunisia and 300,000 in Morocco, there were about a million in Algeria, of French, Italian, Spanish, and Corsican ancestry, many of whose families had lived there for several generations. They could rightly argue that the modernization of Algeria was their work and that of France: roads, rails, agricultural and commercial development, sanitary, medical, and educational advances. That the Arab population of 8 million benefited little from this work but instead, as Germaine Tillion pointed out, were being pauperized by the effects of modernization, did nothing to shake the settlers' conviction that Algeria was their homeland. The few very wealthy landowners (the *gros colons*) were political powers in France, as were the directors of French businesses in Algeria, which had enjoyed an economic boom since the end of the war and returned high profits to a few. Although distrusted by the mass of European petty bourgeois, urban workers, and small farmers, this oligarchy could count on a common Algerian patriotism to help them resist concessions from Paris (including serious land reform) that might endanger their privileges. The city of Algiers in particular often produced crowds of demonstrators to protest softness in official policy.

Vital to this blackmail by demonstration (and attacks on Europeans suspected of weakness) was the sympathy of the army for the settlers and its determination to end the humiliating series of defeats it had suffered since May of 1940. It was not usually a matter of French soldiers won over by the *gros colons;* on the contrary, many hated the wine and grain kings of Algeria and blamed them for the exploitation of land and labor that embittered the Moslem majority and furnished recruits for the Algerian FLN (*Front de Libération National*). Many believed that the fight in Algeria was also part of the fight against Communism. To them the rebels were "Viets," whose hold over the Moslem population was maintained by terror. French army leaders differed on tactics to break this hold. Some, the majority usually upheld from Paris, depended on conventional military operations to crush the FLN; others developed counterguerrilla ideas they adapted from Mao Tse-tung, including night infiltration, surprise attack and ambush by small, highly trained units. Some officers preferred rough counterterror against the Moslem population; some, a minority, went to the other extreme, "going to the people," taking them into their confidence in an effort to revive trust between Moslems and Frenchmen. These attempts were often sabotaged by the FLN, rival French army groups, the settlers' militia, or settlers' organizations powerful in Algiers and Paris. But whatever its methods, the army command cherished a French Algeria of some sort. Even the conscripts were likely to sympathize with the Europeans they came to know; and as the circle of violence, terror, and torture widened, many exhibited a racist, religious, or "anti-Communist" fervor encouraging indiscriminate attacks and reprisals on the Arab population.

Three events in 1956 hardened the forces against moderation and all but ended the Republic's control over Algeria and the army. On February 6th, an Algiers mob greeted Premier Mollet and his choice for Governor-General, the reputedly liberal and pro-Arab General Georges Catroux, with a wild protest demonstration, a shower of rotten eggs and tomatoes. Mollet capitulated, appointed the tough Socialist Robert Lacoste in place of Catroux, and announced his determination first to restore order, then to consider political reforms—a sterile formula, for colonial peoples had learned (as had French workers decades before) that after order was restored, nothing, or worse, might follow. By the summer of 1956 half a million French troops, including conscripts, were in Algeria. Mendès-France resigned in protest over Mollet's surrender to Algiers, but most vocal opinion supported the Premier who, with Lacoste, was applauded as a Socialist strong man.

In October, when Bourguiba and the Sultan of Morocco arranged a conference with FLN leaders in Tunis in the hope of settling the war, the French press was enraged. French authorities in Algiers had Ben Bella and four other FLN spokesmen kidnaped (the French crew of the Sultan's plane landed at Algiers instead of Tunis). Lacoste had accepted the plot and Mollet approved it later, refused Tunisian and Moroccan protests, and jailed the five near Paris. The popular press erupted with praise of Mollet's "virility." Socialists who protested the trick, which ruined any chance of early negotiation and invited Tunisian and Moroccan hostility, were forced out of office or out of the party—the Minister for Protectorates, Alain Savary, André Philip, and Daniel Mayer, whom Mollet had ousted as party leader for insufficient Socialist purity. Not only the power of Algiers but its mood was reflected in France; critical books and newspapers were seized, meetings disrupted by Rightist toughs; a Socialist government prosecuted critics of the war and victims of the bullies, and kept suspects in detention without trial. Europeans in Algeria who plotted, terrorized, and denounced the Republic were rarely molested; the French capital, Mollet's critics said, had moved to Algiers.

The next decisive date was November 5th, when the Mollet government launched its invasion of Suez. For months Algerian resistance had been blamed on Egyptian aid and incitement from Radio Cairo. In a mood of frustrated nationalism, the French public was ready for an assertion of French power; and by late 1956, the usually liberal newspapers *Combat* and *Le Monde* had joined the chorus. But the Anglo-French Suez adventure ended in disaster. Russian threats and United Nations appeals, backed by Washington, forced a cease-fire; although the French hotly resented Eden's surrender, it saved Mollet from taking the same step first. The Moroccan and Tunisian governments were again forced to denounce France, and the FLN was encouraged by French humiliation. Most seriously, French soldiers were furious at the government's marriage of folly and weakness; the paratroops under General Jacques Massu were particularly incensed at having a long-sought victory taken from their grasp. In Paris an Assembly defiant of world opinion stifled the critics of Suez and voted confidence in Mollet. His government lasted until May of 1957, when he was overthrown by the Right and Center for seeking to push ahead with social legislation in the face of budget problems brought on by his Suez operation.

His successor was the Radical Bourgès-Maunoury, who kept Lacoste in Algeria and made the nationalist André Morice Minister of Defense. Like Mollet, Bourgès-Maunoury pressed the Algerian war while seeking a formula for political settlement to follow upon a cease-fire. Since a cease-fire would involve the FLN's surrender of its weapons, no such settlement was remotely possible; neither Mollet nor Bourgès-Maunoury dared go beyond a gradual concession of autonomy to Moslem communities. On the other hand, the Europeans of Algeria denounced Bourgès' proposed Algerian *loi-cadre* (framework law) because of its single electoral college for an Algerian Assembly of limited powers. The Algerian Statute of 1947 had provided separate Moslem and European colleges; elections to the Moslem college had been rigged to elect the most docile, and none of the Statute's reforms in local administration, education, or religion had ever been voted by the European-dominated Assembly. Even so, the European settlers were now hostile to political arrangements that treated Algeria differently from France herself. In 1956, the Assembly was dissolved and the Europeans adopted "integration," with France as their political aim. In this situation, the attempts of Mollet and Bourgès-Maunoury to reach a political compromise were mere exercises in parliamentary maneuver.

# DEATH OF THE FOURTH REPUBLIC

Bourgès-Maunoury was overthrown on the issue of the *loi-cadre* in September of 1957. After a month-long cabinet crisis the young Radical Félix Gaillard succeeded him. A modified *loi-cadre* giving the European population added guarantees was passed in November. Since neither side in Algeria would accept it and the army neither would nor could enforce it, the law was meaningless. The war dragged on, with French soldiers increasingly contemptuous of a government of drift and delay, unable to curb the *gros colons* but unwilling to give up its plans for reform, willing to sacrifice its soldiers' lives and their honor but unwilling to take public responsibility for the harsh methods, including torture, it winked at in private. In early 1958, Gaillard allowed the Algerian struggle to become "internationalized," further angering the Right, the settlers, and the army. After failing in Egypt, these factions had turned to denunciation of Tunisian aid to the FLN. In January, an FLN detachment lured the French into bombing the Tunisian border village of Sakiet-Sidi-Youssef. London and Washington offered their "good offices" to mediate the ensuing Franco-Tunisian crisis, and Gaillard accepted. The Assembly overthrew him in April in an outburst of anti-American and anti-British resentment, nourished on the belief that foreign oil interests were plotting to expel France from all North Africa and seize control of the newly-discovered Sahara deposits. But both Bidault and Pleven failed to win investiture. President Coty turned to another MRP leader, one who had vaguely suggested a negotiated settlement. Pierre Pflimlin presented himself to the Assembly on May 14th, 1958. He was invested by a narrow margin with the support of the Socialists, the Mendès-France group, liberal Radicals, and most of the MRP—not because of a new policy toward Algeria, for his investiture speech contained nothing new, but "in defense of the Republic." On the previous day, Algiers had revolted against the Paris government and appeared to have the support of the military.

The accumulated frustrations of soldiers and settlers boiled over during the search for a successor to Gaillard. Bidault's failure (his own MRP rejected his hard line in Algeria) was taken as proof that the Fourth Republic would never do what was needed for victory; instead, rising criticism of the war in France, and shifts within the SFIO and

MRP, foretold concessions to the FLN. The prospects were intolerable to Europeans, who saw no alternative between an *Algérie française* and abandonment of their homes, and shameful to soldiers, who foresaw the abandonment of pro-French Moslems to FLN reprisals after years of common sacrifice. Sustained by such feelings, several bands of plotters succeeded in turning a protest demonstration of May 13th into insurrection, seized the government building, and proclaimed a Committee of Public Safety. The passive acquiescence of the army and police encouraged the assorted (and armed) factions of *colons,* fascists, Poujadists, Vichyites, students' and veterans' leagues to believe all things possible, ranging from mere pressure on Paris for continuation of the war to Algerian secession or a military dictatorship displacing the Fourth Republic entirely. But it was the Gaullists, led by Léon Delbecque (and later by Jacques Soustelle, who had been a popular "integrationist" Governor-General in Algiers before Lacoste), who won control of the critical force. On May 15th, General Raoul Salan, the army Commander-in-Chief in Algeria (to whom Pflimlin had hopefully delegated civil authority as well), was induced to declare himself publicly for de Gaulle. The latter's answer was prompt: "I am ready to assume the powers of the Republic."

Charles de Gaulle now reaped the rewards of his aloofness and ambiguity. Since his dismissal of the RPF in 1953, he had lived quietly in Colombey-les-Deux-Églises, composing his memoirs and watching the deterioration of the Fourth Republic. Many on each side of the Algerian question no doubt believed that his views were theirs. More important was the confidence of most Frenchmen, including some who claimed to be wholly for war or wholly for peace, that a de Gaulle government would have the strength to take one path or the other and follow it to the end. While the Gaullists consolidated their hold over the cabals and army officers in Algeria, the General succeeded in convincing enough Socialists (including Mollet), Catholic Republicans, and Radicals of his Republicanism to win their consent to his legal investiture as Premier. In his public pronouncements he avoided endorsing either the rebellion or the Pflimlin government, but insisted he would assume office only by legal means. In prestige de Gaulle outshone all possible rivals; apathy toward the Fourth Republic was evident in the failure of CGT strike calls and the Paris procession staged on May 28th by the non-Communist Left. Interior Minister Moch's security forces were undependable; high civil and military officers were patently reluctant to act against old friends in Algiers, with whose feelings and aims many of them sympathized.

Lest Pflimlin delay his resignation and the Assembly its acceptance of de Gaulle, the leaders in Algiers (Delbecque and General Massu) persuaded Salan to send paratroops to seize Corsica on May 24th, and threatened to order a military march on Paris. Pflimlin resigned on the 28th of May. Gaullists argued that there was no choice between the General's return and a paratroop *Putsch,* which might unleash civil war. The President of the Republic, René Coty, now threatened to resign unless the Assembly gave way. On June 1st, de Gaulle was voted into office by 329 to 224, the Communists, *Mendèsistes,* and half the Socialists opposed. On the next day, the Assembly gave him full powers for six months and the authority to draft a new constitution for submission to the voters in a referendum. It then recessed *sine die* and France's Fourth Republic since 1789 was dead.

## ⚜ XIII ⚜

# THE FIFTH
# REPUBLIC

Charles de Gaulle's purpose in 1958 as in 1944 was to rebuild the French state, to restore the nation's confidence and self-respect, its sense of mission and grandeur. But patriots in every party of the Fourth Republic had sought nothing less; their work prepared de Gaulle's way. If a nation's confidence arises from economic vigor and the advent, or expectation, of social well-being, France's revival dated from the mid-1950's, at the very moment of defeat in Indo-China and the outbreak of war in Algeria. From 1954 to 1958 the French national product increased by 5 per cent a year and industrial production by roughly twice that rate. In 1958 real wages were nearly a third higher than in 1949. The French were buying consumer goods, including automobiles, at four times the rate of 1949. Steel production was over a third higher than in the great year of 1929, French use of all types of energy had tripled since then, and the productivity of French labor in such basic industries as coal and steel had passed all European rivals including the Germans.

The Fourth Republic had at last begun to attack its housing shortage, completing more than 200,000 dwellings a year after 1954. In many spheres, Frenchmen were enjoying the long-awaited results of capital investment in the expansion and modernization of their economy. And under the despised Fourth Republic, the French population began rising at a rate unknown for more than a century: from 40 million in 1945 to 44 million in 1956 to 46 million in 1962. Whether out of confidence or heedlessness, it suggested resurgent youth.

The Fourth Republic had also prepared the way in foreign affairs. Not de Gaulle but the Mollet government of 1956 decided to build a French nuclear striking force. Negotiations for France's entry into the European Common Market and the European Atomic Community (Euratom) resulted in the Rome treaties of March, 1957, which were to come into effect in 1958 and 1959. Not only Gaullists but most of the Fourth Republic's coalition cabinets had been wary of political and military supranationalism in Europe, despite the greater vigor of "European" factions, such as the MRP, before 1958. The last governments of the Fourth Republic were also as suspicious of British attempts to block or weaken the Common Market as de Gaulle was to be, and as concerned by the flow of American capital into the French and neighboring economies. The dream of turning France alone or France allied with other European states into a Third Force, whether between America and the Soviet Union or as an equal partner to America, was as old as Liberation and was stirred by neutralism, nationalism, and the "European Idea." Since 1954, successive French governments had worked to bind West Germany to closer cooperation. Fourth Republic Premiers had demanded a greater voice for France in NATO and periodically whittled down military collaboration with the United States, partly out of cost, partly out of distrust of American foreign policy and fear of American inconstancy. In all these matters, and most notably in colonial affairs, General de Gaulle's contribution— like Napoleon's after the Directory—was to lend greater political force to attitudes and initiatives taken by a weaker, troubled regime.

## THE NEW POLITICAL ESTABLISHMENT

The vehicle for this force was a new quasi-presidential system established as the Fifth Republic. But behind it was one man, of towering prestige and strength of character. The referendum of September, 1958, by which 80 per cent of the voters approved the new constitution, was in fact a grant of personal power to de Gaulle, to end the threats of civil war and military dictatorship still hanging over France. His first concern was to cool French tempers on both sides of the

Mediterranean by veiling and postponing the divisive questions, for his first aim was to win the broadest possible support for his new political system. The Algerian crisis, like most divisive questions, was to him more the consequence than the cause of Republican debility. It, like the others, would be solved only by a political authority worthy of the nation's, and of the world's, respect. One elemental task was to restore the army's obedience to Paris. For many reasons, not least the hatred some of its officers had borne for him since before 1940, it would take time. Meanwhile, the crisis that had brought him back to power made him indispensable, free to pursue goals far more exalted than the liquidation of problems he thought should never have arisen.

De Gaulle imagined France, he said, as "the princess in the stories or the Madonna in the frescoes," a creature fated to an exceptional destiny. He believed that only great ventures could suppress the discords "inherent in her people." France's greatness in the second half of the twentieth century would be to lead—by word, example, and action—old Europe back to that world primacy which her numbers, wealth, talents and culture merited. For her role, France required political rejuvenation to match and extend the economic and demographic gains of the Fourth Republic.

The new constitution was written by de Gaulle's cabinet, aided by a parliamentary committee and the Council of State. Its chief author was the Minister of Justice, Michel Debré, a loyal Gaullist, a lawyer, and Councilor of State, who had prepared his ideas since Resistance days. The main provisions, which were his and de Gaulle's, sought to reconcile a strong executive team of President and Premier with the tradition of a parliamentary republic. Debré's regard for the British system was evident, as was his realization that what British society and habit allowed at Westminster could be approached in Paris only by constitutional mechanisms. Of these the most vital was the increased power of the President, an attempt to capture on paper and to fix in the office what de Gaulle himself was: the symbol of national authority, but, unlike the Presidents of the Third and Fourth Republics, with enough prestige and power of his own to act as national guide, arbiter, and guarantor of order. Standing above party quarrels, no longer the creature of parliament but elected by some 80,000 political notables including Deputies, Senators, mayors, and departmental and municipal councilors, the President of the Republic was to intervene at critical moments to prevent deadlock or deterioration in political affairs. Often called the institutionalization of de Gaulle, it was also the institutionalization of a practice frequently resorted to under the Third Republic. In abnormal times, under the burdens of war, inflation or civil strife, parliament had effaced itself and allowed a strong man to cut the knots of *immobilisme* and take command while the crisis raged. Clemenceau and Poincaré were the happier examples. Doumergue and Pétain were warnings of what could happen when parliamentary government waited too long, or failed, out of weakness or jealousy, to call the right man. In 1962, the constitution was revised to provide election of the President by universal suffrage. Henceforth, it was hoped, the nation would choose its savior in advance.

The President and parliament were separate expressions of popular sovereignty for the first time since the ill-fated Second Republic. The President appointed the Premier, who was to be the active executive, choosing his own cabinet, in charge of policy, legislation, administration, and enforcement, responsible to parliament for his acts. But the President had several ways to influence policy and to bolster his chosen Premier against the Deputies. He presided over cabinet meetings, could address messages to parliament, force it to reconsider a bill, and dissolve it on his own authority (though not more than once a year). He also had the right, on approval of either the Premier or the parliament, to submit certain questions to popular referendum and to submit any proposed law to a new Constitutional Council for a binding decision on its constitutionality. Finally, Article 16 gave the President broad emergency powers in times of crisis.

The powers of parliament (National Assembly and Senate) were considerably restricted, when measured against the French republican tradition of parliamentary supremacy. Its sessions were shortened to less than six months a year; special sessions could be called only by the Premier or by a majority of the National Assembly. Deputies were obliged to give up their seats upon accepting cabinet posts. An innovation that could either weaken or strengthen the parliament—depending upon circumstances, the quality of the Deputies or of the parties behind them—was the limit put on its legislative domain, though not on subjects for debate. In effect, it retained power to legislate on fundamental matters (including money bills) but retained almost none to obstruct the orderly consideration of government bills—a British effect achieved by constitutional provisions. Thus, responsibility—and public attention—were to be focused on the Premier and his ministers. Procedures for debate, interpellation, and votes of censure were much stiffened to ease and prolong the lives of cabinets.

The first years of the Fifth Republic offered little evidence on the ultimate workability of the constitution, for de Gaulle as President took direct command of policy on major issues. He chose not only Premiers but cabinet members. The dominant party in the Assembly, the Union for the New Republic (UNR), appeared to be a reflection of one man's prestige with the voters. The referendum of September, 1958, had fortified him; only 20 per cent of the voters opposed the Gaullist constitution. Only 4.6 million votes in opposition showed that the Communists had lost control of many of their habitual followers. The parliamentary elections of late November were fought by *scrutin d'arrondissement,* single-member districts, favored by de Gaulle to prevent what he feared would otherwise be too great a sweep by Rightists and colonialists in the UNR professing to be his men. The UNR nonetheless won a striking victory, attracting 3.6 million votes on the first ballot and, because other voters rallied to its candidates against Communist challengers, 4.8 million (26 per cent) on the second. With its own 188 seats and those of its allies, it commanded the Assembly. The Communists dropped from 145 seats in 1956 to only 10, so solid were the alliances against them; from 25 per cent of the vote in 1956 (5.5 million) they fell to 19 per cent (3.9 million). The Socialists held their 1956 vote at 3.1 million (15 per cent), as did the MRP at 2.4 million (10 per cent), but the former sank from 88 to 40 seats, the latter from 71 to 57. The Radicals and their allies declined from 3.3 million (15 per cent) and 74 seats to 2.7 million (13 per cent) and 37 seats. The Poujadists nearly disappeared, electing only one Deputy. But various other groups on the Right rose from 3 million (14 per cent) and 95 seats to 4 million (20 per cent) and 132 seats. Along with these changes in party strength went the wholesale defeat of men prominent in the Fourth Republic; former Premiers Mendès-France, Ramadier, Laniel, Bourgès-Maunoury, Edgar Faure, and Daladier lost their seats, together with the veteran Communist Jacques Duclos and the Socialists Moch, Pineau, Lacoste, and Gaston Defferre. Only 131 Deputies of the 537 in the previous Chamber were reelected.

The new Assembly was a second endorsement of de Gaulle. The third was his own election as President of the Fifth Republic. In late December, 1958, he won 62,000 votes to the Communist candidate's

10,000 and 6700 for the candidate of the *Union des Forces Démocratiques,* made up of *Mendèsistes,* anti-Mollet Socialists, and other Leftist factions which had campaigned with the Communists against the constitution. In January, de Gaulle named Michel Debré as Premier; he presented himself to the Assembly in the proper Republican tradition to be approved by a majority vote. This bright, devoted, but inflexible and abrasive man bore the brunt of opposition to de Gaulle's policies and to his own determination to keep the Assembly to the rules. His task was much complicated by de Gaulle's early reticence on Algeria. Much of the UNR was colonialist or integrationist and rightly suspected, by 1959, that de Gaulle was neither. Their resentment was the sharper for their knowledge that he enjoyed public confidence and could hardly be opposed by Deputies elected on his name.

## THE ALGERIAN SETTLEMENT

The Algerian crisis still haunted men's consciousness, and de Gaulle's solution of it showed a patience, resourcefulness (his enemies said duplicity), and political acumen most Frenchmen had not expected of him. From the first, he believed that the free consent of the Moslems was necessary to any permanent settlement. His failure to act quickly upon his accession to power dismayed the "men of May 13th," who demanded total force to keep Algeria French, as well as those who hoped he would seek a liberal solution. His speech to the European crowd at Algiers in early June, 1958, began with cruelly ambiguous words: "I have understood you (*Je vous ai compris*); I know what has happened here; I see what you wished to do." For over a year he refused to mention either integration or independence, cloaking his intentions behind compliments to the army, appeals for mutual respect between Europeans and Moslems, promises of great economic and social programs for all Algerians. He bought time by giving hope to all sides; time to disarm the settlers and to restore military discipline.

His first cabinet was nonetheless a sign of moderation and angered the extremists. All parties but the Communist were represented in this last ministry of the Fourth Republic, and the despised Pflimlin was Minister of State. The king-makers were left outside. Neither Soustelle nor Delbecque was appointed (the former was made Minister of Information only in July), nor were other leading exponents of repression: Bidault, Morice, or Duchet. On the other hand, he gave Salan full civil power in Algeria and allowed the army to supervise the constitutional referendum of September. As expected, 80 per cent of the voters dutifully appeared and 95 per cent of them approved the Fifth Republic. Liberals in France denounced what they called an imposed victory for integration. De Gaulle said nothing, but his early actions on other French possessions suggested a decision for gradual decolonization, and the substitution of voluntary cooperation as the means of preserving French influence.

Following the release of Tunisia and Morocco, the Mollet government had granted a measure of autonomy to the colonies south of the Sahara. The Defferre Law of 1956 allowed territorial assemblies chosen by universal suffrage to elect executive councils empowered to deal with local questions. The constitution of the Fifth Republic confirmed the Defferre Law and explicitly recognized the right of territories to become independent, though they would thereby cease to belong to the French Community. Prior to the referendum of September, 1958, de Gaulle announced that a no vote would signify a choice of immediate independence, but also an end to French aid. Only Guinea so chose; the eleven other sub-Saharan states and Madagascar voted overwhelmingly for the constitution and the Community. By 1960, all desired independence, and the French constitution was amended to allow them to remain members of the Community. Six did so, but all made agreements for economic cooperation with France and all were admitted to the United Nations as sovereign states in 1961. Most of them still receive French aid and accept French influence in economic, technical, and educational matters, and are within the French trading bloc. In the short run, it appears that de Gaulle succeeded in liquidating the French empire while preserving certain advantages for France and perpetuating some of what was best in the French colonial tradition.

He very likely had the same hope for Algeria, but the circumstances there were much different. After the September referendum, he proclaimed the Constantine Plan, calling for vast expenditures for economic modernization, for land reform, housing, and education. It was designed to demonstrate to Moslems the benefits of continued association with France and, perhaps, to Frenchmen the prohibitive costs of total integration. He then ordered army officers to resign from the settlers' Committees of Public Safety, whose power had to be throttled before any further steps could be taken. Before the parliamentary elections, which were also to be held in Algeria, de Gaulle dramatically offered a "Peace of the Brave" and invited FLN leaders to talks for a cease-fire. It was rejected by the new Provisional Government of the Algerian Republic (GPRA), led by Ferhat Abbas, and the elections sent only docile or integrationist Moslems to Paris as Deputies. But again de Gaulle moved ahead, transferring Salan to Paris and replacing him with General Challe. After his election as President, he stopped executions, reduced sentences, and released thousands of Algerian prisoners—while lavishing decorations on the French army.

Only in September of 1959 was de Gaulle ready to define his policy on Algeria. By then hundreds of suspected army officers had been removed from their posts and the settlers' Committees were divided among integrationists, moderates who supported economic and social reforms in the hope of "association," and those whom de Gaulle scornfully described as longing only to recapture *l'Algérie de papa*. In a national broadcast, he offered Algerians three choices: integration with France, autonomy in association with France, or outright independence. The last he coupled with a threat of partition, which would have left the coastal regions in French hands, and the end of all French aid. "Secession," he said, would mean "appalling poverty, frightful political chaos, widespread slaughter," and Communist dictatorship. The referendum, moreover, could follow only after pacification, and its results would be subject to ratification by the French electorate. De Gaulle's threats and qualifications did not deceive the Right, the army, or the settlers. The offer of independence had been made. The GPRA had responded with a call for negotiations on a cease-fire and on guarantees of a free expression of Algerian opinion. At home, Bidault and others called de Gaulle a traitor. But most of the UNR and Right Deputies found their constituents favorable to his policy, and in October the Assembly overwhelmingly approved it. When Premier Krushchev vaguely assented, the French Communist party followed suit in November.

Algiers was in ferment. In January of 1960, de Gaulle recalled the idol of the settlers, General Massu, after the latter criticized the Paris government in an interview. The extremists answered with riots, a general strike, and an armed insurrection behind barricades set up in the heart of Algiers. Twenty-one were killed as Frenchmen fired on each other; nineteen were gendarmes under orders to quell the uprising, but left unsupported by paratroops on the scene who were sympathetic to the rebels. At this point de Gaulle appealed to the French people and the army in a moving television address. Loyal troops reluctantly forced the rebels to disband, but most of the leaders were allowed to escape. In Paris, the Assembly gave the President emergency powers for a year.

Optimists believed that the Algerian war would soon be over, but 1960 ended without serious negotiation. Fighting continued, with the French public increasingly restive over its cost, impatient with settlers who refused all compromise, and repelled by revelations of torture used by fellow Frenchmen, of degrading conditions in military prisons and resettlement camps. In January of 1961, a referendum on steps toward self-determination won 15 million votes against 5 million in France and a solid majority in Algeria (1.7 million to 800,000), in spite of the FLN's denunciation of it as a ruse. After a meeting between de Gaulle and President Bourguiba of Tunisia, the French government and the GPRA announced that negotiations would begin in April at Évian-les-Bains.

Now dissident army officers determined to overthrow de Gaulle. On April 22nd, Generals Salan, Challe, Jouhaud, and Zeller and several colonels seized control of Algiers with a few thousand paratroops and French Legionnaires. Several other units in Algeria broadcast their support of the "new Revolution" à la Franco, and for a moment the life of the Fifth Republic seemed to hang in the balance. On April 23rd, Premier Debré appealed to the people to resist airborne insurgents he said were expected to land on Paris. That night Committees of Vigilance sprang up in working-class districts and veteran Resistance fighters gathered in anti-fascist bands. But the paratroops and Legionnaires never came. The air force, navy, and most army conscript units answered de Gaulle's plea for obedience. The *Putsch* collapsed in three days. On May 20th, negotiations opened at Évian. In spite of quarrels, suspensions, and delays, the end drew near when de Gaulle, in September, all but abandoned French demands for sovereignty over the oil lands of the Algerian Sahara. Before this, European extremists and disgruntled soldiers had launched their last campaign to frustrate settlement. Having failed to ignite a popular uprising in January of 1960 and a military revolt in 1961, they turned to terror, sabotage, and subversion. The Secret Army Organization (OAS) and its imitators used every weapon—most often the plastic bomb—to intimidate, maim, and murder liberal Frenchmen on both sides of the Mediterranean and to assult Moslems indiscriminately in the hope of provoking reprisals that would wreck all compromise. They failed, partly because the Moslem community was able to limit retaliations on European civilians. In March, 1962, the French government released Mohammed Ben Bella and the other leaders kidnapped in 1956. On the 19th, an official cease-fire went into effect, ending a war in which some 200,000, mostly Moslem, had lost their lives.

The Évian agreements included guarantees for the safety and personal rights of the Europeans who remained in Algeria, joint exploitation of the Sahara oil fields, wide amnesties on both sides, the continuance of French aid and certain French bases in Algeria, and a free vote on Algerian self-determination. Now the OAS struck out savagely, murdering Moslem teachers, workers, shopkeepers, drivers, dockers, and random passers-by. They bombed, raided, and set fire to schools, public buildings, and hospitals, where patients were shot in their beds; finally they sought out and slaughtered Moslem women. Some of the assassins were mad with frustration, some still hoped for a bloodletting that would upset the peace, others sought to wrest added guarantees for Europeans from the FLN—an object temporarily achieved. Moslem leaders won world acclaim for holding their own people in check and European settlers showed rising disgust, and fear, over the extremists' savagery. A great exodus of Europeans brought hundreds of thousands to France, wretched and often unwelcome intruders. On April 8, 1962, French voters approved the peace terms, 17.5 million to 1.8 million. On July 1st, Algerians voted nearly unanimously for independence; two days later de Gaulle proclaimed the transfer of sovereignty to the Provisional Government of the Algerian Republic.

## DE GAULLE'S FOREIGN POLICY

Despite continuing OAS terror in France, including attempts on his own life, the President moved quickly to reap the political rewards of his singular achievement. He replaced Premier Debré in April with another old associate, Georges Pompidou. The new cabinet lasted only until October, when the Assembly overthrew it on the government's proposal to revise the constitution by popular referendum, providing election of the President by universal suffrage. De Gaulle promptly dissolved the Assembly. The doubtful legality of the referendum and the opposition of all parties but the UNR notwithstanding, de Gaulle's proposal won 62 per cent of the votes. Observers pointed to the high rate of abstentions, giving him less than 50 per cent of eligible voters for the first time since his return to power.

Many expected the parliamentary elections of November, 1962, to return the old parties—and the old Republican system—now that the Algerian crisis which had overthrown them was settled. Instead, the UNR scored an even greater triumph than in 1958, winning 31 per cent of the first-round vote, 40 per cent of the second, with 234 of the 482 Assembly seats. Together with the 33 Gaullist Independent Republicans, the Deputies claiming allegiance to the President easily controlled the new parliament. The non-Gaullist Right (which had opposed Algerian independence) salvaged only 10 per cent of the vote and less than 20 seats. The Socialists and MRP each fell nearly a million votes short of their 1958 mark, but the anti-clerical, anti-Gaullist alliances made by the former with the Communists and Radicals increased their seats from 40 to 67 and dropped the MRP from 57 to 38. The Radicals (Entente Démocratique) also lost votes but rose from 37 to 44 seats. The Communist vote held steady at the 1958 figure of nearly 4 million (21 per cent) but gained 31 seats for a total of 41.

Whatever the reasons for the Gaullist sweep—prosperity, the ending of the war, the abiding charms of stability—it greatly strengthened the President's hand in diplomacy and gave him added time to entrench his new political system. From the first, the summer of 1958, de Gaulle had taken personal command of French foreign policy. Although many of its themes were familiar since Liberation, its style and conduct were henceforth entirely de Gaulle's. Parliament played no role. His cabinet, even his Foreign Ministers, were often surprised by his moves and few were taken into his confidence on larger strategy. In no matter did de Gaulle more stubbornly follow his own prescription for leadership given in the Edge of the Sword (1931): the leader must stand apart, alone, aloof, oracular, permitting neither friendship nor sentiment to distort his vision of reality, to divert his work for the greater good of the nation.

The method tempted rival statesmen, especially in Britain and

America, to see and denounce French diplomacy as one man's willfulness. In so doing, they underestimated both the degree of continuity from the Fourth Republic and the popularity of most of his policies among the French. Worse, for French interests as well as for their own, they were sometimes tempted to take too lightly their own policies affecting France. If French policy was de Gaulle's alone, and if de Gaulle, as they asserted, had always hated Anglo-Saxons, whatever they did could make little difference. Better to await his disappearance before reviewing the place France might occupy in their world. As for his utterances on wider world affairs, such as American policy in Asia, they could be utterly discounted. To the extent that de Gaulle's style allowed others to reason thus, it was a disservice to France and to the world. But to ask that he await, and submerge himself in, a parliamentary consensus on foreign affairs was to ask that he cease being de Gaulle, that he practice what he thought partly responsible for the Fourth Republic's impotence in the world.

De Gaulle had, however, no illusions over great power. Critics who dismiss his decade as a failure in foreign affairs because France did not win world leadership, or leadership in Europe, or failed to build a "Europe of the states," or to achieve a détente in Eastern Europe opening the way for a Europe united "from the Atlantic to the Urals," end by judging unfairly. Wise in the turns and ironies and futilities of history, de Gaulle expected no such tidy end in his lifetime. But he was determined quickly to win a measure of independence for France (and for Europe, should Europe be ready) from the domination of the superpowers. However circumstances might limit action, there remained freedom of thought and speech. France, through de Gaulle, would say things needing to be said, to all nations, and so fulfill a mission. That France was a second-rank power he never doubted. It did not follow that France need utter second-rate ideas or acquiesce docilely in policies which he thought ignored both present reality and future possibilities. The future would not be won in a decade or two; it might never be won. Still, a people's vision could be clear, not wishful; its voice candid, not obsequious; it could find pride, not shame, in its role on earth. In the 1960's as in 1940, power was short, military glory out of reach. But de Gaulle's reverence for France's past rested not on days of glory but on grandeur of mind and spirit, on France not dominant but exemplary. De Gaulle as example to France, France as example to the world. From this extraordinary ambition, so incomprehensible to most, he never wavered, from youth to death. On this ground his foreign policy must, at least in part, be judged.

Americans, for many reasons, were least ready to so judge a man who increasingly opposed their policies, challenged their view of the world. Maddened by crises at home, impatient for quick results and "final" settlements abroad, suspicious of critical allies, and rarely, if ever, comforted by historical perspective, American spokesmen in and out of government too often reacted with abuse and ridicule. His only passion was France, they charged, as though it set him apart from other statesmen, including their own. Rather than consider the kind of world he thought best for France (and for America), it was easier to denounce the man: he was an "antique nationalist," "disloyal," "ungrateful," "obstructionist," "a life-long hater of Anglo-Saxons," all of which in turn only confirmed de Gaulle in dismissing "what it is customary to call opinion" in the United States.

De Gaulle was not anti-American, but history and experience had taught him to doubt the consistency of American foreign policy and the ability of Americans to perceive the interests of France and Europe. This was not condemnation but fact. The United States had its own interests and its own destiny, which were—as often demonstrated—not the same as those of France or Europe, and which the United States, quite rightly, did not dream of subordinating to those of others. It was intolerable, then, and dangerous both to old friendships and to world peace, for the United States to persist in controlling the foreign, military, and economic (which was also to say cultural) affairs of Europe. The weak, dependent governments of the Fourth Republic had failed to give France a voice in making Western policies critical to her interests and Europe's. Without a strong lead from the Fifth Republic, Europe would remain without voice. Britain was content to be a privileged satellite to the United States; she also cherished the Commonwealth. Of the other European states, only West Germany could aspire to a leading role, but she too chose dependence on America, was distracted by the dream (and the fear) of unification, and was still suspect to other Europeans, not least to de Gaulle himself. France alone, then, could begin to speak and act for a Europe which would some day find ways to shape her own destiny.

De Gaulle's view of a "European Europe" was, for the near future, a confederation of sovereign states, cooperating on economic and military matters, not in a supranational political union, but through meetings of national representatives. In this he opposed advocates of the Western European Union, as he did John Kennedy's "Grand Design" for a united Western Europe within an Atlantic Community. He saw such a Community dominated by the United States as unnatural. America herself would continue to be diverted, distracted, by her Pacific and Asian ambitions. More important, the division of Europe was a passing affair. The Europe of nature and history stretched from the Atlantic to the Urals. As ideology faded (and as China rose to challenge Russia in the East), the countries of Eastern and Western Europe would once more come to resemble each other, to re-knit their old associations. Europe would outlive the Cold War as she had outlived the ideological storms of the Reformation and the French Revolution. Then, perhaps, it would be time to think of a European political structure. The American idea of an integrated Western portion would pull greater Europe from her natural course. Nor did it speak to the problem of Germany, which would, one day, demand unification. When that day came, France and Russia must already have forged the closest possible understanding. Cold War must give way to détente.

Meanwhile, de Gaulle pursued his objects according to the changing circumstances of the 1960's. Immediately upon assuming power in 1958, he sought from Eisenhower an equal role for France in the Anglo-American directorate of Western world policy. One pretext was the Lebanon crisis, in which he accused Americans of taking military action in an old French sphere without sufficiently consulting him. It could have been little surprise that Washington refused; de Gaulle was in effect asking for a veto on American action in any part of the globe, a constraint he would not have accepted for France. Most analysts now believe that his demand was not serious (he publicized it without waiting for Eisenhower's reply), but a tactic to justify moves toward independence that he had already decided upon. Soon afterward, de Gaulle withdrew the French Mediterranean fleet from NATO control, and forbade American nuclear warheads and rocket-launching sites in France.

Contrary to the fears of "Europeans," however, de Gaulle quickly announced his intention to honor France's pledges to the Common Market, which was to come into effect on January 1, 1959. The stringent budget and monetary measures taken in late 1958 by his Finance Minister, former Premier Antoine Pinay, were designed in part to prepare the French economy for the impact of European competition. Throughout his tenure, de Gaulle kept the Fifth Republic strictly to the timetable of Common Market development and laid the French economy open to competition to an extent that might have been impossible for the weaker Fourth Republic. There were echoes of the Second Empire in de Gaulle's insistence that freer trade was essential to French modernization, but his view was at once wider and narrower than Napoleon III's. Wider, in that not only France but all Europe required modernization to meet the rapid advance of American investments, and their political and cultural consequences. De Gaulle urged European cooperation against American competition, called for a European patent system, Europe-wide companies, and pooling of scientific and technical efforts. On the other hand, free trade was for some time to be narrowed to the six Common Market countries, excluding Great Britain (America's Trojan Horse) and others who would delay and dilute the effort to build a strong, autonomous economy in Western Europe.

The two crises that de Gaulle forced upon the Common Market followed logically. In early 1963, he abruptly refused further negotiations for Britain's entry into the Market. Others of the Six also feared British membership, suspected British reservations and conditions, worried that Britain would bring in her wake the other nations of the European Free Trade Association, to dilute the Market itself. But the others were content to let de Gaulle assume the responsibility of saying No to London. The Nassau agreement of late 1962, on nuclear arms, between Kennedy and Macmillan gave de Gaulle his excuse, for it appeared to make Britain even more obviously the favored, subservient partner of the United States.

The second crisis followed in 1965, when de Gaulle recalled from Brussels the French delegation to the Common Market meetings, to protest the European Economic Commission's "seizure" of supranational power by taking decisions on majority votes. The French boycott ended in 1966 only when the Commission agreed to respect the right of veto. In 1967, de Gaulle rejected British membership a second time. He insisted that supranational innovations and new memberships await further economic integration of the Six. He argued, not without malice in citing the speeches of British politicians at home, that Britain would find it easier to join a Common Market free of supranational entanglements, that she was having trouble enough as it was deciding to meet the basic economic conditions for membership. Once she had, and once she also had relinquished her special, added ties to America and the Commonwealth, political integration could be considered. The same was true of West Germany, inside the Community. After a successful courtship of Chancellor Adenauer, ending in a Franco-German treaty of cooperation in 1963, de Gaulle had found Adenauer's successor, Erhard, still determined to stress the American connection. That the Germans, with for a time the British, entertained the doubtful American project of a multilateral, seaborne nuclear force under Washington's command proved to de Gaulle that an independent Europe was very far off.

In the world as it was, an independent France required greater military power of her own. In 1960, the first French atomic bomb was exploded in the Sahara. Thereafter, de Gaulle pressed the development of France's own nuclear *force de frappe*. He refused to sign the nuclear test ban treaty, calling it collusion between the superpowers to freeze their world hegemony. In August, 1968, France successfully tested her first H-bomb in the Pacific. The French nuclear force, de Gaulle admitted, could never be a substitute for America's in a confrontation with the Soviet Union. It could, however, give France a voice over where and when American nuclear power would be employed. Given Russia's nuclear capacity to strike the United States, he argued, the Anglo-American deterrent might be doubted in case of a threat to Europe alone unless a European state possessed the power to trigger it. Perhaps more important, though unstated, was de Gaulle's determination to arm France against revival of German military power, especially as he saw unification as inevitable in the long run.

On the world scene, de Gaulle grew increasingly uneasy, and critical, over American policy. The world was changing. He believed that it was Moscow and Washington that were anachronistic, not the Fifth Republic, whose "nationalism" was as nothing when contrasted to the pretensions of the superpowers. Their quarrels, their oppression of neighbors and allies, their global adventures, were as out of date as the old colonial empires, and much more dangerous. Of what significance were these contentions among "Western" nations in the face of the Chinese threat, and of the restless, impoverished billions of the Third World? It was already late to attack what he proclaimed the great problem of the age, "to bring these eight hundred millions to unite in cooperation above and beyond their rivalries, for the development of the two billion others." France set the example, devoting more than twice as much of her national product to foreign aid than did the United States. Three entire continents required massive assistance, self-determination in neutralism, and a high degree of socialist economic organization, none of which America appeared to understand. French cooperation with Algeria on these principles had avoided the American mistake in Cuba of pushing native revolutionaries into the arms of world Communism. In May, 1965, the French at the United Nations denounced American intervention in the Dominican Republic. In 1966, de Gaulle toured South America and other parts of the Third World, to suggest that not all nations of the West were so blind to their aspirations.

France, de Gaulle had said earlier, could no longer be content to remain "a pawn on the American chessboard in the game that the Pentagon certainly does not always win" (though he had quickly supported President Kennedy in the Cuban missile crisis). In 1963, he withdrew French naval forces in the Channel and the Atlantic from NATO command. In 1966, de Gaulle followed by removing all French land and air forces in Europe from NATO and expelling NATO headquarters and bases from France. Although France would remain in the alliance and would fight at the side of her allies in the event of a European war, he announced that she would henceforth reject the consequences of Washington's aggressive policy in Asia. In 1964, he had followed the British in recognizing Communist China, without whose participation, he said, there could be no peace in Asia and no possibility of neutralizing Southeast Asia. It was pointedly at Phnom Penh, capital of then-neutral Cambodia, that in 1966 de Gaulle publicly denounced American action in Vietnam as a threat to world peace. Only a political settlement was possible, he said, followed by neutralization of Southeast Asia. He had long believed that national feeling, by nature, was stronger than ideology. He thus dismissed Washington's claim that it was fighting world Communism in Asia. Instead, it was opening Southeast Asia to Chinese influence, much against the desire of the North Vietnamese themselves.

In France, public opinion polls and the pronouncements of journalists and politicians across the party spectrum generally supported de Gaulle in his distrust of "what the United States calls its leadership" and in his move to a neutral position in world affairs. Since his retirement, in 1969, French spokesmen have softened the tone of their observations (as de Gaulle himself might have done for a time, given a new administration in Washington). French military leaders have been allowed to edge back toward more cooperation in NATO. British entry into the Common Market is apparently considered a counter-weight to Germany. But to the large extent that de Gaulle's foreign policy reflected historic French views of American fitfulness (at least as old as the United States' repudiation of Versailles and the Treaty of Guarantee) and of the consequences of American hegemony, the basic lines of his policy are likely to survive.

## POLITICS AND MODERNIZATION

De Gaulle's preoccupation with French foreign relations and wider aspects of world politics was to be expected from his experience, his view of history, his vision of France and her destiny. In his lifetime, France had suffered two holocausts so ravaging as to render next to meaningless the domestic flurries that had captured men's attention. If they failed once again at international politics, if they stumbled into World War III, domestic affairs would count for nothing. To be sure, internal stability was necessary to steady action abroad. No man for whom the 1930's had been such agony could forget it. But de Gaulle had good reason to believe that his new political system had rescued France from parliamentary *immobilisme* and that economic modernization, eased by social welfare, promised to assuage class resentment and class conflict.

From the end of the Algerian war to May of 1968, the Fifth Republic enjoyed relative serenity at home. The French economy continued its advance; the national product, industrial production, productivity of labor, real wages, and consumption continued to rise, with few interruptions. But under the surface of the "French miracle," as it was called by those who most enjoyed its fruits, discontent was also rising. The assaults of a dynamic, modern economy upon old sections of industry, farming, and commerce destroyed old habits and the livelihoods of many Frenchmen. Farmers saw themselves sharing less than others in the new prosperity; demonstrations and boycotts multiplied. The wages of many workers, notably in the nationalized sectors, lagged behind the cost of living. All workers saw the middle class pull away from them in real income and consumption, ever more conspicuous for the effusions of advertising and the mass media. Despite unprecedented expenditures, new housing and new schools fell short of the need. Critics decried the cost of foreign aid and the *force de frappe;* some blamed de Gaulle's policies in the Common Market, as often for pressing it as for opposing it.

The old parties moved only slowly to exploit resentment. Their programs were dated and contradictory, their alliances uncertain, their party journals and organizations failed to win enthusiasm from the young. Nonetheless, support drained slowly away from the Gaullists. Whether out of growing discontent or apathy born of quiet, they slipped backward in the Presidential election of 1965 and the parliamentary election of 1967. For the first popular election of a President since 1848, de Gaulle faced as his principal opponent François Mitterand, candidate of the newly-formed *Fédération de la gauche démocrate et socialiste* (FGDS), comprising the Socialists (SFIO), some Radicals, and a number of Left clubs and groups. This time the Communists offered no candidate and supported Mitterand. The first round disappointed de Gaulle, who won only 43 per cent of the vote (Mitterand 32 per cent, Jean Lecanuet, the MRP centrist candidate, 16 per cent). In the second-round runoff de Gaulle was elected by only 54 per cent to Mitterand's 46 per cent. That in his first direct appeal as a candidate he did less well than in the referenda of 1958 and 1962 was taken as a sign of trouble for the regime.

The parliamentary elections of March, 1967, left the Gaullists with only the most precarious margin in the National Assembly. Since 1965, the Left parties had moved closer. The Communists, led by Weldeck-Rochet, determined to escape their long isolation, joined an electoral alliance with the FGDS and the *Parti socialiste unifié* (PSU, a smaller group, curiously mixed of Communist and Socialist defectors, Trotskyites, and *réformistes* then including Pierre Mendès-France). To improve their chances, they agreed to present only one of their candidates in the second round. Voters of the Left were stirred by rising unemployment, by several major strikes before elections, as by the government's cuts in welfare and social programs. Premier Pompidou led a vigorous "American-style" campaign; de Gaulle intervened to plead for the UNR, an act greeted by his opponents as another sign of weakness. The results left the Gaullists and their allies with a three-seat majority (down to 244 from 267 in the outgoing Assembly). The Left's alliance gave the Communists 32 more seats for a total of 73 and the FGDS rose from 91 to 116.

Mendès-France predicted a victory for the Left next time and events appeared to support him. In May, a brief general strike greeted Pompidou's proposal to rule economic life by decree for six months, to prepare for the end of Common Market tariffs due in July, 1968. A censure motion in the Assembly failed by only eight votes. In the local elections of September and October, the various Left parties won 55 per cent of the vote. Strikes and violent demonstrations dotted France during the winter. The economy remained sluggish; living costs rose pitilessly; as did unemployment, which by January, 1968, had reached 400,000. As the Left worked for unity, rifts opened among the Gaullists. Valéry Giscard d'Estaing, the conservative leader of the Independent Republicans (43 out of the ruling coalition of 244) attacked the government's spending program as not deflationary enough and questioned de Gaulle's exclusion of the British from the Common Market. Gaullism appeared to many as a spent force and rumors spread of de Gaulle's early retirement. Not quite aptly, a *Le Monde* editor, Viansson-Ponté, declared that "France is bored" but it recalled Lamartine and 1848.

The historical parallel proved only too exact. The "French Revolution of 1968" exploded in May. When it was over, the dreamed-of coalition on the Left lay in ruins and the Gaullist party of order had won the most crushing electoral triumph in French history. The "events of May" grew out of student agitation at the bleak new Nanterre campus of the University of Paris. Since January, small groups of Leftist *enragés* had disrupted classes, seized buildings, and set off riots and demonstrations. According to the now-familiar scenario, they had succeeded in provoking tough police reaction and the closing of the university, which in turn won them wider student sympathy. Well before May, many universities in France had seen similar outbursts. The demands ranged from the end of parietal rules through abolition of examinations, curricular reform, higher budgets, better facilities, university autonomy, and self-government, to the destruction of all existing institutions and the overthrow of capitalist society, with its "hierarchies" and "technocrats," its "enslavement of men" by the "opium of commodities." The university, said the militants, was the architect of an inhumane and socially unjust society. Henceforth, it must devote itself entirely to social needs and—an apparent contradiction which occupied many ensuing debates—the liberation and development of each man's personality.

For the first time in France, the lycée (secondary) students joined in strikes and marches, led by activist committees formed earlier to protest the Vietnam war. In early May, the disturbances spread to Paris. The Sorbonne became the focus of the student rebellion when the Rector called in police to end a protest meeting over arrests at Nanterre. Fighting broke out, and by evening of May 3rd, 500 students had been arrested and the University of Paris was closed. The militants had succeeded beyond their dreams. On May 6th, hundreds of thousands of students and teachers demonstrated in most of France's major cities. In Paris, the Latin Quarter was a battlefield between demonstrators and the *Compagnies Républicaines de Securité* (CRS, heavily armed, mobile riot police with an old reputation for brutality). Paving stones and tear-gas grenades flew across the first barricades built in Paris since 1944; hundreds were injured and scores arrested. By the 10th of May, most lycées and all universities in France were on strike or occupied by action committees. That night, the Latin Quarter saw its worst street fighting. Scores of barricades were levelled by the CRS only after vicious combat; many, on both sides, were gassed, burned, and beaten. The CRS lashed out indiscriminately, winning sympathy for the students from the residents of the Quarter, many of whom opened their apartments to the wounded. Pompidou retreated, withdrew the police, and announced the re-opening of the Sorbonne.

Now the Left parties and labor unions joined in. On Monday, May 13th, a sympathy strike spread over much of the country. The students rushed to occupy the Sorbonne; evening saw more than half a million students and workers march across Paris. In the following days, the Odéon theatre, the Opéra, the Opéra-Comique, the Schools of Medicine and Science, the Beaux-Arts, lycées, post offices, and even hospitals were occupied. Under the red flag and the black flag flying at the Sorbonne, day and night meetings debated the total reformation of the university and society. Despite the endless, strident disputes among Maoists, Stalinists, Trotskyites, Castroites, anarchists, socialists, and moderates, an extraordinary mood of solidarity and exaltation suffused the great student demonstrations of May. As in the first days of 1830, 1848, 1871, and 1936, the young could believe in renewal, change in the very ordering of human life. The courtyard of the

Sorbonne, draped in banners, its walls and columns covered with posters and graffiti, offered a *"kermesse idéologique"*: "Imagination has taken power!"; "It is forbidden to forbid!" Revolutionary fervor called forth as always the better and the baser of human attributes. Reason met and mixed with irrationality; patience with hysteria; devotion with ignobility; generous high humor with enraged utopianism. Attacks on the university made temporary allies of those who were troubled about the quality of their education, those who would make it an instrument of social action, those who sought its destruction as a tool of capitalist society, and those who wanted it only to insure themselves a good job in that society. Projects for the reformation of the university emerged in bewildering profusion, professors joining students in denouncing centralization, hierarchy, over-crowding, out-of-date methods, courses, and requirements. Most called for student–staff co-management. But student militants of the Left derided university reform as futile without social revolution. Throughout, they labored to win the working class to their side, and by the middle of May, they appeared to have succeeded.

Workers struck and occupied factories and offices across the country, sometimes spontaneously, sometimes against the orders of the unions, later at the call of unions anxious not to fall behind. The impulse most often came from young workers and technicians, either not union members or disdainful of the unions as creatures of the older, resigned generation. Beyond the usual material demands, the activists called for "power to the workers," participation, self-management. By mid-May, Paris and most of France lay in the grip of a general strike. Factories, shops, offices, banks, schools, theatres, railways, planes, busses, and subways were shut down. Frenchmen had no mail, newspapers, taxis, or gasoline. Paris streets were heaped with trash and garbage. Trade and industry, ordinary life and work were at a standstill. But as time passed, public anxiety rose. Many who had sympathized with the students' defiance of policemen were less patient with workers who upset their lives and livelihood. As toughs and delinquent gangs took advantage of disorder, their violence discredited the student movement, as did the more rabid or nihilist declarations of rival leaders trying to outbid each other in daring. The threat of a police strike stirred fear of chaos, even of civil war.

With the state's authority in doubt, de Gaulle and Pompidou moved on two fronts, political and economic. As if by force of habit, de Gaulle broadcast on the evening of May 24th his decision to hold a national referendum on the principle of "participation" in all French institutions and basic social reforms, to be carried out by himself. If it lost, he would resign. The seventy-eight-year-old President ("old man, perennial recruit of crisis," he had called himself ten years before) appeared weary, floundering for the first time in a career of meeting calamity. The broadcast was badly received, even among Gaullists, and the Left ridiculed it. Printers announced that they would refuse to prepare the ballots. As de Gaulle spoke, mobs of demonstrators surged through Paris, attacking police stations and setting fire to "capitalist strongholds"; the Bourse burned for hours.

Pompidou's appeasement of the unions was more successful. Negotiations begun on the 25th ended in agreement on a 10 per cent rise in wages, a shorter work week, added union rights within factories, and earlier retirement. But when the proposals were offered to the workers for ratification, most strikes continued as young militants defied the leaders of the CGT (Communist) and CGT-FO (Socialist) as collaborators with the "system." In this they were encouraged by the Left Catholic union (CFDT) leaders, who had refused to sign the agreement and persisted in their demands for decentralization of all economic life and decision-making—a new society with overtones of Proudhon, the Commune, the older syndicalists, and anarchists. Quarrels divided the Left as the Communist party lashed out against "leftist adventurers," the FGDS split internally, and the PSU denounced them both for timidity, while throwing its full support to the student Left and the rebel workers who refused to settle for anything less than revolution.

For three days, between May 27th and 30th, the Fifth Republic seemed near its end. Political leaders hurried to offer themselves to a new regime. Even Gaullists asked for the President's resignation. On the 27th, Giscard d'Estaing suggested himself as a possible presidential candidate. On the 28th, it was Mitterand's turn to call for a provisional government, with himself as candidate for President. On the 29th, Pierre Mendès-France offered to form the provisional government. But they evaded the question of Communist participation; and the Communists would not accept Mendès-France. The Left parties drifted apart; the student–worker action committees had neither time nor means to devise political action of their own; the unions were preoccupied with local revolts against their authority. But reports of de Gaulle's resignation flew about the country and for a moment France appeared to have lost all political direction.

So seriously did de Gaulle take the situation that he turned to the army for support. To make sure of it—and of the voters of the Right—he flew to visit military leaders in eastern France and Germany. For their support in case of insurrection, he promised the release of General Salan and other officers convicted during the Algerian crisis. On the night of the 30th, de Gaulle had returned to Paris, ready to take command once again. With the army assured, he broadcast a second time, renewed in vigor and confidence: "I shall not withdraw, the Republic will not abdicate." He would use force against the enemies of order. He announced the dissolution of parliament and called for new elections. A strong majority, he said, would allow him to carry out reforms and insure "participation" in all French life from schools to industry. As he spoke, crowds of cheering Gaullists filled the Etoile and the Champs-Elysées.

De Gaulle's few, firm words marked the turning point. In the days following, unions gradually asserted their authority, negotiations resumed, and slowly Frenchmen returned to work. To the disgust of militant students, strikes and occupations were progressively abandoned. The political parties turned to the election campaign, ignoring Mitterand's cry that de Gaulle's was "the voice of dictatorship," an "appeal to civil war." Continued unrest played into the Gaullists' hands. The radicals' appeal for "total and permanent opposition" in all spheres of society, their acts of pointless violence, only fortified de Gaulle and Pompidou in their claim that Frenchmen had no choice between order and chaos. Despite the caution of the Communist party and the CGT—their restraint may have saved the regime—the Gaullist campaign was a crusade against "totalitarian Communism." In vain l'Humanité denied that the party had sought to take power; it only earned added denunciation from the radical students and other Leftists, who accused the Communists of betraying the revolution. This time there were no electoral alliances on the Left. With a moderate swing of the vote, the Gaullists won nearly all the close contests they had lost the year before. The results gave a stunning response to all those, in France and abroad, who had hoped for or feared the end of the Fifth Republic. For the first time in French parliamentary history, a single party, the UDR (the UNR renamed Union of Democrats for the Republic) won an absolute majority in the National Assembly.

The old parties were routed. Neither they nor the student groups were able to crown their criticism with a coherent alternative to de Gaulle. Out of the 485-seat Assembly, the UDR won 292, their allies, the Independent Republicans, 57, for a Gaullist gain of 100 seats. The Communists sank from 73 to 33, the *Fédération des gauches* from 116 to 57.

In retrospect, the May events gave de Gaulle's political system a solid chance to survive his retirement. Before May, discontent met by complacency could have further eroded the UNR's strength, especially as the Left appeared to be on the verge of unity. For de Gaulle's successor to start well, he would require a majority in the parliament and active public support. The crisis provided both, on an undreamed-of scale. *L'Humanité* had been largely right in accusing the militants of playing the government's game. The alternatives, possible alternatives, lack of alternatives to the Gaullist system had emerged all too clearly for the good of the opposition. Fever had risen too high for compromise; the entire system was denounced and was to be swept away. Nothing could have served the Gaullists better. Even the scale of violence and the obvious dangers France had barely survived helped save them from temptation to abuse their victory.

De Gaulle set the example for response to the upheaval. In July, he dismissed Pompidou, who had, commentators observed, shown a steadier hand than his chief and who had, during the campaign, demonstrated a considerable personal following of his own. But he was also on the Right wing of Gaullism, identified with big business and conservative policies overall. Maurice Couve de Murville, who became Premier, was more clearly de Gaulle's instrument. The President named René Capitant, a "Left" social Gaullist as Minister of Justice despite Capitant's criticism of the regime in May. To carry out liberal university reform, de Gaulle took former Premier Edgar Faure as Minister of Education and consistently backed him against Gaullist critics who found him too ready to allow decentralization and self-government to the universities. In October, the Assembly passed Faure's program. Schools opened with fewer difficulties than expected; the postponed examinations were held. De Gaulle also sought a middle road in responding to the economic problems raised by increased wages and the massive work stoppages of May and June. Conservatives deplored his spending for education and social programs.

At what moment Charles de Gaulle decided to retire as President of the Fifth Republic is not certain. He admitted to considering it during the May crisis. In January, 1969, he announced his intention to complete his term (to 1972), in response to a premature declaration by Pompidou that he would be a candidate upon de Gaulle's retirement. But in January, also, he began his campaign on a national referendum for the regionalization of France. On the principles of "participation" and modernization, de Gaulle proposed a twin reform. First, regional assemblies organized on functional lines, with representatives from all levels of economic and social life; second, a transformation of the Senate on the same lines. In so linking the two and proposing, in effect, a major constitutional revision by referendum, de Gaulle invited the widest possible opposition.

By the time the referendum was held in April, all parties but his own and most labor, business, and civic associations had declared their opposition. Nearly every well-known politician had joined the chorus, from the Communists (opposed for the same reasons they had opposed the decentralizers of May) through Mitterand and the Centrists to de Gaulle's sometime ally, Giscard d'Estaing. Pompidou himself was cool in his support and as early as February, in the course of major speeches explaining his views on economics and education, managed to remind the voters that he was ready for office if it should become necessary. Even UDR leaders asked that the referendum pose two questions, putting the Senate change apart, but de Gaulle was adamant. Two weeks before the referendum, he announced his immediate retirement should the majority be against him. It was a surprise to nobody, but the opposition cried "plebiscite." That most of de Gaulle's opponents except the Communists had at one time or other espoused some form of regionalism led Gaullists to reply that the politicians had sought a plebiscite months before. Asked by Malraux later why he had resigned on such an issue, de Gaulle replied, "Because of the absurdity of it." For posterity, he left a longer explanation: "I had tried to open wide in France the door to participation," but all the "feudalities" had opposed him, "whether Marxist, liberal, or *immobilistes* . . . breaking at once my power and the chances for reform." But he had also said that his "contract with France" had been broken long before the referendum and the May events. He did not say when. In the end, not even his closest associates could explain why he chose to retire when and how he did.

The referendum lost, 10,515,000 (47 per cent) to 11,940,000 (53 per cent). Before the final votes were in, de Gaulle announced that he would "cease to exercise my functions as President of the Republic effective today at noon" (April 28, 1969). Alain Poher, President of the Senate, was interim President of France. The next day, Pompidou announced his candidacy, quickly seconded by Giscard d'Estaing, who had pointedly said he would vote No soon after de Gaulle's threat to resign. De Gaulle as pointedly left for a vacation in Ireland, to avoid any part in the Presidential campaign. Pompidou worked to retain the Gaullist regulars, and to reach beyond, with promises to defend the middle classes, small commerce, and artisans, to "work for Europe." "The burial of reform," said René Capitant, echoing other social Gaullists, but the mass of the UDR remained faithful. The Left, totally divided, offered three candidates. The first round in June presaged Pompidou's victory: Pompidou 44 per cent, Poher 23 per cent, Jacques Duclos (Communist) 21 per cent, Defferre (Socialist) 5 per cent, and Rocard (PSU) 2 per cent. A united Left would have had the runoff candidate. As it was, Poher won the right to lose the second round with 42 per cent to Pompidou's 58 per cent. Nearly a third of the voters stayed home.

Given his majority in parliament, given the lasting memories of May, 1968, Georges Pompidou could hardly have had a better start. Yet the future of the Fifth Republic's presidential system is still in doubt. Pompidou's majority was elected in crisis, partly on de Gaulle's prestige. Succeeding elections may offer the voters less obvious choices. For all his added paper powers, the President has few advantages over his predecessors of the Fourth and Third Republics once his party loses a majority. The Assembly can overthrow governments (though not so often or so easily as before 1958), it can refuse its approval to nominees for Premier; it votes all basic laws, votes the budget, may refuse even temporary credits. To a weak man, or to any man with a weak party behind him, the power of dissolution can be as dangerous as at any time since MacMahon's failure in the 1870's. Like the emergency powers in Article 16, it strengthens the office only if universal suffrage chooses—is allowed by the parties to choose—men worthy of national confidence.

The future of the parties is also uncertain. De Gaulle hoped that the constitution itself, especially the popular election of the President, coupled with economic modernity would call forth new parties, or force new combinations of the old. But the uniquely personal nature of his power—and thereby, many assumed, of the UNR's—allowed the older parties simply to await his disappearance. Their parliamentary campaigns of 1962, 1967, and 1968 betrayed a dearth of new ideas (the ancient church–school question still split the non-Communist Left in 1962) and an inability to offer the voters any alternative to Gaullism but a return to the Fourth Republic. Nor is it clear how long the UDR itself will remain united. Since de Gaulle's retirement, it has felt the strains of having to govern rather than merely to acquiesce. On those economic and social questions that grow more and more urgent, it is nearly as badly divided within itself as are the older parties among each other. Given the abiding nature of the parties and—Debré's labors notwithstanding—the flexibility of the constitution, the most likely evolution is a return to the parliamentarism and coalition cabinets of the earlier Republics.

Those who deplore this prospect find some hope in the emergence of a new generation of leaders in non-party organizations, now much more numerous in France than before 1940: civic and social-religious groups; new cadres in labor, industry, and commerce; federations of students, farmers, technicians, engineers, and scientists. Others see some promise in the training of new political talent on the local level. But the continued centralization of power in Paris works against it. Regionalization is much talked about and vaguely brandished by politicians, but innumerable difficulties arise. Not least is the growing concentration of French business, requiring not less but more matching power at the center. So far, regionalization has meant little more than the deconcentration of the state's bureaucracy, parceled out to the regions, taking its orders from Paris. The omnipresent civil service not only limits the chances of most Frenchmen to work at public affairs, but stirs them to largely negative, sporadic, sometimes violent, expressions of opposition to national policies that happen to touch their immediate interests. As the May events proved, a modern industrial society is vulnerable to such explosions if they occur on a grand enough scale. France may be more vulnerable than most, Raymond Aron believes, precisely because of her extreme centralization and bureaucracy; there are too few intermediate bodies with power of their own (labor unions, faculties, local governments) to stand between total authority and total collapse of authority. To Aron, France is also more vulnerable for being so divided in spirit between nostalgia and modernism, so lacking in common aspirations.

Future politics will no doubt be affected by the profound economic and social changes France is undergoing in the second half of the twentieth century. Many witnesses have testified to the "new France" or the "new French revolution" of modern mass production, distribution, and consumption. New men, new ideas mark many of the larger enterprises, both private and public. Willingness to risk expansion and innovation has rejuvenated the automobile and aircraft industries, the railroads, coal mines, and chemical laboratories. Entire new industries have grown up in engineering, machine tools, computers, electronics, appliances, and nuclear science. New to France and spreading fast are chain stores and supermarkets, mass advertising, and installment buying. New suburbs rise; new hospitals, clinics, resorts, pools, rinks, and playgrounds are built to meet higher expectations of health and leisure for a growing population. As in America after the First World War, the automobile is both symbol and instrument of a new era of mobility. Its manufacture, nourishment, care, and repair create thousands of new jobs each year. Frenchmen are spending relatively less on food, more on amusement, health, housing, and transportation. Even agriculture, that most conservative of occupations, grows mechanized and industrial. Tractors multiply where animal power ruled only a few years ago. Village life changes, with the automobile and electricity, with employment of village youth in nearby towns and industries, with better chances for education and travel outside the village. Rural areas lose thousands yearly to Paris, but also to provincial cities which are enjoying, and suffering, unprecedented growth. Before 1940, 35 per cent of the people lived on the farms; in 1970, only 18 per cent remained. France, in short, is facing all of the threats and promises of mass technological civilization.

The human effects of this revolution are less simply stated, its political and cultural significance not any clearer in France than in the rest of the industrialized world. Most obviously, the years since the Second World War have seen the men who conceive, plan, finance, build, and manage great enterprises, public and private, assume more and more control over the lives of their fellow men—whether they desire to or not. The experts and directors exercise power out of all proportion to their number. The problem of integrating such power into a political community, of using while limiting it, of allowing its holders freedom without thereby destroying the freedom of others, is hardly new. But in France as elsewhere it daily grows more urgent and more complex. Much of the May revolt is explained by resentment of the new power elite so closely identified, in France, with the old bureaucracy, the new rich, and Gaullist politics.

Modernization and its expected product, affluence, are unevenly spread. Much of the south and west of France remains in the "static" sector of the economy. There small farms, small and antiquated industry and commerce, traditional village and town life persist. There Poujadism had much of its appeal. The peasantry fears—from a century's experience—that modernization will be carried out at its expense, as does labor in small, now-marginal, industries where wages are the lowest. But even in the modern sector, the benefits of economic progress have been badly distributed. As so often before, the stringent financial measures of the early Fifth Republic bore heaviest on the working and lower middle classes. Although the larger national product has raised their standard of living, their share of the whole has not increased but decreased. The disparity between the lowest and highest salaries is nearly the widest in Europe (West Germany's is wider). As in America, the labor unions' rivalries and their failures to organize many workers offer little hope for quick improvement. Nor can the worker expect to see his children move easily upward. Progress toward equality of opportunity lags behind economic expansion. Education is still largely a middle-class preserve, despite the efforts of the Fourth and Fifth Republics. The latter has doubled attendance at the *écoles maternelles* (nursery and kindergarten) from a million in 1958 to two million in 1970. It has doubled yearly school construction. France leads all European countries in percentage of young people in higher education—16 per cent, as opposed to 11 in Sweden, 8 in Germany, 7 in Italy and Great Britain—and leads the world in rate of expansion. No doubt this sudden growth in universities, with its consequent overcrowding and confusions, contributed to student unrest in 1968. Still, relatively fewer lower-class children finish their secondary education; even fewer reach, and succeed in, the university.

Housing is the greatest social problem. The French people pay more for less space than any of their European neighbors. Neither the Fourth nor the Fifth Republic filled a need dating from the First World War. Antiquated building codes and methods raise the cost. Worse, recently, has been speculation in land prices, never checked despite government efforts. As in America, old neighborhoods are razed only to make way for luxury apartments while the old residents are deported to massive housing projects. Paris is ringed with mega-liths, most of them as ugly, as barren, as devoid of regard for human needs as any on earth. The worker forced to live in them spends hours each day commuting to his job in Paris. Few of the new develop-ments have the redeeming qualities of the ancient Paris *quartier*; neighbors are lost, cafés are few, stores and cinema are remote, clustered in garish shopping plazas. The French, for the first time, face the scourge of juvenile delinquency; projects are not safe at night; youthful gangs dominate scarce parks, playgrounds, and cafés.

Like some Americans, many Frenchmen are dismayed at the human costs of affluence, as they are at the predictions of population growth (70 to 80 million Frenchmen in 2000, 16 million in the Paris region). Paris glitters, its buildings are scrubbed clean, but the city is choked with automobiles, their noise and fumes fouling the pleasure of strolls, sidewalk cafés, and conversation. Leisurely restaurants close in favor of quick-lunch cafeterias. Cafés lose their patrons to television, or install pinball machines and jukeboxes. Old corners (like the one opposite Saint-Germain-des-Prés) give way to slick, neon-lighted luxury shops. Supermarkets replace small neighborhood stores, their prices not notably lower for all their impersonality and delay. The country-side around the city is filled with factories and suburbs; the "green belt" laws are regularly evaded. The Seine embankments are crowded with new highways. The Metro staggers under its burdens; the last of the old open-platform busses disappeared in 1970. New sealed, slab-sided office buildings repeat from New York the windowless cubicles, the porous soundproofing, the doubtful air and frequent lapses of mechanical ventilation, and the scientific minimum of space and ceiling height bearable to mortals.

The drive to modernism is dominant in France, perhaps more so than in America for its newness and for the obvious need of so many for a better standard of material life. Few public spokesmen deny the need. Most insist that affluence be more justly distributed, that more humane means of production be devised. Both may require greater participation of workers in the management of business and industry, a certain decentralization of politics, administration, and enterprise. At the same time, many of the same spokesmen (Jean-Jacques Servan-Schreiber, author of *The American Challenge*, is among them) also insist that French business and industry must be concentrated in fewer, larger, more competitive firms, more "scientifically" managed, lest

France and Europe fall behind the United States in the "post-industrial age." They deplore the survival of family business, of smallness anywhere, whether in industry, agriculture, or commerce. A modern economy, they say, does not need it. Whether men and their children need it remains unanswered, as do the apparent contradictions between liberty and efficiency, decentralization and giantism, between humane, meaningful work and the new technology.

The main questions in French life, as the nation nears the 200th anniversary of the great Revolution, are akin to those of all advanced societies, akin to that posed by Alexis de Tocqueville over a century ago: whether a new despotism, more sweeping and less painful than any of the old, may not degrade men without torturing them. Nowhere, one would think, is the question more likely to be debated than in France. Yet most of the intelligentsia appear unready to work at the hard question of somehow reconciling the material and spiritual needs of men. Many still find more pleasure, perhaps more profit, in denouncing the worst of the new society. The cinema is even less promising, choosing to exploit the sensational and the hopeless. The "new politics" of May offered some hope, but the more serious efforts were, perhaps inevitably, eclipsed by the destructive. Yet the questions Frenchmen asked of America decades ago are now theirs to answer. Will France now abandon the ideal of liberty to follow that of prosperity, sacrifice individual freedom to efficient authority, quality to quantity, thought to things, being to having? Will the French barter away much that was most distinctive in their ancient civilization? De Gaulle, like some of the best of his antagonists in May, feared that they would, and sacrifice their pride for "this relative degree of popular welfare and security that one is used to call, on this earth, happiness."

Though Tocqueville's question is still unanswered, the French, with us and the rest of the modern industrial world, face questions that go beyond him. For now men begin to see that even the material side of mass technological society cannot be prolonged, while expanding at its present pace, into the future. Its assault upon the earth's limited supply of air, water, land, and resources is catastrophic. So often believed banished, Malthus' shadow still falls over the end of the road. Industrial society is rushing to the point of inescapable decision. Men will have to do with fewer things, to cease making many of the products they are capable of making, that are profitable to sell and pleasant to use, will have to find satisfaction in other than possession and consumption. The decisions required are staggering in their complexity, all the more so as millions of men in the advanced countries and billions in the backward continents still lack the minimum necessities of life. The choices to be made before the century turns can be no other than political choices, made by men whose authority must be formidable indeed. Whether such authority can be freely established and can remain answerable to the people has yet to be seen. Soon the choice may no longer lie between liberty and prosperity but, if free governments fail, between liberty and survival.

That Frenchmen will pose these questions there can be little doubt. Having moved more slowly, less finally, into mass industrialism, they may enjoy better chances than we to turn their questions into choices. In 1928, Georges Duhamel worried that America was "caught in the meshes of a machine, of which soon no one will know the secrets— the king-bolts, the vulnerable zones, the vital centers." France has not yet reached that point. French history offers some hope that she will not pass it without pause. For two hundred years Frenchmen have again and again resisted and recovered from the most alluring deceptions and cruelest blows that history could devise; they have preserved a generous measure of liberty for thought and action under circumstances more difficult than most Western nations have had to face. But the coming decades will be the most trying they, or we, have seen. Men who do not even now wholly grasp the import of Tocqueville's questions will be asked to work through them and beyond, under conditions of daily life and thought more frenzied and debilitating than he could have feared.

# MAP APPENDIX

DEPARTMENTS
OF
FRANCE

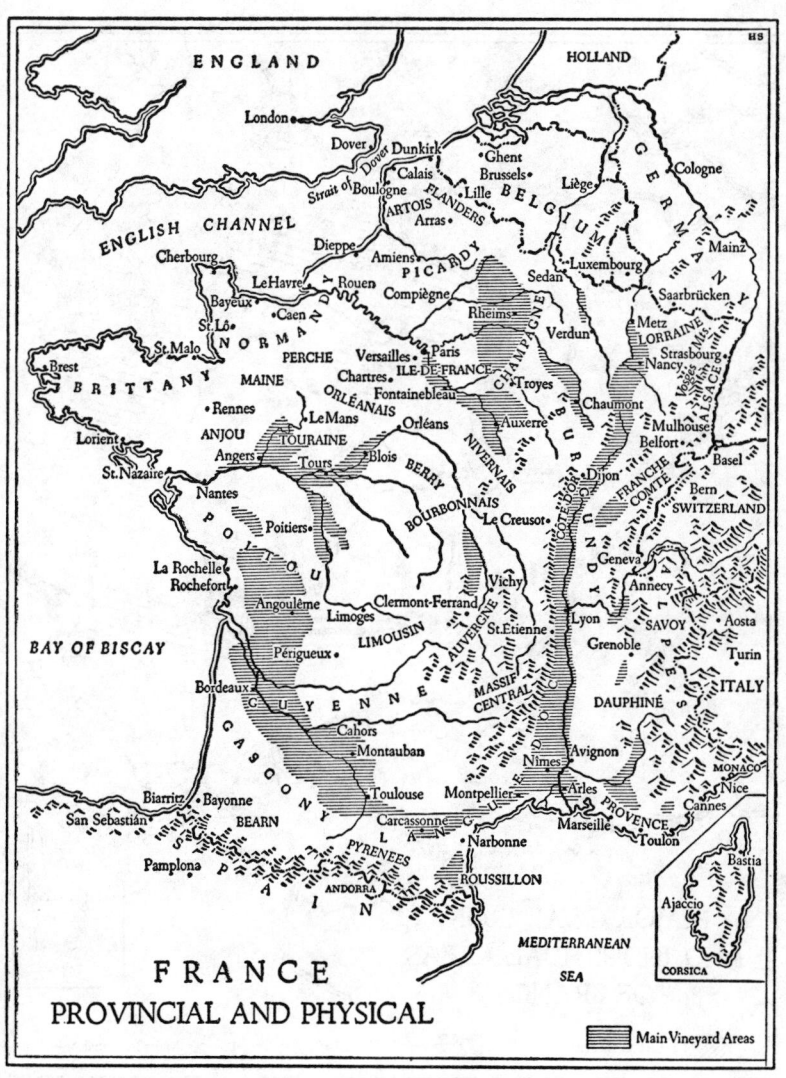

# FRANCE
## PROVINCIAL AND PHYSICAL

Main Vineyard Areas

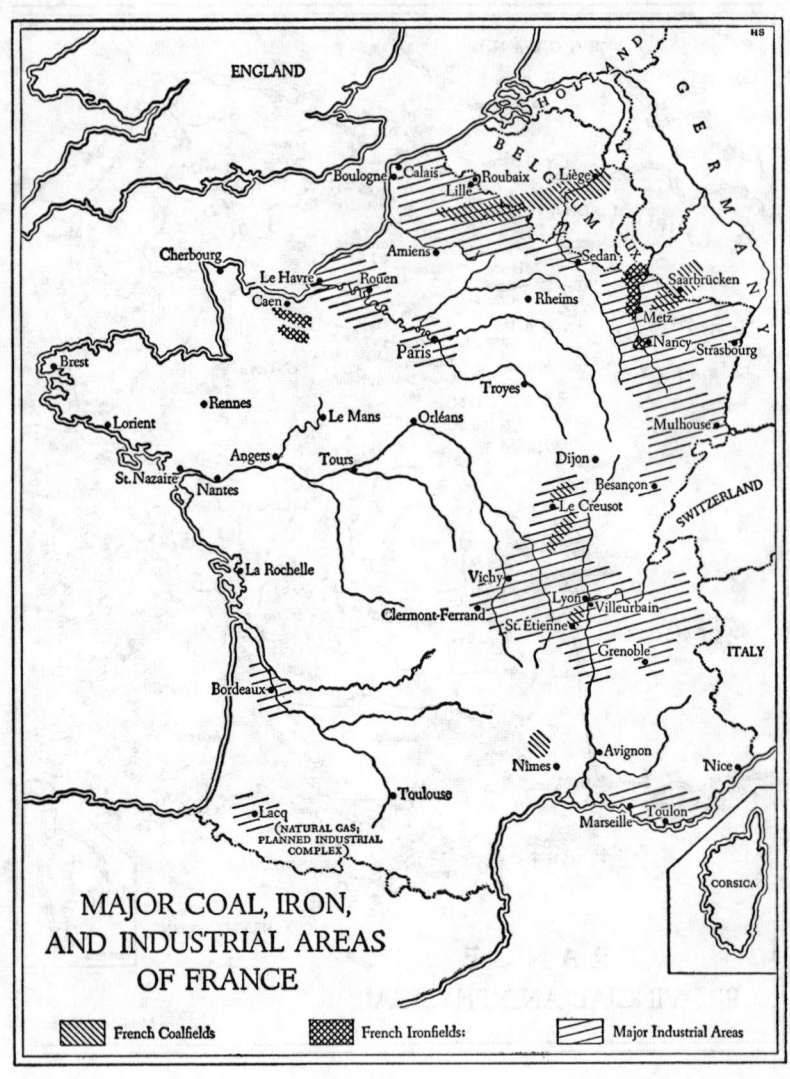

MAJOR COAL, IRON,
AND INDUSTRIAL AREAS
OF FRANCE

French Coalfields     French Ironfields:     Major Industrial Areas

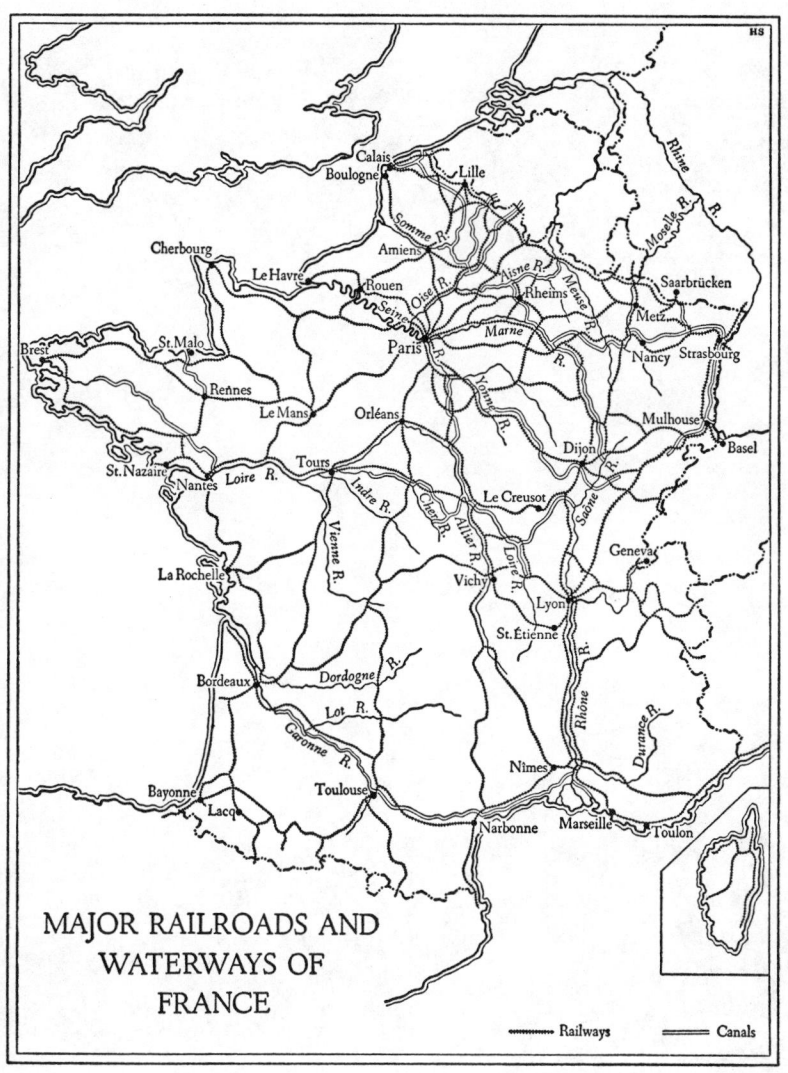

MAJOR RAILROADS AND
WATERWAYS OF
FRANCE

Railways          Canals

# SELECTED
# BIBLIOGRAPHY

An exhaustive listing of primary and secondary works on French history since 1789 would, of course, fill a volume considerably larger than this. The following suggestions are offered only to aid the general reader or the beginning student of French history to widen his acquaintance with important books in the field. Preference is given to works in English and to authors whose ideas have been particularly valuable in the writing of this general history. Many of the following books contain their own bibliographies on the subjects or times concerned; an excellent selection appears in the American Historical Association's *Guide to Historical Literature*, New York, 1961, pp. 464–497. Valuable bibliographies are also to be found in the *Clio* and *Peuples et civilisations* series, both published by the Presses Universitaires de France. Latest works are listed under "Recent Books on French History" in most issues of *French Historical Studies*, published by the Society for French Historical Studies.

## a. GENERAL AND TOPICAL WORKS

Brogan, Denis W., *The French Nation, 1814–1940*, New York, 1957.
Bury, J. P. T., *France, 1814–1940*, London, 1956.
Cameron, Rondo E., *France and the Economic Development of Europe, 1800–1914*, Princeton, 1961.

Chevallier, J.-J., *Histoire des institutions politiques de la France moderne, 1789–1945*, Paris, 1958.

Clapham, J. H., *Economic Development of France and Germany, 1815–1914*, Cambridge (England), 1936.

Clough, Shepard B., *France: A History of National Economics*, New York, 1939.

Cobban, Alfred, *A History of Modern France*, London, 1961, 2 vols.

Dansette, Adrien, *Religious History of Modern France*, New York, 1962, 2 vols.

Freedeman, Charles E., *The Conseil d'État in Modern France*, New York, 1961.

Guérard, Albert, *France: A Modern History*, Ann Arbor, 1959.

Labrousse, Ernest, *Le mouvement ouvrier et les idées sociales en France de 1815 à la fin du XIXᵉ siècle*, Paris, 1948.

McKay, Donald C., *The United States and France*, Cambridge (Massachusetts), 1951.

Manuel, Frank E., *The Prophets of Paris*, Cambridge (Massachusetts), 1962.

Mayer, J. P., *Political Thought in France from the Revolution to the Fourth Republic*, London, 1949.

Moody, Joseph N. (ed.), *Church and Society: Catholic Social and Political Thought and Movements, 1789–1950*, New York, 1953.

Rémond, René, *La droite en France de 1815 à nos jours*, Paris, 1954.

Ruggiero, Guido de, *The History of European Liberalism*, London, 1927.

Sée, Henri, *Histoire économique de la France, 1789–1914*, Paris, 1942, 2 vols.

Soltau, Roger H., *French Political Thought in the 19th Century*, New York, 1959.

Spencer, Philip H., *The Politics of Belief in Nineteenth-Century France*, London, 1954.

Wolf, John B., *France, 1814–1919*, New York, 1963.

Woodward, E. L., *French Revolutions*, Oxford, 1934.

Wright, Gordon, *France in Modern Times: 1760 to the Present*, Chicago, 1960.

### b. REVOLUTION AND EMPIRE

Brinton, Crane, *A Decade of Revolution, 1789–1799*, New York, 1934.

Brinton, Crane, *The Anatomy of Revolution*, New York, 1952.

Bruun, Geoffrey, *Europe and the French Imperium, 1799–1814*, New York, 1938.

Dowd, David L., *Pageant-Master of the Republic: Jacques-Louis David and the French Revolution*, Lincoln (Nebraska), 1948.

Farmer, Paul, *France Reviews Its Revolutionary Origins*, New York, 1944.

Gershoy, Leo, *Bertrand Barère: A Reluctant Terrorist*, Princeton, 1961.

Gershoy, Leo, *From Despotism to Revolution, 1763–1789*, New York, 1944.

Geyl, Pieter, *Napoleon: For and Against*, New Haven, 1949.

Godechot, Jacques, *Histoire des institutions de la France sous la Révolution et l'Empire*, Paris, 1951.

Gottschalk, Louis R., *Jean-Paul Marat, a Study in Radicalism*, New York, 1927.

Harris, Seymour G., *The Assignats*, Cambridge (Massachusetts), 1930.

Latreille, André, *L'Église catholique et la Révolution française*, Paris, 1946–1950, 2 vols.

Lefebvre, Georges, *La Révolution française*, Paris, 1957.

Lefebvre, Georges, *Napoléon*, Paris, 1953.

Lefebvre, Georges, *The Coming of the French Revolution*, Princeton, 1947.

Palmer, R. R., *The Age of the Democratic Revolution, 1760–1800*, Princeton, 1959.

Palmer, R. R., *Twelve Who Ruled*, Princeton, 1941.

Quimby, Robert S., *The Background of Napoleonic Warfare*, New York, 1957.

Rudé, George, *The Crowd in the French Revolution*, Oxford, 1959.

Soboul, Albert, *Les Sans-culottes parisiens en l'an II*, Paris, 1958.

Stewart, John Hall (ed.), *A Documentary Survey of the French Revolution*, New York, 1951.

Thompson, J. M., *Robespierre*, Oxford, 1935, 2 vols.

Thompson, J. M., *The French Revolution*, Oxford, 1944.

## C. NINETEENTH CENTURY TO THE THIRD REPUBLIC

Adhémar, Jean, *Honoré Daumier*, Paris, 1954.

Artz, Frederick B., *France under the Bourbon Restoration*, Cambridge (Massachusetts), 1931.

Barzun, Jacques, *Berlioz and His Century*, New York, 1956.

Bertier de Sauvigny, G. de, *La Restauration*, Paris, 1955.

Blanchard, Marcel, *Le Second empire*, Paris, 1950.

Case, Lynn M., *French Opinion on War and Diplomacy during the Second Empire*, Philadelphia, 1954.

Dunham, A. L., *The Industrial Revolution in France*, New York, 1955.

Duroselle, J. B., *Les Débuts du catholicisme social en France, 1822–1870*, Paris, 1951.

Duveau, Georges, *La Vie ouvrière en France sous le second empire*, Paris, 1946.

Guérard, Albert, *Napoleon III*, Cambridge (Massachusetts), 1943.

Kent, Sherman, *Electoral Procedure under Louis-Philippe*, New Haven, 1937.

Kranzberg, Melvin, *The Siege of Paris, 1870–1871*, Ithaca, 1950.

Lord, Robert H., *The Origins of the War of 1870*, Cambridge (Massachusetts), 1924.

Loubère, Leo, *Louis Blanc: His Life and His Contribution to the Rise of Jacobin Socialism*, Evanston (Illinois), 1961.

McKay, Donald C., *The National Workshops: A Study in the French Revolution of 1848*, Cambridge (Massachusetts), 1933.

Mellon, Stanley, *The Political Uses of History: A Study of Historians in the French Restoration*, Stanford, 1958.

Oncken, Herman, *Napoleon III and the Rhine: The Origin of the War of 1870–71*, New York, 1928.

Pinkney, David, *Napoleon III and the Rebuilding of Paris*, Princeton, 1958.

Robertson, Priscilla, *Revolutions of 1848: A Social History*, Princeton, 1952.

Spitzer, Alan B., *The Revolutionary Theories of Louis Auguste Blanqui*, New York, 1957.

Thompson, J. M., *Louis Napoleon and the Second Empire*, New York, 1955.

Williams, Roger, *Gaslight and Shadow: The World of Napoleon III, 1851–1870*, New York, 1957.

### d. THE THIRD REPUBLIC

Albrecht-Carrié, René, *France, Europe and the Two World Wars*, Paris, 1960.

Baumont, Maurice, *La faillite de la paix, 1919–1939*, Paris, 1951, 2 vols.

Bettelheim, Charles, *Bilan de l'économie française, 1919–1946*, Paris, 1947.

Binion, Rudolph, *Defeated Leaders: The Political Fate of Caillaux, Jouvenel, and Tardieu*, New York, 1960.

Bloch, Marc, *Strange Defeat*, New York, 1949.

Brogan, Denis W., *France under the Third Republic (1870–1939)*, New York, 1940.

Bruun, Geoffrey, *Clemenceau*, Cambridge (Massachusetts), 1943.

Campbell, Peter, *French Electoral Systems and Elections, 1789–1957*, New York, 1958.

Carroll, E. Malcolm, *French Public Opinion and Foreign Affairs, 1870–1914*, New York, 1931.

Challener, Richard D., *The French Theory of the Nation in Arms, 1866–1939*, New York, 1955.

Chapman, Guy, *The Dreyfus Case*, New York, 1955.

Chastenet, Jacques, *Histoire de la Troisième République*, Paris, 1952–1962, 6 vols.

Clouard, Henri, *Histoire de la littérature française du symbolisme à nos jours*, Paris, 1949, 2 vols.

Craig, Gordon A., and Gilbert, Felix (eds.), *The Diplomats, 1919–1939*, Princeton, 1953.

Dansette, Adrien, *Destin du catholicisme français, 1926–1956*, Paris, 1957.

Dupeux, Georges, *Le front populaire et les élections de 1936*, Paris, 1959.

Ehrmann, Henry W., *French Labor from Popular Front to Liberation*, New York, 1947.

Goguel, François, *Géographie des élections françaises, de 1870 à 1951*, Paris, 1951.

Goguel, François, *La politique des partis sous la IIIe république*, Paris, 1958.

Gouault, Georges, *Comment la France est devenue républicaine; les élections générales et partielles à l'assemblée nationale, 1870–1875*, Paris, 1954.

Goutard, Colonel A., *The Battle of France, 1940*, New York, 1959.

Halasz, Nicholas, *Captain Dreyfus: The Story of a Mass Hysteria*, New York, 1958.

Halévy, Daniel, *Péguy et les Cahiers de la Quinzaine*, Paris, 1918.

Hughes, H. Stuart, *Consciousness and Society: The Reorientation of European Social Thought (1890–1930)*, New York, 1958.

Hunter, Sam, *Modern French Painting*, New York, 1956.

Jackson, J. Hampden, *Clemenceau and the Third Republic*, New York, 1948.

Jellinek, Frank, *The Paris Commune of 1871*, London, 1937.

Joll, James (ed.), *The Decline of the Third Republic*, New York, 1959.

Jordan, W. M., *Great Britain, France, and the German Problem, 1918–1939*, London, 1943.

Joughin, Jean T., *The Paris Commune in French Politics, 1871–1880*, Baltimore, 1955.

King, Jere C., *Foch Versus Clemenceau: France and German Dismemberment, 1918–1919*, Cambridge (Massachusetts), 1960.

Lorwin, Val R., *The French Labor Movement*, Cambridge (Massachusetts), 1954.

Marcus, John T., *French Socialism in the Crisis Years, 1933–1936*, New York, 1958.

Mason, Edward S., *The Paris Commune*, New York, 1930.

Mathey, François, *The Impressionists*, New York, 1961.

Mayer, Arno, *Political Origins of the New Diplomacy*, New Haven, 1959.

Micaud, Charles A., *The French Right and Nazi Germany, 1933–1939*, Durham (N. C.), 1943.

Moon, Parker T., *The Labor Problem and the Social Catholic Movement in France,* New York, 1921.

Osgood, Samuel M., *French Royalism under the Third and Fourth Republics,* The Hague, 1960.

Renouvin, Pierre, *La Crise européenne et la première guerre mondiale,* Paris, 1948.

Rihs, Charles, *La Commune de Paris, sa structure et ses doctrines,* Geneva, 1955.

Rollet, Henri, *L'Action sociale des Catholiques en France (1871–1901),* Paris, 1948.

Siegfried, André, *France, a Study in Nationality,* London, 1930.

Simon, Pierre-Henri, *Histoire de la littérature française au XX<sup>e</sup> siècle,* Paris, 1959, 2 vols.

Tannenbaum, Edward R., *The Action Française,* New York, 1962.

Thomson, David, *Democracy in France,* New York, 1958.

Vaussard, Maurice, *Histoire de la démocratie chrétienne,* Paris, 1956.

Warner, Charles K., *The Winegrowers in France and the Government since 1875,* New York, 1960.

Weber, Eugen, *The Nationalist Revival in France, 1905–1914,* Berkeley, 1959.

Werth, Alexander, *The Twilight of France, 1933–1940,* London, 1942.

Wolfers, Arnold, *Britain and France Between Two Wars,* New York, 1940.

### e. SINCE 1940

Ardagh, John, *The New French Revolution,* New York, 1968.

Aron, Raymond, *France, Steadfast and Changing: The Fourth to the Fifth Republic,* Cambridge (Massachusetts), 1960.

Aron, Raymond, *Les désillusions du progrès,* Paris, 1969.

Aron, Raymond, *The Elusive Revolution,* New York, 1969.

Aron, Robert, *An Explanation of de Gaulle,* New York, 1966.

Aron, Robert, *Histoire de la Libération de France, juin 1944–mai 1945,* Paris, 1959.

Aron, Robert, *The Vichy Regime, 1940–1944,* New York, 1958.

Brace, Richard M., and Brace, Joan, *Ordeal in Algeria,* New York, 1960.

Brinton, Crane, *The Americans and the French,* Cambridge (Massachusetts), 1968.

Cairns, John C., *France,* New York, 1965.

Crozier, Michel, *The Bureaucratic Phenomenon,* Chicago, 1964.

De Gaulle, Charles, *Memoirs,* New York, 1958–1960, 3 vols.

De Tarr, Francis, *The French Radical Party; from Herriot to Mendès-France,* New York, 1961.

Duverger, Maurice, *La V<sup>e</sup> République*, Paris, 1959.

Earle, Edward M. (ed.), *Modern France*, Princeton, 1951.

Ehrmann, Henry W., *Organized Business in France*, Princeton, 1957.

Farmer, Paul, *Vichy: Political Dilemma*, New York, 1955.

Fauvet, Jacques, *La Quatrième République*, Paris, 1959.

Furniss, Edgar S., Jr., *France, Troubled Ally: De Gaulle's Heritage and Prospects*, New York, 1960.

Gillespie, Joan, *Algeria: Rebellion and Revolution*, New York, 1960.

Gilpin, Robert, *France in the Age of the Scientific State*, Princeton, 1968.

Goguel, Francois, *France under the Fourth Republic*, Ithaca, 1952.

Grosser, Alfred, *French Foreign Policy under De Gaulle*, Boston, 1967.

Grosser, Alfred, *La IV<sup>e</sup> République et sa politique extérieure*, Paris, 1961.

Hess, John L., *The Case for De Gaulle*, New York, 1968.

Hoffmann, Stanley, *Le mouvement Poujade*, Paris, 1956.

Hoffmann, Stanley, *et al.*, *In Search of France*, Cambridge (Massachusetts), 1963.

Hughes, H. Stuart, *The Obstructed Path*, New York, 1966.

Jeanneny, J. M., *Forces et faiblesses de l'économie francaise*, Paris, 1956.

Kraft, Joseph, *The Struggle for Algeria*, New York, 1961.

Lichtheim, George, *Marxism in Modern France*, New York, 1966.

Liebling, A. J. (ed.), *The Republic of Silence*, New York, 1947.

Luethy, Herbert, *France Against Herself*, New York, 1955.

Macridis, Roy, and Brown, Bernard, *The De Gaulle Republic: Quest for Unity*, Homewood (Illinois), 1960.

Marcus, John T. *Neutralism and Nationalism in France*, New York, 1958.

Matthews, Ronald, *The Death of the Fourth Republic*, London, 1954.

Michel, Henri, *Histoire de la résistance*, (1940–1944), Paris, 1962.

Morin, Edgar, *The Red and the Black: Report from a French Village*, New York, 1970.

Newhouse, John, *De Gaulle and the Anglo-Saxons*, New York, 1970.

Park, Julian (ed.), *The Culture of France in Our Time*, Ithaca, 1954.

Pauchou, Guy, *Oradour-sur-Glane*, Paris, 1945.

Pickles, Dorothy, *France Between the Republics*, London, 1946.

Pickles, Dorothy, *France: The Fourth Republic*, New York, 1958.

Pickles, Dorothy, *The Fifth French Republic*, New York, 1962.

Pierce, Roy, *Contemporary French Political Thought*, New York, 1966.

Posner, Charles (ed.), *Reflections on the Revolution in France, 1968*, London, 1970.

Schoenbrun, David, *As France Goes*, New York, 1957.

Seale, Patrick, and McConville, Maureen, *French Revolution 1968*, London, 1968.

Servan-Schreiber, Jean-Jacques, *The American Challenge*, New York, 1968.

Tannenbaum, Edward R., *The New France*, Chicago, 1961.

Thomson, David, *Two Frenchmen: Pierre Laval and Charles de Gaulle*, London, 1951.

Tillion, Germaine, *Algeria: The Realities*, London, 1958.

Tillion, Germaine, *France and Algeria, Complementary Enemies*, New York, 1961.

Williams, Philip, *Politics in Postwar France*, London, 1954.

Williams, Philip, *The French Parliament*, New York, 1968.

Williams, Philip, and Harrison, Martin, *De Gaulle's Republic*, New York, 1960.

Wright, Gordon, *Rural Revolution in France*, New York, 1964.

Wright, Gordon, *The Reshaping of French Democracy*, New York, 1948.

Wylie, Laurence, *Village in the Vaucluse*, Cambridge (Massachusetts), 1957.

# INDEX

Gouvion Saint-Cyr, Marshal Laurent, 98
GPRA (Gouvernement Provisionale de la République Algérienne), 519–521
Gramont, Duc Agénor de, 195, 196
Grandmaison, Colonel Louis de, 318, 320
Grandval, Gilbert, 502
"Great Fear," 10
Grégoire, Henri, 103
Gregory XVI, 137
Grévy, Jules, 156, 202, 205, 225, 230, 242–246, 248, 379
Griffuelhes, Victor, 279
Gros, Antoine-Jean, 86
Grouchy, Marshal Emmanuel de, 96, 97
Guarantee, Anglo-American Treaty of (1919), 332–334, 360, 529
Guéhenno, Jean, 367, 400
Guesde, Jules, 254, 255, 263, 267, 277, 278, 299, 317
Guesdists, 254, 265, 277
Guibert, Comte de, 71, 72
Guilbert, Yvette, 288
Guise, Jean, Duc de, 442
Guizot, François, 101, 108, 110, 115, 116, 118, 123–125, 127–129, 136, 138–140, 148, 153, 188, 223

Hadj, Messali, 358
Haig, Sir Douglas, 320, 325, 327
Halévy, Daniel, 261
Hanotaux, Gabriel, 307
Hanriot, François, 27, 34
Harmel, Léon, 251
Hashed, Ferhat, 500
Haussmann, Baron Georges, 173, 174, 185, 187, 238, 248, 286
Hébert, Jacques René, 24, 31
Hébertism, 147, 208, 210
Helvetic Republic, 52
Henry, Commandant Hubert, 256–259, 262
Herr, Lucien, 261, 293, 294
Herriot, Édouard, 347, 348, 351, 352, 367, 370–379, 383–387, 424, 431, 432, 503
Hervé, Gustave, 298, 312, 315, 317
Herz, Cornelius, 248
Herzen, Alexander and Nathalie, 144
Hindenburg, Paul von, 350, 384, 387
Hitler, Adolf, 336, 346, 348, 351, 367, 377–380, 387–396, 404, 406, 409–417, 419–423, 427, 428, 431, 432, 436–438, 442, 445–453, 458, 467, 487

Ho Chi Minh, 358, 497, 498
Hoare-Laval Plan, 392
Hoche, General Lazare, 38, 49
Hoffmann, Stanley, 434
Hohenlinden, battle of, 67, 72
"Horizon Blue Chamber," 338
Hôtel de Ville, 34, 118, 119, 141, 149, 150, 152, 153, 163, 197, 200
Howard, Miss Elizabeth, 162
Hué, Treaty of (1883), 241
Hugo, Victor, 87, 107, 108, 114, 115, 144, 148, 150, 155, 159, 163, 164, 177, 181, 189, 198, 204, 205, 236, 237, 291
Humanité, 331, 343, 375, 376, 378, 394, 421, 461, 535, 536
Hundred Days, 84, 87, 95–98, 100, 164
Huntziger, General Charles, 428

Ile de France, 362, 372
Illyrian Provinces, 76
Imperial Conference (1934–1935), 359
Impressionism, 289, 291
Independent Republicans, 522, 531, 536
Index of prohibited books, 294, 354
Indo-China War (1946–1954), 479, 484, 487, 488, 493, 495–499, 501, 505, 512
Industry, under First Empire, 77
  Bourbon restoration, 111
  to 1848, 131–134
  Second Empire, 169–173
  Third Republic, 203, 229, 280–287
  World War I, 321–323, 339, 341, 343, 405–409, 412; losses, 329
  World War II, 419, 422, 437–441, 463
  Fourth Republic, 465, 467, 471, 477, 478, 483–485, 494, 512
  Fifth Republic, 512, 540–543
Institut de France, 62, 63
Inter-Allied Commission on Reparations, 344
Intransigeant, 243
Italian Republic, 69
Italian War (1859), 179–181

Jacobins, 21, 22, 24–45, 52, 53, 59, 85
Jacob, Max, 363
Jansenists, 18
Jarry, Alfred, 363
Jaurès, Jean, 256, 257, 263, 265, 267, 268, 274, 277, 278, 292, 293, 298, 299, 311, 312, 314, 317, 339, 343, 379, 400, 406

71 72 73 74  7 6 5 4 3 2 1